ADVANCED SENIOR MATHEMATICS **11**

MATHEMATICS

PRINCIPLES

PROCESS

Authors

FRANK EBOS, Senior Author
Faculty of Education
University of Toronto

BOB TUCK
Mathematics Consultant
Nipissing Board of Education

WALKER SCHOFIELD
Department Head of Mathematics
Banting Secondary School
London, Ontario

Consultants

Roger Johnston
Assistant Head of Mathematics
South Grenville District High School
Prescott, Ontario

Ronald Reid
Department Head of Mathematics
York Memorial C.I.
Toronto, Ontario

Jim Turcott
Department Head of Mathematics
Levack District High School
Levack, Ontario

NELSON CANADA

Published in 1986 by
Nelson Canada,
A Division of International Thomson Limited
1120 Birchmount Road
Scarborough, Ontario

ISBN 0-17-602522-7

Canadian Cataloguing in Publication Data

Ebos, Frank, 1939–
Mathematics : Principles and Process, Book 1

For use in grade 11.
Includes index.
ISBN 0-17-602522-7

1. Mathematics — 1961–   I. Tuck, Bob, 1941–
II. Title.

QA107.E5 1986   510   C85-099865-4

Project Editor
Sheila Bassett

Editors
Peter Gardiner
Anthony Rodrigues

Technical Art
Frank Zsigo

The symbol for year is a. For the sake of clarity, the word year has been used, in full, in place of a.

Printed and bound in Canada by John Deyell Company
  34567890   JD 8932109876

Photo Credits

p. 19 INCO Canada Limited, p. 22 NASA, p. 29 T. Edward S. Matchette, p. 105 NASA, p. 108 General Telephone and Electronics Corporation, p. 120 Canapress, p. 126 Frank Ebos, p. 130 Canapress/The Globe & Mail, p. 138 Harold Lambert/Miller Services, p. 166 Environment Canada, p. 176 Miller Services/Canadair, p. 190 Bank of Canada, p. 201 (left) Canapress, p. 201 (right) H. Armstrong Roberts/Miller Services, p. 237 Ministry of Transportation and Communication, p. 242 H. Armstrong Roberts/Miller Services, p. 243 Courtesy of Parachute School of Toronto, Ltd. Taken by Jon Latham, p. 261 Saskatoon Star Phoenix, p. 276 General Motors Canada, p. 279 Canapress/Red Deer Advocate, p. 283 (top) Canapress, p. 283 (bottom) Zenon Niewada Pizza with Pizzazz Taken by P. Gardiner, p. 302 H. Armstrong Roberts/Miller Services, p. 323 Canadian Armed Forces, p. 363 (left) H. Armstrong Roberts/Miller Services, p. 363 (right) Murray Wilson/Miller Services, p. 405 National Film Board

The authors wish to express their thanks to Sheila Bassett, Peter Gardiner, Anthony Rodrigues, Frank Zsigo, Andrew Clowes, Sharon Kerr, Bill Allan, Maggie Cheverie, Barbara DeCarlo, Ruta Demery, Lesley Ebos, Michael Ebos, Jeff MacNabb, and Geoffrey Hull.

The authors gratefully acknowledge the advice, assistance or contribution of Barbara Bernstein, Dennis Buck, RoseMary Ebos, John Hopkins, Roger Johnston, Ron Lancaster, Paul Macallum, Tony Pontes, Elwood Sparrow, and Mark Steinhart.

Contents

Using Mathematics: Principles and Process, Book 1

These pages explain how the text is organized. They tell you what to look for in each lesson and in every chapter.

Lesson Features

Identifying the lesson
▶ Look for the lesson number and title.

Teaching
▶ The lesson begins with the information you need to learn. Look for pictures and photos that illustrate uses of mathematics. New words are printed in **bold type**.
▶ Examples and Solutions guide you step-by-step through new material.
▶ Always read the hints and helps printed in red type.

Exercise Features

▶ **Each lesson gives you lots of practice:**

A These questions let you practise the skills and concepts of the lesson. Many of these questions can be done with your teacher and the class.

B These questions give you practice with what you have learned. There are also lots of problems to solve.

C These questions provide an extra challenge, or may involve another approach.

Applications
These sections show how mathematics is a part of the everyday world. You will solve some problems and learn some interesting facts.

4.2 Strategy for Solving Problems: Ratio

To do Example 1, you need to combine your earlier skills with equations and your present skills with ratio.

Example 1 Find the two positive numbers, where
- they are in the ratio 5:4 and
- the sum of their squares is 1025.

Solution Let the numbers be represented by x and y.

$$\frac{x}{y} = \frac{5}{4} \quad \text{or} \quad \frac{x}{5} = \frac{y}{4}.$$

Let $\frac{x}{5} = \frac{y}{4} = k$, $k > 0$, where k is a constant. Then $x = 5k$, $y = 4k$.

Thus
$$(5k)^2 + (4k)^2 = 1025$$
$$25k^2 + 16k^2 = 1025$$
$$41k^2 = 1025$$
$$k^2 = 25$$
$$k = \pm 5$$

Check: $\frac{25}{20} = \frac{5}{4}$ checks ✓

$20^2 + 25^2 = 1025$ checks ✓

Since the numbers are positive, then $k = 5$. The numbers are 20 and 25.

8.1 Exercise

A
Review your skills for factoring trinomials.

1 Factor.
(a) $x^2 - 8x + 12$ (b) $x^2 - x - 6$ (c) $a^2 + 5a - 14$
(d) $2b^2 + 7b + 3$ (e) $3p^2 - 11p - 20$ (f) $6y^2 + y - 1$

2 Write each trinomial as a product of factors.
(a) $x^2 - 8x + 15$ (b) $x^2 - 2x - 8$ (c) $x^2 + 3x - 54$
(d) $3x^2 + 7x + 2$ (e) $2m^2 - 13m - 7$ (f) $8x^2 + x - 7$

Applications: Merchandising

Typically in industry the goal is to maximize profits and yet keep prices competitive. Skills used in finding maxima are applicable to finding solutions to problems in mechandising. Solve each of the following problems.

18 Studies have shown that 500 people attend a high school basketball game when the admission price is $2.00. In the championship game admission prices will increase. For every 20¢ increase 20 fewer people will attend. What price will maximize receipts?

19 The Transit Commission's single-fare price is 60¢ cash. On a typical day approximately 240 000 persons take the transit and pay the single-fare price. To reflect higher costs, single fare prices will be increased, but surveys have

Reviews and Tests

These sections review or test skills and concepts *after* every chapter:

▶ **Practice and Problems: A Chapter Review**
▶ **Test for Practice**

These sections help you review and practise skills from *earlier* chapters:

▶ **Maintaining Skills**
▶ **Cumulative Review**

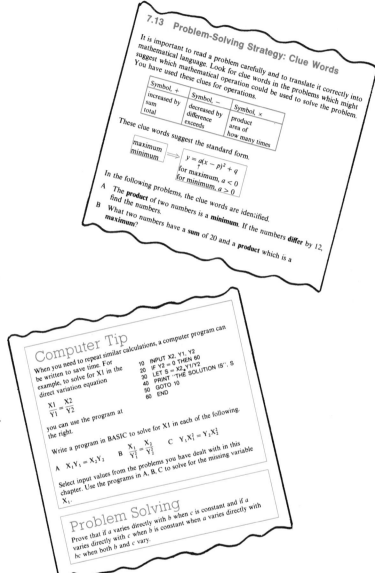

7.13 Problem-Solving Strategy: Clue Words

It is important to read a problem carefully and to translate it correctly into mathematical language. Look for clue words in the problems which might suggest which mathematical operation could be used to solve the problem. You have used these clues for operations.

Symbol, +	Symbol, −	Symbol, ×
increased by sum total	decreased by difference exceeds	product area of how many times

These clue words suggest the standard form.

maximum minimum $\Rightarrow$ $y = a(x - p)^2 + q$
for maximum, $a < 0$
for minimum, $a > 0$

In the following problems, the clue words are identified.

A The **product** of two numbers is a **minimum**. If the numbers **differ** by 12, find the numbers.

B What two numbers have a **sum** of 20 and a **product** which is a **maximum**?

Problem-Solving Features

There are lots of opportunities to learn and practise problem-solving skills — not just in the lessons, but also in special sections based on particular aspects of problem solving.

Solving Problems

Lessons in most chapters give you new problem-solving skills like *Reading Accurately, Deciding on a Strategy* and other strategies.

▶ **Problem Solving** in every chapter give you a chance to do different types of problems and introduce you to interesting aspects of mathematics. Some show new ways to practice your skills.

Computer Tip

When you need to repeat similar calculations, a computer program can be written to save time. For example, to solve for X1 in the direct variation equation

$$\frac{X1}{Y1} = \frac{X2}{Y2}$$

```
10  INPUT X2, Y1, Y2
20  IF Y2 = 0 THEN 60
30  LET S = X2,Y1/Y2
40  PRINT "THE SOLUTION IS", S
50  GOTO 10
60  END
```

you can use the program at the right.

Write a program in BASIC to solve for X1 in each of the following.

A $X_1Y_1 = X_2Y_2$ B $\frac{X_1}{Y_1^2} = \frac{X_2}{Y_2^2}$ C $Y_1X_1^2 = Y_2X_2^2$

Select input values from the problems you have dealt with in this chapter. Use the programs in A, B, C to solve for the missing variable X_1.

Problem Solving

Prove that if a varies directly with b when c is constant and if a varies directly with c when b is constant when a varies directly with bc when both b and c vary.

▶ **Calculator Tips** give you practice with your calculator.

▶ **Computer Tips** will help you learn about micro computers.

Extension Features

Math Tips

Do you like learning shortcuts? Are you interested in who "invented" mathematics? *Math Tips* are for you! They are in every chapter.

1 Concepts, Processes and Polynomials

The importance of the language of mathematics, skills with exponents, meaning of process of mathematics, skills with polynomials; addition, subtraction, multiplication, division, applications and problem-solving, using calculators

Introduction

In studying mathematics, the skills and concepts you learn are applied to solving problems. You use

Skills and concepts you learn are extended to learn new skills and concepts, which in turn provide you with other methods and strategies for solving problems.

The study of mathematics and the process of studying and learning mathematics takes on many aspects. For example:

- When people develop mathematics their results are often named after them in their honour.
- The main purpose of mathematics is to solve problems.
- Often a skill or strategy in mathematics is developed to solve a particular problem. This skill then often extends to solving problems that were not originally intended.
- Skills in mathematics can be used to study the applications of mathematics.
- The development of mathematics has often been furthered by the question. *What if . . .?*
- Patterns play an important role in the study of mathematics. Often they suggest strategies for solving problems or developing skills.

Throughout your study of mathematics you will gain insights into the aspects above and also into other aspects which will be presented to you.

1.1 Language of Mathematics

It is important to learn the vocabulary of mathematics in order to learn the skills needed to work with algebra.

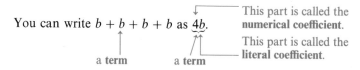

You can write $b + b + b + b$ as $4b$.

a term   a term

Here, you are adding terms.

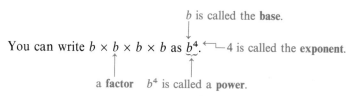

b is called the **base**.

You can write $b \times b \times b \times b$ as b^4. ⟵ 4 is called the **exponent**.

a **factor** b^4 is called a **power**.

Here, you are multiplying factors.

Special words are used to describe algebraic expressions that consist of sums and differences of terms.

Vocabulary   *Example*

*mono*mial ⟵ 1 term ⟶ $4x, 2x^2, 3mn$
*bi*nomial ⟵ 2 terms ⟶ $4x - 3y, 3a^2 + 7, 3x^4 - 6x$
*tri*nomial ⟵ 3 terms ⟶ $3x^2 - 2x + 1, a + b - c$

The above expressions are known collectively as **polynomials**.

In the following algebraic expression, x is called a **variable**. A variable is a placeholder for any member of a given set. The given set is called the **domain**.

$$3x + 4, \quad x \in \{-1, 0, 1, 2\}$$ This set is the domain of the variable x.

x is a variable.

You may evaluate the expression $3x + 4$ for the domain $x \in \{-1, 0, 1\}$.

$x = -1$	$x = 0$	$x = 1$
$3x + 4$	$3x + 4$	$3x + 4$
$= 3(-1) + 4$	$= 3(0) + 4$	$= 3(1) + 4$
$= -3 + 4$	$= 0 + 4$	$= 3 + 4$
$= 1$	$= 4$	$= 7$

When evaluating an expression, you must follow the rules for the order of the operations.

> **Rules for the Order of the Operations**
> 1. Do the calculations within the brackets.
> 2. Then calculate the powers first.
> 3. Then do the multiplications and divisions in the order they appear from left to right.
> 4. Then do the additions and subtractions in the order they appear from left to right.

Example 1 Calculate

(a) $3(8 + 4 - 3)$ (b) $3(8^2 - 2 \times 3)$ (c) $\dfrac{3^2 - 2^3}{8 \div (24 \div 3)}$

Solution

(a)
$$3(8 + 4 - 3)$$
$$= 3(12 - 3)$$
$$= 3(9)$$
$$= 27$$

(b)
$$3(8^2 - 2 \times 3)$$
$$= 3(64 - 6)$$
$$= 3(58)$$
$$= 174$$

(c)
$$\frac{3^2 - 2^3}{8 \div (24 \div 3)} = \frac{9 - 8}{8 \div (8)}$$
$$= \frac{1}{1} = 1$$

The same expression may be evaluated for different values of the variables as shown in the following example.

Example 2 Evaluate $4a + b^2$. Use

(a) $a = 3, b = -2$ (b) $a = -2, b = 3$

Solution

(a) Use $a = 3, b = -2$.
$$4a + b^2 = 4(3) + (-2)^2$$
$$= 12 + 4$$
$$= 16$$

(b) Use $a = -2, b = 3$.   ⌐Use brackets
$$4a + b^2 = 4(-2) + (3)^2 \quad \text{when substituting}$$
$$= -8 + 9 \qquad \text{the value.}$$
$$= 1$$

Symbols are used to write mathematics in a compact form.

Equations	Inequalities
$16 \div 4 + 4 = 8$	$3^2 > 2^3$
$5^2 - 4^2 = 9$	$8 \div 4 - 2 < 3(12 - 3)$

The symbol $\neq$ means "not equal to."

Example 3   Show whether the following are true or false.

A $\quad 8 - (-4 + 1) > 5 + 16 \div 4$ B $\quad \dfrac{1}{2}\left(\dfrac{12 + 3}{20 - 5}\right) \neq \dfrac{12 \div 2}{16 - 4}$

Solution   A $\text{LS} = 8 - (-4 + 1)$

$= 8 - (-3)$

$= 8 + 3 = 11$

$\text{RS} = 5 + 16 \div 4$

$= 5 + 4 = 9$

Since LS > RS then A is true.

B $\text{LS} = \dfrac{1}{2}\left(\dfrac{12 + 3}{20 - 5}\right) \qquad \text{RS} = \dfrac{12 \div 2}{16 - 4}$

$= \dfrac{1}{2}\left(\dfrac{15}{15}\right) \qquad\qquad = \dfrac{6}{12} = \dfrac{1}{2}$

$= \dfrac{1}{2}(1) = \dfrac{1}{2}$

Since LS = RS then B is false.

1.1   Exercise

A 1   Calculate.

(a) $2(6^2 - 3 \times 4)$ (b) $4^2 \times 6 \div (2^2 + 2^2)$ (c) $\dfrac{4^2 - 3^2}{(4^2 + 6 \times 2) \div 4}$

(d) $\dfrac{9 + 3 \times 3}{5^2 - (4^2 - 3^2)}$ (e) $\dfrac{9 \div (2^2 - 3)}{12 \div (6 - 2)}$ (f) $\dfrac{2(1^2 + 2^2 + 3^2)}{16 \div (8 - 2^2)}$

2   Evaluate each expression for the given value of the variable.

(a) $y^2 + y, \quad y = 2$ (b) $x^2 - 3x, \quad x = -1$

(c) $y^2 - 2y + 1, \quad y = -2$ (d) $3x^2 - 2x + 1, \quad x = -3$

3   Find the values of each expression.

(a) $2x + 5, \quad x \in \{-1, 0, 1, 2\}$ (b) $8 - 3y, \quad y \in \{-2, -1, 0, 1\}$

(c) $3p^2 - 1, \quad p \in \{-1, 0, 1\}$ (d) $\dfrac{m^2 - 6m + 9}{m - 3}, \quad m \in \{-1, 0, 1\}$

(e) $(k + 1)(k - 1), \quad k \in \{-1, 0, 1\}$

4   Use a chart or table of values to record the values of the variable and of the expression. Copy and complete each table of values.

(a)
y	$y^2 + 2y$
-1	-1
0	?
1	?
2	?
3	?

(b)
m	$3m^2 - 3m$
-2	?
-1	?
0	?
1	?

(c)
x	$x^2 - 3x + 1$
-1	?
0	?
1	?
2	?

5   If $a = 0$, $b = 1$, $c = -1$, and $d = 2$, find the value of each expression.
    (a) $a + 2b$ (b) $b + 3c$ (c) $3b + 2c - d$
    (d) $9b + cd$ (e) $2a^2 + b^2 - d^2$ (f) $ad - bc$
    (g) $a^2 - 2bc - ad$ (h) $2ab + a^2 - b^2$ (i) $d^2 + b^2 - a^2 - c^2$

B 6   An inequality is given by $4(3 - 1) - \dfrac{1}{2} \ne 3^2 - 2(3 - 2)$.

   (a) Calculate the LS (Left Side).   (b) Calculate the RS (Right Side).
   (c) Is the inequality true or false?

7   An inequality is given by $\left(\dfrac{3}{2}\right)\left(\dfrac{1}{3}\right) + 3 > \left(\dfrac{15}{3}\right)\left(\dfrac{3}{2}\right) - 4$.

   (a) Calculate the LS (Left Side).   (b) Calculate the RS (Right Side).
   (c) Is the inequality true or false?

8   Which of the following are true, (T)? Which are false, (F)?

   (a) $3 - (-2 + 1) \le 5 + (-1)$ (b) $3 + \dfrac{4 + 5}{3} = \dfrac{3 + 5}{4} + 3$

   (c) $\dfrac{1}{4} + \dfrac{3}{5} < \dfrac{4}{9}$ (d) $7 + \dfrac{3}{2} \times \dfrac{1}{3} \ge \dfrac{15}{3} \times \dfrac{3}{2}$ (e) $\dfrac{1}{2} + \dfrac{3}{4} = \dfrac{3}{2} - \dfrac{1}{4}$

   Questions 9 to 11 are based on the following formula.

   The formula for the average mass of a normal adult male is

   $$m = \frac{25(h - 100)}{26}$$

   where m is his mass in kilograms and h is his height in centimetres.

9   (a) Find the mass of an adult male who is 175 cm tall.
   (b) Jackson has a mass of 65 kg. According to the formula, what should be his height?

10   Medical students are carrying out an experiment to see if the formula above is reasonably accurate. The first person in the experiment has a mass of 74 kg.
   (a) What should be the height of this male if the formula is accurate?
   (b) If the male's height is actually 176 cm, how would you assess the formula, based on this single example?

11   The tallest man ever is Robert Wadlow, born in Alton, Illinois. He stood at 272 cm.
   (a) Use the formula to find Wadlow's expected mass at this height.
   (b) His actual mass at this height was 199.5 kg. Can you account for the difference?

1.2 Working with Exponents

You can write the product

$(a)(a)(a)(a)$ as a^4. ←——— 4 is called the exponent.

factors

The exponent tells *how many* factors to multiply.

a is called the *base*.

Exponents occur frequently in your work in mathematics.

Area *A*, of a circle, radius *r*

$$A = \pi r^2$$

You say *r* squared or the second power of *r*.

Volume *V*, of sphere, radius *r*

$$V = \frac{4}{3}\pi r^3$$

You say *r* cubed, or the third power of *r*.

Exponents occur in many subjects. For example:

- The growth of bacteria involves exponents.
- The distance fallen by an object under the influence of gravity is exponential.
- The growth of money is exponential.

Once the definition of exponent is introduced in mathematics, you then examine the properties of exponents. For example, these specific examples suggest the laws of exponents.

Specific Examples

A $a^3 \times a^2 = (a \times a \times a)(a \times a) = a^5$

B $\dfrac{a^5}{a^2} = \dfrac{a \times a \times a \times a \times a}{a \times a} = a^3$

3 factors

C $(a^2)^3 = (a^2)(a^2)(a^2)$
$ = (a \times a)(a \times a)(a \times a) = a^6$

3 factors

D $(ab)^3 = (ab)(ab)(ab)$
$ = (a \times a \times a)(b \times b \times b) = a^3 b^3$

E $\left(\dfrac{a}{b}\right)^3 = \left(\dfrac{a}{b}\right)\left(\dfrac{a}{b}\right)\left(\dfrac{a}{b}\right) = \dfrac{a \times a \times a}{b \times b \times b} = \dfrac{a^3}{b^3}$

> **Laws of Exponents**
>
> A   Multiplication $a^m \times a^n = a^{m+n}$
> B   Division $a^m \div a^n = a^{m-n}$
> C   Power $(a^m)^n = a^{mn}$
> D   Power of a Product $(ab)^m = a^m b^m$
>
> E   Power of Quotient $\left(\dfrac{a}{b}\right)^m = \dfrac{a^m}{b^m}$

The laws of exponents can then be used to simplify algebraic expressions as shown in the following example.

Example 1   Simplify each of the following.

(a) $x^3 \times x^2 \times x$ (b) $y^5 \div y^3$ (c) $(m^2)^3$ (d) $(ab)^3$ (e) $\left(\dfrac{m}{n}\right)^4$

Solution

(a) $x^3 \times x^2 \times x$ Multiplication
$= x^{3+2+1}$ Law
$= x^6$

(b) $y^5 \div y^3$ Division
$= y^{5-3}$ Law
$= y^2$

(c) $(m^2)^3 = m^{2 \times 3}$ Power law
$= m^6$

(d) $(ab)^3 = a^3 b^3$ Power of a Product Law

(e) $\left(\dfrac{m}{n}\right)^4 = \dfrac{m^4}{n^4}$ Power of Quotient Law

In the following example, the laws of exponents are combined to simplify expressions. Your earlier skill of collecting like terms is used to simplify expressions that contain exponents.

Example 2   Simplify   (a) $\dfrac{a^3(b^2)^2}{a^2}\left(\dfrac{a}{b}\right)^3$ (b) $\dfrac{m^{3p+q}m^{3q+p}}{(m^p)^2}$.

Solution

(a) $\dfrac{a^3(b^2)^2}{a^2}\left(\dfrac{a}{b}\right)^3$

$= \dfrac{a^3 b^4}{a^2} \times \dfrac{a^3}{b^3}$

$= \dfrac{a^{3+3}b^4}{a^2 b^3}$

$= a^{6-2}b^{4-3}$

$= a^4 b$

(b) Apply the laws of exponents to rewrite the expression.

$\dfrac{m^{3p+q}m^{3q+p}}{(m^p)^2} = \dfrac{m^{3p+q}m^{3q+p}}{m^{2p}}$

$= \dfrac{m^{4p+4q}}{m^{2p}}$

$\begin{aligned} &3p+q+(3q+p) \\ &= 3p+q+3q+p \\ &= 4p+4q \end{aligned}$

$= m^{4p+4q-2p}$

$= m^{2p+4q}$

1.2 Exercise

A 1 Simplify each of the following. Write with a single base.

(a) $m^3 \times m^2$ (b) $p^4 \times p^3$ (c) $p^2 \times p^3 \times p^4$

(d) $x^3 \times x^2$ (e) $w^3 \times w^5$ (f) 2×2^3

(g) $10^2 \times 10^3$ (h) $(-1)^3(-1)^2$ (i) $(-1)^4(-1)^5$

(j) $(-2)^3(-2)^2$ (k) $(-x)^3(-x)^7$ (l) $(-y)^2(-y)^2$

(m) $(x^{3p})(x^p)$ (n) $y^{2x} \div y^x$ (o) $(m^{3x})(m^{2x})$

2 Remove the brackets from each of the following.

(a) $(3^2)^3$ (b) $(2^3)^2$ (c) $(a^3)^2$ (d) $(y^2)^4$

(e) $[(-1)^3]^2$ (f) $[(-a)^3]^2$ (g) $(my)^2$ (h) $(m^2y)^2$

(i) $(my^2)^3$ (j) $\left(\dfrac{a^2}{b}\right)^3$ (k) $\left(\dfrac{b}{a^2}\right)^2$ (l) $(p^3q^2)^4$

(m) $(w^3xy^2)^3$ (n) $k^2 \times k^4 \times k^2$ (o) $\left(\dfrac{x^2y}{z}\right)^3$ (p) $\left(\dfrac{p^3}{qr^4}\right)^4$

3 Simplify each of the following.

(a) $y^8 \times y^2 \div y^6$ (b) $x^8 \times x^4 \div x^2$ (c) $(m^3)^4 \div m^2$

(d) $(y^3)^2(y^2)^3$ (e) $\left(\dfrac{1}{p^2}\right)^3 (p^3)^2 \div \left(\dfrac{1}{p}\right)^2$ (f) $(s^3)^2 \div s(s^4)^2$

4 Which of the following of each pair is greater? By how much?

(a) $2^3; 3^2$ (b) $3^4; 4^3$ (c) $2^5; 5^2$ (d) $2^4; 4^2$ (e) $5^3; 3^5$

5 Express each of the following as a power of 2. The first one is done for you.

(a) $4^2 = (2^2)^2 = 2^4$ (b) $2^8 \div 2^5$ (c) $2^7 \times 2^5 \div 2^6$ (d) $4^2 \times 2^3$

(e) 8^3 (f) $\left(\dfrac{4}{2}\right)^3$ (g) $(2^m)^3$ (h) $(2^p)^3(2^p)^2$

(i) $32^4 \div 8^3$ (j) 8^{p+1} (k) $4^{2m} \div 2^m$ (l) $\left(\dfrac{16}{2}\right)^m \div (2^m)^2$

(m) 4^{2k+1} (n) 16^{2p-1} (o) $16^{4p} \div 4^{2p+1}$

6 Use $m = -2$ and $n = 1$ to evaluate each of the following.

(a) mn^2 (b) m^2n (c) m^2n^2 (d) $(mn)^2$ (e) m^3n^3 (f) $(mn)^3$

7 Use $x = 4$ and $y = -2$ to evaluate each of the following.

(a) $\dfrac{x^3}{y}$ (b) $\dfrac{x}{y^3}$ (c) $\dfrac{x^3}{y^3}$ (d) $\left(\dfrac{x}{y}\right)^3$ (e) $\dfrac{3x}{y}$ (f) $\dfrac{x}{3y}$

8 (a) Use $x = -3$, $y = 2$ to evaluate expressions A and B.

A: $\dfrac{y^2}{x}\left(\dfrac{x}{y}\right)^3$

B: $\dfrac{x^2}{y}$

(b) Why are the answers in (a) the same?

9 (a) To evaluate $\dfrac{x^3}{y}\left(\dfrac{y}{x}\right)^2 \div \dfrac{y^3}{x}$ when $x = -4$, $y = 3$, what might be your first step?

(b) Evaluate the expression in (a).

B 10 Indicate whether each of the following is true, (T), or false, (F). Be prepared to justify your answer.

(a) $3^3 \times 3^3 = 3^6$

(b) $(5^2)^3 = 5^6$

(c) $9^5 \div 9^4 = 9$

(d) $(-3)^3(-3)^4 = (3)^7$

(e) $(3a^4)^2 = 6a^8$

(f) $\dfrac{27^3}{9^3} = 3^3$

(g) $(5^3)^2 = 3125$

(h) $\left(\dfrac{4}{2}\right)^2 = 2^2$

(i) $\dfrac{27^3}{9^3} = 27$

(j) $(a^2b)^4 = a^8b^4$

(k) $a^n b^n = (ab)^{2n}$

(l) $x^m y^m = (xy)^{m+n}$

(m) $a^x a^y a^{x-y} = a^{2x}$

(n) $\left(\dfrac{x}{py}\right)^c = \dfrac{x^c}{py^c}$

(o) $(x^m y^n)^2 = x^{2m} y^{2n}$

11 Write
(a) $3^5 \times 3^2 \times 3^4$ as a power of 3.
(b) $5^2 \times 5^3 \div 5^2$ as a power of 5.
(c) $2^2 \times 2^3 \div 2$ as a power of 2.
(d) $\dfrac{10^4 \times 10^2}{10^5}$ as a power of 10.
(e) $2^x \times 2^{x+1}$ as a power of 2.
(f) $3^{y-1} \times 3^{y+2}$ as a power of 3.

12 Express each of the following with a single base.
(a) $p^{x+y} p^x$

(b) $y^{2x-p} \div y^p$

(c) $(p^x)^2 (p^3)^x$

(d) $p^{3x-1} \div (p^x)^2$

(e) $(p^3)^m \div p^{2m}$

(f) $\dfrac{a^m}{(a^2)^m}$

(g) $x^{a+b} x^{b+c} x^{a-c}$

(h) $y^{2a-b} y^{b-2c} \div y^{a+b}$

13 Calculate each of the following if $a = 4$, $b = -2$.
(a) $\dfrac{(ab)^2}{ab}$

(b) $\dfrac{3(a^2b)^2}{(a^2)^2}$

(c) $\dfrac{a^2(b^2)^3}{b^3}$

(d) $(a^2)^3 \left(\dfrac{a}{b}\right)^3$

(e) $(a^2b)^3 \left(\dfrac{a}{b}\right)^2$

(f) $\dfrac{a^2 b^3 (ab)^3}{a^2 b}$

14 Express each of the following with a single base.

(a) $\left(\dfrac{a}{b^2}\right)^3 (ab^3)^2$ (b) $(mn^6)\left(\dfrac{m}{n^3}\right)^2$ (c) $(a^k)^2(a^3)^k$

(d) $(x^p)^3 \div (x^p)^2$ (e) $m^k m^{k+2} m^{k+3}$ (f) $\dfrac{p^k(p^{3k})^2}{p^k}$

15 Evaluate each of the following if $a = -2$, $k = 1$.
(a) $(a^3)^k(a^k)^2 a^{2k-1}$ (b) $a^k \times a^{2k-1} \div a^{3k+1}$ (c) $(a^k)^2(a^2)^k \div a^{2k+3}$

C 16 For $y = 2$, $k = 1$, which expression has the greater value, A or B?

A $\dfrac{y^{2k} y^{k+2}}{(y^2)^k}$

B $\dfrac{(y^k)^3 y^{2k-1}}{(y^k)^3}$

17 Simplify each of the following.

(a) $(b^{p+1})^2 \times b^3 \div (b^p)^3$ (b) $\dfrac{p^{3b+2}(p^{b-1})^2}{(p^{b+1})^3}$

(c) Find the value of each of the above when $b = 2$, $p = -1$.

Math Tip

The operation symbols (as well as many others) are intended to simplify the writing and reading of mathematics.

$+, -$ These symbols appeared in print for the first time in 1489, in an arithmetic book.

$=$ This symbol was used for the first time in 1557. The mathematician Robert Recorde used two equal parallel lines ($=$) "because no things can be more equal".

$<, >$ These symbols, first used by Thomas Harriot (1560–1621), were not accepted as suitable symbols by others at the time.

$\times$ The symbol for multiplication was introduced by William Oughtred (1574–1660) but it was not readily adopted since it too closely resembled the variable x.

Problem Solving

Before going on a spare, Michael looked at his watch. After the spare, he noted that the hour hand and the minute hand had exchanged places. How long was the spare?

Applications: Exponents and Pollution

To clean the exhaust from the furnace of a plant, the exhaust is continuously passed through electronic air cleaners. The amount of pollutants left in the exhaust after passing through the air cleaner n times is given by

$$8\left(\frac{1}{2}\right)^n \text{ units.}$$

18   (a) Calculate the amount of pollutants remaining in the exhaust for $n = 1$, $n = 2$, and $n = 3$.

      (b) What is happening to the amount of pollutant in the exhaust as n increases?

19   One factory requires that the amount of pollutants going into the air should not exceed 0.005 units. Find the required value of n.

20   The exhaust from a blast furnace is passed through the air cleaner 9 times.

      (a) Use the above expression. What is the amount of pollutant that goes into the air?

      (b) What is the value of n?

21   At an industrial complex, the amount of pollutants left in the exhaust after passing through the electronic gas cleaner n times is given by the expression

$$6.8(0.63)^n \text{ units.}$$

      (a) Calculate the amount of pollutants remaining in the exhaust for $n = 1$, 2, and 3.

      (b) As n increases, describe the effect on the amount of pollutant in the exhaust.

22   At site A of the industrial complex, it is requested that the amount of pollutants in the exhaust be less than 0.000 25 units. For what value of n will this value be achieved?

1.3 Meaning in Mathematics: x^0 and x^{-m}

In the previous section you established that, for a real number base, a, where $m, n \in N$.

$$a^m a^n = a^{m+n}$$

In the study of mathematics, the question "What if . . .?" is often asked, and in finding the answer, new skills and concepts are developed. For example: "What if the exponent is zero?" Thus, since

$$a^m a^0 = a^{m+0} = a^m$$

then you must define $a^0 = 1$.

Another question that can be asked is: "What if the exponent is negative?" Thus, since

$$a^m a^{-m} = a^{m+(-m)} = a^0 = 1$$

then you must define

$$a^{-m} = \frac{1}{a^m} \quad \text{and} \quad a^m = \frac{1}{a^{-m}}, \quad a \neq 0$$

Thus, $2^0 = 1$, $3^0 = 1$, $(0.5)^0 = 1$, $2^{-1} = \frac{1}{2^1} = \frac{1}{2}$, $2^{-2} = \frac{1}{2^2} = \frac{1}{4}$

Once you have established an understanding of zero and negative exponents you can simplify expressions as shown in the following example.

Example   Find the value of $4^0 + 2^{-2} - 3^0 + 2^{-1}$.

Solution $4^0 + 2^{-2} - 3^0 + 2^{-1} = 1 + \dfrac{1}{2^2} - 1 + \dfrac{1}{2^1}$

$$= 1 + \frac{1}{4} - 1 + \frac{1}{2} = \frac{3}{4}$$

1.3   Exercise

A 1   Find the value of each of the following.
(a) 4^0 (b) 4^{-3} (c) -100^0 (d) -27^0 (e) -2^{-4}
(f) -1.5^0 (g) -100^{-2} (h) $(0.04)^0$ (i) $(0.03)^4$

2   Evaluate.

(a) $2^2 \times 2^{-1}$ (b) $3^{-2} \times 3^0$ (c) $\left(\dfrac{1}{2}\right)^2 \times 2^{-2}$

(d) $4^0 \times 0.3^2$ (e) $(0.001)^0 \times (0.04)^2 \times (0.2)^{-4}$

B 3 Simplify each of the following.

(a) $m^3 \times m^2 \times m^{-1}$ (b) $x^4 \times x^5 \times x^0$ (c) $p^{-2} \times p^3 \times p^4$

(d) $2^3 \times 2^{-2} \times 2^0$ (e) $10^3 \times 10^{-1} \times 10^0$ (f) $(-3)^2(-3)^{-2}(-3)^0$

(g) $(3^{-2})^3$ (h) $[(-a)^3]^{-2}$ (i) $\left(\dfrac{b}{a^{-2}}\right)^2$ (j) $\left(\dfrac{x^{-1}}{y}\right)^{-5}$ (k) $\left(\dfrac{a^2}{2^2}\right)^{-3}$

4 Simplify each of the following.

(a) $\dfrac{3^{-1}}{2^{-1}}$ (b) $3^{-1} + 2^{-1}$ (c) $\dfrac{2^{-1} + 3^{-1}}{6^{-1}}$ (d) $\dfrac{2^{-1}}{2^{-2} - 2^{-3}}$ (e) $\dfrac{2^{-1} - 2^{-3}}{3^{-1} - 2^{-1}}$

5 Express each of the following with a single base.

(a) $\left(\dfrac{a}{b}\right)^{-3}(ab^3)^2$ (b) $(mn^6)\left(\dfrac{m}{n^{-3}}\right)^{-2}$ (c) $(x^k)^{-2}(-x^{-3})^k$ (d) $(x^p)^{-3} \div (x^{-p})^2$

(e) $\left(\dfrac{-b}{a}\right)^{-2}\left(\dfrac{a}{-b}\right)^2$ (f) $\dfrac{(ab^{-1})^3}{a^{-2}}\left(\dfrac{a}{b}\right)^{-3}$ (g) $\dfrac{p^{-k}(p^{3k})^{-2}}{p^0}$

6 Find the value of each of the following if $a = 1$, $b = 2$, $k = 2$.

(a) ab^k (b) $a^k b$ (c) $(ab)^k$ (d) $(ab)^{-k}$ (e) $(-ab)^k$

(f) $(a^{-1}b^{-2})^k$ (g) $(a^{-1}b^{-2})^{-k}$ (h) $(a^k b^k)^k$ (i) $(a^3 b^2)^k$ (j) $a^{-k}(b^k)^3$

7 Express each of the following with positive exponents.

(a) $a^3 b^{-2}$ (b) $\dfrac{3ab^{-2}}{4m^{-2}}$ (c) $\dfrac{3^{-1}a^2 b}{c^{-2}}$ (d) $\dfrac{(5a)^{-1}b}{c^{-2}}$ (e) $\dfrac{a^{-3}b^{-2}}{m^{-1}}$

C 8 For $p = 2$, $k = -1$, which expression has the greater value?

(a) $\dfrac{p^{-2k}p^{-k+2}}{(p^{-2})^k}$ (b) $\dfrac{(p^k)^{-3}p^{-(1-2k)}}{(p^{-k})^3}$

Problem Solving

Blaise Pascal used what he knew to develop what he did not know. Historically, many people have used this method to develop important achievements, not only in mathematics, but also in medicine, science, and astronomy.

$(x + 1)^0 = 1$
$(x + 1) = x + 1$
$(x + 1)^2 = x^2 + 2x + 1$
$(x + 1)^3 = x^3 + 3x^2 + 3x + 1$
$(x + 1)^4 = \qquad ?$
$(x + 1)^5 = \qquad ?$

```
            1
          1   1
        1   2   1
      1   3   3   1
```

Can you continue the next two rows?

1.4 Process of Mathematics: Proving Laws

Many years ago, Copernicus, the founder of modern astronomy, theorized that the sun is at the centre of the planetary system and that the earth and the other planets revolve about it. His theory was based on his many observations while studying the motions of the planets. He arrived at his conclusions *inductively*.

These are the rings of Saturn as photographed from Pioneer 11. Without a telescope, Copernicus could see Saturn but not the rings.

In mathematics, you may also make statements inductively. For example, if you try values of x for $x^2 + x + 41$ it appears that $x^2 + x + 41$ gives values that are prime numbers.

$$x = 1 \quad x^2 + x + 41 = (1)^2 + (1) + 41$$
$$= 1 + 1 + 41$$
$$= 43, \text{ a prime number}$$
$$x = 2 \quad x^2 + x + 41 = (2)^2 + (2) + 41$$
$$= 4 + 2 + 41$$
$$= 47, \text{ a prime number}$$

However, you cannot conclude that $x^2 + x + 41$ represents only prime numbers. (In fact it does not. Try $x = 41$.)

In mathematics, before you can deduce facts or laws, you must understand definitions. Initially, the laws of exponents were suggested inductively by numerical examples. For example, if you remember the definition of a^m,

then since $a^m = \underbrace{a \times a \times a \times \cdots \times a}_{m \text{ factors}}$

and since $a^n = \underbrace{a \times a \times a \times \cdots \times a}_{n \text{ factors}}, m, n \in W$

then $a^m a^n = \underbrace{(a \times a \times a \times \cdots \times a)}_{m \text{ factors}}\underbrace{(a \times a \times a \times \cdots \times a)}_{n \text{ factors}}$ ←——Use the definition again.

$= a^{m+n}$ ←——Use the definition.

Thus $a^m a^n = a^{m+n}$.

1.4 Exercise

A 1   Use the definition of a^m to deduce the law of exponents that for all m, n whole numbers, $m > n$,
$$a^m \div a^n = a^{m-n}.$$

2   Prove that $(a^m)^n = a^{mn}$ for all whole numbers m, n.

3   Deduce that for a, b, real numbers
$$(ab)^n = a^n b^n \quad \text{for all whole numbers, } n.$$

4   Show that for all real numbers a, b
$$\left(\frac{a}{b}\right)^n = \frac{a^n}{b^n} \quad \text{for all whole numbers } n.$$

B   Each of these instructions would accomplish the same result.
- Prove that . . . .
- Show that . . . .
- Deduce that . . . .

5   Show that $\left(\dfrac{ab}{c}\right)^n = \dfrac{a^n b^n}{c^n}$ for all $n \in W$.

6   If $n \in W$, prove that $(abc)^n = a^n b^n c^n$.

7   Deduce that $a^n \times a^n \times a^n = a^{3n}$ for all $n \in W$.

8   Deduce that for all whole numbers, n, m, p, $\dfrac{a^n a^m}{a^p} = a^{n+m-p}$.

9   The following results suggest facts that can be proved about expressions involving the base (-1). Calculate each of the following.
(a) $(-1)^{12}(-1)^{11}$ (b) $(-1)^{15} \div (-1)^{12}$ (c) $(-1)^{20}(-1)^3(-1)^2$
(d) $\dfrac{(-1)^{12}(-1)^5}{(-1)^3}$ (e) $\dfrac{(-1)^6(-1)^8}{(-1)^3(-1)^9}$ (f) $\dfrac{(-1)^3(-1)^5}{(-1)^4} \div (-1)^3$

10   The following results are suggested by the previous question.
(a) Prove that for n an even number, the value of $(-1)^n$ is 1.
(b) Prove that for n an odd number, the value of $(-1)^n$ is -1.
(c) Prove that for m and n even numbers, $(-1)^m(-1)^n$ is positive.
(d) Prove that for consecutive whole numbers m and n, $(-1)^m(-1)^n$ is negative.

1.5 Adding and Subtracting Polynomials

Like terms have the same literal coefficients. **Unlike terms** have different literal coefficients.

like terms: $2x, 3x, -4x, 5x$ **unlike terms:** $3x, -4y, 6x^2, 2xy$

The literal coefficients are the same.   The literal coefficients are different.

To **simplify** expressions, you may collect like terms.

$$12x + 8y - 3x - 5y = 12x - 3x + 8y - 5y$$
$$= 9x + 3y$$

Example 1   Simplify   Simplify means collect like terms.

$(4x + 2y) - (2x - 5y)$.

Solution

$(4x + 2y) - (2x - 5y)$ ⟵ The opposite of $2x - 5y$ is written
$= 4x + 2y - 2x + 5y$ $-(2x - 5y) = -2x + 5y$
$= 4x - 2x + 2y + 5y$ ⟵
$= 2x + 7y$ ⟵   This step would be done mentally.
                $4x - 2x = 2x$
                $2y + 5y = 7y$

Since $2x$ and $7y$ are unlike terms, you cannot simplify further.

When you have to evaluate an expression, you will require fewer calculations if you simplify it first, as shown in the following example.

Example 2   Evaluate $(2a + b - c) + (a - b) - (a - 3b + c)$ for $a = -1$, $b = 2$, $c = -3$.

Solution   Simplify the expression first.

                                     Think:

     $(2a + b - c) + (a - b) - (a - 3b + c)$ Record the given expression.
   $= 2a + b - c + a - b - a + 3b - c$ The expressions
   $= 2a + 3b - 2c$ $(2a + b - c) + (a - b) - (a - 3b + c)$
                                       and $2a + 3b - 2c$ are equivalent
                                       since they are equal for different
                                       values of the variables a, b, and c.

Use $a = -1$, $b = 2$, $c = -3$.

$$2a + 3b - 2c = 2(-1) + 3(2) - 2(-3)$$
$$= -2 + 6 + 6$$
$$= 10$$

Very often, when doing mathematics, you need to know the meanings of special words. To do the following question, you need to know that x^3, x^2, and x are descending powers of x.

Example 3   Simplify and write the resulting expression in descending powers of x.

$$4x(x - 2) - 3(x^2 - 2x + 1) - 3(x - 5)$$

Solution

$$4x(x - 2) - 3(x^2 - 2x + 1) - 3(x - 5)$$
$$= 4x^2 - 8x - 3x^2 + 6x - 3 - 3x + 15$$
$$= 4x^2 - 3x^2 - 8x + 6x - 3x - 3 + 15$$
$$= x^2 - 5x + 12$$

Often, you need to simplify expressions that involve more than one set of brackets.

Example 4   (a) Simplify $4 - 2\,[3x + 5(1 - x)]$.
                    (b) Evaluate the expression in (a) for $x = -2$.

Solution   (a) $4 - 2[3x + 5(1 - x)]$ Simplify the   (b) Use $x = -2$.
                        $= 4 - 2[3x + 5 - 5x]$ inner brackets $4x - 6 = 4(-2) - 6$
                        $= 4 - 2[-2x + 5]$ first. $= -8 - 6$
                        $= 4 + 4x - 10$ $= -14$
                        $= 4x - 6$

1.5 Exercise

A   Questions 1 to 12 practise skills for adding and subtracting polynomial expressions.

1   Write each as a single term.
  (a) $m + m + m + m$ (b) $x + 3x + 2x$
  (c) $5y - 2y + 3y$ (d) $8y - 11y - 3y$
  (e) $12p - 6p + 6p$ (f) $-3q - 2q - q$
  (g) $p - 3p + 5p$ (h) $-r + 3r + r$

2   Simplify each of the following.
  (a) $2x - 3y + 5x$ (b) $3a - 2b + 6a$
  (c) $3x^2 - 2x + 5x^2$ (d) $3xy - y^2 + 2xy$
  (e) $3x + 2x - y + 4y$ (f) $6x - 3x + x + 2y - y + 3y$
  (g) $3x - 2y + 5x + 5y$ (h) $3m + p - 2m + p + 3m$
  (i) $p + 3q - 3q + 3p - 2p$

3   Simplify each of the following.
    (a) $(x + 2y) + (x + 3y)$
    (b) $(p + 2q) - (p + q)$
    (c) $(3m - 2n) - (m + 3n)$
    (d) $(3u + 2w) + (2u - 3w)$
    (e) $(2p - 3q + 5r) - (3p - 2q - 2r)$
    (f) $(x^2 - 3x) - (x^2 - 2x)$
    (g) $(2x^2 - 3x + 5) - (4x^2 - 3x + 5)$

4   (a) Simplify $(2a - 3b) - (3a + b)$.
    (b) Simplify $-(3a - b) + 2a - 5b$.
    (c) Why are the answers to (a) and (b) called equivalent expressions?

B 5   Evaluate each expression if $a = -3, b = 2, c = -1$.
    (a) $(3a - 2b) + (2a - 3c) - (b - c)$
    (b) $(2a + c) + (3a - b) - (2c - b)$
    (c) $(3a - b) - (2b - c) - (2c + a)$
    (d) $(a - b - c) - (a + b - c) - (b - a + c)$

6   Find each product.
    (a) $3(x - 5)$ (b) $-2(2y - 1)$
    (c) $-3(3a - 5)$ (d) $2(6 - 2y)$
    (e) $-3(x - 2y)$ (f) $2(2x + 5y)$
    (g) $3(2x^2 - 3x + 5)$ (h) $-3(2a^2 - 5a - 6)$

7   Expand. ← means to find each product
             Use the distributive law.
    (a) $2x(x - 1)$ (b) $-3a(a - 2)$
    (c) $2m(m^2 - 2m)$ (d) $-3y(y^2 + 4y)$
    (e) $-2t(t^2 - 2t - 1)$ (f) $-3m(m - 2m^2 - 5)$
    (g) $6ab(a^2 + 2ab)$ (h) $-3xy(x^2 + y^2)$

8   (a) Simplify $3(x - 2y) - 2(2x + y)$.
    (b) Simplify $4(x - y) - (5x + 4y)$.
    (c) Why are the answers to (a) and (b) equivalent expressions?

9   (a) What might be the first step in simplifying
    $$3[2x - 3(2x - y)] - 3(x - y)?$$
    (b) Simplify the expression in (a).

10 An operation has been left out for each. What is the missing operation shown by $*$?

(a) $x^2 * x^2 = x^4$ (b) $x^2 * x^2 = 2x^2$ (c) $2x * 2y = 4xy$

(d) $3x * 4x = 12x^2$ (e) $4y * 2y = 6y$ (f) $3k * 3k = 9k^2$

11 Decide what error has been made by a student obtaining each of the following wrong answers.

A $x^2 + x^2 \overset{?}{=} x^4$ C $x^2 \times x^2 \overset{?}{=} 2x^2$ E $3x + 2y \overset{?}{=} 5xy$

B $2x^2 + 3x^2 \overset{?}{=} 6x^4$ D $2x^2 + 3x^2 \overset{?}{=} 6x^2$ F $x^2 + x^3 \overset{?}{=} 2x^5$

12 Simplify (collect like terms).

(a) $x + 2x - 3y - x + 2y$ (b) $x^2 - 2x - 3 - 2x^2 + x + 4$

(c) $3 - ab + 2a - 3ab - 4 + 5a$ (d) $x^2 + 2xy - y^2 - 3x^2 - 6xy - 2y^2$

13 Simplify. Arrange the answers in ascending powers of x.

(a) $x^2 - 3x + 6 - 2x^2 + 5x + 7$

(b) $2x^2 - 8 - 6x^2 + x - 3 + 5x$

14 Find an expression for each perimeter.

(a)   (b)   (c)

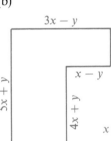

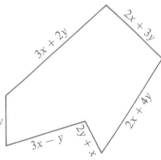

15 Simplify.

(a) $3(4x + 2) + 2(x - 1)$ (b) $2(3a - 2b) - 2(a - b)$

(c) $-2(a - 3b + 4) - 6(a - 2b + 5)$ (d) $3(x - y) - 2(4x - 5y + 6)$

(e) $-2(x^2 - 2x - 3) - (x^2 - 3x)$ (f) $3(3a^2 - 4) - 2(a^2 - 2a - 5)$

16 Simplify. Arrange the answers in ascending powers of y.

(a) $4(y^2 - 2y + 5) - 3(3y^2 - 4y - 6)$

(b) $y(y - 3) - 2y(y + 6) - 6(y - 3)$

(c) $3(y^2 - 1) - 2y(y - 5) - 3y(y - 2)$

17 Simplify each of the following. Which expressions are equivalent?
   (a) $-3(a - b) - 2(b - a) - (a + b)$
   (b) $2(3a - 2b) - 3(a - 5b) - 2a$
   (c) $2(a - 5b) - 5(b - a) - 3(a - 2b)$
   (d) $-2(2b - a) + 3(a - 2b) - (4a - 21b)$

18 Simplify each of the following.
   (a) $2x - 4 - 3[-2(x - 2) + 3]$ (b) $3[(3y - 6) + (-2y - 1)(4)]$
   (c) $b - 2[(1 - 2b) - 5(b + 3)]$

19 (a) Find the value of the expression $x[(5x - 4) - (2 - 3x)]$ if $x = -3$.
   (b) If $x = -1$, find the value of $3(x^2 - 3x - 1) - 2(2x^2 - 3x - 2)$.

20 If $x = 3$, and $y = 2$, which figure has the greater perimeter, A or B?

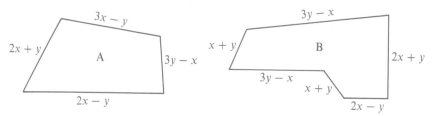

C 21 If $a = -2$, $b = 3$, which expression has the greatest value (maximum value)?
   A $3(a^2 + b^2) - 2ab - 2(a^2 - b^2)$
   B $3(a - b) - 2(b - a) + 3(a - 2b)$ C $b(a - b) - a(2b - a) - ab$

22 If $m = -1$, $n = 3$, which expression has the least value (minimum value)?
   A $2(m - n) - 3(m - 2n) - (m^2 - n^2)$
   B $3m(m - n) - 2n(m + n) - (m^2 - n^2)$
   C $2n(m - 3n) - (m^2 - 2mn) - 3(n^2 - 2mn)$

Math Tip

An important mathematical skill is learning methods of checking our work. One method is to substitute convenient values for the variable (e.g. $a = 1$, $b = 1$) in both the original expression and the simplified expression. The answers should be the same! Try this check in the above.

Applications: Parachuting and Skydiving

It is important to sky divers to know how high up in the sky they are before a jump.

Sky divers can calculate how high they are above ground using the value of this polynomial,

$$A - 4.9t^2$$

where A, in metres, is their initial height above ground and t is the time, in seconds, after the sky divers leave the plane.

If they know how high they will be when they jump and the safe stopping distance for the parachute to bring them to earth, then they will be able to calculate either how long or how far they can free-fall.

23 A skydiving group left the plane at an altitude of 4000 m. Calculate how far above the earth's surface it is after
   (a) 5 s   (b) 10 s

24 Part of the tail section of a 747 Jumbo jet, whose altitude was 3500 m, broke off and fell to the ground.
   (a) What was the height of the tail section after 25 s?
   (b) Between what two consecutive seconds did the tail section hit the ground?

25 The first stage of a rocket is dropped from an altitude of 10 000 m.
   (a) Calculate the height of the first stage after 40 s.
   (b) How far did the first stage drop in the 41st second?
   (c) If the second stage was dropped from the same height as that of the first stage after 43 s, how far apart were the two stages after 44 s?

26 Galileo dropped a large cannon ball from the Leaning Tower of Pisa which is 54.55 m tall. One second later he dropped a smaller cannon ball.
   (a) Find the height of the large cannon ball after 3 s.
   (b) How far apart were the two cannon balls after 3 s?
   (c) Were the balls the same distance apart after 2 s?

1.6 Multiplying a Polynomial by a Monomial

In mathematics, the same skills are used over and over again. You can apply the Laws of Exponents to multiply algebraic expressions by monomials.

Laws of Exponents

$a^m \times a^n = a^{m+n}$

$a^m \div a^n = a^{m-n}$

$(a^m)^n = a^{mn}$

$\left(\dfrac{a}{b}\right)^m = \dfrac{a^m}{b^m}$

$(ab)^m = a^m b^m$

Example 1 Find the product of $-4a^2b^2$ and $-2ab^3$.

Solution $(-4a^2b^2)(-2ab^3) = 8a^3b^5$

Multiply the numerical coefficients. $(-4)(-2)$

Multiply the literal coefficients.
$(a^2)(a) = a^3$
$(b^2)(b^3) = b^5$

In mathematics the Distributive Property is often used to simplify expressions

$$a(b + c) = ab + ac \qquad a(b - c) = ab - ac$$

Remember: multiplication is distributive over addition and subtraction.

Example 2 Expand each product.

(a) $6mn(3mn - 2n)$ (b) $-\dfrac{1}{2}a^4(18ab - 14b^2)$

Solution (a) $6mn(3mn - 2n) = (6mn)(3mn) - (6mn)(2n)$
$= 18m^2n^2 - 12mn^2$

(b) $-\dfrac{1}{2}a^4(18ab - 14b^2) = \left(-\dfrac{1}{2}a^4\right)(18ab) - \left(-\dfrac{1}{2}a^4\right)(14b^2)$
$= -9a^5b + 7a^4b^2$

You need to know certain vocabulary to do mathematics. For example, the **degree** of a polynomial containing one variable is the value of the exponent of the greatest power of the polynomial.

degree 1 $2x$ ←——————— Exponent of the greatest power of the variable is 1.

degree 2 $3x^2 + 2x + 5$ ＼ Exponent of the greatest power of the variable is 2.

degree 3 $4x^3 + 3$ ＼ Exponent of the greatest power is 3.

↑
This is called the **constant term**.

If a polynomial has more than one variable, then find the sum of the exponents of the variables in each term. The greatest of these sums is the degree of the polynomial.

degree 2 $xy \longleftarrow$ Sum of exponents is $1 + 1 = 2$

degree 4 $2x^2y^2 - 3x^2y + 5xy$ Greatest sum is $2 + 2 = 4$

In the following example, it is better to simplify first before evaluating the expression.

Example 3   (a) Find the product $3x^2(x + 5x^2y - 2)$.

(b) Evaluate the expression in (a) for $x = -1$ and $y = 2$.

Solution   (a) $3x^2(x + 5x^2y - 2)$
$= (3x^2)(x) + (3x^2)(5x^2y) + (3x^2)(-2)$
$= 3x^3 + 15x^4y - 6x^2$

(b) Substitute $x = -1$, $y = 2$.
$3x^3 + 15x^4y - 6x^2$
$= 3(-1)^3 + 15(-1)^4(2) - 6(-1)^2$
$= -3 + 30 - 6$
$= 21$

1.6   Exercise

A 1   Find each product.

(a) $(a^2b)(ab^2)$ (b) $(-3a^3b^2)(-2ab^3)$ (c) $(8x^2y^3)(-2xy^2)$

2   (a) Write $(-3x^2y)(-2xy^3)$ as one term.

(b) Evaluate the expression in (a) if $x = -1$, $y = 2$.

3   (a) Find the square of $-4xy$.

(b) Evaluate the expression in (a) if $x = 3$, $y = -2$.

4   Find each product. What is the degree of each polynomial?

(a) $x^2(2y^2 + 3xy)$ (b) $y(ab - a^3b^2)$ (c) $-(3m^2n + 4mn)$

(d) $-3y\left(\frac{1}{3}x^3y^2 + \frac{2}{3}xy^4\right)$ (e) $(10v^3wx - 25vw^2x^4)\left(\frac{1}{5}vwx\right)$

5   (a) Simplify $-5p^3r^2(pr + 2p^2r^2)$.

(b) Evaluate the expression in (a) for $p = -1$, $r = 2$.

6   Find each product. What is the degree of each polynomial?

(a) $p(pq + 2qr + pr)$ (b) $-3m(2mn - 3mn^2 + m^2n^3)$

(c) $(-2a + 3b - 4c)(-2abc)$ (d) $\frac{1}{2}wx(2w^2x + 6wx^2 - 3wx + 4w^2x^2)$

(e) $(3p^2 + 9p^3r^2 + 3pr - r)(5p)$

7   Write each product in simplest terms.
     (a) $(3x)(-2y)$ (b) $(3x)(-4x^2)$
     (c) $(4xy)(2xy)(3x^2y^3)$ (d) $(1 - 3ab)(2ab)$
     (e) $-2x^2y(-3xy^2 + 4xy)$ (f) $-p^2q(4p^2q^2 + pq - 3q^2)$
     (g) $(xy)(-3xy)^2$ (h) $(-2ab)(-a)(ab)$
     (i) $(-3mn)(m^2n)(-m + n)$ (j) $(-pq)(3pq)(p^2 - 2p + 1)$

B 8 Find the value of each of the following if $a = 3$, $b = -2$.
     (a) $(3ab)(-2a^2b)$ (b) $-12(a^2b - 4ab)$
     (c) $3ab^2(18a^3b^2 - 6a^2b)$ (d) $(-2ab^2)(ab)^2$
     (e) $a(b - a^2b + ab^2)$ (f) $(-3a^2b)(-2ab^2)(1 - 8ab^2)$

9   Evaluate each expression for the given values.
     (a) $-4mn(-n + 2m)$ $m = 2, n = 1$
     (b) $(-3a^2b^2)(-3 + 5a - 2b)$ $a = 3, b = -3$
     (c) $(-5mn)^2(-5mn + 2n + 3m)$ $m = -3, n = -2$

10   Find an expression for the area of each figure in simplified form.
     (a)   (b)

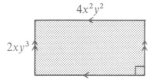
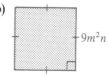

C 11 What is the maximum area of the
     rectangle if $a \in \{1, 2, 3\}$ and
     $b \in \{\frac{1}{2}, \frac{1}{3}, \frac{1}{4}\}$?

$16b^3a^2 - 4ab$

$(a^2b)^2$

Problem Solving

Often, in order to solve a problem, you need to organize all the
facts with care. To solve the following problem you need to use your
clues carefully. Manuel, Curt, and John are married to Michelle,
Tanya and Stacey, but not in this order. Each weekend, they play
tennis doubles but the wives and husbands are not partners. Tanya
and John were partners and Curt was with Manuel's wife. If Curt and
Stacey were partners, who is married to whom?

1.7 Multiplying Binomials

You can use the Distributive Property to learn what the result is when binomials are multiplied.

$$(a + b)(c + d) = (a + b)\;(c + d)$$
$$= (a + b)\,c + (a + b)\,d$$
$$= ac + bc + ad + bd$$

You can use the following diagram to show what $(a + b)(c + d)$ means.

	a	b	
c	ac	bc	c
d	ad	bd	d

Area of whole rectangle is $(a + b)(c + d)$
Sum of the areas of parts of rectangle is

$$ac + bc + ad + bd$$

Thus $(a + b)(c + d) = ac + bc + ad + bd$

You often need to look for more efficient methods of applying skills. For example:

Step 1

Result obtained by applying the Distributive Property.

$$(a + 5b)(a - 3b) = a^2 + 2ab - 15b^2$$

Step 2

Study the result to obtain a more efficient method.

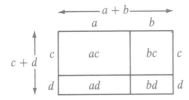

$$(a + 5b)(a - 3b) = a^2 + 2ab - 15b^2$$

Mentally find the result.
$5ab - 3ab = 2ab$

When you square a binomial you are multiplying two binomials. You can apply, again, the Distributive Property. Thus,

$$(a + b)^2 = (a + b)(a + b)$$
$$= (a + b)a + (a + b)b$$
$$= a^2 + ba + ab + b^2$$
$$= a^2 + 2ab + b^2$$

Then you examine your result to obtain a more efficient method.

To square a binomial you add
- the square of the first term
- twice the product of the terms
- the square of the last term.

$\Rightarrow$

$$(a + b)^2 = a^2 + 2ab + b^2$$
$$(a - b)^2 = a^2 - 2ab + b^2$$

To **expand** a product of polynomials means to remove brackets by multiplying and then simplify by adding or subtracting.

Example 1 Expand

(a) $(3x + 1)(2x - 1)$ (b) $(2p + q)^2$ (c) $(4a - 3b)^2$

Solution

(a) $(3x + 1)(2x - 1) = (3x)(2x) + (3x)(-1) + (1)(2x) + (1)(-1)$
$$= 6x^2 - 3x + 2x - 1$$
$$= 6x^2 - x - 1$$

(b) $(2p + q)^2 = (2p)^2 + 2(2p)(q) + (q)^2$
$$= 4p^2 + 4pq + q^2$$

(c) $(4a - 3b)^2 = (4a)^2 + 2(4a)(-3b) + (3b)^2$
$$= 16a^2 - 24ab + 9b^2$$

To check an answer, you could do all the work again, but in doing so you might make the same mistake again. A different strategy is often useful for checking your work, as shown in the following example.

Example 2

(a) Simplify $(a - 3b)(2a + 3b) - 4(a - b)^2$.

(b) Check your answer in (a).

Solution

(a) $(a - 3b)(2a + 3b) - 4(a - b)^2 = (2a^2 - 3ab - 9b^2) - 4(a^2 - 2ab + b^2)$
$$= 2a^2 - 3ab - 9b^2 - 4a^2 + 8ab - 4b^2$$
$$= -2a^2 + 5ab - 13b^2$$

(b) Choose $a = 1$, $b = 2$.

$(a - 3b)(2a + 3b) - 4(a - b)^2$ $-2a^2 + 5ab - 13b^2$
$= (1 - 6)(2 + 6) - 4(-1)^2$ $= -2(1)^2 + 5(1)(2) - 13(2)^2$
$= (-5)(8) - 4$ $= -2 + 10 - 52$
$= -40 - 4$ $= -44$
$= -44$

————————— Answers are the same. —————————

Thus $(a - 3b)(2a + 3b) - 4(a - b)^2 = -2a^2 + 5ab - 13b^2$.

When you solve an equation, always check your answer by substituting your answer in the original equation.

Example 3 Solve $(2a - 1)(3a + 2) - (2a - 1)^2 = 2a(a + 1)$.

Solution
Always begin by writing the original equation.
$$(2a - 1)(3a + 2) - (2a - 1)^2 = 2a(a + 1)$$
$$(6a^2 + a - 2) - (4a^2 - 4a + 1) = 2a^2 + 2a$$
$$6a^2 + a - 2 - 4a^2 + 4a - 1 = 2a^2 + 2a$$
$$6a^2 - 4a^2 - 2a^2 + a + 4a - 2a = 2 + 1$$
$$3a = 3$$
$$a = 1$$

1.7 Exercise

A Questions 1 to 7 develop your skills in working with products of binomials.

1 Find the products.
   (a) $(x + 3)(x + 5)$ (b) $(x - 6)(2x + 1)$ (c) $(3a - 5)(2a + 1)$
   (d) $(3a - b)^2$ (e) $(1 - 2x)^2$ (f) $(2a - b)(2a + b)$
   (g) $(a - 3b)(a - 3b)$ (h) $(xy - 2)(xy - 9)$ (i) $(6 - p)(7 + p)$

   (j) $(x - 4y)(x - 3y)$ (k) $(y^2 - 2)(y^2 + 8)$ (l) $\left(3x - \dfrac{1}{2}y\right)(x + 4y)$

2 Expand.
   (a) $(3y - 1)(3y + 1)$ (b) $(x^2 - 3)(x^2 + 3)$ (c) $(4x - 3y)(4x + 2y)$
   (d) $(8 - 2y)(3 - y)$ (e) $(3k - 2)(3k - 3)$ (f) $(3y - 2)^2$
   (g) $(1 - 3x)^2$ (h) $(m - 3y)(m - 2y)$ (i) $(3y^2 - 1)(2y^2 + 1)$

   (j) $(ab - 2)(ab + 6)$ (k) $\left(2x - \dfrac{3}{2}\right)^2$ (l) $(xy - 6)(xy + 5)$

3 Simplify.
   (a) $2(y - 1)(y - 4)$ (b) $3(y + 6)(y - 5)$ (c) $2(3x - 1)^2$
   (d) $-3(x - y)^2$ (e) $3x(x - y)(x + y)$ (f) $-(3m - n)(3m + 6n)$

   (g) $\dfrac{1}{2}(4x - 3)(2x + 1)$ (h) $-3m(m - n)(m + n)$ (i) $-2(3a - 2b)^2$

4 (a) Simplify $3(a - 2b)^2$.   (b) Simplify $(3a - 2b)^2$.
   (c) Why do the answers in (a) and (b) differ?

5   (a) Simplify $3(x - 3y)^2 + 2(x + 6y)(x - 6y)$.
      (b) Simplify $3(x - 3y)^2 - 2(x + 6y)(x - 6y)$.
      (c) Why do the answers in (a) and (b) differ?

6   (a) Simplify $(4x - 1)^2 - 6(3x + 1)(2x - 3)$.
      (b) Use $x = 1$ to check the answer in (a).

7   (a) Simplify $2(2x - y)(3x + 4y) - 2(x - 2y)^2$.
      (b) Use $x = 1$ and $y = 1$ to check the answer in (a).

B 8   Simplify.
      (a) $(y - 3)(y + 9) - 3(y - 3)(y + 3)$
      (b) $2(x + 6)(x - 2) + 3(x - 4)(x + 6)$
      (c) $(3x - y)(2x + y) - 2(x - y)^2$
      (d) $-3(a - 4b)^2 - 2(a + 5b)^2$
      (e) $(m + 4n)(m - 4n) - 3(m - n)^2$
      (f) $2(3c - d)(2c + d) - 5(c + d)(c - 3d)$
      (g) $3x(x - y)^2 - 2y(x + 2y)^2$

9   Simplify. Check your answers.
      (a) $(x - 1)^2 - (x + 2)^2 - (x - 3)^2$ (b) $2(y - 3)^2 - 3(y - 1)(y + 3)$
      (c) $3m(m - 5) - 2(m + 6)(m - 3)$ (d) $2(x - y)(x + y) - 3(x - y)^2$
      (e) $3(a - b)^2 + 3(2a - b)(a + b) + b(a - b)$

10   Subtract $(x + 3)^2 - (x - 4)^2$ from the sum of $2(x - 1)^2$ and $-3(2x + 2)$.

11   By how much does $2(x - 3)^2 - 5$ exceed $-3(x + 1)^2 - (x - 1)^2$?

12   Find the sum of $(y - x)^2 + 3(x - y)^2$ and $3(x + y)^2 - 2(x + y)^2$.

13   Solve. Verify your answers.
      (a) $(y + 3)(y - 2) = y(y + 4)$
      (b) $y(y + 8) - (y + 2)^2 = 4(2y + 1) - 8(y + 1)$
      (c) $(y + 3)^2 = (y - 1)^2 + 40$ (d) $(m + 3)^2 + (2m - 1)^2 = 5m^2 + 8$
      (e) $(3x + 1)^2 - 6x^2 = 3(x^2 + 1) - 2$ (f) $(2y + 3)^2 - 4y(y + 1) = 5$
      (g) $(5 - 2y)^2 + (y - 3)^2 = 6y^2 - 4 - (y + 4)^2$
      (h) $2x^2 - (7 - 2x)^2 = (x - 3)(4 - 2x) - 37$

C 14   Solve.
      (a) $3(n + 3)(2n - 1) = (3n + 3)^2 - 3(n^2 + 3)$
      (b) $(y + 2)(y - 4) = (y + 3)(y - 4) - 3$

Applications: Permissible Values

Often the variables you use in some problems have certain restrictions. For example, when you use the equation to find the length of the hypotenuse, a restriction must be placed on x. $x > 0$, since distance is always positive.

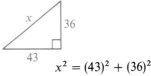

$$x^2 = (43)^2 + (36)^2$$

In the next diagram, the sides are given as variable expressions.

Restrictions:
$2y - 4 > 0$ or $y > 2$
$3x - 6 > 0$ or $x > 2$

Restrictions will occur in many of the topics you will study in mathematics.

15 (a) Find an expression for the area of the shaded region.
    (b) Find the shaded region if $x = 6$.
    (c) Why is the value $x = 1$ not permissible?

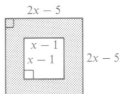

16 Find an expression for the area of each shaded region. Write the expression in simplest terms.

(a)

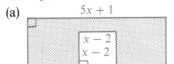

(b)

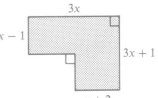

17 The area of a region is given by the expression

$$A(n) = 3(2n - 1)^2 - 2(n + 1)^2, \quad n \in N.$$

Calculate the area for
(a) $n = 2$ (b) $n = 3$ (c) $n = 4$
(d) Why is $n = 1$ not a permissible value?

18 For a computer program, the area of a region is given by

$$A(n) = 2(2n + 1)^2 - (3n - 1)^2, \quad n \in N.$$

Calculate
(a) $A(1)$ (b) $A(2)$ (c) $A(3)$ (d) $A(4)$
(e) Use the pattern in your answers (a) to (d) to predict the value of $A(5)$, $A(6)$, $A(7)$.

1.8 Dividing a Polynomial by a Monomial

You use your laws of exponents to divide a monomial by a monomial.

Example 1   Simplify.   (a) $\dfrac{-8x^6}{2x^4}$ (b) $(-9x^6y^5) \div (x^2y)^2$

Solution   (a) $\dfrac{-8x^6}{2x^4} = -4x^2$ Think: Step 1 $\dfrac{-8}{2} = -4$
Divide the numerical coefficients.

Think: Step 2 $\dfrac{x^6}{x^4} = x^{6-4} = x^2$
Divide the literal coefficients.

(b) $(-9x^6y^5) \div (x^2y)^2 = (-9x^6y^5) \div (x^4y^2)$ ← First, use the exponent law
$$= -9x^2y^3 \quad\quad\quad\quad\quad \text{to simplify.}$$

$x^6 \div x^4 = x^{6-4} = x^2$
$y^5 \div y^2 = y^{5-2} = y^3$

To divide a polynomial by a monomial, you divide each term of the polynomial by the monomial.

Example 2   Evaluate $\dfrac{m^2n - m^3n^3 - 3mn^2}{-mn}$ if $m = 3$, $n = -2$.

Solution $\dfrac{m^2n - m^3n^3 - 3mn^2}{-mn} = \dfrac{m^2n}{-mn} - \dfrac{m^3n^3}{-mn} - \dfrac{3mn^2}{-mn}$ To evaluate, simplify first.
Divide each term by the
same denominator.
$$= -m + m^2n^2 + 3n$$

If $m = 3$, $n = -2$, then $-m + m^2n^2 + 3n = -(3) + (3)^2(-2)^2 + 3(-2)$
$$= -3 + (9)(4) - 6$$
$$= -3 + 36 - 6$$
$$= 27$$

1.8 Exercise

A 1   Find each quotient.

(a) $\dfrac{a^4}{a^2}$ (b) $\dfrac{8a^5}{2a^3}$ (c) $\dfrac{-16a^6}{-4a^3}$ (d) $\dfrac{x^3y^2}{xy}$

(e) $\dfrac{4x^2y^3}{-2xy^2}$ (f) $\dfrac{-8x^5y^2}{2x^3y}$ (g) $\dfrac{-12m^6n^2}{-3mn}$ (h) $\dfrac{25p^3q^5}{-5p^3q^3}$

2   (a) Write $(-9x^3y^2) \div (3x^2y)$ as one term.
     (b) Evaluate the expression in (a) if $x = -1$, $y = 2$.

3   If $a = 3$, calculate each of the following.

(a) $-2a^2$ (b) $-(2a)^2$ (c) $(-2a)^2$ (d) $\dfrac{2a^2}{a}$

(e) $\dfrac{(2a)^2}{a}$ (f) $\left(\dfrac{2a}{a}\right)^2$ (g) $\left(\dfrac{-2a}{a}\right)^2$ (h) $\dfrac{(-2a)^2}{a}$

4   If $a = -2$, $b = 3$, calculate each of the following.

(a) $-2ab^2$ (b) $-2(ab)^2$ (c) $(-2ab)^2$ (d) $\dfrac{2a^2}{b}$

(e) $\dfrac{(-2a)^2}{b}$ (f) $\dfrac{-2a^2}{b}$ (g) $\left(\dfrac{-2ab}{a}\right)^2$ (h) $\dfrac{-2ab^2}{(ab)^2}$

5   (a) Why may $\dfrac{8m^2n + 6mn^2}{2mn}$ be written as $\dfrac{8m^2n}{2mn} + \dfrac{6mn^2}{2mn}$?

(b) Simplify the expression in (a).

6   (a) Why is the area of the square PQRS given by $\left(\dfrac{9a^3b^3}{3ab}\right)^2$?

(b) Simplify the expression in (a).

P ▢▢▢▢▢▢▢ Q
(square PQRS with side labelled $\dfrac{9a^3b^3}{3ab}$)
S ▢▢▢▢▢▢▢ R

B 7   Simplify each quotient.

(a) $\dfrac{-24x^2y}{6xy}$ (b) $\dfrac{-18m^3n^2}{-6m^2n}$

(c) $\dfrac{25a^4b^2}{-5a^2b}$ (d) $(-64x^3y^3) \div (8xy^2)$

(e) $(36p^5q^3) \div (-6p^4q^2)$ (f) $(-72m^4n^2) \div (9mn^2)$

8   Find the value of each of the following if $a = 3$, $b = -2$.

(a) $3ab \div (-2a^2b)$ (b) $(-12a^2b) \div (4ab)$ (c) $\dfrac{18a^3b^2}{-6ab^2}$

(d) $-2ab^2 \div (ab)^2$ (e) $\dfrac{(ab)(a^2b)}{ab^2}$ (f) $\dfrac{(-3a^2b)(-2ab^2)}{6ab^2}$

9   Write each of the following in simplest terms.

(a) $\dfrac{a^2 - ab + ab^2}{a}$ (b) $\dfrac{8y^2 + 16y}{-4y}$ (c) $\dfrac{49m^2n - 14m}{-7m}$

(d) $\dfrac{12ab^2 - 16ab}{-4ab}$ (e) $\dfrac{28a^3b^2 - 7a^5b^3}{-7a^2b}$ (f) $\dfrac{p^2q - p^3q - 3pq^2}{-pq}$

(g) $\dfrac{18m^2n^2 - 12mn^2 - 36m^2n}{-6mn}$ (h) $\dfrac{10a^2b^3 - 20a^3b^2 + 30a^4b^2}{-10a^2b^2}$

10 Evaluate each expression for the given values.

(a) $\dfrac{4mn^2 - 8m^2n}{-4mn}$ $m = 2, n = 1$ (b) $\dfrac{9a^2b^2 - 15a^3b^2}{-3a^2b^2}$ $a = 3, b = -3$

(c) $\dfrac{25m^3n^3 - 10m^2n^3 - 15m^3n^2}{-5m^2n^2}$ $m = -3, n = -2$

11 Simplify each of the following.

(a) $(-3a^2b) \div (15ab)$ (b) $(-48ab^2) \div (-6ab)$

(c) $\dfrac{-56m^2n^3}{-7mn^2}$ (d) $(-2ab)(-3ab) \div (-3a^2b)$

(e) $\dfrac{9a^3b^5}{-3ab}\left(\dfrac{a^2}{b}\right)^3$ (f) $(-3x^3y^2) \div (xy)^2$

(g) $\dfrac{-30a^2b + 5ab}{-5ab}$ (h) $\dfrac{(-3a^2)(6a^2b^3)}{9ab^2}$ (i) $\dfrac{(6a^4)(-2a^2b^3)}{(4ab)^2(-a)^2}$

(j) $\left(\dfrac{ab^2}{b}\right)^2 (a^2b)$ (k) $\dfrac{15x^3y - 30x^2y^2 - 10xy^2}{-5xy}$ (l) $\dfrac{36x^4y^5 - 9x^3y^4}{-9x^2y^3}$

12 Which rectangle has the greater area if $a = 2, b = 3$?

(a)
$\dfrac{24ab^2}{4a^2b}$
$\dfrac{12a^2b^3}{6ab}$

(b)
$\dfrac{6a^3b^2}{4a^2b}$
$\dfrac{2a^2b}{b^2}$

c 13 Which expression, A or B, has the greater value if $a = 1, b = -2$?

A $\dfrac{(-8ab)(-6a^2b^2)}{(-4a)(-2b)}$ B $\dfrac{-8ab}{-4a} - \dfrac{-6a^2b^2}{-2b}$

Math Tip

In arithmetic, we have often learned a shortcut for computing mentally. The following shortcut will help us to multiply binomials mentally.

$(2a + 3b)(4a - b) = 8a^2 - 2ab + 12ab - 3b^2$

First terms · Last terms · Inner terms · Outer terms

F   O   I   L
i   u   n   a
r   t   n   s
s   e   e   t
t   r   r

1.9 Dividing a Polynomial by a Polynomial

The skills you have learned in arithmetic extend to skills in algebra. For example, dividing a polynomial by a polynomial is very much like long division of an integer by an integer. Compare the following.

Arithmetic

Divide $512 \div 36$.

$$
\begin{array}{r}
14 \\
36 \overline{)512} \\
36 \\
\overline{152} \\
144 \\
\overline{8}
\end{array}
$$

Step 1. Divide the first two digits of the dividend by the divisor.

Step 2. Multiply the divisor by the first digit of the quotient.

Step 3. Subtract.

Step 4. Bring down the next digit.

Step 5. Repeat steps 1 to 4.

Step 6. Stop when the remainder is less than the divisor, or is zero.

You can write $512 = \underset{\text{quotient}}{14} \times \underset{\text{divisor}}{36} + \underset{\text{remainder}}{8}$

Algebra

Divide $(a^2 - 2a - 10) \div (a + 2)$.

$$
\begin{array}{r}
a - 4 \\
a + 2 \overline{)a^2 - 2a - 10} \\
a^2 + 2a \\
\overline{-4a - 10} \\
-4a - 8 \\
\overline{-2}
\end{array}
$$

Step 1. Divide the first term of the dividend by the first term of the divisor.

Step 2. Multiply the first term of the quotient by the divisor.

Step 3. Subtract.

Step 4. Bring down the next term.

Step 5. Repeat steps 1 to 4.

Step 6. Stop when the remainder is zero or the degree of the remainder is less than the degree of the divisor.

You can write $a^2 - 2a - 10 = \underset{\text{quotient}}{(a - 4)} \underset{\text{divisor}}{(a + 2)} - \underset{\text{remainder}}{2}$

In general, you can write.

> Dividend = Quotient × Divisor + Remainder

The algebraic skill of dividing a polynomial by a binomial is useful in your study of algebra and mathematics.

Example Divide $6y^3 - 21 - 5y^2$ by $3y - 7$.

Before you divide, think: *Step 1.* Write the dividend and the divisor in descending powers of the variable.

Step 2. If there is a power missing in the dividend or the divisor, represent it using the coefficient 0.

Solution

$$
\begin{array}{r}
2y^2 + 3y + 7 \\
3y - 7 \overline{)\,6y^3 - 5y^2 + 0y - 21} \\
6y^3 - 14y^2 \\
\hline
+\ 9y^2 + 0y \\
+\ 9y^2 - 21y \\
\hline
+\ 21y - 21 \\
+\ 21y - 49 \\
\hline
+ 28
\end{array}
$$

1.9 Exercise

A 1 Arrange each expression in descending powers of the variable.
(a) $m^2 + m^3 - 11m + 3$
(b) $y^4 - 3 + 2y^2 + y^3 - 4y$
(c) $p^2y^2 - 3 + p^3 + pq$
(d) $4 + x - x^5 + \dfrac{1}{x}$

2 (a) To divide $3q^2 - 14q - 5$ by $q - 5$ what is your first step?
(b) Do the division in (a).

3 (a) To do the division $m^4 - 4 - 3m^2 \div (1 + m^2)$ what is the first step you need to do?
(b) Do the division in (a).

B 4 Divide.
(a) $p^2 - 2p - 37 \div (p - 7)$
(b) $2m^2 + 9m + 10 \div (m + 2)$
(c) $6x^2 + 13x + 7 \div (3x + 5)$

5 Find each remainder.
(a) $14w^2 + 31w - 18 \div (2w + 5)$
(b) $12a^2 - 11a + 2 \div (3a - 2)$

6 Find each quotient.
(a) $13x + 14 + 3x^2 \div (x + 2)$
(b) $2p^2 + 5 - 11p \div (2p - 1)$
(c) $20m^2 + m - 12 \div (4 + 5m)$
(d) $-45x + 18x^2 - 8 \div (1 + 6x)$

7   Divide. Check your work by multiplication.   Think:

     Dividend = Quotient × Divisor
                + Remainder

(a) $m^3 + 6m^2 + 10m + 3 \div (m + 3)$

(b) $x^3 + 6x^2 + 11x + 22 \div (x^2 + 2x + 3)$

(c) $6p^3 - 13p^2 - 3p - 5 \div (2p - 5)$

8   Divide.

(a) $1 + p - 3p^2 - 2p^3 \div (1 + 2p)$

(b) $9x^3 - x + 9x^4 - 10 - 7x^2 \div (3x^2 + x + 2)$

(c) $35m^3 - 19m^2 + 9m - 1 \div (1 - 2m + 5m^2)$

(d) $-11p^3 - 5p - 6 + 4p^4 + 16p^2 \div (p^2 + 3 - 2p)$

9   Divide.

(a) $p^6 + p^5 - 2p^4 - p^2 - p + 2 \div (p^4 - 1)$

(b) $a^7 + 3a^5 + 2a^2 + 6 \div (a^5 + 2)$

(c) $w^7 + 2w^4 - 2w^3 + w - 2 \div (w^4 + w - 2)$

(d) $k^6 + 2k^4 - 14k^2 + 5 \div (k^2 + 5)$

(e) $x^5 + x^4 + 4x^3 + 3x^2 - 7x + 2 \div (x^3 + 5x - 2)$

10   When $3x^3 - px - 6$ is divided by $x - 2$, there is no remainder. Find p.

11    $km^3 - 3m^2 - 7m - 6$ is divisible by $m - 3$.

(a) Find the value of k.   (b) Find the other factor.

C 12   The area of a triangle is given by $6x^3 + 18x^2 - 2x - 6$.
If the base of the triangle is given by $3x^2 - 1$,
what is the height of the triangle?

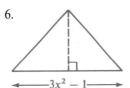

$\longleftarrow 3x^2 - 1 \longrightarrow$

Math Tip

It is important to clearly understand the vocabulary of mathematics
when solving problems. *You cannot solve problems if you don't know
what the clues are.*

- Make a list of all the words you have learned in this chapter.
- Continue to add the remaining new words to your list.
- Provide a simple example to illustrate the meaning of each word.

1.10 Problem-Solving: Using Calculators

The scientific calculator is an invaluable tool for doing complex calculations in mathematical and scientific problems. Calculators have different features. Usually a booklet which comes with the calculator describes the various functions and presents sample calculations. Try the sample problems on your calculator and compare your solutions with those in the booklet to become completely familiar with your calculator.

Throughout this book, look for opportunities to use your calculator to not only check your calculations but also explore extensions of the mathematics you are studying. You will find Calculator Tips which suggest uses for your calculator. Try them.

The examples that follow allow you to apply a few of the many features that are available on a scientific calculator.

1   Exponents often occur in the many formulas from economics, science, space exploration, and so on. A science example is shown.

The radius, r, of the nucleus of the zinc atom is given by the expression

$$r = 1.2 \times 10^{-13}(64)^{\frac{1}{3}}.$$

Calculate the value of r.

2   The mathematics of investment involves the study of sequences and series.

For example, if you invest $100 at 14% per annum compounded quarterly, you would have the following amount, A, of money in 10 years.

$$A = 100\left(1 + \frac{0.14}{4}\right)^{4 \times 10}$$

Calculate the amount, A, to the nearest cent.

3   You already know various ways of calculating the area of a triangle. However, if you are just given the sides of a triangle, you can calculate the area using the following method.

Heron's Formula: For $\triangle ABC$, the semi-perimeter s is defined as

$$s = \frac{a + b + c}{2}.$$

The area, A, of $\triangle ABC$ is given by

$$A = \sqrt{s(s - a)(s - b)(s - c)}$$

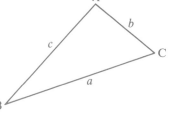

Use the formula to calculate the area of a triangle with dimensions $a = 6.28$ m, $b = 7.35$ m, $c = 8.94$ m.

Practice and Problems: A Chapter Review

At the end of each chapter, this section will provide you with additional questions to check your skills and understanding of the topics dealt with in this chapter. An important step for problem-solving is to decide which skills to use. For this reason, these questions are not placed in any special order. When you have finished the review, you might try the *Test for Practice* that follows.

1 Evaluate.
(a) $-3(-2)^2(-1)^3$ (b) $(-16) \div (-4) + 3$

2 For the formula $d = vt + \frac{1}{2}gt^2$
find v if $d = 93$, $g = 4$, and $t = 3$.

3 Calculate each of the following if $a = 4$, $b = -2$.
(a) $\left(\frac{ab}{b}\right)^2 (ab)^2$ (b) $\left(\frac{b}{a}\right)^2 \left(\frac{a}{b}\right)^2$ (c) $\frac{(ab)^3}{a^2} \left(\frac{a}{b}\right)^3$

4 Simplify.
(a) $\left(\frac{a}{b}\right)^n \left(\frac{b}{c}\right)^n \left(\frac{c}{a}\right)^n$ (b) $\left(\frac{m}{n}\right)^2 \left(\frac{n}{p}\right)^3 \left(\frac{p}{m}\right)^4$

5 Express each with a single base.
(a) $\frac{(ab^{-2})^{-3}}{b^{-2}} \left(\frac{b}{a}\right)^{-3}$ (b) $\frac{p^{-k}p^0(p^{2k})^{-3}}{(p^{-k})^3}$

6 Write a simplified expression which is equivalent to each of the following.
(a) $3(2a - 3b) - 5(2a + 5b) - 6a$ (b) $2(y^2 - 6y + 5) - (2y^2 + 5y - 6)$
(c) $3x(x - 1) - 3(x^2 - 3x) + (x^2 - 2x)$

7 (a) Expand $mn^2(5m - 6n + 2m^2 + 4n^2)$.
(b) Evaluate the expression in (a) for $m = -\frac{1}{2}$ and $n = \frac{1}{2}$.

8 If $x = -2$, $y = 3$, which expression has the greatest value?
(a) $3(x + 2y)(x - y) - (2x - y)(x + 3y)$ (b) $2(x - y)^2 - 3(x - 2y)(x + 2y)$
(c) $3(2x - y)^2 + (x + y)(x + 2y)$ (d) $(x + 2y)^2 - 2(x - y)^2$

9 When $2z^3 + 11z^2 + az + 8$ is divided by $z + 3$, the remainder is 5. What is the value of a?

10 Deduce that $a^m \times a^n \times a^p = a^{m+n+p}$ for $m, n, p \in W$.

Test for Practice

Try this test. Each test is based on the mathematics you have learned in this chapter. Try this test later in the year as a review. Keep a record of those questions that you were not successful with and review them periodically.

1 Which are true (T)? Which are false (F)?

   (a) $-4 - (3 - 1) < 8 \div (-2 + 1)$ (b) $-3(-1)^2 - (6 - 3) \neq \dfrac{18 - 2}{(-2)^2}$

   (c) $-3 + \dfrac{-6 + 3}{-3} > -8 \div \dfrac{4 \div 2}{-6 \div 3}$

2 Express each of the following with a single base.
   (a) $m^x m^y m^{x-y}$ (b) $a^{m+n} a^{m-2n}$ (c) $y^m \times y^n \div y^{2m}$ (d) $(k^2)^m \times (k^3)^n$

3 Simplify. (a) $2^{-4} + 5^0 + (-3)(-2)^{-4}$ (b) $\dfrac{3^{-1}}{3^{-2} - 2^{-3}}$

4 Simplify. Arrange the answers in ascending powers of x.
   (a) $8 - 2x + 6x^2 - 3x - 2x^2 + 16$ (b) $xy^2 - 2x^2y - 3xy^2 - 2x^2y + 4y^2$

5 If $a = -2$ and $b = 3$, by how much does expression A exceed expression B?
   A $3a - 5b - 7[(2a - b) - (b - 2a)]$
   B $9a - (5a - 2b) + 3[1 + 7(a - b) - 4b]$

6 Simplify each of the following.
   (a) $(-3a^2 b)(5ab)$ (b) $(-48ab^2)(1 - 6ab)$
   (c) $(-5ab)^2(6a - 1)$ (d) $(-2ab)(-3ab)(2 - 3a^2 b)$

7 (a) Simplify $2(y - 3)(y + 3) - 2(y - 1)^2 + y^2$.
   (b) If $y = 1$, find the value of the expression in (a).

8 (a) Simplify $\dfrac{36a^3 b^4}{-2ab}\left(\dfrac{a}{b}\right)^3$.
   (b) Evaluate the expression in (a) if $a = -2$, $b = 3$.

9 Divide $a^4 - 5a^3 + 5a^2 + 8a - 12 \div (a - 3)$.

10 The most successful wrestler ever was Strangler Lewis who won all but 33 of 6200 bouts. Lewis wrestled in the 77-kg class. If the mass, m, in kilograms, of a normal adult male is given by $m = \dfrac{25(h - 100)}{26}$ where h is the height in centimetres, determine Strangler's height.

2 Methods of Factoring and Applying Skills

factoring skills, common factors, method of grouping terms, skills with trinomials, using difference of squares, applying skills with factoring, solving quadratic equations, simplifying algebraic expressions, applications, strategies and problem-solving

Introduction

Throughout your study of mathematics, you acquire a variety of strategies and methods of developing mathematics, and of solving problems. Often, you will encounter the following process in the study of mathematics.

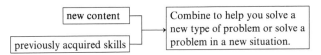

As you learn new skills and concepts you increase your vocabulary, which enables you to make further progress in mathematics. New words lead to the use of new symbols. Many symbols in your everyday activities are universal as shown in the illustrations.

Furthermore, the symbols used to study mathematics are universal. In fact, you may choose a mathematics book in any language and you will notice that you have seen some of the material before, as shown below.

II Ἰδιώτης. Ἐὰν πολλαπλασιάσωμε ἤ διαιρέσωμε καὶ τὰ δύο μέλη μιᾶς ἐξισώσεως μὲ τὸν αὐτὸν μὴ μηδενικὸν ἀριθμόν, αἱ λύσεις τῆς ἐξισώσεως δὲν μεταβάλλονται, ἡ νέα ἐξίσωσις εἶναι ἰσοδύναμος μὲ τὴν ἀρχικήν.

II.χ. ἡ ἐξίσωσις $\dfrac{7x-3}{5} = \dfrac{4x}{3}$

εἶναι ἰσοδύναμος μὲ τὴν

$15 \cdot \dfrac{7x-3}{5} = 15 \cdot \dfrac{4x}{3}$, ἤτοι τὴν $3(7x-3) = 5 \cdot 4x$,

καὶ ἡ ἐξίσωσις

$$8x = 24x$$

εἶναι ἰσοδύναμος μὲ τὴν

$\dfrac{8x}{8} = \dfrac{24x}{8}$, ἤτοι τὴν $x = 3x$.

2.1 Common Factors

To help you remember various skills in mathematics, it is often helpful to look for similarities and differences. For example, examine the meaning of expand and factor.

Expand

To **expand** means to write a product of polynomials as a sum or difference of terms.

$$a(x + y) = ax + ay$$
$$3y(y - 2) = 3y^2 - 6y$$

Factor

To **factor** means to write a sum or difference of terms as a product of polynomials.

$$ax + ay = a(x + y)$$

a is a factor of each term.

$$3y^2 - 6y = 3y(y - 2)$$

$3y$ is a factor of each term.

Thus, expanding and factoring may be thought of as inverse operations.

— expanding ⟶

$$2mn(3m + 2n - 4) = 6m^2n + 4mn^2 - 8mn$$

⟵ factoring —

When factoring expressions, the first step you must take is to find the greatest common factor of the terms, as shown in the following example.

Example Factor each expression

(a) $6x^2 - 12y^2$ (b) $-2a^2x - 4ax - 6x$ (c) $4a^2b + 8ab^2 - 12abc$

Solution (a) $6x^2 - 12y^2 = 6(x^2 - 2y^2)$

└─ 6 is the greatest common factor of the terms.

(b) $-2a^2x - 4ax - 6x = -2x(a^2 + 2a + 3)$

$-2x$ is the greatest common factor of the terms.

(c) $4a^2b + 8ab^2 - 12abc = 4ab(a + 2b - 3c)$

$4ab$ is the greatest common factor.

2.1 Exercise

A 1 Find the missing factor.

(a) $6ab = (3a)(\ ?\ )$ (b) $-16xy = (\ ?\ )(-8y)$ (c) $-8y^4 = (-4y^2)(\ ?\ )$

(d) $6ab^2c = (\ ?\ )(6b^2)$ (e) $-6a^3b^2 = (-3ab)(\ ?\ )$

2 Find the greatest common factor of each of the following.

(a) a^2, ab (b) $-24ab, 8ab$ (c) $ay^2, -by$

(d) $-6x^3, 2x^4, 4x^5$ (e) $3a^4, -3a^3b, 6a^2b^2$ (f) $9a^2, -12ab, -6b^2$

3 (a) Factor the expression $2x^3y - 8x^2y^2 + 6xy^3$.

(b) How would you check your factors is (a)?

B 4 Find the missing factor.

(a) $2mx + 2my = (\ ?\ )(x + y)$ (b) $a^2 - ab = (\ ?\ )(a - b)$

(c) $3x^2 - 12xy = (\ ?\ )(x - 4y)$

(d) $-2m^2n + 2mn^2 - 6mnp = (\ ?\ )(m - n + 3p)$

(e) $2\pi mR - 2\pi mr + 2\pi hm = (\ ?\ )(R - r + h)$

5 Find the greatest common factor of each of the following expressions.

(a) $-13ab - 39ac$ (b) $-15xy + 25xy^2$ (c) $56m^2 - 4mn$

(d) $18x^2 - 9x + 3$ (e) $x^3 - x^2y + xy^2$ (f) $2axy - 4bxy + 6cxy$

(g) $4a^2b^3 - 6a^2b^2 + 2ab^3$ (h) $6m^2n^2 + 3m^3n^2 - 9m^2n^2$

6 Factor.

(a) $4ax - 8bx$ (b) $18y^4 - 27y^3$ (c) $49xy - 14x^2y^2$

(d) $25ab - 10ab^2$ (e) $3y^3 - y^2 + y$ (f) $-6m^2 - 3m^3 - 9m$

(g) $8a^3 + 2a^4 + 8a^5$ (h) $a^3 - a^2b + ab^2$

(i) $2x^2y^3 - 6x^2y^2 + 2xy^3$ (j) $9x^4 - 6x^3y + 12x^2y^2$

Calculator Tip

To use a calculator efficiently, you must plan ahead. For example, to evaluate the expression $ut + \frac{1}{2}gt^2$ for $u = 6.2$, $t = 3.5$ and $g = 9.8$ you need to use the memory keys.

$\boxed{\text{MS}}$ memory store $\boxed{\text{MR}}$ memory recall

Check your calculator. The keys may be labelled in a different way.

Follow these steps.

                                                 Output

$\boxed{\text{C}}\ 3.5\ \boxed{\times}\ 3.5\ \boxed{\times}\ 9.8\ \boxed{\div}\ 2\ \boxed{=}\ \boxed{\text{MS}}\ 6.2\ \boxed{\times}\ 3.5\ \boxed{+}\ \boxed{\text{MR}}\ \boxed{=}$?

- Since each calculator may have different features, refer to the manual given with the calculator.
- On the next page you will use factoring skills which will help you to use a calculator efficiently.

Applications: Factoring and Calculators

You may use your factoring skills to write expressions in a formula in a more convenient form.

	Formula	Factored Form
Co-ordinate Geometry	$y = mx - ma$	$y = m(x - a)$
Area	$A = \dfrac{1}{2}ah + \dfrac{1}{2}bh$	$A = \dfrac{1}{2}(a + b)h$
Physics	$s = \dfrac{ut}{2} + \dfrac{vt}{2}$	$s = \dfrac{1}{2}(u + v)t$

Expressions written in factored form are useful in working with calculators.

7   The area of a trapezoid is given by the formula $A = \dfrac{1}{2}ah + \dfrac{1}{2}bh.$

(a) Use $h = 4$, $a = 3$, $b = 6$ to calculate A.

(b) Factor the expression given above for A. Calculate the value of A using $h = 4$, $a = 3$, and $b = 6$.

(c) Which answer, (a) or (b), requires fewer steps?

(d) Use $h = 6.25$, $a = 3.78$, $b = 8.93$. Calculate A.

8   Rewrite each of the following formula in factored form.

(a) $P = 2l + 2w$ (b) $S = n^2 + n$ (c) $S = 4n^2 + 3n$

(d) $E = Ir + IR$ (e) $S = 180n - 360$ (f) $S = \dfrac{n^2}{2} + \dfrac{n}{2}$

(g) $A = 2\pi rh + 2\pi r^2$ (h) $S_n = \dfrac{3n^2}{2} - \dfrac{n}{2}$

radius, r,

9   The surface area, S, of a cylinder is given by the formula $S = 2\pi r^2 + 2\pi rh$.

(a) Calculate the surface area of a cylinder with height 10 cm and radius 12 cm. Use a factored form. $\pi \doteq 3.14$.

(b) By how much does the area of the cylinder in (a) increase if the radius is increased by 1 cm and the height by 2 cm?

(c) Calculate S for $h = 8.93$, $r = 4.18$.

10   The formula for the sum of n even numbers is $S_n = n^2 + n$
{ Read "S subscript n". The n indicates that the formula gives the sum of n terms.

$2 + 4 + 6 + 8 + \cdots$
n terms.

(a) Calculate the sum of the first 20 even numbers. Use $S_n = n^2 + n$.

(b) Factor the formula in (a). Use the factored form to find the sum of the first 20 even numbers.

2.2 Factoring by Grouping Terms

Often, you can extend a skill you have learned and apply it to a new situation. For example, the distributive property is used to expand an expression.

$$ax + ay = a(x + y)$$

The common factor is a monomial.

Extend this property to a binomial as follows.

$$(\ ? \ )x + (\ ? \ )y = (\ ? \ )(x + y)$$
$$(a + b)x + (a + b)y = (a + b)(x + y)$$

The common factor is a binomial.

Once you have applied the distributive property as shown, you can interpret your result as a method of factoring expressions that have a binomial as a common factor. For example, to obtain a common factor that is a binomial, terms that have a common factor are grouped together.

A: $\quad 2ax + bx + 2ay + by$

$= (2ax + bx) + (2ay + by)$

$= x(2a + b) + y(2a + b)$ Common factor

$= (2a + b)(x + y)$

B: $\quad 2ax + bx + 2ay + by$

$= (2ax + 2ay) + (bx + by)$

$= 2a(x + y) + b(x + y)$ Common factor

$= (x + y)(2a + b)$

In A and B the groupings are different but the same factors are obtained.

Remember, when grouping terms with negative coefficients,

$$-a + b = -(a - b) \quad \text{and} \quad -a - b = -(a + b).$$

This result is needed in the following example.

Example 1   Factor   (a) $3gv + gw + 6hv + 2hw$ (b) $3mp + 2np - 12mq - 8nq$

Solution   (a) $3gv + gw + 6hv + 2hw = (3gv + gw) + (6hv + 2hw)$

$= g(3v + w) + 2h(3v + w)$ Common factor is a binomial.

$= (3v + w)(g + 2h)$

(b) $3mp + 2np - 12mq - 8nq = (3mp + 2np) - (12mq + 8nq)$

$= p(3m + 2n) - 4q(3m + 2n)$

$= (3m + 2n)(p - 4q)$

A common factor can also be a trinomial, as shown in the following example. However, as in your earlier factoring work, before grouping terms, check to see if there is a common factor of all the terms of the expression, and if there is, remove it. Then do the grouping.

Example 2 Factor (a) $2ap - bp + 2aq - bq - 2ar + br$

(b) $8wx^2 + 4vx^2 - 8wxy - 4vxy$

Solution (a) $2ap - bp + 2aq - bq - 2ar + br$
$= (2ap + 2aq - 2ar) - (bp + bq - br)$
$= 2a(p + q - r) - b(p + q - r)$

———————————————— Common factor is a trinomial.

$= (p + q - r)(2a - b)$

(b) $8wx^2 + 4vx^2 - 8wxy - 4vxy$
$= 4x(2wx + vx - 2wy - vy)$

———————————————— greatest common factor of all the terms

$= 4x[(2wx + vx) - (2wy + vy)]$
$= 4x[x(2w + v) - y(2w + v)]$
$= 4x(2w + v)(x - y)$

2.2 Exercise

A 1 (a) What might be your first step in factoring the expression $x(a - b) + 2y(a - b)$?
(b) Factor the expression in (a).

2 (a) Find the factors of $a(x + y) + b(x + y)$.
(b) Find the factors of $x(a + b) + y(a + b)$.
(c) Why are the answers in (a) and (b) the same?

B 3 Factor each of the following.
(a) $2x(a + b) + y(a + b)$ (b) $3m(x - y) - k(x - y)$
(c) $3y(m - n) - 2(m - n)$ (d) $2m(y + 3) + n(y + 3)$
(e) $3x(3m - 2n) + 2y(3m - 2n)$ (f) $4m(4a - 2b) - 3n(4a - 2b)$

4 Find the greatest common factor of each expression.
(a) $4w - 2v$ (b) $-3a^2 - 3ab$
(c) $2x^2y + 4xy - 12xy^2$ (d) $-7m^2n^2 - 14mn^3 + 49mn^2$
(e) $-6px^2y^2 + 12qx^3y - 18rx^4y$ (f) $-3de^3 - 6d^2e^3 + 15d^3e^3 - 9de^2$

5 Factor each of the following.
  (a) $ax + bx + ay + by$ (b) $2ax - 2bx - ay + by$
  (c) $a^2 - ab + ac - bc$ (d) $3bn - 2bm - 9an + 6am$
  (e) $a^2c^2 + acd + abc + bd$ (f) $y^4 + y^3 + 2y + 2$

6 Factor each of the following.
  (a) $a^2 - ac + ab - bc$
  (b) $x^2 + y - xy - x$
  (c) $km^2 + kn^2 + m^2 + km + n^2 + m$
  (d) $10v - 6qv - 5w + 3qw + 4pv - 2pw$
  (e) $5x + 10 - 2z - zx + 5y - zy$
  (f) $-3d^2e - e + 4g - 2de + 8dg + 12d^2g$

7 Factor each of the following.
  (a) $10ap + 5aq + 4bp + 2bq$
  (b) $21m^2p^2 - 42np^2 + 3m^2 - 6n$
  (c) $2xy^5 + 2y^4 + x^2y^3 + xy^2$

C 8 Factor each of the following.
  (a) $3mxy - 6mx - 3nxy + 6nx$ (b) $-2px + 2rx - qy + 2ry - qx - 2py$
  (c) $2g^2h^2 + 8g^3h^4 + 4gh^5 + 4g^4h$ (d) $12uv^2 + 8v^2x^2 - 24uvw - 16vwx^2$
  (e) $\dfrac{1}{4}mp^3 - \dfrac{3}{8}mq - \dfrac{1}{4}np^3 + \dfrac{3}{8}nq$

Problem Solving

To solve some problems we may need to just exhaust all the numbers to find which satisfy the conditions. (A computer works somewhat like this.) Solve the problem.

> The number 121 has the property that by crossing out the digit 2, the remaining number, 11, is the square root of the original number. Find all other numbers less than 1000 that have the same property.

Math Tip

These patterns often occur in studying mathematics. Learn them!

$$(a + b)^2 = a^2 + 2ab + b^2$$
$$(a - b)^2 = a^2 - 2ab + b^2$$
$$(a + b)(a - b) = a^2 - b^2$$

2.3 Factoring Trinomials

Often, when you are developing a strategy for solving a problem, you examine your result and work backwards. For example, you know the following result.

$$(y - 3)(y - 5) = y^2 - 8y + 15$$

But, suppose you are given the expression $y^2 - 8y + 15$ and you want to find the factors. How would you develop a strategy for doing this?

Look at the two example below. Relate the coefficients of the terms of the trinomial to the terms of the binomial factors for the known results.

Known Result A

$$
\begin{aligned}
&(y - 3)(y - 5) \\
&= y(y - 5) - 3(y - 5) \\
&= y^2 - 5y - 3y + (-3)(-5) \\
&= y^2 + (-5 - 3)y + (-3)(-5) \\
&= y^2 - 8y + 15
\end{aligned}
$$

{ This coefficient is the sum of the terms $-3, -5$.

{ This coefficient is the product of the terms $-3, -5$.

Known Result B

$$
\begin{aligned}
&(x + a)(x + b) \\
&= x(x + b) + a(x + b) \\
&= x^2 + bx + ax + ab \\
&= x^2 + (a + b)x + ab
\end{aligned}
$$

{ Sum of the numerical terms, a, b, of the binomial factors.

{ Product of the numerical terms a, b, of the binomial factors.

From A and B you can interpret your results and develop a strategy for factoring a trinomial as shown by the following.

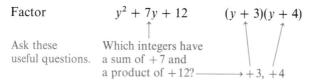

Factor $y^2 + 7y + 12$ $(y + 3)(y + 4)$

Ask these useful questions.   Which integers have a sum of $+7$ and a product of $+12$? ⟶ $+3, +4$

Once you have developed a strategy for factoring a trinomial, you can apply it to find the factors of a given trinomial.

Example 1   Factor $y^2 - 4y - 45$.

Solution   The factors are given by

$$y^2 - 4y - 45 = (y - 9)(y + 5)$$

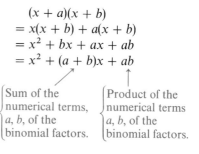

Think:
Which two integers have
• a sum of -4 and • a product of -45?
$(-9) + (+5) = -4$
$(-9)(+5) = -45$

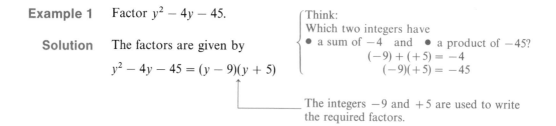

The integers -9 and $+5$ are used to write the required factors.

Factoring by Decomposition

In a similar way, you can use known results to develop a strategy for factoring a trinomial given in the form $ax^2 + bx + c$ where $a \neq 1$. To do so, use a known result and examine how the coefficients of the terms of the trinomial are related to the terms of the binomial factors. Examine the known results carefully.

Observe
$(+6)(+1)(+2)(+3) = +36$

Observe
$(+12)(+3) = +36$

$(6y + 1)(2y + 3) = 12y^2 + 20y + 3$

$+2$

Observe $+18$

$+18 + 2 = +20$

Thus, to find the factors of $12y^2 + 20y + 3$, you may ask the question: Which two integers have • a product of $+36$ and • a sum of $+20$?

Use the answers, $+18$ and $+2$ to *decompose* the given trinomial.

$$12y^2 + 20y + 3 = 12y^2 + 18y + 2y + 3 \qquad \text{20y can be decomposed into } 18y + 2y \text{ or } 2y + 18y$$

$$= 6y(2y + 3) + (2y + 3)$$
$$= (2y + 3)(6y + 1)$$

The strategy developed from known results for factoring a trinomial is called the **method of decomposition**. The strategy is then applied to find the factors of trinomials as shown in the following example.

Example 2 Factor (a) $6y^2 + 5y - 25$ (b) $2x^4 - x^2 - 3$

Solution (a) $6y^2 + 5y - 25$
$= 6y^2 + 15y - 10y - 25$
$= (6y^2 + 15y) - (10y + 25)$
$= 3y(2y + 5) - 5(2y + 5)$
$= (2y + 5)(3y - 5)$

Ask the important question:
Which two integers have
• a sum of $+5$?
• a product of -150
Thus, decompose the trinomial.
Use $+15, -10$.

(b) $2x^4 - x^2 - 3$
$= 2x^4 + 2x^2 - 3x^2 - 3$
$= (2x^4 + 2x^2) - (3x^2 + 3)$
$= 2x^2(x^2 + 1) - 3(x^2 + 1)$
$= (x^2 + 1)(2x^2 - 3)$

Ask yourself:
Which two integers have
• a sum of -1
• a product of -6?
Thus, decompose the trinomial.
Use $-3, +2$.

When factoring any trinomial, always check for a common factor first. For example,

$$3m^2 - 6m - 24 = 3(m^2 - 2m - 8)$$
$$= 3(m - 4)(m + 2)$$

2.3 Exercise

Questions 1 to 6 develop skills for factoring trinomials.

A 1 Find the missing factor.

(a) $x^2 + 8x + 15 = (\ ? \ )(x + 3)$ (b) $y^2 - 12y + 20 = (y - 10)(\ ? \ )$

(c) $a^2 + 4a - 12 = (\ ? \ )(a + 6)$ (d) $m^2 - 17m + 42 = (m - 14)(\ ? \ )$

2 Find the numbers that have the properties shown in the following table. Then write the factors of each trinomial.

	Trinomial	What two numbers have	
		a sum of	a product of
(a)	$b^2 + 6b + 8$	$+6$?	$+8$?
(b)	$y^2 - 12y + 20$	-12?	$+20$?
(c)	$a^2 - 2a - 8$	-2?	-8?
(d)	$m^2 + 7m - 30$	$+7$?	-30?

3 (a) How are the coefficients A, B, and C used in the *method of decomposition* to find the factors of the trinomial $6x^2 - 7x - 3$?

   $\quad\quad\quad\quad\quad\quad\quad\quad\quad\quad\quad\quad\quad\quad\quad$ A $\quad$ B $\quad$ C

   (b) Factor the trinomial.

4 (a) For the trinomial $3y^2 + 10y + 3$, what two integers have a sum of $+10$ and a product of $+9$?

   (b) Use the integers in (a) to write the factors of $3y^2 + 10y + 3$.

5 (a) For the trinomial $3x^2 - 19x - 14$, what two integers have a sum of -19 and a product of -42?

   (b) Use the integers in (a) to factor the trinomial.

6 The *method of decomposition* was used to write each trinomial in the following form. Find the factors.

(a) $2y(y - 1) + (y - 1)$ (b) $3x(x - 3) - 2(x - 3)$

(c) $n(2n - 1) - 3(2n - 1)$ (d) $2x(x - y) - 3y(x - y)$

B 7   Factor. Look for a common factor first.

(a) $x^2 + 13x + 42$ (b) $3m^2 + 7m + 2$

(c) $x^2 - x - 2$ (d) $y^2 + 2y - 3$

(e) $3m^2 + 9m + 6$ (f) $5m^2 + 11m + 2$

(g) $4y^2 - 4y - 3$ (h) $2a^2 + 8a + 8$

8   To find the factors of the following trinomial, Peter used a trial and error method to discover the positive factors as shown.

$$15x^2 - 28x + 5$$

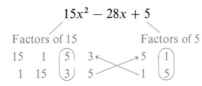

Factors of 15   Factors of 5

(a) Use the circled factors to complete the factors $(5x \quad 1)(3x \quad 5)$.

(b) Why are the signs placed within the factors as shown? $(5x - 1)(3x - 5)$

9   Factor completely.

(a) $a^2 + 3a + 2$ (b) $a^2 + 4a - 12$

(c) $x^2 + x - 56$ (d) $6x^2 + x - 7$

(e) $50 - 20x + 2x^2$ (f) $20x^2 - 19x - 6$

(g) $16m^2 - 8mn + n^2$ (h) $x^2 - 24xy + 144y^2$

(i) $x^3 - 6x^2 + 9x$ (j) $3x^2 - 2x - 1$

(k) $10 + 43x + 28x^2$ (l) $3a^2 + 18a + 27$

(m) $3x^2 + 21x + 36$ (n) $5x^2 - 29x - 6$

10   Express each trinomial in factored form.

(a) $x^2 + 8x + 15$ (b) $a^2 - a - 72$

(c) $b^2 + 6b + 8$ (d) $4x^2 - 16x + 7$

(e) $4x^2 + 8x + 3$ (f) $a^2 + 8a + 16$

(g) $25t^2 - 10t + 1$ (h) $2x^2 + 8x - 10$

(i) $6x^2 - 23x + 21$ (j) $3x^2 - 7x - 6$

(k) $10 + 21x + 2x^2$ (l) $3x^2 - 11x + 10$

11   For each trinomial find the values of k so that two binomials factors are obtained, $0 < k \leq 20$, $k \in I$.

(a) $x^2 + 6x + k$ (b) $x^2 + 7x - k$

(c) $x^2 + kx - 15$ (d) $a^2 + kab + 6b^2$

(e) $x^2 + 5xy + ky^2$ (f) $x^2 - 8xy + ky^2$

Problem-Solving: Working Backwards

You can use a known result to develop a method of solving a problem.

| Use known result to develop a method of solving a problem. | → | Then apply the method to the solution of a given problem. |

For example, the following trinomial was obtained from the product of two factors.

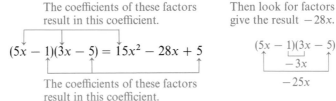

The coefficients of these factors result in this coefficient.

The coefficients of these factors result in this coefficient.

Then look for factors that give the result $-28x$.

$(5x - 1)(3x - 5)$
$-3x$
$-25x$

$(5x - 1)(3x - 5) = 15x^2 - 28x + 5$

You can use known results to develop a method of finding factors.

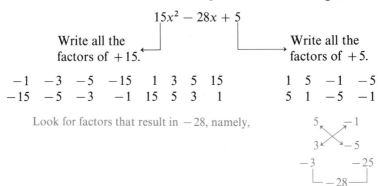

$$15x^2 - 28x + 5$$

Write all the factors of $+15$.

Write all the factors of $+5$.

| -1 | -3 | -5 | -15 | 1 | 3 | 5 | 15 |
| -15 | -5 | -3 | -1 | 15 | 5 | 3 | 1 |

| 1 | 5 | -1 | -5 |
| 5 | 1 | -5 | -1 |

Look for factors that result in -28, namely,

$5 \quad -1$
$3 \quad -5$
$-3 \quad -25$
-28

Once you have developed a method, test the method on examples whose results you know.

12 Factor. Use the method above.
(a) $2y^2 + 11y + 5$ (b) $3 + 4m - 4m^2$ (c) $6x^2 - 19x - 20$

13 (a) Factor $20m^2 + 33m + 10$ by the method of decomposition.
(b) Factor $10m^2 + 21m + 2$ by the method on this page.
(c) Compare the methods in (a) and (b).

14 Factor. Check your answer.
(a) $6x^2 + x - 1$ (b) $4y^2 - 11y - 3$
(c) $3m^2 - 10m + 3$ (d) $21k^2 + 27k + 6$
(e) $24a^2 - 14ab - 5b^2$ (f) $10p^2 - 21p - 10$
(g) $8x^2 - 26xy + 21y^2$ (h) $40p^2 + 61pq + 18q^2$
(i) $27r^2 - 3rs - 10s^2$

2.4 Special Factors

Earlier, you learned to factor polynomials by noticing patterns in the terms of the polynomials to be factored, and by recognizing which skills to use. Recognizing when to use the appropriate skill is an important aspect of solving problems.

For example, you can recognize when to use each of the following skills.

Common Factor

$mx + my = m(x + y)$
$2x^3 - 2x^2 + 2x = 2x(x^2 - x + 1)$

Trinomials

$a^2 + 3ab + 2b^2 = (a + b)(a + 2b)$
$6x^2 - 11xy + 3y^2 = (3x - y)(2x - 3y)$

Factoring a Perfect Square Trinomial

You can use a pattern to recognize the factors of a special trinomial. You already know that

$$(a + b)(a + b) = (a + b)^2 = a^2 + 2ab + b^2$$
$$(a - b)(a - b) = (a - b)^2 = a^2 - 2ab + b^2$$

Now apply the pattern to the following trinomials. Compare the trinomials.

$a^2 + 2ab + b^2 = (a + b)^2 \qquad 9x^2 + 12x + 4 = (3x)^2 + 2(3x)(2) + 2^2$
$$= (3x + 2)(3x + 2)$$
$$= (3x + 2)^2$$

$a \leftrightarrow 3x$

$b \leftrightarrow 2$

A similar comparison is made for the following.

$a^2 - 2ab + b^2 = (a - b)^2 \qquad 16p^2 - 24pq + 9q^2 = (4p)^2 - 2(4p)(3q) + (3q)^2$
$$= (4p - 3q)(4p - 3q)$$
$$= (4p - 3q)^2$$

$a \leftrightarrow 4p$

$b \leftrightarrow 3q$

A trinomial which, when factored, is the square of a binomial is called a **perfect square trinomial**. To use this factoring skill you need to recognize when it can be applied, as shown in the following example.

Example 1   Factor $m^2n^2 - 6m^3n + 9m^4$.

Solution   First, check for a common factor.

$$m^2(n^2 - 6mn + 9m^2) = m^2[(n)^2 - 2(n)(3m) + (3m)^2]$$
$$= m^2(n - 3m)(n - 3m)$$
$$= m^2(n - 3m)^2$$

Factoring a Difference of Squares

If you study the following products, you will notice a pattern that will help you develop a strategy for factoring a special type of polynomial called a **difference of squares**.

$$
\begin{array}{ll}
& \textit{Difference of squares} \\
(x + 3)(x - 3) = x^2 - 9 & (x)^2 - (3)^2 \\
(2m - n)(2m + n) = 4m^2 - n^2 & (2m)^2 - (n)^2 \\
(p - 3q)(p + 3q) = p^2 - 9q^2 & (p)^2 - (3q)^2
\end{array}
$$

Example 2 Factor $9m^2 - n^2$.

Solution
$9m^2 - n^2 = (3m)^2 - (n)^2$ —————— Identify the squares.
$\qquad\qquad = (3m + n)(3m - n)$
$\qquad\qquad\;\;\uparrow\qquad\quad\;\uparrow$
sum of the two terms   difference of the terms

Always remember, when you factor a polynomial, you must

- remove the greatest common factor.
- check the remaining factors to see if any of them can be factored again.

Example 3 Factor completely $3a^4 - 48b^4$.

Solution
$3a^4 - 48b^4 = 3(a^4 - 16b^4)$ —————— Think:
$\qquad\qquad = 3[(a^2)^2 - (4b^2)^2]$ • check: for a common factor.
$\qquad\qquad\qquad\qquad\qquad\qquad$ • check: Can it still be factored?
$\qquad\qquad = 3(a^2 + 4b^2)(a^2 - 4b^2)$ ← Think:
$\qquad\qquad\qquad\qquad\qquad\qquad$ check: Can it still be factored?
$\qquad\qquad = 3(a^2 + 4b^2)(a + 2b)(a - 2b)$ None of the factors can
$\qquad\qquad\qquad\qquad\qquad\qquad\qquad\qquad$ be factored further.

When you factor an expression, you often need to recognize which skills are combined, as shown in the following example.

Example 4 Factor $x^2 + 6xy + 9y^2 - 25x^2$.

Solution
$x^2 + 6xy + 9y^2 - 25x^2 = (x + 3y)^2 - (5x)^2$ Recognize that
$\qquad\qquad\qquad\qquad\quad = (x + 3y + 5x)(x + 3y - 5x)$ $x^2 + 6xy + 9y^2$ is
$\qquad\qquad\qquad\qquad\quad = (6x + 3y)(-4x + 3y)$ a perfect square.

2.4 Exercise

A 1 Expand each of the following. What property do they have in common?

(a) $(p + 4)(p + 4)$
(b) $(3m - 2)(3m - 2)$

(c) $(x + 2y)(x + 2y)$
(d) $\left(a - \dfrac{1}{2}\right)\left(a - \dfrac{1}{2}\right)$

(e) $(2g - 5k)(2g - 5k)$
(f) $(7w + v^2)(7w + v^2)$

2 Expand each of the following. What property do they have in common?

(a) $(a + 5)(a - 5)$
(b) $(2x - 3)(2x + 3)$

(c) $(x + 3y)(x - 3y)$
(d) $(3x + b)(3x - b)$

(e) $(a^2 - 2b^2)(a^2 + 2b^2)$
(f) $(xy - 1)(xy + 1)$

(g) $(x + y + z)(x + y - z)$
(h) $(a + 2b - y)(a + 2b + y)$

3 Find the missing term in each of the following if each is a perfect trinomial square.

(a) $x^2 - 2xy + (\ ?\ )$
(b) $(\ ?\ ) + 4a + 1$

(c) $(\ ?\ ) - 12x + 4$
(d) $4m^2 - 4m + (\ ?\ )$

(e) $4x^2 + (\ ?\ ) + 81$
(f) $9a^2 - (\ ?\ ) + 16$

4 You must be able to identify a difference of squares before you can factor it. Complete each of the following. Then write the factors.

(a) $9a^2 - b^2 = (\ ?\ )^2 - b^2$

(b) $m^2 - 16n^2 = m^2 - (\ ?\ )^2$

(c) $25x^2 - 49y^2 = (\ ?\ )^2 - (\ ?\ )^2$

(d) $(x - y)^2 - 16a^2 = (x - y)^2 - (\ ?\ )^2$

(e) $100m^2 - (2a + b)^2 = (\ ?\ )^2 - (2a + b)^2$

B 5 Write each of the following as a perfect trinomial square.

(a) $m^2 + 6m + 9$
(b) $a^2 - 8a + 16$

(c) $4x^2 + 4x + 1$
(d) $9y^2 - 12y + 4$

(e) $25a^2 - 40ab + 16b^2$
(f) $4 - 20m + 25m^2$

(g) $4p^2 + 12pq + 9q^2$
(h) $\frac{1}{4}w^2 - 3vw + 9v^2$

(i) $m^4n^2 + 4m^2n + 4$
(j) $9c^2 - 12cde + 4d^2e^2$

(k) $49g^2 + 14gh + h^2$
(l) $a^4b^4c^2 - 4a^2b^2c + 4$

(m) $8y^2 - 40y + 50$
(n) $4m^2n - 28mn^2 + 49n^3$

(o) $2x^3y + 8x^2y^2 + 8xy^3$

6 Each of the following trinomials is to be a perfect square. Find k, $k > 0$.

(a) $x^2 - 6x + k$
(b) $x^2 - kx + 121$
(c) $x^2 - 12x + k$

(d) $4x^2 - 4x + k$
(e) $4x^2 + kx + 9$
(f) $4x^2 - kx + 16$

7 For each polynomial, group the terms and write a difference of squares. Then write the factors. The first one has been done for you.

(a) $a^2 + 2ab + b^2 - c^2 \longleftarrow a^2 + 2ab + b^2 - c^2 = (a + b)^2 - c^2$
$$= (a + b - c)(a + b + c)$$

(b) $4x^2 + 4xy + y^2 - c^2$

(c) $x^2 + 6x + 9 - 4y^2$ (d) $4x^2 - a^2 - 2ab - b^2$

(e) $9y^2 - 4a^2 + 4ab - b^2$ (f) $16x^2 - m^2 - 6mn - 9n^2$

(g) $25y^2 - 1 + 6x - 9x^2$ (h) $a^2 - 2ab + b^2 - x^2 - 2xy - y^2$

8 Look at the polynomials $4k^2 - x^2$ and $4(a + b)^2 - x^2$.

(a) How are they alike? How are they different?

(b) Write them in factored form.

9 Look at the polynomials $p^2 - 9k^2$ and $p^2 - 9(q + r)^2$.

(a) How are they alike? How are they different?

(b) Write them in factored form.

10 Write the factors of each of the following.   Remember: regroup to obtain a difference of squares.

(a) $9a^2 - 6ab + b^2 - x^2$ (b) $1 - 2y + y^2 - 4x^2$

(c) $9a^2 + 6a + 1 - 9b^2$ (d) $100x^2 - m^2 - 2m - 1$

(e) $49x^2 - 4m^2 - 4m - 1$ (f) $25y^2 - 1 + 6x - 9x^2$

(g) $x^2 + 2xy + y^2 - a^2 + 2ab - b^2$

(h) $9x^2 - 6x + 1 - 16x^2 + 8xy - y^2$

11 (a) Write the factors of $m^4 - 1$.

(b) Check the factors you wrote in (a). Are they factorable?

12 (a) Write the factors of the trinomial $x^4 - 5x^2 + 4$.

(b) Check the factors in (a). Write the factors of those that are factorable.

13 A square with sides x units is drawn and then a square with sides y units is removed from the original square. Use the diagram to show why $x^2 - y^2 = (x + y)(x - y)$.

14 Factor fully.

(a) $y^2 - 16$ (b) $m^2 - 100$ (c) $36 - x^2$

(d) $18y^2 - 2$ (e) $9 - 4k^2$ (f) $36x^2 - y^2$

(g) $25m^2 - 16a^2$ (h) $1 - 25y^2$ (i) $a^2b^2 - 1$

(j) $m - 16m^3$ (k) $9m^2 - 121$ (l) $98a - 72a^3$

(m) $4a^2 - 9b^4$ (n) $16m^4 - 9n^2$ (o) $x^2y^2 - 4$

15 Factory fully.
    (a) $n^2 - 36$ (b) $9h^2 - 49m^2$ (c) $225m^2 - 1$
    (d) $x^2y^2z^2 - 9$ (e) $-1 + 36m^2$ (f) $(x + y)^2 - 9$
    (g) $(x + y)^2 - m^2$ (h) $y^4 - 81$ (i) $8x^2 - 50y^2$
    (j) $y^2 - (a + h)^2$ (k) $(x - 3y)^2 - 4a^2$ (l) $9m^2 - 4(x - y)^2$
    (m) $\dfrac{1}{4}x^2 - \dfrac{1}{9}y^2$ (n) $a^4 - b^4$ (o) $y^2 - 0.16x^2$
    (p) $2(x - 2y)^2 - \dfrac{1}{2}m^2$ (q) $(x - y)^2 - 4(p - q)^2$
    (r) $(x + y - 3z)^2 - 4k^2$ (s) $(x + y)^2 - 9(a + b - c)^2$

16 Write each of the following in factored form.
    (a) $a^2 - 2ab + b^2 - m^2$ (b) $k^2 - m^2 + 2mn - n^2$
    (c) $a^2 - 2ay + y^2 - 4x^2$ (d) $a^2 - 2ab + b^2 - c^4$
    (e) $x^2 - y^2 - 2yz - z^2$ (f) $m^4 - x^2 + 2xy - y^2$
    (g) $x^2 + 2xy + y^2 - a^2 - 2ab - b^2$
    (h) $x^2 + y^2 - a^2 - b^2 + 2xy + 2ab$
    (i) $x^2 + 2xw + w^2 - y^2 - 2yz - z^2$

17 Factor each of the following completely. Which two cannot be factored?
    (a) $16x^2 - y^2$ (b) $x^2 - 49y^2$ (c) $4x^2 - 1$
    (d) $4x^2 - 25$ (e) $(x + 3)^2 - 25$ (f) $x^2 + 6x + 9 - y^2$
    (g) $2x^2 - 18$ (h) $-75 + 3x^2$ (i) $a^2 + 4bc - 4c^2 - b^2$
    (j) $49 - (x - 2)^2$ (k) $6x^2 - 54y^2$ (l) $27x^2 - 3y^2$
    (m) $9a^2 - 6a + 1 - 9m^2$ (n) $x^2 - 18$ (o) $m^4 - 17m^2 + 16$
    (p) $(x + 2)^2 - (y - 5)^2$ (q) $25x^2 + 16y^2$ (r) $\dfrac{x^2}{16} - \dfrac{y^2}{36}$
    (s) $4a^4 - 37a^2 + 9$ (t) $81m^8n^4 - y^8$
    (u) $a^2 - 2ab + b^2 - 9x^2 - 18xy - 9y^2$
    (v) $m^2 + n^2 - p^2 - q^2 - 2mn - 2pq$

Problem Solving

To go from A to B you can only go right or up. How many different paths are possible from A to B?

Strategy: Factoring Incomplete Squares

In factoring trinomial squares, you learned to identify when the skill can be applied. If you examine the two following expressions, you will notice that these two trinomials are the same, except for the term containing x^2.

$$\underbrace{x^4 + 4x^2 + 16} \qquad x^4 + 8x^2 + 16 = (x^2 + 4)^2$$

This expression is called an *incomplete square*.

To factor the trinomial, $x^4 + 4x^2 + 16$, rewrite its form as follows.

$$x^4 + 4x^2 + 16$$

$$= x^4 + 8x^2 - 4x^2 + 16 \qquad \text{Write } 4x^2 \text{ in a form}$$
$$= x^4 + 8x^2 + 16 - 4x^2 \qquad \text{which will result in a perfect square.}$$
$$= (x^2 + 4)^2 - (2x)^2$$
$$= (x^2 + 4 + 2x)(x^2 + 4 - 2x)$$

18 For what value of m is each of the following a perfect square?
(a) $x^4 + mx^2 + 144$ (b) $9a^4 + ma^2 + 1$
(c) $16k^4 - mk^2 + 9$ (d) $y^4 - my^2 + 25$
(e) $25x^4 - mx^2y^2 + 16y^4$ (f) $9 + mp^2 + 36p^4$

19 The first step in factoring these incomplete squares is shown. Complete the solution.

(a) $x^4 + x^2 + 1$
    $= x^4 + 2x^2 + 1 - x^2$
    $= ?$

(b) $a^4 + 7a^2 + 16$
    $= a^4 + 8a^2 + 16 - a^2$
    $= ?$

(c) $a^4 + 4$
    $= a^4 + 4a^2 + 4 - 4a^2$
    $= ?$

(d) $m^4 - 11m^2n^2 + n^4$
    $= m^4 - 2m^2n^2 + n^4 - 9m^2n^2$
    $= ?$

20 Find the missing term in each of the following. Then complete the solution to find the factors.
(a) $4y^4 - 13y^2 + 1 = 4y^4 - ? + 1 - 9y^2$
(b) $a^4 + 2a^2b^2 + 9b^4 = a^4 + 6a^2b^2 + 9b^4 - ?$

21 Factor each of the following by completing the square.
(a) $y^4 + y^2 + 25$ (b) $x^4 + 2x^2 + 9$
(c) $a^4 + 3a^2 + 4$ (d) $y^4 - 23x^2y^2 + x^4$
(e) $16x^4 - 12x^2 + 1$ (f) $9m^4 + 2m^2 + 1$
(g) $9a^4 - 52a^2b^2 + 64b^4$ (h) $4m^4 - 16m^2 + 9$

2.5 Problem-Solving: Identifying Methods

When solving problems, very often you need to examine carefully the given information and look for clues. In this chapter you have acquired various methods of finding the factors of algebraic expressions. Look for clues to identify the method needed to factor the expressions. For example, the expression

$$m^2 + 6m + 9 - 4n^2$$

appears in a form to which you cannot apply any methods that you know. The square term $-4n^2$ may suggest a difference of squares. Thus, you write

$$(m^2 + 6m + 9) - 4n^2 = (m+3)^2 - (2n)^2$$
$$= (m+3-2n)(m+3+2n)$$

Now you can apply the difference of squares method to factor the expression.

In the following exercise, look for clues to help you identify the method you need to use. Look out for expressions that can not be factored.

2.5 Exercise

1 $4x^3 + x^2$
2 $3x - 9xy$
3 $6x^4 - 12x$
4 $9x^4 - 16y^2$
5 $x^2 + 9x + 20$
6 $5x^2 - 5y^2$
7 $y^2 - 13y + 42$
8 $6x^2 - 13x - 5$
9 $x^2 + xy - 12y^2$
10 $9x^2 + 27x + 8$
11 $-4 + 25x^2$
12 $y^3 - y - 6$
13 $3y^2 - 9y^3$
14 $5 + 6x + x^2$
15 $18x^2 - 25x - 3$
16 $9x^2 + 1$
17 $6x^2 - 28x - 10$
18 $x^4 - 64$
19 $m^4 + 3m^2 + 4$
20 $-(9x^2 - y^4)$
21 $x^4 - 3x^2 - 4$
22 $10x^2 + 7x + 1$
23 $4x^6 - y^6$
24 $x^2 + 4x - 21$
25 $2x^4 - 3x^2 - 2$
26 $y^4 + 2y^2 + 9$
27 $2x^2 - 4xy + 8x$
28 $x^2 - 121$
29 $2x^2 - 2x - 28$
30 $(2x + y)^2 - z^2$
31 $m^4 - 6m^2 - 27$
32 $4y^4 - 16y^2 + 9$
33 $x^4 + 2x^2 - 15$
34 $8y^3 + 1$
35 $9x^{10} - 4$
36 $2y^2 + 24y + 40$
37 $5x^2 - 20$
38 $3x^2 - 27x + 54$
39 $x^4 - 225y^2$
40 $4x^2 - 28x - 32$
41 $x^6 - y^6$
42 $3x^5 + 15x^3 + 12x$
43 $-75 + 12x^4$
44 $3x^2yz^3 + 18xy^2$
45 $y^4 - 17y^2 + 16$
46 $4(x - y)^2 - (x + y)^2$
47 $(x - y)^2 - 9(2x + y)^2$
48 $m^2 + 6m + 9 - 4n^2$
49 $16y^2 - a^2 - 6ab - 9b^2$
50 $x^3 - 2x^2 - 9x + 18$

2.6 Applying Factors: Solving Quadratic Equations

In your study of mathematics, once you learn a skill, you apply the skill to develop other skills. For example, you apply your skills in factoring to solve equations such as $x^2 - 6x + 8 = 0$, $2x^2 - 3x + 1 = 0$, $x^2 - 9 = 0$. Each of the above equations is of *degree* 2 and is called a quadratic equation.

To solve a quadratic equation you use the principle:
If $a \times b = 0$ then either $a = 0$ or $b = 0$.

Thus, to solve quadratic equations, first you need to write factors, as shown in the following example.

Example 1   Solve $x^2 - 4x + 3 = 0$.

Solution
$$x^2 - 4x + 3 = 0 \longleftarrow \text{Step 1: Factor the trinomial expression.}$$
$$(x - 1)(x - 3) = 0 \longleftarrow$$

$$x - 1 = 0 \quad \text{or } x - 3 = 0 \qquad \text{Step 2: Apply the principle:}$$
$$x = 1 \qquad\qquad x = 3 \qquad\quad \text{If } a \times b = 0 \text{ then } a = 0 \text{ or } b = 0.$$

Verify *both* roots in the original equation.   Step 3: Check your answer.

For $x = 1$	For $x = 3$
$RS = 0$	$RS = 0$
$LS = x^2 - 4x + 3$	$LS = x^2 - 4x + 3$
$\quad = (1)^2 - 4(1) + 3$	$\quad = (3)^2 - 4(3) + 3$
$\quad = 1 - 4 + 3 = 0$	$\quad = 9 - 12 + 3 = 0$
$LS = RS$	$LS = RS$

The roots of the equation are $\{1, 3\}$.

The quadratic equation in the following example first needs to be rewritten so that one side of the equation is equal to zero.

Example 2   Find the solution set of $(3x - 1)(2x + 3) = -5$.

Solution
$$(3x - 1)(2x + 3) = -5$$
$$6x^2 + 7x - 3 = -5$$
$$6x^2 + 7x + 2 = 0$$
$$(3x + 2)(2x + 1) = 0 \longleftarrow \text{Equate each factor to zero.}$$

$$3x + 2 = 0 \quad \text{or} \quad 2x + 1 = 0$$
$$3x = -2 \qquad\qquad 2x = -1$$
$$x = -\frac{2}{3} \qquad\qquad x = -\frac{1}{2}$$

Thus the solution set is $\left\{-\dfrac{2}{3}, -\dfrac{1}{2}\right\}$.   Remember to check the answers.

In the preceeding examples, you were given a quadratic equation and you found the roots. If you know what the roots of the quadratic equation are, you can write the equation. For example, if the roots are -3 and 2, then introduce a variable, say x, and write the following, using the reverse procedure.

$$x = -3 \quad \text{or} \quad x = 2$$
$$x + 3 = 0 \quad | \quad x - 2 = 0$$

$$\text{Then } (x + 3)(x - 2) = 0$$
$$x^2 + x - 6 = 0$$

A quadratic equation with roots -3 and 2 is $x^2 + x - 6 = 0$.

In this section, you solved quadratic equations by applying the skills of factoring you learned. In Chapter 7, you will study the quadratic equation in detail to learn more methods and strategies for using them.

2.6 Exercise

A   Questions 1 to 9 develop some essential skills for solving quadratic equations.

1   What are the roots for each of the following equations?
(a) $x + 5 = 0$ (b) $(x - 2)(x + 5) = 0$
(c) $2y + 1 = 0$ (d) $(3y - 2)(2y + 1) = 0$
(e) $(x - 3)(x + 4) = 0$ (f) $(y + 5)(y - 6) = 0$
(g) $(m - 3)(3m + 2) = 0$ (h) $(2y - 1)(3y - 2) = 0$

2   Solve each of the following.
(a) $(x - 3)(x + 2) = 0$ (b) $(y + 5)(y - 5) = 0$
(c) $(3k - 2)(k + 3) = 0$ (d) $a(a - 5) = 0$
(e) $(m - 3)(2m + 1) = 0$ (f) $3y(y - 5) = 0$

3   Factor. Then find the roots.
(a) $x^2 + 8x + 15 = 0$ (b) $m^2 + 7m - 30 = 0$
(c) $m^2 - 25 = 0$ (d) $5x^2 + 17x + 6 = 0$
(e) $3y^2 + 10y + 3 = 0$ (f) $6 + 7y - 5y^2 = 0$

4   (a) What might be your first step in solving $y^2 - 7y = -12$?
(b) Solve the equation in (a).

5   (a) Find the solution set for $x^2 - 4x = 21$.
(b) Verify your results in (a).

6 Solve each of the following.
   (a) $a^2 - 2a = 48$ (b) $3x^2 + 13x = 30$ (c) $3 = 6x^2 - 7x$
   (d) $2x^2 - 7x + 6 = 0$ (e) $15 + x = 2x^2$ (f) $m^2 + 7m = 30$

7 (a) What might be your first step in solving $4x^2 - 4x - 48 = 0$?
   (b) Solve the equation in (a).

8 Solve. Watch for common factors.
   (a) $2y^2 + 12y + 16 = 0$ (b) $3a^2 - 3a - 216 = 0$
   (c) $6x^2 - 23x + 21 = 0$ (d) $2x^2 + 10x + 12 = 0$
   (e) $15 + x - 2x^2 = 0$ (f) $6x^2 - 22x + 20 = 0$

9 (a) To simplify your calculations, what might be your first step in solving
   $$x^2 + \frac{5}{2}x = \frac{33}{2}?$$
   (b) Solve the equation in (a).

B 10 Solve.   Did you check your answers?
   (a) $y^2 - y - 6 = 0$ (b) $x^2 - 2x - 15 = 0$
   (c) $m^2 + 9m + 20 = 0$ (d) $a^2 - 13a + 42 = 0$
   (e) $y^2 - 8y = 0$ (f) $2m^2 + 19m + 35 = 0$
   (g) $y^2 - 16 = 0$ (h) $2y^2 - 10y - 28 = 0$
   (i) $6x^2 - 28x - 10 = 0$ (j) $y^2 + 4y - 21 = 0$
   (k) $5m^2 + 12m + 7 = 0$ (l) $25 - 16y^2 = 0$

11 Solve.   Check your answer.
   (a) $x^2 - 4x = 21$ (b) $y^2 + 7y = 18$
   (c) $15 = 3m^2 + 4m$ (d) $9y = 2y^2 + 7$
   (e) $42 = x^2 - x$ (f) $26x = 5x^2 + 24$
   (g) $y^2 = 9y$ (h) $x^2 = 36$

12 Use your skills with common factoring to solve each of the following.
   (a) $y(y^2 - 4) - 4(y^2 - 4) = 0$ (b) $m^2(m + 1) - 9(m + 1) = 0$
   (c) $4(k^2 - 9) - k(k^2 - 9) = 0$

13 If $x(x - 1)(x - 2) = 0$, then you write $x = 0$ or $x - 1 = 0$ or
   $x - 2 = 0$. Find the roots of each equation.
   (a) $(m - 1)(m - 2)(m - 3) = 0$ (b) $p(p - 1)(p + 3) = 0$
   (c) $x^3 + 5x^2 + 6x = 0$ (d) $2y^3 + 7y^2 - 15y = 0$
   (e) $15y = 3y^3 + 4y^2$ (f) $m^3 - 4m^2 = 21m$

14   (a) Solve and verify $x^4 - 10x^2 + 9 = 0$.

(b) Find the solution set for $x^4 - 13x^2 + 36 = 0$.

15   An important skill in problem-solving is to know when to apply a particular skill to solve a problem. Find all the roots of the following equations.

(a) $5m^2 - 4 = 19m$
(b) $3(x^2 - 5) = -4x$
(c) $x^2 - 16 = 0$
(d) $y^2 + 2y + 1 = 0$
(e) $(2y + 3)(4y + 1) = 18$
(f) $25y^2 - 1 = 0$
(g) $5(2y + 5) + y^2 = 0$
(h) $1 - 7x + 6x^2 = 0$
(i) $x^2 - 10 = \dfrac{x}{3}$
(j) $x^2 + 4x + 4 = 0$
(k) $\dfrac{m + 3}{2} = m^2$
(l) $16x - x^3 = 0$
(m) $4y^2 + \dfrac{11}{3}y = 5$
(n) $2y = 3y^2 + \dfrac{1}{3}$
(o) $16 - 25x^2 = 0$
(p) $12y = y^3 - 4y^2$
(q) $y^3 - 9y^2 = 0$
(r) $25 + 10p + p^2 = 0$
(s) $16(y^2 - 9) - y(y^2 - 9) = 0$
(t) $m(m^2 - 4) - 7(m^2 - 4) = 0$

16   Copy and complete the table.

	Original equation	Equation in factored form	Roots of equation
(a)	$4x^2 - 8x - 5 = 0$	?	?
(b)	?	$(x - 3)(2x + 7) = 0$	?
(c)	?	?	$\dfrac{1}{3}, -3$
(d)	$3x^2 - 10x + 3 = 0$	?	?

17   Construct an equation in the form $ax^2 + bx + c = 0$ that has the following roots.

(a) $3, -2$ (b) $-4, -6$ (c) $3, \dfrac{1}{2}$ (d) $-3, \dfrac{2}{3}$ (e) $0, 4$ (f) $-\dfrac{1}{2}, \dfrac{1}{3}$

18   -6 is a root of the equation $3x^2 + 16x + p = 0$.

(a) Find the value of p.   (b) Find the other root.

19   One root of each equation is given.

• Find the value of p.   • Find the other root.

(a) $3x^2 + 5x + p = 0$, -2 (b) $2x^2 - 9x + p = 0$, 5

(c) $4x^2 - px + 6 = 0$, 6 (d) $px^2 + 24x - 5 = 0$, $\dfrac{1}{5}$

2.7 Simplifying Rational Expressions

In the previous section you applied your skills in factoring to find the roots of a quadratic equation. In this section, you apply your skills with factoring to simplify rational expressions. The word rational has occurred in your earlier work. For two integers, p and q, a rational number is formed when $\frac{p}{q}$ and $q \neq 0$. For example, the following are rational numbers.

$$\frac{5}{2}, \quad 0.75 = \frac{3}{4}, \quad 4 = \frac{4}{1}$$

In the study of mathematics, words used in arithmetic are used in a similar way in algebra. For example, for polynomials F and G, a rational expression is formed when $\frac{F}{G}$, $G \neq 0$. The following expressions are rational expressions.

$$\frac{x + 2}{5}, \quad \frac{x^2 - 3x + 4}{x^4 - 1}, \quad \frac{1}{3 + 2x}$$

Since division by zero is undefined, the denominator cannot be zero. Thus, restrictions must be placed on the value of the variable so that the denominator will not be equal to zero. For the polynomial $\frac{1}{3 + 2x}$, since $3 + 2x \neq 0$, then the restriction on x is given by $2x \neq -3$ or $x \neq -\frac{3}{2}$.

Again, your factoring skills are used, except this time, they are applied to the simplification of rational expressions, as shown in the following example.

Example 1 Simplify $\dfrac{x^2 - 2x - 3}{2x - 6}$. What is the restriction on the variable?

Solution Since the denominator cannot equal zero, then
$$2x - 6 \neq 0$$
$$2x \neq 6$$
$$x \neq 3$$

Thus, the restriction on the variable is $x \neq 3$.

Factor the numerator and denominator.

$$\frac{x^2 - 2x - 3}{2x - 6} = \frac{(x - 3)(x + 1)}{2(x - 3)}, \quad \text{where } x \neq 3$$

$$= \frac{(x - 3)^{1}(x + 1)}{2(x - 3)^{1}}$$

$$= \frac{x + 1}{2}, \quad x \neq 3$$

In the following example, you use your skills in solving a quadratic equation to obtain the restrictions on the variable.

Example 2   Simplify $\dfrac{15 - 3m}{m^2 + 2m - 35}$.

Solution

First, identify the restrictions on the variable.

$m^2 + 2m - 35 \neq 0$ or $(m + 7)(m - 5) \neq 0$

Thus, $m + 7 \neq 0$ or $m - 5 \neq 0$

                            $m \neq -7$ or $m \neq 5$

Thus, the restrictions are $m \neq -7, 5$.

Now simply factor the numerator and the denominator.

$$\frac{15 - 3m}{m^2 + 2m - 35} = \frac{3(5 - m)}{(m + 7)(m - 5)}$$

$$= \frac{-3(m - 5)}{(m + 7)(m - 5)} \qquad \text{Remember}$$
$$\qquad\qquad\qquad\qquad 5 - m = -(m - 5)$$

$$= \frac{-3\overset{1}{\cancel{(m - 5)}}}{(m + 7)\underset{1}{\cancel{(m - 5)}}}$$

$$= -\frac{3}{m + 7} \quad \text{where } m \neq 5, -7$$

Remember, when finding the restrictions on the variable, use the original rational equation, as shown in the previous examples. Finding the restrictions should be your first step of the solution.

2.7   Exercise

A 1   Identify the restrictions on the variable.

(a) $\dfrac{x + 2}{x}$ (b) $\dfrac{5}{x}$ (c) $\dfrac{3}{y - 2}$

(d) $\dfrac{5}{5x - 1}$ (e) $\dfrac{2x}{2x + 5}$ (f) $\dfrac{x}{x^2 + x}$

(g) $\dfrac{k}{(k - 2)(k + 1)}$ (h) $\dfrac{x + y}{(x - y)(x + y)}$ (i) $\dfrac{2x + 3y}{(x - 2y)(2y - x)}$

(j) $\dfrac{(m - 1)(m + 1)}{2m + 1}$ (k) $\dfrac{-m}{x}$ (l) $\dfrac{-x}{m}$ (m) $\dfrac{x - 1}{x^2 - 1}$

2 Which of the following are equivalent to $\dfrac{y-x}{x+y}$?

(a) $-\dfrac{x-y}{x+y}$ (b) $-\dfrac{y-x}{x+y}$ (c) $-\dfrac{-(y-x)}{x+y}$ (d) $-\dfrac{x-y}{y+x}$

3 Simplify.

(a) $\dfrac{a+b}{b+a}$ (b) $-\dfrac{(b-a)}{b-a}$ (c) $\dfrac{a-b}{-(b-a)}$

(d) $\dfrac{-(b+a)}{-(b+a)}$ (e) $\dfrac{-(b-a)}{a-b}$ (f) $\dfrac{-(b-a)}{-(a-b)}$

B 4 Simplify. Remember to list the restrictions on the variable first.

(a) $\dfrac{3}{6x}$ (b) $\dfrac{4p}{2p^2}$ (c) $\dfrac{5y+10}{25y}$ (d) $\dfrac{-25mn^2}{5mn}$

(e) $\dfrac{(x+1)^2}{x+1}$ (f) $\dfrac{2(m-1)^2}{m^2-1}$ (g) $\dfrac{4x+16}{x+4}$

(h) $\dfrac{k^2+3k}{k^3+3k^2}$ (i) $\dfrac{w^2+2w+1}{w^2-2w-3}$ (j) $\dfrac{d^2-5d+6}{2d^2-7d+3}$

5 Simplify.

(a) $\dfrac{4p^2-9q^2}{3q-2p}$ (b) $\dfrac{6a-3}{1-4a^2}$ (c) $\dfrac{4-4a^2}{2+4a+2a^2}$

(d) $\dfrac{5x^4-15x^5}{5-17x+6x^2}$ (e) $\dfrac{p^2-4p-21}{p^2-9}$ (f) $\dfrac{x^2-2x-15}{4x-20}$

(g) $\dfrac{y^2-25}{y^2-3y-10}$ (h) $\dfrac{y^2-8y+15}{y^2-y-6}$ (i) $\dfrac{x^2-4x-5}{5x^2-25x}$

6 Divide.

(a) $\dfrac{3+x-2x^2}{3x^2+4x+1}$ (b) $\dfrac{m^2-n^2}{m^2+2mn+n^2}$ (c) $\dfrac{x^3+7x^2+12x}{x^2+9x+20}$

(d) $\dfrac{4x+16}{x^3+4x^2}$ (e) $\dfrac{4x^2-4xy-15y^2}{4x^2+16xy+15y^2}$ (f) $\dfrac{2w+6}{81-w^4}$

(g) $\dfrac{16-9x^2}{3x^2-x-4}$ (h) $\dfrac{12x^4-8x^3-4x^2}{x^2-1}$

7 Divide.

(a) $\dfrac{x^2+3x-10}{2x^2+10x-x-5}$ (b) $\dfrac{(5-k^2)-1}{2k^2+7k+6}$ (c) $\dfrac{2x(2x+3)+x(2x+5)}{6x^2+5x-11}$

(d) $\dfrac{(a-7b+c)^2-(7b-c)^2}{a^2+2ac}$ (e) $\dfrac{2(2y+3)+(y+9)}{18+3y-y^2}$

(f) $\dfrac{(p-5)+(p+1)(p-5)}{(p-5)(p+2)(2p+1)}$ (g) $\dfrac{x^4+8x^2y+16y^2}{2(x^2+3y)-(x^2+2y)}$

2.8 Multiplying and Dividing Rational Expressions

Concepts and skills developed in arithmetic extend to your work with algebraic expressions. For example, rules that apply to rational numbers also apply to rational expressions.

Addition of Fractions	Subtraction of Fractions
$\dfrac{a}{b} + \dfrac{c}{d} = \dfrac{ad + bc}{bd}$	$\dfrac{a}{b} - \dfrac{c}{d} = \dfrac{ad - bc}{bd}$
Multiplication of Fractions	Division of Fractions
$\dfrac{a}{b} \times \dfrac{c}{d} = \dfrac{ac}{bd}$	$\dfrac{a}{b} \div \dfrac{c}{d} = \dfrac{a}{b} \times \dfrac{d}{c} = \dfrac{ad}{bc}$

However, when working with rational expressions, you must identify any restrictions that apply to the variable, since the denominator cannot be equal to zero.

Example 1 Calculate $\dfrac{1 - 3y}{2y + 1} \times \dfrac{4y^2 - 1}{1 - 9y^2}$ if $y = 5$. What are the restrictions on the variable?

Solution Let $2y + 1 = 0$ and $1 - 9y^2 = 0$ Find the restrictions on the variable

$$2y = -1 \qquad\qquad 1 = 9y^2$$

$$y = -\frac{1}{2} \qquad\qquad \frac{1}{9} = y^2 \quad \text{or} \quad y^2 = \frac{1}{9}$$

$$y = \pm\frac{1}{3}$$

Thus, the restrictions on the variable are $y \neq \pm\frac{1}{3}, -\frac{1}{2}$.

$$\frac{1 - 3y}{2y + 1} \times \frac{4y^2 - 1}{1 - 9y^2} = \frac{1 - 3y}{2y + 1} \times \frac{(2y - 1)(2y + 1)}{(1 - 3y)(1 + 3y)}$$

Step 1: Simplify the rational expression. Use your skills from your previous work.

$$= \frac{\overset{1}{\cancel{1 - 3y}}}{\underset{1}{\cancel{2y + 1}}} \times \frac{(2y - 1)\overset{1}{\cancel{(2y + 1)}}}{{}_{1}\cancel{(1 - 3y)}(1 + 3y)}$$

$$= \frac{2y - 1}{1 + 3y}$$

Use $y = 5$. Then $\dfrac{2y - 1}{1 + 3y} = \dfrac{2(5) - 1}{1 + 3(5)}$

Step 2: Once you have simplified the expression, then substitute.

$$= \frac{10 - 1}{1 + 15}$$

$$= \frac{9}{16}$$

In practising with rational numbers, you have learned to multiply and divide them. These skills and concepts extend to your work with rational expressions, as shown in the following example.

Example 2 Simplify $\dfrac{2x^2 - 7x - 4}{x^2 - 7x + 12} \div \dfrac{4x^2 - 1}{2x - 6}$.

Solution $\dfrac{2x^2 - 7x - 4}{x^2 - 7x + 12} \div \dfrac{4x^2 - 1}{2x - 6} = \dfrac{2x^2 - 7x - 4}{x^2 - 7x + 12} \times \dfrac{2x - 6}{4x^2 - 1}$ Remember, the restrictions $x \neq 3, 4, \pm\frac{1}{2}$.

$$= \dfrac{(2x + 1)(x - 4)}{(x - 3)(x - 4)} \times \dfrac{2(x - 3)}{(2x - 1)(2x + 1)}$$

$$= \dfrac{\overset{1}{\cancel{(2x+1)}}\overset{1}{\cancel{(x-4)}}}{\underset{1}{\cancel{(x-3)}}\underset{1}{\cancel{(x-4)}}} \times \dfrac{2(x - 3)\overset{1}{\cancel{}}}{(2x - 1)\underset{1}{\cancel{(2x+1)}}}$$

$$= \dfrac{2}{2x - 1}$$

2.8 Exercise

A Throughout the exercise, consider the restrictions that occur on the variables.

1 Simplify.

(a) $\dfrac{a^2 - b^2}{b - a}$ (b) $-\dfrac{4x^2 - y^2}{y - 2x}$ (c) $\dfrac{x^2 - 2x + 1}{1 - x}$

2 Simplify each of the following.

(a) $\dfrac{-3a}{10b} \times \dfrac{20b}{-24a}$ (b) $\dfrac{a}{2y} \times \dfrac{-4by}{-10ax}$ (c) $\dfrac{3t^2}{-2y} \div \dfrac{6t^3}{4y^2}$

(d) $\dfrac{3x}{-4y^3} \div \dfrac{-32}{15x^2y}$ (e) $\dfrac{4km}{9m} \times \dfrac{-3m^3k}{6k^2}$ (f) $\dfrac{a}{-2b} \div \dfrac{-a}{4b}$

(g) $\dfrac{6x^3}{-x^2} \times \dfrac{x^5}{18x} \div \dfrac{8}{6x^6}$ (h) $\dfrac{36x^3y^5}{-x} \div \dfrac{12x^2y}{10xy^2} \times \dfrac{-x^4}{15y^4}$

3 Simplify.

(a) $\dfrac{y - 1}{y + 3} \times \dfrac{2y + 6}{1 - y}$ (b) $\dfrac{x - 3}{2 - x} \div \dfrac{2x - 6}{x - 2}$

(c) $\dfrac{x - 1}{3x} \times \dfrac{x}{x^2 - 1}$ (d) $\dfrac{y + 1}{y^2 - 1} \div \dfrac{y - 1}{y}$

B 4 Simplify.

(a) $\dfrac{x^2 + 7x}{x^2 - 1} \times \dfrac{x^2 + 3x + 2}{x^2 + 14x + 49}$ (b) $\dfrac{(x^2 - 9)}{x^2 + 5x + 4} \div \dfrac{x^2 - 4x + 3}{x^2 + 5x + 4}$

(c) $\dfrac{x^2 - 3x + 2}{x^2 + 6x + 9} \times \dfrac{x^2 - 9}{2x - 4}$ (d) $\dfrac{2x^2 - 14x + 24}{4x^2 - 64} \div \dfrac{x^2 - 8x + 15}{2x^2 - 11x + 5}$

5   If $x = -3$, find the value of each of the following.   What is your first step?

(a) $\dfrac{x^2 + 9}{x + 9}$ (b) $\dfrac{x^2 + 3x + 2}{4 - x^2}$ (c) $\dfrac{x^2 - 9}{2x + 1} \div \dfrac{x^2 - 6x + 9}{2x - 6}$

(d) $\dfrac{x^2 + 4x + 4}{x^2 - 4} \times \dfrac{2x - 4}{x^2 - 3x - 10} \div \dfrac{4x + 16}{x^2 - 25}$

6   Write each of the following as a rational expression in lowest terms.

(a) $\dfrac{m^2 + 7m + 12}{m^2 + m - 6} \div \dfrac{2m + 8}{m^2 + 9m + 20}$ (b) $\dfrac{x^2 - 4}{2x^2 + 11x + 5} \times \dfrac{x^2 + 2x - 15}{x^2 - x - 6}$

(c) $\dfrac{a^2 - 4a - 21}{a^2 - 3a - 28} \div \dfrac{a^2 - 9}{a^2 - a - 20}$ (d) $\dfrac{a + 1}{a - 1} \times \dfrac{a + 3}{1 - a^2} \div \dfrac{(a + 3)^2}{1 - a}$

(e) $\dfrac{x^2 - 5x + 6}{2x} \div \dfrac{x - 3}{4x^2} \times \dfrac{4x^2 - 4x - 8}{8x - 16}$

7   (a) How does the value of the expression $\dfrac{2x^2 - 18}{x^2 - 6x + 9} \div \dfrac{3x + 6}{x^2 + 2x}$ change if x increases in value from 1 to 2?

   (b) Now simplify the expression in (a). Then answer: "How does the value of the simplified expression change as x increases in value from 1 to 2?"

   (c) Based on your results in (a) and (b), what should be the first step in answering questions about rational expressions?

   (d) How does the value of $\dfrac{28x - 4x^2}{16x^2 + 4x^3} \times \dfrac{x^2 + 7x + 12}{x^2 - 9x + 14}$ change if x decreases in value from 4 to 3?

8   (a) Find the value of the rational expression $\dfrac{3m^2 - 17m + 20}{3m^2 + 7m - 20} \times \dfrac{m^2 + 9m + 20}{m^2 + m - 20}$

     for $m = 3$ and $m = -2$.

   (b) Find the value of the rational expression $\dfrac{4a^2 + 8ab + 4b^2}{8} \times \dfrac{3a - 3b}{a^2 - b^2}$

     for $a = 0$, $b = -3$.

9   If $f(m) = \dfrac{m^2 - 3m + 2}{2m^2 + 5m + 2} \times \dfrac{2m^2 + 11m + 5}{m^2 + 4m - 5}$ find

(a) $f(-1)$ (b) $f(2)$ (c) $f(0)$ (d) $f(3) - f(-3)$ (e) $3f(-1) - f(-3)$

2.9 Adding and Subtracting Rational Expressions

In your study of mathematics, once you learn a skill or concept, very often you will find that you can relate it to a new topic. For example, how are these simplifications alike? How are they different?

Simplify.

$$\frac{1}{x} + \frac{3}{xy}$$

Restrictions understood are $x, y \neq 0$.

$$= \frac{y}{xy} + \frac{3}{xy}$$

$$= \frac{y + 3}{xy}$$

Simplify.

$$\frac{1}{x - 1} - \frac{2}{x^2 - 1}$$

Restrictions understood are $x \neq \pm 1$

$$= \frac{1}{x - 1} - \frac{2}{(x - 1)(x + 1)}$$

$$= \frac{(x + 1)}{(x - 1)(x + 1)} - \frac{2}{(x - 1)(x + 1)}$$

$$= \frac{x + 1 - 2}{(x - 1)(x + 1)}$$

$$= \frac{x - 1}{(x - 1)(x + 1)}$$

$$= \frac{\overset{1}{\cancel{(x - 1)}}}{\underset{1}{\cancel{(x - 1)}}(x + 1)}$$

$$= \frac{1}{x + 1}$$

Throughout your work with rational expressions, you must always be aware of the restrictions on the variables. In the following example, a rational expression that is expressed in **complex fraction** form is dealt with.

Example   Simplify $\dfrac{\dfrac{a}{1 + a} + \dfrac{1 - a}{a}}{\dfrac{a}{1 + a} - \dfrac{1 - a}{a}}$ and list the restrictions on the variable.

Solution   The expression is undefined for $1 + a = 0$, $a = 0$, and $\dfrac{a}{1 + a} - \dfrac{1 - a}{a} = 0$.

$$\frac{a}{1 + a} = \frac{1 - a}{a}$$

$$a^2 = (1 - a)(1 + a)$$

$$a^2 = 1 - a^2$$

$$2a^2 = 1$$

$$a^2 = \frac{1}{2} \text{ or } a = \pm\frac{1}{\sqrt{2}}$$

Thus the restrictions on the variable are $a \neq 0, \pm\dfrac{1}{\sqrt{2}}, -1$

Once you know the restrictions, simplify the expression. Simplify complex expressions, one step at a time, so that you reduce the risk of major errors.

$$\dfrac{\dfrac{a}{1+a} + \dfrac{1-a}{a}}{\dfrac{a}{1+a} - \dfrac{1-a}{a}} = \left(\dfrac{a}{1+a} + \dfrac{1-a}{a}\right) \div \left(\dfrac{a}{1+a} - \dfrac{1-a}{a}\right)$$

$$= \left(\dfrac{a^2 + (1+a)(1-a)}{a(a+1)}\right) \div \left(\dfrac{a^2 - (1+a)(1-a)}{a(1+a)}\right)$$

$$= \left(\dfrac{a^2 + 1 - a^2}{a(a+1)}\right) \div \left(\dfrac{a^2 - 1 + a^2}{a(a+1)}\right)$$

$$= \dfrac{1}{a(a+1)} \times \dfrac{a(a+1)}{2a^2 - 1}$$

$$= \dfrac{1}{\overset{1}{\cancel{a(a+1)}}} \times \dfrac{\overset{1}{\cancel{a(a+1)}}}{2a^2 - 1}$$

$$= \dfrac{1}{2a^2 - 1} \quad \text{where } a \neq 0, \pm\dfrac{1}{\sqrt{2}}, -1$$

2.9 Exercise

A   Questions 1 to 6 practise essential skills needed to add and subtract rational expressions.

1   Express each of the following in simplest terms.

(a) $\dfrac{16 - b^2}{b^2 - 8b + 16}$ (b) $\dfrac{a^3 - a^2}{3 - 3a^2}$ (c) $\dfrac{2k^2 + k - 1}{2k^2 - 3k + 1}$

2   Remember that $y - x = -(x - y)$. Simplify each of the following.

(a) $\dfrac{16 - y^2}{y + 4}$ (b) $\dfrac{(y - x)^2}{x - y}$ (c) $\dfrac{3 - x}{x^2 - 9}$

(d) $\dfrac{2a^2 - a - 1}{1 - a^2}$ (e) $\dfrac{x^3 + x^2 + x}{x^2 + x + 1}$ (f) $\dfrac{m^2 - 5m}{25 - m^2}$

3   Copy and complete.

(a) $\dfrac{x}{x - 1} = \dfrac{?}{x^2 - 1}$ (b) $\dfrac{3}{a + 2} = \dfrac{?}{a^2 + 4a + 4}$

(c) $\dfrac{m - 2}{m + 2} = \dfrac{?}{4 - m^2}$ (d) $\dfrac{y - 1}{y + 3} = \dfrac{?}{2y^2 + 5y - 3}$

4 (a) Simplify each term of the rational expression $\dfrac{3x-3}{x^2-1} - \dfrac{2x+2}{(x+1)^2}$.

   (b) Find a common denominator for the expression in (a) and simplify.

5 First simplify each term of the expression $\dfrac{3y^2-9y}{y^2-6y+9} - \dfrac{y^2+3y}{y^2-9}$.

   Then simplify the resulting expression.

6 Simplify each of the following.

   (a) $\dfrac{y+1}{5} - \dfrac{y}{4}$

   (b) $\dfrac{6a}{6} - \dfrac{3a}{9} + \dfrac{a}{12}$

   (c) $\dfrac{1}{x} - \dfrac{1}{3x}$

   (d) $\dfrac{1}{y^2} - \dfrac{3}{2y}$

   (e) $\dfrac{4}{a+1} - \dfrac{1}{a}$

   (f) $\dfrac{3}{p} - \dfrac{2}{p(p+1)}$

   (g) $\dfrac{3}{x-2} - \dfrac{4}{x+1}$

   (h) $\dfrac{x-2}{3} - \dfrac{x+1}{4}$

   (i) $\dfrac{2a-3b}{a} - \dfrac{3a+2b}{b}$

   (j) $\dfrac{a}{2a-3b} - \dfrac{b}{3a+2b}$

   (k) $\dfrac{m+x}{m} + \dfrac{m^2-x^2}{mx} - \dfrac{m-x}{x}$

B Throughout the exercise, be sure to identify the restrictions on the variables in the denominators.

7 Find the lowest common denominator of each of the following. Then simplify.

   (a) $\dfrac{2}{x^2-xy} - \dfrac{3}{xy-y^2}$

   (b) $\dfrac{6a}{a^2-9} - \dfrac{2}{a-3} + \dfrac{3}{a+3}$

   (c) $\dfrac{6}{2y-1} - \dfrac{3}{2y+1} - \dfrac{8y-2}{1-4y^2}$

   (d) $\dfrac{3x}{(x+1)(x+2)} - \dfrac{4x}{(x+2)(x+3)} + \dfrac{5x}{(x+3)(x+1)}$

8 Simplify.

   (a) $\dfrac{x-y}{x+y} - \dfrac{2xy}{x^2-y^2}$

   (b) $\dfrac{3a-1}{a^2-9} - \dfrac{5}{a-3}$

   (c) $\dfrac{a-b}{a+b} - \dfrac{a+b}{a-b}$

   (d) $\dfrac{3}{x^2-xy} - \dfrac{3}{xy-y^2}$

   (e) $\dfrac{x-4}{4} + \dfrac{4}{x-4} - \dfrac{1}{4x-16}$

9 (a) Simplify $\dfrac{2y-3}{1-y} - \dfrac{2y+7}{y-1}$.

   (b) Find the value of the expression in (a) when $y = -1$.

10 (a) Simplify $\dfrac{5}{x^2 - 3x - 18} - \dfrac{2}{x^2 + x - 6}$.

(b) Find the value of the expression in (a) if $x = -\dfrac{2}{3}$.

11 Find the value of each expression for $y = -1$.

(a) $\dfrac{y}{y^2 + 3y} + \dfrac{1}{y + 3}$ (b) $\dfrac{y + 2}{y^2 - 4} - \dfrac{3}{2 - y}$

12 Find the value of each of the following for $x = -3$.

(a) $\dfrac{2x}{3x - 3} + \dfrac{3x^2}{5x + 5}$ (b) $\dfrac{4}{3x + 2} + \dfrac{3x - 1}{3x - 2}$

13 Evaluate for $x = -2$, $y = 3$.

$$\dfrac{2y^2 + x^2}{x^4 - y^4} - \dfrac{1}{x^2 - y^2} + \dfrac{1}{y^2 + x^2}$$

14 How does the value of the expression $\dfrac{x^2 - 1}{x^2 + x - 12} \times \dfrac{x^2 + 2x - 8}{x^2 - 3x + 2} \div \dfrac{x + 1}{x - 3}$ change as x increases in value from 9 to 10?

15 If $g(x) = \dfrac{2}{x + 4} - \dfrac{12 - 3x}{x^2 - 16}$, how does the value of $g(x)$ change if x increases in value from -2 to -1?

16 If $f(y) = \dfrac{3 - y}{y + 2} - \dfrac{2y^2 + 7}{2 - y - y^2}$, then how does the value of $f(y)$ change if y increases in value from 3 to 4?

Problem Solving

In the study of mathematics, the following statement is often used to solve equations. If $\dfrac{a}{b} = \dfrac{a}{d}$, then $b = d$, b, $d \neq 0$.

The above statement was used to solve the equation at the right. What went wrong?

$$2 + \dfrac{-8}{x + 2} = \dfrac{2x - 4}{x + 3}$$

$$\dfrac{2x + 4 - 8}{x + 2} = \dfrac{2x - 4}{x + 3} \quad \text{The numerators are equal. Thus}$$
$$\dfrac{2x - 4}{x + 2} = \dfrac{2x - 4}{x + 3} \quad x + 2 = x + 3.$$
$$x + 2 = x + 3$$
$$2 = 3$$

2.10 Problem-Solving: Reading Accurately

In order to follow instructions accurately, you must read the instructions accurately. The misinterpretation of one word in a problem can lead to an incorrect answer. The following questions provide practice in reviewing language and in reading accurately to interpret a problem and translate it correctly into algebra.

2.10 Exercise

B Read each of the following instructions carefully and accurately.

1 Subtract $\dfrac{1}{1 - 9x^2}$ from $\dfrac{2}{1 + 3x}$.

2 Add $\dfrac{3}{x + 2}$ to the sum of $\dfrac{2}{x}$ and $\dfrac{2}{x - 2}$.

3 Decrease the sum of $\dfrac{3x}{x^2 - 9}$ and 1 by $\dfrac{x}{x - 3}$.

4 By how much does $\dfrac{x^2 + 2}{x^2 - 16}$ exceed the sum of $\dfrac{x}{x + 4}$ and $\dfrac{x}{x - 4}$?

5 Subtract the sum of $\dfrac{2}{x + 3}$ and $\dfrac{5}{x - 3}$ from $\dfrac{6}{x^2 - 9}$.

6 Find the result of $\dfrac{x - 3}{x - 3}$ subtracted from $\dfrac{x + 3}{x - 3}$.

7 The product of $x - 1$ and $\dfrac{1}{x + 1}$ is subtracted from $\dfrac{2x}{x^2 + 7x + 6}$.

8 Multiply $\dfrac{x}{x^2 + 7x + 10}$ by the sum of $\dfrac{x^2 + 5x}{x - 3}$ and $\dfrac{x^2 - x - 6}{x}$.

9 $4x^2 - 25$ is divided by $2x - 5$ and then increased by $\dfrac{2}{2x + 5}$.

10 By how much does $x + 1$ divided by $3x^2 + 6x + 3$ exceed $\dfrac{1}{x^2 + 9x + 8}$?

11 $\dfrac{2y}{y + 3}$ is decreased by $\dfrac{3}{4}$ and the result is multiplied by $3(y + 3)$.

12 Divide the difference $\dfrac{2}{3} - \dfrac{1}{6y}$ by the sum $\dfrac{1}{5y} + \dfrac{2}{3}$.

Practice and Problems: A Chapter Review

An important step for problem-solving is to decide which skills to use. For this reason, these questions are not placed in any special order. When you have finished the review, you might try the *Test for Practice* that follows.

1   A square with sides x units is drawn and then a square with sides y units is removed from the original square. Use the diagram to show why $x^2 - y^2 = (x + y)(x - y)$.

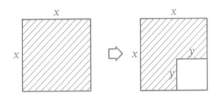

2   Write the following in factored form.

$$9m^2 - 6m + 1 - k^2 - 8ky - 16y^2$$

3   Factor. Then find the roots.
(a) $x^2 - 4x - 21 = 0$ (b) $16m^2 - 1 = 0$
(c) $2m^2 + 7m + 3 = 0$ (d) $2y^2 + 9y + 4 = 0$

4   Factor each of the following.
(a) $2y + by + 2b + b^2$ (b) $6m^2 + 3mn - 2qm - qn$
(c) $y^4 + 2y^2 + 9$

5   Simplify.
(a) $\dfrac{y - y^2}{y^3 - y}$ (b) $\dfrac{x^4 - y^4}{y^2 - x^2}$ (c) $\dfrac{4k^2 - 36k + 72}{k^2 - 36}$

6   Simplify.
(a) $\dfrac{a + 1}{a - 1} \times \dfrac{a + 3}{1 - a^2} \div \dfrac{(a + 3)^2}{1 - a}$ where $a \neq \pm 1$.

(b) $\dfrac{2}{(x - 1)(x + 1)} - \dfrac{3}{(x - 1)^2}$ where $x \neq \pm 1$.

7   Simplify.
(a) $\dfrac{3}{(m + 1)^2} - \dfrac{4}{m^2 - 1} - \dfrac{1}{m^2 - 2m + 1}$ (b) $6x(x - 5)\left(\dfrac{x}{x - 5} - \dfrac{6}{x}\right)$

8   Each trinomial has 2 binomial factors. Find suitable values for f if $0 < f \leq 20$.
(a) $x^2 - fx + 12$ (b) $x^2 - 7xy - fy^2$

Test for Practice

Try this test. Each *Test for Practice* is based on the mathematics you have learned in this chapter. Try this test later in the year as a review. Keep a record of those questions that you were not successful with, get help in obtaining solutions and review them periodically.

1 Examine the polynomials $k^2 - x^2$ and $(a + b)^2 - x^2$.
   (a) How are they alike? How are they different?
   (b) Write them in factored form.

2 Factor fully.
   (a) $36x^2 - y^2$
   (b) $9 - 4k^2$
   (c) $2a^2 - 17a + 21$
   (d) $5x^2 + 22xy - 48y^2$
   (e) $(x - y)^2 - (x + 2y)$
   (f) $x^4 + 3x^2 + 4$

3 (a) Solve $9y^2 - 3y - 6 = 0$.
   (b) Verify your results in (a).

4 Simplify.
   (a) $\dfrac{m^4 - n^4}{m^2 + n^2}$
   (b) $\dfrac{-ab - ac}{2b^2 + bc - c^2}$
   (c) $\dfrac{15x^2}{x^2 + 3x + 2} \times \dfrac{x^2 - 4x - 5}{5x^2 - 25x} \div \dfrac{x^2 - 16}{x^2 + 8x + 16}$

5 Simplify.
   (a) $\dfrac{x + y}{x - y} - \dfrac{x - y}{x - 2y}$
   (b) $\dfrac{3}{2m - 5} - \dfrac{4}{4m^2 - 20m + 25}$

6 Find an expression in simplified form if you decrease the sum of $\dfrac{4}{x^2 - xy}$ and $\dfrac{1}{x - y}$ by $\dfrac{1}{xy - y^2}$.

7 For the trinomial $x^2 - mx - 6$, $0 < m \leq 20$, $m \in W$ find the values of m so that two binomial factors are obtained.

Math Tip

It is important to clearly understand the vocabulary of mathematics when solving problems.

- Make a list of all the words you have met in this chapter.
- Provide a sample example to illustrate each word.

3 Applying Concepts and Skills: Real Numbers

meaning of rationals and irrationals, skills with expressions and exponents, meaning of accuracy and significant digits, using scientific notation, exponential equations, applications and problem-solving

Introduction

Mathematics is the creation of people. Studying mathematics is often like learning about the lasting contributions of famous mathematicians and re-living some of the mathematical ideas and thinking processes which these people developed.

The list of contributors to the development of mathematics goes on and on, and only a partial list is shown here. How many do you know? (They are not listed in any special order.)

Fourier	Descartes	DeMoivre	Plato	Copernicus
Pascal	Pythagoras	Cayley	Aristotle	Recorde
Newton	Archimedes	Euler	Hipparchus	Viète
Thales	Fermat	Abûl Wefâ	Einstein	Galileo
Sacrobosco	Leibniz	Cardan	Ptolemy	Appolonius
da Vinci	Napier	Fibonacci	Al Karkui	

Many of these mathematicians were ordinary people who became interested in someone else's work. As in your own everyday activities, often one mathematician was influenced by the mathematical interests, thinking and thought processes of another. For example, Pythagoras, who has an important theorem named after him, was influenced by the work of Thales, another Greek mathematician.

Pythagoras stated an important relationship among the 3 sides of a right-angled triangle. This law in mathematics advanced the science of surveying and map-making and is used to solve many problems in mathematics.

Not only does mathematics build upon the thoughts of individual people, but also its collective influence touches every aspect of modern society. In so doing, it affects people everywhere. In your study of mathematics, you will share the methods of many great thinkers.

3.1 Rationals, Irrationals and Reals

Fundamental to your work in algebra is the need to know the concepts and skills with numbers. You have already dealt with these sets of numbers.

$$\text{Natural Numbers} \quad N = \{1, 2, 3, 4, \ldots\}$$
$$\text{Whole Numbers} \quad W = \{0, 1, 2, 3, \ldots\}$$
$$\text{Integers} \quad I = \{\ldots, -3, -2, -1, 0, 1, 2, \ldots\}$$

The set of rational numbers is defined as in your earlier work with numbers.

$$\text{Rational Numbers} \quad Q = \left\{\frac{a}{b} \,\middle|\, a, b, \in I, b \neq 0\right\}.$$

Thus, if $a = -6$ and $b = 5$, then, for the set Q, a rational number is $\frac{-6}{5}$.

Any rational may be written in any one of the following equivalent decimal forms.

Terminating decimals: $\quad \dfrac{1}{2} = 0.5, \quad \dfrac{1}{4} = 0.25$ The dot is placed above the first digit and the last digit of the period.

Repeating or Periodic decimals: $\quad \dfrac{1}{3} = 0.333\,33\ldots \quad$ or $0.\overline{3}$, or $0.\dot{3}$

$$\frac{311}{999} = 0.311\,311\ldots \text{ or } 0.\overline{311} \text{ or } 0.\dot{3}1\dot{1}$$

For a periodic decimal, the **length of the period** is the number of digits that repeat, and the **period** is the digits which repeat. Thus, for the periodic decimal $\frac{31}{99} = 0.313131\ldots$ or $0.\overline{31}$ the length of the period is 2, because two digits (3 and 1) repeat, and the period is 31.

Conversely, any periodic decimal can be written as a rational number, as shown in the following example.

Example   Find the rational number, equivalent to each periodic decimal.

(a) $0.\overline{13}$ (b) $0.1\overline{3}$

Solution

(a) Let x represent the periodic decimal.
Then $x = 0.\overline{13}$ or $0.131313\ldots$

$$100x = 13.1313\ldots$$
$$\underline{x = 0.131313\ldots}$$
$$99x = 13$$
$$x = \frac{13}{99}$$

(b) Let y represent the periodic decimal.
Then $y = 0.1\overline{3}$ or $0.13333\ldots$

$$100y = 13.333\ldots$$
$$\underline{10y = 1.333\ldots}$$
$$90y = 12$$
$$y = \frac{12}{90}$$

Some decimals are non-terminating and non-periodic such as
0.393993999399993...

They represent numbers which are not rational. Numbers which are
represented by non-terminating and non-periodic decimals are called
non-rational or **irrational numbers**.
Other numbers such as the following are irrational.

- The decimal for π is non-periodic and non-terminating.
- The decimal for numbers given by $\sqrt{2}$, $\sqrt{3}$, $\sqrt[3]{2}$, and so on, are non-periodic
  and non-terminating.

The set of all irrational numbers is represented by the symbol $\bar{Q}$. All
rationals, Q, and irrationals, $\bar{Q}$, are referred to as the **real numbers, R**.

$$R = Q \cup \bar{Q}$$

Rational numbers: periodic decimals ——↑   ↑—— Irrational numbers: non-periodic,
terminating and non-terminating   non-terminating decimals

To show an irrational number such as $\sqrt{2}$ on the number line, you can use
the construction shown at right which is based on your knowledge of the
Pythagorean Property.

$OB^2 = BC^2 + OC^2$
$OB^2 = 1 + 1$
$OB^2 = 2$
$OB = \sqrt{2}$

Once you have located $\sqrt{2}$, you can then locate $-\sqrt{2}$, as the reflection of
$\sqrt{2}$ through the origin.

In working with mathematics, you often need to invent symbols that
enable you to record information in a more compact form. For example,
to show the absolute value of a real number, you use the symbols as
shown.

$|r| = r$ if $r > 0$ Thus, $|5| = 5$
$|r| = 0$ if $r = 0$ $|0| = 0$
$|r| = -r$ if $r < 0$ $|-5| = -(-5) = 5$

↑
└—— Read this as "the absolute value of r".

3.1 Exercise

A   You may wish to use a calculator to answer some of these questions.

1   Which of the following numbers are
    - rational?   - irrational?

(a) $\dfrac{2}{3}$ (b) $\sqrt{2}$ (c) $-\dfrac{6}{7}$ (d) 2π (e) $\sqrt{7}$

(f) 3 (g) $1+\sqrt{2}$ (h) 0.25 (i) $\sqrt{3}+1$ (j) $-\dfrac{3}{2}$

(k) $\dfrac{\sqrt{3}}{2}$ (l) -3π (m) $\sqrt{19}$ (n) $\sqrt{4}$ (o) $\sqrt{\dfrac{25}{16}}$

2   Express each rational number as a decimal.

(a) $\dfrac{1}{4}$ (b) $\dfrac{3}{8}$ (c) $-\dfrac{2}{5}$ (d) $\dfrac{23}{50}$ (e) $-\dfrac{1}{11}$

(f) $\dfrac{2}{9}$ (g) $\dfrac{11}{9}$ (h) $-2\dfrac{1}{8}$ (i) $\dfrac{53}{100}$ (j) $\dfrac{-7}{15}$

(k) $\dfrac{3}{7}$ (l) $1\dfrac{2}{3}$ (m) $-3\dfrac{1}{8}$ (n) $\dfrac{11}{21}$ (o) $-\dfrac{7}{13}$

3   (a) Write a decimal for each rational $\dfrac{11}{30}, \dfrac{9}{26}$.
    (b) Which rational in (a) is greater?

4   For each pair, which is the greater number?

(a) $\dfrac{1}{6}, \dfrac{6}{29}$ (b) $-\dfrac{3}{13}, -\dfrac{2}{7}$ (c) $\dfrac{2}{13}, \dfrac{11}{57}$

5   Write the period and length of each periodic decimal.
    (a) $0.\overline{6}$ (b) $0.1\dot{6}$ (c) $2.\overline{36}$ (d) $-4.3\overline{8}$ (e) $2.9\overline{16}$
    (f) $-0.1\dot{6}\dot{2}$ (g) $6.3\overline{82}$ (h) $0.00\overline{45}$ (i) $0.\overline{142\,857}$

6   Find the value of each of the following.
    (a) $|2|$ (b) $|-2|$ (c) $|-(-3)|$ (d) $|-3|$
    (e) $|0|$ (f) $|3-2|$ (g) $|-3-2|$ (h) $|3+2|$
    (i) $|-3+2|$ (j) $|-6|+|-3|$ (k) $|6|-|-3|$ (l) $|-6|-|-3|$

7   Use the Pythagorean Theorem to show the length of AB in each triangle.

(a)

(b)

8   To show $\sqrt{5}$ on the number line, the following construction was done.
Show why $OE = \sqrt{5}$.

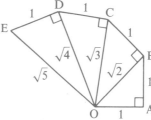

9   Use the above construction to mark each number on the number line.
(a) $-\sqrt{2}$ (b) $\sqrt{6}$ (c) $\sqrt{7}$ (d) $1 + \sqrt{2}$

10 (a) Show why 0.2356 is the decimal equivalent of a rational number.
(b) Show why $0.\overline{2356}$ is the decimal equivalent of a rational number.

11 (a) A decimal is given by 0.431431431431... Is the number, represented
by the decimal, rational or irrational? Give reasons for your answer.
(b) A decimal is given by 0.431433143331... Is the number, represented
by the decimal, rational or irrational? Give reasons for your answer.

B 12 Write the rational number represented by each decimal.
(a) 0.25   (b) $0.\overline{7}$ (c) $-0.\dot{2}\dot{5}$ (d) $0.\overline{13}$
(e) $2.1\overline{3}$ (f) $0.0\dot{1}\dot{3}$ (g) $-3.6\dot{3}$ (h) $2.8\overline{56}$

13 Express each of the following as an equivalent rational number.
(a) 0.18   (b) $0.\dot{1}\dot{8}$ (c) $0.1\overline{8}$
(d) $0.\dot{9}$ (e) $0.1\overline{9}$ (f) $0.11\overline{9}$

14 Construct the decimal for an irrational number between each of the
following.
(a) $\dfrac{1}{8}, \dfrac{2}{15}$ (b) $-\dfrac{4}{5}, -\dfrac{7}{10}$ (c) 0.25, 0.26
(d) 0.01, 0.012   (e) 0.7, $0.7\overline{5}$ (f) 0.63, $0.6\overline{3}$
(g) 0.46, 0.47   (h) -2.315, $-2.31\overline{5}$ (i) -3.63, -3.65

15 Determine the equivalent rational number for
    (a) 0.5   (b) $0.4\overline{9}$
    (c) What do you notice about your answers in (a) and (b)?
    (d) Use your answers above to predict the rational number given by $0.74\overline{9}$.
        Check your answer by finding the rational number represented by $0.74\overline{9}$.

16 Use your results in the previous question. Write 2 different decimal
    equivalents for each of the following.
    (a) $\dfrac{1}{4}$ (b) $\dfrac{3}{8}$ (c) $-1\dfrac{1}{8}$ (d) $\dfrac{3}{20}$ (e) $\dfrac{5}{8}$ (f) $-\dfrac{6}{25}$

17 A periodic decimal such as $0.\overline{7}$ may be written as
    $$0.\overline{7} = 0.7 + 0.07 + 0.007 + 0.0007 + \cdots.$$
    Find the equivalent rational number for each decimal.
    (a) $0.2 + 0.02 + 0.002 + \cdots$ (b) $0.06 + 0.006 + 0.0006 + \cdots$
    (c) $0.4 + 0.04 + 0.004 + 0.0004 + \cdots$ (d) $0.25 + 0.0025 + 0.000\,025 + \cdots$

18 The circumference, C, of a circle is given by $C = 2\pi r$, with radius r, and
    $C = \pi d$, with diameter d. Develop a method of showing how the irrational
    number π may be marked on the number line.

C 19 Mark the position of each number on a number line.
    (a) $\sqrt{3} + \sqrt{2}$ (b) $\sqrt{3} - \sqrt{2}$

20 Show that $\sqrt{3} + \sqrt{2} \neq \sqrt{5}$. Use your constructions on a number line to aid
    you.

Calculator Tip

Does your calculator have a constant feature? If you press any of
the keys $+$ $-$ $\times$ $\div$ twice, you establish a constant. The symbol
K appears in the display. The constant function $+$ $+$ is useful when
you want to add the same number each time to different inputs.

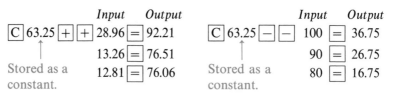

Try the constant feature for $\times$ $\times$ and for $\div$ $\div$.

3.2 Inventory: Skills with Exponents

You have already applied the Laws of Exponents.

Laws of Exponents with $m, n \in I$

product of powers	$a^m \times a^n = a^{m+n}$
quotient of powers	$a^m \div a^n = a^{m-n}, \quad$ for $a \neq 0$
power of a power	$(a^m)^n = a^{mn}$
power of a product	$(ab)^m = a^m b^m$
power of a quotient	$\left(\dfrac{a}{b}\right)^m = \dfrac{a^m}{b^m}, \quad$ for $b \neq 0$

You used these laws to introduce the definitions for a^0 and a^{-m}.

For a^0: $\quad a^2 \times a^0 = a^{2+0} = a^2 \quad$ also $\quad a^2 \times 1 = a^2$

Based on the observations, you can conclude that $a^0 = 1$.

Similarly, for a^{-m} you noted the following.

Step 1 $\quad a^m \times a^{-m} = a^{m-m}$
$$= a^0$$
$$= 1$$

Step 2 $\quad$ Use $a^m \times a^{-m} = 1$.
Divide through by a^m.
$$\frac{a^m \times a^{-m}}{a^m} = \frac{1}{a^m}$$

Based on the observations, you can conclude that for $a \neq 0$, $a^{-m} = \dfrac{1}{a^m}$ or $a^m = \dfrac{1}{a^{-m}}$.

With these laws and definitions, you simplified expressions involving exponents.

Example (a) Simplify $(2^0 + 2^{-1}) \div 3^{-2}$

(b) Simplify $\dfrac{m^{-3}n^4}{m^4 n^{-3}}$. Express the answer with positive exponents.

Solution (a) $(2^0 + 2^{-1}) \div 3^{-2} = \left(1 + \dfrac{1}{2}\right) \div \dfrac{1}{3^2}$

$$= \frac{3}{2} \div \frac{1}{9}$$

$$= \frac{3}{2} \times \frac{9}{1}$$

$$= \frac{27}{2} \quad \text{or} \quad 13\frac{1}{2}$$

(b) $\dfrac{m^{-3}n^4}{m^4 n^{-3}} = m^{-3-4}n^{4-(-3)}$

$$= m^{-7} \times n^7$$

$$= \frac{n^7}{m^7} \qquad m^{-7} = \frac{1}{m^7}$$

3.2 Exercise

A 1 Evaluate.
(a) -3^{-2} (b) $(-3)^{-2}$ (c) -3^0 (d) $(-3)^0$
(e) $2^2 \times 3^{-1}$ (f) $(2^2 \times 3)^{-1}$ (g) $(-3)^2$ (h) $-(-3)^{-2}$

2 Evaluate.
(a) 2^{-3} (b) $3^0 \times 2^{-2}$ (c) 5^{-2} (d) -3×3^{-1} (e) $\left(\dfrac{1}{3}\right)^{-2}$

(f) $(-7)^0$ (g) $3^0 - 3^{-1}$ (h) $-3^{-2} + 3^0$ (i) $8 \div 2^{-2}$ (j) $\left(\dfrac{3^{-1}}{2^{-1}}\right)^{-2}$

3 Express each of the following with a positive exponent.
(a) x^{-2} (b) y^{-3} (c) a^{-7} (d) b^{-5} (e) $\dfrac{1}{x^{-2}}$ (f) $\dfrac{1}{a^{-1}}$

(g) $\dfrac{1}{c^{-4}}$ (h) $2x^{-4}$ (i) ab^{-5} (j) $\dfrac{x^{-3}}{y^{-4}}$ (k) $4a^{-2}$ (l) $\dfrac{3x^{-4}}{2y^{-2}}$

4 Express each of the following with all variables in the numerator.
(a) $\dfrac{1}{x^3}$ (b) $\dfrac{x}{y^4}$ (c) $\dfrac{3a}{b^3}$ (d) $\dfrac{4}{a^{-3}}$ (e) $\dfrac{3}{a^{-2}b^{-1}}$ (f) $\dfrac{3}{(x+y)^{-2}}$

5 Simplify each of the following.
(a) $a^5 \times a^{-3}$ (b) $(m^{-3})^2$ (c) $a^5 \div a^{-8}$ (d) $(3a)^{-1}$
(e) $x^5 \div x^{-1}$ (f) $(xy^2)^{-1}$ (g) $(a^{-1})^3 \div a^{-1}$ (h) $\left(\dfrac{b^3}{b^{-3}}\right)^{-2}$

B 6 Evaluate.
(a) $(3^0 + 3^2)^{-2}$ (b) $2^4 + \left(\dfrac{1}{2}\right)^{-3}$ (c) $4^{-1}(4^2 + 4^0)$

(d) $(3^3 - 3^2)^2 \div 3^2$ (e) $(5^7 \div 5^{-2})(5^0 - 1)$ (f) $\dfrac{2^5}{3^{-2}} \times \dfrac{3^{-1}}{2^4}$

7 Evaluate.
(a) $(-3)^{-2}(3^3 - 3^4)$ (b) $\dfrac{3^{-2} \times 2^{-3}}{3^{-2} + 2^{-3}}$ (c) $\dfrac{4^{-1} + 3^{-2}}{3^{-2} + 2^{-3}}$ (d) $\dfrac{5^{-1} - 2^{-2}}{5^{-1} + 2^{-2}}$

8 Simplify. Write each as a power with a single base.
(a) $(8^{2-2n})(16^{3-n}) \div (4^{2n})^{-1}$ (b) $[3^{-2}(27^m \div 9^{-m})]^{-1}$

C 9 If $x = -1$ and $y = 2$, find the value of each of the following.
(a) $\dfrac{16x^{-3}y^{-2}}{4x^5}$ (b) $(3x^4y^{-2})^{-2}$ (c) $\dfrac{2x^{-5}y^{-2}}{x^{-2}y^{-1}}$ (d) $\dfrac{x^{-2} - y^{-1}}{x^{-2} + y^{-1}}$

3.3 Powers with Rational Exponents

In the development of mathematics, you often look for patterns and similarities. For example:
you know from the Laws of Exponents that

$$3^{\frac{1}{2}} \times 3^{\frac{1}{2}} = 3^{\frac{1}{2}+\frac{1}{2}} = 3^1 = 3. \qquad \text{Result } ①$$

You also know that

$$\sqrt{3} \times \sqrt{3} = 3. \qquad \text{Result } ②$$

You examine the similarity for the two results ① and ②.

$$① \;\; 3^{\frac{1}{2}} \times 3^{\frac{1}{2}} = 3 \qquad ② \;\; \sqrt{3} \times \sqrt{3} = 3$$

Based on these results, it appears you can interpret $3^{\frac{1}{2}}$ as another way of recording $\sqrt{3}$. Thus, it appears that

$$3^{\frac{1}{2}} = \sqrt{3}$$

In general, $\qquad a^{\frac{1}{2}} \times a^{\frac{1}{2}} = a^{\frac{1}{2}+\frac{1}{2}} = a \quad$ and $\quad \sqrt{a} \times \sqrt{a} = a$

Define $a^{\frac{1}{2}} = \sqrt{a}$ for $a \geq 0$.

Similarly, if $a^{\frac{1}{3}} \times a^{\frac{1}{3}} \times a^{\frac{1}{3}} = a^{\frac{1}{3}+\frac{1}{3}+\frac{1}{3}} = a^1 = a$ and if $\sqrt[3]{a} \times \sqrt[3]{a} \times \sqrt[3]{a} = a$

then, define $\qquad\qquad\qquad\qquad a^{\frac{1}{3}} = \sqrt[3]{a}$

To extend your work to n^{th} order radicals, you can state that

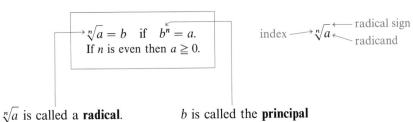

$\sqrt[n]{a} = b \quad$ if $\quad b^n = a$.
If n is even then $a \geq 0$.

index $\longrightarrow \sqrt[n]{a}$ ← radical sign
← radicand

$\sqrt[n]{a}$ is called a **radical**.

b is called the **principal n^{th} root** of a.

Thus, if $\underbrace{2^3 = 8}_{\text{exponential form}} \quad$ then $\quad \underbrace{2 = \sqrt[3]{8}}_{\text{radical form}}$

Exponential and radical forms occur in the following examples.

Example 1 Calculate.

(a) $8^{\frac{1}{3}}$ (b) $(-27)^{\frac{1}{3}}$ (c) $(25y^4)^{\frac{1}{2}}$

Solution (a) $8^{\frac{1}{3}}$ means $\sqrt[3]{8} = 2 \leftarrow 2 \times 2 \times 2 = 8$

(b) $(-27)^{\frac{1}{3}}$ means $\sqrt[3]{-27} = -3 \leftarrow (-3)(-3)(-3) = -27$

(c) $(25y^4)^{\frac{1}{2}}$ means $\sqrt{25y^4} = 5y^2$

By using your algebraic skills you can obtain the following equivalent forms.

Since $\dfrac{m}{n} = m \times \dfrac{1}{n} = \dfrac{1}{n} \times m$ then

$a^{\frac{m}{n}} = a^{m \times \frac{1}{n}}$ or $a^{\frac{m}{n}} = a^{\frac{1}{n} \times m}$

$\quad = (a^m)^{\frac{1}{n}} \qquad\qquad = (a^{\frac{1}{n}})^m$

$\quad = \sqrt[n]{a^m} \qquad\qquad = (\sqrt[n]{a})^m$

> For $m \in I,\ n \in N,$
>
> $$a^{\frac{m}{n}} = \sqrt[n]{a^m} \quad \text{or} \quad a^{\frac{m}{n}} = (\sqrt[n]{a})^m.$$
>
> If n is even, then $a \geq 0$.

These definitions are applied in the following example.

Example 2 Calculate. (a) $8^{\frac{2}{3}}$ (b) $16^{-\frac{3}{4}}$

Solution (a) In terms of radicals, the expression is simplified.

$8^{\frac{2}{3}} = 8^{\frac{1}{3} \times 2}$ or $8^{\frac{2}{3}} = 8^{2 \times \frac{1}{3}}$

$\quad = (8^{\frac{1}{3}})^2 \qquad\qquad = (8^2)^{\frac{1}{3}}$

$\quad = (\sqrt[3]{8})^2 \qquad\qquad = (64)^{\frac{1}{3}}$

$\quad = (2)^2 \qquad\qquad\quad = \sqrt[3]{64}$

$\quad = 4 \qquad\qquad\qquad = 4$

In terms of exponents, the expression can also be simplified.

$8^{\frac{2}{3}} = (2^3)^{\frac{2}{3}}$

$\quad = 2^{3 \times \frac{2}{3}}$

$\quad = 2^2$

$\quad = 4$

(b) In terms of radicals, the expression is simplified.

$16^{-\frac{3}{4}} = \dfrac{1}{16^{\frac{3}{4}}}$

$\quad = \dfrac{1}{16^{\frac{1}{4} \times 3}}$ or $\dfrac{1}{16^{3 \times \frac{1}{4}}}$

$\quad = \dfrac{1}{(16^{\frac{1}{4}})^3}$ or $\dfrac{1}{(16^3)^{\frac{1}{4}}}$

$\quad = \dfrac{1}{(\sqrt[4]{16})^3}$ or $\dfrac{1}{\sqrt[4]{16^3}}$

$\quad = \dfrac{1}{(2)^3}$ or $\dfrac{1}{8}$

In terms of exponents the expression can also be simplified.

$16^{-\frac{3}{4}} = (2^4)^{-\frac{3}{4}}$

$\quad = 2^{4(-\frac{3}{4})}$

$\quad = 2^{-3}$

$\quad = \dfrac{1}{2^3}$ or $\dfrac{1}{8}$

Use these useful relationships in the following exercise

$$a^0 = 1, \quad \sqrt{a} = a^{\frac{1}{2}}, \quad \sqrt[n]{a} = a^{\frac{1}{n}} \qquad \sqrt[n]{a^m} = a^{\frac{m}{n}} \quad \text{and} \quad (\sqrt[n]{a})^m = a^{\frac{m}{n}}$$

$$a^{-n} = \frac{1}{a^n} \quad \text{where} \quad a \neq 0. \qquad \text{If } \sqrt[n]{a} = b \text{ then } a = b^n.$$

3.3 Exercise

A 1 Find the value of each of the following.

(a) 4^0 (b) $4^{\frac{1}{2}}$ (c) $4^{-\frac{1}{2}}$ (d) $27^{\frac{1}{3}}$

(e) $27^{-\frac{1}{3}}$ (f) 27^0 (g) -100^0 (h) $-100^{\frac{1}{2}}$

(i) $-100^{-\frac{1}{2}}$ (j) $(0.04)^0$ (k) $(0.04)^{-\frac{1}{2}}$ (l) $(0.04)^{\frac{1}{2}}$

2 Simplify.

(a) $25^{\frac{1}{2}}$ (b) $\sqrt{25}$ (c) $25^{-\frac{1}{2}}$ (d) 4^2

(e) $(\sqrt{4})^{-1}$ (f) 4^{-2} (g) $16^{\frac{1}{4}}$ (h) $\sqrt[4]{16}$

(i) $-\sqrt[4]{16}$ (j) $-27^{-\frac{1}{3}}$ (k) $-27^{\frac{1}{3}}$ (l) $-\sqrt[3]{27}$

3 Find the value of each of the following.

(a) $32^{\frac{1}{5}}$ (b) $32^{\frac{2}{5}}$ (c) $32^{\frac{3}{5}}$

(d) $\sqrt[5]{32}$ (e) $\sqrt[5]{32^2}$ (f) $\sqrt[5]{32^3}$

4 Find the value of each of the following.

(a) $125^{-\frac{1}{3}}$ (b) $4^{\frac{3}{2}}$ (c) $100^{\frac{1}{2}}$ (d) $16^{-\frac{1}{4}}$

(e) $-27^{\frac{1}{3}}$ (f) $256^{\frac{1}{4}}$ (g) $8^{\frac{2}{3}}$ (h) $64^{\frac{2}{3}}$

(i) $4^{-\frac{3}{2}}$ (j) $-32^{\frac{1}{5}}$ (k) $125^{\frac{2}{3}}$ (l) $-27^{\frac{2}{3}}$

B 5 Write each of the following in a radical form.

(a) $3^3 = 27$ (b) $3^5 = 243$ (c) $(-1)^5 = -1$

(d) $2^4 = 16$ (e) $(-2)^5 = -32$ (f) $4^3 = 64$

(g) $5^4 = 625$ (h) $7^4 = 2401$ (i) $0.04 = (0.2)^2$

6 Which of the following represent rational numbers? Give reasons for your answers.

(a) $\sqrt[3]{-27}$ (b) $\sqrt{-4}$ (c) $(4)^{\frac{1}{2}}$

(d) 10^0 (e) $\sqrt[4]{-16}$ (f) $(-8)^{\frac{1}{2}}$

7 Simplify each of the following. Write with a single base.

(a) $m^3 \times m^2 \times m^{-1}$ (b) $x^4 \times x^5 \times x^0$ (c) $p^{-2} \times p^3 \times p^4$

(d) $2^3 \times 2^{-2} \times 2^0$ (e) $10^3 \times 10^{-1} \times 10^0$ (f) $(-3)^2(-3)^{-2}(-3)^0$

(g) $(3^{-2})^3$ (h) $(2^{-3})^2$ (i) $[(-a)^3]^{-2}$

(j) $\left(\dfrac{b}{a^{-2}}\right)^2$ (k) $\left(\dfrac{x^{-1}}{y}\right)^{-5}$ (l) $\left(\dfrac{a^2}{2^2}\right)^{-3}$

8 Simplify.

(a) $16^{\frac{1}{4}}$ (b) $-125^{\frac{1}{3}}$ (c) $\left(\dfrac{1}{4}\right)^{\frac{1}{2}}$ (d) $\sqrt[4]{16}$

(e) $\left(\dfrac{25}{36}\right)^{\frac{1}{2}}$ (f) $-\sqrt[3]{\dfrac{27}{125}}$ (g) $16^{-\frac{5}{4}}$ (h) $\left(\dfrac{1}{4}\right)^{-\frac{1}{2}}$

(i) $-1000^{\frac{1}{3}}$ (j) $\dfrac{1}{(27)^{\frac{2}{3}}}$ (k) $-125^{\frac{2}{3}}$ (l) $\sqrt[3]{8^2}$

(m) $-\sqrt[4]{16^{-2}}$ (n) $\left(\dfrac{32}{50}\right)^{\frac{1}{2}}$ (o) $16^{\frac{5}{4}}$ (p) $\sqrt[3]{\dfrac{1}{8}}$

(q) $\dfrac{1}{16^{-\frac{3}{4}}}$ (r) $-\sqrt[5]{243}$ (s) $\sqrt[5]{-243}$ (t) $-\sqrt[5]{-243}$

9 Evaluate each of the following and express your answer with denominator 1.

(a) $4^{-\frac{1}{2}}$ (b) $-4^{\frac{3}{2}}$ (c) $16^{-\frac{3}{4}}$ (d) $(\sqrt[4]{16})^{-1}$

(e) $25^{-\frac{3}{2}}$ (f) $\sqrt[3]{-8}$ (g) $(\sqrt{16})^{-1}$ (h) $8^{\frac{2}{3}}$

(i) $-\sqrt[5]{-32}$ (j) $(-\sqrt[3]{27})^{-1}$ (k) $\left(\dfrac{36}{49}\right)^{\frac{1}{2}}$ (l) $(-\sqrt{144})^2$

(m) $\left(\dfrac{100}{196}\right)^{\frac{1}{2}}$ (n) $(25^{\frac{1}{2}})^0$ (o) $(\sqrt[3]{-8})^3$

Problem Solving

How big is big? For example, if you typed five digits every second, how long would it take you to type the number given by the following?

$$9^{9^9}$$

Problem Solving

Use the method of indirect proof to prove that $\sqrt{2}$ is an irrational number.

3.4 Simplifying Expressions Containing Exponents

The skills you learned in the previous section can be applied to the simplification of expressions that contain powers and radicals.

You use the Laws of Exponents and the relationship

$$\sqrt[n]{a^m} = a^{\frac{m}{n}}, \quad m \in I, n \in N, \text{ if } n \text{ is even then } a \geq 0$$

to simplify expressions containing powers.

Example Simplify. (a) $\sqrt[5]{32^2} - \sqrt[3]{8}$ (b) $32^{-\frac{3}{5}} - 32^{\frac{3}{5}}$

Solution (a) Write the terms using exponents. (b) $32^{-\frac{3}{5}} - 32^{\frac{3}{5}} = \dfrac{1}{32^{\frac{3}{5}}} - 32^{\frac{3}{5}}$

$$\sqrt[5]{32^2} - \sqrt[3]{8} = (32^2)^{\frac{1}{5}} - 8^{\frac{1}{3}}$$
$$= [(2^5)^2]^{\frac{1}{5}} - (2^3)^{\frac{1}{3}}$$
$$= (2^{10})^{\frac{1}{5}} - 2$$
$$= 2^2 - 2$$
$$= 4 - 2$$
$$= 2$$

$$= \dfrac{1}{(2^5)^{\frac{3}{5}}} - (2^5)^{\frac{3}{5}}$$
$$= \dfrac{1}{2^3} - 2^3$$
$$= \dfrac{1}{8} - 8$$
$$= -7\dfrac{7}{8}$$

3.4 Exercise

A 1 Simplify.
(a) $49^{\frac{1}{2}} + 16^{\frac{3}{4}}$ (b) $27^{\frac{2}{3}} - 81^{\frac{1}{4}}$ (c) $16^{\frac{3}{4}} + 16^{\frac{3}{4}} - 81^{-\frac{3}{4}}$
(d) $128^{-\frac{2}{7}} - 16^{-0.25}$ (e) $16^{\frac{3}{2}} + 16^{0.75} + 5 - 27^{\frac{2}{3}}$

2 Simplify each of the following.
(a) $81^{\frac{1}{2}} + \sqrt[3]{8} - 32^{\frac{3}{5}} + 32^{-\frac{1}{5}}$ (b) $9^{\frac{1}{2}} - \sqrt[4]{16} + 81^{\frac{1}{4}} - 3(3^{-2})$
(c) $\left(\dfrac{1}{8}\right)^{\frac{1}{3}} - \sqrt[3]{\dfrac{27}{125}} + 2(16^{-\frac{3}{4}}) - (\sqrt{4.01})^0$ (d) $(-125)^{\frac{1}{3}} - 32^{-\frac{3}{5}} + \dfrac{1}{25^{\frac{1}{2}}} + \sqrt[3]{8^{-1}}$

3 Simplify each of the following.
(a) $\dfrac{3^{-1}}{2^{-1}}$ (b) $(9^{-\frac{1}{2}}) \div (16^{-\frac{3}{4}})$ (c) $3^{-2} \div 2^{-3}$

(d) $(3^{-2}) \div (27^{-\frac{2}{3}})$ (e) $\dfrac{3^{\frac{7}{12}}}{3^{\frac{1}{3}} \times 3^{\frac{1}{4}}}$ (f) $\dfrac{64^{\frac{5}{6}} \times 16^{\frac{3}{4}}}{27^{\frac{2}{3}}}$

4   Simplify.

(a) $\dfrac{2^{-1} + 3^{-1}}{6^{-1}}$ (b) $\dfrac{2^{-1}}{2^{-2} - 2^{-3}}$ (c) $\dfrac{2^{-1} - 2^{-3}}{3^{-1} - 2^{-1}}$

(d) $\dfrac{4^{-\frac{1}{2}} + 9^{-\frac{1}{2}}}{27^{-\frac{2}{3}}}$ (e) $\dfrac{8^{\frac{2}{3}} + 8^{\frac{2}{3}}}{8^{\frac{1}{3}} - 8^{\frac{2}{3}}}$ (f) $\dfrac{81^{\frac{1}{4}} + 81^{\frac{1}{4}}}{81^{\frac{3}{4}} - 81^{\frac{1}{4}}}$

B 5   Simplify.

(a) $\dfrac{x^{\frac{1}{2}} \times x^{\frac{2}{3}}}{x^{\frac{1}{4}}}$ (b) $\dfrac{x^{\frac{5}{6}} \times x^{\frac{2}{3}}}{x^{\frac{1}{2}}}$ (c) $(y^{\frac{1}{2}})^3 \div (4y^4)^{\frac{1}{2}}$

(d) $\left(\dfrac{\sqrt[4]{y^2}}{\sqrt{y}}\right)^{10}$ (e) $\left(\dfrac{x^3}{16}\right)^{\frac{1}{4}}\left(\dfrac{81^{\frac{3}{4}}}{x}\right)$ (f) $\dfrac{(x^2y^4)^{\frac{1}{2}}(x^4y^2)^{\frac{1}{2}}}{(x^{\frac{1}{2}}y^{\frac{1}{2}})^4}$

(g) $\sqrt[3]{\dfrac{\sqrt{x}\sqrt{x^3y}}{x^{\frac{4}{3}}}}$ (h) $(\sqrt[3]{x^{3n+1}})(\sqrt[3]{x^{-1}})$ (i) $\left(\dfrac{a^5b^{-2}}{x^{-2}y^3}\right)^2\left(\dfrac{a^{-2}b^{-4}}{x^{\frac{1}{2}}y^{\frac{3}{2}}}\right)$

6   Simplify each of the following.

(a) $\left(\dfrac{a}{b}\right)^{-3}(ab^3)^2$ (b) $(x^k)^{-2}(-a^{-3})^k$ (c) $(x^p)^{-3} \div (x^{-p})^2$

(d) $\left(\dfrac{-b}{a}\right)^{-2}\left(\dfrac{a}{-b}\right)^2$ (e) $\dfrac{(ab^{-1})^3}{a^{-2}}\left(\dfrac{a}{b}\right)^{-3}$ (f) $\dfrac{(a^3)^{-k}(a^{-k})^2}{a^{-5k}}$

7   Find the value of each of the following if $a = 1$, $b = 2$, $k = 2$.
(a) ab^k (b) a^kb (c) $(ab)^k$ (d) $(ab)^{-k}$
(e) $(-ab)^k$ (f) $(a^{-1}b^{-2})^k$ (g) $(a^{-1}b^{-2})^{-k}$ (h) $(a^3b^2)^k$

8   Express each of the following with positive exponents.

(a) a^3b^{-2} (b) $\dfrac{3a^{-1}b}{c^{-1}}$ (c) $\dfrac{3ab^{-2}}{4m^{-2}}$ (d) $\dfrac{3^{-1}a^2b}{c^{-2}}$ (e) $\dfrac{(5a)^{-1}b}{c^{-2}}$

9   Each of the following represents a real number. What are the restrictions on the variables?
(a) $\sqrt{3x + 1}$ (b) $\sqrt{2y - 3}$ (c) $\sqrt{m^2 - 25}$ (d) $\sqrt[3]{3 - p}$ (e) $\sqrt[4]{y + 1}$

10 Find the smallest positive value of the variable so that each of the following represents an integer.
(a) $\sqrt{x + 1}$ (b) $\sqrt{3p - 1}$ (c) $\sqrt{\dfrac{y + 5}{2}}$ (d) $\sqrt{\dfrac{2(x - 5)}{3}}$ (e) $\sqrt{x^2 - 1}$

C 11 For $p = 2$, $k = -1$, which expression has the greater value?

A: $\dfrac{p^{-2k}p^{-k+2}}{(p^{-2})^k}$ B: $\dfrac{(p^k)^{-3}p^{-(1-2k)}}{(p^{-k})^3}$

3.5 Accuracy, Precision and Significant Digits

In solving problems, you have often been asked to express your answer, rounded to a number of decimal places. For example,

0.15 rounded to 1 decimal place is 0.2
3.752 rounded to 2 decimal places is 3.75
201.48 rounded to the nearest whole number is 201

When measurements are given, they are approximations.

For example, when the radius of a circle, r, is given as 0.124 m this means that its actual length lies between 0.1235 m and 0.1245 m

$$0.1235 \leq r < 0.1245$$

For measured or estimated values the **maximum possible error** is half of the place value of the last retained digit. Thus, for the radius of the circle above, this measurement has a maximum possible error of 0.0005 m greater than or less than the given measurement of 0.124 m and can be written $r = 0.124$ m $\pm$ 0.0005 m.

The **precision** of a measurement or an estimated value is given by the unit used. For example:

▶ If you say that the diameter at the equator is 12 800 km to the nearest 100 km then this measurement is precise to 100 km and the maximum possible error is ± 50 km.

▶ If you say that the mass of a Ringtail monkey is 2.7 kg to the nearest tenth of a kilogram then this measurement is precise to one tenth of a kilogram and the maximum possible error in this measurement is ± 0.05 kg.

The **accuracy** of a measurement is often defined in terms of the **relative error**.

$$\text{relative error} = \frac{\text{maximum possible error}}{\text{measurement}}$$

You can compare the accuracy of the previous measurements.

▶ For the equator: measurement = 12 800 km, maximum possible error = 50 km

$$\text{relative error} = \frac{50}{12\ 800} \doteq 0.39\%$$

▶ For the Ringtail monkey: measurement = 2.7 kg, maximum possible error = 0.05 kg

$$\text{relative error} = \frac{0.05}{2.7} \doteq 1.9\%$$

Thus, the measurement of the equator is more accurate than the measurement of the mass of the Ringtail monkey.

Significant Digits

Often, when you express measurements, not all of the digits are significant. For example, when you measure the length of a wire as 91.2 cm, the digits used indicate that the measure is between 91.15 and 91.25. Thus, the digits 9, 1, and 2 in 91.2 cm are **significant**. When a number is written in decimal form, a significant digit is any digit which has a purpose other than just placing the decimal point. For example, the numbers

36   36 000   0.000 36

all have 2 significant digits.

The numbers 4306, 0.043 06 and 4 306 000 all have 4 significant digits. In the number 4306 the 0 digit is not used to indicate the position of the decimal point and thus is a significant digit.

In the measures 25.0 m and 25.00 m, the 0 digits are used to indicate the accuracy of the measure.

Thus 25.0 m has 3 significant digits and 25.00 m has 4 significant digits.

To express a measure to a certain number of significant digits, you use your rounding skills, as shown in the following example.

Example 1   Write 248.6306 kg to

(a) 4 significant digits   (b) 3 significant digits   (c) 2 significant digits.

Solution

(a) The fifth digit is 3 (i.e. less than 5). Thus, the fourth digit is left unchanged. 248.6306 kg to 4 significant digits is 248.6 kg.

(b) The fourth digit is 6 (i.e. 5 or more). Increase the third digit by 1. 248.6306 kg to 3 significant digits is 249 kg.

(c) The third digit is 8 (i.e. 5 or more). Increase the second digit by 1. 248.6306 kg to 2 significant digits is 250 kg.

The zero of 250 kg is not significant, but it is written in, in order to locate the position of the decimal point.

Computations with Measured or Estimated Values

Throughout your work in mathematics, calculations are performed with measurements. In writing your answers to a problem, you must consider the accuracy of the answer you give. When multiplying or dividing measured or estimated values, the number of significant digits in the answer should be no greater than the given measured or estimated value with the least number of significant digits.

The following example illustrates the result stated above.

Example 2   An aquarium has dimensions 52 cm × 28.25 cm × 35.5 cm. What is the capacity of the aquarium in litres, to the nearest litre? (Use 1 cm^3 = 1 mL.)

Solution

Think: 52 cm has 2 significant digits.
28.25 cm has 4 significant digits.
35.5 cm has 3 significant digits.
Thus the answer is to be expressed to 2 significant digits

Volume of aquarium = length × width × height
$$V = 52 \times 28.25 \times 35.5$$
$$= 52\ 149.50 \longleftarrow \text{Express your answer to 2 significant digits.}$$

The volume of the aquarium is 52 000 cm^3.

Thus, the capacity of the aquarium is 52 000 mL or 52 L to the nearest litre.

3.5 Exercise

A 1 What is the maximum possible error for each of the following measures?
(a) 0.0237 m   (b) 0.237 m   (c) 2.37 m   (d) 23.7 m
(e) 23.70 m   (f) 0.02 kg   (g) 2.7 km   (h) 25 370 kg
(i) 37.215 m   (j) 82.01 km   (k) 0.000 03 g   (l) 39.000 29 g

2 Write an expression which includes the maximum possible error for each of the following measures. The first one is done for you.
(a) 37.2 cm   37.2 cm ± 0.05 cm
(b) 21.31 kg   (c) 0.251 m   (d) 27 000 m   (e) 386.4 g
(f) 1.0001 L   (g) 526.02 mL   (h) 1798.7 g   (i) 0.000 02 m
(j) 89 625 000 mL   (k) 15.0 m   (l) 6.032 g   (m) 889.8264 kg

3 What is the precision of each of these measures?
(a) 1.56 m   (b) 113.8 kg   (c) 20.0003 kg   (d) 57 600 m
(e) 1 000 000 g   (f) 50.362 L   (g) 0.000 06 g   (h) 38 127 001 mm
(i) 21.06 mL   (j) 385 L   (k) 28.020 g   (l) 85 126 138.1 m

B 4 Write the precision and the maximum possible error of each of these measures.
(a) 22.05 L   (b) 132.7 mL   (c) 5.021 kg
(d) 17 841.0 m   (e) 38 261 025 g   (f) 5.000 02 km

(g) 221.32 g   (h) 789 326.60 km   (i) 52.7068 mm

(j) 3.26 km   (k) 0.021 L   (l) 0.000 000 02 g

5   What is the accuracy of each of these measures?

(a) 82.02 g   (b) 1378.1 kg   (c) 0.000 006 L

(d) 32 012 692 m   (e) 38.0 g   (f) 3.80 g

(g) 982.026 m   (h) 372 mm   (i) 10.0001 mL

(j) 38 262.005 L   (k) 3.89 cm   (l) 38.602 50 m

6   How many significant digits are shown in each measure?

(a) 0.023 m   (b) 7.01 kg   (c) 85 000 000 cm

(d) 85 000 001 cm   (e) 38.0 g   (f) 38.00 g

(g) 76 032 mm   (h) 38.0060 L   (i) 127 832.0261 L

(j) 380 000.0 cm   (k) 76.0007 g   (l) 0.000 206 0 mL

7   All of the following numbers are approximations. Calculate each to the required accuracy.

(a) 2.65×38

(b) $0.002\ 42 \div 2.36$

(c) $\dfrac{0.0020 \times 2.001}{0.103}$

(d) $27\ 800 \times 1.500 \times 0.275$ (e) $0.326\ 02 \div 16.301$

(f) $\dfrac{3.0 \times 86\ 000 \times 0.12}{0.26}$

8   A laboratory technician is finding the mass of a residue. She first finds its mass to be 0.33 g. When she checks her measurement, she finds the mass to be 0.326 g. Which measurement is more accurate?

Problem Solving

The strategies and skills of solving a problem recur each time we study a different branch of mathematics.

A: In solving a problem we often make the problem more difficult because we don't read carefully or we interpret the problem in only one way. Solve this problem.

A circular field is to be divided into 4 equal parts using 3 fences. If the fences are of equal length, how will you do it?

B: To solve some problems, we often just need to use common sense and not advanced algebraic or geometric skills. Solve this problem.

A hovercraft, travelling at 75 km/h, and a freighter, travelling at 15.5 km/h, head towards each other on open sea for a rendezvous. How far apart are they exactly 1 h before they meet?

3.6 Scientific Notation

These numbers are written in scientific notation.

$$68\ 000 = 6.8 \times 10^4$$

The exponent, 4, indicates that the decimal point has been placed 4 positions to the left.

$$0.000\ 068 = 6.8 \times 10^{-5}$$

The exponent, -5, indicates that the decimal point has been placed 5 positions to the right.

How big is big? How small is small?

Our sun is far larger than any of the planets that orbit it. Its diameter is about 1 392 900 km. Still, it is not large as stars go. For example, the largest known star is IRS$_5$ with a diameter of 14 800 000 000 km (about 10 625 times greater than that of the sun). When you compare the above magnitudes to the mass of an electron (0.000 000 000 000 000 000 000 000 904 g), you may begin to ask yourself whether

---

A number, N, is written in **scientific notation** when it is expressed as a product in the following form.

$$N = n \times 10^p \quad \text{where } 1 \leqq n < 10 \text{ and } p \text{ is an integral value}$$

Example 1   Write the numbers in the newspaper article above to 3 significant digits.

Solution   The diameter of the Sun is

to 3 significant digits

$$1\ 392\ 900 \text{ km} = 1.39 \times 10^6 \text{ km.}$$

The diameter of IRS$_5$ is

$$14\ 800\ 000\ 000 \text{ km} = 1.48 \times 10^{10} \text{ km}$$

The mass of an electron is

$$0.000\ 000\ 000\ 000\ 000\ 000\ 000\ 000\ 000\ 904 \text{ g} = 9.04 \times 10^{-28} \text{ g}$$

Computations in scientific work often involve calculations with very large or very small numbers. The Laws of Exponents enable you to perform calculations in a more convenient form, as shown in the following example.

Example 2 Calculate. Express your answer to the required accuracy.

$$46\ 300\ 000 \times 28\ 900 \div 0.000\ 635$$

Solution Express the numbers in scientific notation.

$$\frac{46\ 300\ 000 \times 28\ 900}{0.000\ 635} = \frac{4.63 \times 10^7 \times 2.89 \times 10^4}{6.35 \times 10^{-4}}$$

The final answer is to be expressed to 3 significant digits.

$$= \underbrace{\frac{4.63 \times 2.89}{6.35}}_{\text{number part}} \times \underbrace{\frac{10^7 \times 10^4}{10^{-4}}}_{\text{exponent part}}$$

$$= 2.11 \times 10^{15} \text{ (to 3 significant digits)}$$

$$\frac{10^7 \times 10^4}{10^{-4}} = 10^{7+4-(-4)} = 10^{15}$$

Some electronic calculators have features built into them so that when you calculate with large or small numbers, the answers are automatically expressed in scientific notation.

$$\boxed{4.8301211 \qquad 36}$$

$1 \leqq n < 10$ exponent p

The number shown on the display of the calculator is $4.830\ 121\ 1 \times 10^{36}$.

3.6 Exercise

A 1 Write each of the following in standard form. Express your answer to 3 significant digits.

(a) 3620×10^4 (b) $0.007\ 380 \times 10^3$ (c) $780\ 000 \times 10^5$

(d) 382.3×10^4 (e) 586×10^{-7} (f) $0.000\ 036\ 200 \times 10^8$

(g) $0.000\ 000\ 057\ 500 \times 10^3$ (h) $0.000\ 730 \times 10^{-6}$

2 Express in scientific notation to 3 significant digits.

(a) 28 000   (b) 0.002 380   (c) 7800

(d) 632 000 000   (e) 0.75   (f) 876 500 000

(g) 0.000 073 800   (h) 0.000 000 042 300   (i) 0.000 000 900 1

3   Express each of the following in scientific notation. Use 2 significant digits.
    (a) 632 000 000 000   (b) 0.000 000 000 480
    (c) 3 800 000 000 000   (d) 0.000 000 000 000 000 053 200
    (e) 8 ÷ 1 000 000   (f) 46 ÷ 1 000 000 000

4   Express each of the following as a decimal numeral.
    (a) 7.21×10^4 (b) 3.6×10^3 (c) 7.31×10^{-3} (d) 4.581×10^{-4}
    (e) 5.67×10^8 (f) 2×10^{-4} (g) 8.7×10^{-6} (h) 21×10^5
    (i) 3620×10^4 (j) $0.007\ 530 \times 10^5$ (k) $750\ 000 \times 10^4$
    (l) 38.6×10^3 (m) 5864×10^{-5} (n) $0.007\ 280 \times 10^5$

5   Express each of the following measures in scientific notation to 2 significant digits.
    (a) The equatorial radius of the earth is 6 380 000 m.
    (b) The polar radius of the earth is 6 360 000 m.
    (c) The earth is approximately 150 000 000 000 m from the sun.
    (d) The mass of a proton is about 0.000 000 000 000 000 000 000 001 660 g.
    (e) The interior temperature of the sun is 15 000 000°C.
    (f) The diameter of an electron is approximately 0.000 000 000 000 400 cm.
    (g) The diameter of the star Mira Ceti is 697 000 000 km.

6   For each of the following, write a decimal numeral for the values given.
    (a) The earth's average distance from the sun is 1.50×10^8 km.
    (b) The average distance between the earth and moon is 3.84×10^5 km.
    (c) The mass of a hydrogen atom is 1.66×10^{-24} g.
    (d) The mass of an electron is 9.04×10^{-28} g.
    (e) The mass of the earth is 5.98×10^{24} kg.

B 7   Each product or quotient involves calculations of numbers expressed in scientific notation. Express the answer to 3 significant digits.
    (a) $(4.63 \times 10^4)(6.91 \times 10^6)$ (b) $(3.89 \times 10^{-8})(4.61 \times 10^6)$
    (c) $(9.86 \times 10^{-3})(4.86 \times 10^8) \div (6.35 \times 10^{-2})$
    (d) $(3.21 \times 10^{-2})(3.86 \times 10^4)^2$ (e) $\dfrac{6.84 \times 10^6}{3.21 \times 10^{-3}}$ (f) $\dfrac{9.62 \times 10^{-3}}{8.79 \times 10^{-6}}$

8   Calculate. Express each answer in scientific notation to 2 significant digits.
    (a) $(4.3 \times 10^6)(2.4 \times 10^{-3})$ (b) $(5\ 900\ 000)(0.000\ 120)$
    (c) $(380\ 000\ 000)(0.000\ 450)$ (d) $(550\ 000)(0.000\ 000\ 006)$

9   Calculate. Express your answer in scientific notation to 2 significant digits.
     (a) $(5.4 \times 10^3)(4.8 \times 10^5)$ (b) $(2.73 \times 10^9)(4.63 \times 10^{-4})$
     (c) $5200 \times 680\ 000$ (d) $0.000\ 000\ 723 \times 7\ 890\ 000$

10   Calculate. Express your answer in scientific notation to 3 significant digits.
     (a) $(2.63 \times 10^{-3})^2 \div (7.82 \times 10^5)$ (b) $2\ 560\ 000 \div (861)^2$
     (c) $(0.000\ 000\ 545) \div (0.004\ 890)$ (d) $(6.38 \times 10^8) \div (5.3 \times 10^4)$

11   Use $m = 0.000\ 483$, $n = 0.000\ 045\ 100$, and $p = 4\ 830\ 000$.
     Calculate each of the following to 2 significant digits.
     (a) mnp (b) m^2np (c) $m^2 \div (np)$ (d) $(mn)^3 \div p^2$

12   The land area of the earth is 149×10^6 km^2 and its ocean area is
     3.61×10^8 km^2. Calculate the ratio of ocean area to land area.

C 13 The diameter of the star Arcturus is $42\ 000\ 000$ km. The diameter of Venus
      is $12\ 100$ km. A space ship can travel completely around Venus in 1.5 min.
      Calculate the time needed to travel around the star Arcturus.

Calculator Tip

The scientific calculator has an exponential key $\boxed{\text{EXP}}$ and a change
sign key $\boxed{+/-}$ that can be used to express numbers in scientific
notation. Also, calculations can be performed in other disciplines
such as chemistry and physics.

Number	Calculator Steps
967 000 000	$\boxed{\text{C}}$ 9.67 $\boxed{\text{EXP}}$ 8
0.000 000 000 967	$\boxed{\text{C}}$ 9.67 $\boxed{\text{EXP}}$ 10 $\boxed{+/-}$

Calculation	Calculator Steps	Output
$(8.4 \times 10^{-7})(9.3 \times 10^6)$	$\boxed{\text{C}}$ 8.4 $\boxed{\text{EXP}}$ 7 $\boxed{+/-}$ $\boxed{\times}$ 9.3 $\boxed{\text{EXP}}$ 6 $\boxed{=}$	?
$(9.3 \times 10^6) \div (8.6 \times 10^{-5})$	$\boxed{\text{C}}$ 9.3 $\boxed{\text{EXP}}$ 6 $\boxed{\div}$ 8.6 $\boxed{\text{EXP}}$ 5 $\boxed{+/-}$ $\boxed{=}$	?

Try these on your calculator.
A $(8.6 \times 10^7)(4.3 \times 10^{-6})$ B $(3.9 \times 10^{-8}) \div (4.6 \times 10^3)$

C $\dfrac{(9.8 \times 10^6)(4.6 \times 10^{-5})}{(4.3 \times 10^8)(6.9 \times 10^{-3})}$

Applications: Stars, Galaxies, and Parsecs

In an average galaxy there are about ten thousand million stars. To measure distances outside of your solar system, a unit of astronomical distance called the **parsec** is used. A parsec is about 30.9 million million kilometres.

$$1 \text{ parsec} = 30.9 \times 10^{12} \text{ km}$$
$$\text{(to 3 significant digits)}$$

14   Proxima Centauri, the nearest star to your solar system, is about 40 000 000 000 000 km away. Express this distance in parsecs to 3 significant digits.

15   The galaxy designated by 3C-295 is one of the most distant galaxies ever photographed. Its distance from earth is 1.5×10^9 parsecs. What is this distance in kilometres to 3 significant digits?

16   The distance of the star Capella is 15.8 parsecs. The distance of Arcturus is 10.9 parsecs. How much further is Capella? Express your answer in kilometres to 3 significant digits.

17   Express each of the following distances in kilometres to 2 significant digits.
      (a) The Andromeda galaxy is 231 000 parsecs away.
      (b) The brightest part of the Andromeda galaxy has a diameter of about 1000 parsecs.
      (c) The average distance between galaxies is about 300 000 parsecs.

18   The speed of light to 4 significant digits is 29 980 000 000 cm/s. A light year is the distance travelled by light in a year. To appreciate how fast light travels, consider the fact that, in one second, light goes a distance equivalent to 7.5 times the circumference of the earth.
      Express the speed of light in scientific notation
      (a) to 4 significant digits.   (b) to 2 significant digits.

19   Calculate, to 3 significant digits, the distance, in kilometres, light travels in
      (a) an hour.   (b) a year.

20   The diameter of the earth measured at the equator is 12 800 km. Show that an object travelling at the speed of light could go about 7.5 times around the earth in a second.

3.7 Solving Exponential Equations

In the previous section, you learned certain properties of exponents. The following two properties are also related to exponents.

A: If two powers are equal and they have like bases, then the exponents are equal.

$$\text{If } m^x = n^y \text{ and } m = n \text{ then } x = y.$$

B: If two powers are equal and they have the same exponents, then the bases are equal.

$$\text{If } m^x = n^y \text{ and } x = y \text{ then } m = n.$$

You can now combine properties A and B with your earlier skills with equations and apply them to solve equations involving exponents.

Example 1 Solve $5^{x^2 - 3x} = 5^{2x - 4}$.

Solution Since the bases of the powers are equal then

$$x^2 - 3x = 2x - 4$$
$$x^2 - 3x - 2x + 4 = 0$$
$$x^2 - 5x + 4 = 0$$
$$(x - 1)(x - 4) = 0$$
$$x = 1 \quad \text{or} \quad x = 4$$

In the equation in the following example you need to recognize the exponents as they occur in a quadratic equation.

Example 2 Solve and verify $5^{2x} - 30(5^x) + 125 = 0$.

Solution Write 5^{2x} as $(5^x)^2$. Then

$$5^{2x} - 30(5^x) + 125 = 0$$
$$\text{becomes} \quad (5^x)^2 - 30(5^x) + 125 = 0$$
$$(5^x - 5)(5^x - 25) = 0$$

$5^x - 5 = 0$ or $5^x - 25 = 0$	Check: Let $x = 1$ and $x = 2$ in the
$5^x = 5 \qquad\qquad 5^x = 25$	original equation.
$x = 1 \qquad\qquad 5^x = 5^2$	For $x = 1$, LS $= 5^{2x} - 30(5^x) + 125$
$x = 2$	$= 5^2 - 30(5) + 125$

For $x = 1$, LS $= 5^{2x} - 30(5^x) + 125$
$= 5^2 - 30(5) + 125$
$= 0$
$= $ RS
$x = 1 \quad$ checks ✓

For $x = 2$, LS $= 5^{2x} - 3(5^x) + 125$
$= 5^{2(2)} - 30(5^2) + 125$
$= 625 - 750 + 125$
$= 0 = $ RS
$x = 2 \quad$ checks ✓

Thus, the solutions are $x = 1$ and $x = 2$.

3.7 Exercise

A   Check you answers in the original equations.

1   Find the solution set.

(a) $2^x = 32$ (b) $5^x = 3125$ (c) $3^x = 81$

(d) $4(2^x) = 256$ (e) $7^{3x+2} = 7^{2x+5}$ (f) $3^{x+3} = 9^x$

2   Find the root of each of the following.

(a) $2^x = 32$ (b) $3^x = 27$ (c) $3^x = 9^{x-1}$ (d) $7^{x+4} = 7^{2x}$

B 3   Solve.

(a) $2^{2x} = 2^8$ (b) $3^{3x+1} = 3^{x-3}$ (c) $5^{4x+1} = 5^{3x+9}$

(d) $10^{3-5x} = 10^{x-9}$ (e) $5^{x^2-3x} = 5^{2x-6}$ (f) $4^{x^2-5x} = 4^{x-5}$

4   (a) Solve $\left(\dfrac{1}{4}\right)^{x+2} = \left(\dfrac{1}{8}\right)^{x+3}$ (b) Verify your answer in part (a).

5   *Equivalent* equations have the same root(s). Which of the following equations are equivalent?

(a) $4^{x+2} = 2^{x+5}$ (b) $25^2 = 5^{x-1}$ (c) $9^{2x-4} = 27^{x-1}$

6   Find the solution set. Verify.

(a) $2^{x^2} = 32(2^{4x})$ (b) $3^{x^2} = 27(3^{2x})$ (c) $9^{x+2} = \left(\dfrac{1}{27}\right)^{x+2}$

7   Solve each of the following.

(a) $27^{-x} = \dfrac{1}{2}$ (b) $2^{x-2} = 4^{x+2}$ (c) $\left(\dfrac{1}{9}\right)^{x-2} = \left(\dfrac{1}{27}\right)^{x+1}$

(d) $4^{x-2} = 8^4$ (e) $9^{2x+1} = 81(27^x)$ (f) $2^{2x+2} + 7 = 71$

(g) $9^{x-2} - 8 = 73$ (h) $2^{x+1} \times 4^{x+1} \times 8^{x+1} = 128^x$

8   Solve each of the following.

(a) $(2^{x-4})^x = 32$ (b) $4^{2-x^2} = 4^x$

(c) $9^{x^2+1} = (27^x) \times (3^x)^x$ (d) $2^{x^2} = (16^{x-1}) \times 2^x$

9   Solve.

(a) $3^{x-y} = 9$ (b) $9^x = \left(\dfrac{1}{3}\right)^{y-1}$

$\quad\quad 27^y = 3^{x+2}$ $2^x = 8^{y-1}$

3.8 Problem-Solving: Computer Awareness

You learn mathematics to develop methods of solving problems in industry, science, business, etc. The computer is a powerful tool for helping people solve problems. Not only does the computer remove some of the drudgery from calculations, but also it provides unique opportunities for exploring mathematics.

There are few things that you do nowadays in which a computer is not involved.

The forerunners of today's computers were bulky. For example, one of the early computers, called ENIAC, invented in 1945, occupied a room about 9 m × 9 m and had a mass of 27 000 kg. The development of electronic technology has resulted in computers that are compact, faster and more reliable. For example, in 1946 it took about 70 h to calculate π to 2037 decimal places; in 1961 it took 8.7 h to calculate π to 100 265 decimal places.

Today's computers can perform 36 000 000 operations in one second.

A computer can work only if it is programmed. A computer cannot think or plan for itself. To plan the work for a computer you must understand the principles and methods of mathematics.

When you prepare instructions for a computer in some computer language you are *writing a program*. There are different computer languages for different families of computers. The computer language used throughout this book is called BASIC.

These symbols are used in computer language.

+ add	↑ exponential	≠ not equal to
− subtract	> greater than	< less than
* multiply	> = greater than or equal to	< = less than or equal to
/ divide		

Examine the following program, written in BASIC.

The following program gives the area of a triangle when the co-ordinates of its vertices are known.

The co-ordinates of the vertices are provided. This information is called the INPUT.

```
10  INPUT X1, Y1, X2, Y2, X3, Y3
20  LET D = X1*Y2 + X2*Y3 + X3*Y1
30  LET U = X2*Y1 + X3*Y2 + X1*Y3
40  LET A = ABS(D − U)/2
50  PRINT "AREA OF TRIANGLE IS"; A
60  END
```

The program ends.

The computer provides the area of a triangle. This is called the OUTPUT.

Each statement is numbered. The computer will do the steps involved in each statement in order. The statement numbers are not written 1, 2, 3, . . . in case other steps are added later. These statements are then coded in computer language on cards, or typed at a terminal which tells the computer what to do.

The history of computers and the skills needed to program a computer are complete studies in themselves. Many books have been written about computers and about BASIC. In subsequent pages you will find other programs, related to a variety of topics, written in the computer language BASIC.

1 (a) Research the meaning of BASIC.
   (b) Research the contribution of Pascal (1642) and Leibniz (1671) towards the science of computing.

2 (a) Explore the pages of this book. List the mathematics involved in the computer programs that occur in the Computer Tips.
   (b) Choose a mathematical topic or problem of your own. Write a computer program to solve the problem.

Computer Tip

The computer may be used to perform calculations in *any* branch of mathematics. For example, in Chapter 9 we will study analytic geometry. The following program finds the co-ordinates of the midpoint of a line segment if we know the co-ordinates of the end points.

```
10  INPUT X1, Y1, X2, Y2
20  LET M1 = (X1 + X2)/2
30  LET M2 = (Y1 + Y2)/2
40  PRINT "MIDPOINT IS" M1, M2
50  END
```

Practice and Problems: A Chapter Review

An important step for problem-solving is to decide which skills to use. For this reason, these questions are not placed in any special order. When you have finished the review, you might try the *Test for Practice* that follows.

1 Express in lowest terms each of the following in the form $\dfrac{a}{b}$, $a, b, \in I$.

   (a) 0.375   (b) $0.\overline{8}$ (c) $0.\overline{12}$ (d) $0.3\overline{4}$ (e) $0.3\overline{9}$ (f) $0.0\overline{48}$

2 Use a construction to mark each number on the number line.
   (a) $\sqrt{2} - 1$ (b) $1 + \sqrt{3}$

3 Arrange the values $\left(\dfrac{4}{5}\right)^{-1}$, $\dfrac{5}{3^{-2}}$, $(-2)^{-3}$, $\left(\dfrac{1}{3}\right)^{-3}$, $\dfrac{7^0}{2^{-3}}$ from least to greatest.

4 Write each expression with the variables in the numerator.
   (a) $\dfrac{x^{-3}y^2}{x^{-2}y^5}$ (b) $\dfrac{ab^{-3}}{a^{-3}b^{-2}}$ (c) $\dfrac{14a^{-3}}{7ab^{-3}}$ (d) $\dfrac{16x^4y^{-2}z^{-6}}{8x^0y^{-3}z^2}$

5 Simplify each of the following.
   (a) $8^{-\frac{1}{3}} + 10^0 + 4^{\frac{1}{2}}$ (b) $2^{-4} + 5^0 - 3(-2)^{-4}$
   (c) $16^{\frac{3}{4}} - (3)^2 + 8^{-\frac{2}{3}} - 3^4 \times 3^{-5}$

6 Simplify.   (a) $(32x^{10}y^{15}z^{20})^{\frac{2}{5}}$ (b) $\sqrt[4]{\dfrac{1}{y}(y^{-\frac{3}{4}})}$

7 What is the maximum possible error for each measure?
   (a) 36.82 kg   (b) 179.6 g   (c) 5.068 m   (d) 1.003 L

8 Each of these calculations represents an approximation. Calculate each to the appropriate accuracy.

   (a) 6.98×43.2 (b) $0.003\,65 \div 4.96$ (c) $\dfrac{0.0050 \times 4.003}{0.205}$

9 Solve.   (a) $12^{3x-9} = 1$ (b) $2^{x-2} + 2^x - 640 = 0$

Problem Solving

A golf hole has a diameter of 8 cm. What are the dimensions of the greatest square pole that can be placed in the hole?

Test for Practice

Try this test. Each test is based on the mathematics you have learned in this chapter. Try this test later in the year as a review. Keep a record of those questions that you were not successful with and review them periodically.

1 Find the equivalent rational number represented by each decimal, in lowest terms.
   (a) 0.36 (b) $0.\overline{36}$ (c) $0.3\overline{6}$

2 Which of the following expressions are equal in value?

   A $\dfrac{3^0 \times 8}{2 \times 9^0}$ B $\dfrac{5 + 5^0}{4 - 4^0}$ C $\dfrac{3^0(6 + 2^0) + 6^0}{2^0 + 3^0}$ D $\dfrac{3^{-1}}{2^{-3} + 2^{-2}}$

3 Simplify each of the following.
   (a) $8^{\frac{2}{3}}$ (b) $27^{-\frac{1}{3}}$ (c) $3^0 - 16^{\frac{3}{4}} + 2^{-2}$
   (d) $-\sqrt{49} + \left(-\dfrac{1}{27}\right)^{\frac{1}{3}} + (-8)^{-\frac{2}{3}}$

4 Express each of the following with a single base.
   (a) $(mn^6)\left(\dfrac{m}{n^{-3}}\right)^{-2}$ (b) $\dfrac{p^{-k}(p^{3k})^{-2}}{p^0}$

5 Write the precision and the maximum possible error for each measure?
   (a) 36.08 L   (b) 229.76 g   (c) 0.0036 mm   (d) 16 821.0 m

6 Use $p = 0.000\ 365$, $q = 0.000\ 483$, $r = 9\ 625\ 000$. Calculate each of the following to 2 significant digits.
   (a) p^2qr (b) $pr \div q$ (c) $p^2r \div q$

7 Solve. (a) $3^{x-3} = 9^{x-2}$ (b) $2^{2x} - 33(2^x) + 32 = 0$

Math Tip

It is important to clearly understand the vocabulary of mathematics when solving problems. *You cannot speak the language of mathematics if you don't know the vocabulary.*

- Make a list of all the words you review and learn in this chapter.
- Provide a simple example to illustrate the meaning of each word.

Looking Back: A Cumulative Review

1 Factor.
(a) $4 - 9x^4$ (b) $x^4 + 4y^4$ (c) $3x^2 - 2xy - y^2$
(d) $3y^3 + 5y^2 + 3y + 5$ (e) $2mx^2 + 3mxy - 2nxy - 3ny^2$

2 Simplify. $\dfrac{3m + 9}{m^2 - 4m - 21} - \dfrac{12 - 3m}{2m^2 - 7m - 4}$

3 Simplify each of the following.
(a) $2^3 \times 2^4$ (b) $3^8 \div 3^4$ (c) $10^3 \times 10^2$
(d) $\dfrac{a^9}{a^2}$ (e) $3^2 \times 3^4 \times 3$ (f) $2^8 \times 2^2 \div 2^5$
(g) $4^2 \times 4 - 4^2$ (h) $y^3 \times y^2$ (i) $m^5 \div m^2$
(j) $p^2 + p^5 \div p^3$

4 Write each of the following without brackets.
(a) $(m^5)(m^4)$ (b) $(xy)^4$ (c) $\left(\dfrac{x}{y}\right)^5$ (d) $(p^3)^5$
(e) $\left(\dfrac{a}{2}\right)^3$ (f) $(2k)^3$ (g) $\left(\dfrac{2}{3}\right)^3$ (h) $(mn)^3(mn)^2$

5 Find the coefficient of x and z in each of the following expressions.
(a) $3z + 6x - ax - 3ax + 2bx - 5bz$
(b) $-3ax - 4mz - 5az + 3mx - 8z + 9x$

6 Write $\dfrac{x^4 - y^4}{x^4 + 2x^2y^2 + y^4} \times \dfrac{x^2 + y^2}{-x^2 + y^2}$ as a rational expression in lowest terms.

7 Find k so that $x^4 - kx^2 + 36$ is divisible by $x - 2$.

8 An important skill in problem solving is to know when to apply a particular skill to a problem. Find all roots of the following equations.
(a) $x(6x + 11) = 10$ (b) $\dfrac{3}{2}(p + 2) = 9p^2$

9 Divide $d^4 + 50d^3 + 9d^2 - 34d - 5$ by $(d^2 + 7d + 1)$.

10 Remember that $y - x = -(x - y)$. Simplify each of the following.
(a) $\dfrac{16 - y^2}{y + 4}$ (b) $\dfrac{2x + 1}{2x^2 - 5x - 3}$ (c) $\dfrac{25 + 20a + 4a^2}{4a^2 - 25}$

4 Applications with Ratio and Variation

essential skills with ratio, working with direct variation, direct squared variation, inverse variation, inverse squared variation, joint variation, partial variation, applications, strategies and problem-solving

Introduction

Certain recurring themes can give you insight into the nature of mathematics. One such theme has to do with questions that arise in problem solving. In mathematics, as well as in many other disciplines, the two most important problem-solving questions are those below.

> - What are you asked to find?
> - What are you given?

These questions occur in a larger framework called *Steps for Solving Problems*. This framework, which appears below, is designed to help you organize your work: to keep track of your goal and the stages through which you must progress to attain that goal.

Steps for Solving Problems

Step A: Understand the problem.
- What are you asked to find?
- What are you given?

This is the time to introduce variables for what is unknown. Record the information on a diagram.

Step B: Decide on a method.
This is the time to write your variables into equations.

Step C: Find the answer.
This is the time to solve the equations.

Step D: Check your answer.
- Is it reasonable?
- Are your calculations correct?

Step E: Write a final statement.
- Have you used the correct units?
- Have you rounded correctly?

Throughout your work in this chapter and in others, you must use some method of organizing your solution to a problem. The more mathematics you do and the more problems you solve, the more likely you are to begin to apply your skills of organizing the solution to a problem. You must develop skills for writing solutions, whether they be your own or whether they be from suggestions such as the one shown above.

4.1 Skills and Concepts with Ratios

Ratios occur in many situations.

- In business you compare profits to losses.
- In sports you compare wins to losses.
- In science you compare amounts of material, such as oxygen to nitrogen.

A comparison of two or more numbers is a **ratio**. The 2-term ratio 3:2 is read as "3 is compared to 2" or "3 to 2". The numbers 3 and 2 are called the **terms** of the ratio.

You can write a 2-term ratio in fractional form when the second term is non-zero.

$$\text{Thus,} \qquad a:b = \frac{a}{b}, \qquad b \neq 0.$$

Often, you compare more than two numbers. In sports, you make comparisons.

wins to losses to ties is 8:3:2.

To solve problems about ratios, you need to know the following.

- The order of the terms of a ratio is important. If the order of the terms is changed, then the meaning of the ratio changes. Thus, the ratio

3:8:2

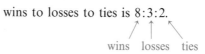

  means losses to wins to ties.
- A ratio is in **lowest terms** or **simplest form** if the terms of the ratio have no integral common factor. Thus, to write 4:8:12 in lowest terms, you divide each term by the greatest common factor of the terms.
  Thus, 4:8:12 = 1:2:3 in lowest terms.
- When you equate two ratios you are writing a **proportion**. Thus, $a:b = c:d$ and 4:8:12 = 1:2:3 are proportions.

Proportions containing 2-term ratios can be written from proportions containing 3-term ratios. For example, from the proportion 4:8:12 = 1:2:3 you can write the following to include

$$4:8 = 1:2, \quad 4:12 = 1:3, \quad 4:1 = 8:2, \quad 8:12 = 2:3, \quad 3:12 = 2:8.$$

$$\frac{4}{8} = \frac{1}{2}, \qquad \frac{4}{12} = \frac{1}{3}, \qquad \frac{4}{1} = \frac{8}{2}, \qquad \frac{8}{12} = \frac{2}{3}, \qquad \frac{3}{12} = \frac{2}{8}$$

To solve problems about proportions, you need to know the following vocabulary and concepts.

For the proportion $a:b = c:d$,

- a, b, c, d are the first, second, third, and fourth terms in the proportion, and as such are called the first, second, third, and fourth proportionals.
- a, d are called the **extremes** of the proportion.
- b, c are called the **means**.

  The product of the extremes equals the product of the means

$$\text{If } \frac{a}{b} = \frac{c}{d}, b \neq 0, d \neq 0 \qquad \text{then } bd \times \frac{a}{b} = bd \times \frac{c}{d}$$

$$ad = bc$$

- If $\frac{a}{b} = \frac{b}{c}$, then b is called the **mean proportional** between a and c.

To solve problems, you need to combine your earlier skills with algebra with your skills with ratio and proportion.

Example 1   (a) Write $(x^2 - y^2):(ax + ay)$ in lowest terms.

(b) Find the mean proportional between 3 and 75.

Solution   (a) Factor the terms of the ratio. Thus

$$(x^2 - y^2):(ax + ay) = (x - y)(x + y):a(x + y)$$
$$= (x - y):a \quad \text{provided } x + y \neq 0, a \neq 0$$

Thus $(x^2 - y^2):(ax + ay) = (x - y):a$.

(b) Let x represent a mean proportional. Then

$$\frac{3}{x} = \frac{x}{75}$$
$$x^2 = 225$$
$$x = \pm 15$$

Thus, the mean proportional is 15 or -15.

Example 2   Find $x:y$ if $(x + 9)(y - 2) = (x + 3)(y - 6)$.

Solution   Expand the products.

$$xy + 9y - 2x - 18 = xy + 3y - 6x - 18$$
$$9y - 2x = 3y - 6x$$
$$4x = -6y$$

Divide by $4y$.

$$\frac{4x}{4y} = \frac{-6y}{4y}$$

$$\frac{x}{y} = \frac{-3}{2} \quad \text{or} \quad x:y = -3:2$$

4.1 Exercise

A 1 Write each ratio in lowest terms.
   (a) 120 cm to 20 cm   (b) 2 m to 25 cm   (c) 1.5 km to 200 m
   (d) 4 h to 30 min   (e) 2 min to 30 s   (f) $5 to 25¢

2 Express each of the following in lowest terms.
   (a) $36a:72a$ (b) $28ab:14b$ (c) $30a^2b:60ab^2$
   (d) $-16xy:32y$ (e) $(8k - 2k):2k$ (f) $4p:(6p + 2p)$
   (g) $\dfrac{3}{p}:\dfrac{q}{6}$ (h) $\dfrac{x}{3}:\dfrac{9}{y}$ (i) $(2x + 4y):2x$
   (j) $(ap + aq):(bp + bq)$ (k) $(p^2 - q^2):(p + q)$
   (l) $(a^2 - b^2):(a - b)$ (m) $(ma^2 + mb^2):(ma + mb)$

3 Find the missing value (?) for each of the following.
   (a) If $\dfrac{x}{y} = \dfrac{2}{3}$ then $\dfrac{y}{x} = ?$ (b) If $\dfrac{3}{b} = \dfrac{2}{a}$ then $\dfrac{b}{a} = ?$
   (c) If $\dfrac{m}{n} = \dfrac{4}{5}$ then $\dfrac{m + 1}{n} = ?$ (d) If $7t = 4s$ then $\dfrac{s}{t} = ?$
   (e) If $\dfrac{a}{b} = \dfrac{4}{5}$ then $\dfrac{a + 1}{b - 1} = ?$

B 4 Find the missing terms for each proportion.
   (a) $x:7 = 5:2$ (b) $2:5 = 4:x$ (c) $4:3x = 45:63$
   (d) $3s:36 = 9:16$ (e) $8:4 = 20:4x$ (f) $6:2x = 7:4$

5 Find the value of the variables that satisfy the proportions.
   (a) $\dfrac{y}{45} = \dfrac{2}{3}$ (b) $\dfrac{12}{y} = \dfrac{16}{9}$ (c) $\dfrac{m}{24} = \dfrac{3}{10}$ (d) $\dfrac{3}{7p} = \dfrac{1}{2}$

6 (a) If $x = 3k$ and $y = 4k$, find $x:y$.
   (b) If $p = 5k$ and $q = -2k$, find $q:p$.

7 Find the ratio $x:y$ for each of the following.
   (a) $2x = 3y$ (b) $4x - 5y = 0$ (c) $2x + 3y = 3x$
   (d) $2x - y = 3y - x$ (e) $\dfrac{2x}{3} - \dfrac{y}{2} = 0$ (f) $\dfrac{x - y}{x + y} = \dfrac{2}{3}$ (g) $\dfrac{y + 2x}{x - y} = \dfrac{5}{4}$

8 Find the values of the variables that satisfy the proportions.
   (a) $\dfrac{x}{2} = \dfrac{y}{5} = 3$ (b) $\dfrac{m}{3} = \dfrac{4}{n} = 5$ (c) $\dfrac{30}{p} = \dfrac{25}{q} = \dfrac{5}{4}$

9 If $\dfrac{m}{n} = \dfrac{2}{3}$, what is the value of each of the following?

(a) $\dfrac{m - n}{m}$ (b) $\dfrac{m - n}{n}$ (c) $\dfrac{m - n}{m + n}$ (d) $\dfrac{m + n}{m - n}$

10 Find the value of each variable that satisfies the proportion.

(a) $\dfrac{4}{y + 1} = \dfrac{2}{3}$ (b) $\dfrac{2}{3} = \dfrac{3}{x - 3}$ (c) $5:7 = 2:(p + 3)$

11 Solve each proportion.

(a) $\dfrac{x + 3}{x + 2} = \dfrac{2}{3}$ (b) $\dfrac{y + 3}{y - 2} = \dfrac{2}{3}$ (c) $(2 + y):2 = (2 - y):3$

(d) $\dfrac{y + 6}{6} = \dfrac{y + 2}{2}$ (e) $\dfrac{a + 5}{6} = \dfrac{a + 6}{7}$ (f) $(b - 7):(b + 5) = 5:3$

12 Solve.

(a) $\dfrac{3}{5m - 9} = \dfrac{-7}{21}$ (b) $\dfrac{2x - 7}{2x + 7} = \dfrac{7}{5}$ (c) $\dfrac{2p - 8}{6} = \dfrac{p + 3}{24}$

(d) $(2x - 3):3 = 3:1$ (e) $(p - 1):1 = (p + 1):3$ (f) $(4y + 3):5 = y:2$

13 Find the ratio $x:y$ in each of the following.
(a) $(x + 4)(y - 4) = (x - 8)(y + 2)$ (b) $(x - 9)(y - 4) = (x - 12)(y - 3)$
(c) $(4x + 3)(y + 8) = (2x + 6)(2y + 4)$
(d) $(3x + 3)(2y + 2) = (2x - 3)(3y - 2)$

14 Solve for the ratio $x:y$ in each of the following.
(a) $x^2 - 4xy + 3y^2 = 0$ (b) $x^2 + 3xy - 10y^2 = 0$
(c) $2x^2 - 7xy + 3y^2 = 0$ (d) $10x^2 - 9xy + 2y^2 = 0$

15 Find the mean proportionals between
(a) $4, 9$ (b) $3, 27$ (c) m, mn^2 (d) $3m, 12m^3$
(e) $2ab^2, 8a$ (f) $4p^2, 16p^4$ (g) $\sqrt{3}, 3\sqrt{3}$ (h) $2\sqrt{2}a^2, \sqrt{2}a$

16 Find the fourth proportional for each of the following.

(a) $3, 4, 12$ (b) $5, 4, 25$ (c) $3, 8, 12$ (d) $\dfrac{1}{2}, \dfrac{2}{3}, \dfrac{3}{4}$

17 If $x:y = 2:1$, find the value of each of the following.

(a) $\dfrac{x + y}{x - y}$ (b) $\dfrac{x^2}{y^2}$ (c) $\dfrac{x^2 - 2y^2}{x^2}$ (d) $\dfrac{x^2 - y^2}{x^2 + y^2}$ (e) $\dfrac{x^2 - y^2}{(x - y)^2}$

C 18 If $m:n = -3:5$, $n:p = 6:7$ and $p:q = -10:21$, then find the ratio of $m:q$.

19 If $a:b = 6:5$, $b:c = -2:9$, and $c:d = 10:3$, then find the ratio $a:d$.

Problem-Solving Strategy

To solve some problems, you need to introduce an additional symbol, called a parameter. A parameter represents a constant, shown by a letter such as k. To solve the following problem, the parameter k is introduced.

Example If $x:y = a:b$ prove that $\dfrac{x + a}{y + b} = \dfrac{a}{b}$.

Solution Since $x:y = a:b$ then $\dfrac{x}{y} = \dfrac{a}{b}$ or $\dfrac{x}{a} = \dfrac{y}{b}$.

Let $\dfrac{x}{a} = \dfrac{y}{b} = k$, where k is a parameter and $k \neq 0, -1$.

Then $x = ak$, $y = bk$.

By substitution, $\text{LS} = \dfrac{x + a}{y + b} = \dfrac{ak + a}{bk + b}$

$$= \frac{a(k + 1)}{b(k + 1)}, \qquad k \neq -1$$

$$= \frac{a}{b}$$

$$= \text{RS}$$

Thus $\dfrac{x + a}{y + b} = \dfrac{a}{b}$.

20 (a) If $\dfrac{x}{y} = \dfrac{a}{b}$ and $x, y, a, b \neq 0$, show that $\dfrac{a}{x} = \dfrac{b}{y}$.

(b) Prove your result in (a) using a different method.

21 If $x:y = a:b$, $x, y, a, b \neq 0$, prove that

(a) $\dfrac{x}{a} = \dfrac{y}{b}$ (b) $bx = ay$ (c) $bx - ay = 0$ (d) $\dfrac{y}{x} = \dfrac{b}{a}$

22 If $\dfrac{x}{y} = \dfrac{a}{b}$, $x, y, a, b \neq 0$, prove that

(a) $\dfrac{x + y}{y} = \dfrac{a + b}{b}$ (b) $\dfrac{x - y}{y} = \dfrac{a - b}{b}$

(c) $\dfrac{x + a}{a} = \dfrac{y + b}{b}$ (d) $\dfrac{x + a}{y + b} = \dfrac{a}{b}$

23 If $\dfrac{x}{a} = \dfrac{y}{b}$, $x, y, a, b \neq 0$, prove that

(a) $\dfrac{x + a}{x - a} = \dfrac{y + b}{y - b}$ (b) $\dfrac{x + y}{x - y} = \dfrac{a + b}{a - b}$

4.2 Strategy for Solving Problems: Ratio

To do Example 1, you need to combine your earlier skills with equations and your present skills with ratio.

Example 1   Find the two positive numbers, where

- they are in the ratio 5:4 and
- the sum of their squares is 1025.

Solution   Let the numbers be represented by x and y.

$$\frac{x}{y} = \frac{5}{4} \quad \text{or} \quad \frac{x}{5} = \frac{y}{4}.$$

Let $\frac{x}{5} = \frac{y}{4} = k$, $k > 0$, where k is a constant. Then $x = 5k$, $y = 4k$.

Thus $(5k)^2 + (4k)^2 = 1025$

$25k^2 + 16k^2 = 1025$

$41k^2 = 1025$ *Check:* $\frac{25}{20} = \frac{5}{4}$ checks ✓

$k^2 = 25$

$k = \pm 5$ $20^2 + 25^2 = 1025$ checks ✓

Since the numbers are positive, then $k = 5$. The numbers are 20 and 25.

You may use your skills with proportions to solve the next problem.

Example 2   In carrying the Olympic Torch, Samuel, Jerome, and Donna ran a total of 6000 m. The ratio of Samuel's distance to Jerome's distance was 5:4 and Donna's distance to Jerome's distance was 3:4. How far did each person run?

Solution   Let s, j, and d represent the number of kilometres run respectively by Samuel, Jerome, and Donna.

Then $\frac{d}{j} = \frac{3}{4} \quad d = \frac{3}{4}j \quad \frac{s}{j} = \frac{5}{4} \quad s = \frac{5}{4}j$

The total distance travelled was 6000 m.

Thus $j + \frac{3}{4}j + \frac{5}{4}j = 6000$

$4j + 3j + 5j = 24\ 000$

$12j = 24\ 000$

$j = 2000$

Thus, $d = \frac{3}{4}j = 1500$, $s = \frac{5}{4}j = 2500$.

Thus, the distances run by Samuel, Jerome, and Donna are respectively 2500 m, 2000 m, and 1500 m.

4.2 Exercise

A 1 A pleasing ratio of the width to the length of a picture frame is 5:8. What should be the width of the picture frame shown in the diagram?

2 The ratio of the number of strikeouts to walks of a baseball pitcher is 5:4.
   (a) Express the number of strikeouts and the number of walks in terms of a constant, k.
   (b) The pitcher gave up 60 walks. Write an equation to show this using the number of walks from part (a).
   (c) Find the number of strikeouts the pitcher would have if he gave up 60 walks.

3 John and Tim invest in a company in the ratio 4:3. If John's profit in 1 year from the company is $28 360, how much will Tim receive?

4 In creating a wood filler substitute, clean sawdust and white glue are mixed in the ratio 5:2 by volume. How much glue must be added to 22 mL of sawdust to form this substitute?

5 The ratio of the circumference of a circle to its diameter is 3.14:1. What is the circumference of a bicycle wheel which has a 65-cm diameter?

6 One season the Montreal Canadiens outscored their opponents by a ratio of 8:5. If the Canadiens scored 328 goals, how many goals did the opponents score?

For 30 years the Montreal Canadiens have maintained a top position in Canadian Hockey. They have won the Stanley Cup more than 20 times.

7   Two numbers, in the ratio 2:3, have a sum of 140. What are the numbers?

B 8   In a basketball game, Tony, Colin and André scored a total of 72 points. The ratio of Tony's points to Colin's points was 2:7 and Colin's points to André's points was 7:3. How many points did each score?

9   Jane, Karen and Rose share the rent on their townhouse. Due to differences in room sizes, the ratio of Jane's rent to Karen's rent is 4:3 and Jane's rent to Rose's rent is 2:1. Find each girl's rent if the monthly rent is $540.

10   The ratio of two positive numbers is 2:3. Their product is 96. Find the numbers.

11   The ratio of two positive numbers is 3:5. Twice their product when added to the sum of their squares is 256. Find the numbers.

12   The ratio of two numbers is 5:4. If the sum of their squares is 1025, find the numbers.

13   The difference of the squares of two numbers is 180. If the numbers are in the ratio 7:2, find the numbers.

14   The square of one number exceeds the square of a second number by 612. Find the numbers if their ratio is 13:4.

15   A ratio is given by 2:9. What number added to each term of the ratio will result in a ratio equivalent to 3:4?

16   Find the number such that when it is doubled and then added to each term of the ratio 3:10 the resulting ratio is equivalent to 3:4.

17   Bill, Chris and Ann work at the Pizza Palace. They share 50 h of counter work so that
   • Ann's share:Bill's share is 3:5.
   • Bill's share:Chris' share is 10:9.
   How long did each person work at the counter?

18   A will divides 300 shares of IBM stock among 3 brothers as follows.
   • Bill's share:Brad's share is 3:2
   • Bill's share:Bob's share is 6:5
   How many shares did each brother receive?

C 19   If $a:b = b:c$, prove that $(ac + b^2):b = 2b:1$.

20   If b is a mean proportional for a and c, prove that $(a - b^2):b = (b - bc):c$.

Applications: Chemicals and Ratios

When pure substances combine in a chemical reaction they do so in certain ratios. For example, dry ice is solid carbon dioxide. Carbon dioxide is a combination of carbon and oxygen in the ratio 3:8 by mass. Thus, 3 g of carbon combine with 8 g of oxygen to produce (3 + 8) g or 11 g of carbon dioxide.

21 Carbon dioxide consists of carbon and oxygen which have combined in the ratio 3:8 by mass. What mass of oxygen is needed to produce 55 g of carbon dioxide?

22 Laughing gas consists of nitrogen and oxygen combined in the ratio 28:16 by mass. How much oxygen can be obtained from 22 g of gas?

23 Heavy water or deuterium consists of hydrogen and oxygen which have combined in the ratio 1:4 by mass. What mass of oxygen can be obtained from 60 g of heavy water?

24 Silver iodide, used in "seeding" clouds in rain making, consists of silver and iodine combined in a ratio of about 108:127 by mass. What mass of silver is contained in 705 g of silver iodide?

25 Sodium fluoride consists of sodium and fluorine in a ratio of 23:19 by mass. This compound is sometimes added to a city's water supply in an effort to reduce tooth decay. What mass of fluorine is found in 21 g of sodium fluoride?

26 Silicon and oxygen combine in the ratio 7:8 by mass to produce ordinary sand. What mass of silicon can be extracted from 45 g of sand?

27 Common salt consists of sodium and chlorine in the ratio 23:35.5 by mass. What mass of chlorine can be obtained from 117 g of salt?

28 Moth balls consist of carbon and hydrogen which have combined in the ratio 15:1 by mass. If the carbon from 48 g of moth balls could be obtained, what would be its mass?

29 Magnesium is used in flares and fireworks because it gives off a dazzling white light when it burns. The resulting compound, magnesium oxide, consists of magnesium and oxygen combined in a ratio of 3:2 by mass. How many grams of magnesium would have to be burned to produce 75 g of magnesium oxide?

4.3 Ratios and Proportions: Three Terms

A symbol or form in mathematics represents a lot of useful information. For example, if you are given the two-term proportions you can write them in a compact form.

$$\frac{a}{2} = \frac{b}{3} \quad \text{and} \quad \frac{b}{3} = \frac{c}{4} \Rightarrow \frac{a}{2} = \frac{b}{3} = \frac{c}{4} \quad \text{or} \quad a:b:c = 2:3:4$$

Thus, to solve problems about ratios, you must remember what hidden information occurs in the proportion. For example, finding the values of k and m in the proportion

$$\frac{20}{m} = \frac{4}{1} \rightarrow m = 5 \qquad \frac{k}{5} = \frac{4}{1} \rightarrow k = 20$$

The skills you learned in the previous section extend to your work with 3-term ratios, as shown in the following example.

Example 1 Solve for a and b if $(a + 2):2:3 = 7:-14:(2b - 3)$.

Solution Write

$$\frac{a + 2}{7} = \frac{2}{-14} = \frac{3}{2b - 3}.$$

From the proportion

$$\frac{a + 2}{7} = \frac{2}{-14} \qquad \frac{3}{2b - 3} = \frac{2}{-14}$$

$$\frac{a + 2}{7} = -\frac{1}{7} \qquad \frac{3}{2b - 3} = -\frac{1}{7}$$

$$7(a + 2) = -7 \qquad 21 = -(2b - 3)$$
$$7a + 14 = -7 \qquad 21 = -2b + 3$$
$$7a = -21 \qquad 2b = -18$$
$$a = -3 \qquad b = -9$$

You may, as you did in the previous section with 2-term ratios, introduce a parameter k, to evaluate expressions.

Example 2 Three positive numbers are in the ratio $2:3:4$. If the sum of their squares is 116, find the numbers.

Solution Let the numbers be x, y, z. Thus, $x:y:z = 2:3:4$ or $\frac{x}{2} = \frac{y}{3} = \frac{z}{4}$.

Let $\frac{x}{2} = \frac{y}{3} = \frac{z}{4} = k$, $k \neq 0$. Then, $x = 2k$, $y = 3k$, $z = 4k$.

$$(2k)^2 + (3k)^2 + (4k)^2 = 116$$
$$4k^2 + 9k^2 + 16k^2 = 116$$
$$29k^2 = 116$$
$$k^2 = 4$$
$$k = \pm 2$$

Since the numbers are positive use $k = 2$.
Thus, $2k = 4$, $3k = 6$, $4k = 8$ and the required numbers are 4, 6, and 8.

4.3 Exercise

A   Express your answers as required to 1 decimal place.

1   Express each ratio in lowest terms.
(a) $8:12:16$ (b) $15:-5:10$ (c) $3a^2b:6ab^2:9ab$
(d) $(a^2 - b^2):(a - b):(a^2 - 2ab + b^2)$
(e) $(x^2 + 2xy + y^2):(x + y):(x^2 - y^2)$

2   Solve for a and b.
(a) $3:a:12 = 6:4:b$ (b) $a:3:b = 5:15:10$ (c) $7:5:a = 14:b:4$
(d) $a:10:16 = 3:b:8$ (e) $3:a:b = 6:20:24$ (f) $a:4:10 = 9:6:b$

3   (a) If $x = 6k$, $y = 2k$, $z = 8k$, find $x:y:z$.
(b) If $a = 9k$, $b = -3k$, $c = -12k$, find $a:b:c$.

4   Find the values of a and b.
(a) $7:(a + 3):2 = 14:10:(b - 1)$ (b) $(a + 2):12:8 = 3:(2b + 1):6$
(c) $(3a + 2):3:7 = 8:12:(3b + 1)$ (d) $3:6:(4a + 1) = -2:(b + 1):10$

5   Solve each of the following for m and n.
(a) $\dfrac{2m + 2}{2} = \dfrac{1 - 6m}{-3} = \dfrac{m}{n}$ (b) $\dfrac{3m - 1}{2} = \dfrac{6m + 3}{3} = \dfrac{m}{n + 1}$

6   A football team had a win-loss-tie record in the ratio of $4:2:1$. In that season, they played 21 games. How many games were won, lost and tied?

7   For a triangle the measures of the angles are in the ratio $2:2:5$. Find the measure of each angle.

8   Three numbers are in the ratio $3:2:5$. If the sum of the numbers is 300, find the numbers.

9   The analysis of skim milk powder reveals that the ratio of protein to carbohydrates to water is $7:10:1$ by mass. How many grams of each is contained in a 500-g box of powder?

10   Jenny, Lori and Alex have formed a pool to buy lottery tickets. Respectively, they contribute $5, $7.50, and $12.50. How should they divide the $100 000 cash prize?

B 11   The sum of the squares of 3 positive numbers is 1368. If the ratio of the numbers is $2:3:5$, find the numbers.

12   Three positive numbers are in the ratio of $3:4:5$. When the square of the middle number is subtracted from the product of the other 2 numbers, the answer is -9. Find the numbers.

13   Silver, tin, and lead are used in the ratio $10:8:12$ to forge an alloy for costume jewellery. How much silver is required to forge a bracelet which has mass 40.0 g?

14   A sidewalk is built using gravel, cement and sand in the ratio $14:4:8$ by mass. How much gravel is needed to produce 42.0 kg of this mixture?

15   The ratio of three positive numbers is $3:4:6$. The sum of the squares of the first 2 numbers is 44 less than the square of the third number. Find the numbers.

16   Sugar consists of carbon, hydrogen and oxygen combined in the ratio $72:11:88$. What mass of hydrogen can be obtained from 1 kg of sugar?

17   In Krug Township the ratio of blood types O to A to B to AB is $25:20:4:1$. In a town of 2650 people, how many people would you expect to have type B blood?

18   Glucose or dextrose is a compound of carbon, hydrogen and oxygen combined in the ratio $84:12:96$. How much of each of carbon and oxygen is required to react with 3 g of hydrogen?

19   If $x:y:z = 1:2:3$, find the values of each of the following.

(a) $\dfrac{x - 2y}{2x - z}$ (b) $\dfrac{x^2 - y^2}{y^2 + z^2}$

C 20   If $x:y:z = 2:5:3$, find the values of

(a) $\dfrac{x + y + z}{x + z}$ (b) $\dfrac{x^2 + y^2 + z^2}{x^2 + y^2 - z^2}$

Math Tip

The proportion $x:y = a:b$ or $\dfrac{x}{y} = \dfrac{a}{b}$ may be written in other useful equivalent forms.

$$\frac{x}{a} = \frac{y}{b}, \quad bx = ay, \quad \frac{y}{x} = \frac{b}{a}, \quad \frac{a}{x} = \frac{b}{y}.$$

Can you show that they are indeed equivalent forms?

Applications: The Fertilizer Ratio

Each of the terms of the ratio as shown on a bag of fertilizer has a special significance. The ratio indicates the relative amounts of nitrogen, phosphoric acid, and potash in the fertilizer.

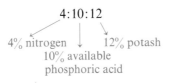

4:10:12

4% nitrogen   12% potash
10% available
phosphoric acid

In the bag shown, the active ingredients of nitrogen, phosphoric acid and potash account for a total of 26% of the mass.

21 A plant fertilizer contains nitrogen, phosphoric acid and potash in the ratio 14:14:12. If a bag of this fertilizer has 21 kg of nitrogen, how much of the other two ingredients does it contain?

22 Lawn Booster gives lawns an early feeding and provides vigorous growth. If a bag contains nitrogen, phosphoric acid and potash in the ratio 20:5:5, how much nitrogen and phosphoric acid is in such a bag containing 2 kg potash?

23 All-Purpose Fertilizer is applied in the late spring when lower nitrogen content is needed. This fertilizer contains nitrogen, phosphoric acid, and potash in the ratio 14:7:7. If the bag contains 2 kg of nitrogen, how much potash does it contain?

24 4-12-8 Garden Special has a high proportion of phosphoric acid and potash for large, healthy flowers and fruits. A bag of this fertilizer contains nitrogen, phosphoric acid and potash in the ratio 4:12:8. How much potash and nitrogen is contained in a bag which has 4 kg of phosphoric acid?

25 A bag of Super Pro fertilizer contains nitrogen, phosphoric acid, and potash in the ratio 21:3:3. If the mass of all the active ingredients is 5 kg, what is the mass of each active ingredient in the bag, to 1 decimal place?

26 Fertilizer for rose bushes contains nitrogen, phosphoric acid, and potash in the ratio 18:24:16. In the spring, each rose bush is to receive 5 g of fertilizer. If only 58% of the fertilizer contains nitrogen, phosphoric acid and potash, how much of each ingredient is applied to one rose bush?

4.4 Ratios in Geometry: Similar Triangles

Often, algebraic skills are used in many topics of mathematics. For example, skills with ratios are used to study similar triangles. Earlier, you learned that two triangles are similar if corresponding angles are congruent or if the ratio of corresponding sides is constant. This means that

If $\angle A = \angle D$, $\angle B = \angle E$, $\angle C = \angle F$, then
  $\triangle ABC \sim \triangle DEF$ and thus,
                                            is similar to

$$\frac{AB}{DE} = \frac{AC}{DF} = \frac{BC}{EF}$$

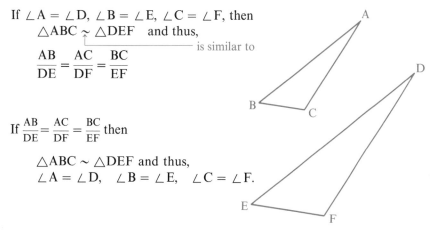

If $\frac{AB}{DE} = \frac{AC}{DF} = \frac{BC}{EF}$ then

  $\triangle ABC \sim \triangle DEF$ and thus,
  $\angle A = \angle D$, $\angle B = \angle E$, $\angle C = \angle F$.

In the following example, your skills with equations are applied to the solution of a problem involving similar triangles.

Example $\triangle ABC \sim \triangle ADE$.
Find the value of x.

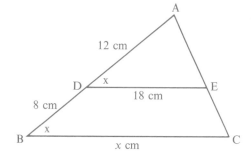

Solution   Since $\triangle ABC \sim \triangle ADE$ then $\frac{AB}{AD} = \frac{BC}{DE} = \frac{AC}{AE}$.

Thus, $\dfrac{20}{12} = \dfrac{x}{18}$

$\qquad x = \dfrac{18 \times 20}{12}$

$\qquad\quad = 30$

Thus x is 30 cm.

4.4 Exercise

A In order to solve problems involving similar triangles, you need to interpret carefully the information given on a diagram.

1 Find the value of the variables.

(a)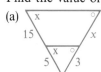

(b)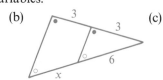

(c)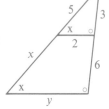

(d)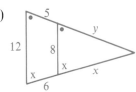

(e)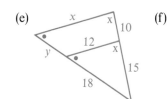

(f)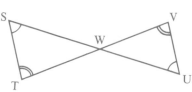

2 $\triangle ADE \sim \triangle ABC$, $AE = 6$, $EC = 4$, $DE = 9$.
Find BC.

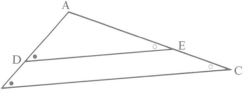

3 $\triangle STW \sim \triangle UVW$, $SW = 6$, $WV = 2.5$, $UW = 4$, Find TW.

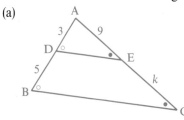

4 Find k for each of the following.

(a)

(b)

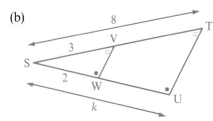

5 Find the value of x and y in the diagram.

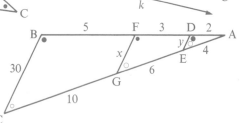

B To solve these problems, you need to record the given information on a diagram. The diagram has been given in Questions 7 and 8. Round answers to 1 decimal place.

6 A clubhouse has a roof whose slant height is 13 m and whose base is 24 m. Two extra supports, 2 m and 3 m from the peak, and perpendicular to the base of the peak, need to be constructed. Find the length of each support.

7 Gene is 1.7 m above the ground and stands 1.3 m from a puddle. The puddle is 20.0 m from a pole. The light is reflected in the puddle. The reflection property of a puddle gives $\angle PDM = \angle BDF$. With this information find **PM**, the height of the pole.

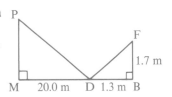

8 In a lumberjack contest two poles are secured for a pole-climbing event. The poles are of different heights. The wires from the top of the poles to the ground make equal angles as shown in the diagram. If the smaller pole is 8.0 m with its wire secured 9.2 m from the base, and the guide wire to the taller pole is 16.0 m, find the height of the taller pole.

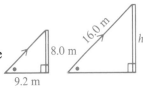

9 For light hitting a mirror, the angle of incidence equals the angle of reflection. The top of a street light pole is reflected into a puddle 25.0 m away. A person 5 m away on the other side of the puddle sees the reflection. If the person's eyes are 2.1 m above street level, how high is the light?

10 A plane climbs 30 m for every 100 m the plane travels forward. If the plane is travelling at 225 km/h, how high will the plane be after 12 s?

11 Two people attached to kites jump from two different heights. Their angles of descent are equal. If Ian's cliff was 28 m high and he lands 52.8 m from his cliff, find the height of the cliff Shelly jumped from if she landed 120 m from her cliff.

C 12 In 600 B.C. the Greek mathematician, Thales, used the following method to find the height of the Great Pyramid. The shadow of the top of the pyramid of Cheops, Son of Seneferu, was 280 m (to the centre of the pyramid). At the tip of the shadow a stick 2.2 m was placed having a shadow 4.2 m long. Calculate the height of the Great Pyramid to the nearest metre.

4.5 Working with Direct Variation

Cindy swam at an average rate of 3 km/h across the English Channel. The distance she travelled is shown in the chart.

t	v	d
Time to swim (h)	Rate (km/h)	Distance (km)
1	3	3
2	3	6
3	3	9
4	3	12

Use the formula $d = vt$. When $v = 3$, $d = 3t$.

The relationship between the distance travelled (d) and the time taken (t) is given by $d = 3t$.
From the equation $d = 3t$ note that
- if d increases then t increases.   • if d decreases then t decreases.

Thus d is said to vary directly with t or simply varies with t. This is written in symbols as $d \propto t$ ___ varies directly with

In general, if y varies directly with x, then you may write the direct variation as $y \propto x$, or $\dfrac{y}{x} = k$ where k is a constant, ($k \neq 0$), called the **constant of variation** or **constant of proportionality**.

If the ordered pairs (x_1, y_1) and (x_2, y_2) satisfy the equation

$$\frac{y}{x} = k, \quad k \text{ is a constant}$$

the ordered pairs are then said to satisfy the direct variation.

Thus you may write the following, where k is a constant.

$$\frac{y_1}{x_1} = k \quad \text{①} \qquad \text{and} \qquad \frac{y_2}{x_2} = k \quad \text{②}$$

From ① and ② the following proportion for a direction variation can be written.

$$\frac{y_1}{x_1} = \frac{y_2}{x_2} = k$$

Note the relative positions of the x and y terms of the proportion.

There is often more than one strategy which can be used to solve a problem in mathematics. For example, problems with direct variation can be solved using different strategies, as shown in the following example.

Example If y varies directly with x and $y = 384$ when $x = 192$, find the value of y when x is 48.

Solution *Step 1:* Find k, the constant of variation.   *Step 2:* Solve for y if $x = 48$.
Write $y = kx$, where k is constant, $k \neq 0$.
$$y = 2x$$
Use $y = 384$, $x = 192$.
$$y = 2(48)$$
$$y = kx$$
$$= 96$$
$$384 = k(192)$$
$$2 = k$$
Thus $y = 96$ when $x = 48$.

The equation for the direct variation is $y = 2x$.

To solve the previous example, you could have used an alternative strategy.

Use the proportion statement $\dfrac{y_1}{x_1} = \dfrac{y_2}{x_2}$.

From the given information, record $y_1 = 384$, $x_1 = 192$, $y_2 = ?$, $x_2 = 48$.

Thus, $\dfrac{384}{192} = \dfrac{y_2}{48}$

$\dfrac{48(384)}{192} = y_2$

$96 = y_2$

Thus $y = 96$ when $x = 48$.

4.5 Exercise

Questions 1 to 7 develop skills for solving problems involving direct variation.

A 1 (a) If A varies directly with W, then write an equation to express the direct variation.
(b) If $A = 720$ when $W = 12$, find A when $W = 15$.

2 (a) If H is directly proportional to A, then write an equation to express the direct variation.
(b) If $H = 40.3$ when $A = 6.5$, find H when $A = 9.5$.

3 Determine the constant of variation for each direct variation.
(a) m varies directly with n and $m = 12$ when $n = 72$.
(b) p varies directly with q and $p = 36$ when $q = 3$.
(c) L is directly proportional to T and $L = 225$ when $T = 15$.
(d) y varies directly with x and $y = 300$ when $x = 30$.
(e) m varies directly with n and $m = 28$ when $n = 14$.

4   Which ordered pairs belong to each direct variation?
   (a) $P = 4T$ (T, P); $(1, 16), (8, 34), (3, 12)$
   (b) $S = 6P$ (P, S); $(3, 18), (1, 48), (10, 68)$
   (c) $y = 15x$ (x, y); $(5, 70), (10, 150), (2, 40)$
   (d) $\dfrac{d}{t} = 12$ (t, d); $(5, 60), (2, 20), (10, 120)$

5   For each of the following, calculate the constant of variation first.
   (a) A direct variation is given by $P = kV$, k is constant. Find the value of V when $P = 1500$ if $P = 600$, when $V = 3$.
   (b) If d varies directly with t and $d = 325$ when $t = 6.5$, find d when $t = 12$.
   (c) h is directly proportional to t. If $t = 8$ when $h = 288$, find h when $t = 20$.

6   For each direct variation, find the missing value.
   (a) $d_1 = 375$ $t_1 = 5$ $d_2 = ?$ $t_2 = 9$
   (b) $P_1 = 1560$ $T_1 = ?$ $P_2 = 1586$ $T_2 = 12.2$
   (c) $W_1 = ?$ $t_1 = 129.2$ $W_2 = 3.5$ $t_2 = 8.5$
   (d) $h_1 = ?$ $t_1 = 3.2$ $h_2 = 209.1$ $t_2 = 8.2$

7   Introduce suitable variables and express each of the following as a direct variation in the form $y = kx$, k is constant.
   (a) The perimeter of a square varies directly with the length of a side.
   (b) The crop yield of a corn field is directly proportional to the amount of rainfall during the season.
   (c) The mass of a metal ball varies directly with the cube of its diameter.

8   Sam can do 70 situps in 1 min.
   (a) How many situps can he do in 2.5 min?
   (b) How long will it take him to do 14 situps?
   (c) What assumptions do you make in finding your answers in (a) and (b)?

B 9   The mass of a cylinder rod is directly proportional to its length.
   (a) Write an equation to express the direct variation.
   (b) The mass of the cylinder is 100 kg when its length is 6 m. Find the mass of a cylinder 15 m in length.

10   The amount of stretch of a spring is directly proportional to the mass added.
   (a) The spring stretched 2 cm when 6 g was added. How many grams must be added to stretch the spring 7 cm?
   (b) What will be the stretch on the spring when 10 g are added?

11   The distance a car travels varies directly with the volume of fuel the tank holds. If a car can travel 500 km on 30 L of gas, how far can the car travel if there is 20 L of gas in the tank?

12   The maximum speed of a car varies directly with the size of its engine. If a car with a 1400 cm^3 engine has a maximum speed of 120 km/h, what size of engine would you need to reach a maximum speed of 88 km/h?

13   Parking fees in a downtown lot vary directly with the length of time parked. If Juan paid $3.90 for 6.5 h, how long could he have parked his car for $1.20?

14   The annual interest earned on a savings account varies directly with the amount on deposit. If Janet earns $13 on a deposit of $200, how much should she earn on a $500 deposit?

15   At a constant speed, the amount of gas consumed varies directly with the distance travelled by the car. When Tania travelled 375 km from Prince George to Kamloops, her car used 12.5 L of fuel. At the same speed, how far could she travel on 15 L of gas?

16   The amount of chlorine needed for a pool is directly proportional to the size of the pool. If 27 units of chlorine are used for 15 kL of water, how much chlorine is required for 25 kL of water?

Problem Solving

If $\frac{a}{b} = \frac{a}{d}$, then $b = d$ was used to solve the following equation. What went wrong?

$$3 - \frac{12}{x + 1} = \frac{3x - 9}{x - 2}$$

$$\frac{3x + 3 - 12}{x + 1} = \frac{3x - 9}{x - 2}$$

$$\frac{3x - 9}{x + 1} = \frac{3x - 9}{x - 2} \longleftarrow \text{Equal numerators.}$$
$$x + 1 = x - 2$$

$$x + 1 = x - 2$$
$$1 = -2$$

Math Tip

These equivalent forms are useful to know.

Can you prove these results?

If $\frac{a}{b} = \frac{c}{d}$ then

$$\frac{a + b}{b} = \frac{c + d}{d} \quad \text{or} \quad \frac{a - b}{b} = \frac{c - d}{d}.$$

4.6 Direct Squared Variation

There are many phenomena that involve a squared relationship. For example,

- The area A of a circle varies directly with the square of the radius r.

$$A \propto r^2$$

- The value, V, of a diamond, varies directly with the square of its mass, M.

$$V \propto M^2$$

Make the following comparison.

Direct variation

- $y \propto x$
- $y = kx$, k constant
- y varies directly with x.
- y is directly proportional to x.
- $\dfrac{y_1}{x_1} = \dfrac{y_2}{x_2} = k$

Direct squared variation

- $y \propto x^2$
- $y = kx^2$, k, constant
- y varies directly with the square of x.
- y is directly proportional to the square of x.
- $\dfrac{y_1}{x_1{}^2} = \dfrac{y_2}{x_2{}^2} = k$

Again, to solve a problem on variation, you can use either strategy. Once you have completed both solutions, compare them and determine why the strategies used are really the same, even though they appear to be different.

Example The volume of water rushing from a hose in a unit of time varies directly with the square of the diameter of the hose (if the water pressure is constant). From a fire hose, with a diameter of 8 cm, 400 kL of water were obtained. For the same amount of time, how much water could be obtained from a garden hose 2 cm in diameter?

Solution Strategy 1 Let V represent the volume of water, in kilolitres, obtained in a unit of time. Let d represent the diameter of the hose, in centimetres.

Then $V = kd^2$, where k is a constant, $(k \neq 0)$.

Record the information given in the problem in a chart. ⟶

V (kL)	d (cm)
400	8
?	2

Step 1: Use $V = kd^2$.

$$400 = k(8)^2$$

$$\frac{400}{8^2} = k \quad \text{or} \quad k = \frac{25}{4}$$

Thus, the variation equation is given by $V = \dfrac{25}{4} d^2$.

Step 2: Solve for V, using $d = 2$.

$$V = \frac{25}{4} d^2$$

$$V = \frac{25}{4} (2)^2 \quad \text{or} \quad V = 25$$

Thus, the volume of water obtained from the garden hose is 25 kL.

Solution
Strategy 2

Let V represent the volume of water, in kilolitres obtained in a unit of time. Let d represent the diameter of the hose, in centimetres.

Then, $\dfrac{V_1}{d_1{}^2} = \dfrac{V_2}{d_2{}^2}$

Given information
$V_1 = 400 \quad d_1 = 8$
$V_2 = ? \quad d_2 = 2$

To solve any problem, record all the given information before you begin the solution.

Use the given information to solve for V_2.

$$\frac{400}{(8)^2} = \frac{V_2}{(2)^2}$$

$$\frac{400}{64} = \frac{V_2}{4}$$

$$\frac{4(400)}{64} = V_2$$

$$25 = V_2$$

Thus the volume of water obtained from the garden hose is 25 kL.

4.6 Exercise

A 1 If b is directly proportional to c^2, then find the constant of variation if $b = 72$ when $c = 12$.

2 (a) If s varies directly as p^2, then write a variation equation to express the relationship.
   (b) If $s = 9$ when $p = 6$, then find s when $p = 10$.

3 If R is directly proportional to the square of V and $R = 50$ when $V = 15$, then find V when $R = 200$.

4 If air resistance is neglected the distance a meteor travels through the atmosphere varies directly with the square of the time of falling.
   (a) Find the constant of variation if a meteor takes 12 s to travel 2304 m.
   (b) How long does it take a meteor to travel 6400 m?

5 The mass of a china plate is directly proportional to the square of the diameter of the plate.
   (a) Write a proportion to express the above variation.
   (b) A plate, 24 cm in diameter, has a mass of 64 g. What is the mass of a plate that is 30 cm in diameter?

B 6 When a vehicle moves, the resistance of air to it varies directly with the square of its speed. For a car travelling at 10 km/h, the resistance to it is 4 units. Find the resistance to the car when the speed is 25 km/h.

7   The distance a car rolls down a hill from a stand-still is directly proportional to the square of the time it rolls. If a car rolls 135 m in 6 s, how far will it roll in 10 s?

8   (a) The value, in dollars, of a diamond is directly proportional to the square of its mass. If a diamond, worth $6300, is 200 mg, then find the mass of a diamond that is worth $25 200.
    (b) Calculate the value of the diamond with a mass of 28 mg.

9   The number of bacteria in a culture is directly proportional to the square of the time the bacteria have been growing. A culture growing for 16 min has 600 bacteria. How long will it take to grow 15 000 bacteria?

10 The amount of leather needed to cover a ball is directly proportional to the square of the radius. A ball of radius 9 cm requires 162 cm^2 of leather. What is the radius of a ball if the amount of leather used is 144.5 cm^2?

11 On an ice surface, the distance, in metres, travelled by a frozen puck before it stops is directly proportional to the square of its initial speed, in metres per second.
    (a) Find the constant of variation if a puck with initial speed of 8 m/s could travel 320 m.
    (b) The initial speed of a puck in some National Hockey League games may be as high as 42 m/s. How far would a puck go before it stops? Express your answer to the nearest kilometre.

For Questions 12 to 14 use the following.

The distance an object falls from a height varies directly with the square of the time the object has been falling.

12 (a) Write a proportion statement for the above variation.
    (b) A ball falls 312 m in 8 s. How far would a ball fall in 10 s?

13 Calculate the distance a ball would fall in
    (a) 3 s   (b) 4 s
    (c) Use the information in (a) and (b) to determine the distance fallen during the 4th second.

C 14 A parcel is dropped in the Arctic from an airplane, but its parachute does not open.
    (a) How far will the parcel drop in the 4th second?
    (b) How far will the parcel drop in the 5th second?
    (c) How much farther will the parcel drop in the 5th second than in the 4th second?

Applications: Driving Safely

The distance, d, in metres, a car travels after braking is directly proportional to the square of its speed, v, in kilometres per hour, at the time of braking.

The two graphs show how the distance for braking increases as the speed of a car increases, on different surfaces.

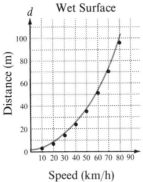

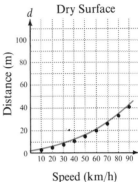

15 The distance, d, in metres, a truck needs to come to a full stop varies directly with the square of its speed, v km/h.

(a) Write a proportion to show this direct squared variation.

(b) A truck requires 8 m to come to a full stop when travelling at 20 km/h. At what distance will the truck come to a stop travelling at 30 km/h?

16 The distance, d, in metres a car travels to a full stop is directly proportional to the square of its speed, v km/h, at the time of braking. At an initial speed of 60 km/h a car travels 36 m before stopping. If the car required 81 m to stop, at what initial speed was it travelling?

17 On a wet surface the distance a car travels upon braking is directly proportional to the square of its speed at the time of braking. A car at an initial speed of 80 km/h travels 90 m before stopping. If the car was travelling at 60 km/h, how far would it travel before stopping? Express your answer to 1 decimal place.

18 The distance required for a truck to come to a full stop is directly proportional to the mass of the truck. At a speed of 60 km/h, a 10 t truck required 55 m to come to a full stop safely. A truck traveling at 60 km/h enters an intersection and at the same time a car stops 38.5 m directly in front of the truck. If the truck has a mass of 7.5 t, will there be a collision? Give reasons for your answer.

19 The braking distance of a car varies directly with its mass. A compact car with a mass of 1135 kg requires 45 m to go from 100 km/h to 0 km/h. A luxury car travelling at 100 km/h is able to come to a complete stop in 50 m. To the nearest kilogram, what is the mass of the luxury car?

4.7 Inverse Variation and Its Applications

The baseball team marked out a course of 16 km for its workouts. The formula is used to complete the chart.

$$vt = 16$$

speed ↙ ↓ ↘ course
time   is 16 km
taken

Speed, v	Time, t	
16 km/h	1 h	← Bicycle
8 km/h	2 h	← Jogging
4 km/h	4 h	← Walking
1 km/h	16 h	

From the above chart, note that
• if the speed is increased, the time taken to travel 16 km is decreased.
• if the speed is decreased, the time taken to travel 16 km is increased.

From $vt = 16$, write $v = \dfrac{16}{t}$.

You say that
• v varies inversely with t.   Write $v \propto \dfrac{1}{t}$.
• v is inversely proportional to t.

In general, an inverse variation is given as

$$xy = k \quad \text{or} \quad y = \frac{k}{x}$$

Where k is the constant of variation, $k \neq 0$.

If (x_1, y_1) and (x_2, y_2) satisfy the inverse variation, then you may obtain a proportion as follows.

$$x_1 y_1 = k \qquad x_2 y_2 = k$$

Thus $x_1 y_1 = x_2 y_2 \quad \text{or} \quad \dfrac{x_1}{x_2} = \dfrac{y_2}{y_1}$

This proportion statement provides an alternative strategy for solving problems involving variation, as shown in the following example.

In your study of mathematics, look for similarities in the topics you study. For example, the strategies you learned for direct variation extend in a similar way to learning strategies for solving problems involving inverse variation.

Example If s varies inversely with t and $s = 30$ when $t = 25$, then find the value of s when t is 150.

Solution Write $s = \dfrac{k}{t}$, k constant $\qquad$ or $\quad s_1 t_1 = s_2 t_2$

When $s = 30$, then $t = 25$.

$$s = \frac{k}{t}$$

$$30 = \frac{k}{25}$$

$$k = 750$$

The variation equation is $s = \dfrac{750}{t}$.

Use $t = 150$ to solve for s.

$$s = \frac{750}{t} = \frac{750}{150} = 5$$

Thus $s = 5$ when $t = 150$.

$\qquad\qquad\qquad s_1 t_1 = s_2 t_2$

$\qquad\qquad\qquad s_1 = 30, \qquad t_1 = 25,$

$\qquad\qquad\qquad s_2 = ?, \qquad t_2 = 150$

$$s_1 t_1 = s_2 t_2$$
$$30(25) = s_2(150)$$

$$\frac{30 \times 25}{150} = s_2$$

$$5 = s_2$$

Then $s = 5$ when $t = 150$.

4.7 Exercise

A The following questions develop skills for working with inverse variation.

1 Calculate the constant of variation for each of the following inverse variations.
   (a) m varies inversely with n and $m = 25$ when $n = 2$.
   (b) P is inversely proportional to T and $T = 16$ when $P = 4$.
   (c) x varies inversely with y and $x = 8$ when $y = 12$.

2 Which ordered pairs in columns A, B, C, satisfy each inverse variation?

	A	B	C
(a) $sp = 60$, (s, p):	(4, 15)	(3, 30)	(2, 30)
(b) $t = \dfrac{100}{q}$, (q, t):	(2, 50)	(10, 10)	(4, 30)
(c) $P = \dfrac{72}{T}$, (T, P):	(2, 36)	(3, 24)	(4, 18)

3 If P varies inversely with T and $P = 108$ when $T = 3$, then find
   (a) the constant of variation. $\qquad$ (b) T if $P = 18$. $\qquad$ (c) P if $T = 54$.

4 H is inversely proportional to S.
   (a) Write a proportion to express the inverse variation.
   (b) If $H = 9$ when $S = 140$, then find S when $H = 60$.

B 5 Use the proportion $x_1 y_1 = x_2 y_2$ to solve each of the following.

(a) $S_1 = 10$, $T_1 = 100$, $S_2 = ?$, $T_2 = 40$

(b) $x_1 = 10$, $x_2 = ?$, $y_1 = 20$, $y_2 = 20$

(c) $P_1 = 6$, $Q_1 = ?$, $P_2 = 24$, $Q_2 = 2$

6 (a) T is inversely proportional to P. If $T = 50$ then $P = 2$. Find P when $T = 20$.

(b) If x varies inversely with y, and $x = 30$ when $y = 15$, then find x when $y = 90$.

(c) An inverse variation is given by $PT = k$, k is constant. Find P_1 when $T_1 = 50$, $P_2 = 125$ and $T_2 = 5$.

7 Write a proportion for each of the following variations. Introduce appropriate variables.

(a) The value of a car varies inversely with the age of the car.

(b) The frequency of sound waves is inversely proportional to the wave length of the sound waves.

(c) If the temperature of a gas is constant, then the volume of the gas is inversely proportional to the pressure.

8 The time required to cook a roast varies inversely with the oven temperature. If a 3-kg roast takes 3 h to cook at 175°C, how long will it take the same roast to cook at 210°C?

9 Boyle's Law states that at a fixed temperature the volume of the gas is inversely proportional to the pressure. If the volume of the gas is 30 L when the pressure is 8 units, determine the pressure when the gas expands to 80 L.

10 A baseball pitcher throws a fastball at a speed of 15 m/s. If it takes 1.5 s for the ball to cross the plate, how long will it take to return the ball if the catcher has a sore elbow and can only throw the ball at a speed of 10 m/s?

11 The effect of a sunlamp is inversely proportional to the distance from the source. When a person is 2 m from the source the tanning power is 40 units. What is the tanning power at 0.5 m?

12 Richard rode his "pedal power" bicycle to visit a friend. The trip takes 3 h pedalling at 8 km/h. How much time would he have saved if he had taken his 10-speed bicycle which travels at 12 km/h?

C 13 A noise pollution researcher found that the sound level of heavy traffic varies with the distance from the road. At a distance of 5 m the sound level is 120 dB. At what distance would the sound level be a soft 30 dB?

4.8 Inverse Squared Variation

When you show a film on a screen, the intensity, I, of the beam decreases quickly as you move the projector away from the screen. In fact, the intensity, I, varies *inversely as the square* of the distance, d.

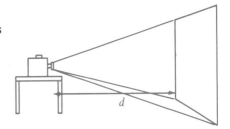

You can write the *inverse squared variation*.

$$I \propto \frac{1}{d^2} \quad \text{or} \quad I = \frac{k}{d^2} \qquad \text{Where } k \text{ is the constant variation}$$

Compare the following.

Inverse Variation

$$y = \frac{k}{x}$$

- y varies inversely as x.
- y is inversely proportional to x.
- $y_1 x_1 = y_2 x_2$

Inverse Squared Variation

$$y = \frac{k}{x^2}$$

- y varies inversely as x^2.
- y is inversely proportional to x^2.
- $y_1 x_1^2 = y_2 x_2^2$

The strategies and skills you learned earlier for other types of variation now readily extend to solving problems about inverse squared variation.

Example
The force of gravity between two bodies in the solar system is inversely proportional to the square of the distance between them. The moon is now about 400 000 km from the earth. If the moon were only 100 000 km from the earth, what would be the change in the force of gravity between the earth and the moon?

Solution
Let the present force of gravity between the earth and the moon be represented by F units. Let d represent the distance, in kilometres, between the bodies. Write the proportion statement as follows.

$$F_1 d_1^2 = F_2 d_2^2 \qquad \begin{array}{ll} F_1 = F & d_1 = 400\ 000 \\ F_2 = ? & d_2 = 100\ 000 \end{array}$$

Thus, $F(400\ 000)^2 = F_2(100\ 000)^2$.
Solve for F_2.

$$\frac{F(400\ 000)^2}{(100\ 000)^2} = F_2$$

$$16F = F_2 \quad \text{or} \quad F_2 = 16F \qquad \text{Original force between the bodies.}$$

Since the original force was F units, then the force between the bodies has increased by a factor of 16, (namely $16F$).

4.8 Exercise

A 1 Calculate the constant of variation if P varies inversely with the square of T and $P = 6$ when $T = 8$.

2 Calculate the constant of variation if y is inversely proportional to the square of x, and $y = 0.25$ when $x = 4$.

3 R varies inversely with the square of S. If $R = 24$ when $S = 15$, then find
(a) the constant of variation.
(b) R when $S = 5$.   (c) S when $R = 150$.

4 An inverse squared variation is given by $a_1 b_1{}^2 = a_2 b_2{}^2$. If $a_2 = 6$ when $b_2 = 30$, then find a_1 when $b_1 = 6$.

5 A variation is given by $ST^2 = k$, k is constant. If $S = 36$ when $T = 2$ then find T when $S = 16$.

B In solving any problem you must read carefully. The following questions include not only inverse squared variations but also other types of variations. Be sure to read carefully.

6 (a) An inverse squared variation is given by $rs^2 = k$, k is constant. If $r_1 = 15$ when $s_1 = 9$ then find r_2 when $s_2 = 6$.
(b) P varies directly with V^2. If $P = 16$ when $V = 10$, find P when $V = 4$.
(c) Q varies inversely with the square of T. If $Q = \frac{7}{2}$ when $T = 5$, then find T when $Q = 14$.
(d) If $\dfrac{P}{V} = k$, k is constant, and we know $P_1 = 15$, $P_2 = 25$, and $V_2 = 125$, find the value of V_1.

7 The volume of a cylinder is directly proportional to the square of its radius. If a cylinder of radius 3 cm holds 49.5 L, what is the radius of the cylinder that would hold 137.5 L?

8 The price of a diamond ring varies directly with the square of the mass of the stone. A stone, whose mass is 40 mg costs $1000. What is the mass of a stone which costs $1500?

9 The mass of commercial soup cans varies directly with the square of the radius. A large can with radius 3 cm has a mass of 300 g. What is the mass of a similar can with radius 5 cm?

10 The time needed to fill the gas tank of a car varies inversely with the square of the diameter of the hose. If a hose of diameter 2 cm takes 10 min to fill the tank, how long will it take to fill the same tank if the hose has a diameter of 5 cm?

11 The exposure time required for a photograph is inversely proportional to the square of the diameter of the camera lens. If the lens diameter is 5 cm, the exposure time needed is $\frac{1}{625}$ s. Find the diameter of the lens if an exposure time of $\frac{1}{3600}$ s is needed.

12 The value of fine china is inversely proportional to the square of the thickness of the porcelain. Calculate the value of a plate 4 mm in thickness if a plate 1.5-mm thick, costs $50.00.

C 13 If the height of a right circular cone is kept constant, the volume varies directly with the square of the radius of the base. If a cone with a base radius 6 cm has a volume of 189 cm^3, what is the volume of a cone with a base radius 4 cm?

Problem Solving

Three freighters leave St. John's, Newfoundland, for Montreal, Quebec, at the same time. One ship takes 20 d to make the round trip, another ship takes 16 d, and the final ship takes 12 d. If these three ships continuously make this round trip between St. John's and Montreal, how many trips would each freighter have to make so that all three ships are again in port at the same time?

Calculator Tip

Use your calculator to do lengthy computations throughout your work in mathematics. For example, there are 30 horses eligible for a race, but only 12 horses can enter the race. A draw is made to decide which horses will run in the race. Belmont Stables has 3 eligible horses. The probability, P, that all three of Belmont's horses will be drawn is given by the expression

$$P = \frac{(27 \times 26 \times \cdots 2 \times 1)(12 \times 11 \times 10 \times \cdots \times 2)}{(9 \times 8 \times \cdots \times 2 \times 1)(30 \times 29 \times \cdots \times 2 \times 1)}.$$

Calculate the value of P.

4.9 Applications with Joint Variation

A large, heavy boat coming into a dock slowly can cause considerable damage if it accidentally bumps the dock. At the same time, a very small bullet travelling at a tremendously high speed can also cause a lot of damage. This property of an object is called its **momentum**.

The momentum of an object varies directly with its mass and its velocity. Momentum illustrates an example of **joint variation**.

To understand the principle of joint variation, consider a rectangle. If the width of a rectangle is constant, the area, A, varies directly with the length, L; or simply the greater the length, the greater the area. Thus if L, W, and A represent the number of consistent units of length, width, and area respectively,

$A \propto L$ when
W is constant.

Similarly

$A \propto W$ when
L is constant.

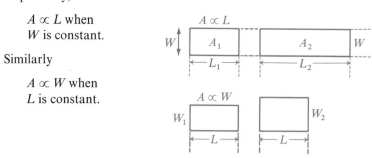

Thus, the area of a rectangle varies directly with its length *and* its width. You say that the area of the rectangle varies *jointly* with its length and its width.

$A \propto L \times W$ and $A = kL \times W$ where k is the constant of variation.

You may also write
$$\frac{A_1}{A_2} = \frac{L_1 W_1}{L_2 W_2}$$

and if the area is constant $L_1 W_1 = L_2 W_2$.

The equation of joint variation can be used to solve the following problem. The skills and the strategies you learned earlier for the other types of variation now extend to your work with joint variation.

Example   The cost of publishing a sailing magazine varies directly with the number of pages and inversely with the number of advertisements in the magazine. A magazine with 50 advertisements and 125 pages costs $2.00 to publish. How many advertisements are necessary for a 250-page magazine so that it costs $2.50 to publish?

Solution   Let C represent the cost of the magazine, in dollars; p the number of pages, and n, the number of advertisements. Then $C \propto p \times \dfrac{1}{n}$ or $C \propto \dfrac{p}{n}$.

Step 1: Write the proportion.

$$\frac{C_1 n_1}{p_1} = \frac{C_2 n_2}{p_2}$$

Record the information given.

$C_1 = 2 \quad n_1 = 50 \quad p_1 = 125$
$C_2 = 2.5 \quad n_2 = ? \quad p_2 = 250$

Thus, the number of advertisements is 80.

Step 2: Substitute given information into the proportion.

$$\frac{2(50)}{125} = \frac{2.5 n_2}{250} \quad \leftarrow \text{Solve for } n_2.$$

$$80 = n_2$$

← Always make a final statement to answer the original problem.

4.9 Exercise

Questions 1 to 9 develop skills for solving problems involving joint variation.

A 1 Write a variation statement involving a constant $k \neq 0$ for each of the following joint variations.
(a) V varies directly with T and Q.
(b) R varies directly with T and inversely with P.
(c) U varies inversely with S and directly with the square of T.
(d) E varies directly with M and the square of v.
(e) Q varies directly with M and inversely with the square of P.

2 Write a proportion to express each of the following joint variations.
(a) J varies directly with T and inversely with P.
(b) P varies directly with Q and inversely with the square of R.
(c) A varies directly with B and the square of C.
(d) R varies inversely with the square of S and directly with G.

3 A varies directly with T and inversely with M^2. If $A = 75$ and $T = 15$, then $M = 2$.
(a) Find the constant of variation.
(b) Use the value found in (a) to find a value of T if $A = 100$ when $M = 5$.

4 R varies directly with L and inversely with D^2. If $R = 14$ and $D = 3$, then $L = 0.8$.
(a) Write a proportion.
(b) Use the proportion obtained in (a). Find R if $D = 6$ when $L = 0.4$.

5   A joint variation is given by $P \propto \dfrac{S}{R}$. Which of the following are equivalent variation statements for the above?

   (a) $\dfrac{P_1 R_1}{S_1} = \dfrac{P_2 R_2}{S_2}$ (b) $\dfrac{P_2}{P_1} = \dfrac{S_1}{R_1} \times \dfrac{S_2}{R_2}$

   (c) $\dfrac{P_1}{P_2} = \dfrac{S_1 S_2}{R_1 R_2}$ (d) $\dfrac{P_1}{P_2} = \dfrac{S_1}{R_1} \times \dfrac{R_2}{S_2}$

6   Q varies directly with R and V. If $Q = 192$ and $R = 3$ when $V = 16$, then find R when $Q = 96$ and $V = 4$.

7   E varies directly with F and inversely with the square of G. If $E = 75$ and $F = 60$ when $G = 12$ then find F when $E = 12$ and $G = 15$.

8   For the joint variation $Q \propto RV$, find the missing value if $Q_1 = 840$, $R_1 = 2$, $V_1 = 30$, $R_2 = 12$, $V_2 = 15$.

9   For $R \propto \dfrac{Q}{T^2}$ we know that $R = 20$ and $Q = 15$ when $T = 21$. Find R when $Q = 60$ and $T = 14$.

B   Solve the following problems involving joint variation.

10   The area of a triangle varies directly with its base and altitude. The area of a triangle with base 8 cm and altitude 12 cm is 48 cm². Find the area when the base is 11 cm and the altitude is 22 cm.

11   The resistance of a wire to an electric current is directly proportional to the length of the wire and inversely proportional to the square of the wire's diameter. If 3.2 km of wire with a diameter of 6 mm has a resistance of 14 units, then find the resistance for 8.4 km of wire with a diameter of 7 mm.

12   The energy of a moving billiard ball is directly proportional to the mass of the ball and the square of its speed. A 150-g billiard ball moving at 2 m/s has an energy of 300 units. Calculate the speed of a 140-g ball that has an energy of 630 units.

C 13   The destructive force of a falling object varies directly with the mass of the object and the height from which the object is dropped. From a height of 75 m, a 20-kg rock has a destructive force of 15 000 units. Calculate the destructive force of a 40-kg rock dropped from a height 25 m less than in the first case.

4.10 Partial Variation

The total cost, C, of placing an advertisement in the newspaper partly depends on a fixed cost, and partly varies directly with the number of words in the ad.

The total amount is based on two parts.

- a part that is fixed
- a part that varies.

This is an example of **partial variation**.

School District...

TEACHERS REQUIRED
SECONDARY (8-10)
Science, Math, Social Studies, French
EARLY FRENCH IMMERSION
(K-7) — General
Apply in person Thursday, January 30; Friday, January 31; or Saturday, February 1, 1986 at the Holiday Inn, Toronto Downtown. For more information and appointment times, please call ...oss (604) 374- ...a January 25,

Example

The total cost of running an advertisement in the newspaper is partly constant and partly varies directly with the number of words in the advertisement. An advertisement with 20 words costs $7.00 and an advertisement with 30 words costs $9.50. How many words would be in an advertisement that costs $13.50?

Solution

Let the total cost, T, in cents, be represented by a constant part, C cents, and vary directly with the number of words, n.

Then $T = C + kn$ where k is a constant of variation.

Then
$$700 = C + k(20) \quad ①$$
$$950 = C + k(30) \quad ②$$

Solve equations ① and ②.
Subtract ② − ①.
$$250 = 10k$$
$$25 = k$$

Use $k = 25$ in ①.
$$700 = C + (25)(20)$$
$$700 = C + 500$$
$$200 = C$$

Thus the partial variation is given by the equation $T = 200 + 25n$.

Use $T = 1350$.
$$1350 = 200 + 25n$$
$$1150 = 25n$$
$$46 = n$$

Thus the number of words in an advertisement that costs $13.50 is 46.

4.10 Exercise

A 1 A partial variation is given by $y = p + mx$. If $y = 22$ when $x = 3$ and $y = 64$ when $x = 17$, find m and p.

2   A partial variation is given by $C = K + pb$. If $C = 200$ when $b = 8$ and $C = 140$ when $b = 5$, find K and p.

3   The total expenses, E, in cents, of a basketball tournament are partly constant, C, in cents, and partly vary directly with the number of players, n.
   (a) Use the variation statement $E = C + kn$, k is constant.
       Find the constant of variation for the above tournament if the fixed cost is $60 and the total expenses are $240 when 120 players attend.
   (b) Find the total expenses of the above tournament if the number of players is 230.
   (c) Find the number of players that attended the above tournament if the total expenses were $511.50.

B   Solve the problems.

4   The cost of producing handbills is partly constant and partly varies directly with the number printed. To produce 50 copies, the total cost is $13.60 and the fixed cost is $9.80. Find the cost of producing 1000 copies.

5   The cost of renting a motor home for a week is partly constant and partly varies directly with the distance travelled. To travel 2000 km in the motor home the total cost is $750, and the fixed cost is $100. Find the total rental cost to travel 3000 km.

6   The toll charge over the Humber Skyway is partly constant and partly varies directly with the number of people in the vehicle. The Walker family paid $2.50 with 4 persons in the car, while the Driver family in the next car had 6 people and was charged $3.00. How many persons were in the next vehicle if the charge was $2.00?

7   The value of a car is partly constant and partly varies inversely with the age, in years, of the car. A 2-year-old car is worth $3800, but after 4 years it is worth $2500. What would be the value of the car after 8 years?

8   The cost of auto repairs at Lethbridge Auto is partly constant and partly varies directly with the length of time of repair. Melissa's compact car was in for an oil change and other services which took 45 min. The bill was $19.25. Later an 8 h transmission overhaul cost $171.50. Calculate the hourly rate in the shop.

9   Cooking time for roast beef is partly constant and partly varies directly with the mass of the roast. If it takes Betty 3 h to cook a 3 kg roast, and 4 h to cook a 5 kg roast, how soon before dinner is to be served should Betty start cooking a 6 kg roast?

4.11 Problem Solving: Deciding on a Strategy

In the previous sections you have solved problems involving each of the following types of variation.

- direct variation
- direct squared variation
- inverse variation
- inverse squared variation
- joint variation
- partial variation

Although the types of variation are different, the strategies you have used to solve the problems are similar.

- introducing a constant of variation, k
- using the proportion statement of the variation

In problem solving you need to first decide what strategy you will use. To solve a problem involving variation, you must recognize which type of variation is involved. Once the type of variation is noted then you need only apply the steps you have learned to solve the problem.

In the exercise that follows, you need to interpret the question carefully so that you know what information you have to find. Remember to organize your solution. Use the *Steps for Solving Problems*.

Steps for Solving Problems

A Ask yourself:
   I What information am I asked to find?
   II What information am I given?

B Decide on a method.

C Do the work.

D Check your work.

E Make a final statement.
   Answer the original problem.

4.11 Exercise

A 1 (a) Decide what type of variation occurs in this problem:

The amount of interest earned in a year in a savings account is directly proportional to the amount of money in the account. If $36.75 interest is earned on $350, how much interest will be earned on $420?

(b) Solve the problem.

2 (a) Decide what type of variation occurs in this problem:

When Todd sits 2 m away from the TV screen he notices that the intensity bothers his eyes. By what factor is the intensity decreased when he sits twice as far away if intensity varies inversely as the square of the distance from the source?

(b) Solve the problem.

3 (a) Decide what type of variation occurs in this problem:

   The sales of coffee on a given day are inversely proportional to the price per kilogram. A 1-kg jar costs $2.50 on Tuesday and 2000 jars were sold. If the price was increased by $1.50 on Friday, how many jars would you expect to be sold?

   (b) Solve the problem.

B 4 The number of chairs in a row varies inversely as the distance between them. If 45 seats are needed when they are 6 cm apart, what would be the distance between the seats if only 27 are needed?

5 At a given speed the distance that a car travels varies directly as the amount of gasoline consumed. A driver notices that on a certain day she drove 216 km and used 54 L of gas. How much gas will she need for a night run of 296 km at the same speed on roads that have no gas stations open?

6 The cost of operating a boat varies directly as the cube of the speed of the boat. If a trip of 300 km at 50 km/h costs $150, find the cost of the trip at 60 km/h.

7 After a fixed length of time, the interest generated by a movie varies inversely as the square of time the movie continues. For an additional 6 min the interest level is 25 units. How much time beyond the fixed length does the movie continue to be interesting if 4 units indicates boredom setting in?

8 The spring factor of car shock absorbers varies inversely as the square root of the distance the car has travelled. After 2500 km of travel, the spring factor is 9 units. How far can the car go before getting new shock absorbers if a spring factor of less than 2 is considered unsafe?

9 To play a hockey tournament in another city the expenses are partly constant and partly vary directly with the number of players that go to the tournament. If 10 hockey players were to go, they would each have to pay $14. However, if 20 players were to go, then each player would need to pay $10.25. What would it cost each player if 40 players were to go?

10 The volume of a cylinder varies directly with the height of the cylinder and with the square of the radius of the cylinder. A circular swimming pool, with a radius of 4 m and a depth of 2.5 m has a capacity of 125 600 L. What is the depth of a pool whose capacity is 235 500 L and whose radius is 5 m?

11 The amount of rubber needed to make a racquet-sport ball varies directly as the square of the radius of the ball. A squash ball of radius 2 cm requires 20 cm² of rubber. How much rubber is required for a racquet ball which has a radius of 4 cm?

12 On a 289-cm swing Jason takes 3.4 s for one swing. He then goes to a swing that is 625 cm in length. If the time for one swing is proportional to the square root of the length, find the time for one swing on the longer swing.

13   The expenses of a basketball tournament are partly constant and partly vary directly with the number of players that attend the tournament. If 12 players attend, each player will pay $15.00. For 24 players, the price will be $11.00 each. What will it cost each player if 30 players attend?

14   A stereo turntable spins at a constant speed so that the number of revolutions varies directly with time. If the turntable makes 666 revolutions during the 20 min of one side of a record, how many revolutions will it take to play a song 6 min in length?

15   The gas efficiency of a car varies inversely with the mass of the car. If a 2000-kg car obtains a gas efficiency of 9 km/L, what will the gas efficiency be for a 1500-kg car?

C 16   Donna discovers that when she shines her flashlight at an object the intensity of illumination varies inversely as the square of the distance from that object. When standing 4 m from an object she notices the intensity is 3 units. At what distance from the object will the intensity be doubled?

Computer Tip

When you need to repeat similar calculations, a computer program can be written to save time. For example, to solve for X1 in the direct variation equation

$$\frac{X1}{Y1} = \frac{X2}{Y2}$$

you can use the program at the right.

```
10    INPUT X2, Y1, Y2
20    IF Y2 = 0 THEN 60
30    LET S = X2*Y1/Y2
40    PRINT "THE SOLUTION IS", S
50    GOTO 10
60    END
```

Write a program in BASIC to solve for X_1 in each of the following.

A $X_1Y_1 = X_2Y_2$ B $\dfrac{X_1}{Y_1^2} = \dfrac{X_2}{Y_2^2}$ C $Y_1X_1^2 = Y_2X_2^2$

Select input values from the problems you have dealt with in this chapter. Use the programs in A, B, C to solve for the missing variable X_1.

Problem Solving

Prove that if a varies directly with b when c is constant and if a varies directly with c when b is constant then a varies directly with bc when both b and c vary.

Practice and Problems: A Chapter Review

An important step for problem-solving is to decide which skills to use. For this reason, these questions are not placed in any special order. When you have finished the review, you might try the *Test for Practice* that follows.

1 If $\frac{x}{y} = \frac{m}{n}$ then find an equivalent expression for each of the following.

(a) $\frac{y}{x}$ (b) my (c) $\frac{x}{m}$

2 Find the value of the variable which satisfies the proportion.
(a) $(x - 3):2 = (x + 2):3$ (b) $4:(3 - y) = 3:4$
(c) $3:(2s + 3) = 2:(3s + 2)$ (d) $4a:5 = (a + 3):2$

3 Ammonia consists of nitrogen and hydrogen combined in the ratio $14:3$ by mass. How many grams of ammonia were used to obtain 56 g of nitrogen?

4 If $x:y:z = 2:5:7$, find the value of each of the following.

(a) $\frac{x + y}{x - y}$ (b) $\frac{(x + y + z)^2}{x^2 + y^2 + z^2}$ (c) $(x + 2y - 3z)^2 \div y^2$

5 For each direct variation, find the missing value.
(a) $h_1 = ?$ $t_1 = 4$ $h_2 = 240$ $t_2 = 15$
(b) $P_1 = 750$ $V_1 = ?$ $P_2 = 1250$ $V_2 = 10$

6 (a) An inverse variation is given by $VT = k$, where k is constant. If $V = 75$ when $T = 36$, then find V when $T = 50$.
   (b) T is inversely proportional to the square of s. If $T = 150$ when $s = 6$, then find the value of T when $s = 30$.

7 The surface area of a sphere varies directly with the square of its radius. The surface area of a basketball, with radius 15 cm, is 900π cm^2. What would be the surface area of a ball with a radius 12 cm?

8 The temperature of a location on the earth's surface varies inversely with the distance from the equator. On a given day, the temperature is $36°$ C at a place 5250 km from the equator. What is the temperature 7500 km from the equator?

9 The owner of a concession booth at a stadium has discovered that the amount of sales varies directly with the attendance at football games. If $5540 worth of food and soft drinks was sold at a game attended by 22 160 fans, how much would you expect to be sold at the next game if the expected attendance is 30 000?

Test for Practice

Try this test. Each *Test for Practice* is based on the mathematics you have learned in this chapter. Try this test later in the year as a review. Keep a record of those questions that you were not successful with, get help in obtaining solutions and review them periodically.

1   (a) If $\dfrac{m}{15} = \dfrac{n}{8} = 2$, find the values of m and n.

   (b) Solve $(y + 3):2 = (2 - y):3$.

2   If $x:y = 2:1$, find the value of (a) $\dfrac{2x}{3y}$ (b) $\dfrac{2x^2 - y^2}{y^2}$

3   Solve $\dfrac{3m - 1}{4n - 1} = \dfrac{6m}{8n + 2} = \dfrac{3 - 6m}{1 - 4n}$ for m and n.

4   (a) Sand is composed of silicon and oxygen in the ratio 7:8 by mass. What mass of oxygen could be obtained from 90 g of sand?

   (b) Dry ice consists of carbon and oxygen in the ratio 3:8 by mass. Using the oxygen obtained in part (a), what mass of dry ice would be created if sufficient carbon were available?

5   (a) A direct variation is given by $y = kx$, k is constant. If $x = 12.2$ when $y = 183$, find x when $y = 300$.

   (b) If $ab = $ constant and $a = 3$ when $b = 32$, then find a when $b = 12$.

6   If the height of a cone is constant, then the volume of the cone varies directly with the square of the radius of its base. The volume of cone is 2464 cm^3 when the radius is 14 cm. What is the volume when the radius is 21 cm?

7   The number of chairs on a lift at a ski resort varies inversely with the distance between them. When they are 16 m apart the ski lift can accommodate 45 chairs. If the distance between chairs is 12 m, how many more chairs can be placed on the ski lift?

8   The distance a car travels from rest is directly proportional to the acceleration and the square of the time elapsed. If the car travels 400 m in 4 s with an acceleration of 50 m/s^2, find the acceleration of a car that travels 1080 m in 6 s.

9   The amount of water a humidifier releases into the air varies directly as the square of the radius of the wheel in the humidifier. A wheel of radius 20 cm releases 5 L of water over a fixed period of time. How many litres will be released during the same period if the radius of the wheel is 25 cm?

Maintaining Skills: Reading Accurately

To do mathematics well you need to practise, regularly, skills in mathematics. *Maintaining Skills* sections will review not only skills you develop in each chapter, but also skills you need for developing more mathematics. You may wish to refer to this *Maintaining Skills* more than once to review these skills.

For Questions 1 to 12 write your answers in simplest terms. Read carefully.

1 Write the square of $-3ab^2$.

2 Find the quotient when $-3xy^2 + 9x^2y$ is divided by $-3xy$.

3 What is the resulting numerical coefficient when $-3xy^3$ is multiplied by $-6x^3y^4$?

4 Find the sum of $3x - 2y$ and $2(3x - 2y)$ decreased by the product of 2 and $-3x + 2y$.

5 What is the exponent of b when the product of $6a^2b$ and $-5a^3b^3$ is written in simplest terms?

6 Find the missing factor of $-18x^3y^5$ if the other factor is $-6xy^3$.

7 Decrease the sum of $6x - 12y$ and $-8x + 5y$ by the product of -3 and $2x - 6y$.

8 By how much does $(12x^2) \div (-4xy)$ exceed $2(3x - 5y)$?

9 One factor of $16a^3b^2$ is $-4ab^2$. Find the other factor.

10 What is the exponent of q when the quotient of $-16p^2q^9$ divided by $-4pq^3$ is written in simplest terms?

11 What is the numerical coefficient of the square of $(-3x^2y)^3$?

12 What is the greater exponent when the square of $-2x^3y^2$ is divided by $2xy^2$?

Math Tip

It is important to clearly understand the vocabulary of mathematics when solving problems. Make a list of all the new words you have met in this chapter. Provide a simple example to illustrate each word.

5 The Linear Function: Solving Systems of Equations

concepts and skills with linear functions, solving linear systems, method of substitution, comparison method, method of addition-subtraction, strategies for solving problems, solving problems, applications, making decisions

Introduction

Almost all of the major achievements of mankind involved mathematics in some way. Many years ago, the development of the formula for the principle of the lever required a knowledge of mathematics.

Archimedes' formula is the basis on which many of the principles of engineering have been developed.

In more recent years, the development of Albert Einstein's famous formula $E = mc^2$ required a knowledge of mathematics. Albert Einstein's formula relates mass, m, and energy, E. His formula states that a small mass can be converted into a great amount of energy, the principle behind nuclear energy.

One of the main reasons for learning mathematics is to acquire skills and strategies to solve problems. The more problems you solve, the better you will be able to solve problems you have never met before.

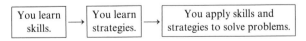

You learn skills. → You learn strategies. → You apply skills and strategies to solve problems.

Throughout your study of mathematics, you, like other people who have developed mathematics, will learn organizational skills that can be applied and used to solve problems.

5.1 Inventory: The Linear Function

A relation is defined by the equation $3x - 2y - 6 = 0$ where x, y are real numbers. In your earlier work you drew the graphs of relations by first finding ordered pairs for the relation, as follows:

A table of values is set up for the relation defined by

$$3x - 2y - 6 = 0$$

and the graph is drawn.

Use $3x - 2y - 6 = 0$

$$2y = 3x - 6$$

$$y = \frac{3}{2}x - 3$$

x	y
-2	-6
-1	$-4\frac{1}{2}$
0	-3
1	$-\frac{3}{2}$
2	0
3	$\frac{3}{2}$

Graph of $3x - 2y - 6 = 0$

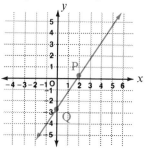

The function $y = \frac{3}{2}x - 3$ is a linear function because the graph of $y = \frac{3}{2}x - 3$ is a straight line. The graph intersects the x-axis at $(2, 0)$ and intersects the y-axis at $(0, -3)$. Function notation is also used to represent the linear function as shown.

$$f : x \rightarrow \frac{3}{2}x - 3$$

The **x-intercept** of a graph is the directed distance from the origin to the point where the graph crosses the x-axis. Since the directed distance, OP, is 2 units, then the x-intercept of $3x - 2y - 6 = 0$ is 2.

The **y-intercept** of a graph is the directed distance from the origin to the point where the graph crosses the y-axis. Since the directed distance, OQ, is -3 units, then the y-intercept of $3x - 2y - 6 = 0$ is -3.

The y co-ordinate of the point at which the x-intercept occurs is zero. Thus, the x-intercept can be found algebraically by equating $y = 0$. Similarly, the x co-ordinate of the point at which the y-intercept occurs is zero. Thus, the y-intercept can be found algebraically by equating $x = 0$, as shown in the following example.

Example Find the x- and y-intercepts of the graph of the linear function given by $2x - 6 = y$, x, $y \in R$.

Solution To find the x-intercept, use $y = 0$.

$$2x - 6 = y$$
$$2x - 6 = 0$$
$$2x = 6$$
$$x = 3$$

The x-intercept is 3.

To find the y-intercept, use $x = 0$.

$$2x - 6 = y$$
$$2(0) - 6 = y$$
$$-6 = y$$

The y-intercept is -6.

5.1 Exercise

A 1 Which of the following represent linear functions?

(a) $2x - y = 6$ (b) $x = \dfrac{3}{y}$

(c) $y - 2x = 4$ (d) $f(x) = x - 5$

(e) $g{:}x \rightarrow \dfrac{2x - 1}{3}$ (f) $y = x^2$

(g) $f(x) = 2x^2 - 1$ (h) $y = \sqrt{x}, \quad x \geq 0$

2 Write the equation of a line parallel to the y-axis that passes through

(a) $(-3, 1)$ (b) $(5, -3)$ (c) $(2, 0)$

3 Write the equation of a line parallel to the x-axis that passes through

(a) $(-2, 1)$ (b) $(3, -4)$ (c) $(0, -3)$

B 4 Write each of the following defining equations in the form $Ax + By + C = 0$.

(a) $y - 3 = 2(x - 1)$ (b) $\dfrac{x}{3} - y = 5$

(c) $y = \dfrac{2x - 1}{3}$ (d) $\dfrac{x - 3}{2} - y = 6$

(e) $\dfrac{x}{2} - \dfrac{y}{3} = 6$ (f) $2(x - 1) - 3(y + 1) = 1$

(g) $\dfrac{y - 1}{3} - \dfrac{x + 1}{2} = 6$ (h) $\dfrac{x + 1}{2} - \dfrac{3y - 1}{4} = 3$

5 Find the x- and y-intercepts for each of the following.

(a) $3x - y = 2$ (b) $2x - 5y = 10$

(c) $3x = \dfrac{y - 1}{2}$ (d) $\dfrac{y - 2x}{3} = 4$

(e) $f(x) = \dfrac{2x - 1}{3}$ (f) $x = 5$

(g) $y = -6$ (h) $2y = -\dfrac{3x - 1}{2}$

(i) $f{:}x \rightarrow 3x - 1$ (j) $g{:}x \rightarrow \dfrac{2x - 1}{3}$

6 Find the range for each of the following.

(a) $3x + y = -6, \quad 0 \leq x \leq 3$ (b) $x - 2y = 8, \quad -2 \leq x \leq 2$

(c) $y = \dfrac{-x + 1}{3}, \quad -3 \leq x \leq 0$ (d) $3x = \dfrac{2y - 1}{2}, \quad -5 \leq x \leq -2$

7 Find the value of k if the given point lies on the graph defined by each equation.
   (a) $3x + ky = 2$ $(1, -1)$ (b) $y + kx = 8$ $(-3, 2)$
   (c) $2x - 3y = k$ $(-1, 5)$ (d) $2x - k = 4y$ $(2, 0)$

8 Find the value of k if the lines have equal y-intercepts.

$$3x + y - 4 = 0, \qquad x + ky + 2 = 0$$

9 Find the value of k if the lines have equal x-intercepts.

$$3x - y = 6, \qquad kx - 2y = 8$$

10 A linear function is given by $x + ky = 6$. Find the value of k if the x-intercept is 5 more than the y-intercept.

11 For the linear function given by $2x - ky = 3$, find the value of k if the x-intercept exceeds the y-intercept by 3.

C 12 A linear function is defined by $Ax + By + C = 0$, $A, B, C \in R$, $A, B \neq 0$.

   (a) Prove that the x-intercept is given by $-\dfrac{C}{A}$.

   (b) Prove that the y-intercept is given by $-\dfrac{C}{B}$.

13 Use the results in the previous question to write the x- and y-intercepts for each of the following.
   (a) $3x + 6y - 9 = 0$ (b) $2x - y + 4 = 0$ (c) $3x - y - 6 = 0$
   (d) $2x + y = 8$ (e) $3x - y = -6$ (f) $y - 3x + 5 = 0$

14 For the linear function given by $px + qy = 6$, prove that $p = \dfrac{3q}{3 + q}$ if the x-intercept exceeds the y-intercept by 2.

> # Math Tip
>
> A linear function may be defined in different forms as follows:
>
> - by an equation $y = 2x + 1$
> - by ordered pairs $(x, 2x + 1)$
> - by a mapping notation $f : x \rightarrow 2x + 1$
> - by function notation $f(x) = 2x + 1$
>
> Be sure to recognize the linear function that may be written in these different ways.

5.2 Concepts and Skills: Linear Functions

You can use the Cartesian plane to show relations between pairs of numbers that satisfy the following condition:

> The sum of one integer and twice another integer is always 6. What are the integers?

First of all, translate the question into mathematics, by choosing variables to represent numbers.

Find x, y so that $x + 2y = 6$, $x, y \in I$.

To find the graph of this linear function, you again find ordered pairs that satisfy the equation. For example, use $x = 2$ to find y.

$$x + 2y = 6 \qquad \text{Substitute 2 for } x$$
$$2 + 2y = 6 \longleftarrow \text{in the equation.}$$
$$2y = 4$$
$$y = 2$$

Thus, one ordered pair that satisfies $x + 2y = 6$ is $(x, y) = (2, 2)$.

Write other ordered pairs.

Use the co-ordinate plane to plot these ordered pairs.

$x + 2y = 6$
(x, y)
$(6, 0)$
$(4, 1)$
$(0, 3)$
$(-2, 4)$
$(-4, 5)$

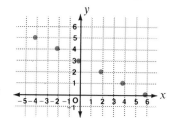

All the possible ordered pairs (x, y) that satisfy the equation $x + 2y = 6$ can not possibly be listed. Thus, it is not possible to show all the points on the graph. Thus, the graph drawn above for the linear function

$$\underline{x + 2y = 6}, \quad x, y \in I \quad \text{is a } partial \ graph.$$

This is the *defining equation* of the above graph.

Two important concepts which are fundamental to the study of graphs of linear functions are:

I The co-ordinates of any point of a graph satisfy the equation of the graph.

The values $x = -8$ and $y = 7$ satisfy the equation of the graph defined by

$$x + 2y = 6.$$

II Any ordered pair, (x, y), which satisfies the equation of the graph represents a point on the graph.

The values $x = 8$ and $y = -1$ satisfy the equation of the graph defined by $x + 2y = 6$.

The point with co-ordinates $(8, -1)$ lies on the graph.

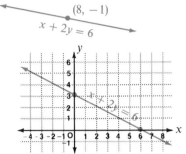

If the domain of the function defined by $x + 2y = 6$ is the real numbers, R, rather than the integers, I, then the graph of this relation $x + 2y = 6$, $x, y \in R$ appears as a solid line as shown.

The equation $x + 2y = 6$, $x, y \in R$ defines this relation among numbers:

The sum of a number and twice another number is always 6.

Example   (a) Draw the graph of $3x - y = 9$, $x, y \in R$.

(b) Find the value of the missing co-ordinate in each of $(x, 9)$ and $(-2, y)$.

Solution   (a) Since the domain and the range are both R then you need find only two points to draw the line given by the equation $3x - y = 9$. Find the co-ordinates of a third point on the graph as a check on your accuracy.

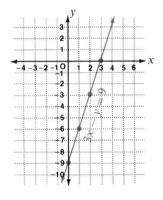

x	y
0	-9
3	0
1	-6
2	-3

Use $x = 0$
Then $3x - y = 9$
$0 - y = 9$
$y = -9$

(b) The partial graph drawn in (a) does not include the points of the graph $(x, 9)$ and $(-2, y)$. Thus, you must find the missing co-ordinates, using algebra.

To find x for $(x, 9)$, use the value $y = 9$ in the defining defining

$3x - y = 9$
$3x - 9 = 9$
$\quad 3x = 18$
$\quad\quad x = 6$

Thus the point $(6, 9)$ is on the line $3x - y = 9$.

To find y for $(-2, y)$, use the value $x = -2$ in the defining equation.

$3x - y = 9$
$3(-2) - y = 9$
$-6 - y = 9$
$-y = 15$
$y = -15$

5.2 Exercise

A Throughout this exercise, all variables represent real numbers unless otherwise indicated.

1 The graph of $3x - 2y = 6$, $x, y \in R$ is drawn. Which of the following points satisfy the equation? Which do not?

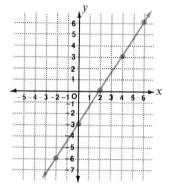

(a) $(6, 6)$ (b) $(3, 4)$

(c) $(-2, 6)$ (d) $(2, 0)$

(e) $(-3, 0)$ (f) $(-6, -1)$

2 The equation of a graph is given by $2x + y = 10$, $x, y \in R$. Indicate which of the following points lie on the graph.

(a) $(6, -2)$ (b) $(2, 8)$ (c) $(2, 6)$

(d) $(-3, 16)$ (e) $(-6, 18)$ (f) $(-6, 22)$

3 For each equation, indicate which points lie on the graph of the equation. Do not draw the graph.

(a) $x - y = 8$ A(10, 2)   B$(-2, -10)$ C(4, 4)

(b) $y = 3x - 6$ D$(0, -6)$ E(3, 15)   F(2, 0)

(c) $2x - y = 12$ G$(7, -2)$ H(6, 0)   I$(-4, -20)$

4 (a) Find x if $(x, -3)$ is a point on the graph given by $3x - y = -6$.

(b) Find y if $(-4, y)$ is a point on the graph given in (a).

5 A linear relation is given by the equation $y = -3x + 7$ where $x, y \in R$. Find the missing co-ordinates if each of the following satisfies the above relation.

(a) $(x, -2)$ (b) $(0, y)$ (c) $(x, -5)$

(d) $(-1, y)$ (e) $(6, y)$ (f) $(x, -8)$

B 6 (a) Draw the graph of the equation $2x - y = 12$.

(b) Use your graph in (a) to decide which of the following points are on the graph.

A$(0, -12)$ B$(2, -6)$ C$(5, -2)$

7   A linear relation is given by $y = 3x + b$, $b \in R$, b is a parameter.
    Using the same axes, draw the graph of the above relation for
    (a) $b = -3$ (b) $b = 2$ (c) $b = -1$
    What do you notice about your results?

8   Draw the graph of each of the following equations using the same axes.
    (a) $y = 3x + 3$ (b) $2x - y = -3$ (c) $2x = 3 - y$
    (d) What property do the above graphs have in common?

9   A linear relation is given by the equation
    $$y = mx + 5, \quad m \in R. \quad m \text{ is a parameter.}$$

    Using the same axes, draw the graph of the above relation for
    (a) $m = 1$ (b) $m = 3$ (c) $m = -1$
    What do you notice about your results?

10 Draw the graph of each of the following equations using the same axes.
    (a) $4x - 2y = 5$ (b) $2x - y = -8$ (c) $y = 2x + 5$
    (d) What property do the above graphs have in common?

11 Find the 2 intercepts of the graph for each linear function. Draw the graph.

    (a) $3x + y - 9 = 0$ (b) $y = \dfrac{2}{3}x - 4$ (c) $3x + 5y - 15 = 0$

    (d) $x = 3(y + 3)$ (e) $2x - 4 = x + y$ (f) $y = \dfrac{3x - 1}{2}$

    (g) $f(x) = 2x - 3$ (h) $g{:}x \rightarrow \dfrac{2x - 3}{3}$

C 12 Draw the graph of each of the following. $x \in R$.
    (a) $y = 2x - 1, \quad -1 \le x \le 2$ (b) $2x - y = 3, \quad -3 \le x \le 0$
    (c) $y = -8x + 5, \quad -2 \le x \le 2$ (d) $3x - y = 2, \quad -3 \le x \le -1$
    What is the range for each of the above?

Problem Solving

We should have a plan when solving a problem. To devise a plan for some problems, it is often helpful to draw a diagram for the given conditions. Draw a diagram for the following problem.

A quadrilateral has vertices $P(3, -8)$, $Q(10, -5)$, $R(7, 2)$, $S(0, -1)$. What type of quadrilateral is it?

Now use the diagram to plan your work.

5.3 Solving Linear Systems of Equations Graphically

In order to draw the graphs defined by $x + y = 4$, $x, y \in R$ and $x - 2y = 10$, $x, y \in R$, you can construct a table of values for each equation and then plot the points.

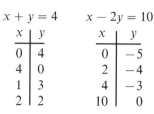

$x + y = 4$	
x	y
0	4
4	0
1	3
2	2

$x - 2y = 10$	
x	y
0	-5
2	-4
4	-3
10	0

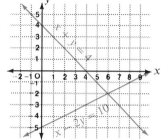

From the graph, the co-ordinates of the intersection point of the lines is $(6, -2)$. This is the only point which lies on both lines.

Since the ordered pair $(6, -2)$ satisfies both $x + y = 4$ and $x - 2y = 10$, then $(6, -2)$ is said to be a **solution** of the linear system of equations. To **solve** a linear system of equations means to find the values of the variables which satisfy *all* the equations of the system. You can write the solution as $(x, y) = (6, -2)$. You can check or verify that you have obtained the correct solution to the above system by substituting $x = 6$ and $y = -2$ into each of the original equations.

For $x + y = 4$
$$LS = x + y \qquad RS = 4$$
$$= (6) + (-2)$$
$$= 6 - 2 = 4$$
LS = RS Solution checks ✓

For $x - 2y = 10$
$$LS = x - 2y \qquad RS = 10$$
$$= 6 - 2(-2)$$
$$= 6 + 4 = 10$$
LS = RS Solution checks ✓

Another ordered pair such as $(x, y) = (5, -1)$ may satisfy one equation but *not* the other. Thus, for non-parallel lines the solution of a linear system is unique and may be seen graphically as the intersection point of the lines.

5.3 Exercise

A 1   A co-ordinate system is used to determine the position of an island at $(-4, 5)$. The following equations define the paths of various recent hurricanes. Which hurricanes crossed the island?

(a) Hurricane Arnold; $4x + 2y = -6$ (b) Hurricane David; $\dfrac{x}{2} - y = 7$

(c) Hurricane Hazel; $3x - y = -17$ (d) Hurricane Gloria, $2x = 3y + 10$

2 The position of a sinking freighter is $(6, -8)$. Four rescue planes travel paths defined by the following equations. Which of the planes will make the rescue?

A: Piper Cub; $x - 3y = 20$ B: Cherokee; $y = 4 - 2x$

C: Wingstar; $30 + 2y = 3x$ D: Starcraft; $y + 10 = \dfrac{x}{3}$

3 A weather station uses a co-ordinate system to locate places in Alberta, as shown. A major storm is travelling along the path given by the equation $x + 4y = -18$.

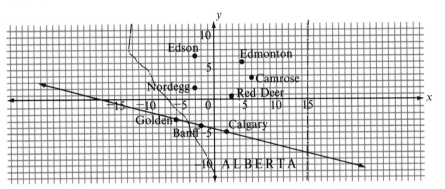

Which of the following places are in the path of the storm?

(a) Edson $(-3, 7)$ (b) Golden $(-6, -3)$ (c) Nordegg $(-3, 2)$

(d) Red Deer $\left(3, \dfrac{1}{2}\right)$ (e) Calgary $(2, -5)$ (f) Edmonton $\left(\dfrac{9}{2}, 6\right)$

(g) Banff $(-2, -4)$ (h) Camrose $\left(6, \dfrac{7}{2}\right)$

B 4 Which places in the previous question will be hit by a storm travelling along the path given by $y = \dfrac{11}{2}x - 16$?

5 What is the intersection point of each of the following systems of equations?

(a)
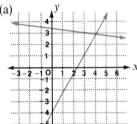

(b)
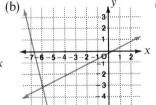

(c)
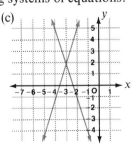

6   Use a graphical method to solve each of the following linear systems of equations.

(a) $3x - y = 7$
$x + 2y = 7$

(b) $y = 3x + 13$
$2x + y = -2$

(c) $x + y = -2$
$5x - 3y = -2$

(d) $x - 3y = 13$
$2x + 3y = -1$

(e) $y = 2x + 10$
$x + y + 8 = 0$

(f) $4x + y = 0$
$y = 2x + 6$

7   Write the co-ordinates of the point of intersection of the lines defined by the following systems of equations.

(a) $6x + y = 0$
$x + \dfrac{3}{2}y = 8$

(b) $4x - 3y = -1$
$6x + 9y = 39$

(c) $2y + x - 8 = 0$
$3 + y - 3x = 0$

(d) $y = -0.5x + 3.5$
$y = 0.5x + 6.5$

(e) $2t = 11 - m$
$3m - t - 5 = 0$

(f) $3a - b = 11$
$2a + 5b = -4$

8   The equations of the sides of quadrilateral ABCD are

AB: $x + 6y = 15$ BC: $4x - y = 10$
DC: $3x + 7y = -8$ AD: $x - y = -6$

Find the co-ordinates of the vertices of the quadrilateral.

C 9   A tangent with equation $2x + 3y = 13$ meets the radius with equation $3x = 2y$ at point M. What are the co-ordinates of M?

Problem Solving

To solve a problem, we must understand the meaning of each word. Otherwise we will not be able to solve the problem. Read the following problem. Why can it not be solved?

A line given by $2x + y = 4$ intersects the axes to form a triangle. How many lattice points are inside the triangle?

Lattice points on the co-ordinate plane are those that have integral co-ordinates. $(3, 4)$, $(-2, 0)$, and $(-3, -4)$ are examples of lattice points. Now solve the problem!

Math Tip

To solve problems you must understand the meaning of each mathematical word. Make a list of all the new words you meet in this chapter. Use an example to illustrate the meaning of each word.

Applications: Plotting Storms

The weather office collects data in order to predict the weather. The principles used in plotting the path of a storm are similar to those used in the following questions.

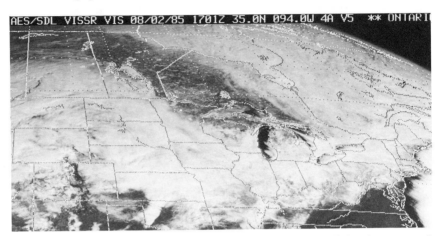

AES/SDL VISSR VIS 08/02/85 1701Z 35.0N 094.0W 4A V5 ** ONTARI

Information is forwarded to a weather centre where data are recorded and summarized in charts. Based on the forwarded information, a forecast of the weather is made for the short term and for the long term.

10   A cruiser is on a course given by the equation $4x - 3y = 6$, while a tugboat follows the course given by $2x + 3y = 12$.
      (a) Find the co-ordinates of the point where their paths will cross.
      (b) A buoy is located at $(-3, 6)$. Which ship will need to alter its course?
      (c) Which ship will come closest to a shoal located at the point $(\frac{1}{2}, -2)$?

11   In Canada's Arctic, a co-ordinate system is one way of locating position. Two surveying crews trek along the following paths.

             A: Survey crew Hollander: $6x + y = 0$
             B: Survey crew Williams: $2x - y = -8$

At which point might the two crews meet?

12   A tornado is following a path plotted by the weather office as given by $x - 2y = -8$. At the same time the centre of a thunderstorm is on the path given by $y = 7 - x$. Indicate which towns with the given co-ordinates will experience: I   a thunderstorm
                           II   a tornado
                       III   a thunderstorm and a tornado

      (a) Delhi $(-4, 2)$ (b) Marysville $(7, 0)$ (c) Everett $(0, 4)$
      (d) Norwich $(2, 5)$ (e) Walton $(-1, 8)$ (f) Vernon $(8, 8)$

5.4 Equivalent Linear Systems

Linear systems are equivalent if they have the same solution. All of the following systems of equations are equivalent, since the graphs all intersect at the point $(-4, -2)$.

A: $x = 2y$
  $3x + y = -14$

B: $x + 4y = -12$
  $x = -4$

C: $2x - y = -6$
  $y = -2$

D: $x = -4$
  $y = -2$

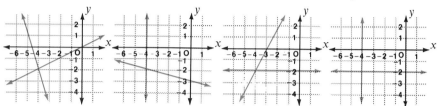

Thus, the method of finding the solution of a linear system is to reduce the given linear system

  A: Solve $x = 2y$ $3x + y = -14$

to an equivalent linear system that can easily be solved by inspection, such as the system D.

  D: $x = -4$ $y = -2$

From D, the solution of the original system A is quickly seen to be

  $(x, y) = (-4, -2)$.

The solution must be verified in the original given equations, system A.

5.4 Exercise

A 1 (a) Draw the graph of each system of equations using the same axes. Label each line clearly.

  A: $2x - y = 8$
    $x + y = 1$

  B: $3x + y = 7$
    $3x - 2y = 13$

(b) Why are systems A and B equivalent?

2 (a) The solution of systems, C and D, is given as $(x, y) = (3, 0)$.

  C: $3x - 2y = 9$
    $x + y = 3$

  D: $x - y - 3 = 0$
    $2x - y = 6$

Verify the given solution.

(b) Why are systems C and D equivalent?

3   (a) Which system has $(x, y) = (-2, 3)$ as its solution?

P: $x + y = 1$ Q: $2y - x = -4$
     $2x - y = -7$ $y = 3x + 3$
R: $x = 7 - 2y$ S: $x = 2y - 8$
     $2x - 3y = 0$ $3 + y = -3x$

(b) Which systems in (a) are equivalent?

(c) Find the solution for the other equations not named in (b).

4   The following lines pass through the same intersection point. One system of equations is

$$x + 5y = 11$$
$$3x - 2y = -18$$

Write 2 different linear systems that are equivalent.

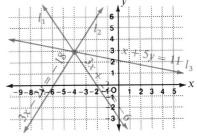

5   (a) From the graph shown write pairs of equations that give equivalent systems.

(b) Which linear system equivalent to those in (a) has the simplest form?

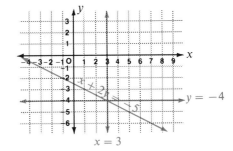

6   (a) Draw the graph given by $3x + y = 6$.

(b) Draw the graph given by $6x + 2y = 12$.

(c) What do you notice about the graphs in (a) and (b)?

(d) How are these equations related?

B 7   Based on your results in the previous question, describe how each of the graphs in Column A is related to the corresponding graph in Column B.

Column A   Column B

(a) $x - y = 3$ $2x - 2y = 6$

(b) $-x + 2y = 6$ $x - 2y = -6$

(c) $x + 5y = 1$ $3x + 15y = 3$

(d) $x + y = 2$ $\dfrac{1}{2}x + \dfrac{1}{2}y = 1$

8   (a) Draw the graphs of the lines given by
       A: $x + y = 3$ B: $2x - 3y = 1$
    (b) Draw the graph of equation C obtained as follows.

       A: $x + y = 3$ Equations A and B are added
       B: $2x - 3y = 1$ to obtain equation C.
       ――――――――――――
       C: $3x - 2y = 4$

    (c) Draw the graph of equation D obtained as follows.

       A: $x + y = 3$ Equations A and B are subtracted
       B: $2x - 3y = 1$ to obtain equation D.
       ――――――――――――
       D: $-x + 4y = 2$

    (d) What do you notice about the intersection point of the graphs of
        equations A, B, C, and D?

9   Repeat the procedure outlined in the previous question,
    with the following equations.

       A: $x - y = -7$ B: $3x + y = -9$

10 Use your results in the previous two questions. For each of the following
    systems, write another equation that passes through the same intersection
    point.
    (a) $x - y = 7$ (b) $x - 2y = 0$ (c) $2x + y = 1$
        $x + 2y = -2$ $2x + y = -5$ $x - 2y = -17$

C 11 For each system, another equation is given. Why does the other equation
      pass through the same intersection point?

    (a) $\left.\begin{array}{l} 2x + y = 1 \\ x + y = 2 \end{array}\right\}$ A $3x + 2y = 3$

    (b) $\left.\begin{array}{l} 3x - y = 9 \\ x - 2y = 8 \end{array}\right\}$ B $2x + y = 1$

    (c) $\left.\begin{array}{l} x - 2y = -1 \\ x + 2y = -5 \end{array}\right\}$ C $2x = -6$

Problem Solving

Often the answer to a problem is surprising; one we do not expect.
Solve the following problem.

> An island is in the shape of an equilateral triangle. Where should
> a cottage be built so that the sum of the distances from the
> cottage to all shores is a minimum?

5.5 Classifying Linear Systems

The linear system
$$x + y = 4$$
$$x - 2y = -2$$

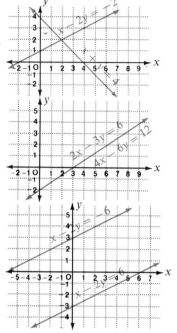

has one intersection point and thus exactly one solution. This system is classified as a **consistent** but **independent system**.

The linear system
$$2x - 3y = 6$$
$$4x - 6y = 12$$

has more than one solution. This system is **consistent**, but since one equation is derived from the other it is also classified as a **dependent system**.

The linear system
$$x - 2y = -6$$
$$x - 2y = 6$$

has no solution, since the graph is a pair of parallel lines which, of course, do not intersect. This system is classified as an **inconsistent system**.

5.5 Exercise

A 1 (a) Draw the graph of each equation. A: $2x - y = 8$ B: $4x - 2y = 16$

(b) Why is the system in (a) dependent?

2 (a) Draw the graph of each equation.   C: $x + 2y = 6$ D: $x + 2y = 10$

(b) Why is the system in (a) inconsistent?

B 3 The graphs of equations are drawn. Write 1 linear system that is
(a) consistent but independent
(b) inconsistent
(c) consistent but dependent

4 Classify each of the following.

(a) $y = 3x - 5$
$y = 3x + 8$

(b) $x - 2y = 1$
$x + y = 4$

(c) $2x - 3y = 3$
$6 + 6y = 4x$

(d) $x + 3y = 9$
$x + 3y = -2$

(e) $x + y = -1$
$x - y = -3$

(f) $4x + y = 8$
$4 - \dfrac{1}{2}y = 2x$

5.6 Solving Linear Systems of Equations: Substitution Method

To solve this system of 2 equations in 2 variables, you could use your skills in co-ordinate geometry.

System of 2 equations in 2 variables

$$x + y = 1$$
$$4x - 8y = 49$$

Graph of the system of 2 equations in 2 variables.

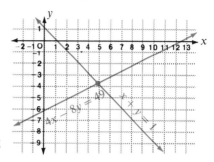

From the graph, you can only estimate the solution of the above system of equations.

Thus, a more exact method of solving a system of 2 equations in 2 variables needs to be developed.

Another system is shown on the graph at the right. To solve this system, you can substitute the given value of x into the remaining equation to find the value of y.

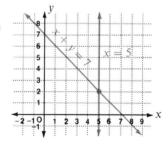

$$x = 5 \qquad ①$$
$$x + y = 7 \qquad ②$$

From equation ① use the value of x in equation ②.

$$x + y = 7$$
$$5 + y = 7$$
$$y = 2$$

Thus, $x = 5$ and $y = 2$.

From the graph of this system, you can see that the lines given by $x = 5$ and $x + y = 7$ intersect at (5, 2).

You saw above that a value for x from one equation was substituted into the remaining equation. The remaining equation was then solved for y.

In the following example, an expression is found for y in terms of x. This expression is then substituted into the remaining equation.

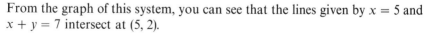

Example   Solve $3x + y = 2$
                     $2x + 5y = 23$

Solution

$$3x + y = 2 \qquad \text{①}$$
$$2x + 5y = 23 \qquad \text{②}$$

From equation ① obtain an expression for y in terms of x.

$$3x + y = 2 \qquad \text{①}$$
$$y = 2 - 3x \qquad \text{③}$$

Substitute the expression for y in equation ③ into equation ②.

$$2x + 5y = 23$$
$$2x + 5(2 - 3x) = 23 \qquad \text{④}$$

Equation ④ is in 1 variable, which is solved for x.

$$2x + 5(2 - 3x) = 23$$
$$2x + 10 - 15x = 23$$
$$10 - 13x = 23$$
$$-13x = 13$$
$$x = -1 \qquad \text{⑤}$$

Now substitute $x = -1$ in equation ①.

$$3x + y = 2 \qquad \text{Remember: to avoid errors}$$
$$3(-1) + y = 2 \longleftarrow \text{use brackets when substituting.}$$
$$-3 + y = 2$$
$$y = 5$$

Thus, the solution is $x = -1$, $y = 5$.

Check the solution.

For equation $3x + y = 2$	For equation $2x + 5y = 23$
LS $= 3x + y$ RS $= 2$	LS $= 2x + 5y$ RS $= 23$
$= 3(-1) + 5$	$= 2(-1) + 5(5)$
$= -3 + 5$	$= -2 + 25$
$= 2$	$= 23$
LS $=$ RS	LS $=$ RS
checks ✓	checks ✓

In the previous method you choose one of the equations and express one variable in terms of the other variable. Then substitute into the remaining equation. This algebraic method of solving a system of 2 equations in 2 variables is called the **substitution method**.

5.6 Exercise

A 1 Express y in terms of x.
  - (a) $3x + y = 4$
  - (b) $5x + y = 8$
  - (c) $y - 3x = 8$
  - (d) $y - 2x = -6$
  - (e) $2x = y + 4$
  - (f) $3x = 4 - y$
  - (g) $2x + y - 7 = 0$
  - (h) $2x - y + 5 = 0$
  - (i) $4x = 3y$

2 Express x in terms of y.
  - (a) $x + 3y = 8$
  - (b) $x - 2y = 6$
  - (c) $x + y - 5 = 0$

B 3 (a) Use the *method of substitution* to solve this system.

$$x = 2y - 1 \qquad 2x + y = 3$$

  (b) Verify your solution in (a).

4 Use the *method of substitution* to solve each system.
  - (a) $x = 3$
    $3x - 2y = 11$
  - (b) $y = 5$
    $2x + 3y = 11$
  - (c) $3a - b = -6$
    $a = -2$
  - (d) $2b - 5a = 14$
    $b = -3$
  - (e) $m = 3n - 8$
    $2n - m = 5$
  - (f) $3a - 2b = 1$
    $a = b + 1$

5 (a) Draw a graph to find the co-ordinates of the point of intersection of the lines given by $\qquad x - y = -1 \qquad 2x - y = -1$

  (b) How can you check your answer in (a) by using an algebraic method? Find the algebraic solution.

6 Find the co-ordinates of the point of intersection of each of the following systems.
  - (a) $2x - 3y = -9$
    $x + y = -2$
  - (b) $x - y = 1$
    $3x + y = 7$
  - (c) $y - x + 1 = 0$
    $x - 2y = 1$
  - (d) $x + 3y = 4$
    $2x - y = 8$

7 Solve each system.
  - (a) $x + y = 2$
    $2(x - 1) - y = -7$
  - (b) $3x - y = 16$
    $2x + 3 = y + 16$
  - (c) $x - 2y = 2$
    $2(x - 3) - 3(y - 1) = 0$

C 8 To solve the system of equations given by

$$A: \ y + \frac{3}{4}x = -1 \qquad x - \frac{1}{4}y = 5$$

  Jean wrote the following:

$$B: \ 4y + 3x = -4 \quad \text{and} \quad 4x - y = 20$$

  (a) Show why the equations in A are equivalent to those in B.
  (b) Solve the system.

5.7 Solving Linear Systems of Equations: Comparison Method

You can extend the method of substitution and from each equation obtain an expression for one of the variables. For example, to solve this system

$$x - 2y = -3 \qquad ①$$
$$x + 4y = 3 \qquad ②$$

You can obtain from equation ①

$$x - 2y = -3$$
$$x = -3 + 2y \qquad ③$$

You can obtain from equation ②

$$x + 4y = 3$$
$$x = 3 - 4y \qquad ④$$

Equate the two expressions for x from equations ③ and ④ and then solve the resulting equation in 1 variable.

$$-3 + 2y = 3 - 4y$$
$$2y + 4y = 3 + 3$$
$$6y = 6$$
$$y = 1$$

Use the value of $y = 1$ in equation ① (or ②) to obtain a value of x.

$$x - 2y = -3$$
$$x - 2(1) = -3$$
$$x - 2 = -3$$
$$x = -1$$

Thus you obtain $x = -1$, $y = 1$ as the solution of the system.

In the above method, you obtain expressions for one of the variables from both equations and then *compare* them to obtain 1 equation in 1 variable. This method is called the **comparison method**.

In deciding which variable to work with, you choose the variable that can more readily be expressed in terms of the remaining variable.

5.7 Exercise

A 1 For each expression, express the variable indicated in terms of the remaining variable.

(a) $2m - n = 6$, n (b) $3y = 8 + x$, x (c) $4a - b - 6 = 0$, b

(d) $3x = y - 8$, y (e) $3y - x = 8$, x (f) $5a = 8 - b$, b

(g) $2m + 3n - 5 = 0$, m (h) $4x + 3y = 0$, y

2 (a) Use the *method of comparison* to solve this system.

$$a = b - 1, \qquad 3a + b = 3$$

(b) Verify your solution in (a).

B 3 Use the *method of comparison* to solve each system.

(a) $m = 1 - n$ (b) $-3 - 2y = x$ (c) $m = 3 - 2n$
    $m = 1 - 2n$ $1 + 2y = x$ $n + 3 = m$

(d) $n = m - 1$ (e) $x = 2y + 3$ (f) $b + a = 0$
    $2 - 2m = n$ $x + y = 0$ $2b = 3 + a$

4 Find the co-ordinates of the point that lies on both lines given by the following systems.

(a) $x = 2y + 1$ (b) $3x - 2y = -5$ (c) $2x + 3y = 0$
    $y - x = -1$ $x = y - 2$ $2x + y = -4$

5 (a) Solve this system using the *method of substitution*.

$$3x - 2y = 9 \qquad x + y = -2$$

(b) Solve the system in (a) using the *method of comparison*.

(c) Which method do you prefer, (a) or (b)? Why?

6 For each of the following systems, *first* decide which method to use to solve each system.

- Method of Substitution • Method of Comparison

Then, solve each system.

(a) $b = 8 - 3a$ (b) $x = 3y - 10$ (c) $a - b = 2$
    $-b = 7 - 2a$ $y - 4 = x$ $a + 3b = -10$

(d) $13 - 9x = y$ (e) $3x - y = -9$ (f) $3m - n = 4$
    $3x - 5y = -33$ $y - 2x = 7$ $m = 2n + 3$

7 Solve each system.

(a) $x + y = -3$ (b) $\dfrac{1}{3}x - y = 1$
    $3(x + 1) - 2(y - 1) = -4$

                                 $\dfrac{2}{3}x + y = 5$

(c) $2a + \dfrac{1}{2}b = 8$ (d) $\dfrac{1}{3}a - b = -5$ (e) $\dfrac{m}{6} + \dfrac{n}{2} = -\dfrac{1}{2}$

    $a - \dfrac{1}{2}b = 1$ $a - \dfrac{2}{3}b = -1$ $\dfrac{m}{3} - 3n = 7$

Applications: Using Co-Ordinates

In order to rescue people, the pilot of the helicopter or the rescue crew must know the exact co-ordinates of the people needing to be rescued.

The line of sight of a forest fire is given from one observation post as $x - y = 1$. From another observation post the line of sight is given by the equation $x + 3y = 21$.

The fire is located at the co-ordinates of the point of intersection of the two lines of sight.

In real life, more advanced methods are used to determine the positions of wrecked ships, forest fires, survivors, but the principles needed to calculate their position are the same.

8 (a) Solve the equations $x - y = 1$ and $x + 3y = 21$ for the forest fire?

   (b) Where is the fire located?

9 The lines of sight for a forest fire are given.
   From Observation Deck A: $3x + y - 9 = 0$
   From Observation Deck B: $2x + 3y - 13 = 0$
   What are the co-ordinates of the forest fire?

10 The position of a wrecked oil tanker is given at the intersection of $2x - y = 2$ and $3(2x - 1) - 2(y - 1) = 9$. Find the co-ordinates of its position.

11 A piper cub crashed in the desert and was located by the lines given by $x - y = -2$ and $3y - 4 = x$. Find the co-ordinates of its position.

12 The coasts of a triangular island are given by the following equations.

   (a) Find the co-ordinates of the northern tip.
   (b) Find the co-ordinates of the farthest west point.

5.8 Solving Linear Systems of Equations: Addition-Subtraction Method

A method of solving a linear system is based on the following properties of equivalent systems.

Property I: You can perform operations on an equation such that the resulting equation and the original equation are equivalent. For example, equations $x + y = 4$ and $2x + 2y = 8$ are equivalent, since the second equation is obtained by multiplying the first equation by a factor of 2.

Property II: For any linear system, adding or subtracting the equations results in an equation that passes through the same intersection point as the original system.

Add the given equations.

$$3x + 2y = 12$$
$$\underline{2x + 3y = 13}$$
$$5x + 5y = 25$$

Subtract the given equations.

$$3x + 2y = 12$$
$$\underline{2x + 3y = 13}$$
$$x - y = -1$$

Thus, the equations $5x + 5y = 25$ and $x - y = -1$ have the same intersection point as the original system.

The above two properties of a linear system of equations allow you to develop an algebraic method of solving a pair of linear equations. Namely, you can add or subtract the linear equations to obtain a simpler system of equations that is equivalent to the original system. This procedure of solving a linear system of equations is shown in Example 1 and is known as the **addition-subtraction method.**

Example 1 Solve the system $x + 2y = 11$

$$3x - 2y = 9$$

Solution

$x + 2y = 11$ ①   Note that the numerical coefficients of y are the same
$3x - 2y = 9$ ②   except for the sign. Use Property II.

Add ① and ② to eliminate the y variable.

$$4x = 20$$
$$x = 5 \quad ③$$

Use $x = 5$ in ① to obtain
a value for y.

$$x + 2y = 11$$
$$5 + 2y = 11$$
$$2y = 6$$

Be sure to check
your work.
See next page.

Thus, $(x, y) = (5, 3)$.

$$y = 3$$

Remember. Verify in the original equation.

Verification: Use $x = 5$, $y = 3$.

$$x + 2y = 11$$
$$\begin{aligned} LS &= x + 2y & RS &= 11 \\ LS &= 5 + 2(3) \\ LS &= 5 + 6 \\ LS &= 11 \\ LS &= RS \quad \text{Checks} \checkmark \end{aligned}$$

$$3x - 2y = 9$$
$$\begin{aligned} LS &= 3(5) - 2(3) & RS &= 9 \\ LS &= 15 - 6 \\ LS &= 9 \\ LS &= RS \quad \text{Checks} \checkmark \end{aligned}$$

In the following example, Property II of equations is used to change the form of one of the equations so that you end up with a system of equations in which one of the variables has the same numerical coefficients, except for the sign, in both equations. In this way they are readily eliminated by adding.

Example 2 Solve $3x - 2y = 13$
$$x + y = 1$$

Solution

$$\begin{aligned} 3x - 2y &= 13 & &① \\ x + y &= 1 & &② \end{aligned}$$

Multiply ② by a factor 2.

$$2x + 2y = 2 \qquad ③$$

Add ① and ③ to eliminate the variable y.

$$\begin{aligned} 3x - 2y &= 13 & &① \\ 2x + 2y &= 2 & &③ \\ \hline 5x &= 15 \\ x &= 3 \end{aligned}$$

Use $x = 3$ in ①

$$\begin{aligned} 3x - 2y &= 13 & &① \\ 3(3) - 2y &= 13 \\ 9 - 2y &= 13 \\ -2y &= 4 \\ y &= -2 \end{aligned}$$

Thus, $(x, y) = (3, -2)$. ⟵ Don't forget to check your solution!

5.8 Exercise

A 1 How are the equations in Column B obtained from those in Column A?

Column A	Column B
(a) $x + 3y = 6$	$\longrightarrow \quad 2x + 6y = 12$
(b) $2p - 3q = 12$	$\longrightarrow \quad 6p - 9q = 36$
(c) $6a + 10b = 12$	$\longrightarrow \quad 3a + 5b = 6$
(d) $2y - 3x = 8$	$\longrightarrow \quad 6x - 4y = -16$
(e) $-m + 4n = -11$	$\longrightarrow \quad 3m - 12n = 33$

Why are the equations in columns A and B equivalent?

2 For each system, how is equation ③ obtained from equations ① and ②?

(a) $a + 3b = 6$ ①   (b) $5x - 3y = 14$ ①
      $2a - b = 5$ ② $2x - y = 6$ ②
      $2a + 6b = 12$ ③ $6x - 3y = 18$ ③

3 (a) Which variable of the following system is more easily eliminated?

$$2x - y = -1 \qquad 3x + y = -9$$

(b) Solve the system in (a).

4 (a) Which variable of the following system is more easily eliminated?

$$3a - 5b = 10 \qquad a - 2b = 4$$

(b) Solve the system in (a).

5 • Decide which variable is more easily eliminated in each of the following systems.
• Solve the system.

(a) $2m + n = -1$ (b) $x + 3y = 2$ (c) $a + 2b = -7$
      $3m - n = -4$ $x - 2y = 2$ $3a - 2b = -5$

(d) $3p - q = 14$ (e) $3x + 2y = -15$ (f) $4m - 3n = 23$
      $3p + 2q = 8$ $x - 3y = 6$ $2m + 5n = 5$

B 6 • First decide which method to use to solve each of the following systems.
• Then solve each system.

(a) $y = 2x + 5$ (b) $3m - 2n = 8$ (c) $2a + 3b = -6$
      $2x - 3y = -11$ $7m + 2n = 32$ $5a - 2b = -15$

7 Solve.   In solving systems, be sure to look ahead and decide *first* which method is preferable. Save yourself tedious calculations.

(a) $a + 4b = 6$
    $2a - b = 3$

(b) $2m = 6 + n$
    $3m + n = 9$

(c) $2p - 3q = -1$
    $2p + 6q - 8 = 0$

(d) $b - 3a = 0$
    $2a + 5b = 17$

(e) $2m = 3 - 3n$
    $6n + 10m + 3 = 0$

(f) $5p = 2q$
    $2p = 5q$

(g) $6y = 21 - 9x$
    $3y - 2x = 4$

(h) $2x - 18y = 0$
    $3x - 5y = 22$

(i) $3x - 2y - 5 = 0$
    $4x + 14y - 15 = 0$

8 (a) What might be your first step in solving this system? Why?

$$\frac{x}{2} - y = 5 \qquad 2x - \frac{y}{3} = 9$$

(b) Solve the system in (a).

9 (a) A system is given by $3(a - 2) - 3(b + 6) = -9$ and $2a + 3b = -5$.
     What might be your first step in solving the system?
   (b) Solve the system. Then verify your solution.

10 Solve.

(a) $\frac{a}{2} + b = -4$

    $a - \frac{2b}{3} = 8$

(b) $x - \frac{3}{4}y = -5$

    $x - \frac{y}{4} = -1$

(c) $2(x + 1) - 3y = 5$

    $2x + y = 7$

(d) $3x - y = 7$
    $5x - 2(y - 3) = 18$

(e) $2a = 4(2b + 2)$
    $3(a - 3b) + 2 = 17$

(f) $2(m - 1) + n = 1$
    $m - 3n = 5$

11 Two lines are defined by $2x - 3y = -25$ and $3x + y = -21$.
    Find the co-ordinates of the point of intersection.

12 Find the co-ordinates of the intersection of each pair of lines.

(a) $2x + 5y = 19$
    $3x - y = 3$

(b) $3x - 2y = 13$
    $2x + y = 4$

(c) $2x + 14 = 3y$
    $48 = 3x + 7y$

(d) $7x = 5 + 3y$
    $2y + 4 = 5x$

(e) $x - 3 = 2y$
    $5x + 4y - 8 = 0$

(f) $4x - 10y = -13$
    $4y - 3x - 8 = 0$

C 13 Find the co-ordinates of the vertices of the triangle shown.

5.9 Linear Systems of Equations: Simplifying First

Earlier, when you solved equations of the type $\dfrac{m-5}{3} - \dfrac{2m+6}{2} = -4$

you first simplified by eliminating the fraction form.

To simplify the equation, you can multiply both sides of the equation by the lowest common multiple of 2 and 3, namely 6.

$$6\left(\frac{m-5}{3}\right) - 6\left(\frac{2m+6}{2}\right) = 6(-4)$$

Remember: Multiply *each* term of the equation on *both* sides.

$$2(m-5) - 3(2m+6) = -24$$
$$-4m - 28 = -24$$
$$-4m = 4$$
$$m = -1$$

Example 1 Solve the linear system given by $\dfrac{x-2}{3} - \dfrac{y+5}{2} = -3$ and $x + y = 8$.

Solution

$$\frac{x-2}{3} - \frac{y+5}{2} = -3 \qquad ① $$

Simplify the first equation by multiplying it by the least common multiple of 3 and 2 which is 6.

$$6\left(\frac{x-2}{3}\right) - 6\left(\frac{y+5}{2}\right) = 6(-3)$$

$$\overset{2}{6}\left(\frac{x-2}{3_1}\right) - \overset{3}{6}\left(\frac{y+5}{2_1}\right) = 6(-3)$$

$$2(x-2) - 3(y+5) = -18$$
$$2x - 4 - 3y - 15 = -18$$
$$2x - 3y = 1 \qquad ②$$

Now solve the simplified system.

$$2x - 3y = 1 \qquad ②$$
$$x + y = 8 \qquad ③$$

Substitute $y = 8 - x$ from ③ into ②.

Thus
$$2x - 3y = 1$$
$$2x - 3(8-x) = 1$$
$$2x - 24 + 3x = 1$$
$$5x = 25$$
$$x = 5$$

Use $x = 5$ in the *original* equation ③ to obtain the value of y.

$$x + y = 8$$
$$5 + y = 8$$
$$y = 3$$

To verify your solution use the original equation ①. This is left for you to try.

Thus the solution is $(x, y) = (5, 3)$.

In doing mathematics, look for methods of saving tedious or cumbersome calculations. This is illustrated in the following example.

Example 2 Solve the linear system $\dfrac{3}{x} + \dfrac{4}{y} = 10$ $\qquad \dfrac{2}{x} - \dfrac{1}{y} = 3$ $\qquad x, y \neq 0$

Solution Use $\dfrac{1}{x} = a$ and $\dfrac{1}{y} = b$. The equations are then rewritten as

$$\dfrac{3}{x} + \dfrac{4}{y} = 10 \qquad ① \qquad \longrightarrow \qquad 3a + 4b = 10 \qquad ③$$

$$\dfrac{2}{x} - \dfrac{1}{y} = 3 \qquad ② \qquad \longrightarrow \qquad 2a - b = 3 \qquad ④$$

$$
\begin{aligned}
& 3a + 4b = 10 && ③ \\
4 \times ④ \quad & 8a - 4b = 12 && ⑤ \\
\cline{2-2}
③ + ⑤ \quad & \;\;\;11a = 22 && \\
& \qquad a = 2 && ⑥
\end{aligned}
$$

Use $a = 2$ in equation ④.

$$
\begin{aligned}
2a - b &= 3 \\
2(2) - b &= 3 \\
4 - b &= 3 \\
-b &= -1 \quad \text{or} \quad b = 1
\end{aligned}
$$

Thus $a = 2$, $b = 1$. Use $\dfrac{1}{x} = a$ and $\dfrac{1}{y} = b$ to write $\dfrac{1}{x} = 2$ and $\dfrac{1}{y} = 1$.
Thus $x = \frac{1}{2}$, $y = 1$ or $(x, y) = (\frac{1}{2}, 1)$.

5.9 Exercise

A 1 How are the equations in Column B obtained from those in Column A?

Column A	Column B
(a) $3x - \dfrac{1}{2}y = 4$	$6x - y = 8$
(b) $\dfrac{2}{3}x + y = -3$	$2x + 3y = -9$
(c) $3(x - 1) + y = -2$	$3x + y = 1$
(d) $y - 2(x + 5) = 6$	$y - 2x - 10 = 6$
(e) $\dfrac{x - 1}{2} + y = 4$	$x - 1 + 2y = 8$

2 (a) What might be your first step in solving this linear system? $\dfrac{x - 1}{2} + y = 5 \qquad x + y = 8$

(b) Solve the system in (a).

3 (a) How is the least common multiple of 3 and 4 used to simplify the following system?

$$\frac{(2x + 1)}{3} - \frac{(y + 5)}{4} = -3 \qquad 2x + y = -1$$

(b) Solve the system in (a).

B 4 Solve each of the following systems.

(a) $\dfrac{x + 1}{5} = 2y - 3$

$x + \dfrac{y + 7}{4} = -4$

(b) $\dfrac{4x - 5}{3} - 3y = 22$

$3x - \dfrac{(y + 1)}{6} = 7$

(c) $5x - \dfrac{(5y - 2)}{3} + 11 = 0$

$\dfrac{x + 3}{2} + 4y = -8$

(d) $2x + \dfrac{(4y + 3)}{2} = 2$

$\dfrac{3x + 1}{3} = y + \dfrac{5}{4}$

5 (a) Solve the system. $\dfrac{x - 1}{2} + y = -2 \qquad 3y + \dfrac{2x + 11}{5} = 1.$

(b) Verify the answers you obtained in (a).

6 Solve and verify.

(a) $\dfrac{x + 1}{2} + \dfrac{3y - 3}{8} = 0$

$\dfrac{2x + 3}{3} + 6y = -1$

(b) $\dfrac{x}{7} - \dfrac{2y + 1}{5} = 0$

$\dfrac{x - 2}{9} + \dfrac{y}{3} + 2 = 0$

7 (a) What is the first step needed to solve the following system?

$$\frac{1}{x} + \frac{4}{y} = 3 \qquad \frac{2}{x} - \frac{2}{y} = 1$$

(b) Solve the system in (a).

8 Solve each system. Verify your answer

(a) $\dfrac{2}{x} + \dfrac{8}{y} = 0$

$\dfrac{3}{x} + \dfrac{4}{y} = -2$

(b) $\dfrac{7}{x} = 15 - \dfrac{1}{y}$

$\dfrac{14}{x} - \dfrac{2}{y} = -14$

9 Solve and verify.

(a) $\dfrac{6}{y} = 5 + \dfrac{2}{x}$

$\dfrac{3}{y} = 15 - \dfrac{4}{x}$

(b) $\dfrac{2}{x} - \dfrac{1}{y} - 13 = 0$

$\dfrac{3}{x} + \dfrac{2}{y} = 2$

Applications: Computer Program For Linear Systems

A computer is often used to solve complex systems of equations. A general system of linear equations can be given by

$$Ax + By = C \qquad\qquad Dx + Ey = F$$

The solution of the general system of linear equations such as the one above can be given by

$$x = \frac{CE - BF}{AE - BD}, \quad AE \neq BD \qquad y = \frac{CD - AF}{BD - AE}, \quad BD \neq AE$$

This computer program in BASIC will solve all linear systems of 2 equations in 2 unknowns.

```
10  PRINT     "SOLVE TWO EQUATIONS IN TWO VARIABLES"
20  INPUT A
30  INPUT B
40  INPUT C
50  INPUT D
60  INPUT E
70  INPUT F
80  LET Q = AE - BD
90  IF Q = 0,     THEN 20
100 LET X = (C * E - B * F)/(A * E - B * D)
110 LET Y = (C * D - A * F)/(B * D - A * E)
120 PRINT X; Y;
130 PRINT DO YOU WANT TO INPUT ANY MORE VALUES?
140 IF YES THEN 20
150 END
```

10 A system of equations is given by $3x - 4y = 5$, $x + 5y = 8$.
(a) What are the values of A, B, C, D, E, and F?
(b) Use the program to calculate the value of x and y.
(c) Solve the above system to verify your answers in (b).

11 For each system of equations, use the computer program to obtain the values of x and y.
(a) $4x + 5y = 7$ (b) $8x - 9y = 41$ (c) $2x - y = -7$
    $3x + 4y = 6$ $4x + 3y = 3$ $y + 3x = -8$

(d) $3x = 9 - 4y$ (e) $3x = 12 - y$ (f) $3x + 4 = 2y$
    $4 + 8y = 5x$ $2x + 5y = 21$ $6x = 3y$

12 For each system of equations, make the appropriate changes in the computer program to obtain the values of x and y.
(a) $2x + ay = -2$ (b) $ax - by = e$
    $bx - 3y = 5$ $cx - dy = f$

13 A system is given by $\frac{x + 7}{5} + \frac{y + 13}{3} = 7$ and $\frac{1}{2}x + \frac{3}{4}y = 3$.

Change the form of the above equations so that the computer program may be used. Then use the program to obtain the values of x and y.

5.10 Steps For Solving Problems

In order to be successful in solving problems you must organize your work
Refer to the *Steps For Solving Problems*.

Steps for Solving Problems

Step A Read the problem carefully. Answer these two important questions:
  I What information am I asked to find? (information I don't know)
  II What information am I given? (information I know)
  Be sure to understand what it is you are to find, then introduce the variables.

Step B Translate from English to mathematics and write the equations.

Step C Solve the equations.

Step D Check the answer in the original problem.

Step E Write a final statement as the answer to the problem.

- To solve any problem an important step is to translate correctly from English to mathematics.

- As you read the following example and solution, identify where *Steps A, B, C, D,* and *E* occur.

Example Bob and Kevin bought a lottery ticket and won $100 000. Since they paid different amounts for the winning ticket, Bob received $10 000 more than twice what Kevin received. How much did each person receive?

Solution Let b represent Bob's share of the lottery and k Kevin's share.

Bob's share, plus Kevin's share in $100 000.

Write $b + k = 100\ 000$ ①

Bob's share is $10 000 more than twice Kevin's share.

Write $b = 10\ 000 + 2k$ ②   Now solve the equations. Use the skills you have developed in your earlier work.

$b + k = 100\ 000$ ①
$b - 2k = 10\ 000$ ③   Check in the original problem.
$3k = 90\ 000$ ① − ③
$k = 30\ 000$

Check		
Amount received by Bob		$70 000
Amount received by Kevin		$30 000
checks ✓	Total	$100 000

Use $k = 30\ 000$ in equation ①.

$b + k = 100\ 000$
$b + 30\ 000 = 100\ 000$
$b = 70\ 000$

Twice Kevin's share + $10 000		$60 000
Bob's share		$10 000
	checks ✓	$70 000

Thus Bob received $70 000 and Kevin received $30 000 of the lottery winnings.

5.10 Exercise

A 1 Find the value in cents of each of the following.

(a) 6 dimes   (b) t dimes

(c) $2m$ dimes   (d) $(k + 2)$ quarters

(e) t dimes, k quarters   (f) s quarters, t dimes

(g) a nickels, b quarters   (h) d pennies, e quarters

2 Find the amount of interest paid on each of the following investments. (The rate of interest is yearly and the money is invested for a year.)

(a) \$$s$ at 8% and \$$y$ at 9%   (b) \$$k$ at 15% and \$$y$ at 10%

(c) \$$(y - 1)$ at 10% and \$$(m + 1)$ at 12%

3 Find the total distance travelled.

(a) Lori walked for 14 h at y km/h.

(b) A jet travelled 12 h at m km/h.

(c) A truck travelled at 90 km/h for x min.

4 For each of the following statements
  • use two variables of your own choice.
  • write an equation in 2 variables.

(a) The sum of Barb's age and three times Frank's age is 160 years.

(b) The interest on an amount of money invested at 9% exceeds the interest on another amount of money invested at 12% by \$190.

(c) When twice the width of a rectangle is added to half the length the sum is 126 m.

(d) A car travelled for y h at 40 km/h and x h at 65 km/h and covered a total of 480 km.

B 5 There were 52 more girls than boys at the last school dance at Vernon High. Total attendance at the dance was 420. How many boys and girls attended?

6 Two numbers differ by 25. If 3 times the smaller exceeds the larger by 3, find the two numbers.

7 Alex and Sam won \$2000 in a television game show. If Sam received twice as much as Alex less \$100, how did they share their prize?

8 1400 students attended a concert at Stoney Creek High School. The cost for students with activity cards was \$2.00 and \$2.50 for those without activity cards. If \$3025 was collected, how many students had activity cards?

9   The Book Store cash register had $30 in $1- and $2-bills. If there were 3 times as many $1-bills as $2-bills, how many of each were there?

10   The fishery stocked a lake with 9000 pike and salmon. If it had stocked the lake with twice as many pike and three times as many salmon as it did, it would have placed 23 500 fish. How many of each type of fish did it place in the lake?

11   Lori purchased 5 boxes of chocolates and 3 bags of candies for $12.05. If the cost of a box of chocolates and a bag of candies were reversed then it would have cost Lori $11.07 for the same order. What is the cost of a box of chocolates?

12   Brass is a mixture of copper and zinc. A brass block containing 60% zinc and a brass bar containing 40% zinc are melted together. The resulting mixture is 51% zinc. If 400 kg of the new mixture is obtained, what was the original mass of the block?

13   Michael has a total of $580. He has 76 bills, in all, consisting of $5-bills and $10-bills. How many of each type of bill does he have?

14   Jackson collected 70 coins, consisting of quarters and nickels. If the total value of the coins is $9.50, how many of each type of coin does he have?

Calculator Tip

If you need to solve systems of equations frequently, you can develop these formulas and use your calculator.

$$Ax + By = C \qquad x = \frac{CE - BF}{AE - BD} \qquad y = \frac{CD - AF}{BD - AE}$$
$$Dx + Ey = F$$

List the steps you would use on your calculator to efficiently calculate x and y for the system of equations given by

$$2.3x + 6.5y = 19.9 \qquad 6.8x - 4.3y = 11.8$$

Math Tip

It is important to clearly understand the vocabulary of mathematics when solving problems. Make a list of all the new words you have met in this chapter. Provide a simple example to illustrate each word.

5.11 Using Charts to Solve Problems

There are several tools you can use which will help you solve a problem

- You can use variables that remind you of the given information.

- You can organize the information given in a problem under these headings:

A: | What You Are Asked to Find | B: | Facts You Are Given |

- Often, you can use a chart to organize the information given in a problem.

Example
From the yearbook receipts the student council deposited part of the $1200 in a savings account receiving 9% interest per annum, and the remainder in a chequing account receiving 4% interest per annum. If the total interest received for a year is $88, how much money was deposited in each account?

Solution
Let $\$s$ represent the amount of money deposited in the savings account and $\$c$ in the chequing account.

	Amount of money deposited	Rate of interest	Interest paid
Savings Account	$\$s$	9%	$0.09s
Chequing Account	$\$c$	4%	$0.04c

Add to obtain total amount deposited.   Add to obtain total interest.

$$s + c = 1200 \quad \text{①}$$
$$0.09s + 0.04c = 88 \quad \text{②}$$

$100 \times$ ②
$4 \times$ ①
③ − ④

$$9s + 4c = 8800 \quad \text{③}$$
$$4s + 4c = 4800 \quad \text{④}$$
$$5s = 4000$$
$$s = 800$$

Use $s = 800$ to find c in ①

$$s + c = 1200$$
$$(800) + c = 1200$$
$$c = 400$$

Check
I Total amount $800 + $400 = $1200
II 9% of $800 = $72
4% of $400 = $16   ✓ checks
Total interest $88   checks ✓

Thus $800 was deposited in the savings account and $400 was deposited in the chequing account.

5.11 Exercise

A 1 (a) Read the problem and then complete the chart.

Simco Gas sells regular gas at 49¢/L and premium gas at 51¢/L. It also sells a mixture of the regular gas and the premium gas at a medium price of 50.2¢/L. If a 10 000-L tanker is to be filled with the medium price gas, how much regular and premium gas should be used?

Gas Type	Amount of gas (L)	Value of gas ($)
Regular	r	$0.49r$
Premium	p	$0.51p$
Medium	$r + p$	?

(b) Solve the problem.

2 (a) Read the problem and then complete the chart.

A chemical firm produces an 80% iron alloy by combining 90% iron ore A and 60% iron ore B by mass. If the company wishes to fill an order for 150 kg of this alloy, how much of each type of ore must be used?

Ore Type	Amount of ore (kg)	Amount of iron (kg)
90% iron	a	$0.90a$
60% iron	b	$0.60b$
80% iron	?	?

(b) Solve the problem.

B 3 Susan invested part of her $1800 savings at 9% per annum and the remainder at 6% per annum. In one year, the 9% investment earned $102 more than the 6% investment. How much did she invest at each rate?

4 Steven won $10 000 in a lottery. He invested his winnings, part at 10% per annum and part at 11% per annum. If the total interest earned was $1060, how much was invested at each rate?

5 Premium gasoline sells at 53¢/L. Regular gasoline sells at 51.5¢/L. To boost sales, a middle octane gasoline is formed by mixing premium and regular. If 1000 L of this middle octane gasoline is produced and sold at 52.1¢/L, how much of each type of gasoline was used?

6 Total sales on Tuesday at Balmoral Pharmacy were $4200. A profit of 4% was realized on part of these sales and a profit of 5% on the rest. If the profit from the 4% part exceeded the profit on the 5% part by $51, how much of sales were realized at each of the two profit rates?

Applications: Working with Gold

Many ancient relics found by archeologists are pure gold. The purest gold nugget ever found was discovered in Victoria, Australia and was 98.59% pure gold. To show the purity of jewellery in terms of the amount of gold in it, the term carat (k) is used. 1 carat represents one 24th part. Pure gold is described as 24 k gold. Thus, to say a bracelet is 10 k gold means it is made of an alloy consisting of

10 parts gold   14 parts of another metal or alloy.

A coin that is 14 k gold means it is 14 parts gold and 10 parts alloy.

7   A 14 k gold statue was found at an auction by an antique dealer. In order to maximize profits from this statue, it was melted down with cheap 6 k gold trinkets to produce an 8 k gold antique replica. If the replica has a mass of 3.2 kg, what were the masses of the statue and trinkets used?

8   Bing Crosby won an Oscar Award in 1951, for his role in the movie "Going My Way". This award is 0.5 k gold (bronze with a gold plate). If this award were melted together with raw ore of 5 k gold, a cheap costume jewellery with 2 k gold could be made. Find the mass of the Oscar if 5.25 kg of this new structure is formed.

9   Alan wants to have a pin made for his girlfriend. For sentimental reasons he decides to have a jeweller melt some gold coins from his collection to make the pin. One coin was 18 k gold and the other was 11 k gold. If the pin is 14 k and has a mass of 17.5 g, what was the mass of each coin?

10 The largest gold nugget was the Holtermann Nugget found in Hill End, Australia in 1872. The nugget was 23 k. This nugget was melted with 10 k gold alloy to produce jewellery of 14 k gold. If 702 kg of this alloy was melted, find the mass of the nugget.

11 Chains and Things Limited sold a 12 k gold chain. After many complaints, the owner realized that the chain was too soft. It was decided to melt it down with a bar of 6 k gold and make a new harder chain of 10 k gold. If the new chain has a mass of 31.5 g, find the mass of

(a) the original chain.   (b) the amount of 6 k gold used.

5.12 Strategy for Solving Problems: Diagrams

Another strategy which helps you solve problems is to use a diagram to record the information and visually interpret the problem. For example:

Problem

A cleanser containing 20% ammonia is mixed with another cleanser containing 10% ammonia to dilute its strength. If 100 L of this 17% ammonia mixture is obtained, how much of each cleanser was used?

Diagram   A diagram is drawn to help you better interpret the problem.

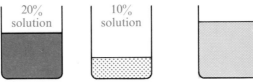

Original Solutions   Mixture Solution

Chart   The chart, an earlier skill, is used to organize the given information.

	20% solution	10% solution	Mixture
Amount of liquid	x L	y L	100 L
Concentration	20%	10%	17%
Amount of ammonia	0.20x L	0.10y L	0.17(100) = 17 L

The equations needed to solve the problem are constructed from the above information.

$$x + y = 100 \qquad ①$$
$$0.20x + 0.10y = 17 \qquad ②$$

Multiply ② by 10 in order to remove the decimal fractions

$$2x + y = 170 \qquad ③$$

Subtract ① from ③. Thus

$$③ - ① \qquad x = 70 \qquad ④$$

Substitute ④ into ①. Thus

$$70 + y = 100$$
$$y = 100 - 70$$
$$y = 30.$$

Remember: Check your answer in the original problem.

Thus 70 L of the 20% cleanser plus 30 L of the 10% cleanser were used.

5.12 Exercise

- Draw a diagram to illustrate the physical situation in the problem.
- Then construct a chart, record the information, and solve the problem.

A 1 (a) Construct a diagram to illustrate the information in the following problem:
A 50% lime solution is mixed with a 30% lime solution to produce 300 L of a 46% solution. How much of each solution was used?

(b) Solve the problem.

2 (a) Construct a diagram to illustrate the information in the following problem.
A window wash solution consists of windshield fluid and water. How much windshield fluid should Rick add to 5 L of a 20% window wash solution to increase its concentration to 75%?

(b) Solve the problem.

B 3 A nut mixture contains 20% peanuts by mass and another contains 40%. The two mixtures are combined to obtain 100 kg which contains 36% peanuts by mass. What quantities of each of the original mixtures were used?

4 Terry made 10 L of orange juice using 70% water. How much orange concentrate should be added to bring the water concentration down to 50%?

5 The coffee trucks sell 250 mL of coffee containing 2% cream. How much hot water should be added to each portion of coffee to decrease the cream concentration to 1.5%?

6 How much sugar should be added to 100 mL of tea to increase its sugar concentration from 7% to 10%?

7 Two nut mixtures were not selling. To increase sales, a retailer mixed one type selling at $2.20/kg with another selling at $2.40/kg. If 100 kg were mixed and sold for $2.28/kg, how much of each type of nut mixture was used?

8 Dick left a 500-mL pot of solution boiling on the stove. Originally the pot had contained 2% salt, but now contains 5% salt. How much water had evaporated?

9 A quantity of 50% silver alloy is melted together with a quantity of 70% silver alloy to produce 500 g of alloy containing 65% silver. How much of each alloy was used?

5.13 Strategy for Solving Problems: Special Facts

To solve any problem, you need to identify the answers to these two important questions.

    I What information does the problem ask you to find?

    II What information is given in the problem?

However, to answer Question II, often you need to use information that is not given in the problem. For example; to solve a problem involving time, distance, and rate, you must understand the time-distance-rate formula and its different forms.

$$d = vt, \qquad \frac{d}{v} = t, \qquad \frac{d}{t} = v, \quad \text{where } d \text{ is distance, } t \text{ is time, } v \text{ is speed.}$$

In the following example, you need to use the above formulas to solve the problem.

Example   Sue drove her car from Pembroke to North Bay in 3 h while Peter drove his truck for 2 h in the opposite direction to Ottawa. Sue drove 20 km/h faster than Peter. If the distance between North Bay and Ottawa is 400 km, find the speed of the car and the truck.

Solution   Let s km/h represent Sue's speed and p km/h represent Peter's speed. You can use a chart to record the information.

	Distance (km)	Speed (km/h)	Time (h)
Sue	$3s$	s	3
Peter	$2p$	p	2

From the chart and the given information in the problem, write the equations needed to solve the problem.

$$3s + 2p = 400 \qquad \text{①} \longleftarrow \text{The total distance is 400 km.}$$
$$s = p + 20 \qquad \text{②} \longleftarrow \text{Sue drove 20 km/h faster than Peter.}$$

Substitute ② into ①. Thus

$$3(p + 20) + 2p = 400$$
$$3p + 60 + 2p = 400$$
$$5p = 340$$
$$p = 68 \qquad \text{③}$$

Substitute ③ into ②

$$s = 68 + 20$$
$$s = 88$$

Remember: Check your answer in the original problem.

Thus the speed of the car was 88 km/h and the speed of the truck was 68 km/h.

In the previous example, you could have also used a combination of diagram and chart to help you visualize the problem and organize the given information.

North Bay   Pembroke   Ottawa

Diagram:
Use a diagram to
help you visually
understand the problem.

	Sue	Peter
speed (km/h)	s	p
time (h)	3	2
distance (km)	$3s$	$2p$

5.13 Exercise

Use a chart to help you organize the given information.

A 1 (a) Read the problem. Find the missing information for the diagram.
Grant and John jog every Saturday. Grant runs 0.2 m/s faster than John. After 20 min, Grant got a stitch and stopped for rest for 5 min while John kept running. At the end of the rest period John was 1200 m ahead of Grant. How fast was each person running?

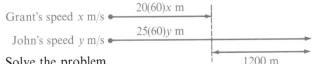

Grant's speed x m/s $20(60)x$ m

John's speed y m/s $25(60)y$ m

1200 m

(b) Solve the problem.

2 (a) Read the problem. Find the missing information for the diagram.
Two trains are 750 km apart and start towards each other (on different lines) at the same time. One train travels 24 km/h faster than the other. If they passed each other after 3 h how fast was each train travelling?

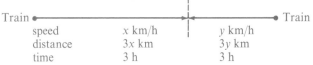

Train

speed	x km/h	y km/h
distance	$3x$ km	$3y$ km
time	3 h	3 h

Train

(b) Solve the problem.

B 3 Two trucks leave Edmonton with one going north and the other heading south. The truck going north had a heavier load so it drove 10 km/h slower. In 8 h the trucks were 1840 km apart. Find the speeds of the trucks.

4 Two birds flew towards each other from two trees which are 240 m apart. One bird flew 2 m/s faster than the other. If they met in 12 s, how fast was each bird flying?

5 Two sailboats leave their clubhouses and sail toward each other. One boat sails 1 km/h faster than the other and they pass each other in 4 h. If the clubhouses are 164 km apart, find the speed of each sailboat.

Applications: Headwinds and Tailwinds

If you look at an airline schedule you will
see the times of departure and arrival of
flights across Canada. However, very often
a flight time is different than the one in the
schedule because of the air current.

In a similar way, the river current helps
you downstream, but works against
you upstream.

Speed of airplane in still air	Tailwind or headwind	Speed of airplane with respect to the ground
450 km/h	tailwind 120 km/h	570 km/h
450 km/h	headwind 90 km/h	360 km/h
V km/h	tailwind W km/h	$(V + W)$ km/h
V km/h	headwind H km/h	$(V - H)$ km/h

6 A Piper Cub plane leaves Prince Albert for Estevan, flying into the wind.
The trip takes 2.5 h. The return trip, with this tailwind, takes only 2 h. If
the distance between the two cities is 350 km, what is the speed of the
wind?

7 A traffic helicopter pilot finds that with a tailwind a 120-km distance takes
45 min. but that the return trip, into the wind, takes 1 h. What is the speed
of the helicopter? What is the speed of the wind?

8 A twin engine plane flies into the wind from Windsor to the Quebec Winter
Carnival in 5 h 20 min. The return flight with the wind is done in 4 h 24 min.
Windsor and Quebec City are 1760 km apart. What is the rate of the wind
and the rate of the plane?

9 A canoeist takes 5 h to deliver a telegram to an outpost 85 km downstream.
Returning upstream with the reply the canoeist takes 1 h to travel 10 km.
What is the rate of the canoeist in still water? What is the rate of the
current?

10 At the Pan-Am Games, the Canadian kayak team averaged 40 km/h
downstream but only 6 km/h upstream, in the white water obstacle course.
What was the rate of the kayak in still water? What was the rate of the
current?

5.14 Problem Solving: Supply and Demand

To help analyze profit and loss, and solve problems, a simple model using graphs can be used. For example, from recorded data, a firm has determined that the amount, A, in dollars, received from the sale of goods can be represented by $A = 0.5n + 100$, where n is the number of items. The cost, C, in dollars, of producing the items is given by $C = 0.25n + 250$, where n is the number of items. The graph provides a visual model for analyzing sales and costs of production. When the

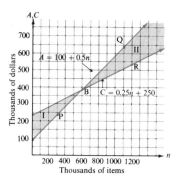

amount of money received equals the cost, there is neither profit nor loss. The point at which this condition occurs is represented by the intersection of the two curves and is called the **break-even point**.

Graphs can be used to illustrate, simply, some very complex concepts. If you are a manufacturer, you learn that many factors affect the selling price of your goods. One of these factors is the relationship between **supply and demand**. Thus, if the supply of manufactured goods exceeds the buyers' demand, then you may need to lower the price to stimulate sales. On the other hand, if the demand for your goods exceeds the supply available, then the buyers may be willing to pay more for the goods so that they can supply their customers. This complex process can be illustrated with graphs.

Demand In the diagram below the buyer, B, knows, in general, that the more items bought, the lower will be the price per item. The graph can be used as a straight line model to illustrate the buyers strategy.

Supply In the diagram below the seller, S, knows, in general, that to create a larger volume of sales the price per item is decreased (quantity buying). This strategy is again illustrated by the straight line model.

When the graphs of supply and demand are drawn on the same set of axes, the diagram can be used to analyze the selling and buying strategies. E is the point at which supply equals demand and is called the **equilibrium point**. At this point the buyer will pay the asking price and the seller will supply the number of items required.

5.14 Exercise

B 1 Refer to the Break-Even Point graph.
  (a) What are the co-ordinates of the break-even point B? Interpret the significance of the point B.
  (b) Interpret (i) shaded region I (ii) shaded region II
  (c) Interpret the co-ordinates of points P, Q, and R.

2 A computer system company decides to manufacture computers and install computing systems. From the data collected, the company determines

  ▶ The profit P, in dollars, is represented by $P = -13\,000 + 700n$, where n represents the number of computing systems.
  ▶ The expenses, E, in dollars, is represented by $E = 23\,000 + 300n$, where n is the number of computing systems.

  (a) Draw a graph for the equations on the same set of axes. What are the co-ordinates of the break even point?
  (b) Interpret your graph. Where does expenses exceed profit? Where is profit greater than the expenses?
  (c) 145 computing systems are sold and installed. What is the profit?
  (d) Create a question based on the graph. Write a solution to the question.

3 Refer to the Supply-Demand diagram. Interpret the graphs that occur
  (a) before equilibrium is reached.   (b) after the equilibrium point.

4 Refer to the Supply-Demand graph. What change would occur in the graph in each of the following situations?
  (a) The seller offered an additional fixed discount on each item sold, regardless of the quantity purchased.
  (b) The buyer is willing to pay an additional fixed amount for each item.
  (c) The seller offered an additional 2% discount on the purchase of goods.
  (d) The buyer is willing to pay 2.7% more for the goods.

5 For each situation, how is the Supply-Demand graph affected? Illustrate your answer by sketching an appropriate graph.
  (a) There is more than one supplier selling the same item to buyers.
  (b) One of the manufacturers selling the goods has gone bankrupt.
  (c) An advertising campaign has increased the demand for the goods.
  (d) The supplier has increased the prices to more than that of a competitor.
  (e) There is a greater demand for the goods in winter than in summer.

Practice and Problems: A Chapter Review

An important step in problem-solving is to decide which skills to use. For this reason, these questions are not placed in any special order. When you have finished this review, you might try the *Test for Practice* that follows.

1   Find the co-ordinates of a rendezvous for two submarines on the courses shown.   Sub A: $y = 10 - 4x$ Sub B: $2x = y - 7$

2   (a) Solve the system. $x + y = 344$ $x - y = 108$
      (b) Why have you used an algebraic method rather than a graphical method to obtain your answers in (a)?

3   Solve and verify.   (a) $\dfrac{5(x + 1)}{3} - \dfrac{3(y - 1)}{2} = 8$ (b) $4(x + 2) - 5(3y - 1) = -46$
                                   $y - x = -3$ $5(2x - 1) + 4(y + 2) = 63$

4   Solve each system for x and y.
      (a) $x + y = m + n$ (b) $px + qy = 1 + q^2$
         $mx - ny = m^2 - n^2$ $p^2x + y = p + q$

5   A flour mill mixes a 40% whole wheat flour with a 70% whole wheat flour to obtain a 60% whole wheat flour. If 45 kg of the final product was obtained, how much of each type of flour was used? Use the chart.

Flour type	Amount of flour (kg)	Amount of whole wheat (kg)
40% Whole Wheat	x	$0.40x$
70% Whole Wheat	y	$0.70y$
60% Whole Wheat	$x + y$	$0.60(x + y)$

6   Ad-Place in Saskatoon processed 1200 advertisements. The cost of delivering them locally was 10¢ each, but out-of-province deliveries cost 14¢ each. If the total budget was $152, how many were delivered out of Saskatchewan?

7   Janet wishes to invest $660 so that the interest from a 10% investment is equal to the income from a 12% bond. How much should be invested at each rate?

8   To increase sales, vegetable seeds selling at $1.40/kg were mixed with seeds selling at 80¢/kg. 400 g of seeds were mixed and sold at $1.22/kg. How much of each type of seed were mixed?

9   Two joggers running in opposite directions pass each other. Sarah jogs at 3 m/s while Janet runs at 5 m/s. After how long will they be 1000 m apart?

Test for Practice

1   The graph of an equation is given by $3x - 2y = 12$. Which of the following points do not lie on the line?
    (a) $(2, -3)$ (b) $(6, 2)$ (c) $(4, 0)$

2   (a) Draw the graph of the following equations using the same axes.
$$3x + 2y + 10 = 0, \qquad x + \frac{3}{2} = \frac{1}{4}y, \qquad 7y = 3x - 8$$
    (b) What do the lines have in common?

3   Write the co-ordinates of the intersection point for each of these systems.
    (a) $\dfrac{x + y}{2} - \dfrac{2y}{3} = \dfrac{5}{2}$ (b) $12(x - 2) - (2y - 1) = 14$
    $\dfrac{3}{2}x + 2y = 0$ $5(x - 1) + 2(1 - 2y) - 14 = 0$

4   Solve each system. Verify your answers.
    (a) $2x + 3y = -3$ (b) $a = 3 + 2b$
    $\quad 3x - y = -10$ $\quad 5a + 4b - 8 = 0$

5   Solve and verify.
    (a) $\dfrac{3}{a} - \dfrac{4}{b} - 15 = 0$ (b) $\dfrac{3(a + 5)}{5} - \dfrac{2(b - 3)}{4} = 4$
    $\dfrac{3}{a} + \dfrac{4}{b} = \dfrac{15}{2}$ $2a + b = -15$

6   Solve for x and y.
    (a) $3x = 6b - 2y$ (b) $ax - by = 1$
    $\quad 4x - 3y = 25b$ $\quad 4x + 9y = 4$

7   Jeremy earns 10¢ per week for each newspaper subscription he delivers and 6¢ per week for each business flyer he delivers. If Jeremy earned $24 in one week for delivering 320 items, how many business flyers did he deliver?

8   Two rare herbs are mixed together to form a cold remedy. One herb costs $5.50/kg and the other herb costs $7.00/kg. 600 kg of this mixture is produced and sold at $6.25/kg. How much of each herb was used?

9   A showboat travelled up the Mississippi River and back to its dock in 25 h. Travelling upstream, the boat could only manage a speed of 20 km/h but gained 10 km/h downstream. How far upstream did the boat travel?

10 Ruth runs at 4 m/s over flat land and 3 m/s over rough terrain. On Saturday, she ran 3000 m in 13 min over flat and rough terrain. What distance did she run over flat land?

Looking Back: A Cumulative Review

1 Simplify $3mn - 2mp + 3np - 2mp - 3mn - 2np$.

2 Subtract the polynomial in Column B from that in Column A.

Column A	Column B
(a) $2(x - y) - 3x$	$2(y - x) - 4y$
(b) $2(x^2 - 2x + 5)$	$3(x^2 - 3x - 6)$
(c) $-3(a + b) - 2b$	$-2(a - 3b) - 6b$
(d) $2(x^2 - 3x) - 4x^2$	$-3(x^2 - 2x) - 4x$

3 Find the missing factor.

(a) $(-ab)(\ ? \ ) = 3abc$ (b) $(\ ? \ )(-5m) = -25mn$

(c) $(9ab)(\ ? \ ) = -18a^2b$ (d) $(\ ? \ )(-4mn) = 16m^2n$

4 (a) How are these equations alike? different?

$$m^2 - 3m + 2 = 0$$
$$(x - 1)^2 - 3(x - 1) + 2 = 0$$

(b) Solve $(x - 1)^2 - 3(x - 1) + 2 = 0$.

5 Simplify $\dfrac{3 - \dfrac{2}{3y}}{5 - \dfrac{1}{2}y}$.

6 For each of the following, which is greater, A or B?

A	B
(a) $(3^{-2} \times 4^{-1})^{-1}$	$4^8 \times 2^{-12}$
(b) $\dfrac{27^{-1}}{3^{-9}}$	$\dfrac{(3^7 \times 4^2 \times 3^4)^0}{3^{-1}}$
(c) $3^{-1} \times 2^0 \times 4^2 \times 5^{-1}$	$(2^4 \times 4^{-1})^{-3}$

7 Nitroglycerine is a compound of carbon, hydrogen, nitrogen and oxygen in the ratio $36:5:42:48$. What mass of each of oxygen, carbon, and hydrogen will react with 6 g of nitrogen to form this compound?

8 Write the missing value for each inverse squared variation

$P \propto \dfrac{1}{Q^2}$.

	P_1	Q_1	P_2	Q_2
(a)	36	25	225	?
(b)	?	12	16	30

9 The fuel efficiency of a car is inversely proportional to its speed. A car travelling at 80 km/h has a fuel efficiency of 50 km/L. If the car was travelling at 100 km/h, what would the fuel efficiency be?

6 Functions and Transformations

vocabulary of relations and functions, skills and concepts, development of skills related to $y = f(x)$, $y = f(x) + q$, $y = f(x + p)$, $y = af(x)$, $y = f(bx)$, $y = f(-x)$, $y = -f(x)$, $y = af(x + b) + c$, properties of functions, inverse of a function and equations, applying skills

Introduction

Relations are common in everyday life.

- When you drive a car, the distance you travel is related to how fast you drive for how long.

- The amount of an iceberg above water is related to the amount below the surface.

- How high you can jump is related to your speed at the point of take off, to your skill at jumping, and to your level of training.

Relations are also common in the various disciplines that you study. Social sciences, applied sciences, and pure sciences (such as mathematics) are permeated with relations.

Often in mathematics you will see a relation described as a function, a relation with a special property. The concepts you learn and the skills you gain in this chapter will provide a basis for your study of many important mathematical topics related to the nature and aspects of functions.

6.1 Vocabulary of Relations

- You may use a **table of values** to show how numbers of one set are related to numbers of another set.

Length of spring (cm)	Mass added (g)
12	4.5
12.8	4.8
13.6	5.1
14.4	5.4
15.2	5.7

- You may also show a relationship among numbers by using a **mapping diagram** such as the one at the right. The number 0 is mapped into the number 2. In symbols, this is shown as
$$0 \rightarrow 2$$

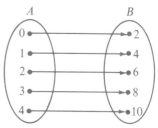

- You may also use **ordered pairs** to show the relation between the numbers in sets. The ordered pairs are written to show the relation.

From A   From B

(0, 2),   (1, 4),   (2, 6),   (3, 8),   (4, 10)

The relation, S, is written as
$$S = \{(0, 2), (1, 4), (2, 6), (3, 8), (4, 10)\}$$

The following vocabulary is used in working with relations.

Domain   The set of all first elements of the ordered pairs of a relation is called the **domain** of the relation. The domain for the relation S above is given by
$$\text{domain} = \{0, 1, 2, 3, 4\}$$

Range   The set of all second elements of the ordered pairs of the relation is called the **range** of the relation. The range for the relation S above is given by
$$\text{range} = \{2, 4, 6, 8, 10\}$$

A relation may also be defined as a set involving a **defining equation**. For example,

$$P = \{(x, y) \,|\, y = 2x + 2, \, -2 \le x \le 3, x \in R\}$$

ordered pairs of relation   defining equation of the relation   domain of the relation

You can draw a graph for the relation P on the previous page by constructing a table of values given by the equation,

$$y = 2x + 2, \qquad -2 \le x \le 3$$

Table of Values

Choose integral values for x.

x	y
-2	-2
-1	0
0	2
1	4
2	6
3	8

Plot the points in the table of values.

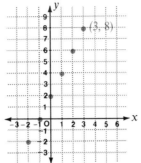

Draw the complete graph as shown.

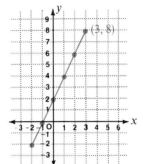

Since the domain of P is $\{x \mid -2 \le x \le 3,\ x \in R\}$, the graph of P is a line segment with end points $(-2, -2)$, $(3, 8)$.

From the graphs, you can see that for $-2 \le x \le 3$, the interval of values for y is given by $-2 \le y \le 8$. The graph of relation P is a straight line. Thus a relationship such as P is called a **linear relation**.

6.1 Exercise

A 1   For the relation shown in the graph, write
(a) the domain.   (b) the range.

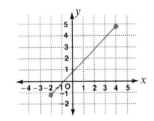

2   For the relation shown in the graph, write
(a) the domain.   (b) the range.

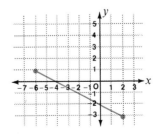

3   For each relation given by the arrow diagram, write
    (i) the domain.   (ii) the range.

(a)   (b)   (c)

(d)   (e)   (f)

B 4   A relation is given by

x	-1	0	1	2	0	1	2	1	2
y	-2	-2	-2	-2	-1	-1	-1	0	0

(a) Write the domain; range.
(b) Draw a graph of the relation.

5   (a) Draw a mapping diagram for the relation given by the ordered pairs
        (0, 1), (1, 2), (2, 3), (3, 4).
    (b) Write the domain; range.

6   A relation is defined by

$$y = 3x - 1, \quad x \in \{0, 1, 2, 3, 4\}.$$ ←——the domain of the relation

(a) Find the ordered pairs of the relation.
(b) Write the range of the relation.

Problem Solving

Steven, Brian and Jason are married to Barbara, Jackie and Gale, but not in this order. On Saturday night they played bridge, but the wives and husbands were with different partners. Jackie played with Jason, and Brian played with Steven's wife. If Brian and Gale played together, then who is married to whom?

6.2 Skills and Concepts: Functions

In the previous section, you drew the graphs of linear relations. You may follow the same procedure when drawing the graphs of **non-linear relations**.

Example 1   Draw the graphs defined by   A: $y = x^2 - 3$ B: $x = y^2 - 3$ $x, y \in R$

Solution   Construct a table of values for each of A and B. Plot the corresponding points showing the ordered pair associated with each point. Draw a smooth continuous curve through the points.

A: Graph the relation defined by $y = x^2 - 3$. Choose representative values for x.

B: Graph the relation defined by $x = y^2 - 3$. Choose representative values for y.

x	y
-3	6
-2	1
-1	-2
0	-3
1	-2
2	1
3	6

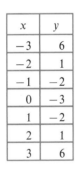
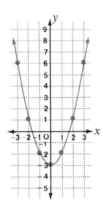

x	y
6	-3
1	-2
-2	-1
-3	0
-2	1
1	2
6	3

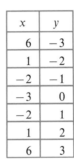
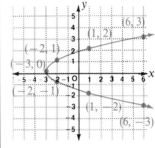

Note: The bold dots are plotted to locate the position of the graph.

The graphs in Example 1 are called **parabolas**. Only part of each graph has been drawn, that is, the part of the graph which turns about a point called the **turning point**. In Graph A, the turning point is $(0, -3)$ and in Graph B, the turning point is $(-3, 0)$. As a rule, the part of the parabola which contains the turning point is the part which is plotted.

The following observations about the graphs of A and B will help you understand an important concept.

- In graph A, for every x co-ordinate there is *only one* corresponding y co-ordinate.
- In graph B, for some x co-ordinates there is more than one y co-ordinate.

These observations introduce the following concept.

> A relation is a **function** such that for every x co-ordinate there is one and only one corresponding y co-ordinate.

In other words, no two ordered pairs in the function have the same first element. Thus the relation shown in graph A is a function. The relation shown in graph B is *not* a function.

The Vertical Line Test

To determine whether or not a relation is a function, draw a line parallel to the y-axis to intersect the graph.

- If the vertical line cuts the graph at most once, the relation is a function.
- If the vertical line cuts the graph more than once, the relation is not a function.

Example 2   (a) Graph the relations

A: $\{(x, y)\,|\,x^2 + y^2 = 9, \ x \in R\}$
B: $\{(x, y)\,|\,y = (x - 1)^2 - 2, \ x \in R\}$

Decide whether or not they are functions.
(b) What is the domain and range for each relation?

Solution   (a) A: The graph for the relation
$\{(x, y)\,|\,x^2 + y^2 = 9, x \in R\}$ is shown.

Draw a line parallel to the y-axis to intersect the graph. Since this vertical line intersects the graph in two points, then the relation $\{(x, y)\,|\,x^2 + y^2 = 9, \ x \in R\}$ is not a function.

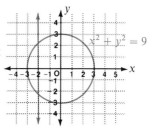

B: The graph for the relation
$\{(x, y)\,|\,y = (x - 1)^2 - 2, x \in R\}$ is shown.

Draw a line parallel to the y-axis to intersect the graph. Since this vertical line intersects the graph at most once, then the relation $\{(x, y)\,|\,y = (x - 1)^2 - 2, \ x \in R\}$ is a function.

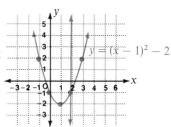

(b) A: Domain $\{x\,|-3 \leq x \leq 3, \ x \in R\}$
    Range $\{y\,|-3 \leq y \leq 3, \ y \in R\}$

B: Domain $= R \longleftarrow$ The domain is all
                               the real numbers.
    Range $= \{y\,|\,y \geq -2, \ y \in R\}$

A relation, or function, may also be denoted by using an arrow or mapping notation. For example, an equivalent form of the function defined by $y = 2x - 2$, $x \in R$ is

$$f : x \longrightarrow 2x - 2, \quad x \in R \longleftarrow \text{Read this as}$$
$$f \text{ maps } x \text{ into } 2x - 2.$$

It is useful to have different ways of denoting a function. For example, these two forms are also equivalent.

$$\longrightarrow f(x) = 2x - 2, \quad x \in R$$

Read this as "f at x".

$$f : x \longrightarrow 2x - 2, \quad x \in R$$

$f(-1)$ means the value of $f(x)$ when $x = -1$.

$$f(x) = 2x - 2 \qquad f(-1) = 2(-1) - 2$$
$$= -2 - 2$$
$$= -4$$

Thus, for two sets A and B, a function or relation, shown by f, may be thought of as a rule or correspondence shown as follows.

f associates each element x in A, (the domain), with an element $f(x)$ in B (the range).

> You can say that f maps x onto its image $f(x)$ and that x is the pre-image of $f(x)$.

6.2 Exercise

A 1 For the relation shown by the graph, write the
(a) domain   (b) range
(c) Is the relation a function?
   Give reasons for your answer.

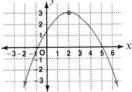

 2 For the relation shown by the graph, write the
(a) domain   (b) range
(c) Is the relation a function?
   Give reasons for your answer.
(d) With which axis is the domain associated?
(e) With which axis is the range associated?

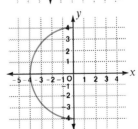

3   For the following:
    A: use the vertical line test to determine which represent a function;
       which do not.
    B: write the domain and range.

(a)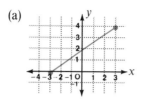

(b)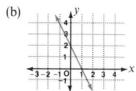

(c)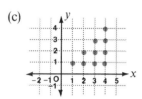

(d)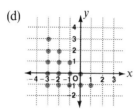

(e)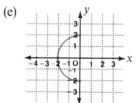

(f)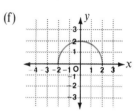

(g)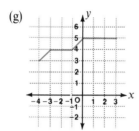

(h)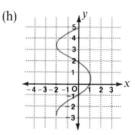

(i)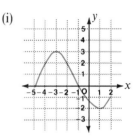

4   • Write the domain and range for each of the following.
    • Which relations represent functions? Which do not?

(a)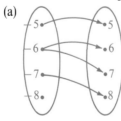

(b)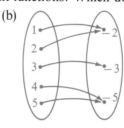

(c)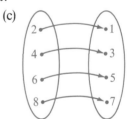

B 5   For the relation given by the ordered pairs, determine which are functions
         and which are not. Give reasons for your answer.
         (a) $(4, 0)$ $(3, 0)$ $(-2, 0)$ $(4, 1)$ $(2, 1)$
         (b) $(1, 3)$ $(6, 8)$ $(5, 7)$ $(4, 6)$ $(0, 2)$
         (c) $(-1, 4)$ $(0, 4)$ $(1, 3)$ $(-1, 5)$ $(2, 2)$
         (d) $(8, 5)$ $(5, 2)$ $(3, 0)$ $(-1, -4)$ $(-3, -6)$

6   A relation is defined by $y^2 = x, \ x \in R$.
     (a) Write the range of the relation.
     (b) Is the relation a function? Why or why not?

7   A function is given by $f : x \longrightarrow 2x + 5, \ x \in R$. Write three other ways of representing the function.

8   For each function, the domain is $\{-2, -1, 0, 3\}$. Write the function values for each of the following.
     (a) $f(x) = 3x + 1$ (b) $H(u) = 1 - 2u$ (c) $f(m) = m^2$

     (d) $g(k) = k^2 - 3$ (e) $k(t) = \dfrac{1}{t}, t \neq 0$ (f) $F(x) = \dfrac{1}{3x - 1}$

9   (a) Draw the graph of the relation defined by $f : x \longrightarrow 3x^2 + 1, \ x \in R$.
     (b) Write the domain and range of the relation.
     (c) Is f a function? Why or why not?

10   (a) Draw the graph of the relation defined by $y = \dfrac{1}{x}, \ x \in R$.
     (b) Write the domain and range of the relation.
     (c) Is the relation a function? Why or why not?

11   (a) Draw the graph of the relation defined by $y^2 - 3 = x, \ x \in R$.
     (b) Write the domain and range of the relation.
     (c) Is the relation a function? Why or why not?

12   Draw the graph of each of the following relations. $x, y \in R$.

     (a) $y = 3x + 2$ (b) $x^2 - 1 = y$ (c) $y = \dfrac{1}{x^2}$

     (d) $f(x) = x(x - 1)$ (e) $h : x \longrightarrow x^2 + 3$ (f) $f : x \longrightarrow x(x - 3)$
     (g) $g(x) = 2x^2 - 3$ (h) $y = 3x - 3, \ -2 \leq x \leq 5$
     (i) $x^2 + y^2 = 25$ (j) $f(x) = 2x^2 + 1, \ 0 \leq x \leq 2$
     (k) $f : x \longrightarrow x(x + 1), \ -1 \leq x \leq 3$

Math Tip

To Leonhard Euler (1707–1783) we owe a lot of the development of mathematics. He used, as a convention, the following symbols.

- i, a complex number ($i^2 = -1$).
- $f(x)$, functional notation
- a, b, c for the sides of $\triangle ABC$

6.3 Function Notation: f(x)

In order to speak a language you must learn the vocabulary. To do mathematics, you also need to learn the vocabulary. Symbols such as $f(x)$ or $g(x)$ are used to represent expressions in the variable x.

$$f(x) = x + 3 \qquad\qquad g(x) = 2x^2 - 3x + 5$$

    Read f at x equals $x + 3$ Read g at x equals $2x^2 - 3x + 5$.

You can evaluate $f(x)$ and $g(x)$ for values of the variable.

If $x = 2$, then
$$f(x) = x + 3$$
$$f(2) = 2 + 3$$
$$= 5$$

If $x = -3$
$$g(x) = 2x^2 - 3x + 5$$
$$g(-3) = 2(-3)^2 - 3(-3) + 5$$
$$= 18 + 9 + 5$$
$$= 32$$

You will find many symbols used in the same way such as $h(x)$, $H(x)$, $K(x)$, and $P(x)$.

Example 1   For the function $f(x) = 3x^2 - 2x + 1$ find

(a) $f(1)$ (b) $f(-1)$ (c) $f\left(\dfrac{1}{2}\right)$

Solution   (a) $f(x) = 3x^2 - 2x + 1$
$$f(1) = 3(1)^2 - 2(1) + 1$$
$$= 3 - 2 + 1$$
$$= 2$$

(b) $f(x) = 3x^2 - 2x + 1$
$$f(-1) = 3(-1)^2 - 2(-1) + 1$$
$$= 3 + 2 + 1$$
$$= 6$$

(c) $f(x) = 3x^2 - 2x + 1$
$$f\left(\frac{1}{2}\right) = 3\left(\frac{1}{2}\right)^2 - 2\left(\frac{1}{2}\right) + 1$$
$$= 3\left(\frac{1}{4}\right) - 1 + 1$$
$$= \frac{3}{4}$$

If two functions are given by $f(x) = 2x^2 - 1$ and $g(x) = 3x - 1$ then you can calculate $f[g(2)]$.

Find $g(2)$ first.
$$g(2) = 3(2) - 1$$
$$= 6 - 1$$
$$= 5$$

Then find $f[g(2)]$
$$f[g(2)] = f(5) \longleftarrow \text{since } g(2) = 5$$
$$= 2(5)^2 - 1$$
$$= 49$$

Example 2   If $h(x) = 2x + 5$ and $k(x) = \frac{1}{2}x^2 + 2$ find

(a) $h[k(4)]$ (b) $h(-3) - k(-2)$ (c) $2h(3) \times k(1)$

Solution   (a) First find $k(4)$.

$$k(x) = \frac{1}{2}x^2 + 2$$

$$k(4) = \frac{1}{2}(4)^2 + 2$$

$$= 8 + 2$$

$$= 10$$

Thus, $h[k(4)] = h(10)$

$$h(x) = 2x + 5$$

$$h(10) = 2(10) + 5$$

$$= 20 + 5$$

$$= 25$$

Thus, $h[k(4)] = 25$.

(b) $h(x) = 2x + 5$

$$h(-3) = 2(-3) + 5$$

$$= -6 + 5$$

$$= -1$$

$$k(x) = \frac{1}{2}x^2 + 2$$

$$k(-2) = \frac{1}{2}(-2)^2 + 2$$

$$= 2 + 2$$

$$= 4$$

Thus,

$$h(-3) - k(-2)$$

$$= -1 - 4$$

$$= -5$$

(c) $h(x) = 2x + 5$

$$h(3) = 2(3) + 5$$

$$= 6 + 5$$

$$h(3) = 11$$

$$2h(3) = 2 \times 11$$

$$= 22$$

$$k(x) = \frac{1}{2}x^2 + 2$$

$$k(1) = \frac{1}{2}(1)^2 + 2$$

$$= \frac{5}{2}$$

$$2h(3) \times k(1)$$

$$= 22 \times \frac{5}{2}$$

$$= 55$$

6.3   Exercise

A 1   If $f(x) = 2x + 5$, find

(a) $f(0)$ (b) $f(-1)$ (c) $f(3)$

2   If $f(x) = 3x^2 - 6x + 5$, find

(a) $f(3)$ (b) $f(-3)$ (c) $f(0)$

3   A function is given by $G(p) = p^2 + 2p$. Find each of the following.

(a) $G(0)$ (b) $G(1)$ (c) $G(2)$

(d) $G(-2)$ (e) $G(3)$ (f) $G\left(\frac{1}{2}\right)$

4   For each function, find the values as shown.

(a) $f: x \longrightarrow 5x - 2$, $f(2), f(-3)$

(b) $g: x \longrightarrow 5 - 2x$, $g(-2), g(-3)$

(c) $F: x \longrightarrow 2x^2 - 1$, $F(-2), F(2)$

B 5   If $H(y) = \dfrac{y^2 - 2}{4}$ find

(a) $H(2)$ (b) $H(0)$ (c) $H(-2)$

6 · Given that $f(s) = s^2 - 3s + 1$, calculate

(a) $f(2)$ (b) $3f(2)$ (c) $-2f(3)$ (d) $\dfrac{f(2)}{2}$ (e) $\dfrac{f(-2)}{-2}$

7 If $f(x) = 2x^2 - 1$ and $g(x) = 3x - 1$, calculate

(a) $g(2)$ (b) $f(2)$ (c) $g[f(2)]$ (d) $f[g(2)]$
(e) $g(-3)$ (f) $f(-3)$ (g) $g[f(-3)]$ (h) $f[g(-3)]$

8 If $g(x) = 3x^2 - 5x$ find

(a) $g(0)$ (b) $g(-3)$ (c) $g(3)$
(d) $g(-3) - g(3)$ (e) $g(-3) + g(3)$ (f) $g(3) - g(-3)$
Find $g(-3), g(3)$. Then find the sum.⏎

9 If $f(x) = 4 - x^2$, $g(x) = 2x^2 - 1$, find

(a) $f(3)$ (b) $g(3)$ (c) $f(3) + g(3)$
(d) $f(-1)$ (e) $g(-1)$ (f) $f(-1) + g(-1)$

(g) $3[f(2) - g(2)]$ (h) $\dfrac{1}{2}[g(-2) - f(2)]$

10 The notation $f^2(x)$ means $f(x) \times f(x)$. If $H(x) = 2x^2 - 3$, then find
(a) $H(3) + H(-3)$ (b) $H^2(-3)$ (c) $H^2(3)$

Use your earlier skills with equations to solve the following problems.

11 If $f(x) = 3x - 8$, find the value of x that makes $f(x)$ equal to
(a) 7   (b) -2 (c) 0

12 If $g(x) = 16 - 3(x - 5)$, find the value of x that makes $g(x)$ equal to
(a) 34   (b) 22   (c) -5

13 A function is given by $g: x \longrightarrow 3x - 1$. Find a value of k so that
(a) $g(k) = 8$ (b) $g(k) = -4$

14 If $f(x) = 3x + 2$ and $g(x) = 2x - 3$, for what value of x is $f(x) = g(x)$?

15 If $H(x) = 2(x - 5) + 3$ and $F(x) = 3(x - 1) - 3$ for what value of x
is $F(x) = H(x)$?

C 16 Use the functions in Question 14 to prove that $f[g(x)] \neq g[f(x)]$ for all x.

17 $f(x) = x + 1$ and $g(x) = 2x^2$. Find a value, k, such that $f[g(k)] = g[f(k)]$.

6.4 Functions: Sketching $y = f(x) + q$, $y = f(x + p)$

The example below demonstrates some of the skills which you will find helpful when investigating the effect of these transformations on a function, f, defined by $y = f(x)$.

$$y = f(x) + a \qquad y = af(x) \qquad y = -f(x)$$
$$y = f(x + a) \qquad y = f(ax) \qquad y = f(-x)$$

To do the following investigations, you must develop your skills in working with graphs, as shown in the following example.

Example
(a) A diagram of the graph of $y = f(x)$ is given. What is the value of $f(2)$, $f(-3)$, $f(0)$?

(b) Draw the graph of the function given by $y = f(x + 1)$.

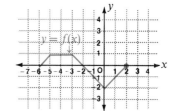

Solution
(a) From the graph,
if $x = 2$, then $f(2) = 0$.
if $x = -3$, then $f(-3) = 1$.
if $x = 0$, then $f(0) = -2$.

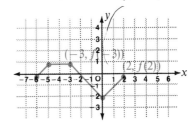

(b) To draw the graph of $y = f(x + 1)$ construct a table of values.

x	-7	-6	-5	-4	-3	-2	-1	0	1	2
$x + 1$	-6	-5	-4	-3	-2	-1	0	1	2	3
$f(x + 1)$	0	1	1	1	0	-1	-2	-1	0	0

If $x = -6$, $x + 1 = -5$,
$f(x + 1) = f(-5)$
$= 1$ Use the value for the given graph.

Use the table of values to draw the graph of $y = f(x + 1)$.

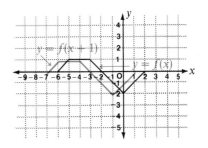

In each of the following investigations of transformations, you will use a graph to determine other function values. The following exercise investigates the skills needed to sketch $y = f(x) + q$ and $y = f(x + p)$.

6.4 Exercise

B Questions 1 to 5 investigate the relationship between $y = f(x)$ and $y = f(x) + q$, q is constant.

1. The graph defined by $y = f(x)$ is shown. On the same set of axes, draw the graphs of

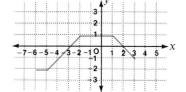

(a) $y = f(x) + 3$ (b) $y = f(x) + 2$
(c) $y = f(x) - 1$ (d) $y = f(x) - 2$

2. Study the graphs you drew in Question 1.
   (a) What is the relationship between the graph of $y = f(x)$ and $y = f(x) + q$, if $q > 0$? If $q < 0$?
   (b) Describe the effect on the graph of $y = f(x) + q$ if q increases. Decreases.
   (c) Write a mapping to relate the graph of $y = f(x)$ and $y = f(x) + q$.
   (d) Why may the mapping in (c) be described as a translation?
   (e) Are there any invariant points of the mapping?

3. Use the graph $y = f(x)$ defined by $f(x) = 2x$. Sketch the graphs of $y = f(x) + 3$, $y = f(x) - 1$.

4. Use the graph of $y = f(x)$ defined by $f(x) = \frac{1}{2}x^2$ to sketch the graphs of $y = f(x) + 4$, $y = f(x) - 2$.

5. Use the graph of $y = f(x)$ defined by $f(x) = 2x + 3$ to sketch the graphs of $y = f(x) + 2$, $y = f(x) - 3$.

Questions 6 to 10 investigate the relationship between $y = f(x)$ and $y = f(x + p)$, p is constant.

6. The graph defined by $y = f(x)$ is shown. On the same set of axes draw the graphs of

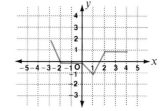

(a) $y = f(x + 3)$ (b) $y = f(x + 2)$
(c) $y = f(x - 1)$ (d) $y = f(x - 2)$

7   Study the graphs you drew in Question 6.
    (a) What is the relationship between the graph of $y = f(x)$ and $y = f(x + p)$ if $p > 0$? If $p < 0$?
    (b) Describe the effect on the graph of $y = f(x + p)$ if p decreases.
    (c) Write a mapping to relate the graph of $y = f(x)$ and $y = f(x + p)$.
    (d) Why may the mapping in (c) be described as a translation?
    (e) Are there any invariant points of the mapping?

8   Use the graph of $y = f(x)$ defined by $f(x) = -3x$ to sketch the graphs of $y = f(x + 3)$, $y = f(x - 1)$.

9   Use the graph of $y = f(x)$ defined by $f(x) = -\frac{1}{2}x^2$ to sketch the graphs of $y = f(x + 4)$, $y = f(x - 2)$.

10 Use the graph of $y = f(x)$ defined by $f(x) = 2x + 1$ to sketch the graphs of $y = f(x - 1)$, $y = f(x - 3)$.

11 Use your results in Questions 1 to 10 to answer the following questions.
    (a) How is the graph of $y = f(x)$ related to the following graphs?

    A: $y = f(x) + q$ B: $y = f(x + p)$ C: $y = f(x + p) + q$

    (b) Use a mapping to relate the graph of $y = f(x)$ to each of A, B, and C above.
    (c) Use the above results to sketch the graph of

    A: $y = x^2 + 4$ B: $y = (x - 2)^2$ C: $y = (x - 2)^2 + 4$

C 12 Draw a sketch of each graph.
    (a) $y = (x - 1)^2 + 3$ (b) $y = (x + 1)^2 - 2$

Problem Solving

A tape is placed snugly around the earth's equator. Of course, if 2 m more of tape are added, the tape will no longer be snug.
Suppose this same tape is placed a uniform distance, d, in centimetres, from the earth's surface. Then which of the following would you agree with?

The distance, d, is
$\begin{cases} \text{A less than 1 cm.} \\ \text{B equal to 1 cm.} \\ \text{C greater than 1 cm.} \end{cases}$

Now, prove your result.

6.5 Sketching $y = af(x)$ and $y = f(bx)$

In the previous section, you investigated the skills needed to sketch graphs $y = f(x) + q$, q a constant and $y = f(x + p)$, p a constant. This was stated simply as;

Given the graph of $y = f(x)$.   A: Draw the graph of $y = f(x) + q$.
                                   B: Draw the graph of $y = f(x + p)$.

In this section, you will investigate the transformation given as follows.

Given the graph of $y = f(x)$.   A: Draw the graph of $y = af(x)$.
                                   B: Draw the graph of $y = f(bx)$.
                                             a, b are constants.

6.5 Exercise

I Sketching $y = af(x)$

B   Questions 1 to 4 investigate the relationship between $y = f(x)$ and $y = af(x)$, a is constant.

1   Use the graph defined by $y = f(x)$ as shown. On the same set of axes, draw the following graphs.

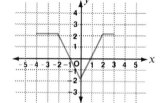

(a) $y = 2f(x)$ (b) $y = 3f(x)$
(c) $y = -2f(x)$ (d) $y = -3f(x)$

2   Study the graphs you drew in Question 1.
     (a) What is the relationship between $y = f(x)$ and $y = af(x)$ if $a > 0$? If $a < 0$?
     (b) Describe the effect of the graph of $y = af(x)$ if

     A: $a > 0$ and a increases   B: $a < 0$ and a decreases.

     (c) Write a mapping to relate the graph of $y = f(x)$ and $y = af(x)$.
     (d) Are there any invariant points of the mapping?

3   Use the graph of $y = f(x)$ defined by $f(x) = 3x$ to sketch the graphs of $y = 2f(x)$, $y = -3f(x)$.

4   Use the graph of $y = f(x)$ defined by $f(x) = x^2$ to sketch the graph of $y = 2f(x)$, $y = -2f(x)$.

II Sketching $y = f(bx)$

Questions 5 to 9 investigate the relationship between $y = f(x)$ and $y = f(bx)$, $b > 0$, b is constant.

5 Use the graph defined by $y = f(x)$ as shown. Draw the graphs of

(a) $y = f(2x)$ (b) $y = f(3x)$

on the same set of axes.

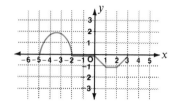

6 Use the graph defined by $y = f(x)$ as shown. Draw the graphs of

(a) $y = f\left(\dfrac{1}{2}x\right)$ (b) $y = f\left(\dfrac{1}{3}x\right)$

on the same set of axes.

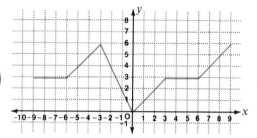

7 Study the graphs you drew in Questions 5 and 6.

(a) What is the relationship between $y = f(x)$ and $y = f(bx)$ if $b > 0$?

(b) Describe the effect on the graph of $y = f(bx)$ if $b > 0$ and b increases; b decreases.

(c) Write a mapping to relate the graph of $y = f(x)$ and $y = f(bx)$.

(d) Are there any invariant points of the mapping?

8 Use the graph of $y = f(x)$ defined by $f(x) = 4x$ to sketch the graphs of $y = f(2x)$, $y = f\left(\dfrac{1}{2}x\right)$.

9 Use the graph of $y = f(x)$ defined by $f(x) = x^2$ to sketch the graph of $y = f(2x)$, $y = f\left(\dfrac{1}{2}x\right)$.

10 Use your results in Questions 1 to 9 to answer the following questions.

(a) How is the graph of $y = f(x)$ related to the following graphs, $b > 0$?

A: $y = af(x)$ B: $y = f(bx)$ C: $y = af(bx)$

(b) Use a mapping to relate the graph of $y = f(x)$ to each of A, B, and C on the previous page.

(c) Use the results in (a) and (b) to sketch the graph of each of the following if $f(x) = x^2$.

$$\text{A: } y = 2f(x) \qquad \text{B: } y = f\left(\frac{1}{2}x\right) \qquad \text{C: } y = 2f\left(\frac{1}{2}x\right)$$

11   Draw a sketch of each graph.
(a) $y = 3x^2$ (b) $y = 2(x + 1)$ (c) $y = -2x^2$ (d) $y = -3(x - 2)$

III   Sketching $y = f(-x)$ and $y = -f(x)$

Questions 12 to 16 investigate the relationship of $y = f(x)$ to $y = f(-x)$ and $y = -f(x)$.

12   The graph defined by $y = f(x)$ is shown. On the same set of axes draw the graphs of
(a) $y = -f(x)$ (b) $y = f(-x)$

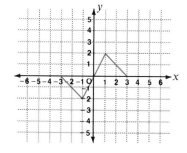

13   Look at the graphs you drew in Question 12.
(a) What is the relationship of $y = f(x)$ to $y = -f(x)$ and to $y = f(-x)$?
(b) Write a mapping to relate the graph of $y = f(x)$ and $y = -f(x)$.
(c) Write a mapping to relate the graph of $y = f(x)$ and $y = f(-x)$.
(d) Are there any invariant points of the mapping?

14   Use the graph of $y = f(x)$ defined by $f(x) = x^2$ to sketch the graphs of $y = -f(x)$ and $y = f(-x)$.

15   Use the graph of $y = f(x)$ defined by $f(x) = 2x$ to sketch the graphs of $y = -f(x)$ and $y = f(-x)$.

16   Sketch the graph of $f(-x)$ and of $-f(x)$ for each function defined by
(a) $f(x) = -x^2$ (b) $f(x) = 3x$ (c) $f(x) = x + 1$

(d) $f(x) = -x + 2$ (e) $f(x) = 3x^2$ (f) $f(x) = -\frac{1}{2}x^2$

IV Sketching $y = af(x + b) + c$

A combination of the methods used in I, II, and III can be used to sketch a graph of a function defined by $y = af(x + b) + c$. For example, if you graph the function $y = x^2$ then you can use a combination of the methods used in I, II, and III to graph

$$y = -\frac{1}{2}(x - 3)^2 + 4.$$

A: Sketch the graph of the fundamental or basic curve

$y = x^2$.

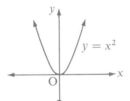

B: Apply the methods used in II, to sketch the curve given by

$y = \frac{1}{2}x^2$.

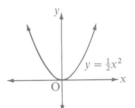

C: Apply the methods used in III, to sketch the curve given by

$y = -\frac{1}{2}x^2$.

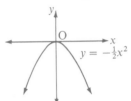

D: Apply the methods used in I, where applicable, to sketch the curve given by

$$y = -\frac{1}{2}(x - 3)^2.$$

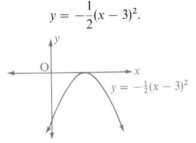

E: Apply the methods used in I again, where applicable, to sketch the curve given by

$$y = -\frac{1}{2}(x - 3)^2 + 4$$

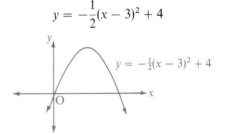

17 Sketch the graphs of each of the following on the same set of axes.
(a) $y = x^2$ (b) $y = 3x^2$ (c) $y = -3x^2$
(d) $y = 3(x - 1)^2$ (e) $y = 3(x + 2)^2$
(f) $y = -3(x - 1)^2$ (g) $y = 3(x + 2)^2 - 4$

C 18 Sketch the graph of each of the following.

(a) $y = 2(x - 1)^2 + 1$ (b) $y = -3(x + 1)^2 - \dfrac{1}{2}$

6.6 Properties of Functions

One-To-One Relations

If each image of a relation has only one pre-image, and if each pre-image of the relation has only one image, then the relation is said to be a one-to-one relation. The diagram at right illustrates a one-to-one relation. Algebraically, for a one-to-one relation you can write:

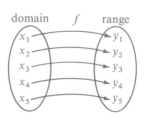

if $x_1 \neq x_2$, then $f(x_1) \neq f(x_2)$, or $y_1 \neq y_2$.

To test whether a function is one-to-one, draw a line parallel to the x-axis. If the line intersects the graph of the function in at most one point, then the function is one-to-one.

The function shown is one-to-one.   The function shown is not one-to-one.

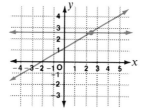   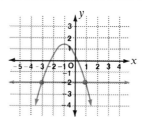

The above is often referred to as the **horizontal line test**.

Example   Which of the following is one-to-one?

(a) $f(x) = x^2 - 3x + 2$ (b) $g(x) = 2x^3$

Solution   Draw a graph.

(a) 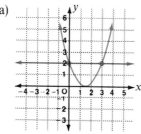   (b)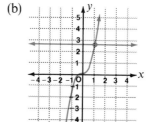

A horizontal line meets the graph in 2 points. The function is not one-to-one.

A horizontal line meets the graph in 1 point. The function is one-to-one.

You can find values for f algebraically to show that the relation in Example (a) is not one-to-one.

$$f(1) = (1)^2 - 3(1) + 2 \qquad f(2) = 2^2 - 3(2) + 2$$
$$= 0 \qquad\qquad\qquad = 0$$

f is not one-to-one since $x_1 \neq x_2$, but $f(x_1) = f(x_2)$.

One-To-Many Relations
When a relation has a number of images with the same pre-image, then the relation is said to be a one-to-many relation. The diagram at right illustrates a one-to-many relation.

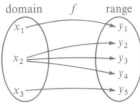

Many-To-One Relations
When a relation has a number of pre-images with the same image, then the relation is said to be a many-to-one relation. The diagram at right illustrates a many-to-one relation.

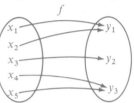

6.6 Exercise

A 1 Describe each of the following relations as many-to-one, one-to-many, or one-to-one.

(a)

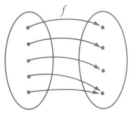

(b)

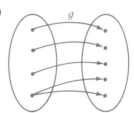

(c)

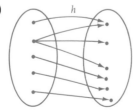

(d)

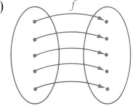

2 The graphs of various relations are shown. Which are one-to-one?

(a)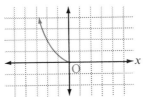

(b)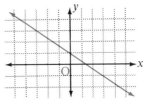

(c)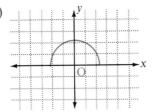

(d)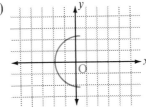

3 Which of the following relations are functions? Give reasons for your answer.
- f is a many-to-one relation.
- g is a one-to-many relation.
- h is a one-to-one relation.

4 A relation is defined by $f(x) = x^2 + x - 6$. Calculate the following.
(a) $f(2)$ (b) $f(-3)$
(c) Why is the relation not one-to-one?

5 The defining equations for various relations are given. Which of them are one-to-one?

(a) $f(x) = x + 2$ (b) $f(x) = 2x$ (c) $f(x) = 4 - x$

(d) $f(x) = 2x^2$ (e) $f(x) = (x - 1)^2$ (f) $f(x) = \dfrac{2}{x}$

(g) $f(x) = 2\sqrt{x}$ (h) $f(x) = \dfrac{1}{x^2}, x > 0$

Calculator Tip

Very often different strategies are used to solve a problem or obtain an answer. For example, to find the value of the constant e, the expression E is used.

$$E = \left(1 + \frac{1}{n}\right)^n$$

As n increases, the value of E approaches the value of e. If $e = 2.718\ 281$ (to 6 decimal places), what value of n is needed? Use your calculator.

6.7 Special Functions

The following diagrams will help you understand the vocabulary of functions.

A function f is said to be **increasing** over an interval if, for any $x_1 < x_2$ in the interval, $f(x_1) < f(x_2)$.

A function f is said to be **decreasing** over an interval if, for any $x_1 < x_2$ in the interval, $f(x_1) > f(x_2)$.

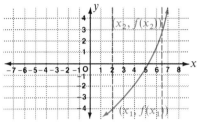

$$x_1 < x_2 \rightarrow f(x_1) < f(x_2)$$
f is an increasing function.

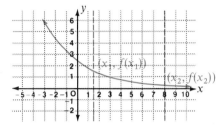

$$x_1 < x_2 \rightarrow f(x_1) > f(x_2)$$
f is a decreasing function.

A function that neither increases nor decreases for different values of the domain is a **constant** function.

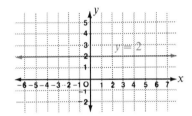

$$x_1 < x_2 \rightarrow f(x_1) = f(x_2)$$
f is a constant function.

A function is said to be **piecewise linear** if it is linear for certain intervals, but the equation of the function changes within each interval. Thus, the function

$$f : x \rightarrow \begin{cases} x + 1, & 0 \le x \le 3 \\ -x + 7, & 3 < x \le 7 \\ 0, & 7 < x \le 10 \end{cases}$$

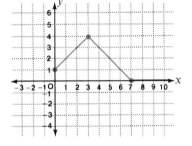

is a piecewise linear function.

To determine whether a function is increasing, decreasing, or constant for $x_1 < x_2$ calculate $f(x_1) - f(x_2)$.

- If $f(x_1) - f(x_2)$ is positive, f is *decreasing*.
- If $f(x_1) - f(x_2)$ is negative, f is *increasing*.
- If $f(x_1) - f(x_2)$ is zero, f is *constant*.

Example   For the interval $2 \leq x \leq 4$, determine whether the function f is increasing or decreasing. $f(x) = x^2 - 3x + 2$

Solution   Choose $x_1 < x_2$ in the interval $(x_1 \neq x_2)$.

$$\begin{aligned} f(x_1) - f(x_2) &= [(x_1)^2 - 3x_1 + 2] - [(x_2)^2 - 3x_2 + 2] \\ &= (x_1)^2 - (x_2)^2 - 3x_1 + 3x_2 \\ &= (x_1 - x_2)(x_1 + x_2) - 3(x_1 - x_2) \\ &= (x_1 - x_2)(x_1 + x_2 - 3) \end{aligned}$$

$$\begin{bmatrix} \text{For } 2 \leq x \leq 4, x_1 \text{ and } x_2 \geq 2. \\ \text{Thus } x_1 + x_2 \geq 4 \\ \text{and thus } x_1 + x_2 - 3 \geq 0. \end{bmatrix} \quad \textcircled{1}$$

$$\begin{bmatrix} \text{Since } x_1 < x_2, x_1 - x_2 < 0. \end{bmatrix} \quad \textcircled{2}$$

From ① and ② you have a negative expression multiplied by a positive expression. The product is thus negative, and $f(x_1) - f(x_2) < 0$. Since $f(x_1) - f(x_2) < 0$, then f is increasing in the interval.

6.7 Exercise

A 1   Which of the following are the graphs of

A: increasing functions?   B: decreasing functions?

(a) 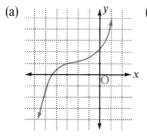   (b) 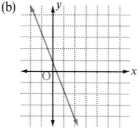   (c)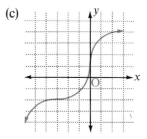

2   Over which interval is the graph
(a) increasing?
(b) decreasing?
(c) neither of the above?

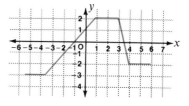

3   For which intervals are the graphs   A: increasing?   B: decreasing?
    (a) 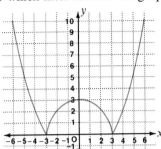   (b)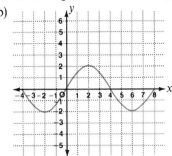

4   A function is defined by $y = x^2 - 4x + 3$.
    (a) What is its domain? its range?
    (b) What are its intercepts?
    (c) Sketch its graph.
    (d) Over which interval(s) is the graph increasing?
    (e) Over which interval(s) is the graph decreasing?

5   Over which interval(s) is the graph
    (a) decreasing?
    (b) increasing?
    (c) constant?

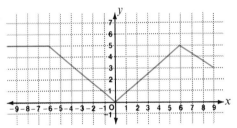

B 6   For each of the following functions,
    • draw its graph.
    • identify intervals for which the function is decreasing or increasing.
    (a) $y = 2x - 3$ (b) $y = 3x^2$ (c) $y = 2 - x^2$
    (d) $y = \sqrt{x}$ (e) $y = \sqrt{x^2 - 1}$ (f) $y = \dfrac{1}{x}$

7   (a) Prove that for all x, the function f, defined by $f(x) = \dfrac{1}{2 - x}, x \geq 3$ is
        increasing.
    (b) Prove that the function given by $f(x) = \dfrac{2}{x + 1}, x > 0$ is a decreasing
        function.

8   For each of the following prove that the function is an increasing function.
    Do not use a graph to show your work.
    (a) $f(x) = 2x - 1$ (b) $g(x) = 3x^2, \quad x \geq 0$ (c) $h(x) = x^2 - 2x, \quad x \geq 1$
    (d) $f(x) = \dfrac{1}{1 - 2x}, \quad x \geq 2$ (e) $h(x) = 3 - (x - 1)^2, \quad x \leq 1$

9   For each of the following prove that the function is a decreasing function.
    Do not use a graph to show your work.
    (a) $f(x) = 3 - x$ (b) $g(x) = 2x^2, \quad x \leq 0$ (c) $h(x) = 2x^2 - 8x, \quad x \leq 2$
    (d) $f(x) = \dfrac{1}{1 + x}, \quad x \geq 0$ (e) $g(x) = 5 + 4x + x^2, \quad x \leq -2$

10 A relation is defined by $y = 3 - (x - 1)^2$.
    (a) Sketch the graph.   (b) List the properties of the graph.

11 For each of the following relations
    • draw the graph.
    • list the properties observed from the graph.
    (a) $y = 3x - 1$ (b) $y = 2 - x$ (c) $y = 4 - x^2$
    (d) $y = x(x - 1)$ (e) $y = 4x - x^2$ (f) $y = x^2 + 3x$

12 A function is defined by $f(x) = 3x + 1$.
    (a) Calculate $f(x + 3) - f(x)$.
    (b) Use your answer in (a). What change occurs in $f(x)$ when x increases by 3?

13 A function is defined by $f(x) = x^2 - 9$.
    (a) Calculate $f(x + 1) - f(x)$.
    (b) Use your answer in (a). What change occurs in $f(x)$ when x increases by 1?

14 (a) For $f(x) = 5x + 1$, calculate $f(x + 2) - f(x)$.
    (b) For $g(x) = 3x + 1$, calculate $g(x + 2) - g(x)$.
    (c) Which function, f or g, has the greater change when x increases by 2 and $2 \leq x \leq 5$?

15 (a) If $f(x) = 3x^2 - 2$, calculate $f(x + 1) - f(x)$.
    (b) If $g(x) = 2x^2 - 2$, calculate $g(x + 1) - g(x)$.
    (c) Which function f or g has the greater change when x increases by 1 and $1 \leq x \leq 3$?

C 16 For each interval which function has the greater change when x increases by 1?
    (a) $f(x) = x^2 - 1, \quad g(x) = x - 1, \quad 2 \leq x \leq 5$
    (b) $f(x) = \dfrac{1}{x}, \quad g(x) = \dfrac{1}{2x}, \quad 1 \leq x \leq 3$
    (c) $f(x) = 4x - 2x^2, \quad g(x) = 2 + 2x - x^2, \quad -2 \leq x \leq 0$.

6.8 Inverse of a Function

Three arrow diagrams are drawn. Each represents a function.

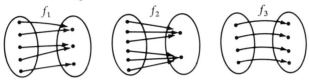

What if the arrows were reversed? Do the arrow diagrams then represent functions?
If the arrows are reversed, not all of them produce a function.

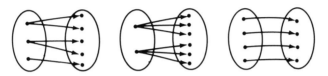

In the mapping diagrams representing the relations $f_1, f_2,$ and f_3, the relations represented by reversing the arrows are called **inverse relations**.

The diagram illustrates the relationship in general.

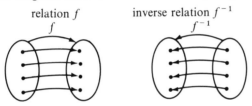

relation f inverse relation f^{-1}

From the above diagram, $f(a) = b$ and $f^{-1}(b) = a$.

If the domain of f is D and has range R then f^{-1} has domain R and range D.

In general, the **inverse** of a relation f is the relation f^{-1} obtained by interchanging the components of each ordered pair. (x, y) becomes (y, x).

$$f^{-1} \text{ is read } inverse \text{ } of \text{ } f.$$
$$f^{-1}(x) \text{ is read } f \text{ } inverse \text{ } of \text{ } x.$$

It is important to note that f^{-1} does not mean $\dfrac{1}{f}$, and $f^{-1}(x)$ does not mean $\dfrac{1}{f(x)}$.

Notice the mapping for function f_3 is one-to-one. When the arrows are reversed, another function is obtained. Thus, if f is a *one-to-one function*, then f^{-1} is a *function*. Thus, if you wish the inverse of a function to be a function also, the domain of the function must be restricted, if necessary, to make the function a one-to-one function.

An important property is shown when you draw the graph of a function f and its inverse f^{-1}.

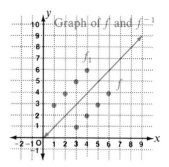

A function f is given by the ordered pairs $(3, 1), (4, 2), (5, 3)$, and $(6, 4)$. A graph is drawn. The diagram at the right shows that the graphs of f and f^{-1} are symmetrical with respect to the line $y = x$.

Thus, the graph of the inverse, f^{-1}, of a function, f, is the reflection of the graph of f through the line $y = x$. This principle will help you to draw the graph of an inverse function f^{-1}.

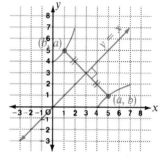

Example A relation f is defined by $y = 3x - 2$. Draw the graph of f and f^{-1}.

Solution Use a table of values.

x	y
0	-2
1	1
2	4

$P(0, -2)$
$Q(1, 1)$
$R(2, 4)$

To sketch the graph of f^{-1}, find the reflection of f in the line $y = x$.
$P(0, -2) \rightarrow P'(-2, 0)$
$Q(1, 1) \;\; \rightarrow Q'(1, 1)$
$R(2, 4) \;\; \rightarrow R'(4, 2)$

Graph of f Graph of f^{-1}

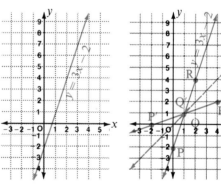

6.8 Exercise

A 1 Each point is reflected in the line given by $y = x$. Find the co-ordinates of the image.
(a) $(4, 1)$ (b) $(-3, 2)$ (c) $(-4, -5)$
(d) $(6, -3)$ (e) $(0, 4)$ (f) $(-5, 0)$

2   A relation k is given by $k = \{(-3, 2), (0, 1), (2, 1), (3, 6), (7, 7)\}$.
   (a) Graph k. Is it a function?
   (b) Graph k^{-1}. Is it a function?
   (c) Is the inverse of a function necessarily a function? Why or why not?

3   For each of the following
   • Draw its graph and the graph of its inverse.
   • Which inverses are functions?
   (a) $f = \{(-2, 1), (-1, 2), (0, 3), (1, 4), (2, 5)\}$
   (b) $g = \{(-1, 4), (-2, 4), (-3, 4), (-4, 4)\}$
   (c) $h = \{(2, 5), (2, 4), (3, 2), (3, 1)\}$
   (d) $k = \{(2, 5), (-1, 5), (-1, 4), (2, -4)\}$

B 4   A relation is shown in each of the following.

   A: What is the domain and range?   B: Copy the original graph.

   C: Draw the graph of its inverse. What is the domain and range?

(a)   (b)   (c)

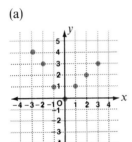   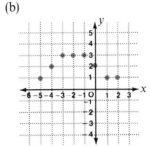   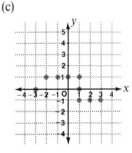

5   A: Construct the graph of the inverse relation, f^{-1}, of each relation, f.
   B: List the domain and range for f and f^{-1} in each of the following.
   C: Which of the relations, f, and its inverse, f^{-1} are functions?

(a)   (b)   (c)

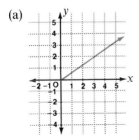   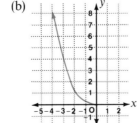   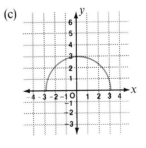

6   For each relation, f,   A: Draw its inverse, f^{-1}.
                             B: Which of f and f^{-1} are functions?
                             C: List the domain and range of each f and f^{-1}.

(a) 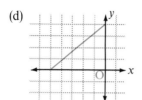   (b) 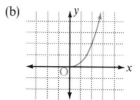   (c)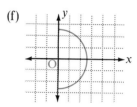

(d) 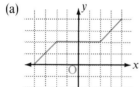   (e) 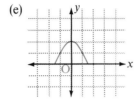   (f)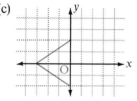

7   Which of the following relations have an inverse that is a function?

(a) 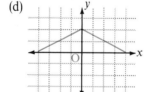   (b) 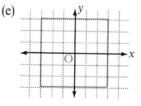   (c)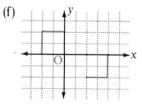

(d) 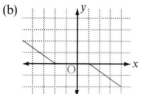   (e)   (f)

8   Which of the following functions have an inverse that is also a function?
(a) $f: x \rightarrow 2x - 3$ (b) $g: x \rightarrow 3x + 2$ (c) $h: x \rightarrow 2x^2$ (d) $f: x \rightarrow 3x^2$

(e) How is the domain and range of a one-to-one function, f, related to
the domain and range of its inverse?

9   Which of the following points is not on the inverse of $y = x^2 - 3$?
A(1, 2)   B(-2, 1)   C(6, 4)

10 Which of the following points is not on the inverse of $y = 2x - 3$?
A(-7, -2)   B(1, -1)   C(-3, 0)

6.9 Equations for f^{-1}

In the previous section, you drew the graph of the inverse relation f^{-1} and examined some of its properties. To find the defining equation of the inverse relation you use your earlier algebraic skills.

A function, f, is defined as $f: x \rightarrow 3x - 2$.
You can also write $y = 3x - 2$, and any ordered pair of the function, f, is given by (x, y).

To find the defining equation of f^{-1}, you interchange the components.

Defining equation, f $\begin{pmatrix} \text{Compare the positions} \\ \text{of the variables.} \end{pmatrix}$ Defining equation, f^{-1}
(x, y) (y, x)
$y = 3x - 2$ $x = 3y - 2$

To express f^{-1} in mapping notation you need to solve the equation for y.

$$x = 3y - 2 \quad \text{or} \quad 3y - 2 = x$$
$$3y = x + 2$$
$$y = \frac{x + 2}{3} \qquad \text{Thus, } f^{-1}: x \rightarrow \frac{x + 2}{3}.$$

The above skills are applied in the following example.

Example   A function f is defined by $y = x^2 - 1$, $x \geq 0$. ⟵ With this restriction the function f is one-to-one.

(a) Sketch the graph of f^{-1}.
(b) Find the defining equation of f^{-1}.

Solution   (a) To draw the graph of f^{-1},   Find the reflection of f in the
first draw the graph of f.   reflection line $y = x$.

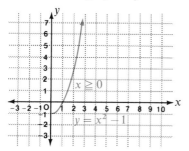   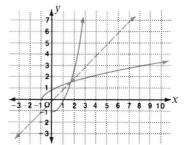

(b) To find the defining equation, solve $y = x^2 - 1$ for x.
$$x^2 - 1 = y, \qquad x \geq 0$$
$$x^2 = y + 1, \quad x \geq 0$$
$$x = \sqrt{y + 1}$$
The defining equation for f^{-1} is given by $y = \sqrt{x + 1}$.

6.9 Exercise

A 1 A relation is given by $f: x \rightarrow 2x + 3$.
(a) Draw the graph of the inverse relation.
(b) What is the equation for f? For f^{-1}?
(c) Express f^{-1} in mapping notation.

2 A relation f is defined by $y = 2x - 1$. Which of the following is the equation of its inverse f^{-1}?

(a) $x = \dfrac{y + 1}{2}$ (b) $x = 2y - 1$ (c) $y = \dfrac{x - 1}{2}$

B 3 A relation is given by $f: x \rightarrow 2x^2 - 1$, $x \geq 0$.
(a) Draw the graph of its inverse f^{-1}.
(b) Write the defining equation of f.
(c) Write the equation of f^{-1}.

4 If $y = x^2 - 3$ defines the relation f, which of the following defines the inverse relation f^{-1}?

(a) $x = y^2 - 3$ (b) $x = \pm\sqrt{y + 3}$ (c) $x = \sqrt{y + 3}$

5 For each of the following, write the equation of f^{-1}. What is the domain and range?

(a) $f(x) = 3 - 2x$ (b) $f(x) = 3x^2, \quad x \geq 0$

(c) $f(x) = \dfrac{1}{2x}$ (d) $f(x) = \dfrac{1}{2}x^3$

6 Write the equation of the inverse for each of the following. What are the intercepts of each relation and its inverse?

(a) $f: x \rightarrow \dfrac{1}{2}(x - 4)$ (b) $g: x \rightarrow 8 - 2x^3$

(c) $h: x \rightarrow \sqrt{2x - 1}$ (d) $f: x \rightarrow 1 - \dfrac{1}{x}$

7 A function is given by $f(x) = x^2 - 3$, $x \geq 0$.
(a) Construct the graph of f and f^{-1}.
(b) What are the intercepts of the graph of f and f^{-1}?
(c) What are the domains and ranges of f and f^{-1}?
(d) Express f^{-1} in function notation.

8   The function, $f: x \rightarrow \sqrt{x - 2}$ is given.
      (a) Construct a graph of f.
      (b) Use the graph in (a) to construct the graph of f^{-1}.
      (c) Compare the properties of f and f^{-1}.

9   For each of the following,   • write the equation of f^{-1}.
                                       • write the domain and range of f^{-1}.
      (a) $y = 3x - 2$ (b) $y = \sqrt{2x - 1}$ (c) $y = x^2 - 3, \quad x \geq 0$
      (d) $y = 2 - x^2, \quad x \leq 0$ (e) $y = \sqrt{9 - x^2}, \quad x \geq 0$ (f) $y = \dfrac{1 - x}{x}$

10   For each of the following,
      • impose restrictions on the variable so that the function is one-to-one.
      • express the defining equation for f^{-1} in the form in which f is given.
      (a) $f: x \rightarrow 2x - 7$ (b) $y = \dfrac{3x - 2}{4}$ (c) $f(x) = 3(x - 2)$
      (d) $f: x \rightarrow x^2$ (e) $y = x^3$ (f) $y = \sqrt{x}$
      (g) $f(x) = (x - 1)^2$ (h) $y = 2x^2 - 3$
      (i) $f: x \rightarrow 2\sqrt{x - 3}, \quad x \geq 3$ (j) $f: x \rightarrow 4(x - 3)^2 + 2$

C 11   For each of the following relations, f, what restrictions are needed so that each represents a one-to-one function?
      (a) $y = 3x^2 - 2$ (b) $y = 3 - 2x^2$
      (c) $x^2 + y^2 = 16$ (d) $4x^2 + 9y^2 = 16$

12   (a) Draw the graph of each f in the previous question.
      (b) Use each graph in (a) to draw the graph of f^{-1}.

Computer Tip

A computer is an invaluable tool in helping scientists construct a table of values for various functions. Use each program below. Choose your own values of A, B, and C. What can you tell about each graph from the table of values?

```
10 INPUT A,B,C
20 FOR X = -20 TO 20
30 LET Y = A*X↑2 + B*X + C
40 PRINT "VALUE OF X", X
50 PRINT "VALUE OF Y", Y
60 NEXT X
70 END
```

• Modify the program to print the values of x and y in increments of 0.1 from -10 to 10.
• Write a program for $y = ax^3 + bx^2 + cx + d$.

Practice and Problems: A Chapter Review

An important step for problem-solving is to decide which skills to use. For this reason, these questions are not placed in any special order. When you have finished the review, you might try the *Test for Practice* that follows.

1 A relation is given by
$$y = 2x + 3, \quad x \in \{-2, -1, 0, 1, 2\}.$$
(a) Write the ordered pairs for the relation.
(b) What is the range?

2 Write the function values for each of the following. $x \in \{-1, 0, 1, 2\}$.
(a) $f(x) = 6x - 5$ (b) $f(x) = x^2 + 1$ (c) $f(x) = \dfrac{1}{5x + 2}$

3 Given that $f(p) = p^2 + 5p - 3$, calculate
(a) $f(-3)$ (b) $[f(3)]^2$ (c) $-3f(0)$ (d) $\dfrac{[f(-1)]^2}{2}$

4 If $g(x) = 3x^2 + 2$ and $f(x) = x + 1$, calculate
(a) $g[f(-2)]$ (b) $f[g(2)]$ (c) $g[f(0)]$

5 (a) How is the graph of $y = f(x)$ related to each of the following graphs?
$$y = f(x) + q \qquad y = f(x + p)$$
(b) Illustrate your answer in (a) by using the graph given by $y = x^2$.

6 Two relations are given by $f(x) = 3x - 2$ and $g(x) = 2x^2 + 3x$.
(a) Find expressions for $f[g(x)]$ and $g[f(x)]$.
(b) Calculate $f[g(-1)]$ and $g[f(0)]$.

7 If $f : x \to \dfrac{2x + 1}{3}$ and $g : x \to \dfrac{x - 1}{2}$, determine m so that $f(m) = g(m)$.

8 Find the equation of the inverse for each of the following, $a \neq 0$.
(a) $f(x) = \dfrac{a}{x}$ (b) $f(x) = \dfrac{1}{x + a}$ (c) $f(x) = \dfrac{x + a}{x}$ (d) $f(x) = \dfrac{x}{x + a}$

Test for Practice

Try this test. Each *Test for Practice* is based on the mathematics you have learned in this chapter. Try this test later in the year as a review. Keep a record of those questions that you were not successful with, find out how to answer them, and review them periodically.

1   Refer to the relation shown. Write
    (a) the domain   (b) the range

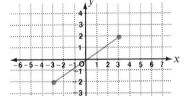

2   A relation is given by $y^2 = 2x$, $x \in R$.
    (a) Write the range of the relation.
    (b) Is the relation a function?
        Give reasons for your answer.

3   A function is defined by $g(y) = y^2 - 3y$. Calculate
    (a) $g(0)$ (b) $g(-3)$ (c) $g\left(\dfrac{1}{2}\right)$ (d) $g\left(-\dfrac{2}{3}\right)$

4   $G(x) = 2x^2 - 3$ and $F(x) = 2x + 1$. Find the value of $G[F(-2)]$, $F[G(-2)]$.

5   A function $y = f(x)$ is given by $f(x) = x^2$. Sketch the graph of
    (a) $y = f(x + 2)$ (b) $y = f(x - 2)$

6   (a) How is the graph of $y = f(x)$ related to the graph of $y = f(2x)$ and
        $y = 2f(x)$?
    (b) Illustrate your answer in (a) by using the graph of $y = x^2$.

7   Refer to the graph given in
    the diagram. Sketch the graph
    of each of the following.
    (a) $y = f(x) + 2$ (b) $y = f(x) - 2$
    (c) $y = f(2x)$ (d) $y = 2f(x)$
    (e) $y = -f(x)$ (f) $y = -f(x) + 3$

8   Use an example to illustrate the meaning of each of the following terms.
    (a) constant function   (b) increasing function   (c) one-to-one function

9   (a) Find the equation of f^{-1} if $f(x) = 2x^2 + 3$.
    (b) What is the domain and range of f^{-1}?

10 Show that the function given by $2f(x) = 3 - \dfrac{2}{x}$ is an increasing function
    for $x > 0$.

Maintaining Skills: Solving Equations

To solve problems about ratio, we need to solve equations and proportions. Solve each of the following.

1   Find the missing term for each of the following.
   (a) $5:x = 7:3$ (b) $45:25 = 9:x$ (c) $15:y = 3:2$
   (d) $2:3 = k:45$ (e) $s:3 = 24:18$ (f) $4:8 = y:10$
   (g) $3:x = 5:8$ (h) $8:4 = 5:x$

2   Solve for a and b.
   (a) $2:3:a = 14:b:49$ (b) $a:2:6 = 6:18:b$
   (c) $4:a:30 = b:3:5$ (d) $20:a:b = 4:3:7$

3   Solve each of the following.
   (a) $\dfrac{x+2}{5} = \dfrac{4-x}{7}$ (b) $\dfrac{x-1}{3} = \dfrac{5x-1}{5}$ (c) $\dfrac{8-x}{5} = \dfrac{x+16}{10}$

   (d) $\dfrac{x+7}{x+17} = \dfrac{-3}{7}$ (e) $\dfrac{3-x}{2} = \dfrac{x+12}{4}$ (f) $\dfrac{x+3}{x-3} = \dfrac{7}{6}$

4   Solve for m and n.
   (a) $6:(m+n):12 = 2:5:m$ (b) $4:2:1 = (m+3):(n+2):1$
   (c) $(m+n):3:8 = 2:6:m$

5   Solve for a and b.   (a) $\dfrac{2}{a} = \dfrac{b}{12} = \dfrac{7}{21}$ (b) $\dfrac{2a}{12} = \dfrac{3b}{1} = \dfrac{7}{3}$

6   Solve for a, b, and c, if $\dfrac{a}{6} = \dfrac{b}{2} = \dfrac{c+1}{3} = 3.$

7   Solve for m and n. $\dfrac{m+n}{3n+2} = \dfrac{2m}{2n+3} = \dfrac{4m-1}{5+4n}$

Math Tip

How is the graph of $y = f(x)$ related to each of the following graphs, where a, b, p, and q are constants?

$$y = f(x+p) \qquad y = af(x) \qquad y = -f(x)$$
$$y = f(x+q) \qquad y = f(bx) \qquad y = f(-x)$$

---

7 Quadratic Functions and Their Applications

skills with graphing, applying transformational techniques, sketching graphs, writing defining equations, method of completing the square, formulas and quadratic functions, working with maximum and minimum, inverses and regions, solving problems, applications, strategies and problem-solving

Introduction

Earlier you studied the linear function $y = mx + b$ and its properties. However, many functions are not linear in nature. For example, the path of a motor cycle leap or the shape of the arches of many bridges are not linear in nature. They are examples of curves represented by quadratic functions. The general form of the equation is $y = ax^2 + bx + c, a \neq 0$.
    └ second degree

Equations involving the variable in the second degree occur in many branches of science and also in economics, as shown by the following.

interest	energy	free fall in space	orbits of space probes
$I = P(1 + i)^n$	$E = mc^2$	$s = ut + \dfrac{1}{2}gt^2$	$y = ax^2$

To study the quadratic function you may now apply your earlier mathematical skills, such as analytic geometry and transformations.

The concepts and skills relating to the quadratic function occur frequently in your study of mathematics.

7.1 Quadratic Functions and Their Graphs

When an object is dropped from a building or when a parachutist jumps from a plane, the distance fallen, in metres, and the length of time, in seconds, are related mathematically.

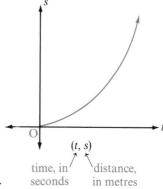

If measurements are made and the results plotted, a graph, showing the relationship, is drawn. The relationship shown in the graph is **non-linear**, and is given in general by

$$f : x \rightarrow ax^2 + bx + c, \quad a \neq 0, \quad a, b, c \in R.$$

The above function is a **quadratic function** (*quadratus* is Latin for "square").

A table of values can be used to draw the graph of a quadratic function, as shown in Example 1. In this example, $a = 1$, $b = 0$ and $c = 0$.

Example 1   A function, f, is given by $f : x \rightarrow x^2$, $x \in R$.

Draw the graph of f for $-3 \leq x \leq 3$.

Solution   Choose selected points.

x	$f(x) = x^2$
-3	9
-2	4
-1	1
0	0
1	1
2	4
3	9

From the table of values, the points are plotted. A smooth curve is drawn through the points.

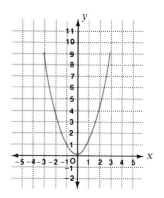

From the above graph of f, note the following:

domain   The domain is $-3 \leq x \leq 3$.

range   The range is $0 \leq y \leq 9$. If the domain for f was $x \in R$, then the range would be $0 \leq y$, $y \in R$.

axis of symmetry   For every point $A(a, b)$ on the curve there is a corresponding point $A'(-a, b)$. The equation $y = (-x)^2$ defines the same curve as $y = x^2$. Thus the graph of f is a reflection of itself in the y-axis. The y-axis is the **axis of symmetry** of the graph of f.

vertex The point $(0, 0)$ shows a **minimum point**. The point $O(0, 0)$ is called a **vertex**. Thus, function f is said to have a **minimum value** since the minimum value of all the ordinates, y, is 0.

The curve in Example 1 is called a **parabola**. The vertex is a minimum point and the curve **opens upwards**.

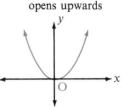
opens upwards

The parabola has a minimum point.

Example 2   (a) Draw a graph of g, defined by $y = -x^2 + 6x - 5$, $-1 \leqq x \leqq 7$.

(b) Write the domain, range, co-ordinates of the vertex and equation of the axis of symmetry.

Solution   Choose selected points.

x	$g(x)$
-1	-12
0	-5
1	0
2	3
3	4
4	3
5	0
6	-5
7	-12

From the table of values, the points are plotted. A smooth curve is drawn through the points.

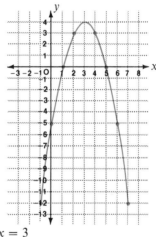

From the graph

domain: $\{x \mid -1 \leqq x \leqq 7\}$
range: $\{y \mid -12 \leqq y \leqq 4\}$
co-ordinates of vertex: $(3, 4)$
equation of axis of symmetry: $x = 3$

From the above graph, notice that for all x the **maximum value** of the ordinate y is 4. Since $y \leqq 4$ for all y then the graph of g has a **maximum point**. The maximum value of g is 4.

The vertex of the previous graph of a quadratic function is a maximum point, and the graph **opens downwards**.

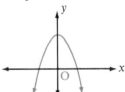
opens downwards

The parabola has a maximum point.

Zeroes of a Function   The zeroes of a quadratic function are the values of x which make the quadratic function zero. These values of x are called the **x-intercepts** of the graph and occur where the graph crosses the x-axis.

In Example 2, the graph crosses the x-axis at the points $(1, 0)$ and $(5, 0)$. Thus, the zeroes of the function are $x = 1$ and $x = 5$ since g is zero for these values of x. You can also say that the x-intercepts of g are 1 and 5.

7.1 Exercise

A Throughout the exercise, the domain of each quadratic function is R unless indicated otherwise.

1 Which of the following define a quadratic function? Give reasons for your answer.

(a) $f: x \rightarrow 3x^2$

(b) $g: x \rightarrow 2x^3 - 5$

(c) $h: x \rightarrow 2x^2 - x + 1$

(d) $F: x \rightarrow 3x - \dfrac{1}{x}$

2 A graph of a quadratic function is shown.

(a) What is the domain? range?

(b) What are the co-ordinates of the vertex?

(c) Write the equation of the axis of symmetry.

(d) What are the zeroes of the function, g?

(e) What are the x-intercepts of the graph?

(f) Does the curve have a maximum or minimum point?

(g) Does the curve open upwards or downwards?

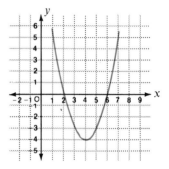

3 For each of the following, write the domain, the range, the co-ordinates of the vertex, the equation of the axis of symmetry, and the maximum or minimum value.

(a)

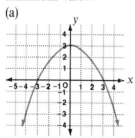

(b)

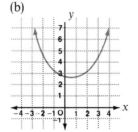

(c)

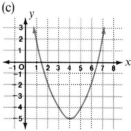

(d)

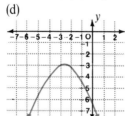

(e)

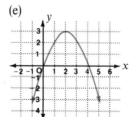

(f)

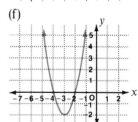

4 Express the following quadratic functions in the form $y = ax^2 + bx + c$.

(a) $y = 3(x - 1)^2$

(b) $y = 2(x + 1)^2$

(c) $y = -2(x - 3)^2 - \dfrac{4}{3}$

(d) $y = \dfrac{1}{2}(x - 4)^2 + 5$

5   For each equation, the co-ordinates of two points are given. Which points satisfy the equation?

		A	B
(a)	$f(x) = 3x^2 - 2$	$(-1, -1)$	$(-1, 1)$
(b)	$f(x) = -x^2 + 3$	$(-2, -1)$	$(-2, 7)$
(c)	$f(x) = x^2 - 2x + 1$	$(-1, 2)$	$(1, 0)$
(d)	$f(x) = \frac{1}{2}x^2 - 2$	$(2, 0)$	$(-2, 0)$
(e)	$f(x) = (x - 1)^2$	$(-2, 1)$	$(-1, 0)$

B   List the words used to describe the properties of a quadratic function. You *must* understand their meanings before you can use them.

6   (a) Draw a sketch of each parabola.   A: $y = x^2$ B: $y = -x^2$
    (b) Which parabola has a minimum point? maximum point?
    (c) Which curve opens upwards?

7   For each function, determine which graph opens upwards (U), or opens downwards (D).

   (a) $f: x \rightarrow 2x^2 + \dfrac{1}{2}$ (b) $g: x \rightarrow -3x^2 + 1$ (c) $h: x \rightarrow 2(x - 1)^2 - 1$

8   (a) Draw a sketch of the parabola given by the equation $y = \frac{1}{2}x^2 - 3$.
    (b) What are the co-ordinates of the intersection of the axis of symmetry and the curve?
    (c) Does the graph have a minimum or maximum point? Write its co-ordinates.

9   (a) Draw the graph of the function defined by $f: x \rightarrow 3x^2 + 2$.
    (b) What are the domain, range, co-ordinates of the vertex and the equation of the axis of symmetry?

10   (a) Sketch the parabola $y = x^2 - 3$.
    (b) Use the graph in (a) to obtain a maximum or minimum value of the expression $x^2 - 3$.
    (c) What are the co-ordinates of the vertex?

C 11   (a) Which of the following points are on the parabola given by $y = 2x^2 - 1$?

   A(1, 1)   B(2, 8)   C(−2, 7).

   (b) Write the equation of the axis of symmetry of the graph in (a).
   (c) Write the co-ordinates of the mirror image of the points in (a) which are on the parabola.

Applications: Sports and Quadratics

If an object is thrown vertically upwards with a starting speed of v metres per second, from an altitude of H metres, then the height h metres after time t seconds is given by

$$h = vt - 4.9t^2 + H$$

The height of a basketball player after jumping in the air obeys the above mathematical law. If the player jumps at a speed of 6 m/s then $v = 6$. Since the player began on the floor then $H = 0$. Thus, the equation describing the height, h, of the player above the floor at time t is given by

$$h = 6t - 4.9t^2 \quad (v = 6, H = 0)$$

12 Find the height of the player above the floor after
(a) 0.5 s   (b) 1 s

13 Use the equation to determine how long it will take the player to return to the floor. (Use $h = 0$.)

14 A ball is thrown upward with a velocity of 14.7 m/s by a person 1.4 m tall. How long is the ball in the air before it is caught again?

15 A missile is launched vertically with a velocity of 2450 m/s from a base 500 m above sea level. How long will it be before the missile descends to an altitude of 500 m above sea level?

16 A diver jumps from a tower 30 m above the water with a velocity of 4.9 m/s. How long does it take for the diver to reach a point 0.6 m above the water?

17 Wilbur was crop dusting in his single engine plane at an altitude of 50 m when the propeller fell off. The height, h, of a falling object is given by

$$h = A - 4.9t^2 \quad \text{where } A \text{ is the initial height of the object and}$$
$$t \text{ is the number of seconds elapsed.}$$

(a) How far above the ground is the propeller after 3 s?
(b) Will the propeller have hit the ground after the 4th second?

7.2 Solving Problems: Using Graphs

Many phenomena may be described by quadratic functions.

- stopping distances for cars   • cooling of substances

The distance, h in metres, of a skydiver above the earth's surface is given by $h = A - 4.9t^2$, where t is the time (in seconds) after leaving the plane, and A is the altitude of the plane (in metres) at the time of the jump.

The quadratic function used to describe the height of the skydiver is also used to describe the height of an object dropped from a building.

Example

A ball is dropped from the top of a building which is 70 m high. The height of the ball at time, t (in seconds) is given by $h = A - 4.9t^2$, where A is the height in metres of the ball before it is dropped.

(a) Draw a graph of the function.

(b) What is the height of the ball after 3 s have elapsed?

(c) Will the ball strike the ground after 4 s?

Solution

(a) To draw the graph use time, t as the variable for the horizontal axis and height, h as the variable for the vertical axis.

$h = 70 - 4.9t^2$

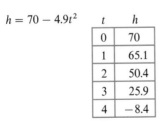

t	h
0	70
1	65.1
2	50.4
3	25.9
4	−8.4

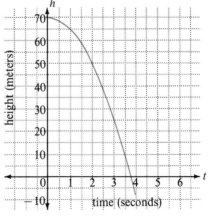

(b) From the graph, the height of the ball is about 26 m after 3 s.

(c) $h = 0$ represents the ball striking the ground. Since $h = 0$ when $t = 3.8$, the ball strikes the ground in about 4 s (to the nearest second).

7.2 Exercise

B   Questions 1 to 4 are based on the following information.

The path of a ball thrown forward is a familiar sight.
As the ball travels forward, gravity acts on it and makes the ball return to earth. At any time, t, in seconds, the height, h, in metres, of a ball thrown at a certain speed is given by $h = 8 + 6t - 2t^2$
If the ball is thrown at different angles or speeds the equation will vary.

1   (a) Draw a graph of the ordered pairs (t, h) when $t \geq 0$.
    (b) From the graph estimate the maximum height reached by the ball.

2   (a) Find the height, h, when $t = 0$.
    (b) How high was the ball above the earth before it was thrown?

3   Estimate from the graph the height of the ball after each amount of elapsed time.
    (a) 1 s   (b) 2 s   (c) 1.5 s   (d) 2.5 s

4   When $h = 0$, the ball has returned to earth. Estimate from the graph how long the ball is in the air.

5   During a stunt, the power dive of a plane is given by the equation,

$h = t^2 - 10t + 80$ where h (in metres) is the height of the plane after time, t (in seconds).

    (a) Draw a graph of the path of the plane.
    (b) How high is the plane at the start of the dive?
    (c) How high above ground level is the plane at its minimum point?

6   In a cooling experiment, it is found that the ordered pairs, $(x, f(x))$ satisfy the equation, $f(x) = 2.3x^2 - 1.5x - 3.1$.
    (a) Draw a graph of f.
    (b) From the graph estimate the values for which $f(x) = 0$.

7   (a) Two values of x at which a propeller vibrates are the zeroes of the function $P(x) = 1.2x^2 - 0.6x - 10.2$. Draw a graph defined by the equation.
    (b) Read from your graph the zeroes of the function P.

C 8   From an experiment, it is found that the ordered pairs $(x, f(x))$ satisfy the functional relationship $f(x) = 2.1x^2 + 3.5x + 1.2$. Draw a graph of f, and estimate the values of x to 1 decimal place for which $f(x) = 0$.

7.3 Applying Transformations to Quadratic Functions

The first step in exploring the properties of quadratic functions is to draw their graphs.

The exercise that follows leads you through an investigation of certain properties of quadratic functions, which will provide you with skills for sketching their graphs.

7.3 Exercise

A 1 (a) Draw the graph of the parabolas $y = 2x^2$ and $y = -2x^2$.
   (b) Which parabola opens upwards?
   (c) Which parabola opens downwards?

2 (a) Which of the points P(4, 0), Q(0, −4), R(3, −7) are on the graph of the function given by $y = x^2 - 16$?
   (b) Draw the graph of the function given by $y = x^2 - 16$.
   (c) What are the x-intercepts of the graph?
   (d) What are the zeroes of the function?
   (e) In which direction does the parabola open?

3 (a) Which of the points A(1, 1), B(2, 10), C(3, 7) are on the parabola given by $y = 3x^2 - 2$?
   (b) Draw the graph of the function given by $y = 3x^2 - 2$.
   (c) Write the equation of the axis of symmetry of the graph.
   (d) What are the co-ordinates of the vertex?
   (e) In which direction does the parabola open?

4 (a) Draw the graph of each quadratic function. $y = x^2 - 3$, $y = -x^2 + 3$
   (b) Which graph opens upwards?   (c) Which graph opens downwards?

Effect of a in $y = ax^2$ — Questions 5 to 7 examine the effect on the graph as the value of a varies for $y = ax^2$.

5 Draw the graph of each of the following functions. Use the same co-ordinate axes for all curves.

   (a) $y = x^2$ (b) $y = 3x^2$ (c) $y = 4x^2$ (d) $y = \frac{1}{2}x^2$ (e) $y = \frac{1}{3}x^2$

   (f) How are the graphs given by (a) to (e) the same? How are they different?

6   Draw the graph of each of the functions defined by the following. Use the same co-ordinate axes for each curve.

(a) $y = -x^2$ (b) $y = -2x^2$ (c) $y = -3x^2$

(d) $y = -4x^2$ (e) $y = -\frac{1}{2}x^2$ (f) $y = -\frac{1}{3}x^2$

(g) How are the graphs given by (a) to (f) the same? How are they different?

7   The general equation that describes the quadratic functions in Questions 5 and 6 is given by $y = ax^2$, $a \neq 0$.

(a) What is the direction of the opening of the graph if $a > 0$?

(b) What is the direction of the opening of the graph if $a < 0$?

(c) If $a > 0$, does $y = ax^2$ have a maximum or minimum point?

(d) If $a < 0$, does $y = ax^2$ have a maximum or minimum point?

Effect of b in   Questions 8 to 11 examine the effect on the graph as the value of b varies
$y = ax^2 + b$ for $y = ax^2 + b$.

8   Draw the graphs given by (a), (b) and (c).

(a) $y = x^2$ (b) $y = x^2 - 1$ (c) $y = x^2 + 1$

(d) How are the graphs given by (a), (b), and (c) the same? How are they different?

(e) Write the co-ordinates of the vertex for each curve.

(f) Write the equation of the axis of symmetry for each curve.

9   Draw the graphs given by (a), (b) and (c).

(a) $y = -x^2$ (b) $y = -x^2 - 1$ (c) $y = -x^2 + 1$

(d) How are the graphs given by (a), (b), and (c) the same? How are they different?

(e) Write the co-ordinates of the vertex for each curve.

(f) Write the equation of the axis of symmetry for each curve.

10   Draw the graphs given by (a) and (b).

(a) $y = 2x^2 - 8$ (b) $y = 2x^2 + 8$

(c) How are the graphs given by (a) and (b) alike? How are they different?

11   Based on your results in Questions 8 to 10, answer the following.
A quadratic function f, is defined by $f : x \rightarrow ax^2 + b$, $a \neq 0$.
Describe the graph of f if

(a) $a > 0$ and $b > 0$ (b) $a > 0$ and $b < 0$

(c) $a < 0$ and $b > 0$ (d) $a < 0$ and $b < 0$

B Use the properties you have explored to complete the following questions.

12 (a) Draw the graph of $y = 2(x - 3)^2 - 5$, $x \in R$.
  (b) What is the minimum value of y?
  (c) What is the equation of the axis of symmetry?
  (d) What are the co-ordinates of the vertex?
  (e) How are your answers in (b), (c), and (d) related to the equation $y = 2(x - 3)^2 - 5$?

13 (a) Draw the graph of $y = -3(x + 2)^2 + 4$, $x \in R$.
  (b) What is the maximum value of y?
  (c) What is the equation of the axis of symmetry?
  (d) What are the co-ordinates of the vertex?
  (e) How are your answers in (b), (c), and (d) related to the equation $y = -3(x + 2)^2 + 4$?

14 Draw the graphs of the quadratic functions given by (a), (b), (c), and (d).
  (a) $y = 2(x - 1)^2 - 4$ (b) $y = 3(x - 2)^2 + 1$
  (c) $y = -2(x + 1)^2 - 3$ (d) $y = 3(x - 2)^2 + 2$
  (e) For each graph how does the equation of the axis of symmetry seem to relate to the equation?
  (f) For each graph, how do the co-ordinates of the vertex seem to relate to the equation?

15 (a) Draw the graphs of the following quadratic functions.

  A: $y = x^2$ B: $y = (x + 2)^2$ C: $y = (x - 2)^2$

  (b) How are the graphs of A, B, and C alike? How do they differ?

16 (a) Draw the graphs of the following functions.

  A: $y = 3x^2 - 1$ B: $y = 3(x - 2)^2 - 1$ C: $y = 3(x + 2)^2 - 1$

  (b) How are the graphs of A, B, and C alike? How do they differ?

C 17 Use your results to answer the questions about the graph of the function, f, given by $f: x \rightarrow a(x - p)^2 + c$.
  (a) If $p = 0$ and $c = 0$, describe the position of the graph when $a > 0$; when $a < 0$.
  (b) If $a > 0$ and $c > 0$, describe the position of the graph of f.
  (c) If $a > 0$ and c increases in value, describe the effect on the graph of f.
  (d) If $a < 0$ and $c > 0$, describe the position of the graph.
  (e) If $a < 0$ and c increases in value, describe the effect on the graph of f.

7.4 Sketching Graphs: Transformations

In the previous section, you examined the properties of the graphs of quadratic functions. The skills for sketching graphs you learned in Chapter 6 may also be applied to sketching the graphs of quadratic functions.

Example   Sketch the graph given by $y = (x + 2)^2 - 3$.

Solution   A: The graph of $y = x^2$ is drawn.

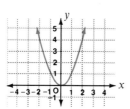

B: To obtain the graph of $y = (x + 2)^2$ *apply a horizontal shift of 2 units to the left* to the graph in Step A.

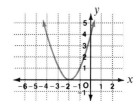

C: To obtain the graph of $y = (x + 2)^2 - 3$, *apply a vertical shift of 3 units downwards* to the graph in Step B.

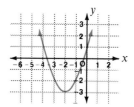

Thus, the graph of $y = (x + 2)^2 - 3$ is obtained.

7.4   Exercise

A 1   (a) Sketch the graph of $y = x^2$.

(b) Use your sketch in (a) to help you sketch the graph of

      A: $y = x^2 - 3$ B: $y = x^2 + 1$

2   (a) Sketch the graph of $y = (x + 3)^2$.

(b) Use your sketch in (a) to help you sketch the graph of

      A: $y = (x + 3)^2 + 2$ B: $y = (x + 3)^2 - 4$

3   (a) Sketch the graph of $y = -x^2$.

(b) Use your sketch in (a) to help you sketch the graph of

      A: $y = -x^2 + 6$ B: $y = -x^2 - 3$

4   (a) Sketch the graph of $y = -(x + 1)^2$.

(b) Use your sketch in (a) to help you sketch the graph of

      A: $y = -(x + 1)^2 + 3$ B: $y = -(x + 1)^2 - 2$

B 5 Sketch the graph of each of the following.

    (a) $y = x^2 - 3$ (b) $y = x^2 + 1$ (c) $y = (x - 1)^2$ (d) $y = (x + 2)^2$

6 Sketch the graph of each of the following.

    (a) $y = (x + 3)^2 - 2$ (b) $y = (x - 3)^2 + 2$
    (c) $y = (x + 3)^2 + 2$ (d) $y = (x - 3)^2 - 2$

7 Sketch each of the following graphs.

    (a) $y = (x - 1)^2 + 3$ (b) $y = (x + 3)^2 - 1$
    (c) $y = (x + 4)^2 - 5$ (d) $y = (x - 4)^2 - 2$

8 Sketch the graph of $y = 2x^2$. Use the graph to sketch each of the following.

    (a) $y = 2x^2 + 3$ (b) $y = 2x^2 - 3$ (c) $y = 2(x - 3)^2$
    (d) $y = 2(x + 2)^2$ (e) $y = 2(x - 1)^2 - 3$ (f) $y = 2(x + 3)^2 + 2$

9 Sketch each of the following graphs.

    (a) $y = 3(x - 1)^2$ (b) $y = 3(x + 2)^2 - 3$ (c) $y = \frac{1}{2}(x + 3)^2$

    (d) $y = \frac{1}{2}(x - 2)^2 + 3$ (e) $y = 4(x - 2)^2 - 1$ (f) $y = 4(x + 1)^2 + 3$

10 Sketch each of the following graphs.

    (a) $y = x^2$ (b) $y = -x^2$ (c) $y = x^2 + 3$
    (d) $y = -x^2 - 2$ (e) $y = -(x - 1)^2$ (f) $y = -(x + 3)^2$

11 Sketch the graph of each of the following.

    (a) $y = -2x^2$ (b) $y = -2x^2 + 3$ (c) $y = -2(x - 1)^2$
    (d) $y = -2(x + 2)^2$ (e) $y = -2(x + 1)^2 + 2$ (f) $y = -2(x - 3)^2 - 1$

12 (a) Sketch the graph of the function given by $y = (x - 1)^2 - 4$.

    (b) What are the zeroes of the function?

13 (a) Sketch the graph given by $y = (x + 2)^2 - 1$.

    (b) What is the y-intercept?

    (c) What are the x-intercepts?

14 (a) Which of the following open upwards (U)? Which open downwards (D)?

        A: $y = (x - 1)^2 - 3$ B: $y = -2(x + 4)^2 - 1$

        C: $y = -\frac{1}{2}(x + 3)^2 + 2$ D: $y = 3(x - 2)^2 - 5$

    (b) Sketch each graph. What are the co-ordinates of the maximum point or minimum point?

7.5 Writing Equations: Using Locus

In the previous section, you found the standard form of the quadratic function to be given by

$$y = a(x - p)^2 + q.$$

The equation of the axis of symmetry is $x = p$.

The co-ordinates of the vertex are (p, q).

These properties enabled you to sketch the graphs of quadratic functions. The points of a quadratic function satisfy the equation of the curve. The graph of the quadratic function is an example of a **locus** of points.

Properties of the locus are important in the study of functions. The **locus** is the set of points which satisfy the conditions listed below. For any locus,

A: if a point is on the graph, the co-ordinates of the point satisfy the equation of the locus, and

B: if a point has co-ordinates that satisfy the equation of a locus, the point is on the graph.

Properties A and B allow you to write the defining equation of a locus, or in this particular case, the defining equation of a quadratic function.

Example A quadratic function is defined by $y = a(x - 1)^2 - 12$ and passes through the point $(3, -1)$.

(a) Find the defining equation.

(b) Does the function have a maximum or minimum value?

Solution (a) Since $(3, -1)$ is a point on the graph, then the co-ordinates $(3, -1)$ satisfy the equation.

$$y = a(x - 1)^2 - 12$$
$$-1 = a(3 - 1)^2 - 12$$
$$-1 = 4a - 12$$
$$11 = 4a \quad \text{or} \quad a = \frac{11}{4}$$

The equation of the quadratic function is

$$y = \frac{11}{4}(x - 1)^2 - 12.$$

(b) Since $a = \frac{11}{4}$, then $a > 0$. Thus the quadratic function has a minimum value of -12, which occurs when $x = 1$.

7.5 Exercise

A 1 Each equation is given in the form $y = a(x - p)^2 + q$.
  - What are the co-ordinates of the vertex?
  - What is the equation of the axis of symmetry?

(a) $y = 2x^2 + 3$ (b) $y = -3x^2 - 8$ (c) $y = 2(x + 1)^2 + 3$

(d) $y = -3(x - 1)^2 - 8$ (e) $y = \frac{1}{2}(x - 3)^2 - 6$ (f) $y = 3(x - 3)^2 + 8$

(g) $y = 0.8(x - 1)^2 - 7.2$ (h) $y = -62(x + 1)^2 - 3.6$

2 For each quadratic function,
  - does the curve open upwards or downwards?
  - what is the range of the function?

(a) $y = 4x^2 - 3$ (b) $y = -\frac{1}{2}x^2 + 6$ (c) $y = -9(x + 3)^2 - \frac{1}{2}$

(d) $y = \frac{3}{2}(x - 2)^2 + 5$ (e) $y = 1.5(x - 3)^2 - 0.5$ (f) $y = -0.8(x + 4)^2 + 1.6$

3 A quadratic function is given by $y = 3(x - 1)^2 + 6$.

(a) What are the co-ordinates of the vertex?

(b) What is the equation of the axis of symmetry?

(c) Use the information in parts (a) and (b) to sketch the graph.

4 Sketch the graph of each quadratic function without using a table of values.

(a) $y = 3(x - 1)^2$ (b) $y = 3(x - 1)^2 + 5$ (c) $y = -2(x - 3)^2 - 3$

(d) $y = -2(x - 3)^2 + 6$ (e) $y = \frac{1}{2}(x - 1)^2 - 2$

5 Without using a table of values, sketch the graph of each of the following.

(a) $y = x^2$ (b) $y = x^2 + 2$ (c) $y = x^2 - 3$

(d) $y = 2(x - 1)^2$ (e) $y = 2(x - 1)^2 - 4$ (f) $y = -3(x + 2)^2$

(g) $y = -3(x + 2)^2 + 5$ (h) $y = 2(x - 3)^2 - 1$ (i) $y = -2(x + 3)^2 + 1$

6 Write an equation in the form $y = a(x - p)^2 + q$ for each quadratic function, given the co-ordinates of the vertex and the value of a.

	vertex	value of a
(a)	$(-2, 3)$	-3
(c)	$(-3, -2)$	2
(e)	$(-8, -1)$	$\frac{1}{2}$
(g)	$(4, -3)$	0.5

	vertex	value of a
(b)	$(6, 3)$	-2
(d)	$(0, -3)$	-10
(f)	$(3, -4)$	$-\frac{3}{2}$
(h)	$(6, 2)$	-1.5

B   Learn the significance of a, p, and q in the equation $y = a(x - p)^2 + q$.

7   The standard form of the equation of a parabola is given by $y = a(x - p)^2 + q$.
    (a) A parabola has its vertex at (2, 6). If the same curve passes through (1, 7), find the value of a for $y = a(x - p)^2 + q$.
    (b) Which does the function have: a maximum or minimum value?
    (c) Write the equation of the parabola.

8   (a) A parabola has its vertex at (3, 5). If the same curve passes through (2, 4), find the value of a for $y = a(x - p)^2 + q$.
    (b) Does the function have a maximum or minimum value?
    (c) Write the equation of the parabola.

9   A quadratic function is given by $y = ax^2 + b$.
    (a) If the two points P(1, 5) and Q(2, 11) are on the graph of the function, then find a and b.
    (b) What are the co-ordinates of the vertex?

10   The equation of a locus is given by $y = ax^2 + b$.
    (a) If the points A(1, -1) and B(2, -7) are points on the locus, find the defining equation.
    (b) Describe the locus given by the equation in part (a).

11   A locus is defined by the equation $y = a(x - 2)^2 + q$.
    (a) The points (0, 17) and (2, 5) are on the locus. Find the equation of the locus.
    (b) Describe the locus given by the equation in part (a).

12   The equation of a parabola is given by $y = ax^2 + b$. The points $R\left(1, \dfrac{11}{4}\right)$ and $Q\left(-1, \dfrac{11}{4}\right)$ are on the parabola. Find its defining equation, if the vertex is at the origin.

13   The function $y = ax^2 + b$ may be written in function notation as $f(x) = ax^2 + b$. If $f(2) = 2$ and $f(3) = -3$, then calculate a and b.

C 14   If $f(x) = a(x - 1)^2 + q$, and $f(-1) = -9$ and $f(1) = 1$, then
    (a) calculate the values of a and q.
    (b) find the defining equation of the function f.
    (c) describe the graph of the function f.

7.6 The Method of Completing the Square

The **general form** of the equation of a quadratic function is

$$f : x \rightarrow ax^2 + bx + c, \quad x \in R.$$

The general form can be rewritten in **standard form**

$$y = a(x - p)^2 + q$$

by completing the square as shown in Example 1.

Example 1   Express $y = x^2 - 4x + 3$ in the standard form $y = a(x - p)^2 + q$.

Solution
$$y = x^2 - 4x + 3$$
$$= x^2 - 4x + 4 - 4 + 3 \qquad \text{Add a value that completes the square}$$
$$= x^2 - 4x + 4 - 1 \qquad\quad x^2 - 4x + 4 = (x - 2)^2$$
$$\qquad\qquad\qquad\qquad\qquad\quad \text{Remember } 4 - 4 = 0.$$
$$= (x - 2)^2 - 1$$

Thus $y = (x - 2)^2 - 1$.

In Example 1 in order to decide what expression to add to $x^2 - 4x$ to make a perfect square you must note that $x^2 - 4x = x^2 - 4x + 4 - 4$

Think of these steps:

Compute half of the coefficient of x and find its square. $\quad \dfrac{1}{2}(-4) = -2 \qquad$ Thus use the expression $4 - 4$.

$$(-2)^2 = 4$$

This procedure is known as **completing the square**.

Example 2   Use the method of completing the square to write $y = 2x^2 - 12x + 13$ in the form $y = a(x - p)^2 + q$.

Solution
$$y = 2x^2 - 12x + 13 \qquad\qquad \text{Add the expression } 9 - 9 \text{ to complete the square.}$$
$$= 2(x^2 - 6x) + 13 \qquad\qquad x^2 - 6x = x^2 - 6x + 9 - 9$$
$$= 2(x^2 - 6x + 9 - 9) + 13 \qquad\qquad = (x - 3)^2 - 9$$
$$= 2[(x - 3)^2 - 9] + 13 \qquad\quad \text{Note: The expression added to the}$$
$$= 2(x - 3)^2 - 18 + 13 \qquad\quad \text{original expression is equal to zero.}$$
$$= 2(x - 3)^2 - 5 \qquad\qquad\quad 9 - 9 = 0.$$

In the previous section, you explored the properties of the quadratic function. When you use the method of completing the square, you can readily translate information when the equation is in the form

$$y = a(x - p)^2 + q.$$

For example, each of the following graphs are sketched.

Graph 1 $y = (x - 2)^2 - 1$ Graph 2 $y = -2(x - 3)^2 + 8$

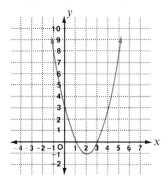   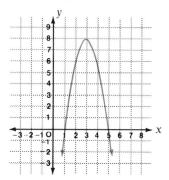

Compare the observations in the chart above with the equations of the graphs of the functions.

	Graph 1	Graph 2
Equation	$y = (x - 2)^2 - 1$	$y = -2(x - 3)^2 + 8$
Axis of Symmetry	$x - 2 = 0$ or $x = 2$	$x - 3 = 0$ or $x = 3$
Direction of opening	$a > 0$, thus upwards	$a < 0$, thus downwards
Value of function	-1, minimum	8, maximum
Co-ordinates of vertex	$(2, -1)$	$(3, 8)$

In general, for the quadratic function, f, given by
$$f : x \rightarrow a(x - p)^2 + q \quad \text{or} \quad y = a(x - p)^2 + q$$

you can obtain the equation of the axis of symmetry and the co-ordinates of the vertex for the equation by inspection.

Axis of symmetry: $x - p = 0$ or $x = p$.
Co-ordinates of vertex: (p, q).

Furthermore, from the standard form of the equation:

If $a > 0$, then the function has a minimum value of q.
If $a < 0$, then the function has a maximum value of q.

But one of the most useful results of the standard form is the following: once the equation for a function is expressed in the form $y = a(x - p)^2 + q$, you can draw a sketch of the curve without constructing a table of values.

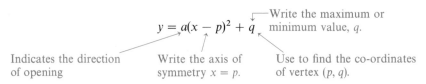

Write the maximum or minimum value, q.

Indicates the direction of opening

Write the axis of symmetry $x = p$.

Use to find the co-ordinates of vertex (p, q).

7.6 Exercise

A 1 Find the value of c that will make each of the following a perfect square.

(a) $x^2 + 4x + c$ (b) $x^2 - 4x + c$ (c) $x^2 - 6x + c$

(d) $x^2 + 8x + c$ (e) $x^2 + 5x + c$ (f) $x^2 - 3x + c$

(g) $2x^2 + 4x + c$ (h) $3x^2 + 6x + c$ (i) $2x^2 - 5x + c$

(j) $\dfrac{1}{2}x^2 - 5x + c$ (k) $\dfrac{1}{2}x^2 + 5x + c$ (l) $\dfrac{2}{3}x^2 - 3x + c$

2 What is the value of m so that each is a perfect square?

(a) $y = x^2 + 2x + m$ (b) $y = x^2 + 8x + m$ (c) $y = x^2 - 6x + m$

(d) $y = x^2 - 10x + m$ (e) $y = x^2 + 3x + m$ (f) $y = x^2 + 9x + m$

(g) $y = x^2 - 11x + m$ (h) $y = x^2 - 5x + m$ (i) $y = x^2 - \dfrac{5}{2}x + m$

3 Find the values of p and q that will make each of the following true.

(a) $x^2 + 4x = (x - p)^2 + q$ (b) $x^2 - 6x = (x - p)^2 + q$

(c) $x^2 - 9x = (x - p)^2 + q$ (d) $x^2 + 5x = (x - p)^2 + q$

4 For what values of a, p, and q is each of the following true?

(a) $2x^2 + 8x + 4 = a(x - p)^2 + q$

(b) $-3x^2 - 12x + 5 = a(x - p)^2 + q$

(c) $\dfrac{1}{2}x^2 - 3x + 5 = a(x - p)^2 + q$

(d) $4 - 6x - x^2 = a(x - p)^2 + q$

(e) $-2x^2 + 4x - 2 = a(x - p)^2 + q$

5 Write each of the following in the form $y = a(x - p)^2 + q$.

(a) $y = x^2 + 6x$ (b) $y = x^2 + 6x - 4$ (c) $y = 2x^2 - 3x + 5$

(d) $y = 8 - 3x - x^2$ (e) $y = -2x^2 + 8x + 5$ (f) $y = 15 - 3x - 3x^2$

(g) $y = 4x^2 - 10x - 3$ (h) $y = \dfrac{2}{3}x^2 - 3x + 9$

B 6 For each of the following, what is
- the equation of the axis of symmetry?
- the co-ordinates of the vertex?
- the maximum or minimum value?

(a) $y = 3(x - 1)^2 - 2$ (b) $y = -2(x + 1)^2 + 5$ (c) $y = 2(x - 1)^2 - \dfrac{3}{2}$

(d) $y = -\dfrac{2}{3}(x + 2)^2 + 6$ (e) $y = -3(x - 3)^2$ (f) $y = \dfrac{3}{4}(x + 5)^2 - \dfrac{3}{2}$

7   (a) A function, f, is given by $y = x^2 - 2x - 3$.
        Write an equation in the form $y = a(x - p)^2 + q$.
    (b) Write the equation of the axis of symmetry.
    (c) Write the co-ordinates of the vertex.
    (d) What is the minimum or maximum value of f?
    (e) What is the range of the function?
    (f) Draw a sketch of the graph of f.

8   Sketch the curve of each of the following. Do not use a table of values.
    (a) $y = x^2 - 2x + 3$ (b) $y = x^2 + 4x + 7$ (c) $y = 8 - 6x - x^2$
    (d) $y = 5 + 3x - x^2$ (e) $y = 2x^2 + 8x + 7$ (f) $y = 7 + 8x - 2x^2$
    (g) $y = 2x(x - 2) - 5$ (h) $y = -2(x^2 - 4x - 5)$

9   For each parabola find the equation of the axis of symmetry and the
    co-ordinates of the vertex.
    (a) $y = x^2 + 4x + 3$ (b) $y = x^2 - 6x + 5$ (c) $y = 3x^2 - 6x - 1$
    (d) $y = -2x^2 + 4x - 3$ (e) $y = -x^2 - 4x - 2$ (f) $y = 2x^2 - 4x - 1$

10 Draw a sketch of each of the following parabolas.
    (a) $y = 3x^2 - 6x$ (b) $y = -2x^2 - 4x$
    (c) $y = x^2 + 6x + 8$ (d) $y = -x^2 + 4x + 5$

    (e) $y = \dfrac{1}{2}x^2 + 2x - 3$ (f) $y = -8 - 6x - x^2$ (g) $y = 12 - 6x - \dfrac{3}{2}x^2$

11 A ball is thrown and follows the path given by $y = x - 3x^2$.
    (a) What are the co-ordinates of the vertex?
    (b) What is the equation of the axis of symmetry?

12 A comet enters the solar system on a locus given by $y = 3x^2 - 2x + 1$. Are
    the points in (a), (b), and (c) on the curve?
    (a) $(2, 9)$ (b) $(-2, 7)$ (c) $(-1, 6)$
    (d) What are the co-ordinates of the vertex?
    (e) What is the equation of the axis of symmetry?

C 13 A space probe is sent on a trajectory given by the equation
       $y = 9x^2 - 30x + 25$.
    (a) Meteors are expected to pass through points $(3, -16)$, $(1, -4)$ and
        $(-5, 400)$. Is there any danger of a collision? If so, at what
        co-ordinates does the danger lie?
    (b) What are the co-ordinates of the vertex?
    (c) What is the equation of the axis of symmetry?

7.7 Formulas for Quadratic Functions: Computer Programming

A formula for the equation of the axis of symmetry and for the co-ordinates of the vertex can be found from the general form of the defining equation.

Numerical Case

$y = 2x^2 + 3x + 4$

$= 2\left(x^2 + \dfrac{3}{2}x\right) + 4$ Complete the square.

$= 2\left(x^2 + \dfrac{3}{2}x + \dfrac{9}{16} - \dfrac{9}{16}\right) + 4$

$= 2\left[\left(x + \dfrac{3}{4}\right)^2 - \dfrac{9}{16}\right] + 4$

$= 2\left(x + \dfrac{3}{4}\right)^2 - \dfrac{9}{8} + 4$

$= 2\left(x + \dfrac{3}{4}\right)^2 + \dfrac{23}{8}$

Axis of symmetry   Minimum value $\dfrac{23}{8}$,

$x = -\dfrac{3}{4}$ since $a > 0$.

General Case

$y = ax^2 + bx + c$

$= a\left(x^2 + \dfrac{b}{a}x\right) + c$ Complete the square.

$= a\left(x^2 + \dfrac{b}{a}x + \dfrac{b^2}{4a^2} - \dfrac{b^2}{4a^2}\right) + c$

$= a\left[\left(x + \dfrac{b}{2a}\right)^2 - \dfrac{b^2}{4a^2}\right] + c$

$= a\left(x + \dfrac{b}{2a}\right)^2 - \dfrac{b^2}{4a} + c$

$= a\left(x + \dfrac{b}{2a}\right)^2 + \dfrac{4ac - b^2}{4a}$

The maximum or minimum value occurs where $x = -\dfrac{b}{2a}$.

The maximum or minimum value is $\dfrac{4ac - b^2}{4a}$.

Thus,

(i) the equation of the axis of symmetry is $x = -\dfrac{b}{2a}$

(ii) the maximum or minimum value is $\dfrac{4ac - b^2}{4a}$

(iii) the co-ordinates of the vertex are $\left(-\dfrac{b}{2a}, \dfrac{4ac - b^2}{4a}\right)$

Once you have found the general expressions, you can use the values of a, b, and c from a specific quadratic equation and find the maximum or minimum, co-ordinates of the vertex, etc. For example, in the previous numerical example, you can check your work.

(i) $y = 2x^2 + 3x + 4$, $a = 2, b = 3, c = 4$

(ii) Axis of symmetry $x = -\dfrac{b}{2a}$, $x = -\dfrac{3}{4}$ Checks ✓

(iii) $a > 0$, thus the minimum value is given by

$$\dfrac{4ac - b^2}{4a} = \dfrac{4(2)(4) - (3)^2}{4(2)} = \dfrac{32 - 9}{8} = \dfrac{23}{8} \quad \text{Checks ✓}$$

Computer Programming

A computer program can be written for these formulas which will use the values of a, b, and c of a given quadratic function to calculate the values needed to draw the curve of the quadratic function. The computer program shown uses the language of BASIC. With this program you can determine, for any quadratic function,

- the maximum or minimum value,
- the value of x at which the maximum or minimum occurs.

From these two values you also know the axis of symmetry and the co-ordinates of the vertex.

```
10    INPUT A, B, C
20    IF A = 0 GOTO 120
30    LET M = (4*A*C − B ↑ 2)/(4*A)
40    LET X = (−B)/(2*A)
50    IF A > 0 GOTO 100
60    IF A < 0 GOTO 70
70    PRINT "MAXIMUM IS", M
80    PRINT "VALUE OF X IS", X
90    GOTO 120
100   PRINT "MINIMUM IS", M
110   PRINT "VALUE OF X IS", X
120   END
```

7.7   Exercise

B 1   For each of the following, use the formula to determine a minimum or maximum value.

(a) $y = x^2 − 3x + 1$ (b) $y = 3 − 2x + x^2$
(c) $y = 5x^2 + 10x − 1$ (d) $y = −3x^2 + 5x − 1$
(e) $y = x^2 − 6x + 8$ (f) $y = −x^2 + 4x − 6$
(g) $y = 4x^2 − 8x + 3$ (h) $y = −6x^2 + 12x − 10$

2   Use the formula.   • What is the equation of the axis of symmetry?
                       • What are the co-ordinates of the vertex?

(a) $y = x^2 − 3x − 3$ (b) $y = 2 − 3x + 2x^2$
(c) $y = 3x^2 − 2x + 1$ (d) $y = 5 − x − 3x^2$
(e) $y = x^2 + 2x − 1$ (f) $y = 3x^2 − 6x + 4$
(g) $y = −3x^2 + 6x + 1$ (h) $y = 4x^2 − 8x + 6$

3   Use the formula. Draw a sketch of each of the following parabolas.

(a) $y = x^2 + 6x + 5$ (b) $y = 3 + 2x − x^2$
(c) $y = 2x^2 − x − 15$ (d) $y = 2 + 3x − 2x^2$
(e) $y = 3x^2 + 12x + 12$ (f) $y = 6 + 5x − 2x^2$
(g) $y = 2x^2 − 5x + 3$ (h) $y = 15 − 5x − 3x^2$

4   Collect the values of a, b, and c from the quadratic functions in Questions 1 to 3. Use the computer program given above to check the values needed to draw the quadratic functions.

7.8 Writing Defining Equations for Functions

Consider a function whose graph has the following properties.
- It is a parabola.
- The co-ordinates of the vertex are $(-3, \frac{11}{2})$.
- P(0, 1) is a point on the graph.

The defining equation of the function can be written. Use the co-ordinates of the vertex, $(-3, \frac{11}{2})$, in the general formula.

$$y = a(x - p)^2 + q.$$

Thus, $\quad y = a[x - (-3)]^2 + \dfrac{11}{2} \longleftarrow$ From the above, $p = -3$ and $q = \dfrac{11}{2}$.

or $\quad y = a(x + 3)^2 + \dfrac{11}{2}$

Since P(0, 1) is a point on the graph, the co-ordinates of P satisfy the equation.

In $y = a(x + 3)^2 + \dfrac{11}{2}$, $\qquad 1 = a(0 + 3)^2 + \dfrac{11}{2}$

$x = 0$ and $y = 1$.

$$1 = 9a + \frac{11}{2}$$

$$2 = 18a + 11$$

$$-9 = 18a$$

$$-\frac{1}{2} = a$$

The defining equation is $y = -\dfrac{1}{2}(x + 3)^2 + \dfrac{11}{2}$.

7.8 Exercise

A 1 (a) For the equation, $y = -\frac{1}{2}(x + 3)^2 + \frac{11}{2}$, what information is given by $a = -\frac{1}{2}$?

(b) Sketch the graph of the above function.

2 Find the defining equation of each function for the following information.

	Co-ordinates of the vertex	Point on the graph
(a)	$(-3, 1)$	$(2, 0)$
(b)	$(0, 4)$	$(-2, 0)$
(c)	$(-1, -3)$	$(3, 1)$
(d)	$(2, -\frac{1}{2})$	$(-2, 3)$
(e)	$(3, -\frac{3}{2})$	$(-2, -5)$

B 3   The graph of the quadratic function, f,

$$f(x) = a(x - p)^2 + q,$$

passes through the point $(-2, 0)$.

(a) Find the defining equation if the co-ordinates of the vertex are $(-3, 5)$.

(b) Sketch the function, f.

4   A parabola is defined by the equation $y = a(x - p)^2 + q$ and passes through the point $(-1, -1)$.

(a) If the vertex of the parabola has co-ordinates $(3, -\frac{1}{2})$, find the equation.

(b) Sketch the parabola in part (a).

5   The range of a parabola is given by $\{y \mid y \geq -2, y \in R\}$. The equation of the parabola is in the form $y = a(x - p)^2 + q$.

(a) The equation of the axis of symmetry is $x = 3$. Find the equation of the parabola which goes through $(5, 0)$.

(b) Draw a sketch of the parabola.

6   Find the defining equation of each function in the form $y = a(x - p)^2 + q$.

(a)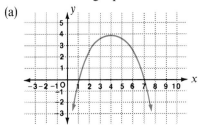

(b)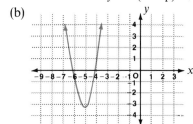

(c)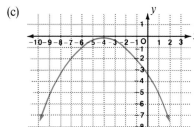

(d)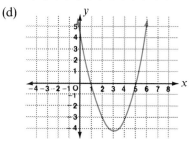

7   Write the conditions on a, p, and q so that the parabola $y = a(x - p)^2 + q$ will

(a) be concave upward, intersecting the x-axis in two distinct points.

(b) be concave upward, not intersecting the x-axis.

(c) be concave downward, touching the x-axis at one point.

(d) be concave downward, intersecting the x-axis in two distinct points.

(e) be concave upward, passing through the origin.

Applications: Curves of Strength

Parabolic curves are common in bridges. One reason for this is that such curves are very aesthetic, arching across rivers and highways in a graceful, pleasing manner. Another reason is that certain building materials become very strong when cast in the form of a parabolic curve. To find the equation that defines a parabolic curve, in a bridge or elsewhere, begin with the standard form of parabolic equations $y = a(x - p)^2 + q$.

For the above bridge, the origin is placed at one end as shown. The information gained is then used to solve the equation for a, p, and q. *Take the origin at the left end of the curve, in the following questions.*

8   Use the data shown in the photo above. Find the defining equation of the parabola.

9   The arch of a bridge is in the shape of a parabola with highest point 40 m above ground level. The width of the arch is 200 m. Determine the equation of the parabola.

10   To obtain maximum strength, engineers often design tunnels as parabolic arches. In such a design, if the highest point of the arch is 19 m above the road and the road is 20 m wide, determine the equation of the parabolic arch.

11   A parabolic reflector has a maximum displacement of 20 cm, as shown, and a width of 30 cm. Find an equation for the parabola.

12   The inside surface of a car headlight is in the shape of a parabola with maximum displacement 10 cm and width 40 cm. Find an equation of the parabolic surface.

7.9 Maxima and Minima

You can find the maximum value of the function given by

$$h = 1 + 3t - 2t^2$$

by completing the square.

From the expression at the right

$$\left(t - \frac{3}{4}\right)^2 \geq 0,$$

$$-2\left(t - \frac{3}{4}\right)^2 \leq 0 \text{ for all } t.$$

Thus, the maximum value of the expression occurs for $t = \frac{3}{4}$, namely, when $-2(t - \frac{3}{4})^2 = 0$.
Thus, the maximum value of h is $\frac{17}{8}$.

$$h = -2t^2 + 3t + 1$$

$$= -2\left(t^2 - \frac{3}{2}t\right) + 1$$

$$= -2\left(t^2 - \frac{3}{2}t + \frac{9}{16} - \frac{9}{16}\right) + 1$$

$$= -2\left[\left(t - \frac{3}{4}\right)^2 - \frac{9}{16}\right] + 1$$

$$= -2\left(t - \frac{3}{4}\right)^2 + \frac{9}{8} + 1$$

$$= -2\left(t - \frac{3}{4}\right)^2 + \frac{17}{8}$$

Example 1 The height, h, in metres, after the launching of a projectile, on the earth's surface at any time, t, in seconds is defined by $h = \dfrac{81}{4} + 9t - 3t^2$.

(a) Find the maximum height reached by the projectile. At what time, t, does this occur after the launching?

(b) Find the values of t when $h = 0$. What is the significance of the result?

Solution (a) $h = -3t^2 + 9t + \dfrac{81}{4}$

$$= -3(t^2 - 3t) + \frac{81}{4}$$

$$= -3\left(t^2 - 3t + \frac{9}{4} - \frac{9}{4}\right) + \frac{81}{4}$$

$$= -3\left[\left(t - \frac{3}{2}\right)^2 - \frac{9}{4}\right] + \frac{81}{4}$$

$$= -3\left(t - \frac{3}{2}\right)^2 + \frac{27}{4} + \frac{81}{4}$$

$$= -3\left(t - \frac{3}{2}\right)^2 + 27$$

Since $-3(t - \frac{3}{2})^2 \leq 0$ for all t, then h has a maximum value, $h = 27$ when $t = \frac{3}{2}$. Thus, the maximum height reached is 27 m at 1.5 s.

(b) For $h = 0$, then

$$-3\left(t - \frac{3}{2}\right)^2 + 27 = 0$$

$$-3\left(t - \frac{3}{2}\right)^2 = -27$$

$$\left(t - \frac{3}{2}\right)^2 = 9$$

$$t - \frac{3}{2} = \pm 3$$

$$t - \frac{3}{2} = 3 \quad \text{or} \quad t - \frac{3}{2} = -3$$

$$t = \frac{9}{2} \qquad\qquad t = -\frac{3}{2}$$
$$\text{inadmissible}$$

Thus $\frac{9}{2}$ s or 4.5 s after launching, $h = 0$. Since h represents the height of the projectile after t seconds then 4.5 s after launching, the projectile strikes the earth's surface.

Very often, a diagram is very useful for visualizing the problem and then solving it.

Example 2 In a conservation park, a lifeguard has used 620 m of marker buoys to rope off a safe swimming area. If one side of the park is adjacent to the beach, calculate the dimension of the swimming area so that it is a maximum.

Solution Let w, in metres, represent the width of the swimming area. Then the length, in metres, is given by $620 - 2w$.

The area, A, is given by

$$\begin{aligned} A &= w(620 - 2w) \\ &= -2(w^2 - 310w) \\ &= -2(w^2 - 310w + 24\,025 - 24\,025) \\ &= -2[(w - 155)^2 - 24\,025] \\ &= -2(w - 155)^2 + 48\,050 \end{aligned}$$

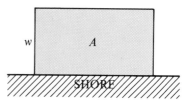

Since $-2(w - 155)^2 \leqq 0$ for all w, then A is maximum for $w = 155$. The value of A is 48 050. Thus, the maximum swimming area is obtained if the dimensions are 310 m by 155 m.

7.9 Exercise

A 1 What is the minimum or maximum value for each of the following? Give reasons for your answer.

(a) $y = 3(x - 2)^2 - \dfrac{3}{2}$ (b) $y = -2(x - 5)^2 + \dfrac{12}{5}$

(c) $y = -\dfrac{3}{2}(x - 1)^2 - 25$ (d) $y = \dfrac{4}{3}(x - 3)^2 + 16$

2 (a) Find the maximum value of V if $V = 4m - 3m^2 + 12$.
   (b) For what value of m is the maximum obtain?

3 (a) Find the minimum value of P if $P = 2k^2 - 3k + 5$.
   (b) For what value of k is the minimum obtained?

4 For what value of t is H a minimum?
   (a) $H = t^2 - 2t + 5$ (b) $H = 2t^2 - 3t + 16$

5 For what value of t is H a maximum?
   (a) $H = 3t - 2t^2$ (b) $H = -3t^2 + 6t + 9$

B 6 Find two numbers which have a difference of 7 and a product that is a minimum.

7 Find two numbers whose difference is 13 and whose squares when added together yield a minimum.

8 Two numbers are related in the manner $3x + y = 42$. Find the values of x and y so that their product is a maximum.

9 A fence is to be built around an area such as the one shown in the diagram.
What must be the values of x and y if the area is to be a minimum and the perimeter is to be 300 m?

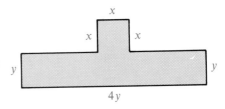

10 A frisbee is thrown straight up in the air from a position 2 m above ground level. Because of the wind pattern, the height, h, in metres, after time, t, in seconds, is given by the formula $h = 2 + 6t - 2t^2$.
(a) What is the maximum height the frisbee will reach?
(b) If it is caught 2 m above the ground, how long will it have been in the air?

11 On a sloping street, Lori gives Michael, who is on a skateboard, an abrupt push uphill. After time, t, in seconds, the distance, s, in metres, that Michael travels from the starting point is determined by the equation $s = 16t - 2t^2$.
(a) Find the farthest distance Michael travels uphill before he starts to roll back down.
(b) After how many seconds will he start to roll back down the street?

12 The Northern Resources Department wants to mark off an area as a conservation park. One side of the rectangular-shaped area will be a large lake. Not including this side, the lengths of the remaining 3 sides must not total more than 36 km. What must be the dimensions of the conservation park in order to obtain a maximum size?

13 A handball court is to be surrounded by plastic stripping 30 m long. One side of the court does not need the stripping because it is a brick wall. What must be the dimensions of the court in order to obtain a maximum?

14 A landscaper wishes to enclose a rectangular rest area with trees planted 1 m apart along the boundary. The perimeter of the area is to be 120 m. What will be the maximum area of the rest area?

Applications: Heights

In order to determine a projectile's displacement h, in metres, at any particular time, t, in seconds the formula $h = H + v_i t - 4.9t^2$ is used, where v_i is the initial velocity, in metres per second, and H is the initial height, in metres, from which the projectile is launched.

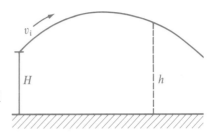

15 At Ralph's Rifle Range the clay pigeons are fired upward from ground level at an initial velocity of 14.7 m/s. What is the maximum height achieved by the clay pigeons?

16 Babe Ruth, the all-time Yankee slugger, was renowned for hitting high fly balls. One day he made contact with a ball 1 m above the ground and hit the ball at a speed of 29.4 m/s. Determine the maximum height of the fly ball.

17 A human cannonball is fired from a cannon at an initial speed of 9.8 m/s from a height of 6 m above the ground. If the cannonball is to pass through a hoop at the top of the flight, how high must the hoop be above the ground?

18 The height, h, of the trajectory of a football (in metres) is given by

$$h(t) = 2 + 28t - 4.9t^2,$$

where t (in seconds) is the time in flight.
(a) What is the maximum height, h, reached by the ball?
(b) At what time, t, is the maximum height reached?

19 In the Olympics a hammer was thrown according to the curve given by

$$h(t) = 0.975 - 4.9t^2 + 14.7t$$

where h is the height reached by the hammer, in metres, and t was the time taken in seconds. How long did the hammer take to reach its maximum height?

20 An arrow is released with an initial speed of 39.2 m/s. It travels according to

$$h(t) = 39.2t + 1.3 - 4.9t^2$$

where h is the height reached, in metres, and t is the time taken, in seconds. How long is the arrow in the air?

7.10 Inverse of a Quadratic Function

For any relation, f, the inverse relation, f^{-1}, is obtained by interchanging the components of corresponding ordered pairs. Remember that the inverse of a function is not necessarily a function.

The graph of the function $y = x^2$ is shown.

x	y
0	0
± 1	1
± 2	4
± 3	9
± 4	16

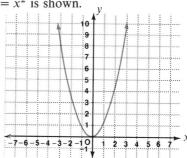

The graph of the inverse, f^{-1}, of this function is $x = y^2$ or $y = \pm\sqrt{x}$, $x \geq 0$.

x	y
0	0
1	± 1
4	± 2
9	± 3
16	± 4

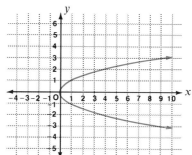

In particular, f^{-1} above is not a function since for every x, $x \geq 0$, there are two corresponding values of y. But the equation of each branch of the curve of the relation $y = \sqrt{x}$, $x \geq 0$, defines a function as shown.

$y = \sqrt{x}, \quad x \geq 0$

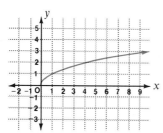

$y = -\sqrt{x}, \quad x \geq 0$

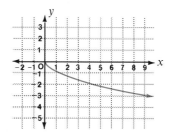

Remember too that the graph of the inverse of a function is the reflection of the graph of the function when the line $y = x$ is the line of reflection.

To sketch the graph of $y = f^{-1}(x)$ where $f(x) = x^2 - 1$, you can use a table of values.

Find the equation of the inverse relation. Since $f(x) = x^2 - 1$ or $y = x^2 - 1$ then the equation for the inverse relation is

$$x = y^2 - 1$$
$$x + 1 = y^2$$
$$\sqrt{x + 1} = y \quad \text{or} \quad y = \sqrt{x + 1}$$

Since the domain of $f(x)$ is all the real numbers and the range of $f(x)$ is $y \geq -1$ then the domain of $f^{-1}(x)$ is $x \geq -1$ and the range of $f^{-1}(x)$ is all the real numbers. Set up a table of values and plot the ordered pairs.

x	y
-1	0
0	± 1
3	± 2
8	± 3

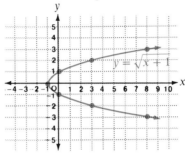

An alternative strategy is to use your earlier skills in sketching a curve to draw the graph of the inverse.

Step 1 Draw the graph of $y = x^2 - 1$.

Step 2 Use the graph in Step 1 to draw the graph of $y = f^{-1}(x)$ or $y = \sqrt{x + 1}$ by reflecting $y = x^2 - 1$ through the line $y = x$.

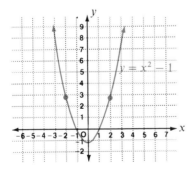

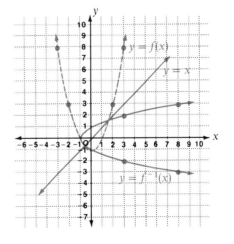

7.10 Exercise

B 1 What is the defining equation of the inverse of each of the following?
  (a) $f(x) = 9x^2$ (b) $f(x) = 3(x^2 + 2)$
  (c) $f(x) = (x + 1)^2 - 1$ (d) $f(x) = -3(x - 2)^2 + 5$

2 A function, f is given by $f(x) = 2x^2 - 8$, $x \geq 0$.
  (a) Construct the graphs of f and f^{-1}.
  (b) What is the domain and range of f and of f^{-1}?

3 (a) Draw the graph of $f(x) = (x + 1)^2 - 1$.
  (b) Use the graph in (a) to construct the graph of f^{-1}.

4 A function is defined by $f: x \rightarrow x^2 - 16$.
  (a) Draw the graph of the inverse.
  (b) Write the defining equation of the inverse.
  (c) Is the inverse a function? Give reasons for your answer.

5 A function is defined by $h: x \rightarrow 25 - x^2$.
  (a) Draw the graph of the inverse.
  (b) Write the defining equation of the inverse.
  (c) Is the inverse a function? Give reasons for your answer.

6 A function is given by $f(x) = x^2 - 4$. Draw the graph of its inverse, namely, $y = f^{-1}(x)$.

7 Draw the graph of the inverse of each of the following.
  (a) $f(x) = x^2 - 4$ (b) $f(x) = 9 - x^2$
  (c) $f: x \rightarrow (x - 1)^2 + 3$ (d) $f: x \rightarrow 2x(x^2 + 2)$

Math Tip

Remember: a very serious, and very common, error when working with inequalities is to forget to do the following.

$$-x < 3$$
$$(-1)(-x) > (-1)(3)$$
$$x > -3$$

$$-x < 3$$
$$\frac{-x}{-1} > \frac{3}{-1}$$
$$x > -3$$

Review your skills with inequalities.

7.11 Quadratic Regions

The graph of a quadratic function divides the Cartesian plane into three regions as shown.

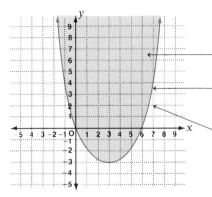

First region: the interior region consisting of points "above" the graph.

Second region: the points on the curve.

Third region: the exterior region consisting of points "below" the graph.

Five inequations can be written for the regions above.

$$y > \frac{1}{3}x^2 - 2x \qquad\qquad y \geqq \frac{1}{3}x^2 - 2x \qquad\qquad y = \frac{1}{3}x^2 - 2x$$

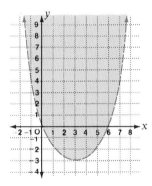
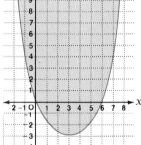
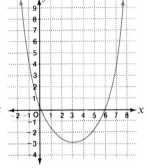

$$y \leqq \frac{1}{3}x^2 - 2x \qquad\qquad\qquad\qquad\qquad y < \frac{1}{3}x^2 - 2x$$

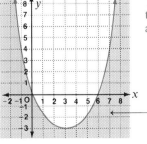

The broken line indicates that points on the curve are excluded

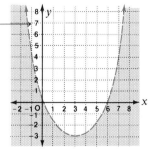

The solid line indicates that the points on the curve are included.

To check whether a given point is in a region, substitute the co-ordinates of the given point into the equation of the region. Thus, to see if the point (3, 1) is in the region $y > \frac{1}{3}x^2 - 2x$ substitute $x = 3$, $y = 1$ in the equation. Use $y > \frac{1}{3}x^2 - 2x$. Substitute.

$$1 > \frac{1}{3}(3)^2 - 2(3)$$

$$1 > \frac{1}{3}(9) - 6$$

$1 > 3 - 6$ Which is true.
$1 > -3$ Thus, (3, 1) checks. ✓

Thus, the point (3, 1) satisfies $y > \frac{1}{3}x^2 - 2x$ and is therefore in the region.

Example 1 Sketch the graph of the region defined by

(a) $y > 1 - 4x - x^2$ (b) $y \leq 1 - 4x - x^2$

Solution To sketch each region, express the equation in the form $y = a(x - p)^2 + q$.

$$
\begin{aligned}
y &= 1 - 4x - x^2 \\
&= -x^2 - 4x + 1 \\
&= -(x^2 + 4x) + 1 \\
&= -(x^2 + 4x + 4 - 4) + 1 \\
&= -[(x + 2)^2 - 4] + 1 \\
&= -(x + 2)^2 + 4 + 1 \\
y &= -(x + 2)^2 + 5
\end{aligned}
$$

The graph of $y = -(x + 2)^2 + 5$, above, is used to sketch the graph of the required regions.

(a) Region: $y > 1 - 4x - x^2$ (b) Region: $y \leq 1 - 4x - x^2$

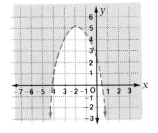
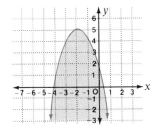

7.11 Exercise

B 1 (a) Sketch a graph of $y = x^2 - 4x$.
(b) Sketch a graph of the region given by $y > x^2 - 4x$.
(c) Sketch a graph of the region given by $y < x^2 - 4x$.

2 (a) Sketch the graph of $y = x^2 - 2x$.
  (b) Use the graph in (a) to sketch the region given by $y \leqq x^2 - 2x$.

3 (a) Draw a graph of the region defined by $y > x^2 - 6$.
  (b) Which of the points A(1, 3), B(10, 2), C(4, 12) are in the region?

4 (a) Draw a graph of the region given by

  P: $y < -2x^2 + 7$ Q: $y < -x^2 - 4$ R: $y > -x^2 + 5$

  (b) To which regions does each point belong?

  A(2, 3)   B(-1, 5)   C(-2, 4)

5 Sketch and shade a region defined by each of the following.
  (a) $y < (x - 2)^2 + 6$ (b) $y > 4x^2 - 6$ (c) $y \leqq (x - 3)^2 + 8$
  (d) $y \geqq 3x^2 - 2$ (e) $y < -4(x - 3)^2$ (f) $y \geqq -5(x + 2)^2 - 3$

6 (a) Sketch the graph of $y < x^2 - 6x + 7$.
  (b) Choose a point in the region. Check whether the co-ordinates of the
      point satisfy the inequation $y < x^2 - 6x + 7$.

7 (a) Sketch the graph of $y \geqq 1 + 4x - x^2$.
  (b) Choose a point in the region. Check whether the co-ordinates of the
      point satisfy the inequation $y \geqq 1 + 4x - x^2$.

8 Sketch the region defined by each of the following.
  (a) $y < 6x^2 - 3x$ (b) $y > x^2 - 6x + 4$ (c) $y \leqq 2x^2 - 12x + 6$
  (d) $y \geqq 2x^2 + 4x - 1$ (e) $y > 2x^2 + 8x - 3$ (f) $y > 3x^2 - 6x + 2$

9 Write the defining inequation that describes each region.

  (a) 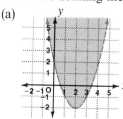   (b) 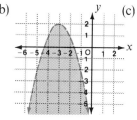   (c)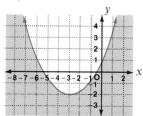

  (d) 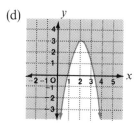   (e) 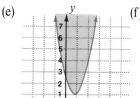   (f)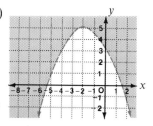

7.12 Solving Problems: Organizing the Steps

Solving problems requires a well-organized plan.

In sports you organize the practice of skills carefully and repeat them many times. In the actual game, you use these skills to make instant decisions and thus solve the problems with which you are confronted. Similarly, in solving problems, you practise organizing your solution to help you make proper decisions. You have used the following plan.

Steps for Solving Problems

Step A   Identify the two main parts of the problem.
          I What information are you asked to find?
          II What information are you given?
Step B   Decide on a method. Translate the problem into mathematics. Introduce variables if necessary.
Step C   Solve the mathematical problem.
Step D   Go to the original problem to see if the answer seems reasonable. Have you answered the question asked?
Step E   Write a final statement to answer the problem.

The *Steps for Solving Problems* above are applied to the solution of Example 1.

Example 1   Find two numbers such that   • their difference is 24
                                              • their product is a minimum.

Solution

Think:
Step A   I Find two numbers.
          II Their difference is 24, their product is a minimum.
Step B   Translate the problem into mathematics.

Let the numbers be represented by n and $n + 24$. Let the product be represented by P. Thus, $P = n(n + 24)$.

$$P = n(n + 24)$$
$$= n^2 + 24n$$
$$= n^2 + 24n + 144 - 144$$
$$= (n + 12)^2 - 144$$

Think:
Step C   Solve the mathematical problem.

Since $(n + 12)^2 \geqq 0$ for all n, then P is a minimum for $n + 12 = 0$ or $n = -12$. Thus, n is -12 and from $n + 24 = -12 + 24 = +12$.

Think:
Step D   Check the answer.
        $12 - (-12) = 24$ Thus, they differ by 24. Checks ✓
        Also, P is a minimum for $n = -12$.

Think:
Step E   Write a final statement.

The numbers are 12 and -12.

Algebraic skills with maxima and minima can be used to solve problems about profit.

Example 2 Vehicles Incorporated currently sells an average of 20 compact cars each week at a price of $6400 each. The sales department wants to increase the price, but the marketing department predicts that for every $300 increase, sales will fall by one car. If the dealer cost (cost to the dealer) for each car is $4000, what price will maximize profits for Vehicles Incorporated?

Solution The profit on each car is: selling price − dealer cost = profit
$6400 − $4000 = $2400

Each $300 increase will add directly to profits. The profit on one car will be $(2400 + 300n)$, where n represents the number of $300 increases. But for each increase, the number of cars sold weekly drops by one. Then the number of cars sold is $(20 - 1n)$. The total profit, P, is

$P = (2400 + 300n)(20 - n)$
$\quad = -300n^2 + 3600n + 48\ 000$
$\quad = -300(n^2 - 12n) + 48\ 000$
$\quad = -300(n^2 - 12n + 36 - 36) + 48\ 000$
$\quad = -300(n - 6)^2 + 58\ 800 \longleftarrow$ The maximum value of P is 58 800 when $n = 6$.

The price that will maximize profits is

old price + 6(increases of $300 each) = $6400 + 6($300)
$\qquad\qquad\qquad\qquad\qquad\qquad\qquad\qquad\quad = $8200

For maximum profit, Vehicles Incorporated can price the cars at $8200 each.

7.12 Exercise

A Remember: You must clearly understand when a maximum or a minimum occurs.

1 What are the maximum or minimum values of each expression? For what value of the variable does the maximum or minimum occur?

(a) $2(x - 3)^2 + 5$

(b) $-3(x - 2)^2 - 25$

(c) $\frac{1}{2}(a - 2)^2 + 6$

(d) $-\frac{3}{2}(m - 3)^2 + 8$

(e) $16 - 2(m - 4)^2$

(f) $3(y - 2)^2 - 3$

(g) $36\left(d - \frac{2}{3}\right)^2 - 16$

(h) $\dfrac{2(9 - a)^2 - 8}{3}$

2   What are the maximum or minimum values of each expression? For what value of the variable does the maximum or minimum value occur?
    (a) $x^2 + 6x + 12$ (b) $8m^2 - 3m + 4$ (c) $3m^2 - 6m + 8$
    (d) $12 - 9a - a^2$ (e) $16 - 3a - 2a^2$ (f) $3m^2 - 4m$

    (g) $6y^2 - 3y - 8$ (h) $16 - m(m - 6)$ (i) $16 - \dfrac{1}{2}y(4y - 3)$

3   What is the maximum or minimum value of each function? For what value of the variable is the function a maximum or a minimum?
    (a) $f(x) = 3x^2 - 4x$ (b) $f(x) = 16 - 2x - 3x^2$
    (c) $A(t) = 2t^2 - 4t + 6$ (d) $s(t) = 12 + 6t - 5t^2$
    (e) $m(s) = 16 - 20s - 2s^2$ (f) $f(y) = 3y(y - 3) + 8$

4   Two numbers satisfy the condition $2x + y = 28$.
    (a) Solve the equation for y.
    (b) Write an expression for the product of the two numbers.
    (c) Solve the equation so the product is a maximum. What are the values x and y?

5   Two numbers are related by the equation $4x + y = 64$. Find the values of the numbers so that their product is a maximum.

6   Two numbers are given by m and $m - 3$. Find the numbers if the sum of their squares is a minimum.

7   y and $y + 8$ are two numbers. Find their values if the sum of their squares decreased by their sum is a minimum.

8   An enclosure is constructed with the shape shown and with a perimeter of 600 m.

    What are the values of x and y so that the area of the enclosure is a maximum.

B   For each problem, be sure to organize your solution. Refer to the *Steps for Solving Problems*.

9   Find two numbers whose difference is 9 and whose product is a minimum.

10 What are the values of two positive numbers whose sum is 60 and whose product yields a maximum.

11 In a newspaper contest a problem is posed. The last two numbers for a combination to open a safe add up to 44. As an additional clue, the product of the two numbers is a maximum. What are the last two numbers?

12 What is the maximum area of a sand lot that can be enclosed by 200 m of fencing.

13 A parking lot is to be fenced in on three sides with the fourth side bounded by a building. If 400 m of fencing are available, what is the maximum area of the parking lot?

14 An isosceles triangle has base 6 m and height 4 m. Find the maximum area of the rectangle placed as shown in the diagram.

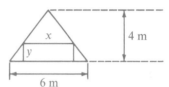

15 From preliminary computer results, it is found that two required numbers have a sum of 121. Before the computer breaks down, it indicates that the product of the numbers is a maximum. What are the numbers?

16 The Environment Group wants to designate an area as a natural habitat. One side of the rectangular-shaped area is a large lake. Not including this side the group is allowed to have the remaining 3 sides total 48 km. What dimensions will ensure a maximum area for the natural habitat?

C 17 For positive numbers, prove that the sum of a number and its reciprocal is at least 2.

Problem Solving

Prove that $f(x) = (x - a)^2 + (x - b)^2$ has a minimum when $x = \dfrac{a + b}{2}$.

Calculator Tip

Review the use of each of the following keys on your calculator. Remember: refer to the manual provided with your calculator.

$\boxed{\sqrt{}}$ $\boxed{x^2}$ $\boxed{1/x}$ $\boxed{x^y}$ $\boxed{\pi}$ $\boxed{\%}$ $\boxed{\,.\,}$ $\boxed{MR}$ $\boxed{+/-}$ $\boxed{EXP}$

Which of the above did you use in this chapter?

Applications: Merchandising

Typically in industry the goal is to maximize profits and yet keep prices competitive. Skills used in finding maxima are applicable to finding solutions to problems in mechandising. Solve each of the following problems.

18 Studies have shown that 500 people attend a high school basketball game when the admission price is $2.00. In the championship game admission prices will increase. For every 20¢ increase 20 fewer people will attend. What price will maximize receipts?

19 The Transit Commission's single-fare price is 60¢ cash. On a typical day approximately 240 000 persons take the transit and pay the single-fare price. To reflect higher costs, single fare prices will be increased, but surveys have shown that every 5¢ increase in fare will reduce ridership by 5000 riders daily. What single-fare price will maximize income for the commission based on single fares?

20 Slacks Incorporated sold 6000 pairs of slacks last month at an average price of $44 each. The store is going to increase prices in order to increase profits. Sales forecasts indicate that sales will drop by 200 for every dollar increase in price. On the average, the company pays $25 for each pair of slacks it sells. What price will maximize profits?

21 An auto parts store currently sells 300 spark plug packages each week at a price of $6.40 each. To increase sales and reach more customers the parts outlet decides to reduce the price of the package, knowing that every 10¢ decrease in price will result in 5 more sales. What price will maximize total revenue?

22 Tri Electronics sells radios for $50 each. 40 radios are sold daily. A survey indicates that a price raise of $1.00 will cause the loss of one customer. If the cost of producing the radios is $18.00, how much should the company charge to maximize the profit?

23 A company selling cassette tape recorders for $80.00 each sells 60 each day. A survey indicates that for each dollar the price is raised one customer will be lost. The cost of making the recorders is $54.00 each. How much should the company charge to maximize the profit?

7.13 Problem-Solving Strategy: Clue Words

It is important to read a problem carefully and to translate it correctly into mathematical language. Look for clue words in the problems which might suggest which mathematical operation could be used to solve the problem. You have used these clues for operations.

Symbol, +	Symbol, −	Symbol, ×
increased by	decreased by	product
sum	difference	area of
total	exceeds	how many times

These clue words suggest the standard form.

$$\boxed{\begin{array}{c}\text{maximum}\\ \text{minimum}\end{array}} \Longrightarrow \boxed{\begin{array}{l} y = a(x - p)^2 + q \\ \quad\uparrow \\ \text{for maximum, } a < 0 \\ \text{for minimum, } a > 0 \end{array}}$$

In the following problems, the clue words are identified.

A The **product** of two numbers is a **minimum**. If the numbers **differ** by 12, find the numbers.

B What two numbers have a **sum** of 20 and a **product** which is a **maximum**?

Throughout this section, when you are doing the problems, do the following.

Step 1 Look for clue words as you read. Be sure you understand
• what information the problem is asking you to find.
• what information you are given.

Step 2 Then, once you understand the problem, solve it. Refer to the *Steps for Solving Problems* to organize your solution.

7.13 Exercise

A For Questions 1–9, first identify all the clue words and list the information needed to solve the problem. Then solve the problem.

1 Find the number x so that $x - x^2$ is a maximum.

2 Find two numbers whose sum is 25 and whose product is a maximum.

3 Determine two numbers whose difference is 25 and whose product is a minimum.

4   One number subtracted from another is 11. The product of the two numbers is a minimum. What are the numbers?

5   Two numbers have the sum 29. Their product is a maximum. What are the numbers?

6   Determine two numbers which add up to 20 such that the sum of their squares is a minimum.

7   Determine two numbers that add up to 16 such that their product is a maximum.

8   Two consecutive odd numbers and a third number add up to 48. What are the numbers so that the sum of their squares is a minimum?

9   A holding compound for livestock beside a riverside dock is fenced as shown. If 600 m of fencing is used, what are the values of a and b so that the area is a maximum.

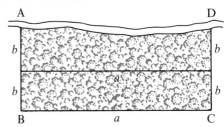

B 10   Warren and Rajni have fifty dollars between them. How should they divide the money so that the product of the amounts is a maximum?

11   A rectangular field is to be fenced along the four sides with another fence parallel to the shorter side. If 900 m of fencing are available, what dimensions of the field give maximum area?

12   A designer wishes to enclose a rectangular parking area with trees planted one metre apart on the boundary. The perimeter of the area is to be 150 m.
(a) What is the maximum area of the parking area?
(b) How many trees are required?

13   The function $f(x) = 2000 - (40 - 2x)(50 - 2x)$ represents the area of grass cut after a strip of width x has been cut around the perimeter of a lawn. Simplify the expression and use it to find the following.
(a) The width of strip needed to cut an area of 800 m^2.
(b) How many times you have to go around with a 50 cm mower to cut 1800 m^2?

14   In an experiment a function, g, is given by $g(t) = -0.2t^2 + 8t - 1$.
(a) What is the maximum or minimum value of g?
(b) What are the co-ordinates of the minimum or maximum point?

15 (a) Find the area of a triangle with maximum area for which the sum of the base and corresponding altitude is 36 cm.

(b) What are the dimensions of the triangle with maximum area?

16 Calculate the dimensions of a rectangular parking lot of maximum area if its boundary is 500 m in length.

To solve Questions 17 to 19 use the following formula.

The approximate height of an object h, in metres, thrown vertically into the air, after time, t(in seconds), is given by
$h(t) = h_0 + vt + 5t^2$,
where h_0 is the initial height (in metres) from which the object is thrown and v is the speed (in metres per second) at which the object is thrown.

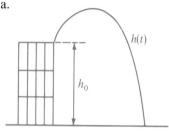

17 A rock is thrown upward from a cliff 15 m high, at a speed of 10 m/s. Determine the maximum height reached by the rock.

18 At the Suburban Rifle Range the clay pigeons are fired upward from ground level at an initial speed of 19.6 m/s. What is the maximum height reached by a clay pigeon?

C 19 For the photo, the height, h, in metres, of the driver above the ground is given by the equation on the photograph, where t is the time taken, in seconds.

$$h(t) = 13.3t - 4.9t^2$$

Find the maximum height reached by the driver.

Practice and Problems: A Chapter Review

1   (a) Draw the graph of the function given by $g(x) = -2x^2 + 4$.
   (b) What are the domain, range, co-ordinates of the vertex and the equation of the axis of symmetry?
   (c) Does the graph have a minimum or maximum point?

2   The data from an experiment verified the hypothesis that the ordered pair $(x, f(x))$ satisfies the relationship given by the equation

$$f(x) = 3.5x^2 + 4.8x - 2.1$$

   (a) Draw the graph of f.
   (b) For what values of x, to 1 decimal place, is $f(x) = 0$?

3   (a) Sketch the graph of $y = x^2$.
   (b) Use your result in (a) and sketch the graph of
      A: $y = 3x^2$ B: $y = -3x^2$ C: $y = 3(x - 1)^2$ D: $y = -3(x - 1)^2 + 2$

4   (a) Write the quadratic function given by $y = x^2 - 6x - 7$ in the form $y = a(x - p)^2 + q$.
   (b) From your answer in part (a), what is the range of the function?

5   Sketch the graph of each curve.
   (a) $y = 3x^2 - 6x + 1$ (b) $y = -2x^2 + 4x + 1$

6   Sketch the following regions. What property do they have in common?
   (a) $y \leq x^2 - 6x + 4$ (b) $y \geq 2x^2 - 12x + 13$
   (c) $y \geq -x^2 + 6x - 14$ (d) $y \leq -2x^2 + 12x - 23$

7   What is the maximum value of A in each of the following?
   (a) $A = 24x - x^2$ (b) $A = 5 - 12x - x^2$ (c) $A = 16 - 3x - 2x^2$

8   Two numbers n and $n + 8$ are given. What are the numbers if their product is to be a minimum?

9   A baseball player threw a ball that travelled according to the equation
$$h(t) = 9.8t + 1.1 - 4.9t^2$$
   where h is the height reached, in metres, and t is the time taken, in seconds. What was the maximum height reached by the ball?

10   A length of 60 cm of gold braid is available. The gold braid is to be cut into two pieces to form two squares. If the area of each square is to be minimum, what are the dimensions of the squares?

Test For Practice

1   Draw the graph of $g: x \rightarrow x^2 - 9$. Write the co-ordinates of
   (a) the vertex .
   (b) the intersection of the graph of g with the x-axis.
   (c) What are the zeroes of the function g?

2   Find the zeroes of the function, g, defined by the equation
   $$g(x) = 1.9x^2 + 6.2x - 3.1$$

3   Sketch the graph of each of the following.
   (a) $y = x^2$ (b) $y = -x^2$ (c) $y = 2x^2$ (d) $y = x^2 + 3$ (e) $y = (x + 1)^2$

4   For each parabola the vertex and a point on the parabola are shown. Find
   the equation of the parabola in standard form: $y = a(x - p)^2 + q$, $x \in R$.
   (a) point $(-1, -1)$, vertex $(4, 7)$ (b) point $(-1, 9)$, vertex $(-2, 7)$

5   Draw a sketch of the parabola passing through the point $(1, -18)$ with
   vertex $(-1, -6)$. Find its defining equation.

6   For each parabola find the equation of the axis of symmetry and the
   co-ordinates of the vertex.
   (a) $y = 5x^2 - 10x + 4$ (b) $y = -3x^2 + 6x - 2$

7   (a) Sketch the graph of $y = 2x^2 + 8x - 7$. Identify
       (i) the region of $y \geq 2x^2 + 8x - 7$.   (ii) the region $y > 2x^2 + 8x - 7$.
   (b) How are the graphs in (i) and (ii) alike? How do they differ?

8   Determine the values of two positive numbers whose sum is 80 and whose
   product yields a maximum.

9   An arrow shot with a crossbow with an upward velocity of v m/s achieves
   a height, h, in metres, after time, t, in seconds, given by the formula
   $$h = vt - \frac{1}{2}gt^2, \quad (g = 9.8).$$
   (a) How long will the arrow take to return to earth if it is shot with an
       upward velocity of 14.7 m/s?
   (b) What is the maximum height reached?

10   A rectangular waiting area is to be separated by 40 m of enclosure. One
    side of the waiting area does not require the material because it is a brick
    wall. What dimensions will ensure the maximum floor space?

Looking Back: A Cumulative Review

1   What is the coefficient of x in the expression $ax - ay + bx + by - cx + cy$?

2   Simplify.

   (a) $3(x - 2) - 5x + 3$ (b) $3a - 2b - 2(3a + 2b)$

   (c) $-(3x - 2y) - 3(x - y)$ (d) $2(m - n) - 3(2m - 3)$

3   Find the least common multiple for each of the following.

   (a) $2x - 5$, $4x^2 - 20x + 25$ (b) $y^2 + y - 2$, $y^2 + 3y + 2$

   (c) $2m^2 - 5m - 3$, $3m^2 + 5m - 12$ (d) $a^2 - 25, a + 5$, $a - 5$

   (e) $12p^2 + 3p - 42$, $12p^3 + 30p^2 + 12p$

4   Solve.

   (a) $\dfrac{1}{2}a - b = 8$ (b) $p + 3q = 2$

                           $3(p - 2q) = 1$

       $a + \dfrac{1}{3}b = 2$

5   Solve the following system. Verify your answers.

$$\frac{2}{x} + \frac{4}{y} = 10 \qquad \frac{4}{x} + \frac{6}{y} = 23$$

6   Nitro Superturf 21-8-9 contains a high proportion of slow releasing nitrogen for prolonged feeding and less risk of burning the lawn. If each bag contains nitrogen, phosphoric acid and potash in the ratio given in its name, how much phosphoric acid is in a bag containing 4 kg of potash?

7   Jim is always thinking about food. He had bacon and eggs for breakfast and noticed there were twice as many pieces of bacon as eggs. If he had eaten 1 more egg, he would have had two-thirds the number of pieces of bacon. How many eggs and pieces of bacon were on his plate?

8   The sum of two numbers is -16. Determine the maximum product of the two numbers.

9   Find two numbers whose sum is 8 and the sum of whose cubes is a minimum.

10   A senior lifeguard at a conservation area locates 620 m of markers in the water to mark out a rectangular safe-swimming area. One side of the safe area is the beach, which does not need markers. What are the dimensions of the safe-swimming area?

8 Study of Quadratic Equations

strategies for solving quadratic equations, method of completing the square, quadratic formula, approximate roots, solving problems, organizational strategies, nature of the roots, applications, strategies, problem solving

Introduction

In the previous chapter, you studied the quadratic function and its graph. The solution of the quadratic equation in the general form, $ax^2 + bx + c = 0$ is useful in solving many problems.

- In sports, quadratic equations occur in the scheduling of games and events.

In a hockey league there are n teams. Each team plays every other team twice, once at home and once on the road. How many games are necessary?

- In business, quadratic equations occur in the analysis of profit and loss.

The price of pizzas depends upon the cost of the ingredients, as well as the cost of staff, heat, lights, and other expenses of running a restaurant. How does the owner of the business decide what price to charge?

The solutions of quadratic equations provide answers to many problems, including those above.

8.1 Strategies: Solving Quadratic Equations

The path of a space probe shown on a screen is given by the equation $y = x^2 + x - 12$.

An **x-intercept** is the directed distance from the origin to one point where the curve crosses the x-axis. The x-intercepts for the curve shown are 3 and -4. Note that the value of y at the point where the curve crosses the x-axis is zero. Thus, the curve shown crosses the x-axis at $(3, 0)$ and $(-4, 0)$.

To find the x-intercepts, algebraically, let $y = 0$, and solve the resulting equation for the value(s) of x, as shown in the following example.

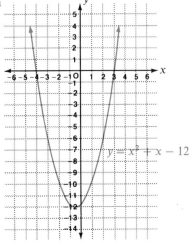

$y = x^2 + x - 12$

Example 1 Find the x-intercepts for curves defined by

(a) $y = x^2 + x - 12$.   (b) $y = 2x^2 + 3x - 2$.

Solution Along the x-axis, $y = 0$. To solve for x-intercepts, let $y = 0$.

(a) $y = x^2 + x - 12$
$(x - 3)(x + 4) = 0$
So, $x - 3 = 0$ or $x + 4 = 0$
$\qquad x = 3 \qquad\quad x = -4$
The x-intercepts are 3 and -4.

(b) $y = 2x^2 + 3x - 2$
$(2x - 1)(x + 2) = 0$
So, $2x - 1 = 0$ or $x + 2 = 0$
$\qquad 2x = 1 \qquad\quad x = -2$
$\qquad x = \dfrac{1}{2}$

The x-intercepts are $\frac{1}{2}$ and -2.

In the previous example, those values of x which make the quadratic equation zero are also known as the **roots** of the equation. Also, the **zeroes of a function** are those values of x which make $f(x) = 0$. Thus, the zeroes of the function $y = x^2 + x - 12$ are 3 and -4 since $f(3) = 0$, and $f(-4) = 0$.

Thus, the skill of solving the quadratic equation may be interpreted in different ways:

- finding the roots of the equation
- finding the x-intercepts of the graph
- finding the points of intersection of the graph and the x-axis
- finding the zeroes of the function.

Example 2 What are the points of intersection of the graph given by
$y = x^2 - 1 - 5(x - 1)$ and the x-axis?

Solution Let $y = 0$. $x^2 - 1 - 5(x - 1) = 0$ ← To find the points of intersection
$$x^2 - 1 - 5x + 5 = 0$$ write the corresponding quadratic
$$x^2 - 5x + 4 = 0$$ equation.
$$(x - 4)(x - 1) = 0$$
$$x - 4 = 0 \quad \text{or} \quad x - 1 = 0$$
$$x = 4 \qquad\qquad x = 1$$

The x-intercepts are 4 and 1. Thus, the points of intersection of the graph
of $y = x^2 - 1 - 5(x - 1)$ and the x-axis are $(4, 0)$ and $(1, 0)$.

In the previous example, the quadratic equation was rewritten in a form
that could be solved. Remember to do so each time.

Finding the y-intercept

To find the x-intercept, you let $y = 0$. In a similar way, to find the
y-intercept, use $x = 0$. The y-intercept is the directed distance from the
origin to the point where the curve crosses the y-axis. The y-intercept is
another important point of the curve of a quadratic function. Finding the
y-intercept will help you draw the graph of the function.

Example 3 Find the y-intercept of $y = x^2 - 1 - 5(x - 1)$.

Solution $y = x^2 - 1 - 5(x - 1)$.
Let $x = 0$.
$$y = 0^2 - 1 - 5(0 - 1)$$ Remember, let $x = 0$ to find the y intercept.
$$= -1 + 5$$ Note the distinction.
$$y = 4$$ The y-intercept is 4, but the co-ordinates of the
curve where the graph crosses the y-axis is $(0, 4)$.
The y-intercept is 4.

8.1 Exercise

A Review your skills for factoring trinomials.

1 Factor.
(a) $x^2 - 8x + 12$ (b) $x^2 - x - 6$ (c) $a^2 + 5a - 14$
(d) $2b^2 + 7b + 3$ (e) $3p^2 - 11p - 20$ (f) $6y^2 + y - 1$

2 Write each trinomial as a product of factors.
(a) $x^2 - 8x + 15$ (b) $x^2 - 2x - 8$ (c) $x^2 + 3x - 54$
(d) $3x^2 + 7x + 2$ (e) $2m^2 - 13m - 7$ (f) $8x^2 + x - 7$

3   What are the x-intercepts of each graph?

(a)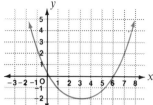

(b)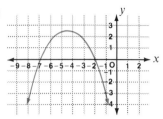

4   What are the roots of each of the following?

(a) $(x - 1)(x + 3) = 0$ (b) $(a - 4)\left(a + \dfrac{1}{2}\right) = 0$

(c) $(2x - 4)(3x + 1) = 0$ (d) $(4b - 1)(7b - 6) = 0$

(e) $(3y - 1)(y + 4) = 0$ (f) $(2m - 1)(3m - 1) = 0$

(g) $(4y - 3)(2y - 1) = 0$ (h) $(3y + 2)(5y - 2) = 0$

5   Solve each equation by factoring.

(a) $a^2 + 4a - 12 = 0$ (b) $b^2 + 5b - 24 = 0$ (c) $6b^2 - b - 2 = 0$

(d) $15a^2 + 26a + 8 = 0$ (e) $4a^2 - 24 = 10a$ (f) $6a^2 = 3a + 3$

(g) $2x^2 - x = 0$ (h) $4a^2 = 8a$

6   Which of the following quadratic equations have 2 as a root?

(a) $x^2 + 2x - 8 = 0$ (b) $y^2 - y - 6 = 0$ (c) $2m^2 + 7m - 4 = 0$

(d) $3x^2 - 7x + 2 = 0$ (e) $2q^2 - 5q + 2 = 0$ (f) $2p^2 + 9p + 10 = 0$

7   Find the roots of each quadratic equation. Check the roots.

(a) $x^2 + 4x - 21 = 0$ (b) $x^2 - 7x + 10 = 0$ (c) $2x^2 - x - 15 = 0$

(d) $6x^2 + 19x - 7 = 0$ (e) $6x^2 - 7x + 2 = 0$ (f) $5x^2 - 6x = 0$

8   (a) Find the roots of $x^2 - 5x + 4 = 0$.

(b) What are the x-intercepts of the graph given by $y = x^2 - 5x + 4$?

(c) How are your answers in parts (a) and (b) related?

9   (a) Find the roots of $2x^2 + 7x - 4 = 0$.

(b) What are the x-intercepts of the graph given by $y = 2x^2 + 7x - 4$?

(c) How are your answers in parts (a) and (b) related?

B 10   Find the x-intercepts of the graph given by each of the following.

(a) $y = x^2 - x - 6$ (b) $y = x^2 + 3x - 40$

(c) $y = 6 + x - x^2$ (d) $y = 2x^2 - 5x - 3$

(e) $y = 15 + 2x - 8x^2$ (f) $y = -2x^2 - 11x + 21$

11 For each of the following • Find the x- and y-intercepts.
                              • Sketch a graph of the curve.
(a) $y = 2x^2 - x - 10$ (b) $y = 2x^2 - 5x - 3$
(c) $y = 2x^2 + 13x + 15$ (d) $y = 6x^2 - 5x - 6$

12 Which of the following graphs have the same x-intercepts?
(a) $y = x^2 + 2x + 1$ (b) $y = x^2 + 3x - 4$ (c) $y = 2x^2 + 3x - 2$
(d) $y = -x^2 - 3x + 4$ (e) $y = -2x^2 - 3x + 2$ (f) $y = -x^2 - 2x - 1$

13 (a) Write the equation $x^2 - 3x = -9(x - 3)$ in general form.
    (b) Solve the equation in part (a). Check your answer.

14 Solve each of the following. Check your answer.
(a) $6x^2 - 5x = 4$ (b) $9 - 6x = -x^2$ (c) $2(x + 4) = x^2$
(d) $2(x^2 - 6) = 5x$ (e) $\frac{1}{2}x^2 + 4x = -\frac{7}{2}$ (f) $(2x + 1)^2 = 8x$
(g) $(m + 2)^2 + 5(m + 2) + 6 = 0$

15 Solve each of the following. Check your answer.
(a) $3y^2 = y + 4$ (b) $3(2x^2 - 3) = 25x$
(c) $2x(5 - 4x) = -3$ (d) $\frac{1}{3}x^2 - \frac{10}{3}x + 7 = 0$
(e) $(x - 5)(x + 5) - x = -19$ (f) $3x(2 - x) + x(x + 1) = 5$

16 (a) Find the roots of $x^2 + (x + 1)^2 - 13 = 0$.
    (b) What are the x-intercepts of $y = x^2 + (x + 1)^2 - 13$?
    (c) How are your answers in parts (a) and (b) related?

17 For each of the following
    • Find the x-intercepts of each graph.
    • Sketch the graph of the curve.
(a) $y = (x + 3)(x - 3) - 7(x + 3)$ (b) $y = x^2 - 1 - 5(x - 1)$
(c) $y = (2x - 1)^2 + (x - 2)(x + 1) + x$

18 (a) What restrictions are needed to solve $\dfrac{3}{3 - x} + \dfrac{4}{x + 2} = 4$?
    (b) Solve the equation in part (a).

19 Solve each of the following. List the restrictions.
(a) $\dfrac{5x + 7}{2 + 3x} + 1 - x = 0$ (b) $\dfrac{1 - 5x}{-3x} - \dfrac{x + 1}{2} = 0$ (c) $\dfrac{6}{x + 1} - \dfrac{5}{1 - x} = 7$

Strategy: Interpreting the Question

To solve a problem, you must read the question carefully. Often in mathematics, the same question may be asked in different ways. The actual solutions may be similar, but the interpretation of the answer may be different.

The solution

Curve $y = x^2 - 3x + 2$

Solution $\quad x^2 - 3x + 2 = 0$

$\quad\quad (x - 1)(x - 2) = 0$

$\quad x - 1 = 0 \quad$ or $\quad x - 2 = 0$

$\quad\quad x = 1 \quad$ or $\quad x = 2$

The interpretations

A: The zeroes of the function
$\quad f(x) = x^2 - 3x + 2$ are 1 and 2.

B: The x-intercepts of
$\quad y = x^2 - 3x + 2$ are 1 and 2.

C: The curve crosses the x-axis at the points $(1, 0)$ and $(2, 0)$.

20 (a) Solve the quadratic equation $x^2 - x - 12 = 0$.

(b) What are the x-intercepts of the graph $y = x^2 - x - 12$?

(c) What are the co-ordinates of the points where the graph of $y = x^2 - x - 12$ crosses the x-axis?

(d) What are the zeroes of the function, f, where $f(x) = x^2 - x - 12$?

21 (a) What are the roots of $2x^2 + 3x - 2 = 0$?

(b) What are the x-intercepts of the graph $y = 2x^2 + 3x - 2$?

(c) What are the co-ordinates of the point where $y = 2x^2 + 3x - 2$ crosses the x-axis?

(d) What are the zeroes of the function $f(x) = 2x^2 + 3x - 2$?

22 Find the x-intercepts of each of the following.

(a) $y = x^2 + 2x - 15$ (b) $y = 3x^2 - 9x$ (c) $y = 2x^2 - 9x - 5$

Interpret your answers in parts (a) to (c) in 2 other ways.

23 Find the zeroes of each function.

(a) $f(x) = x^2 + 3x - 40$ (b) $f(x) = 4 + 5x - 6x^2$ (c) $y = -x^2 + 4x$

Interpret your answers in parts (a) to (c) in 2 other ways.

24 Which of the following functions have 4 as a zero?

(a) $f(x) = 2(4 - 11x) + 5x^2$ (b) $f(x) = 2x^2 + 4x - 4$

(c) $f(x) = 3x^2 + 2(7x + 4)$ (d) $f(x) = 3x^2 - 11x - 4$

Interpret your answers in parts (a) to (d) in 2 other ways.

25 Find the co-ordinates of the point(s) where the graph crosses the x-axis.

(a) $y = x^2 + 8x + 15$ (b) $y = 64 - x^2$ (c) $y = x - x^2$

Interpret your answers in parts (a) to (c) in 2 other ways.

8.2 Solving Quadratic Equations: The Method of Completing the Square

In the study of mathematics, you often use the solution to a question to help you develop a solution to another type of problem. For example: to find the x-intercepts of the graph defined by $f(x) = x^2 - 4x - 1$ you find the roots of the *corresponding quadratic equation* $x^2 - 4x - 1 = 0$. But this equation cannot be factored. To develop a solution, you examine the solution to a question that *can* be done. For example, to find the roots of $x^2 - 4x - 1 = 0$, examine the solution of a simpler equation such as $x^2 - 6 = 0$, which cannot be factored. The equation can be solved as follows:

$$x^2 - 6 = 0$$

Place the variables on one side and the numbers on the other side.

This side is a perfect square. $\longrightarrow x^2 = 6 \longleftarrow$ This side is a number.

$$x = \pm\sqrt{6}$$

The above solution suggests the method of completing the square to solve $x^2 - 4x - 1 = 0$.

Example 1   Solve $x^2 - 4x - 1 = 0$ by completing the square.

Solution

$$x^2 - 4x - 1 = 0$$
$$x^2 - 4x = 1$$

To solve the problem, make the variable side a perfect square.

$$x^2 - 4x + 4 = 1 + 4$$

To complete the square use $\frac{1}{2}(-4) = -2$. Then $(-2)^2 = 4$.

$$(x - 2)^2 = 5$$
$$x - 2 = \pm\sqrt{5}$$
$$x = 2 \pm \sqrt{5}$$

Thus $x = 2 + \sqrt{5}$ or $x = 2 - \sqrt{5}$.

The solution obtained can be interpreted in different ways. Thus, for the function, f, defined by $y = x^2 - 4x - 1$,

- the x-intercepts are $2 + \sqrt{5}$ and $2 - \sqrt{5}$.
- the zeroes of the function are $2 + \sqrt{5}$ and $2 - \sqrt{5}$.
- the co-ordinates of the points where the graph crosses the x-axis are $(2 + \sqrt{5}, 0)$ and $(2 - \sqrt{5}, 0)$.

To find the x-intercepts, you need to use many of the skills you learned in algebra, as shown in the following example.

Example 2   (a) Solve $3x^2 - 6x - 1 = 0$.   (b) Interpret your answer.

Solution   (a) $3x^2 - 6x - 1 = 0$

$3x^2 - 6x = 1$

$x^2 - 2x = \dfrac{1}{3}$

$x^2 - 2x + 1 = 1 + \dfrac{1}{3}$

$(x - 1)^2 = \dfrac{4}{3}$

$x - 1 = \pm\dfrac{2}{\sqrt{3}}$

$x = 1 \pm \dfrac{2}{\sqrt{3}}$ or $\dfrac{3 \pm 2\sqrt{3}}{3}$.

(b) The x-intercepts are $\dfrac{3 \pm 2\sqrt{3}}{3}$;

the zeroes of the function, f,

are $\dfrac{3 \pm 2\sqrt{3}}{3}$;

the co-ordinates of the points where the graph of

$y = 3x^2 - 6x - 1$

crosses the x-axis are

$\left(\dfrac{3 + 2\sqrt{3}}{3}, 0\right)$ and $\left(\dfrac{3 - 2\sqrt{3}}{3}, 0\right)$.

Before you use the method of completing the square, be sure you check whether the quadratic equation can be factored.

8.2 Exercise

A   Unless indicated otherwise, express the roots in radical form.

1   Solve each equation by factoring.
(a) $x^2 - x - 6 = 0$ (b) $x^2 - 2x - 15 = 0$ (c) $x^2 - 10x + 21 = 0$
(d) $2x^2 + x - 1 = 0$ (e) $3x^2 - 7x + 4 = 0$ (f) $2x^2 - 11x + 15 = 0$

2   The method of completing the square has been used to rewrite each equation. Solve.
(a) $(x - 1)^2 = 3$ (b) $(x - 2)^2 = 5$ (c) $2(x + 1)^2 = 8$
(d) $\left(x - \dfrac{2}{3}\right)^2 = \dfrac{5}{9}$ (e) $2\left(x - \dfrac{1}{2}\right)^2 = \dfrac{3}{4}$ (f) $\dfrac{1}{2}\left(x - \dfrac{1}{3}\right)^2 = \dfrac{5}{16}$

3   (a) Show that $-4 - \sqrt{13}$ is a root of $x^2 + 8x + 3 = 0$.
(b) Show that one root of $x^2 + 5x - 3 = 0$ is $\frac{1}{2}(-5 + \sqrt{37})$.

4   (a) Solve the equation $x^2 - 10x + 4 = 0$.
(b) Verify your roots in (a).   (c) Interpret your answer in (a).

B   Check first to see if you need to use your factoring skills.

5   Solve each equation. Interpret your results in each of the following.
(a) $x^2 - 3x + 1 = 0$ (b) $2x^2 - 5x + 1 = 0$
(c) $2c^2 - 3c - 2 = 0$ (d) $y^2 = 5 - 5y$

6   Solve each of the following.
    (a) $x^2 + 5x - 3 = 0$ (b) $x^2 + 2x - 15 = 0$ (c) $3x^2 + 8x - 3 = 0$
    (d) $2x^2 + 8x + 1 = 0$ (e) $3x^2 - 17x + 10 = 0$ (f) $6x^2 + 5x - 1 = 0$

7   (a) Find the roots of $x^2 - 3x + 1 = 0$ by completing the square.
    (b) What is the relationship between your answer in (a) with the function
        defined by $y = x^2 - 3x + 1$? Interpret your answer in (a) in another way.

8   A function is defined by $y = x^2 + 8x + 3$.
    (a) Find the x-intercepts.
    (b) Interpret your answer in (a) in another way.

9   The function, g, is given by $g: x \rightarrow 5x^2 + 3x - 2$. Find the co-ordinates of
    the points where the parabolic curve meets the x-axis.

10 (a) Find the zeroes of the function, f, defined by $f(x) = 2x^2 - 3x - 5$.
    (b) Interpret your answer in (a) in another way.
    (c) Show that one zero of the function, f, defined by $f(x) = x^2 - x - 5$
        is $\frac{1}{2}(1 + \sqrt{21})$.

11 Find the x-intercepts for each of the following curves.
    (a) $y = x^2 - 2x - 6$ (b) $y = 3 - 2x - x^2$
    (c) $y = 2x^2 - 5x - 1$ (d) $y = 3 - x - 3x^2$

12 For the function, f, defined by $f(x) = x^2 - 14x + 48$ find k so that
    (a) $f(k) = 0$ (b) $f(k) = 8$ (c) $f(k) = 3$

13 The formula $S_n = \dfrac{n^2 + n}{2}$ represents the sum of the numbers 1, 2, 3, 4, 5, . . . , n.
    How many numbers are needed so that
    (a) $S_n = 36$?   (b) $S_n = 120$?   (c) $S_n = 465$?

14 (a) A function, g, is defined by $g(x) = x^2 - 3x - 15$. Find the values of k if
        $g(k) = k$.
    (b) If $f(x) = x^2 - 3x + 1$, then find m if $f(m - 1) = f(2m)$.
    (c) If $h(x) = x^2 - 2x + 14$, then find the values of m if
        $h(3m - 2) = 3\, h(m) - 2$.

15 Show that one root of $x^2 + bx - 4 = 0$ is $\dfrac{-b + \sqrt{b^2 + 16}}{2}$.

C 16 Find the roots of each of the following equations.
    (a) $x^2 + 2x + c = 0$ (b) $x^2 + bx - 3 = 0$
    (c) $ax^2 + 4x + 1 = 0$ (d) $x^2 + bx + c = 0$

8.3 Expressing the Roots of a Quadratic Equation in Decimal Form

From the graph of $y = x^2 - 4x - 1$, the values of the x-intercepts may be estimated to be -0.25 and 4.25. But if you wish the values, to be more accurate, you can use the method of completing the square. To find the x-intercepts of $y = x^2 - 4x - 1$, let $y = 0$.

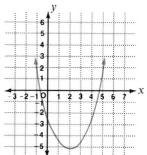

$$x^2 - 4x - 1 = 0$$
$$x^2 - 4x = 1$$
$$x^2 - 4x + 4 = 1 + 4$$
$$(x - 2)^2 = 5$$
$$x - 2 = \pm\sqrt{5}$$
$$x = 2 \pm \sqrt{5} \longleftarrow$$

Once the x-intercepts are found in radical form you can find a value for $\sqrt{5}$.

Use $\sqrt{5} = 2.236$ (to 3 decimal places) to approximate decimal values for the x-intercepts.

$$x \doteq 2 \pm 2.236 \longleftarrow$$
$$x \doteq 2 + 2.236 \quad \text{or} \quad x \doteq 4.236$$
$$x \doteq 2 - 2.236 \quad \text{or} \quad x \doteq -0.236$$

The x-intercepts are -0.236 and 4.236 (to 3 decimal places).

You can now combine the above skill with your graphical skills to solve problems. For example, in the following problem, you can interpret the equation given as follows.

A sketch is used to visualize the problem, when an object is shot in the air.

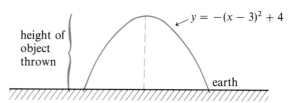

height of object thrown

$y = -(x - 3)^2 + 4$

earth

Example   An object is shot into the air. After time t, in seconds, the height, h (in metres), is given by $h = 2 + 30t - 5t^2$.

Find the time it takes to reach a height of 10 m to the nearest tenth of a second.

Solution   The height is 10 m. Set $h = 10$.

$$h = 2 + 30t - 5t^2$$
$$10 = 2 + 30t - 5t^2$$
$$5t^2 - 30t + 8 = 0$$
$$5t^2 - 30t = -8$$
$$t^2 - 6t = -\frac{8}{5}$$
$$t^2 - 6t + 9 = 9 - \frac{8}{5}$$
$$(t - 3)^2 = \frac{37}{5}$$
$$t - 3 = \pm\sqrt{\frac{37}{5}}$$

$$t - 3 = \sqrt{\frac{37}{5}} \qquad \text{or} \qquad t - 3 = -\sqrt{\frac{37}{5}}$$

$$t = 3 + \sqrt{\frac{37}{5}} \qquad\qquad t = 3 - \sqrt{\frac{37}{5}} \qquad \text{Think}$$

$$t = 3 + \frac{\sqrt{185}}{5} \qquad\qquad t = 3 - \frac{\sqrt{185}}{5} \qquad \sqrt{\frac{37}{5}} \times \sqrt{\frac{5}{5}} = \frac{\sqrt{185}}{5}$$

Use $\sqrt{185} = 13.601$ (to 3 decimal places).   Use a calculator to do
                                                      the computation.

$$t = 3 + \frac{13.601}{5} \qquad \text{or} \qquad t = 3 - \frac{13.601}{5}$$

$$t = 5.720 \; t \qquad\qquad\qquad t = 0.280$$

The object reaches the height of 10 m in 0.3 s and in 5.7 s.

You may wonder why there are two
answers. The physical interpretation
of the mathematical result is as
follows.

From the graph of $s = 2 + 30t - 5t^2$
you can see that the object is 10 m
high at two points.

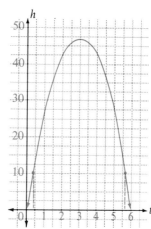

8.3 Exercise

A   Unless indicated otherwise, express answers correct to 1 decimal place.

1   Estimate the values of the x-intercepts of each of the following graphs.

(a) 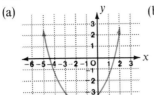   (b) 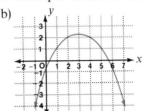   (c)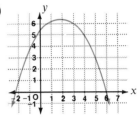

2   (a) Estimate the value of the
        x-intercept from the graph.
    (b) Use $y = x^2 - 3x + 1$ to find
        the values of the x-intercepts.
        Use the approximation
        $\sqrt{5} \doteq 2.236$.

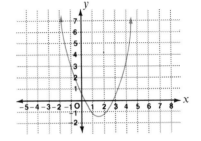

3   (a) Draw the graph of $y = x^2 - 4x - 7$.
    (b) Estimate the values of the x-intercepts from the graph in part (a).

4   (a) Express the x-intercepts of $y = x^2 - 4x - 7$ in radical form.
    (b) Use $\sqrt{11} \doteq 3.317$ to calculate the value of the x-intercepts in part (a).
    (c) Compare your answers in Questions 3(b) and 4(b).

5   (a) Draw the graph of $y = 2x^2 + 4x - 7$.
    (b) Estimate the value of the x-intercepts from the graph in part (a).
    (c) Express the x-intercepts in radical form.
    (d) Use $\sqrt{2} \doteq 1.414$ to calculate the x-intercepts to 2 decimal places.

6   (a) Draw a graph. Estimate the zeroes of the function given by
        $f(x) = x^2 + 6x + 2$.
    (b) Express the zeroes of f in radical form.
    (c) Use your answer in part (b). Calculate the zeroes. Use $\sqrt{7} \doteq 2.646$.

7   (a) Estimate the zeroes of the function, g, given by $g(x) = 2x^2 - 5x - 1$.
    (b) Find the zeroes of g, expressed in radical form.
    (c) Use the values from part (b) to obtain the zeroes to 2 decimal places.
        Use $\sqrt{33} \doteq 5.745$.

B 8 Find the x-intercepts correct to 2 decimal places
(a) $y = x^2 + 5x + 1$ (b) $y = 2x^2 - 11x + 1$ (c) $y = 3(x^2 - 2) - 2$
Refer to the answers above. Interpret them in 2 different ways.

9 A parabola given by $y = 2x^2 + 8x + 1$ intersects the x-axis. Give the co-ordinates of the points of intersection correct to 2 decimal places.

10 Find the zeroes of each function accurate to 2 decimal places.
(a) $f(x) = x^2 - 4x - 6$ (b) $f(x) = x^2 + 3x - 8$
(c) $f(x) = 4x^2 - 3x - 2$

11 A baseball player throws a ball and the height, h (in metres) after time, t (in seconds) is approximated by the formula,

$$h = 2 + 28t - 5t^2.$$

(a) Calculate the time required for the ball to reach a height of 15 m.
(b) What is the maximum height reached?

12 The safe stopping distance, d (in metres) of a motorcycle on a wet pavement is given by

$$d = 0.02(3v^2 + 20v + 1000),$$

where v is the speed of the motorcycle (in metres per second). Find the speed at which the safe stopping distance is 50 m.

Computer Tip

The following computer program, written in the language of BASIC, calculates the roots of the quadratic equation $ax^2 + bx + c = 0$ using

$$x = \frac{-b \pm \sqrt{b^2 - 4ac}}{2a}.$$

Use the program to find the roots for the work you have done on this page.

```
10 INPUT A, B, C
20 LET D = B ↑ 2 − 4 * A * C
30 IF D < 0 THEN 80
40 LET X1 = (−B + SQR(D))/(2 * A)
50 LET X2 = (−B − SQR(D))/(2 * A)
60 PRINT "THE ROOTS ARE", X1, X2
70 GOTO 90
80 PRINT "THE ROOTS ARE NOT REAL"
90 END
```

Math Tip

It is important to clearly understand the vocabulary of mathematics when solving problems. Make a list of all the new words you learn in this chapter. Provide a simple example to illustrate each word.

8.4 The Quadratic Formula

An important strategy in developing mathematics is to examine the solution to specific problem in order to organize a general method of solving further problems. For example, you have solved equations such as $x^2 - 3x + 1 = 0$.

A formula can be found for the roots of a quadratic equation given in the general form $ax^2 + bx + c = 0$.

Compare the steps of a specific quadratic equation and a general quadratic equation.

Specific Case

$$2x^2 + 5x + 1 = 0$$
$$2x^2 + 5x = -1$$
$$x^2 + \frac{5x}{2} = -\frac{1}{2}$$
$$x^2 + \frac{5}{2}x + \frac{25}{16} = \frac{25}{16} - \frac{1}{2}$$
$$\left(x + \frac{5}{4}\right)^2 = \frac{17}{16}$$
$$x + \frac{5}{4} = \frac{\pm\sqrt{17}}{4}$$
$$x = -\frac{5}{4} \pm \frac{\sqrt{17}}{4}$$
$$x = \frac{-5 + \sqrt{17}}{4} \quad \text{or} \quad x = \frac{-5 - \sqrt{17}}{4}$$

General case

$$ax^2 + bx + c = 0, \quad a \neq 0$$
$$ax^2 + bx = -c$$
$$x^2 + \frac{b}{a}x = -\frac{c}{a}$$
$$x^2 + \frac{b}{a}x + \frac{b^2}{4a^2} = \frac{b^2}{4a^2} - \frac{c}{a}$$
$$\left(x + \frac{b}{2a}\right)^2 = \frac{b^2 - 4ac}{4a^2}$$
$$x + \frac{b}{2a} = \frac{\pm\sqrt{b^2 - 4ac}}{2a}$$
$$x = \frac{-b}{2a} \pm \frac{\sqrt{b^2 - 4ac}}{2a}$$
$$x = \frac{-b + \sqrt{b^2 - 4ac}}{2a} \quad \text{or}$$
$$x = \frac{-b - \sqrt{b^2 - 4ac}}{2a}$$

In general, the roots of a quadratic equation, $ax^2 + bx + c = 0, a \neq 0$,

are $\quad x = \dfrac{-b + \sqrt{b^2 - 4ac}}{2a} \quad$ or $\quad x = \dfrac{-b - \sqrt{b^2 - 4ac}}{2a}$.

The roots, written compactly, are given in the form $\quad x = \dfrac{-b \pm \sqrt{b^2 - 4ac}}{2a}$.

Now that the solution has been found for a general quadratic equation, you can apply the results to finding the roots of a specific quadratic equation as shown in the following example. To solve the problem always record the given information first. For example, in the following example, list $a = 2$, $b = 5$ and $c = -3$.

Example Use the quadratic formula to solve
(a) $2x^2 + 5x - 3 = 0$.   (b) $3x^2 - 5x + 1 = 0$.

Solution (a) $2x^2 + 5x - 3 = 0$
$a = 2, b = 5,$ and $c = -3$

$$x = \frac{-b \pm \sqrt{b^2 - 4ac}}{2a}$$

$$x = \frac{-5 \pm \sqrt{25 - 4(2)(-3)}}{2(2)}$$

$$x = \frac{-5 \pm \sqrt{25 + 24}}{4}$$

$$x = \frac{-5 \pm \sqrt{49}}{4}$$

$$x = \frac{-5 \pm 7}{4}$$

$$x = \frac{-5 + 7}{4} \quad \text{or} \quad x = \frac{-5 - 7}{4}$$

$$x = \frac{1}{2} \quad \text{or} \quad x = -3$$

The roots are $\frac{1}{2}$ and -3.

(b) $3x^2 - 5x + 1 = 0$
$a = 3, b = -5, c = 1$

$$x = \frac{-b \pm \sqrt{b^2 - 4ac}}{2a}$$

$$x = \frac{+5 \pm \sqrt{25 - 4(3)(1)}}{2(3)}$$

$$x = \frac{+5 \pm \sqrt{25 - 12}}{6}$$

$$x = \frac{+5 \pm \sqrt{13}}{6}$$

$$x = \frac{+5 + \sqrt{13}}{6} \quad \text{or} \quad x = \frac{+5 - \sqrt{13}}{6}$$

The roots are $\frac{5 \pm \sqrt{13}}{6}$.

Before you solve an equation, you must express the equation in the standard quadratic form, namely, $ax^2 + bx + c = 0$, where the terms are on one side of the equation and are equated to zero. Watch for equations which can be solved by factoring.

8.4 Exercise

A 1 Compare each of the following equations to $ax^2 + bx + c = 0$. What are the values of a, b, and c?
(a) $3x^2 - 2x - 7 = 0$ (b) $2x^2 - 6x + 11 = 0$ (c) $4x^2 + 5x + 1 = 0$
(d) $-3x^2 - x - 10 = 0$ (e) $2x^2 - 11 = 0$ (f) $3x^2 + 8x = 0$

2 For each quadratic equation, what are the values of a, b, and c?
(a) $2x^2 - 3x - 2 = 0$ (b) $x^2 = 4x + 2$ (c) $3x^2 = 4x - 2$
(d) $2x^2 = 5x + 1$ (e) $2x^2 = 3x + 1$ (f) $3x^2 - 2x = 5$

3 Write each equation in general form. What are the values of a, b, and c?
(a) $2(2 - x^2) = 8x$ (b) $x^2 = 3(x - 2) + 5x$
(c) $2x(x - 1) = 3$ (d) $2x(x - 3) = 4x(x - 1)$
(e) $2(x - 1)^2 = 3x - 2$ (f) $(x - 1)(x + 1) = 3x(x - 2)$

4   (a) Find the roots of the quadratic equation $3x^2 - 5x + 2 = 0$,
    • by factoring   • by using the quadratic formula
    (b) Which method of finding the roots do you prefer?

5   Use the quadratic formula to solve each of the following equations.
    Check your answer by factoring.
    (a) $x^2 - 5x + 6 = 0$ (b) $6x^2 - x - 1 = 0$
    (c) $x^2 - 9 = 0$ (d) $x^2 - 6x = 0$

6   (a) Use the formula to find the roots of $2y^2 + 5y - 2 = 0$.
    (b) Verify your roots in part (a).

7   (a) Use the formula to find the roots of $x^2 - 4x - 1 = 0$.
    (b) Verify your roots in part (a).

B 8 Solve each of the following. Use the quadratic formula.
    (a) $x^2 + 3x - 4 = 0$ (b) $x^2 + x - 12 = 0$
    (c) $2x^2 - x - 6 = 0$ (d) $3x^2 - 4x - 15 = 0$
    What do you notice about your answers?

9   (a) Solve $2x^2 + 6x + 1 = 0$.
    (b) Based on your answer in part (a), what information do you know
        about the graph defined by $y = 2x^2 + 6x + 1$?

10 For the graph given by each equation find the x-intercepts.
    (a) $y = 3x^2 - 7x + 1$ (b) $y = 2x^2 - 9x + 2$ (c) $y = 2 - 5x - 2x^2$

11 Find the zeroes of the function, f, defined by the following.
    (a) $f(x) = 2x^2 - 3x - 2$ (b) $f(x) = 4x^2 - x - 3$
    (c) $f(x) = 2x^2 + 6x + 1$

12 Find the roots of each of the following.
    (a) $x^2 - 4x - 1 = 0$ (b) $x^2 + 5x + 2 = 0$ (c) $x^2 - 7x - 2 = 0$
    (d) $2x^2 - x - 3 = 0$ (e) $2x^2 + 7x + 1 = 0$ (f) $5x^2 - 6x - 2 = 0$

13 Solve each of the following.
    (a) $-4a^2 - 3a = -5$ (b) $4b^2 - 2 = 3b$ (c) $y^2 - 8y = +6$
    (d) $4(m^2 - 2) = -3m$ (e) $\dfrac{3}{a} = \dfrac{4}{a^2 - 2}$ (f) $\dfrac{b-1}{b^2 - 2} = \dfrac{2}{3}$
    (g) $(2x + 1)^2 + x^2 + (x - 1)^2 = 10$

C 14 Solve for x.
    (a) $2x^2 + 3ax - 1 = 0$ (b) $4ax^2 + 4x + 3 = 0$
    (c) $3m^2 + 8mx - 2 = 0$ (d) $x^2 + 2ax - b^2 = 0$
    (e) $2mx^2 = 1 - (2 - m)x$

8.5 Approximate Roots, Inadmissible Roots

In solving a quadratic equation, answers left in radical form are **exact** roots.

$$x = 5 \pm \sqrt{3}$$

If $\sqrt{3} \doteq 1.732$ is substituted then the answers are given as decimal **approximations**. For example:

$$x = 5 + \sqrt{3} \longleftarrow \text{exact roots} \longrightarrow x = 5 - \sqrt{3}$$
$$x \doteq 5 + 1.732 \longleftarrow \text{approximate roots} \longrightarrow x \doteq 5 - 1.732$$
$$x \doteq 6.732 \qquad\qquad\qquad\qquad\qquad x \doteq 3.268$$

Example 1 (a) Calculate the exact roots of the quadratic equation.

$$\frac{2 - x}{x} = \frac{3(4 - x)}{2 + x}$$

(b) Find the values of the roots to the nearest tenth. $\sqrt{7} \doteq 2.646$.

Solution (a) $\dfrac{2 - x}{x} = \dfrac{3(4 - x)}{2 + x}$ $\longleftarrow$ Write the quadratic equation in general form. Record the restrictions on the variable.

$$(2 + x)(2 - x) = 3x(4 - x) \qquad x \neq 0, -2.$$
$$4 - x^2 = 12x - 3x^2$$
$$2x^2 - 12x + 4 = 0 \longleftarrow \text{Remember: Check first to see if the}$$
$$x^2 - 6x + 2 = 0 \qquad\qquad \text{quadratic equation can be factored.}$$

Use $a = 1, b = -6,$ and $c = 2$.

$$x = \frac{-b \pm \sqrt{b^2 - 4ac}}{2a}$$

$$x = \frac{-(-6) \pm \sqrt{(-6)^2 - 4(1)(2)}}{2(1)}$$

$$x = \frac{6 \pm \sqrt{36 - 8}}{2}$$

$$x = \frac{6 \pm \sqrt{28}}{2}$$

$$x = \frac{6 \pm 2\sqrt{7}}{2} \longleftarrow \begin{array}{l} \sqrt{28} = \sqrt{4 \times 7} \\ = 2\sqrt{7} \end{array}$$

$$x = 3 \pm \sqrt{7}$$

(b) Use $\sqrt{7} \doteq 2.646$. $x = 3 + \sqrt{7}$ or $x = 3 - \sqrt{7}$
$$\doteq 3 + 2.646 \qquad\qquad \doteq 3 - 2.646$$
$$\doteq 5.646 \qquad\qquad\qquad = 0.354$$

The roots are 5.6 and 0.4 to the nearest tenth.

Inadmissible Roots

Sometimes one of the roots of a quadratic equation may not lead to a solution that satisfies the original problem. Such a root is called an **inadmissible root**. In the next example an inadmissible root is obtained because width cannot be negative.

Example 2   The width (in metres) for the most efficient wind tunnel is given by the equation $w^2 + 1.40w - 7.35 = 0$
Solve the equation to obtain the width, to 1 decimal place.

Solution $w^2 + 1.40w - 7.35 = 0$
Use $a = 1, b = 1.40,$
$c = -7.35$

$$w = \frac{-b \pm \sqrt{b^2 - 4ac}}{2a}$$

$$w = \frac{-1.40 \pm \sqrt{(1.40)^2 - 4(1)(-7.35)}}{2(1)}$$

$$w = \frac{-1.40 \pm \sqrt{1.96 + 29.40}}{2}$$

$$= \frac{-1.40 \pm \sqrt{31.36}}{2} \qquad \text{Obtain the value of the square root using a calculator.}$$

$$w = \frac{-1.40 \pm 5.6}{2}$$

Thus

$$w = \frac{-1.40 + 5.6}{2} \quad \text{or} \quad w = \frac{-1.40 - 5.6}{2} \longleftarrow \text{This root is inadmissible because the width cannot be negative}$$

$$w = 2.1$$

The width of the wind tunnel is 2.1 m, to 1 decimal place.

8.5 Exercise

A   1   The exact roots of a quadratic equation are $4 \pm \sqrt{3}$. Use $\sqrt{3} \doteq 1.732$ to find the approximate value of the roots
(a) rounded to the nearest tenth .   (b) rounded to 2 decimal places.

2   (a) Use the quadratic formula. Find the roots of $x^2 - 4x - 1 = 0$.
(b) Use $\sqrt{5} \doteq 2.236$. Find the value of the roots to 1 decimal place.

3   (a) Find the exact roots of the quadratic equation $x^2 + x - 3 = 0$.
(b) Use $\sqrt{13} \doteq 3.606$. Find the value of the roots to 2 decimal places.

4   (a) Use the quadratic formula to find the exact roots of $4x^2 + 2x - 1 = 0$.
    (b) Use $\sqrt{5} \doteq 2.236$. Find the value of the roots to the nearest hundredth.

5   (a) Find the x-intercepts of the function, f, given by $f(x) = 3x^2 - 2x - 2$.
    (b) Use $\sqrt{7} \doteq 2.646$. Find the value of the x-intercepts to 2 decimal places.

B   Use a calculator or tables to find the approximate roots as needed.

6   (a) Find the x-intercepts of the graph given by $y = x^2 + 3x + 1$,
        (i) to 1 decimal place.   (ii) to 2 decimal places.
    (b) Show why the zeroes in part (a)(ii) provide a better approximation
        than those in part (a)(i). Verify.

7   (a) Find the zeroes of the function given by $f(p) = 2p(p - 3) - 3$,
        (i) to 1 decimal place.   (ii) to 2 decimal places.
    (b) Show why the x-intercepts in part (a)(ii) provide a better approximation
        than those in part (a)(i). Verify.

8   Find the value of the roots of each equation correct to 1 decimal place.
    (a) $x^2 + 3x - 2 = 0$ (b) $t^2 - t - 5 = 0$ (c) $2p^2 - 5p + 1 = 0$
    (d) $4k^2 + 3k - 5 = 0$ (e) $10n^2 - 3n - 3 = 0$ (f) $7m^2 + 8m + 2 = 0$

9   A computer program for finding the roots of a quadratic equation using
    the quadratic formula is written as follows in BASIC language

```
10 INPUT A,B,C
20 LET D = B↑2 − 4∗A∗C
30 IF D < 0 THEN 80
40 LET X1 = (−B + SQR(D))/(2∗A)
50 LET X2 = (−B − SQR(D))/(2∗A)
60 PRINT "THE ROOTS ARE", X1, X2
70 GOTO 90
80 PRINT "THE ROOTS ARE NOT REAL"
90 STOP
```

How many digits will
your computer show?

    Use the computer program to verify the values of the roots found in the
    previous question.

10 Express each quadratic equation in the general form. Then find its roots
    correct to the nearest tenth.
    (a) $a(a - 1) - 3 = 5a$ (b) $(k - 1)^2 + (k - 2) = 0$
    (c) $\dfrac{t + 2}{t} - \dfrac{4t}{3} + 2 = 0$ (d) $\dfrac{1 - x}{2x} = \dfrac{5x}{3x + 1}$
    (e) $\dfrac{n + 1}{2} - \dfrac{n - 1}{3n} = \dfrac{2n + 3}{4n}$ (f) $\dfrac{3(a - 2)}{a + 1} - \dfrac{6a}{a - 2} = \dfrac{(a - 1)^2}{a^2 - a - 2}$

Applications: Equations from Engineering

In engineering, equations do not usually have whole number coefficients. However, the same principles are used to solve these equations as those used to solve quadratic equations with whole number coefficients.

11 In the specifications for a solar dish for heating purposes, the depth (in centimetres) is given by the equation $1.10d^2 - 10.66d - 40.32 = 0$. Find the required depth.

12 At a residential construction project, it is found that the insulation thickness in centimetres needed to obtain efficiency in cost and energy control for the piping is given by the root(s) of the equation $2.5x^2 + 9.5x - 124.2 = 0$. Find the insulation thickness for the piping.

13 By experiments, it is found that the most efficient pedestrian tunnel is given by $y = -0.04x^2 + 0.88x - 0.84$ where the width of the floor of the tunnel, in metres, is considered to be the x-axis. Determine the width of the tunnel.

14 After experimentation, it was found that the safe stopping distance, d (in metres) for a heavy aircraft that taxis at v km/h is given by
$$d = 0.003(6v^2 + 400v + 50\ 000).$$
(a) What is the safe stopping distance of the aircraft taxiing at 100 km/h?
(b) Use the equation to determine the speed at which the aircraft is taxiing to take 200 m to stop safely.

15 After various tests, it is found that the safe stopping distance, d (in metres) for a boat in calm water travelling at v km/h is given by
$$d = 0.002(2v^2 + 10v + 3000).$$
(a) What is the safe stopping distance of a boat in calm water travelling at 12 km/h?
(b) Use the equation to determine the speed at which the boat is travelling to take 15 m to stop safely.

8.6 Solving Problems: Quadratic Equations

In the study of mathematics, very often the same procedure can be used to solve different problems. It is important to be able to recognize which procedure or skill in particular is needed to solve the problem.

The *Steps for Solving Problems* can be used to help you organize your work. You can use these steps to organize your solution of a quadratic equation or problems based on quadratic equations.

Remember, you may also apply other strategies to the solution of a problem. Some of these strategies are shown.

Steps for Solving Problems

A Ask yourself:
   I What information am I asked to find?
   II What information am I given?

B Decide on a method.

C Do the work.

D Check your work.

E Make a final statement.

   Answer the original problem.

Some Problem-Solving Strategies
▶ Estimating an answer and asking yourself, "Is my answer reasonable?"
▶ Checking whether an answer is reasonable by using estimation.
▶ Identifying essential information needed to solve a problem.
▶ Recording the information on a diagram.
▶ Solving the problem by thinking of a simpler problem.
▶ Solving a problem by using a combination of skills.

In the example a diagram helps you not only to visualize the problem, but also to organize your solution.

Example
For Curran Park, a landscaper wishes to plant a boundary of tulips within a rectangular garden with dimensions 18 m by 12 m. To obtain a pleasing look the area of the tulip border should be half of the area of the garden. How wide should the border be, to 1 decimal place?

Solution
Let w, in metres, represent the width of the border. Area of ABCD is given by 12 m × 18 m or 216 m². Area of HEFG given by $(18 - 2w)(12 - 2w)$ m².

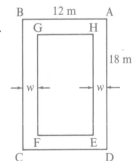

Use area of HEFG $= \dfrac{1}{2}$(Area ABCD)

$$(18 - 2w)(12 - 2w) = \frac{1}{2}(216)$$

$$216 - 60w + 4w^2 = 108$$
$$4w^2 - 60w + 108 = 0$$
$$w^2 - 15w + 27 = 0$$

Use $w = \dfrac{-b \pm \sqrt{b^2 - 4ac}}{2a}$ $a = 1, b = -15, c = 27.$

$w = \dfrac{15 + \sqrt{225 - 108}}{2}$ or $w = \dfrac{15 - \sqrt{225 - 108}}{2}$

$w = \dfrac{15 - \sqrt{117}}{2}$ $\sqrt{117} = 10.82$ $w = \dfrac{15 - \sqrt{11}}{2}$

$w = \dfrac{15 + 10.82}{2}$ $w \doteq \dfrac{15 - 10.82}{2}$

$w \doteq 12.91$ ⟵ inadmissible root $w \doteq 2.09$ (to 2 decimal places)

Thus, the width of the boundary is 2.1 m to 1 decimal place.

Throughout your work in solving problems, you must record a final statement which interprets your algebraic results and translates them into a statement that answers the original question.

8.6 Exercise

A In this exercise, remember to use a diagram when needed to help you translate the problem into mathematics. Express your answers to 1 decimal place, as needed.

1 Use the following problem.

Two numbers differ by 4 and the sum of their squares is 208. What are the numbers?
(a) Use n and $n + 4$ to represent the numbers. Write the appropriate equation.
(b) Solve the equation in (a). Are your answers reasonable?
(c) Check your answers. Verify your answers in the original problem.
(d) What are the numbers?

2 A package designer wants to protect an expensive square book with a 5-cm wide cardboard rim. The area of the rim of the front cover is equal to the area of the front cover of the book. What is the length of the book?

cardboard

3 The perimeter of a right triangle is 60 cm. The lengths of 2 sides of a right triangle, in centimetres, are shown. Find the lengths of all sides of the triangle.

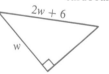

4   In travelling from Arcola to Beamsville you can use either the super highway or connect through Pasqua as shown. On the super highway you can travel 20 km/h faster, and take 2 h less time. What is the average speed for each route?

B 5   When two consecutive integers are squared and the squares added their sum is 421. What are the possible numbers?

6   A right-angled triangle has a height 8 cm more than twice the length of the base. If the area of the triangle is 96 cm², find the dimensions of the triangle.

7   For a certain model of a jet plane, aerodynamics requires that the tail have the profile of a right-angled triangle with area 7.5 m². If the height must be 2 m less than the base length for attachment purposes, calculate the base length of the tail.

8   A rectangular solar heat collecting panel has a length 3 m more than its width. If the area of the solar panel is 28 m², how long is the panel?

9   A right-angled triangle has a perimeter of 120 cm. If the hypotenuse is 50 cm, find the lengths of the other two sides.

10   A matte of uniform width is to be placed around a painting so that the area of the matted surface is twice the area of the picture. If the outside dimensions of the matte are 40 cm and 60 cm, find the width of the matte.

11   A square swimming pool with a side measuring 16 m is to be surrounded by a uniform rubberized floor covering. If the area of the floor covering equals the area of the pool, find the width of the rubberized covering.

12   In the annual 60-km charity Walk-A-Thon, Mark and Tina leave at the same time. Tina walks 0.8 km/h faster than Mark, but stops to have her feet taped, thus losing 0.5 h. Even with this delay Tina finishes the race 2 h before Mark.
(a) How fast was each person walking?
(b) How long did it take each to walk the course?

C 13   A television screen is 40 cm high and 60 cm long. Using the vertical and horizontal control buttons, the picture is compressed to 62.5% of its original area, leaving a uniform dark strip around the outside. Find the dimensions of the smaller picture.

8.7 Organizing the Given Information: A Strategy

You have already learned a number of strategies for helping you to organize your solutions and for obtaining the answers to word problems. In some problems, the given information can be organized more visually by using a chart.

Example   Each trip, a fishing trawler sails 120 km from shore to the Grand Banks. With a full cargo, the ship returns at a speed 10 km/h slower. If the return trip takes 2 h longer, find the total travelling time for each trip to the Grand Banks.

Solution   Let t, in hours, represent the time taken to travel to the Grand Banks. Then $t + 2$, in hours, is the return time.

From the chart, the difference in the rate is given by

	Distance (km)	Rate (km/h)	Time (h)
Out	120	$\dfrac{120}{t}$	t
In	120	$\dfrac{120}{t + 2}$	$t + 2$

$$\frac{120}{t} - \frac{120}{t + 2} = 10$$
$$120(t + 2) - 120t = 10t(t + 2)$$
$$120t + 240 - 120t = 10t^2 + 20t$$
$$10t^2 + 20t - 240 = 0$$
$$t^2 + 2t - 24 = 0$$
$$(t - 4)(t + 6) = 0$$
$$t = 4 \quad \text{or} \quad t = -6 \longleftarrow \text{inadmissible}$$

Thus, the time out is 4 h and the time in is 6 h. The total travelling time is 10 h.

8.7 Exercise

A 1   (a) Read the problem.

The Caldwells start out on a 1520-km car trip to Wascana Park. On the first day they cover 960 km. On the second day they complete the trip, but a heavy rain storm causes them to reduce their average speed by 10 km/h. If the 2-d trip took a total of 20 h, what was the average speed on each day?

(b) What headings could be used to organize the information in the chart.

(c) Copy and complete the chart.

(d) Solve the problem.

B For each of the following problems, decide on the strategy you will need to use to solve the problem.

2 Each side of a square house is 6 m longer than each side of the square garage. If the combined area of house and garage is 180 m², find the dimensions of the house and the garage.

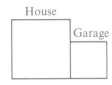

3 John and Petra leave the cottage by two separate roads, each 3 km in length, to go to town. Petra walks 0.5 km/h faster than John. Along the road John meets a friend and stops to talk for 5 min so that Petra has to wait in town 10 min for John to arrive.
(a) How fast do John and Petra walk?
(b) How long does it take John and Petra to travel the distance?

4 Find 3 consecutive positive odd integers such that the sum of the squares of the first two is 15 less than the square of the third.

5 The "Fashion Up" magazine prints square photographs in two sizes. The larger photographs have sides 2 cm longer than the smaller photographs. The combined area of 3 of the smaller photographs is 12 cm² more than one larger photograph. Find the dimensions of each size of photograph.

6 Davidson is on a cross Canada motorcycle trip and has just arrived at the foothills of the Rockies. He plans to take 1 h longer on the 245-km trip up the east side than on the 225-km trip down the west side. To do this he will have to average 20 km/h faster on the downhill side. How long will the trip through the Rockies take?

7 Janet swims lengths at a local pool every morning. Last week she swam a total of 12 000 m. This represented 20 more lengths than the length of the pool. What is the length of the pool?

8 If a guitar maker increases the production rate by 3 guitars per month he will finish an order for 65 guitars in 2 months less time. What is the original output of the guitar maker (to the nearest whole guitar)?

C 9 Amy loves pizza crust and Bill likes the cheese that gathers in the middle. They want to split a pizza with radius 30 cm so that Amy gets the outside ring and Bill gets the centre, yet they each get the same amount of pizza. How wide should Amy's ring be?

8.8 Nature of the Roots of Quadratic Equations

The general quadratic equation

$$ax^2 + bx + c = 0$$

has roots m and n, defined by the following equations.

$$m = \frac{-b + \sqrt{b^2 - 4ac}}{2a} \qquad n = \frac{-b - \sqrt{b^2 - 4ac}}{2a}$$

The expression $b^2 - 4ac$ provides information about the roots of the quadratic equation. The expression $D = b^2 - 4ac$ is called the **discriminant**. By examining the values of $D = b^2 - 4ac$ you can learn about the characteristics of the roots without necessarily finding the roots. Look for patterns in the example.

Example 1 Find the roots of each quadratic equation. Describe the value of the discriminant, D, for each equation.

(a) $x^2 - 8x + 16 = 0$ (b) $3x^2 - 7x + 2 = 0$ (c) $3x^2 + 2x + 4 = 0$

Solution (a) $x^2 - 8x + 16 = 0$ Calculate the roots.

$a = 1, b = -8, c = 16$

$$m = \frac{8 + \sqrt{0}}{2} = 4, \quad n = \frac{8 - \sqrt{0}}{2} = 4$$

$D = b^2 - 4ac$
$D = (-8)^2 - 4(1)(16)$
$D = 64 - 64 = 0$

The roots are real and equal.

The discriminant is equal to zero.

(b) $3x^2 - 7x + 2 = 0$ Calculate the roots.

$a = 3, b = -7, c = 2$

$$m = \frac{7 + \sqrt{25}}{6} = \frac{7 + 5}{6} = \frac{12}{6} = 2$$

$D = b^2 - 4ac$
$D = (-7)^2 - 4(3)(2)$
$D = 49 - 24 = 25$

$$n = \frac{7 - \sqrt{25}}{6} = \frac{7 - 5}{6} = \frac{2}{6} = \frac{1}{3}$$

The discriminant is a perfect square.

The roots are real, unequal and rational.

(c) $3x^2 + 2x + 4 = 0$ Calculate the roots.

$a = 3, b = 2, c = 4$

$$m = \frac{-2 + \sqrt{-44}}{6}, \quad n = \frac{-2 - \sqrt{-44}}{6}$$

$D = b^2 - 4ac$
$D = (2)^2 - 4(3)(4)$
$D = 4 - 48 = -44$

$\sqrt{-44}$ is not a real number.

The discriminant is negative.

Thus, the roots are not real.

The chart shows the nature of the roots related to the value of the discriminant.

Value of Discriminant $D = b^2 - 4ac$	Nature of the Roots		
	real or not real	equal or unequal	rational or irrational
I $D > 0$ (not a perfect square)	real	unequal	irrational
II $D > 0$ (perfect square)	real	unequal	rational
III $D = 0$	real	equal	rational
IV $D < 0$	not real	unequal	does not apply

Example 2   Describe the nature of the roots for each of the following.
(a) $3x^2 + 6x + 1 = 0$ (b) $x^2 - 5x + 7 = 0$

Solution   (a) $D = b^2 - 4ac$
$D = 6^2 - 4(3)(1)$
$D = 36 - 12 = 24$

$D > 0$ and not a perfect square.
Thus, the roots are real, unequal, and irrational.

(b) $D = b^2 - 4ac$
$D = (5)^2 - 4(1)(7)$
$D = 25 - 28 = -3$

$D < 0$. There are no real roots.

Example 3   Find the value(s) of k so that $x^2 + (k - 1)x - k = 0$ has equal roots.

Solution   *Step 1*
For the equation, $a = 1$,
$b = (k - 1)$, and $c = -k$.

$D = b^2 - 4ac$
$D = (k - 1)^2 - 4(1)(-k)$
$D = k^2 - 2k + 1 + 4k$
$D = k^2 + 2k + 1$

Step 2
For equal roots, $D = b^2 - 4ac = 0$.

$k^2 + 2k + 1 = 0$
$(k + 1)(k + 1) = 0$
$k + 1 = 0$
$k = -1$

Thus, for equal roots, $k = -1$.

8.8 Exercise

A 1   (a) For each equation, calculate $D = b^2 - 4ac$.
(i) $x^2 - x - 12 = 0$ (ii) $x^2 - 2x - 24 = 0$
(iii) $2x^2 + x - 3 = 0$ (iv) $6x^2 - 7x - 3 = 0$
(b) Describe the nature of the roots of the above equations.

2   (a) For each equation, calculate $D = b^2 - 4ac$.
   (i) $x^2 - 3x - 2 = 0$ (ii) $2x^2 - 5x - 1 = 0$
   (iii) $2x^2 - 7x + 1 = 0$ (iv) $x^2 - 2x - 1 = 0$
   (b) Describe the nature of the roots of the above equations.

3   (a) For each equation, calculate $D = b^2 - 4ac$.
   (i) $x^2 + 6x + 9 = 0$ (ii) $x^2 - 12x + 36 = 0$
   (iii) $16x^2 + 8x + 1 = 0$ (iv) $4x^2 - 12x + 9 = 0$
   (b) Describe the nature of the roots of the above equations.

4   (a) For each equation, calculate $D = b^2 - 4ac$.
   (i) $x^2 - 2x + 9 = 0$ (ii) $x^2 - 3x + 7 = 0$
   (iii) $3x^2 + x + 6 = 0$ (iv) $4x^2 + 2x + 1 = 0$
   (b) Describe the nature of the roots of the above equations.

5   The discriminants for various quadratic equations are listed below. In each
   case describe the nature of the roots.
   (a) 25   (b) 12   (c) -3 (d) 4.5   (e) 0
   (f) 64   (g) 0.36   (h) -18 (i) 96   (j) 100

6   (a) For the equation $x^2 - 6x + 2 = 0$, calculate the discriminant. Describe
       the nature of the roots.
   (b) Check your answers in part (a) by finding the roots of the equation.

B Remember: to find values for a, b, and c, the quadratic equation must be
   in the form $ax^2 + bx + c = 0$.

7   Find the discriminant for each of the following equations and describe the
   nature of the roots.
   (a) $x^2 - 5x + 1 = 0$ (b) $x^2 - 6x + 5 = 0$
   (c) $x^2 - 4 = 0$ (d) $x^2 - 11 = 0$
   (e) $5x^2 + 10x + 9 = 0$ (f) $7 + 10x - 15x^2 = 0$

8   Express the roots of each equation in terms of k.
   (a) $x^2 - 4kx + 2k^2 = 0$ (b) $kx^2 - (k - 1)x - 1 = 0$

9   Express the discriminant of each equation in terms of k.
   (a) $x^2 - 4kx + 4k^2 = 0$ (b) $2kx^2 + kx - (k - 1) = 0$
   (c) $4k^2x^2 - 4kx + 1 = 0$ (d) $kx^2 - (k - 2)x - 2 = 0$

10   Describe the nature of the roots of the following.
   (a) $(x + 3)(x - 2) = 5$ (b) $5(x^2 - 5x) + 2 = 0$
   (c) $\dfrac{x - 2}{3} + x^2 + 2 = 0$ (d) $\dfrac{1}{x + 1} + \dfrac{1}{x + 2} = 2$

11 Describe the nature of the roots of each equation.

(a) $\dfrac{2}{1-x} + 1 = \dfrac{3}{x+2}$ (b) $\dfrac{2}{x} - 1 = \dfrac{3}{x+1}$

(c) $\dfrac{1}{x} - \dfrac{1}{x-3} = 1$ (d) $\dfrac{1-2x}{3} = \dfrac{7}{x-5}$

12 (a) For the quadratic equation $kx^2 + 2x + 4 = 0$, find the value of k so that the roots are equal.

(b) The roots of $x^2 + (k+8)x + 9k = 0$ are equal. What are the values of k?

13 Each equation has two real and distinct roots. What value or values does k have?

(a) $kx^2 + 3x + 6 = 0$ (b) $x^2 + kx + 4 = 0$

14 Each equation has non-real roots. What value or values does k have?

(a) $kx^2 - 5x + 6 = 0$ (b) $4x^2 + 4x + k = 0$

15 For what values of m does each equation have real and unequal roots?

(a) $mx^2 - 2x - 4 = 0$ (b) $4x^2 - 5x + m + 1 = 0$

C 16 Find the value or values for k, $k \neq 0$, so that $(k+2)x^2 - kx - 2 = 0$ will have real, rational roots.

17 Find two values for k, $k \neq 0$, so that $x^2 + (k-3)x - k + 2 = 0$ will have real, rational roots.

Calculator Tip

You can use a calculator in problems about structures. For examples, many bridges have circular arches. To calculate the radius, r of a circular arch of a bridge you can use the formula

$r = \dfrac{h}{2} + \dfrac{2s^2}{h}$

where h, s are given in the diagram.

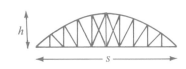

▶ Calculate the radius of a circular arch if the length of the bridge is 8.562 m long and the height of the arch is 2.365 m.
▶ Write a computer program to calculate the radius r.

Problem Solving: Finding Conditions

You can use your skills with the nature of the roots of quadratic equations to determine various conditions imposed on it as shown by the following.

What condition is true about the coefficients of the quadratic equation $mx^2 - 6nx + p = 0$ if it has real and unequal roots?

To answer the question, you need to examine the question for clues. Ask yourself "What is the condition for real and unequal roots?"

For real and unequal roots $b^2 - 4ac > 0$. In the equation, $a = m$, $b = -6n$, and $c = p$.

Find an expression.	Apply the condition.
$D = b^2 - 4ac$	$36n^2 - 4mp > 0.$
$D = (-6n)^2 - 4(m)(p)$	$9n^2 > mp$
$D = 36n^2 - 4mp$	$n^2 > \dfrac{mp}{9}$

Thus, the roots are real and unequal for $n^2 > \dfrac{mp}{9}$.

18 Find the conditions that must be true if the equation $px^2 + (2p + 1)x + p = 0$ has equal roots.

19 If $h^2x^2 - 5hx = -c^2$ has real and unequal roots for $h \neq 0$, prove that $-\dfrac{5}{2} < c < \dfrac{5}{2}$.

20 If $6a^2x^2 + 10bx + \dfrac{2}{3} = 0$ has imaginary roots, $a, b \neq 0$, prove that $\dfrac{a^2}{b^2} > \dfrac{25}{4}$.

21 (a) Show that $a^2 + (b + 1)a + b = 0$ has rational roots for rational values of b.

(b) Prove that $(k + 1)x^2 - x - (k + 2) = 0$ has real roots for all values of k.

(c) Prove that no real value of k exists for which the quadratic equation $x^2 - 10 = k(x - 2)$ has equal roots.

22 (a) Prove that $(x^2 + 1)y = (x + 1)^2$ will have real roots if $0 \leq y \leq 2$.

(b) Prove that $(x^2 + 2)y = (x + 2)^2$ will have equal roots if $y = 0$ or $y = 3$.

23 Show that $(x^2 - 1)k = (x - 1)^2$ will have equal roots for only one value of k.

24 For what condition on a, b, and c will the equation $ax^2 - (ac + b)x = 2cb$ have equal roots?

8.9 Sum and Product of the Roots of a Quadratic Equation

The quadratic equation $ax^2 + bx + c = 0$, $a, b, c \in R$, $a \neq 0$ has the roots

$$m = \frac{-b + \sqrt{b^2 - 4ac}}{2a}, \qquad n = \frac{-b - \sqrt{b^2 - 4ac}}{2a}.$$

Addition of the Roots

Let's see what happens when you add the roots.

$m + n$

$= \dfrac{-b + \sqrt{b^2 - 4ac}}{2a} + \dfrac{-b - \sqrt{b^2 - 4ac}}{2a}$

$= \dfrac{-b + \sqrt{b^2 - 4ac} - b - \sqrt{b^2 - 4ac}}{2a}$

$= \dfrac{-2b}{2a} = \dfrac{-b}{a}$

Product of the Roots

There is a similar result when you find the product of the roots.

mn

$= \left(\dfrac{-b + \sqrt{b^2 - 4ac}}{2a}\right)\left(\dfrac{-b - \sqrt{b^2 - 4ac}}{2a}\right)$

$= \dfrac{(-b)(-b) - (\sqrt{b^2 - 4ac})(\sqrt{b^2 - 4ac})}{(2a)(2a)}$

$= \dfrac{b^2 - (b^2 - 4ac)}{4a^2} = \dfrac{c}{a}$

Thus, if m, n are the roots of $ax^2 + bx + c = 0$, $a \neq 0$

- the sum $m + n$ is given by $-\dfrac{b}{a}$,
- the product mn is given by $\dfrac{c}{a}$.

Example 1   What are the sum and product of the roots for each equation?

(a) $3x^2 - 6x + 8 = 0$ (b) $\dfrac{2}{x - 1} + \dfrac{3}{x + 2} = 3$

Solution   (a) $3x^2 - 6x + 8 = 0$ $a = 3, b = -6, c = 8$

The sum is given by $-\dfrac{b}{a} = -\dfrac{-6}{3} = 2$.   The product is given by $\dfrac{c}{a} = \dfrac{8}{3}$.

(b) *Step 1*
Express the equation in the general form $ax^2 + bx + c = 0$.

$\dfrac{2}{x - 1} + \dfrac{3}{x + 2} = 3, \quad x \neq 1, -2$

$2(x + 2) + 3(x - 1) = 3(x - 1)(x + 2)$
$2x + 4 + 3x - 3 = 3(x^2 + x - 2)$
$5x + 1 = 3x^2 + 3x - 6$
$0 = 3x^2 - 2x - 7$

Step 2
For $3x^2 - 2x - 7 = 0$,
$a = 3, b = -2, c = -7$.

The sum is given by $-\dfrac{b}{a} = -\dfrac{-2}{3}$

$= \dfrac{2}{3}$.

The product is given by $\dfrac{c}{a} = \dfrac{-7}{3}$.

Once you know the sum and product of the roots, you can relate them in terms of the original equation as follows.

$$ax^2 + bx + c = 0 \longleftarrow \text{Divide by } a.$$

$$x^2 + \frac{b}{a}x + \frac{c}{a} = 0$$

$$x^2 - \left(-\frac{b}{a}\right)x + \frac{c}{a} = 0$$

$$\underset{\text{sum}}{\uparrow} \qquad \underset{\text{product}}{\uparrow}$$

Thus if the roots of a quadratic equation are known, the equation can be quickly constructed, as follows.

$$x^2 - (\text{sum of roots})x + (\text{product of roots}) = 0$$

Roots	Sum	Product	Equation
5, −8	−3	−40	$x^2 - (-3)x - 40 = 0$ or $x^2 + 3x - 40 = 0$

If one root of an equation is known the other can be quickly determined.

Example 2 One root of $3x^2 + 13x - 10 = 0$ is -5. Find the other root.

Solution Let the other root be m.

$$3x^2 + 13x - 10 = 0$$

$$x^2 + \frac{13}{3}x - \frac{10}{3} = 0$$

$$x^2 - \left(-\frac{13}{3}\right)x - \frac{10}{3} = 0$$

$$\underset{\text{sum of the roots}}{\uparrow}$$

Then, $m + (-5) = -\dfrac{13}{3}$

$$m = 5 - \frac{13}{3}$$

$$m = \frac{2}{3}$$

Thus, the other root is $\dfrac{2}{3}$.

8.9 Exercise

A 1 (a) For the quadratic equation $3x^2 + 5x - 2 = 0$, what is the sum of the roots? What is the product of the roots?

(b) Use your answer in part (a) to decide which set of values forms the roots of the equation.

$$\text{A: } \frac{2}{3} \text{ and } \frac{-7}{3} \qquad \text{B: } \frac{1}{3} \text{ and } -2$$

(c) Why do you need to check the *sum* and *product* to determine whether two given values are the roots of a quadratic equation?

2   Two values are given for each quadratic equation. Check whether they are the roots.

	Quadratic Equation	Values
(a)	$x^2 - 11x + 30 = 0$	5, 6
(b)	$30x^2 + 13x - 10 = 0$	$\dfrac{2}{5}, \dfrac{-5}{6}$
(c)	$130x^2 - 72x + 25 = 0$	$\dfrac{7}{8}, \dfrac{-15}{2}$
(d)	$x^2 + 1.3x - 3 = 0$	$1.2, -2.5$

3   Without solving, find the sum and product of the roots of each equation.
(a) $x^2 + 5x + 2 = 0$ (b) $x^2 + 6x + 9 = 0$
(c) $3x^2 + 2x - 7 = 0$ (d) $5x^2 - 3x - 1 = 0$
(e) $11x^2 + 19x = 7$ (f) $2\pi x^2 + \sqrt{6}x - 8 = 0$
(g) $\dfrac{1}{x-1} + \dfrac{1}{x-2} = 3$ (h) $\dfrac{2}{1-2x} - \dfrac{1}{1+2x} = 1$

4   Find an expression for the sum and product of the roots of each equation.
(a) $dx^2 - 2ex - 3f = 0$ (b) $4px^2 - 3gx + 5 = 0$

5   Construct a quadratic equation which has the following roots. Express your equation in the form $ax^2 + bx + c = 0$.
(a) $3, 9$ (b) $3, -3$ (c) $\dfrac{1}{4}, -\dfrac{3}{4}$ (d) $\dfrac{1}{3}, 3$ (e) $3 + \sqrt{3}, 3 - \sqrt{3}$,

6   For a quadratic equation, the sum and product of the roots are $\frac{1}{9}$ and $-\frac{1}{3}$ respectively.
(a) Construct the quadratic equation.   (b) What are the roots?

7   For a quadratic equation $2x^2 + kx + 8 = 0$ one root is 2.
(a) Find the value of k.   (b) What is the other root?

8   For each quadratic equation a root is given. Find the other root.

	Equation	Root
(a)	$x^2 + 6x + m = 0$	-3
(b)	$x^2 + 8x + p = 0$	2
(c)	$x^2 + bx + 4 = 0$	-2
(d)	$2x^2 + px + 3 = 0$	$\frac{1}{2}$
(e)	$3x^2 + 2x + k = 0$	-1

B 9 For the quadratic equation $x^2 + kx + 6 = 0$, the value $3 - \sqrt{3}$ is a root.
(a) Find the value of k. (b) What is the other root?

10 The roots of $2kx^2 + (3k + 6)x - 12 = 0$ are p and q. If $p + q = 0$, find k.

11 The roots of $px^2 - 25x + 12 = 0$ are reciprocals. What is the value of p?

12 For the quadratic equation $2x^2 + 3mx + 4m = 0$, the sum of the roots is represented by S, and P represents the product. If $S + P = 8$, find m.

13 A quadratic equation is given by $kx^2 - (k - 6)x + 2 = 0$.
The roots of the equation are m and n. For each relationship between m and n given, find the corresponding value of k.
(a) $m + n = 6$ (b) $mn = 8$ (c) $m^2n^2 = 10$
(d) $\dfrac{1}{mn} = 12$ (e) $3(m + n) = 9$ (f) $(4m)(4n) = 24$

14 For the quadratic equation $(m + 1)x^2 + (2m + 1)x - 2 = 0$ find m so that
(a) the roots are numerically equal but opposite in sign.
(b) the roots are reciprocals of each other.
(c) the roots are negative reciprocals of each other.

15 (a) The quadratic equation $ax^2 + bx + c = 0$ has roots that are negative reciprocals. What is the relationship between a and c?
(b) What is the relationship between the roots of $ax^2 + bx + c = 0$ and $cx^2 + bx + a = 0$.

C 16 If one root of $px^2 + qx + r = 0$ is three times as great as the other root, write an equation relating p, q, and r.

17 For the quadratic equation $2x^2 - 3x - 1 = 0$, the roots are m and n. *Without solving*, find the value of $m^2 + n^2$.

Problem Solving

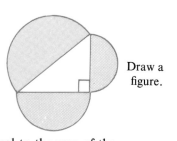

Is the following statement true or false?

Draw a figure.

In a right-angled triangle, the area of the semi-circle drawn on the hypotenuse as the diameter is equal to the sum of the areas of the semi-circles drawn on the other sides as diameters.

Practice and Problems: A Chapter Review

1 Solve each of the following. Check your answer.

    (a) $(a - 5)(2a + 3) = -2a - 3$ (b) $(1 - x)(x + 4) + \frac{2}{3}(2x + 1)^2 = 6$

2 (a) Write the equation in general form.

$$3(1 - x)(x + 2) + (x + 1)^2 - 4 = 0$$

    (b) Solve the equation in part (a). Check your answer.

3 (a) For $f(x) = x^2 - 2x$, find k if $f(k) = 5$.

    (b) If $g(x) = x^2 - 3x$, find k if $g(k) = k + 1$.

4 Use the method of completing the square to find x.
    (a) $x^2 - 6x + 2 = 0$ (b) $2x^2 - 5x + 1 = 0$
    (c) $2x^2 + 8x + 1 = 0$ (d) $3x^2 - 2x - 1 = 0$

5 Find the x-intercepts of $y = 3(x^2 - 2) - 2$, correct to 2 decimal places.

6 Solve each of the following.

    (a) $(x - 2)^2 = 2(x - 1)^2$ (b) $\dfrac{x - 1}{4} + \dfrac{1}{2} = \dfrac{2}{x}$

7 (a) For the equation, $25x^2 - 20x + 4 = 0$, calculate the discriminant and describe the nature of the roots.

    (b) Check your answer in part (a) by finding the roots of the equation.

8 For what values of p does the equation $4x^2 + px + 9 = 0$ have non-real roots?

9 The quadratic equation

$$4x^2 + 6x + k + 3 = 0$$

has real and unequal roots. Find the value(s) of k.

10 If $(k + 2)x^2 - kx - 2 = 0$ has equal, real roots, find the value of k.

11 Dave and Jim entered the annual spring canoe race last year. The number of times they paddled the course during practice was one fewer than the number of kilometres in the course. If they paddled a total of 72 km during practice, how long was the course?

Test For Practice

1   Find the x-intercepts of the graph of $y = 5 - (x - 3)(2x + 3)$.

2   Match the quadratic equations with the roots.

   (a) $2x^2 - 11x + 5 = 0$ A $\left\{-\dfrac{5}{2}, 1\right\}$

   (b) $2x^2 - 9x - 5 = 0$ B $\left\{\dfrac{1}{2}, 5\right\}$

   (c) $2x^2 - 3x - 5 = 0$ C $\left\{-\dfrac{1}{2}, -5\right\}$

   (d) $2x^2 + 3x - 5 = 0$ D $\left\{-\dfrac{1}{2}, 5\right\}$

   (e) $2x^2 + 11x + 5 = 0$ E $\left\{\dfrac{5}{2}, -1\right\}$

3   Use the method of completing the square to find x for $2x^2 - 5x - 1 = 0$.

4   Verify that $1 + \sqrt{1 - c}$ is a root of $x^2 - 2x + c = 0$.

5   Find the zeroes of the function $f(x) = x^2 - 4x - 6$ accurate to 2 decimal places.

6   (a) Solve $5x^2 - 6x - 2 = 0$.
   (b) Based on your answer in part (a), what information do you know about the function $f(x) = 5x^2 - 6x - 2$?

7   For what values of p does the equation $(p - 2)x^2 + 2px + p + 3 = 0$ have non-real roots?

8   Describe the nature of the roots of the following.

   (a) $(x + 1) + \dfrac{1}{x} = 2$ (b) $\dfrac{x}{2} + \dfrac{1}{x + 1} = 7$

9   A football is kicked and the height, h, of the football (in metres) after time, t, (in seconds), is approximated by the formula $h = 24t - 5t^2$.
   Calculate the time required for the ball to reach a height of 10 m.

10   The perimeter of a right-angled triangle is 36 cm. If the hypotenuse is 15 cm, find the length of the other two sides.

11   On a spending spree contest John spends $330 in 2 h less than his competitor Susan. Susan spends money at a rate of $15/h less than John. Find the rate of spending of each person, in dollars per hour, to 1 decimal place.

9 Concepts and Skills: Analytic Geometry

finding distance, internal and external division, equations of circles at the origin and not at the origin, solving linear quadratic systems of equations, strategies with analytic geometry, tangent to circles, applications, problem solving

Introduction

In air navigation, geological surveying, mapmaking, weather forecasting and in many other ways, being able to locate the position of a landmark accurately depends on the mathematics-based concept of latitude and longitude.

The skills required to locate a position are analagous to the skills you developed earlier which are required to find the position of a point on the co-ordinate plane, given either one of the two facts about the point.

- you know the x co-ordinate and the y co-ordinate
- you know two lines l_1 and l_2 which intersect at the point

Although the mathematics involved is far more complex, the same basic principle of determining a point of intersection has been used to successfully guide unmanned satellites towards the most distant planets in your solar system.

Scientists used mathematics to calculate a course for the spacecraft that would *intersect* the orbit for Saturn at exactly the right moment.

The study of intersecting lines and intersecting curves is very important in the study of mathematics. You will learn to extend earlier skills to find the co-ordinates of a point of intersection if you know the equations of the two intersecting lines. The principles you will learn about finding the points of intersection of intersecting curves can be applied when you want to find the points of intersection of more complex curves, in the study of future advanced mathematics.

9.1 Distance Between Two Points

You can find a general formula to show the distance between any two points.

$P_1(x_1, y_1)$ and $P_2(x_2, y_2)$ are any two points on the plane.
Locate the point $P_3(x_2, y_1)$ as shown in the diagram.

From the diagram, $\angle P_1P_3P_2 = 90°$.

$$P_1P_3 = \underbrace{|x_2 - x_1|}_{\text{represented by } |\Delta x|} \qquad P_3P_2 = \underbrace{|y_2 - y_1|}_{\text{represented by } |\Delta y|}$$

Since $\triangle P_1P_3P_2$ is a right-angled triangle then

$$(P_1P_2)^2 = (P_1P_3)^2 + (P_3P_2)^2$$
$$= (|x_2 - x_1|)^2 + (|y_2 - y_1|)^2$$
$$= (x_2 - x_1)^2 + (y_2 - y_1)^2$$
$$P_1P_2 = \sqrt{(x_2 - x_1)^2 + (y_2 - y_1)^2}$$
$$\text{or} \quad P_1P_2 = \sqrt{|\Delta x|^2 + |\Delta y|^2} \quad \text{where } |\Delta x| = |x_2 - x_1|$$
$$|\Delta y| = |y_2 - y_1|$$

The distance between points $P_1(x_1, y_1)$ and $P_2(x_2, y_2)$ is given by
$$P_1P_2 = \sqrt{(x_2 - x_1)^2 + (y_2 - y_1)^2}$$

The formula is used in the following example to find the distance between two points when the co-ordinates of the points are given.

Example 1   Find the length of the line segment joining $P(-4, -2)$ and $Q(2, 2)$.

Solution   From the diagram

length of PC $= |2 - (-4)|$
$\qquad\qquad = |2 + 4| = 6$

length of CQ $= |2 - (-2)|$
$\qquad\qquad = |2 + 2| = 4$

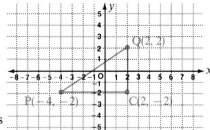

In $\triangle PQC$, $\angle C$ is a right angle. Thus

$PQ^2 = PC^2 + CQ^2 \qquad PQ = \sqrt{52}$
$\qquad = 36 + 16 \qquad\qquad\quad = 2\sqrt{13} \quad \text{(length is positive)}$
$\qquad = 52$

Thus the length of the line segment joining P and Q is $2\sqrt{13}$ units.

When solving a problem, it is useful to draw a diagram to help you visualize the problem as illustrated in the next example.

Example 2 Find a point on the x-axis which is equidistant from $A(-1, 5)$ and $B(6, -2)$.

Solution Let the co-ordinates of the point on the x-axis be $P(x, 0)$. Use $PA = PB$.

Remember: Draw a diagram to help you interpret what the problem asks.

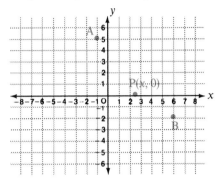

$$PA = \sqrt{[x - (-1)]^2 + (0 - 5)^2}$$
$$= \sqrt{x^2 + 2x + 1 + 25}$$
$$= \sqrt{x^2 + 2x + 26}$$
$$PB = \sqrt{(x - 6)^2 + [0 - (-2)]^2}$$
$$= \sqrt{x^2 - 12x + 36 + 4}$$
$$= \sqrt{x^2 - 12x + 40}$$

Use $PA = PB$.

$$\sqrt{x^2 + 2x + 26} = \sqrt{x^2 - 12x + 40}$$

Square both sides and collect terms.

$$2x + 12x = 40 - 26$$
$$14x = 14$$
$$x = 1$$

Check this answer. Is $(1, 0)$ equidistant from A and B?

Thus the point P with co-ordinates $(1, 0)$ is equidistant from A and B.

9.1 Exercise

A Throughout this exercise, unless indicated otherwise, you may leave your final answer in simplified radical form.

1 Refer to the diagram. Find the length of each line segment.
   (a) AH   (b) CD   (c) OF
   (d) OA   (e) DJ   (f) EI
   (g) DF   (h) AC

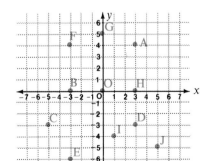

2 Find the distance from each point to the origin.

(a) $(6, 8)$ (b) $(-1, 8)$ (c) $\left(\dfrac{3}{4}, 1\right)$

(d) $(\sqrt{3}, 1)$ (e) $\left(\dfrac{-\sqrt{2}}{2}, \dfrac{\sqrt{2}}{2}\right)$

3   Find the length of the line segment joining each pair of points.
    (a) (0, 0), (8, 6)   (b) (0, 2), (3, 3)   (c) $(-3, 0), (8, -5)$
    (d) $(-2, -2), (8, 0)$ (e) $(8, -8), (4, -1)$ (f) $(6, 8), (-6, -8)$

4   Find the distance from each point to (1, 4).
    (a) $(-1, 7)$ (b) $(-2, 6)$ (c) (4, 6)
    (d) What do you notice about your answers?

B 5   Find the perimeter of each triangle.
    (a) $\triangle ABC$ A(1, 5)   B(1, 2)   C(5, 2)
    (b) $\triangle PQR$ P(4, 2) $Q(-5, -10)$ $R(4, -10)$
    (c) $\triangle DEF$ D(8, 10) $E(-7, -10)$ $F(-7, 10)$
    (d) $\triangle STU$ S(2, 9) $T(9, -15)$ U(9, 9)

6   A triangle has vertices $P(-1, 2), Q(2, 6), R(-4, 4)$.
    (a) Find the perimeter.
    (b) Classify the triangle as scalene, isosceles, or equilateral.

7   Three vertices of rectangle ABCD are $A(-8, 0).$ B(4, 4), and $C(6, -2)$.
    (a) Find the lengths of the sides.   (b) Find the length of the diagonal.

8   Calculate the area of the rectangle whose co-ordinates are $P(-3, 2),$
    $Q(2, 4), R(4, -1)$, and $S(-1, -3)$.

9   Decide whether the points $P(-2, -1)$ and $Q(5, -8)$ lie on the same circle
    with centre $C(1, -5)$. Give reasons for your answer.

10 Find the co-ordinates of the point on the x-axis which is equidistant from
    $A(-4, 6)$ and B(4, 10).

11 Find the length of the line segment with end points given by the points
    where the line $3x - 4y + 24 = 0$ cuts the x-axis and the y-axis.

12 Given that $P(2, -1), Q(-4, 7)$ and R(3, 6) lie on a circle, show that the
    point $C(-1, 3)$ is the centre of that circle.

13 The vertices of an isosceles triangle are given by A(1, 7), $B(-5, 1)$, and
    C(7, 1). Determine whether the triangle formed by joining the midpoints
    of the sides of $\triangle ABC$ is also isosceles.

C 14 If (x_1, y_1) and (x_2, y_2) are two points on the line $y = mx + b$, then show
    that the distance between the two points is given by the expression
    $|x_2 - x_1|\sqrt{1 + m^2}$.

Applications: Decisions and Co-ordinates

Often, if you know where you are, and can pinpoint your position exactly, you can make useful decisions.

The principle of air and sea rescue missions combine the need for much mathematics. Information is fed into a computer, interpreted, and the results are relayed to ships and helicopters as to the approximate co-ordinates for the position of a sinking ship or a downed aircraft.

To make an important decision, as shown in the following problems, you need to use the information, carry out calculations, and interpret your answers.

15 The airport control tower locates two planes on its radar screen. Plane A is located at $(-3, 7)$ and plane B at $(8, 2)$. If the two planes are travelling at the same speed and the control tower is located at $(1, 2)$, which plane should be instructed to land first?

16 A small pleasure boat located at $(1, 6)$ breaks its rudder and sends out a distress signal to the coast guard. Rescue boat A is at $(4, -2)$ and rescue boat B is at $(6, 3)$. Which rescue boat should the coast guard send out to aid the distressed boat?

17 A boat sails from its harbour at $(6, 1)$ to an island at $(12, -5)$. It then sails from the island to meet another sailboat anchored at $(3, 4)$.
   (a) How far has the boat sailed in reaching the second sailboat?
   (b) How much farther did the boat sail than it would have if it had headed directly for the second boat?

18 A group of canoeists must find a campsite before it gets much darker. Their map indicates two possible campsites: camp A $(1, 7)$ and camp B at $(8, -1)$. If the canoeists are at $(-1, 1)$, which campsite should they choose?

19 The pilot of a training mission calculates that there is just enough fuel to fly 17 km. The plane's location is at $(12, 3)$ and the closest airport is at $(17, -9)$. Does the plane have enough fuel to reach the airport, or should the pilot return to its base at $(2, 18)$?

9.2 Internal and External Division of a Line Segment

In your study of mathematics, you often extend your knowledge when earlier skills are combined with new concepts.

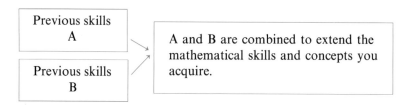

For example, in this section the concepts of internal and external division of a line segment are dealt with. In the next section, these concepts are combined with your previous skills with co-ordinates.

Line segment AB is 12 units long. Suppose C is a point on the line segment AB, and lying between A and B such that AC is 4 units and CB is 8 units. Then C divides the line segment AB internally in the ratio 4:8.

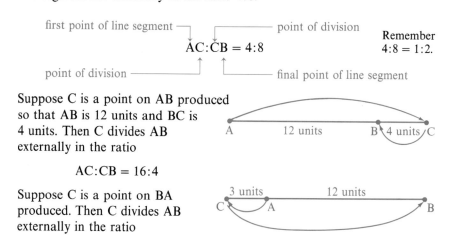

first point of line segment ⌐   ⌐——— point of division

$$\text{AC:CB} = 4:8$$

Remember
$4:8 = 1:2.$

point of division ————⌐   └——— final point of line segment

Suppose C is a point on AB produced so that AB is 12 units and BC is 4 units. Then C divides AB externally in the ratio

$$\text{AC:CB} = 16:4$$

Suppose C is a point on BA produced. Then C divides AB externally in the ratio

$$\text{AC:CB} = 3:15$$

For the 3 collinear points X, Y, and Z you can say

- X divides YZ externally in the ratio YX:XZ = 2:7

- Y divides XZ internally in the ratio XY:YZ = 2:5

- Z divides XY externally in the ratio XZ:ZY = 7:5

The ratio determines on what side of the segment the point of division, T, is placed.

T divides MN externally in the ratio MT:TN = 5:2 (MN is produced to T).	T divides MN externally in the ratio MT:TN = 2:5 (NM is produced to T).

Example 1   Line segment AD is divided as shown in the diagram.

A X   B   Y   C   D

1   2   3   4   5

(a) In what ratio does B divide

   (i) AX?   (ii) AY?   (iii) AC?   (iv) DX?   (v) DA?   (vi) DY?

(b) What point divides AY
   (i) internally in the ratio 1:5?   (ii) externally in the ratio 15:9?
   (iii) internally in the ratio 3:3?   (iv) externally in the ratio 10:4?

Solution   (a) (i) AB:BX = 3:2, externally   (ii) AB:BY = 3:3, internally
              (iii) AB:BC = 3:7, internally   (iv) DB:BX = 12:2, internally
               (v) DB:BA = 12:3, internally   (vi) DB:BY = 12:3, externally
        (b) (i) AX:XY = 1:5 Thus X.   (ii) AD:DY = 15:9 Thus D.
              (iii) AB:BY = 3:3 Thus B.   (iv) AC:CY = 10:4 Thus C.

As in your earlier work, you often need to introduce a variable to solve some problems, as shown in the following example.

Example 2   C divides AB externally in the ratio AC:CB = 7:2.
(a) Find the ratio AB:BC.   (b) If CB is 10 cm, what is the length of AC?

Solution   Use AC:CB = 7:2.

(a) AC is 7 units, and BC is 2 units.
    Thus, AB is 5 units. B lies between A and C. Thus, AB:BC = 5:2.
(b) From the diagram you can see AC:CB = 7:2. Suppose AC is x cm and you are given CB = 10 cm.

$$AC:CB = x:10 \quad \text{or} \quad x:10 = 7:2$$
$$\frac{x}{10} = \frac{7}{2}$$
$$2x = 70$$
$$x = 35$$

Thus, AC is 35 cm long.

9.2 Exercise

A 1 Indicate whether the following ratios describe an internal or external division of PQ.

(a) PM:MQ   (b) PT:TQ   (c) PS:SQ   (d) PN:NQ

2 Write the ratio for each of the following.

(a) MN:NP   (b) MN:NQ   (c) MP:PN   (d) MQ:QP
(e) QP:PN   (f) PQ:QN   (g) NM:MQ   (h) NP:PM
(i) NQ:QP   (j) MQ:QN   (k) QP:PM   (l) MP:PQ

3 PQ is divided externally at R in the ratio 5:3. Find the ratios for
(a) PR:RQ   (b) PQ:QR   (c) RQ:QP   (d) RP:PQ

4 Refer to line segment AB as shown.

What is the ratio when
(a) X divides YB?   (b) A divides XZ?   (c) Y divides BA?
(d) B divides AY?   (e) Z divides AB?   (f) Y divides ZA?

5 For the line segment PQ, give the point which divides

(a) PR internally in the ratio 2:2.   (b) QM externally in the ratio 8:1.
(c) NQ externally in the ratio 1:7.   (d) QP internally in the ratio 6:2.
(e) RQ externally in the ratio 3:7.   (f) MQ internally in the ratio 3:4.

6 C divides AB internally in the ratio 4:5.

A _____ C _____ B
          4   5

If AC is 8 cm long, find the length of CB and of AB.

7 If RT is 25 cm long and S is a point on RT, find the length of RS and of ST where RS:ST = 7:3.

B 8 Point D divides the line EF internally in the ratio 8:3. The length of EF is 44 cm. What are the lengths of ED and DF?

9   If a line AB, 28 m in length, is divided internally at point C in a ratio of 6:4, what are the lengths of AC and CB?

10   The length of a line DF is 16 cm. If E divides DF externally in the ratio 5:3, what are the lengths of DE and EF?

11   S divides UT externally in the ratio 8:5. If ST is longer than TU and if the difference in the lengths of ST and TU is 8 cm, what are the lengths of ST, TU, and SU?

12   C divides AD internally in the ratio 4:1. D divides CB internally in the ratio 2:5. AD is 60 cm long.

     (a) What is the ratio AC:CD:DB?
     (b) What are the lengths of AC, CD, and DB?

13   Base QR of $\triangle$PQR is divided internally at N in the ratio 4:1 and externally at M in the ratio 6:1. Write the ratio for

     (a) $\dfrac{\triangle PQN}{\triangle PNM}$ (b) $\dfrac{\triangle PQR}{\triangle PQM}$ ← $\triangle$PQR means the area of $\triangle$PQR.

     (c) $\dfrac{\triangle PRN}{\triangle PRM}$ (d) $\dfrac{\triangle PQM}{\triangle PQN}$

14   In $\triangle$PQR, base QR is divided internally at S in the ratio 5:2. Write the ratio for

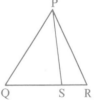

     (a) $\dfrac{\triangle PQS}{\triangle PSR}$ (b) $\dfrac{\triangle PQS}{\triangle PQR}$

15   In $\triangle$MNP, NP is divided internally at Q in the ratio 3:7. Write the ratio for

     (a) $\dfrac{\triangle MQN}{\triangle MNP}$ (b) $\dfrac{\triangle MQN}{\triangle MPQ}$ (c) $\dfrac{\triangle MPQ}{\triangle MNP}$

16   YZ of $\triangle$XYZ is divided externally at T in the ratio YT:TZ = 7:3. Write the ratios for

     (a) $\dfrac{\triangle XYZ}{\triangle XYT}$ (b) $\dfrac{\triangle XYZ}{\triangle XZT}$ (c) $\dfrac{\triangle XZT}{\triangle XYT}$

C 17 $\triangle$PQR has perimeter 30 cm. If the ratio of 3 sides is PQ:QR:RP = 5:3:7, construct the triangle.

9.3 Co-ordinates and Point of Division

In this section, the skills you have learned with co-ordinates are used with your skills of dividing line segments at a point of division.

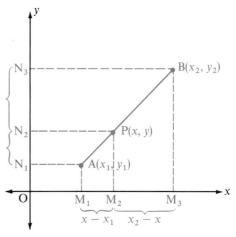

The point P divides the line segment AB into the ratio

$$AP:PB = k:m \quad \text{or} \quad \frac{AP}{PB} = \frac{k}{m}$$

What are the co-ordinates of P?

To find the co-ordinates of P, you first need to do some constructions with the diagram as shown.

Mathematicians like to express a result in terms of the given information. Thus the task is to express the co-ordinates of P in terms of the given information.

Perpendiculars are dropped from A, P, and B to meet the x-axis at M_1, M_2, and M_3 respectively and to meet the y-axis at N_1, N_2, and N_3 respectively.

M_2 divides the line M_1M_3 in the ratio

$$\frac{M_1M_2}{M_2M_3} = \frac{k}{m}$$

N_2 divides the line N_1N_3 in the ratio

$$\frac{N_1N_2}{N_2N_3} = \frac{k}{m}$$

The x co-ordinate of M_2 is also the x co-ordinate of P. The y co-ordinate of N_2 is also the y co-ordinate of P. From the diagram, $M_1M_2 = x - x_1$, $M_2M_3 = x_2 - x$, $N_1N_2 = y - y_1$ and $N_2N_3 = y_2 - y$.

Thus,
$$\frac{x - x_1}{x_2 - x} = \frac{k}{m}$$
$$m(x - x_1) = k(x_2 - x)$$
$$mx - mx_1 = kx_2 - kx$$
$$mx + kx = mx_1 + kx_2$$
$$x(m + k) = mx_1 + kx_2$$
$$x = \frac{mx_1 + kx_2}{m + k}$$

$$\frac{y - y_1}{y_2 - y} = \frac{k}{m}$$
$$m(y - y_1) = k(y_2 - y)$$
$$my - my_1 = ky_2 - ky$$
$$my + ky = my_1 + ky_2$$
$$y(m + k) = my_1 + ky_2$$
$$y = \frac{my_1 + ky_2}{m + k}$$

Thus, the co-ordinates of the point P are $P(x, y) = \left(\dfrac{mx_1 + kx_2}{m + k}, \dfrac{my_1 + ky_2}{m + k} \right)$.

If $P(x, y)$ divides a line with end points $A(x_1, y_1)$ and $B(x_2, y_2)$ into the ratio $\dfrac{k}{m}$ then the co-ordinates

of $P(x, y)$ are given by $\quad P(x, y) = \left(\dfrac{mx_1 + kx_2}{m + k}, \dfrac{my_1 + ky_2}{m + k} \right)$

Once you have derived the previous result, it can be applied to find the co-ordinates of P directly in a problem, as shown in the following example.

Example 1 C divides the line segment with end points A(1, 7) and B(4, 1) internally into the ratio 1:2. What are the co-ordinates of C?

Solution Let the co-ordinates of C be (x, y). The ratio $k:m = 1:2$, $(x_1, y_1) = (1, 7)$ and $(x_2, y_2) = (4, 1)$. Use the formula to find the co-ordinates.

$$x = \frac{mx_1 + kx_2}{m + k} \qquad x = \frac{2(1) + 1(4)}{1 + 2} \qquad y = \frac{my_1 + ky_2}{m + k} \qquad y = \frac{2(7) + 1(1)}{1 + 2}$$

$$= \frac{2 + 4}{3} = 2 \qquad\qquad\qquad = \frac{14 + 1}{3} = 5$$

Thus, $(x, y) = (2, 5)$. The point (2, 5) divides AB internally into the ratio 1:2.

In dividing line segments on the co-ordinate plane, you need to interpret your results.

Internal Division

The point P divides P_1P_2 internally at P.

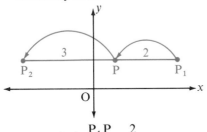

The ratio is $\dfrac{P_1P}{PP_2} = \dfrac{2}{3}$

External Division

The point P divides P_1P_2 externally at P.

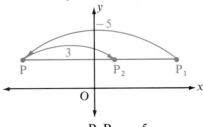

The ratio is $\dfrac{P_1P}{PP_2} = \dfrac{-5}{3}$

From the formula
- if k and m are both positive, then P divides the line segment P_1P_2 internally in the ratio $\dfrac{k}{m}$.
- if either of k and m is negative, then P divides the line segment P_1P_2 externally in the ratio $\dfrac{k}{m}$.

In the following example, you need to interpret your results.

Example 2 Into what ratio does the point R(10, 9) divide the line segment with end points P(4, 6) and Q(−2, 3)?

Solution Given $(x_1, y_1) = (4, 6)$, $(x_2, y_2) = (-2, 3)$ and $(x, y) = (10, 9)$. Substitute in the formula.

$$x = \frac{mx_1 + kx_2}{m + k} \qquad \text{or} \qquad y = \frac{my_1 + ky_2}{m + k}$$

$$10 = \frac{m(4) + k(-2)}{m + k} \qquad\qquad 9 = \frac{m(6) + k(3)}{m + k}$$

$$10m + 10k = 4m - 2k \qquad\qquad 9m + 9k = 6m + 3k$$

$$6m = -12k \qquad\qquad\qquad 3m = -6k$$

$$\frac{6}{-12} = \frac{k}{m} \qquad\qquad\qquad \frac{3}{-6} = \frac{k}{m}$$

$$\frac{k}{m} = \frac{1}{-2} \qquad\qquad\qquad \frac{k}{m} = \frac{1}{-2}$$

Thus, point R divides PQ externally in the ratio 1:2.

9.3 Exercise

A Remember: To do mathematics, you must understand clearly the meaning of internal and external division.

1 P is a point on each line. What are the co-ordinates of P if P divides
   (a) AB internally in the ratio 1:1?
   (b) CD internally in the ratio 1:2?
   (c) EF externally in the ratio 5:3?
   (d) HG externally in the ratio 5:7?
   (e) IJ internally in the ratio 3:2?
   (f) KL externally in the ratio 2:1?

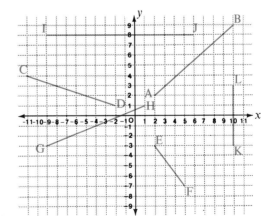

2 Into what ratio does C(4, 6) divide the line segment with end points A(2, 4) and B(10, 12)?

3   C(-35, 13) lies on a line segment with end points A(10, -2) and B(1, 1).
    (a) What is the ratio AC:CB?   (b) Interpret your result.

B   Remember to organize your solution. Refer to the *Steps for Solving Problems*.

4   R divides the line segment joining the points P(2, $-\frac{1}{2}$) and Q(1, 1) externally into the ratio 4:3. What are the co-ordinates of R?

5   X lies on the line segment formed by V(-2, 6) and W(8, -1). If X divides VW internally into the ratio 2:3, what are the co-ordinates of X?

6   A(8, -6), B(3, 4), and C($\frac{9}{2}$, 1) are collinear.
    (a) Into what ratio does A divide CB?   (b) Interpret your result.

7   K divides LM externally into the ratio 3:2. If K has co-ordinates (10, 5) and M has co-ordinates (4, 3), what are the co-ordinates of L?

8   A, P, and Q are collinear points. If A divides the line segment with end points P(2, -5) and Q(-1, 8) internally into the ratio 2:3, what are the co-ordinates of A?

9   Into what ratio does the point (-2, -10) divide the line segment with end points (-20, -34) and (10, 6)?

10   P($\frac{7}{2}$, 0) divides AB, with co-ordinates A(0, 0) and B(m, n), internally into the ratio 7:5. What are the values of m and n?

11   C(3, p), D(q, -5) and E(33, 11) are collinear. If E divides CD externally into the ratio 3:4, what are the values of p and q?

12   Find the co-ordinates of the points of trisection of the line segment joining the points G(-8, 8) and H(4, -1).

C 13   A(2, 8), B(10, 12) and C(9, 2) are the vertices of a triangle. P, Q, and R are the midpoints of AB, BC, and AC respectively. AQ, BR, and CP are the medians of $\triangle$ABC and intersect at point T.
    (a) Find the co-ordinates of P, Q, and R.
    (b) T divides the line segment BR internally into the ratio 2:1. Find the co-ordinates of T.
    (c) Into what ratio does T divide the line segments AQ and CP?
    (d) What do you notice about your answers to (b) and (c)?

9.4 Strategy: Midpoint of a Line Segment

A special case of the formula developed in the previous section occurs when P is the midpoint. The result you obtain has been derived from a different point of view.

The midpoint of a line segment divides a line into two equal parts. In such a case the midpoint divides the line segment AB into the ratio AP:PB = 1:1.

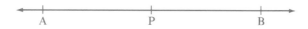

Use the formula for the co-ordinates of a point. For a midpoint, $k = 1$, $m = 1$. Thus

$$x = \frac{x_1 + x_2}{1 + 1} \qquad\qquad y = \frac{y_1 + y_2}{1 + 1}$$

$$= \frac{x_1 + x_2}{2} \qquad\qquad = \frac{y_1 + y_2}{2}$$

If P(x, y) is the midpoint of a line segment joining A(x_1, y_1) and B(x_2, y_2), then the co-ordinates of P are given by

$$P(x, y) = \left(\frac{x_1 + x_2}{2}, \frac{y_1 + y_2}{2} \right)$$

The formula can then be applied, as shown in the following example.

Example What is the midpoint of the line segment joining S(3, −4) and T(−16, 2)?

Think: Sketch a diagram to help you plan the solution.

Solution $(x_1, y_1) = (3, -4)$ $(x_2, y_2) = (-16, 2)$

Thus, $x = \dfrac{3 - 16}{2}$ $y = \dfrac{-4 + 2}{2}$

$\qquad = \dfrac{-13}{2}$ $\qquad = \dfrac{-2}{2}$

$\qquad = -6\dfrac{1}{2}$ $\qquad = -1$

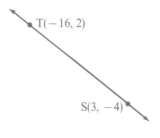

Thus, the co-ordinates of the midpoint are $(-6\frac{1}{2}, -1)$.

9.4 Exercise

A 1 Find the co-ordinates of the midpoint of each line segment.

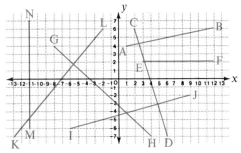

2 Find the co-ordinates of the midpoint of the line joining each pair of points.

(a) $(2, 4), (6, 8)$

(b) $(-6, 4), (-8, 8)$

(c) $(-6, -2), (4, -6)$

(d) $(-3, 5), (5, -3)$

(e) $\left(-3\frac{1}{2}, 7\right), \left(5\frac{1}{2}, -4\right)$

(f) $(-3, -6), (3, 6)$

(g) $(a, b), (0, 0)$

(h) $(2a, 0), (0, 4b)$

3 The points where the diameter meets a circle have co-ordinates $(-11, -4)$ and $(5, 6)$. What are the co-ordinates of the centre of the circle?

4 The endpoints of the diameter of a circle are $(-14, -2)$ and $(-2, 3)$. What are the co-ordinates of the centre of the circle?

B 5 Two points are $S(-2, 5)$ and $H(4, -7)$. Show that SH is a diameter of a circle with centre $(1, -1)$.

6 The centre of a circle has co-ordinates $(7, -4)$. If one endpoint of a diameter of this circle has co-ordinates $(4, 1)$, what are the co-ordinates of the other endpoint of this diameter?

7 The midpoint of AB is given by $M(-1, 7)$ for the points $A(-5, 8)$ and $B(x, y)$. Find x and y.

8 Two points are given by $P(-4, x)$ and $Q(y, -2)$. If the midpoint is given by $M(2, 3)$, find x and y.

9 What are the co-ordinates of the points which divide a line with endpoints $(-10, -16)$ and $(2, 24)$ into 4 equal parts?

10 $\triangle ABC$ is given by $A(-8, 1)$, $B(-2, 7)$, and $C(6, -1)$. Median AP is to be drawn. What are the co-ordinates of the endpoints of median AP?

C 11 Prove that the line joining the midpoints of any two sides of $\triangle ABC$ where $A(4, 7)$, $B(-2, 5)$, and $C(-10, -1)$, is parallel to the third side. (Hint: The slopes of parallel lines are equal.)

9.5 Equation of a Circle with Centre the Origin

The skills you have learned with co-ordinate geometry can be applied to various figures on the plane, such as the circle.

> A circle is the set of points in a plane that are a fixed distance (called the radius) from a fixed point (called the centre).

Co-ordinate skills are used to find the equation of a circle, as shown in the following example.

Example 1   Find the equation of the circle with radius 5 units and centre the origin O(0, 0).

Solution   Let P(x, y) represent any point on the circle.

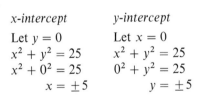

Then $OP = \sqrt{(x - 0)^2 + (y - 0)^2}$

$OP = \sqrt{x^2 + y^2}$

But $OP = 5$

Thus $\sqrt{x^2 + y^2} = 5$ or $x^2 + y^2 = 25$.

The equation of the circle with centre O(0, 0) and radius 5 units is $x^2 + y^2 = 25$.

For the circle in the previous example defined by $x^2 + y^2 = 25$, you can examine its properties.

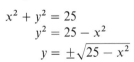

x-intercept	*y-intercept*
Let $y = 0$	Let $x = 0$
$x^2 + y^2 = 25$	$x^2 + y^2 = 25$
$x^2 + 0^2 = 25$	$0^2 + y^2 = 25$
$x = \pm 5$	$y = \pm 5$

Domain

The domain is the set of all x values for $x^2 + y^2 = 25$ for all real values of y.

$$x^2 + y^2 = 25$$
$$y^2 = 25 - x^2$$
$$y = \pm\sqrt{25 - x^2}$$

Since $25 - x^2 \geq 0$ then $25 \geq x^2$. The domain is $\{x \mid -5 \leq x \leq 5\}$.

Range

Similarly, the range is given by $\{y \mid -5 \leq y \leq 5\}$.

In Example 1, the equation was obtained for a particular circle. In Example 2, the equation of any circle with radius r is obtained in **standard form**.

Example 2   Find the equation of the circle with radius r units and centre the origin $O(0, 0)$.

Solution   Let $P(x, y)$ represent any point on the circle.

Then $OP = \sqrt{(x - 0)^2 + (y - 0)^2}$
$\quad\quad OP = \sqrt{x^2 + y^2}$

But $OP = r$

Thus $\sqrt{x^2 + y^2} = r$ or $x^2 + y^2 = r^2$.

The equation of the circle with radius r units and centre the origin is $x^2 + y^2 = r^2$.

This equation for the circle is said to be expressed in **standard form**.

In general, the equation of the circle with radius, r, and centre the origin is given by $x^2 + y^2 = r^2$, $r > 0$.

This equation represents a family of circles with radius, r. In this case, r is a parameter. For the circle with defining equation $x^2 + y^2 = r^2$

you know

x-intercepts $\pm r$
y-intercepts $\pm r$
Domain $\{x \mid |x| \leq r\}$ or $\{x \mid -r \leq x \leq r\}$
Range $\{y \mid |y| \leq r\}$ or $\{y \mid -r \leq y \leq r\}$

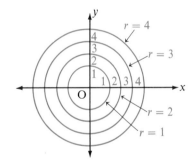

9.5   Exercise

A   Questions 1 to 7 examine skills needed to study the analytic properties of circles.

1   The radius is given for a circle with centre $(0, 0)$. Write its equation.
(a) 3   (b) $\sqrt{3}$ (c) $2\sqrt{5}$ (d) $2r$

2   Two circles with centre $(0, 0)$ are given by

A: $x^2 + y^2 = 16$ and   B: $x^2 + y^2 = 50$. For each circle write the
(a) radius.   (b) x-intercepts.
(c) y-intercepts.   (d) domain.   (e) range.

3   The equation of a circle with centre the origin is given by $x^2 + y^2 = 100$.
Find the values of the missing co-ordinates.
(a) $(-6, ?)$ (b) $(?, 8)$ (c) $(10, ?)$ (d) $(0, ?)$ (e) $(?, 5)$ (f) $(?, 5\sqrt{2})$

4   Which points are *not* on the circle defined by $x^2 + y^2 = 25$?
(a) $(-5, 0)$ (b) $(0, 25)$ (c) $(0, 5)$
(d) $(3, -4)$ (e) $\left(12\frac{1}{2}, 12\frac{1}{2}\right)$ (f) $(-2\sqrt{2}, 4)$

5   The equation of the circle with centre $(0, 0)$ and radius r is given by
$x^2 + y^2 = r^2$. Find the equation of each circle with centre $(0, 0)$ and
passing through each point.
(a) $(6, 0)$ (b) $(0, -3)$ (c) $(-3, 4)$ (d) $(1, -\sqrt{2})$

6   Copy and complete chart.

Equation	Centre	Domain	Range	x-intercept(s)	y-intercept(s)
(a) $x^2 + y^2 = 4$	?	?	?	?	?
(b) $x^2 + y^2 = 16$	?	?	?	?	?
(c) $x^2 + y^2 = 100$	?	?	?	?	?

7   Find the equation of each circle.
(a) centre $(0, 0)$, radius $\dfrac{1}{2}$ (b) centre $(0, 0)$, radius $\dfrac{1}{3}$
(c) centre $(0, 0)$, radius $\sqrt{2}$

B 8   The equation of a circle is given by $4x^2 + 4y^2 = 1$.
(a) Explain why this is the equation of a circle with centre the origin.
(b) What is the radius of the circle?

9   Write an equation of the circle, centre $(0, 0)$, which satisfies each of the
following conditions.
(a) with radius 8 units   (b) passing through the point $(-4, 3)$
(c) passing through the point $(\sqrt{3}, -2)$
(d) with x-intercept -5 (e) with y-intercept 4

10   The equation of a circle is given by $x^2 + y^2 = 36$.
(a) Find m if the point $(m, 3)$ is on the circle.
(b) Find k if the point $(-\sqrt{6}, k)$ is on the circle.
(c) Show why the point with co-ordinates $(8, k)$ cannot be a point on the
circle.

11 Two points on a circle have co-ordinates P(-3, -2) and Q(3, 2).
    (a) Calculate the length of the chord PQ.
    (b) If the centre of the circle is (0, 0), what other name is given to the chord PQ?

12 A diameter of a circle has end points (-6, -2) and (6, 2). Find the equation of the circle.

13 The equation of a circle is given by $9x^2 + 9y^2 = k^2$.
    If the circle passes through the point (0, $\frac{2}{3}$) find the radius of the circle.

C 14 A diameter RS of a circle has co-ordinates R(3, 4), S(-3, -4). If T(5, 0) is a point on the circle show that $\angle$ RTS is a right angle.

Problem Solving

A numerical pattern for a particular example may suggest a conjecture that applies to all general situations. This is shown by the following example.

polygon	number of sides	sum of the interior angles
triangle	3	180°
quadrilateral	4	360° = 2 × 180°
pentagon	5	540° = 3 × 180°
hexagon	6	720° = 4 × 180°

Given the above pattern, follow these steps.

Step A: Make a conjecture about the sum of the interior angles for a polygon of n sides.

Step B: Now test your conjecture for some specific polygons.

Step C: Unless you can prove the result, it will remain a conjecture. Is your conjecture true? (You can answer this question by proving or disproving the result.)

Problem Solving

A sequence of numbers is shown.   1, 2, 6, 24, 120, 720, ...

Find the next two numbers in the sequence.

9.6 Equation of a Circle with Centre (*h*, *k*)

In the previous section, the equation of a circle with centre at (0, 0) and with radius *r* was derived, and the result $x^2 + y^2 = r^2$ was obtained. In the study of mathematics, you often ask the general question, "*What if* . . . ?" In your study of the circle, you might ask, "*What if* the centre of the circle is not at the origin and I wish to obtain its defining equation?" This section investigates this particular question, as shown in Example 1.

Example 1 Find the equation of the circle with centre (4, −1) and radius 6 (units).

Solution *Step 1*

Let P(*x*, *y*) be any point on the curve. *x*, *y* ∈ R.

Step 2

Any point P is 6 units from centre C. CP = 6.

Step 3 $CP = \sqrt{(x - 4)^2 + (y + 1)^2}$

Thus, $\sqrt{(x - 4)^2 + (y + 1)^2} = 6$.

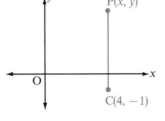

centre (4, −1) ⟶   radius = 6

$$(x - 4)^2 + (y + 1)^2 = 36 \quad \text{Each side of the expression is squared.}$$

$$x^2 - 8x + 16 + y^2 + 2y + 1 = 36 \quad \text{The equation is expanded.}$$
$$x^2 + y^2 - 8x + 2y - 19 = 0$$

The previous example shows that the steps used to derive the equation of a circle with the centre not at the origin are the same steps used when the centre was at the origin. Similarly, the same steps are used to obtain the general form of the equation of a circle with its centre at (*h*, *k*), as shown in the next example.

Example 2 Find the equation of the circle with centre C(*h*, *k*) and radius *r* units.

Solution Let P(*x*, *y*) be any point on the circle, *x*, *y* ∈ R. P is *r* units from C. Thus,

$$CP = r$$
$$CP = \sqrt{(x - h)^2 + (y - k)^2}$$

Thus, $\sqrt{(x - h)^2 + (y - k)^2} = r$ Square each side of the equation.

$$(x - h)^2 + (y - k)^2 = r^2 \quad \left[\begin{array}{l}\text{This equation is referred to}\\ \text{as the \textbf{centre-radius} form.}\end{array}\right.$$

centre (*h*, *k*)   radius = *r*

To obtain the co-ordinates of the centre and the length of the radius, you need to express the equation of a circle in the centre-radius form, as shown in the following example.

Example 3   Find the centre and radius of the circle given by $x^2 + y^2 - 6x - 8y - 39 = 0$.

Solution   Write the given equation in the centre-radius form.

$$x^2 + y^2 - 6x - 8y - 39 = 0$$
$$x^2 - 6x + y^2 - 8y - 39 = 0$$
$$(x^2 - 6x + 9) + (y^2 - 8y + 16) - 25 - 39 = 0$$

Complete the square for the x- and y-terms as shown.

$$9 + 16 - 25 = 0$$

$$(x - 3)^2 + (y - 4)^2 - 64 = 0$$
$$\text{or} \quad (x - 3)^2 + (y - 4)^2 = 64$$

From the centre-radius form, the centre of the circle is given by C(3, 4) and the radius is 8 units.

In general, the equation of a circle is written as shown. P(x, y) is any point on the circle.

Circle with centre the origin (0, 0), and radius, r units.

Circle with centre (h, k), and radius r units.

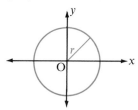

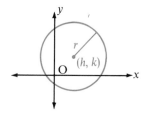

$$\sqrt{(x - 0)^2 + (y - 0)^2} = r$$

standard form $x^2 + y^2 = r^2$

$$\sqrt{(x - h)^2 + (y - k)^2} = r$$

centre-radius form $(x - h)^2 + (y - k)^2 = r^2$

9.6   Exercise

A   Remember: Use the centre-radius form. Review the meaning of the symbols h, k, r.

1   What is the centre and radius for each circle (defined by the following equations)?

(a) $x^2 + y^2 = 49$

(b) $x^2 + (y - 3)^2 = 16$

(c) $(x - 3)^2 + y^2 = 49$

(d) $x^2 + (y - 2)^2 = 64$

(e) $(x - 5)^2 + (y + 3)^2 - 16 = 0$

(f) $(x + 4)^2 + (y - 2)^2 = 100$

2   Write the equation of each circle for the following properties, centre C, radius r.

(a) $C(0, 0), r = 2$ (b) $(0, -2), r = 5$ (c) $C(4, 0), r = 3$

(d) $C(3, 2), r = \dfrac{2}{3}$ (e) $C(5, -3), r = 2\sqrt{2}$ (f) $C(h, k), r = p$

3   The equation of a circle is given by $x^2 + y^2 - 8x + 8y + 22 = 0$. Which of the following points are on the locus?

(a) $P(3, -7)$ (b) $Q(5, -1)$ (c) $R(1, -4)$

4   The equation of a circle is given by $x^2 + y^2 + 8x - 4y + 3 = 0$. Which of the following points are not on the locus?

(a) $M(-3, -2)$ (b) $N(-2, 1)$ (c) $S(1, 2)$

5   The equation of a circle is given by $x^2 + y^2 - 4x + my - 18 = 0$. If $A(7, 3)$ is a point on the circle, find the value of m.

B 6   Find the equation of a circle for each property.

(a) The centre is at $(0, 0)$ and the x-intercept is 4.

(b) The diameter has end points $(2, -7)$ and $(4, 3)$.

(c) The centre is at $(2, 3)$ and the circle passes through the point $(4, -1)$.

7   Find the centre and radius of the circles defined by the following equations.

(a) $x^2 + y^2 - 6y - 3 = 0$ (b) $x^2 + y^2 - 10x - 1 = 0$

(c) $x^2 + y^2 - 4x - 2y + 1 = 0$ (d) $x^2 + y^2 + 6x - 8y + 19 = 0$

(e) $3x^2 + 3y^2 - 18x + 30y + 100 = 0$

8   Find the equation of each circle.

(a) with centre $C(4, -3)$ and passing through $A(6, 1)$

(b) with centre $(-3, -4)$ and passing through the point of intersection of $2x + y = 3$ and $5x - 3y = 2$

9   Find the equation of the circle that has its centre on the y-axis and passes through the points $A(3, 0)$ and $B(-5, 4)$.

10   A circle passes through the points $A(6, -1)$, $B(2, -9)$, and $C(2, -1)$.

(a) Find the equation of the circle.

(b) Find the co-ordinates of the end points of a horizontal diameter.

C 11   A circle has its centre on the line given by $2x + y - 6 = 0$. Find the equation of the circle if it passes through the points $A(7, 3)$ and $B(3, 7)$.

9.7 Solving Linear-Quadratic Systems

Many of the strategies you learn in mathematics can be applied in new situations. For example, you have learned skills to solve a linear system of equations. The method of substitution now extends to solving a system where both equations are not linear. For example, a line and a circle can have no point, one point, or two points of intersection, as shown in the diagrams.

No point of intersection

1 point of intersection

2 points of intersection

When a system of equations consists of a linear equation and a quadratic equation it is referred to as a **linear-quadratic system**.

Example 1 Solve the linear-quadratic system $x + 2y + 5 = 0$ and $x^2 + y^2 = 25$.

Solution

$x + 2y + 5 = 0$ ①
$x^2 + y^2 = 25$ ②

From equation ①, $x = -2y - 5$ ③

Substitute for x in equation ②.

$$(-2y - 5)^2 + y^2 = 25$$
$$4y^2 + 20y + 25 + y^2 = 25$$
$$5y^2 + 20y = 0$$
$$y(y + 4) = 0$$

Thus, $y = 0$ or $y + 4 = 0$.   Check in the original equations.

For, $y = 0$ or $y = -4$.
In equation ①,   In equation ①,
$x + 0 + 5 = 0$. $x + 2(-4) + 5 = 0$
      $x = -5$ $x = 3$

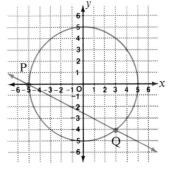

Thus, the solution for the linear quadratic system is given by $(-5, 0)$ and $(3, -4)$.

On a graph, the solution is shown as the intersection points P and Q.

The solution of a linear-quadratic system can be applied to solve a word problem, as shown in the following example.

Example 2   A large rectangular wood frame has a diagonal length of $\dfrac{\sqrt{106}}{2}$ m. If the difference in the dimensions of the frame is 2 m, what are the dimensions of the frame?

Solution   *Step 1:* Write the linear-quadratic system.

Draw a diagram. Let the length of the frame be x m and the width of the frame be y m. Since the diagonal length is $\dfrac{\sqrt{106}}{2}$ m, then, using the

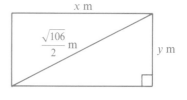

Pythagorean Property, $x^2 + y^2 = \dfrac{106}{4}$ ①

The difference in the dimensions is 2 m.

$$x - y = 2 \qquad ②$$

Step 2: Solve the linear-quadratic system.

$$x^2 + y^2 = \dfrac{106}{4} \qquad ①$$

$$x - y = 2 \qquad ②$$

From ② $x = y + 2$ ③

Substitute ③ into ①. $(y + 2)^2 + y^2 = \dfrac{106}{4}$

Simplify. $y^2 + 4y + 4 + y^2 = \dfrac{106}{4}$

$$2y^2 + 4y + 4 = \dfrac{106}{4}$$

Multiply both $8y^2 + 16y + 16 = 106$
sides by 4. $8y^2 + 16y - 90 = 0$
$$4y^2 + 8y - 45 = 0$$
$$(2y + 9)(2y - 5) = 0$$

$$2y + 9 = 0 \quad \text{or} \quad 2y - 5 = 0$$
$$2y = -9 \quad \text{or} \qquad 2y = 5$$

Inadmissible. $y = -\dfrac{9}{2}$ or $y = \dfrac{5}{2}$

Substitute $y = \dfrac{5}{2}$ in ②. $x - \dfrac{5}{2} = 2$ $x = \dfrac{5}{2} + 2$ $x = \dfrac{9}{2}$

Use this result to check your answer
in the original *word* problem.

Thus, the dimensions of the wood frame are 2.5 m × 4.5 m.

9.7 Exercise

A 1 What is the solution set for each linear-quadratic system?

(a)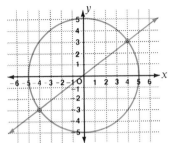

(b)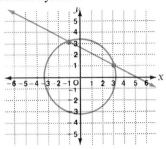

2 (a) Draw the graph of $x^2 + y^2 = 100$ and $3x - 4y = 0$.
(b) What are the co-ordinates of the intersection points?
(c) What is the solution set for the linear-quadratic system of equations, $x^2 + y^2 = 100$ and $3x - 4y = 0$?

3 A line given by $3x + 4y = 20$ intersects the circle defined by $x^2 + y^2 = 25$.
(a) Solve the linear-quadratic system.
(b) Interpret your solution in (a) graphically.

4 (a) Solve $x^2 + y^2 = 10$ and $y = 3x - 10$.
(b) Interpret your solution in (a) graphically.

B 5 Solve and verify.

(a) $x^2 + y^2 = 25$ (b) $3x - y = 1$ (c) $y = 4 - 2x$
    $3x - 4y = 0$ $x^2 + y^2 = 10$ $x^2 + y^2 = 9$

6 Solve each system. Illustrate your solution by sketching the system.

(a) $x - y = -2$ (b) $x = 4 + y$ (c) $2y + x = -15$
    $x^2 + y^2 = 10$ $x^2 + y^2 = 40$ $x^2 + y^2 = 90$
(d) $x - y = -1$ (e) $x^2 + y^2 = 18$
    $(x - 1)^2 + (y + 2)^2 = 9$ $x = y$

7 A circle defined by $x^2 + y^2 = 10$ is intersected by the line defined by $2x - y = 5$. Find the co-ordinates of the intersection points.

8 A linear-quadratic system is given by

$$x^2 + y^2 + 6x - 2y - 31 = 0 \qquad x - 9y = -53$$

(a) Sketch a graph of the system. Find the co-ordinates of the intersection points.
(b) Verify your answers in (a) by solving the system algebraically.

9 A circle is defined by $x^2 + y^2 + 2x - 6y - 39 = 0$. It is intersected by the line defined by $x + 5y = 39$. What are the points of intersection?

10 If a perpendicular is drawn from a point to a line, then the length of the perpendicular, d, is called the distance between the point and the line.

A circle is defined by $x^2 + y^2 = 25$. A line, defined by $x - y + 1 = 0$, intersects the circle at P and Q.
(a) Find the co-ordinates of P and Q.   (b) Find the length of PQ.
(c) Find the co-ordinates of the midpoint, M, of PQ.
(d) What is the measure of $\angle$OMP?   (e) Find the length OM.

11 A circle is defined by $x^2 + y^2 + 2x - 4y = 48$. A line, defined by $5x + 9y = 66$, intersects the circle at E and F. Find how far the chord EF is from the centre of the circle.

12 A weather satellite travels a circular orbit given by $x^2 + y^2 = 25$. A space probe, travelling in a straight line defined by $x - y = 2$, is on a collision course with the satellite. Find the co-ordinates of the points to 2 decimal places where a collision might take place.

13 Find the lengths of the sides of a right triangle which has a hypotenuse of 50 cm and a perimeter of 112 cm.

14 The sum of the squares of two integers is 53. Twice the greater integer, minus the lesser integer is 11. What are the integers?

15 The sum of the squares of two integers is 146. If half of their difference is 3, what are the integers?

16 A rectangular garden has a diagonal length of 13 m. If the perimeter of the garden is 34 m, what are the dimensions of the garden?

17 A farmer has two square fields which are not adjacent to each other (i.e. they have no side in common). These two fields are sown with wheat at the rate of 1 kg/10 m². It is also necessary to install fencing around these fields. If the farmer orders 185 kg of wheat and 240 m of fencing, what are the dimensions of each field?

C 18 What are the conditions on a, b, and m, so that the graphs given by

$$ax + y = b \quad \text{and} \quad x^2 + y^2 = m^2$$

(a) intersect in 2 points?   (b) intersect in 1 point?   (c) do not intersect?

9.8 Another Strategy: Chords of a Circle

In your earlier work in geometry, you used your skills to prove various properties about the chords of a circle.

> I   The right bisector of any chord passes through the centre of the circle.
>
> II   The line joining the mid-point of any chord of a circle and the centre of the circle, is perpendicular to that chord.
>
> III The line perpendicular to any chord of a circle and passing through the centre of the circle, bisects that chord.
>
> IV   The angle subtended at the circumference of a circle by a diameter is a right angle.

You can now use strategies with co-ordinates to prove these properties from a different point of view, an analytic point of view.

Example   Prove that the right bisector of any chord of a circle passes through the centre of the circle.

right or perpendicular bisector

Solution   Show that the equation of the right bisector of a chord of a circle in standard position is a line passing through the origin.
Let the circle be given by $x^2 + y^2 = a^2$ and AB be any chord of the circle with end points A(r, s), B(p, q).

The midpoint of AB is given by $\left(\dfrac{r+p}{2}, \dfrac{s+q}{2} \right)$.

The slope of AB is given by $m_{AB} = \dfrac{q-s}{p-r}$.

The slope of the right bisector of chord AB is the negative reciprocal of the slope of the chord AB. Thus, the slope of the right bisector is

$$-\frac{p-r}{q-s}.$$

Use the slope-point form of a straight line, to derive the equation of the right bisector.
$$\frac{y - y_1}{x - x_1} = m$$

Thus, the equation of the right bisector of any chord, AB, is derived and simplified.

$$\frac{y - \dfrac{s+q}{2}}{x - \dfrac{r+p}{2}} = -\frac{p-r}{q-s}.$$

The equation is simplified.

$$\frac{2y - (s + q)}{2x - (r + p)} = -\frac{p - r}{q - s}$$

$$2y(q - s) - (s + q)(q - s) = -2x(p - r) + (p - r)(p + r).$$
$$2x(p - r) + 2y(q - s) + s^2 + r^2 - (q^2 + p^2) = 0 \qquad ①$$

Since (r, s) and (p, q) are points on the circle, each point satisfies the equation of the circle. Thus, $r^2 + s^2 = a^2$ and $p^2 + q^2 = a^2$. Use these substitutions to simplify equation ①.

$$2x(p - r) + 2y(q - s) + a^2 - a^2 = 0$$
$$x(p - r) + y(q - s) = 0$$

This is the equation of a line passing through the origin because $(0, 0)$ satisfies the equation.

Thus, the right bisector of any chord of a circle passes through the centre of the circle and it is a diameter of the circle.

Be sure to make a final statement!

9.8 Exercise

A   Questions 1 to 5 review skills with co-ordinate geometry.

1   A circle is defined by the equation $x^2 + y^2 = 64$.
(a) Show that P(8, 0) and Q$(-4\sqrt{2}, 4\sqrt{2})$ are points on the circle.
(b) Find the co-ordinates of the midpoint M of the chord PQ.
(c) Write the equation of the line through M and perpendicular to PQ.
(d) Show that the line in (c) passes through the centre of the circle.

2   A circle is defined by $x^2 + y^2 = 10$.
(a) Show that AB is a chord of the circle where A(1, -3) and B(-3, 1).
(b) Find the equation of the right bisector of AB.
(c) Show that the right bisector of AB passes through the centre of the circle.

3   A chord PQ is given in a circle with centre O(0, 0) with co-ordinates P(-6, 4) and Q(4, -6).
(a) Find the co-ordinates of the midpoint M of PQ.
(b) Calculate the slopes of OM and PQ. What do you notice about your results?
(c) Write a probable conclusion based on your work in (a) and (b).

4 A circle is defined by $x^2 + y^2 = 68$.
   (a) Show that RS is a chord of the circle where R($-2, 8$) and S($-8, -2$).
   (b) Show that the line joining the centre to the midpoint of RS is perpendicular to the chord RS.

5 A circle with centre O is defined by $x^2 + y^2 = 20$. A line from centre O, perpendicular to chord LM meets LM at P.
   (a) Show that L($2, 4$) and M($2, -4$) lie on the circle.
   (b) Find the slope of chord LM.
   (c) Find the slope of the perpendicular OP.
   (d) Find the equation of the line segment OP.
   (e) P is the point of intersection of line segment OP and chord LM. Find the co-ordinates of P.
   (f) Find the midpoint, Q, of chord LM.
   (g) What do you notice about the co-ordinates of P and Q?

B Review your skills with analytic geometry. Think of your work with analytic geometry as a strategy for solving problems.

6 A circle is given by $x^2 + y^2 = 26$. D($1, 5$) and E($-5, -1$) are points on the circle. Show that the right bisector of DE passes through the centre of the circle.

7 A circle is given by $x^2 + y^2 - 10x - 10y + 25 = 0$.
   (a) Show that the line joining A($2, 1$) and B($5, 0$) is a chord of the circle.
   (b) Show that the right bisector of AB passes through the centre of the circle.

8 A circle is defined by $x^2 + y^2 = 10p^2$.
   (a) Show that RQ is a chord of the circle where R($3p, p$) and Q($p, -3p$).
   (b) Show that the line segment joining the centre of the circle to the midpoint of RQ is perpendicular to RQ.

9 A circle with centre ($0, 0$) has diameter AB where A($-6, -8$) and B($6, 8$). If C($-8, -6$) is another point on the circle, show that $\angle$ BCA is a right angle.

10 A circle is given by the equation $x^2 + y^2 = 20$. For the points A($-4, -2$) and B($-2, -4$), prove that the line segment perpendicular to AB and passing through the centre of the circle, bisects chord AB.

11 A circle with centre C($-5, 3$) passes through the points A($-5, 0$) and B($-2, 3$).
   (a) Find the equation of the right bisector of AB.
   (b) Show that C lies on the right bisector of AB.

12 Show that the line drawn through the centre of the circle defined by $x^2 + y^2 + 6x + 8y = 0$, and perpendicular to the chord with endpoints P(-6, -8) and Q(2, -4) bisects the chord PQ.

13 On a circle, centre (0, 0), points P(2, -3), Q(3, 2), R(-3, -2) are given.
(a) Draw a sketch of the circle.
(b) Find the equation of the perpendicular bisector of PQ.
(c) Find the equation of the perpendicular bisector of RQ.
(d) Find the intersection point given by the equations in (b) and (c).
(e) Based on (d), suggest a method of locating the centre of a circle.

14 The **circumcircle** of a triangle is the circle that passes through all the vertices of the triangle.
The **circumcentre** is the centre of the circumcircle.

The vertices of $\triangle$PQR are P(2, -2), Q(0, 10) and R(-6, 0). What is the radius of the circumcircle?

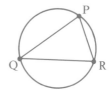

15 A triangle has vertices A(4, 6), B(8, 14) and C(16, 2).
(a) Find the equation of the right bisector of AB and of BC.
(b) Solve the equations in (a) to find the co-ordinates of the circumcentre.

C 16 (a) Prove that more than one circle can be drawn through any two points.
(b) Show that only one circle can be drawn through any three non-collinear points.
(c) Prove that the intersection of the right bisectors of any two chords of a circle intersect at the centre of the circle.
(d) Prove that a line drawn through the centre of a circle perpendicular to the chord of the circle bisects the chord.
(e) Prove that the angle subtended by a diameter is a right angle.
(f) Prove that the circles C_1 and C_2 defined by $C_1 : x^2 + y^2 = r^2$, and $C_2 : x^2 + y^2 - 2ax - 2by + a^2 + b^2 - r^2 = 0$ are congruent.

Calculator Tip

A constant that appears in the study of mathematics is the irrational number $e = 2.718\ldots$ As n increases, the expression $\left(1 + \dfrac{1}{n}\right)^n$ approaches the constant e. With a scientific calculator, you can almost do impossible calculations.

- For what range of values of n does the expression $\left(1 + \dfrac{1}{n}\right)^n$ approximate the value of e to 2 decimal places?
- Use your calculator. What is the next decimal place value of e?
  Hint: Try values of n such as 50 000, 100 000 and so on.

9.9 Tangent at a Point *on* the circle.

The following are the properties of a tangent to a circle.

> I   The line drawn from the centre of a circle to the point where a tangent touches the circle, is perpendicular to the tangent.
>
> II If a line is perpendicular to a circle at the end point of a radius, then it is a tangent to that circle.
>
> III A line drawn perpendicular to a tangent at the point of contact with a circle, passes through the centre of the circle.
>
> IV Tangents to a circle from an external point of the circle are equal.

You can use Property I to find the equation of a tangent to a circle.

Example 1   Find the equation of the tangent to the circle $x^2 + y^2 = 25$ at the point $A(-4, 3)$.

Draw a sketch to show the information.

Solution   The slope of OA $= -\dfrac{3}{4}$. Thus, slope of a tangent at A is $\dfrac{4}{3}$. The equation of the tangent is $\dfrac{y-3}{x+4} = \dfrac{4}{3}$ or $3y - 4x = 25$.

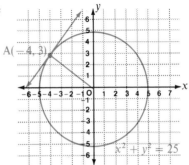

Example 2   Find the equation of the tangent to the circle $x^2 + y^2 = r^2$ at the point $T(x_1, y_1)$.

Solution $P(x, y)$ represents any point on the tangent. $T(x_1, y_1)$ represents the point of contact of the tangent with the circle with centre $O(0, 0)$.

OT is a radius. Slope of OT $= \dfrac{y_1}{x_1}$.

OT $\perp$ PT. Thus slope of PT is $-\dfrac{x_1}{y_1}$.

Equation of tangent is given by $\dfrac{y - y_1}{x - x_1} = -\dfrac{x_1}{y_1}$

This can be simplified to
$$x_1(x - x_1) = -y_1(y - y_1)$$
$$x_1 x - x_1^2 = -y_1 y + y_1^2$$
$$x_1 x + y_1 y = x_1^2 + y_1^2 \qquad \textcircled{1}$$

Since point $T(x_1, y_1)$ lies on the circle $x^2 + y^2 = r^2$ then $T(x_1, y_1)$ satisfies $x^2 + y^2 = r^2$. Thus, $\qquad x_1^2 + y_1^2 = r^2 \qquad ②$

Substitute ② into ①. $\quad x_1 x + y_1 y = r^2$

> The equation of a tangent to a circle with centre $O(0, 0)$ and radius, r, at the point $T(x_1, y_1)$ is $\qquad x_1 x + y_1 y = r^2$.

In Example 1, $(x_1, y_1) = (-4, 3)$ and $r = 5$. Thus, the equation of the tangent at the point $A(-4, 3)$ is $-4x + 3y = 25$ or $3y - 4x = 25$.

The strategy used in Example 2 can be used again to develop the equation of a tangent to a circle with its centre not at the origin. The result follows.

> The equation of the tangent to the circle $(x - a)^2 + (y - b)^2 = r^2$ at the point $T(x_1, y_1)$ is given by $(x_1 - a)(x - a) + (y_1 - b)(y - b) = r^2$.

Example 3 Find the equation of the tangent to the circle $(x - 1)^2 + (y + 2)^2 = 100$ at the point $(9, -8)$.

Solution Point of contact of tangent with circle is $(9, -8)$. Thus, $x_1 = 9$, $y_1 = -8$.

Radius of the circle is 10. Thus, $r = 10$.
Centre of the circle is $(1, -2)$. Thus, $a = 1$, $b = -2$.
Substitute these values into $(x_1 - a)(x - a) + (y_1 - b)(y - b) = r^2$.
$$(9 - 1)(x - 1) + [-8 - (-2)][y - (-2)] = 100$$
$$8(x - 1) + (-6)(y + 2) = 100$$
$$8x - 8 - 6y - 12 = 100$$
$$8x - 6y = 120$$
$$4x - 3y = 60$$

Thus, the equation of the tangent to the circle $(x - 1)^2 + (y + 2)^2 = 100$ at the point $(9, -8)$ is $4x - 3y = 60$.

9.9 Exercise

A 1 A circle is defined by $x^2 + y^2 = 20$.
(a) Show that $A(2, -4)$ is a point on the circle.
(b) Find the slope of the radius OA.
(c) Find the slope of the tangent to the circle at A.
(d) Find the equation of the tangent to the circle at A.

2 (a) Show that $B(-8, -7)$ is a point on the circle $x^2 + y^2 = 113$.
(b) Find the equation of the tangent to the circle $x^2 + y^2 = 113$ at B.

3   Find the equation of the tangent to the circle $x^2 + y^2 = 13$ at $(-3, -2)$.

4   Find the equation of the tangent to the circle $x^2 + y^2 = 145$ at $(-8, 9)$.

B 5   A circle is defined by $(x + 1)^2 + (y + 2)^2 = 25$.
(a) Show that $C(2, -6)$ is a point on the circle.
(b) Find the slope of the tangent to the circle at C.
(c) Find the equation of the tangent to the circle at C.

6   Find the equation of the tangent to the circle $(x - 2)^2 + (y + 3)^2 = 181$ at the point $(-7, -13)$.

7   A tangent meets a circle defined by $(x + 3)^2 + (y - 5)^2 = 40$ at the point $(-9, 3)$. Find the equation of the tangent.

8   Find the equation of the tangent to each circle at the given point P.
(a) $x^2 + y^2 = 25$, $P(-4, 3)$ (b) $x^2 + y^2 = 17$, $P(4, -1)$
(c) $x^2 + y^2 - 4x - 2y = 0$, $P(0, 0)$
(d) $x^2 + y^2 + 6x + 6y - 8 = 0$, $P(2, -4)$
(e) $x^2 + y^2 + 8x - 6y = 25$, $P(3, 4)$
(f) $x^2 + y^2 + 6x - 14y + 6 = 0$, $P(-7, 1)$
(g) $4x^2 + 4y^2 - 4x + 24y - 687 = 0$, $P\left(\dfrac{21}{2}, 6\right)$
(h) $2x^2 + 2y^2 + 2x - 2y - 15 = 0$, $P\left(\dfrac{3}{2}, -\dfrac{3}{2}\right)$

9   Tangents are drawn to the circle defined by $x^2 + y^2 = 25$ at the points $(3, k)$. Prove that $k = \pm 4$.

10   A circle with centre at the origin is tangent to the line $2x - y - 9 = 0$. Find the radius of the circle.

11   A circle with centre at the origin is tangent to the line passing through the points $(4, -2)$ and $(2, -6)$. Find the radius of the circle.

C 12   Prove that the line drawn from the centre of the circle given by $x^2 + y^2 = 25$ to the point where the tangent line $3x + 4y = 25$ touches the circle is perpendicular to the tangent.

Problem Solving

A function, f, has the property that for all $a, b \in R$

$$f(a + b) = f(a) + f(b)$$

A: Explore what some of the properties of this function might be.
B: Find an example of a function which has these properties.

9.10 Equations of Tangents to a Circle

In the previous section, you found the equation of a tangent that was drawn to a point *on* the circle. The question can be asked, "*What if* the tangent is drawn from any point to the circle?"

To find the equation of a tangent *from a point outside* of the circle, you can use your earlier skills in solving quadratic equations.

Example 1 Derive the equations of the tangents to the circle $x^2 + y^2 = 4$ from the point (0, 8).

Solution Solve the system.

$$y = mx + 8 \quad \textcircled{1}$$
$$x^2 + y^2 = 4 \quad \textcircled{2}$$

Substitute $\textcircled{1}$ in $\textcircled{2}$.

$$x^2 + y^2 = 4$$
$$x^2 + (mx + 8)^2 = 4$$
$$x^2 + m^2x^2 + 16mx + 64 = 4$$
$$(1 + m^2)x^2 + 16mx + 60 = 0 \quad \textcircled{3}$$

When possible, draw a diagram to check a solution that may arise. The family of lines passing through (0, 8) is given by $y = mx + 8$ with slope m. There are two possible lines as tangents.

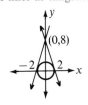

Think:
Since the required line is a tangent to the circle then it intersects in one point. Thus, equation $\textcircled{3}$ must have only one numerical solution. This occurs when the two roots are equal and the discriminant is zero.

The discriminant $b^2 - 4ac = 0$

For $\textcircled{3}$ $a = (1 + m^2)$, $b = 16m$, $c = 60$

$$b^2 - 4ac = (16m)^2 - 4(1 + m^2)60$$
$$= 256m^2 - 240 - 240m^2$$
$$= 16m^2 - 240$$

But $D = 0$.

$$16m^2 - 240 = 0$$
$$m^2 - 15 = 0$$
$$m = \pm\sqrt{15}$$

The equations of the required tangents are

$$y = \sqrt{15}x + 8 \quad \text{and} \quad y = -\sqrt{15}x + 8.$$

To show that a line is tangent to a circle, the line must intersect the circle at only one point. This property of tangents is used to solve the following problem.

Example 2   Show that $3x + 4y = 25$ is a tangent to a circle defined by $x^2 + y^2 = 25$.

Solution   To find the point of tangency, solve the system of equations.

$$3x + 4y = 25 \qquad ①$$
$$x^2 + y^2 = 25 \qquad ②$$

From ① $x = \dfrac{-4y + 25}{3}$ ③

Substitute ③ into ②. $\dfrac{(-4y + 25)^2}{9} + y^2 = 25$

Multiply by 9. $(-4y + 25)^2 + 9y^2 = 225$
Expand. $16y^2 - 200y + 625 + 9y^2 = 225$
$$25y^2 - 200y + 400 = 0$$
$$y^2 - 8y + 16 = 0$$
$$(y - 4)^2 = 0$$
$$y = 4 \qquad ④$$

To find x substitute ④ into ①. $3x + 4(4) = 25$
$$3x + 16 = 25$$
$$3x = 9$$
$$x = 3$$

Thus, the point of intersection of the line $3x + 4y = 25$ and the circle $x^2 + y^2 = 25$ is (3, 4). Since there is only one point of intersection, then the line $3x + 4y = 25$ must be tangent to the circle $x^2 + y^2 = 25$.

9.10   Exercise

A   Remember: A tangent meets a circle at one point. Review the equation of tangents to circles.

1   Show that $3x - 2y - 13 = 0$ is a tangent of the circle with equation $x^2 + y^2 = 13$.

2   Show that $y = 5 - 2x$ is not a tangent of the circle defined by $x^2 + y^2 = 10$.

3   Lines with slope $\dfrac{3}{4}$ are drawn tangent to the circle $x^2 + y^2 = 4$.

(a) Find the equations of the tangents.
(b) How can you check that the lines are tangent to the circle?

4   (a) Show that $x - y = -4$ is a tangent to the circle $9x^2 + 9y^2 = 72$.
(b) Draw a sketch of your result in (a).

B Remember: Your skills with analytic geometry are essential for working with tangents and circles.

5 Find the equation of the tangents
(a) to the circle $x^2 + y^2 + 2x - 4y - 4 = 0$ with slope 1.
(b) from the point $(6, -8)$ to the circle $x^2 + y^2 - 4x + 6y - 12 = 0$.

6 Lines drawn to the circle defined by $x^2 + y^2 = 8$ are tangents. If the lines have slope 3, find the defining equations.

7 Find the equations of the tangents drawn to the circle

$$4x^2 + 4y^2 + 4x - 8y - 27 = 0 \text{ with } y\text{-intercept } -3.$$

8 (a) Show that $x + 2y = 11$ is a tangent to the circle
$x^2 + y^2 - 6x + 2y - 10 = 0$.
(b) Find another tangent to the circle having the same slope as the line in (a).

9 (a) Find the distance from $(-3, 4)$ to the line $2x - 3y = 6$.
(b) Use the information in (a) to find the equation of a circle with centre $(-3, 4)$ that is tangent to the line $2x - 3y = 6$.

10 The line $9x - 10y = 29$ is tangent to the circle $x^2 + y^2 - 4x + 6y = 168$. Find the equations of the tangents to the circle which are perpendicular to the tangent $9x - 10y = 29$.

C 11 The points A(2, 1) and B(0, -7) lie on the circle $x^2 + y^2 - 2x + 6y = 7$ with centre C.
(a) Show that A, B, and C are collinear.
(b) What do you call line segment ACB?
(c) Find the equations of the tangents to the circle at A and B.
(d) Show that lines tangent at the end points of a diameter of a circle are parallel.

Problem Solving

Often a problem may have more than one answer. Sometimes it is possible to draw more than one diagram which satisfies the conditions of the problem. For the following problem, draw the different possible diagrams to predict how many answers might be obtained. Then solve the problem.

$\triangle$PQR has vertices P(-5, 1), Q(-1, 1) and R(x, y). If the area of $\triangle$PQR is 10 square units, calculate y.

9.11 Length of a Tangent

In your study of mathematics, there are certain concepts that occur over and over again to solve problems, as well as to develop further mathematics. One of these is the property of right triangles, namely, the Pythagorean Property. If you use the formula for the distance between two points and the Pythagorean Property, you can find an expression for the length of a tangent from a point to a circle.

Example 1

Find an expression for the length of a tangent from a point $P(x_1, y_1)$ to the point of tangency $T(x, y)$ of a circle $(x - a)^2 + (y - b)^2 = r^2$.

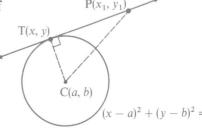

Solution

PT is a tangent to a circle with centre $C(a, b)$. Thus, $PT \perp TC$.
Use the Pythagorean Property.
$$CP^2 = CT^2 + PT^2 \quad \text{or} \quad PT^2 = CP^2 - CT^2$$
$$PT = \sqrt{CP^2 - CT^2} \qquad \text{①}$$

You can use the distance formula to write expressions for the lengths CP and CT.

$CP = \sqrt{(x_1 - a)^2 + (y_1 - b)^2}$ or $CP^2 = (x_1 - a)^2 + (y_1 - b)^2$
$CT = r$ or $CT^2 = r^2$.

Substitute for CP^2 and CT^2 in ①. $PT = \sqrt{CP^2 - CT^2}$
$$PT = \sqrt{(x_1 - a)^2 + (y_1 - b)^2 - r^2}$$

The length, PT, of a tangent from a point $P(x_1, y_1)$ to the point of tangency, $T(x, y)$ of the circle $(x - a)^2 + (y - b)^2 = r^2$ is given by
$$PT = \sqrt{(x_1 - a)^2 + (y_1 - b)^2 - r^2}$$

When the equation of the circle given is $x^2 + y^2 = r^2$, then the centre is the origin $O(0, 0)$. Thus, the expression above is simplified for a circle with centre the origin as the following.

The length, PT, of a tangent from a point $P(x_1, y_1)$ to the point of tangency, $T(x, y)$ of the circle $x^2 + y^2 = r^2$ is given by
$$PT = \sqrt{x_1^2 + y_1^2 - r^2}$$

Example 2 Calculate the length of the tangent from the point P(3, 7) to the circle $(x + 4)^2 + (y - 1)^2 = 25$.

Solution $P(x_1, y_1) = P(3, 7)$. Equation of the circle is $(x + 4)^2 + (y - 1)^2 = 25$. Thus, $x_1 = 3, y_1 = 7, a = -4, b = 1, r^2 = 25$.

Use these values to calculate the length of the tangent.

$$PT = \sqrt{(x_1 - a)^2 + (y_1 - b)^2 - r^2}$$
$$PT = \sqrt{[3 - (-4)]^2 + (7 - 1)^2 - 25}$$
$$PT = \sqrt{49 + 36 - 25}$$
$$PT = \sqrt{60} = 2\sqrt{15}$$

Thus, the length of the tangent from the point P(3, 7) to the circle $(x + 4)^2 + (y - 1)^2 = 25$ is $2\sqrt{15}$ units.

9.11 Exercise

A You may express your answers in radical form as needed.

1 Find the length of the tangent from the point $(-6, -8)$ to the circle given by $x^2 + y^2 = 25$.

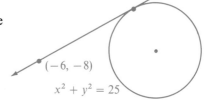

$(-6, -8)$

$x^2 + y^2 = 25$

2 Show that the length of the tangent from $(-8, 10)$ to the circle $x^2 + y^2 = 50$ is $\sqrt{114}$ units.

3 Find the length of the tangent from each given point to the given circle.
(a) $x^2 + y^2 = 17$,   P(5, -2)
(b) $x^2 + y^2 = 65$,   Q(-10, 7)
(c) $(x + 3)^2 + (y - 2)^2 = 16$,   A(-8, 5)
(d) $(x - 2)^2 + (y - 5)^2 = 82$,   B(5, 16)
(e) $(x + 7)^2 + (y + 2)^2 = 13$,   K(-11, -5)
(f) $(x - 3)^2 + (y + 4)^2 = 49$,   L(9, 0)
(g) $x^2 + y^2 - 6x + 12y = 19$,   M(5, 4)
(h) $x^2 + y^2 - 6x + 10y = 3$,   N(-5, -6)

(i) $2x^2 + 2y^2 + 2x - 2y = 19$, $X\left(-\dfrac{15}{2}, \dfrac{5}{2}\right)$

(j) $4x^2 + 4y^2 - 12x + 40y + 81 = 0$, $Y\left(\dfrac{11}{2}, -8\right)$

B 4 Two concentric circles are given by $x^2 + y^2 + 8x - 10y + 16 = 0$ and $x^2 + y^2 + 8x - 10y - 59 = 0$. Find the length of the chord of the outer circle which is tangent to the inner circle at the point $(-1, 9)$.

5 Points A(5, 1) and B(1, -5) lie on the circle given by $x^2 + y^2 = 26$.
(a) Find the equation of the tangent at point A.
(b) Find the equation of the tangent at point B.
(c) Find the point, P, at which these two tangents intersect.
(d) Find the lengths of PA and PB.

6 Points $(-5, 0)$ and $(-5, -4)$ lie on the circle given by $x^2 + y^2 - 2x + 4y = 35$.
(a) Find the point of intersection of the tangents drawn to the circle at these points.
(b) Show that tangents drawn from a point to a circle are equal in length.

C 7 A circle, given by $x^2 + y^2 = 36$, is inscribed in a hexagon. The circle is tangent to the hexagon at the points $(-3, 5)$, $(3, 5)$, $(6, 0)$, $(3, -5)$, $(-3, -5)$, $(-6, 0)$.
(a) Find the equation of each side of the hexagon.
(b) Show that the hexagon is regular.

Computer Tip

Over the years, the size of computing devices has decreased tremendously. The early computers were bulky. For example, one of the forerunners of today's computers, ENIAC, was invented in 1945, occupied a room 10 m × 16 m, and had a mass of about 27 000 kg. The development of electronic technology has resulted in new generations of machines that are faster and more reliable. For example, in 1946 it took about 70 h to calculate π to 2037 places; in 1961 it took 8.7 h to calculate to 100 265 decimal places. Today's computers can perform 36 million operations in one second, and with the rapid progress of computer technology and techniques the subject of numerical analysis has become a major study in itself. Obtain information about the field of computer technology and numerical analysis.

Math Tip

It is important to clearly understand the vocabulary of mathematics when solving problems. *You cannot speak the language of mathematics if you don't know the vocabulary.*

• Make a list of all the words you review and learn in this chapter.
• Provide a simple example to illustrate the meaning of each word.

9.12 Problem-Solving: Using Principles

In the study of mathematics, many principles you learn are applied to new situations. For example, you have used a co-ordinate system with two axes to draw a line in two dimensions. For three dimensions, you introduce another co-ordinate axis. To show a point in space you use the following co-ordinates.

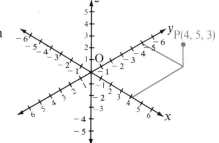

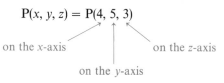

A line is given by an equation such as $2x - y = 5$ using the x-y co-ordinate system. When you solved 2 equations in 2 variables, you found the co-ordinates of the intersection, namely, a point.

A plane in space is given by an equation such as $2x + y + 6z = 4$. The principles involved in solving A and B below are the same.

A: Solving equations on the plane.

Solve $\quad 2x - y = 6$
$\qquad\quad x + y = 0$

Solution $(x, y) = (2, -2)$ represents a point on the plane.

B: Solving equations in space.

Solve $\qquad x + y + z = 2$
$\qquad\quad 3x + y - 2z = 5$
$\qquad\qquad x - y + z = 6$

Solution $(x, y, z) = (3, -2, 1)$ represents a point in space.

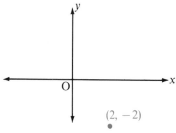

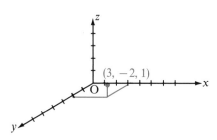

To solve the system of three equations given in B you apply the principles you learned in working with equations in two variables.

Solve
$$x + y + z = 2 \qquad ①$$
$$3x + y - 2z = 5 \qquad ②$$
$$x - y + z = 6 \qquad ③$$

Subtract ② from ①. $\qquad -2x + 3z = -3 \qquad ④$

Add ② and ③. $\qquad\qquad 4x - z = 11 \qquad ⑤$

Now you may solve ④ and ⑤ in the same way as you learned to do earlier.

$$2 \times \text{④} \qquad\qquad -4x + 6z = -6 \quad \text{⑥}$$
$$4x - z = 11 \qquad \text{⑤}$$
$$\text{⑥} + \text{⑤} \qquad\qquad \overline{5z = 5}$$
$$z = 1$$

Use the value $z = 1$ in ⑤. $\quad 4x - z = 11$
$$4x - 1 = 11$$
$$4x = 12$$
$$x = 3$$

Use the values $x = 3$ $\qquad x + y + z = 2$
and $z = 1$ in ①. $\qquad\quad 3 + y + 1 = 2$
$$y = -2$$

Thus you obtain the solution $(x, y, z) = (3, -2, 1)$.

As before, be sure to check your solution in the *original* equations.

9.12 Exercise

B 1 (a) Solve the system of
3 equations in 3 variables.

$$x - y + 2z = 1$$
$$2x + 3y - 2z = -6$$
$$3x - y + z = -1$$

(b) Draw a graph of your solution in (a).

2 Solve each of the following for x, y, and z.

(a) $x - 2y - z = -6$ (b) $x - 3y + 2z = 5$ (c) $3x - 2y + z = -5$
$\ x - y + z = 2$ $2x + y - z = -5$ $2x - 4y - z = -7$
$\ 2x + y - z = 1$ $x - y + 2z = 5$ $-x + 2y + 3z = 6$

3 You may again extend your skills
to the solution of a linear system of
4 equations in 4 variables. Solve.

$$a + 2b + 3c + d = 9$$
$$a - b + c - d = -5$$
$$a + b - c + 2d = 6$$
$$3a - b + 2c - d = -6$$

Computer Tip

Write a computer program in BASIC language to solve the following systems of equations.

A: $ax + by = c$ B: $ax + by + cz = d$
$\ dx + ey = f$ $ex + fy + gz = h$
 $jx + ky + mz = n$

Practice and Problems: A Chapter Review

1 Which line segment is longer?
   AB: A(-3, 1), B(3, 3)   CD: C(-1, -6), D(1, 1)

2 A co-ordinate system is superimposed on a billiard table. Jack has a red ball at co-ordinates (0, 0) and is going to "bank" it off the side rail at (4, 2) and into the pocket at (0, 4). How far will the red ball travel?

3 Point Z divides the line OP externally in the ratio 6:2. If OP is 44 cm in length, what are the lengths of OZ and ZP?

4 The midpoint of a line has co-ordinates $(8, -\frac{1}{2})$. If one endpoint of the line has co-ordinates (4, 9), what are the co-ordinates of the other endpoint?

5 The centre of each circle is at (0, 0). Find the equation of the circle passing through the point.
   (a) (6, 8)   (b) (-3, 2)   (c) (-4, 3)
   (d) ($\sqrt{2}$, 3)   (e) (-1, -1)   (f) ($-\sqrt{3}$, $-\sqrt{5}$)

6 For each circle, copy and complete the chart.

	Centre	Radius	Equation	x-intercept(s)	y-intercept(s)
(a)	(3, 3)	2	?	?	?
(b)	(0, 4)	10	?	?	?
(c)	(-3, 4)	5	?	?	?

7 Write an equation for the curve of all points that are 6 units from (0, 0).

8 (a) Find the equation of the tangent from (-1, 1) to the circle defined by $x^2 + y^2 + 6x - 4y + 9 = 2$.
   (b) How would you check your work in (a)? Check your work.

9 (a) Solve the linear-quadratic system given by
   $$x^2 + y^2 - 4x - 2y = 60 \qquad x - y = 8$$
   (b) Verify your answers in (a).

10 A circle passes through the points P(-4, 0), Q(-6, -6), R(-2, -6) and S(-8, -4). Find the equation of the line
   (a) through the midpoint of PQ and perpendicular to PQ.
   (b) through the midpoint of RS and perpendicular to RS.
   (c) Solve the equations in (a) and (b) to obtain the co-ordinates of the centre of the circle.

Test for Practice

1 If $A(-2, 2)$, $B(7, 5)$, $C(9, -3)$ and $D(-4, -2)$ are the vertices of a quadrilateral, determine which diagonal is longer.

2 If PQ is 28 cm long and N is a point on PQ, find the length of PN and NQ where $PN:NQ = 9:2$.

3 The line BK is 11 cm and C is a point that divides it externally in the ratio $9:4$. What is the length of BC?

4 Show that $P(-1, 2)$ is the midpoint of the line segment AU given by $A(6, -1)$ and $U(-8, 5)$.

5 Find the equation of the circle if the end points of the diameter AB are given by the co-ordinates $A(-7, 24)$ and $B(7, -24)$.

6 Write an equation of the curve containing all the points equidistant from $(0, 0)$ and passing through $(-3, 2)$.

7 A circle is defined by $x^2 + y^2 = 25$. The line given by $y = 2x + 5$ intersects the circle. Find the points of intersection.

8 Find the solution set of the linear quadratic system $x - y = 1$ and $y^2 = 36 - x^2$.

9 A diameter RS of a circle has co-ordinates $R(-3, 8)$, $S(-5, -4)$. If $T(2, 3)$ is a point on the circle, show that $\angle RTS$ is a right angle.

10 A circle defined by $x^2 + y^2 - 4x + 6y = 52$, passes through the points $G(9, 1)$ and $H(-2, -10)$.

   (a) Find the centre of the circle.

   (b) Find the midpoint of chord GH.

   (c) Show that the line joining the centre of the circle to the midpoint of GH is perpendicular to GH.

11 (a) Show that $x + 4y + 31 = 0$ is a tangent to the circle
   $$x^2 + y^2 + 4x + 6y - 4 = 0.$$

   (b) Draw a sketch of your result in (a).

Looking Back: A Cumulative Review

1 Susan, Marilyn, and Nancy drove 1530 km on their vacation. If they shared the driving according to the ratio 3:2:5, how far did each girl drive?

2 If $a:b = b:c$, prove that $(abc^2 - b^2):(b^2c^2) = (bc - 1):c^2$.

3 Find the value of k if A(k, -1) is equidistant from B(-2, -5) and C(5, -1).

4 A line segment with end points A(k, -5) and B(2, 3) has slope $-\frac{3}{4}$. Find k.

5 Find k if the line passing through $(k, -5)$ and $(4, -4)$ is parallel to the line joining $(k, 4)$ and $(-2, 3)$.

6 The sides of a quadrilateral are defined by the lines

$$3x - 2y + 4 = 0 \qquad 2x + 3y - 4 = 0$$
$$2x + 3y + 8 = 0 \qquad 3x - 2y - 8 = 0$$

Is the quadrilateral a rhombus or a square? Give reasons for your answer.

7 Tom must propel his boat very slowly between two shallow points in the lake. If his starting point is (2, 1) and the shallow points are at (1, 4) and (5, 2), determine the path he must steer his boat along in order to pass between these two shallow points.

8 Sketch a graph of each function.

(a) $y = x^2 + 3x$ (b) $y = x^2 - 8x$ (c) $y = x^2 - \frac{5}{2}x$

(d) $y = 3x - x^2$ (e) $y = 2x^2 - 6x + 3$ (f) $y = -3x^2 - 6x$

(g) $y = 2x^2 - 4x$ (h) $y = 6x^2 - 5x + 2$ (i) $y = -x^2 - 6x - 1$

(j) $y = 3x^2 + 10x - 2$ (k) $y = -2x^2 + 5x - 1$ (l) $y = 6x - 2x^2$

9 Two consecutive odd numbers and a third number total 42. What must the numbers be so that the sum of their squares is a minimum?

10 A soccer ball is kicked into the air with an initial speed of 8.8 m/s. The height, h, of the ball, in metres, is given by

$$h(t) = -4.9t^2 + 8.8t + 0.2, \quad \text{where } t \text{ is the time taken, in seconds.}$$

(a) How high does the ball go?   (b) How long is the ball in the air?

11 The volume of a cylinder of a car varies directly with the height of the cylinder and the square of its radius. For a height of 20 cm and a radius of 5 cm, the volume is 1500 cm^3. Find the radius if the height is 8 cm and the volume is 6936 cm^3.

10 Aspects of Sequences, Series

working with the vocabulary of sequences, arithmetic and geometric sequences, solving problems, introduction to series, arithmetic series, geometric series, strategies for solving problems, applications, problem solving

Introduction

Numbers have always intrigued people.

- Some people find 7 a lucky number.
- Some people find 13 an unlucky number.

The use of the word, **sequence** occurs often in your everyday language: *a sequence of events; a sequence of time* and so on.

Number sequences occur throughout the study of mathematics and take on a special variety of applications, and one of them is the applications in the mathematics of investment that you will deal with in the next chapter.

In Science

The numbers of seeds in each row of a daisy have a definite pattern.

In Economics

The value of invested money can be computed with sequences.

In Discoveries

The sequence   0.4, 0.7, 1, 1.6, 2.8, 5.2, 10. . .

led to the discovery of Ceres, the largest asteroid in the solar system.

10.1 The Vocabulary of Sequences

The first number sequence you encountered was probably the natural number sequence. Each number in a sequence is called a *term* of the sequence.

$$1, 2, 3, 4, 5, \ldots, n, \ldots$$

The following symbols are used to represent the terms of any sequence:

$$t_1, t_2, t_3, \ldots, t_n, \ldots$$

Thus for the natural numbers,

$$t_1 = 1, t_2 = 2, \ldots, t_n = n.$$

A **sequence** is a function of the natural numbers. To describe any term of a sequence an expression is used for t_n, $n \in N$. This term is called the *general term*. In the following example, the general term is given by the following.

$$t_n = 3n - 1 \qquad n \in N. \leftarrow \text{ Often, the domain of a sequence is understood to be the set of natural numbers, and is thus not indicated.}$$

Example 1 If $t_n = 3n - 1$, find t_1, t_3, and t_{k+1}.

Solution

$$t_n = 3n - 1$$

For $n = 1$,   For $n = 3$,   For $n = k + 1$,
$t_1 = 3(1) - 1$. $t_3 = 3(3) - 1$. $t_{k+1} = 3(k + 1) - 1$.
$= 2$ $= 8$ $= 3k + 3 - 1$
  $= 3k + 2$

The terms of this sequence are

$$2, 5, 8, 11, \ldots, 3n - 1, \ldots \leftarrow \text{ The symbol ``\ldots'' is read ``and so on''} \text{ and is used to show there are more terms in the sequence.}$$

$t_1, t_2, t_3, \ldots, t_n$ suggests a *finite* sequence. The domain is a subset of the natural numbers.

$t_1, t_2, t_3, \ldots, t_n, \ldots$ suggests an *infinite* sequence. The domain is the set of natural numbers.

Function notation may also be used to show the terms of a sequence. In Example 1, the general term given by $t_n = 3n - 1$ can also be written as $t_n = f(n)$. Thus,

$$f(n) = 3n - 1$$
Use $n = 2$. $f(2) = 3(2) - 1$
$$= 5$$
Thus, $t_2 = f(2) = 5$

The *terms* of the sequence are the *values* of the function.

Example 2   Find the terms of the sequence $f(n) = 3n^2 - 2n$.

Solution $f(n) = 3n^2 - 2n$ A sequence is a function of the
natural numbers. Let $n = 1, 2, 3, \ldots$

$f(1) = 3(1)^2 - 2(1)$ $f(2) = 3(2)^2 - 2(2)$ $f(3) = 3(3)^2 - 2(3)$
$ = 1$ $ = 8$ $ = 21$

The terms of the sequence are $1, 8, 21, \ldots, 3n^2 - 2n, \ldots$

$\qquad\qquad\qquad\qquad\qquad\qquad\qquad\qquad$ The general term is listed.

Sometimes a **recursive formula** can be used to define a sequence. A recursive formula defines each term with reference to the previous term or terms.

Look at the sequence from Example 1.

$$t_1 = 2 \qquad t_2 = 5 \quad \text{or} \quad t_1 + 3$$
$$t_3 = 8 \quad \text{or} \quad t_2 + 3$$
$$t_4 = 11 \quad \text{or} \quad t_3 + 3$$
$$\vdots \qquad\qquad \vdots$$
$$t_n = t_{n-1} + 3 \quad \text{for } n \in N, n > 1.$$

Thus, the sequence $2, 5, 8, 11, \ldots, 3n - 1, \ldots$ can be defined recursively by

$$t_1 = 2, t_n = t_{n-1} + 3, \qquad n \in N, n > 1.$$

The first term of the sequence is given by t_1. Thus, in the general term,

$$t_n = t_{n-1} + 3, \qquad n = 2, 3, 4, \ldots$$

The restriction $n > 1$ is used to indicate which terms the formula applies to.

Example 3   (a) Find the first four terms of the sequence defined recursively by

$$t_1 = -3, \qquad t_n = t_{n-1} + 2n \quad \text{for } n \in N, n > 1.$$

(b) Find a recursive formula for $3, 0, -3, -6, -9, \ldots$.

Solution   (a) $t_1 = -3 \qquad t_n = t_{n-1} + 2n, \qquad n \in N, n > 1$

$t_2 = t_1 + 2(2)$ $t_3 = t_2 + 2(3)$ $t_4 = t_3 + 2(4)$
$ = -3 + 4$ $ = 1 + 6$ $ = 7 + 8$
$ = 1$ $ = 7$ $ = 15$

The first four terms are $-3, 1, 7, 15$.

(b) $t_1 = 3$ Remember: to define a sequence
$t_2 = 0 \qquad \text{or} \quad t_2 = t_1 - 3$ recursively, you must indicate
$t_3 = -3 \quad \text{or} \quad t_3 = t_2 - 3$ the restrictions on the variable n,
$t_4 = -6 \quad \text{or} \quad t_4 = t_3 - 3$ $n \in N$, and $n > 1$.

The recursive formula is $t_1 = 3, t_n = t_{n-1} - 3, n \in N, n > 1$.

10.1 Exercise

A   Unless otherwise indicated, the variables represent natural numbers.

1   Determine the first four terms of each sequence. The general term is given.
(a) $t_n = 3n$
(b) $t_n = 1 - n$
(c) $t_n = 2^n$
(d) $t_n = 3^{n-1}$
(e) $t_n = 2n^2$
(f) $t_n = 5(2^n)$
(g) $t_n = 2 + 3n$
(h) $t_n = 2 + 3(n - 1)$
(i) $t_n = \dfrac{n + 2}{n}$

2   Write the first four terms of each sequence.
(a) $t_n = 2n - 3$
(b) $g(n) = (-2)^n$
(c) $f(n) = \dfrac{2}{n}$
(d) $k_n = 2^{n-1}$

(e) $h(n) = \dfrac{n(n + 1)}{2}$
(f) $t_n = 2\left(\dfrac{1}{3}\right)^n$
(g) $f(n) = \sqrt{n + 1}$
(h) $g(n) = n^2$

3   (a) If $t_k = k - 2$, find t_{k+1}.
(b) If $t_k = 3k - 2$, find t_{k+1}.
(c) If $t_k = 3 - k$, find t_{k+1}.
(d) If $t_k = k^2 + 2k$, find t_{k+1}.

The subscript need not always be n.

4   The recursive formula is given for $k \in N$, $k > 1$. Write the first four terms of each sequence.
(a) $t_1 = 2, t_k = 2(t_{k-1})$
(b) $t_1 = 3, t_k = t_{k-1} + 2k$
(c) $t_1 = -2, t_k = t_{k-1} - (2k + 1)$
(d) $t_1 = 2, t_k = 3(t_{k-1}) + 1$

5   Find the fifth term of each sequence defined recursively for $n \in N$ and $n > 1$.
(a) $t_1 = 3$
    $t_n = t_{n-1} + 2$
(b) $t_1 = -2$
    $t_n = 2(t_{n-1}) + 1$
(c) $t_1 = 32$
    $t_n = \dfrac{1}{2}(t_{n-1})$

6   Find the fifth term of each of the following sequences, $k \in N$ and $k > 2$.
(a) $t_1 = 2, t_2 = 3, t_k = 2(t_{k-1}) + 3(t_{k-2})$
(b) $t_1 = -1, t_2 = 4, t_k = (t_{k-1})(t_{k-2})$
(c) $t_1 = 2, t_2 = 3, t_k = t_{k-1} + t_{k-2} + k$
(d) $t_1 = 5, t_2 = 3, t_k = (t_{k-1})^2 + (t_{k-2})^2$

B 7   Based on your work in the previous questions, what is a disadvantage of finding terms of sequences defined recursively?

8   Write the next three terms of these sequences. Find the possible general terms.

(a) $1, 3, 5, 7, \ldots$
(b) $-10, -8, -6, -4, \ldots$
(c) $\dfrac{-1}{2}, \dfrac{2}{3}, \dfrac{-3}{4}, \ldots$

9   Write the next three terms. Develop a possible recursive formula for each.
(a) $2, 5, 11, 23, \ldots$
(b) $1, 2, 4, 8, \ldots$
(c) $-1, 1, -1, 1, \ldots$

10   Each sequence is defined recursively. Find its general term for $k \in N, k > 1$.

(a) $t_1 = 2, t_k = 3(t_{k-1})$ (b) $t_1 = 3, t_k = 2(t_{k-1}) + 3k$

(c) $t_1 = 2, t_k = (t_{k-1})^2$ (d) $t_1 = 5, t_k = 2(t_{k-1}) + 3$

11   Find a possible recursive formula for each of the following sequences.

, (a) $5, 6, 7, 8, \ldots$ (b) $2, \dfrac{1}{2}, 2, \dfrac{1}{2}, \ldots$ (c) $2, 5, 26, 677, \ldots$

(d) $1, 0, 1, 0, \ldots$ (e) $5, 11, 23, 47, \ldots$ (f) $2, -3, 7, -13, \ldots$

12   A bacterial culture starts with ten bacteria and doubles every hour.

(a) Write the sequence for the first ten hours.

(b) Write the general term of the sequence.

(c) Write a recursive formula to define the sequence.

13   In an atomic reaction the energy released multiplies by a factor of r every second. For the reaction with first term 1,

(a) write the sequence for the first 6 s.

(b) write the general term of the sequence.

(c) write a recursive formula to define the sequence.

14   A checker player places a checker on the first square of a chess board, two checkers on the second square, four on the third square, and so on.

(a) Write the sequence to represent the checkers on the first row of eight squares.

(b) Write the general term of the sequence.

(c) Write a recursive formula that defines the sequence.

15   A sequence has a first term of -3 and each succeeding term is two more than the preceding term.

(a) Find the first four terms.   (b) Find t_n.

(c) Give a recursive definition.   (d) Find the fiftieth term.

(e) Which formula did you use to answer (d), t_n or the recursive definition? Why?

16   Write an expression for the nth term of each of the following sequences.

(a) The first term is 4 and each term is three more than the preceding term.

(b) The first term is 7 and each succeeding term is two less than the preceding term.

(c) The first term is -2 and each succeeding term is three more than the preceding term.

17   The first four triangular numbers are shown.

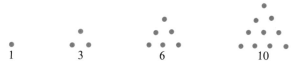

1   3   6   10

(a) Write a definition to define the terms of the sequence.

(b) What are the fifth and tenth triangular numbers?

18   The sequence of square numbers is shown.

1   4   9   16

(a) Find an expression for the nth term of the sequence.

(b) A square number can be expressed in terms of two triangular numbers as shown. Write a recursive definition of square numbers in terms of triangular numbers.

$$9 = 3 + 6$$

$$16 = 6 + 10$$

19   For each diagram the number of non-overlapping equilateral triangles is shown.

1   4   7   10

(a) Construct the diagrams for the next two terms of the sequence.

(b) Define the sequence.

(c) Use your answer in part (b) to find t_9 and t_{30}.

20   The number of line segments drawn for a given number of points determines the following sequence.

Number of Points	2	3	4	...
Number of Line Segments	1	3	6	...

(a) Construct the diagram for the next three terms of the sequence.

(b) Define the sequence.

(c) Use your answer in part (b) to find t_{10}.

(d) How many line segments are required to join twenty points?

Applications: Fibonacci Sequences

Throughout nature certain sequences occur more than others. For example, the stems branching from the main stock of a plant reveal a number sequence.

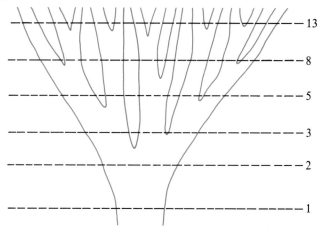

What is the pattern in the number sequence

$$1, 1, 2, 3, 5, 8, 13, \ldots ?$$

The above number sequence is named the Fibonacci sequence after the mathematician Leonardo Fibonacci (say Fee-bo-notch'ee).

Seed growth, leaves on stems, petals on flowers, and rabbit reproduction seem to model themselves after this sequence.

21 List the following terms of the Fibonacci sequence.
    (a) t_3 (b) t_5 (c) t_6 (d) t_8 (e) t_9 (f) t_{10}

22 Which term of the Fibonacci sequence is each of the following?
    (a) 5   (b) 55   (c) 233   (d) 987   (e) 4181   (f) 10 946

23 (a) Write a recursive formula to determine the Fibonacci sequence.
    (b) Describe the sequence in words.

24 The male bee [♂] has only one parent, a mother. The female bee [♀] has two parents, a mother and a father.
    (a) Complete the family tree of the male bee for five generations.
    (b) What sequence describes the family tree of the male bee?

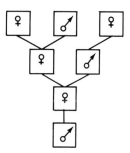

10.2 Arithmetic Sequences

The speed at which sound travels depends on the temperature of the air.

Temperature (°C)	1	2	3	4
Speed of sound (m/s)	332.1	332.7	333.3	333.9

The terms of the above sequence increase by 0.6 each time.

332.1   332.7   333.3   333.9

Difference is given   Difference   Difference
by $332.7 - 332.1 = 0.6$.   is 0.6.   is 0.6.

Each pair of consecutive terms has a common difference of 0.6. Such a sequence with a common difference between consecutive terms is called an **arithmetic sequence**. Thus, the various speeds of sound given in the chart form an arithmetic sequence.

An arithmetic sequence with **first term**, a, and a **common difference** d, can be written in general as

$$a, \quad a + d, \quad a + 2d, \quad a + 3d, \quad \ldots$$
$$t_1 \qquad t_2 \qquad\quad t_3 \qquad\quad t_4 \qquad \ldots$$

The general term, t_n, for the arithmetic sequence with the first term, a, and a common difference, d, is written as

$$t_n = a + (n - 1)d \qquad$$ Note how the subscript n is related to the coefficient $(n - 1)$.

Thus, for the arithmetic sequence $-1, 2, 5, \ldots$ where $a = -1$ and $d = 3$, the tenth term $(n = 10)$ is given as follows.

I Record the given information.

$t_n = a + (n - 1)d$
and $a = -1, d = 3$
$t_n = -1 + (n - 1)3$

II Do the calculation.

$n = 10$ $t_n = -1 + (n - 1)3$
$t_{10} = -1 + (10 - 1)3$
$= -1 + 9 \times 3$
$= -1 + 27$
$= 26$

Example 1   In the arithmetic sequence $0, 4, 8, \ldots, 44$, which term is 44?

Solution   Use $t_n = a + (n - 1)d$.   *Notice $a = 0, d = 4, t_n = 44$.*

Thus $44 = 0 + (n - 1)4$
$= 4n - 4$
$48 = 4n \qquad 12 = n$

Remember: the general term of an arithmetic sequence is $t_n = a + (n - 1)d$
What is a? What is d? What is n?

Thus, 44 is t_{12}, the twelfth term.

Your skills for solving linear equations in two variables are used to solve the following problem.

Example 2 For an arithmetic sequence, $t_7 = 9$ and $t_{12} = 19$. What is the first term and the general term of the sequence?

Solution Let a represent the first term and d the common difference.

$t_n = a + (n - 1)d$ is the general term.

$$t_7 = a + (7 - 1)d \qquad t_{12} = a + (12 - 1)d \qquad \text{Given } t_7 = 9$$
$$t_7 = a + 6d \qquad t_{12} = a + 11d \qquad \text{Given } t_{12} = 19$$

Solve. $a + 6d = 9$ ① $\qquad\qquad\qquad\qquad a + 6d = 9$ ①
$\quad\;\; a + 11d = 19$ ② $\qquad\qquad\qquad\quad a + 6(2) = 9$
②$-$① $\quad\; 5d = 10$ $\qquad\qquad\qquad\qquad\quad a + 12 = 9$
$\qquad\qquad d = 2$ ③ $\quad$ Use $d = 2$ in ① $\qquad a = -3$

The general term is given by $\quad t_n = -3 + (n - 1)(2)$
$$= -3 + 2n - 2$$
$$t_n = 2n - 5$$

A number m is called the **arithmetic mean** between the numbers a and b if a, m, and b form an arithmetic sequence. Namely,

$$m - a = b - m = \text{the common difference}$$

For example, -1 is the arithmetic mean between -5 and 3 because -5, -1, and 3 form an arithmetic sequence.

10.2 Exercise

A 1 Determine which of the following sequences are arithmetic.
(a) $2, 5, 8, 11, \ldots$ $\quad$ (b) $-2, 0, 2, 4, \ldots$ $\quad$ (c) $-5, -1, 3, 7, \ldots$

(d) $2, 5, 7, 10, \ldots$ $\quad$ (e) $101, 94, 87, 80, \ldots$ $\quad$ (f) $2, 1\frac{1}{2}, 1, \frac{1}{2}, 0, \ldots$

2 For each arithmetic sequence, what is the common difference?
(a) $1, 4, 7, 10, 13$ $\qquad$ (b) $15, 11, 7, 3, -1$ $\quad$ (c) $2, 9, 16, 23, 30$

(d) $1, -1, -3, -5, -7$ $\quad$ (e) $\frac{5}{6}, 1, \frac{7}{6}, \frac{4}{3}, \frac{3}{2}$ $\qquad$ (f) $2, -5, -12, -19, -26$

3 Each sequence is an arithmetic sequence. What are the next two terms?
(a) $4, 7, 10, \ldots$ $\qquad$ (b) $7, 4, 1, \ldots$ $\qquad$ (c) $-5, -2, 1, \ldots$

(d) $-1, 0, 1, \ldots$ $\qquad$ (e) $\frac{1}{4}, \frac{1}{3}, \frac{5}{12}, \ldots$ $\qquad$ (f) $a, a + 2b, a + 4b, \ldots$

4   The nth terms of various sequences are shown. Which sequences are arithmetic?

(a) $t_n = 3n - 1$ (b) $t_n = 1 - 3n$ (c) $t_n = \dfrac{1}{3n}$ (d) $t_n = 3n^2$ (e) $t_n = \dfrac{3}{n}$

5   For each sequence   (i) write two more terms,   (ii) find the general term.
(a) $2, 5, 8, \ldots$ (b) $7, 5, 3, \ldots$ (c) $16, 22, 28, \ldots$
(d) $5\sqrt{2}, 4\sqrt{2}, 3\sqrt{2}, \ldots$ (e) $a, a + 2b, a + 4b, \ldots$
(f) $3x - 2, 3x - 5, 3x - 8, \ldots$ (g) $\dfrac{2}{x}, \dfrac{4}{x}, \dfrac{6}{x}, \ldots$

6   What are the first three terms of each arithmetic sequence?
(a) $a = 8, d = -3$ (b) $a = \dfrac{1}{2}, d = -\dfrac{1}{3}$ (c) $a = 2m, d = m - 1$
(d) $t_1 = 2, t_n = t_{n-1} + 4$, for $n \in N$ and $n > 1$
(e) $t_1 = -2, t_n = t_{n-1} + 3$, for $n \in N$ and $n > 1$

7   The nth term of an arithmetic sequence is given as $t_n = 3n - 2$ or written as $f(n) = 3n - 2$. Find each of the following.
(a) $f(1)$ (b) $f(8)$ (c) $f(n + 1)$ (d) $f(n + 1) - f(n)$

8   A sequence is defined by $f(n) = 3n + 2, n \in N$.
(a) Draw a graph of the function. The domain is the set of natural numbers.
(b) What type of sequence is represented by f?

B 9   Determine the indicated term for each of the following sequences.
(a) $3, 7, 11, \ldots, t_9$ (b) $-1, -3, -5, \ldots, t_{11}$
(c) $x, x + y, x + 2y, \ldots, t_{30}$ (d) $-3a, a, 5a, \ldots, t_{40}$

10   Determine the first term, the common difference and the general term for each of the following arithmetic sequences.
(a) $t_{10} = 29$ and $t_{14} = 41$ (b) $t_9 = -6$ and $t_{12} = -12$
(c) $t_{20} = 68$ and $t_{14} = 44$ (d) $t_8 = -23$ and $t_{15} = -54$
(e) $t_9 = 50$ and $t_{13} = 74$

11   Determine the first three terms and the general term of the sequence defined by $t_1 = 2, t_k = t_{k-1} + 4$, for $k > 1$.

12   A sequence is defined by $t_1 = 4$, $t_k = t_{k-1} + 2, k > 1, k \in N$. Show that the sequence is arithmetic.

13 A sequence is defined by $t_n = 3n - 7$. What are each of the following?
   (a) $t_1, t_2,$ and t_3 (b) t_{40} (c) n, if $t_n = 83$
   (d) t_{n-1} (e) $t_{n-1} - t_n$ (f) n, if $t_n = 173$

14 (a) The terms given by $x + 2$, $3x - 1$, and $4x - 1$ form an arithmetic sequence. Find the value of x.
   (b) Find x given that $x + 4$, $3x$, and x^2 form an arithmetic sequence.

15 How many terms are in each sequence?
   (a) $3, 7, 11, \ldots, 39$ (b) $-5, -2, 1, \ldots, 28$ (c) $12, 9, 6, \ldots, -30$
   (d) $-2, -4, -6, \ldots, -24$ (e) $x, x + 2y, x + 4y, \ldots, x + 18y$
   (f) $5a - 3b, 4a - 2b, 3a - b, \ldots, -5a + 7b$

16 The nth term of an arithmetic sequence is given by $f(n) = 2n - 99$.
   (a) Find the value of the first positive term.
   (b) Which term is it?

17 Find the arithmetic mean between
   (a) 3 and 27   (b) -3 and -11

18 Five arithmetic means are inserted between 5 and 29. What are they?

19 Two numbers are such that their arithmetic mean is 7 and the sum of their squares is 148. What are the numbers?

C 20 Three numbers a, x, and b form an arithmetic sequence, $x = 7$, and $a^2 + b^2 = 148$. Find a, x, and b.

21 For an arithmetic sequence, the sum of t_1 and t_3 is 10. The sum of t_2 and t_4 is 24. Find the common difference.

Computer Tip

Before the computer there had been a number of other computing devices that had been invented to reduce the drudgery of tedious calculations, such as the following.

- John Napier (1550–1617) invented Napier's Bones, and later logarithms.
- Pascal, in 1642, invented the first calculating machine. This machine had a limited number of operations.
- Leibniz, in 1671, invented calculating machines that could multiply.

In what years, did each of the following, make a contribution to the development of computing machines: Samuel Morland, Frank Baldwin, Charles Babbage? What contribution did they make?

10.3 Solving Problems Involving Arithmetic Sequences

The distances fallen each second by an object under the influence of gravity are the terms of an arithmetic sequence. The distances fallen during each second are 4.9 m, 14.7 m, 24.5 m, . . .

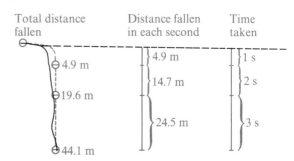

Total distance fallen

4.9 m

19.6 m

44.1 m

Distance fallen in each second

4.9 m

14.7 m

24.5 m

Time taken

1 s

2 s

3 s

Example 1 A watch dropped from the Eiffel Tower falls 4.9 m in the first second, 14.7 m in the next second, 24.5 m in the third second, and so on. How far does the watch fall in the seventh second?

Solution (a) The terms of the sequence are 4.9, 14.7, 24.5, . . .

$$a = 4.9, \qquad d = t_2 - t_1 \qquad\qquad n = 7 \qquad\qquad \text{I} \boxed{\text{Record the given information}}$$
$$= 14.7 - 4.9$$
$$= 9.8 \qquad\qquad \text{the seventh second.}$$

Use $t_n = a + (n - 1)d$
$$= 4.9 + (7 - 1)9.8 \qquad\qquad \text{II} \boxed{\text{Then do the calculations.}}$$
$$= 4.9 + 6(9.8)$$
$$= 63.7$$

Thus, the watch falls 63.7 m in the seventh second.

When a car gets older, the cost of maintenance and repairs increases, often as the terms of a sequence. This is shown in the next example.

Example 2 For a compact car, the cost of maintenance and repairs increased by $85.00 each year. If in the first year the amount was $120, how much was the maintenance at the end of year five?

Solution The terms of the sequence are 120, 205, 290, ...

$t_n = a + (n - 1)d,$ $t_n = 120 + (n - 1)85$
where $a = 120$, and $d = 85$. $= 120 + 85n - 85$
Thus, $t_n = 120 + (n - 1)85$ $= 35 + 85n$
                            For $n = 5$, $t_5 = 35 + 85(5)$.
                                       $= 460$

Thus, the amount of maintenance and repairs was $460.00 at the end of year five.

10.3 Exercise

A 1   To repay the bank for a loan a customer agrees to increase each payment by $11.50. If the first payment is $32.50, how much is the ninth payment?

2   A plane descends 12 m in the first second, 16 m in the second second, and 20 m in the third second. How far would you expect the plane to descend in the eighth second?

3   In a certain lottery the winner of the first ticket drawn receives $10. Each succeeding ticket drawn is $15 more than the previous ticket. How much does the holder of the tenth ticket drawn receive?

4   Carol's minibike cost $2500. After 7 years of operation its resale value was $700. If the bike depreciated by $80 more each year, how much did it depreciate in the first year?

5   The population of the earth in 1975 was 3.9 billion. If the population increased by 203 000 each day, what was the population one year later?

6   The speed of sound in air is approximately 332 m/s at 1°C. This speed decreases at the rate of 0.6 m/s for every 1°C drop in air temperature. What was the speed of sound in the air in the Siberian Village of Oymyakon when the temperature fell to a record -36°C?

7   A jogger running along a course with a slight uphill grade covers 350 m in the first minute, but due to fatigue covers 25 m less in each succeeding minute. What distance is covered in the eighth minute?

B 8   A merchant buys 100 articles. The first 50 cost $100 each. The next 50 decrease in cost at a rate of $1 for each article. How much did the hundredth article cost?

9   Liz paid $2100 for an antique juke box for her new apartment. The juke box appreciated $180 in value each year. After a certain number of years she sold it for $5000. About how long had she owned the juke box?

10   A car purchased for $6000 depreciated $2000 the first year and $500 each of the following years. After how many years was the car worth $1500?

11   Dave's salary is presently $16 500. If he is guaranteed an annual raise of $850, how many years will it take for his salary to reach $23 300?

12   An environmental officer has a starting salary of $18 500. Each year the officer is guaranteed a minimum raise of $1500.00. What will the minimum salary be in 12 years?

13   A stunt driver drives a car over a cliff into the sea. The car falls 4.9 m in the
     the first second, 14.7 m in the next second, 24.5 m in the third second, etc.
     (a) How far does the car fall in the fifth second?
     (b) How much further does it fall in the sixth second?

14   Murray built a home in 1970 for $18 000. Each year the value of the house
     appreciates $2000. By how much did the house appreciate in 11 years?

15   Elaine bought a Barnowsky painting for $1800. After 7 years the artist
     became world famous, and her painting sold for $14 000. Determine the
     annual amount of appreciation if the painting appreciates arithmetically.

16   When you apply the brakes steadily in stopping a vehicle, your speeds at
     the end of each second are often the terms of an arithmetic sequence. Jean's
     speed was 110 km/h, when she applied the brakes. Her speed decreased by
     12.5 km/h each second.
     (a) What was her speed after 5 s?
     (b) How long did it take her to stop?

17   Each year a car decreased in value. It decreased by $1650 after the first year.
     For each year after that the car decreased by $525.50.
     (a) If the new car cost $9650.80, what was the value of the car after 4 years?
     (b) In how many years will the car be worth one-quarter of its original
         value?

C 18 At the end of its fourth year a high school had 1334 students. At the end of
      the thirteenth year the school had 2036 students. The increases each year
      were arithmetic.
      (a) Find the number of students in the school during the first year.
      (b) Find the increase in student population each year.

19   A stamp is purchased through
     an investment club for $275.00.
     The buyer is guaranteed an
     increase in value of 12% each
     year based on the original value.
     What is the value of the stamp
     after the sixth year?

20   Jennifer purchases a rare painting, as an investment, for $9600. If the minimal
     return guaranteed to her is 9.5% each year calculated on the original value,
     what is the value of her painting after she owns it for 8 years?

10.4 Geometric Sequences

If a radioactive substance has a half-life of 12 h, then at the end of 12 h, only half of the radioactive material remains. If you begin with 100 g, then the amount of radioactive material is shown in the chart.

time (h)	0	12	24	36	48
amount of material (g)	100	50	25	12.5	6.25

For the sequence in the chart, 100, 50, 25, 12.5, 6.25, . . . , the ratio of consecutive terms, as shown, is constant. Namely,

$$\frac{50}{100} = \frac{1}{2}, \quad \frac{25}{50} = \frac{1}{2}, \quad \frac{12.5}{25} = \frac{1}{2}.$$

This constant ratio is called the **common ratio** and is denoted by the variable, r. Thus, in general,

$$\frac{t_n}{t_{n-1}} = r.$$

Such a sequence with a *common ratio* between consecutive terms is called a **geometric sequence**.

Compare the definition of the arithmetic and geometric sequence.

Arithmetic Sequence   A sequence of numbers is an arithmetic sequence if the *difference* of any two consecutive terms is constant.

Geometric Sequence   A sequence of numbers is a geometric sequence if the *ratio* of any two consecutive terms is constant.

A geometric sequence with first term, a, and common ratio, r, can be written in general as

$$\begin{array}{ccccc} a, & ar, & ar^2, & ar^3, & \dots \\ t_1, & t_2, & t_3, & t_4, & \dots \end{array}$$

The general term for the geometric sequence is given by

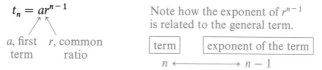

$t_n = ar^{n-1}$

a, first term r, common ratio

Note how the exponent of r^{n-1} is related to the general term.

term	exponent of the term

$n \longleftrightarrow n - 1$

Example 1   A geometric sequence is given by 5, 10, 20, 40, ...
(a) Find the nth term.   (b) Find the seventh term.
(c) What term in the sequence is 5120?

Solution   Find r. $r = \dfrac{t_2}{t_1} = \dfrac{10}{5} = 2$

The sequence is then represented by $a, ar, ar^2, ar^3, \dots, ar^{n-1}, \dots$
$a = 5$, and $r = 2$. Now solve the problem as follows.

(a) The nth term is given by
$$t_n = ar^{n-1}$$
$$= 5(2)^{n-1}$$

(b) Use $n = 7$ to find the 7th term.
$$t_7 = 5(2)^{7-1}$$
$$= 5(2)^6$$
$$= 5(64)$$
$$= 320$$

(c) Let 5120 be the nth term.
$$t_n = 5120$$
$$5(2)^{n-1} = 5120 \qquad \text{Divide by 5.}$$
$$2^{n-1} = 1024$$
$$2^{n-1} = 2^{10}$$
$$n - 1 = 10$$
$$n = 11$$
Thus, 5120 is the eleventh term of the geometric sequence.

Example 2   The fifth term of a geometric sequence is 1050 and the seventh term is 26 250. Find the first term.

Solution   Let the terms of the sequence be represented by $a, ar, ar^2, ar^3, \ldots, ar^{n-1}$.

Thus, if $t_5 = ar^{5-1} = ar^4$ and $t_5 = 1050$, then $\qquad ar^4 = 1050 \qquad ①$
Thus, if $t_7 = ar^{7-1} = ar^6$, and $t_7 = 26\,250$, then $\qquad ar^6 = 26\,250 \qquad ②$

Eliminate one variable by dividing ② by ①.

$$\frac{ar^6}{ar^4} = \frac{26\,250}{1050} \qquad \begin{array}{l} \text{Use } r = \pm 5 \text{ in } ① \\ ar^4 = 1050 \end{array}$$

$$r^2 = 25 \qquad\qquad 625a = 1050$$
$$r = \pm 5 \qquad\qquad a = 1.68$$

The first three terms of the sequence are,

for $a = 1.68, r = 5$: $1.68, 8.4, 42, \ldots$ Note: There are two
for $a = 1.68, r = -5$: $1.68, -8.4, 42, \ldots$ different sequences.

A number m is called the **geometric mean** between the numbers a and b, if a and b form a geometric sequence. Namely,

$$\frac{m}{a} = \frac{b}{m} = r \leftarrow \text{common ratio}$$

For example, 6 is the geometric mean between -3 and -12 because -3, 6, -12 form a geometric sequence.

10.4   Exercise

A 1   Which of the following are geometric sequences? Name the common ratio.

(a) $1, 3, 9, \ldots$

(b) $2, 5, 10, \ldots$

(c) $-4, 8, -15, \ldots$

(d) $a, \dfrac{ab}{2}, \dfrac{ab^2}{2}, \ldots$

(e) $ay, ay^3, ay^5, \ldots$

(f) $-1, -2, -4, \ldots$

(g) $-7, -4, -1, \ldots$

(h) $0.2, 0.02, 0.002, \ldots$

2   Identify each of the following sequences as geometric or arithmetic. Write the next two terms.
   (a) $3, 6, 12, \ldots$ (b) $7, 9, 11, \ldots$ (c) $-2, 2, -2, \ldots$
   (d) $16, 4, 1, \ldots$ (e) $-5, -7, -9, \ldots$ (f) $1, -2, 4, \ldots$
   (g) $\dfrac{1}{2}, 1, \dfrac{3}{2}, \ldots$ (h) $4, 2, 1, \ldots$ (i) $m, 2m^2, 4m^3, \ldots$
   (j) $\dfrac{1}{27}, \dfrac{1}{9}, \dfrac{1}{3}, \ldots$ (k) $p, 3p, 5p, \ldots$ (l) $\sqrt{3}, 3, 3\sqrt{3}, \ldots$

3   For the geometric sequence $2, 4, 8, \ldots$ find
   (a) t_5.   (b) t_7.   (c) t_n.

4   The nth term of a geometric sequence is given by $t_n = 3(-2)^{n-1}$. Find the following.
   (a) t_1 (b) t_5 (c) t_{2k} (d) $t_{n-1} \div t_n$

5   For each geometric sequence, find the term indicated.
   (a) t_8 $1, 2, 4, \ldots$ (b) t_7 $\dfrac{2}{3}, \dfrac{2}{9}, \dfrac{2}{27}, \ldots$ (c) t_7 $-\dfrac{1}{6}, \dfrac{1}{3}, \dfrac{-2}{3}, \ldots$
   (d) t_{15} $2^{50}, 2^{48}, 2^{46}, \ldots$ (e) t_{10} $\dfrac{p^2}{q}, \dfrac{p^3}{2q}, \dfrac{p^4}{4q}, \ldots$ (f) t_9 $\sqrt{3}, \sqrt{6}, 2\sqrt{3}, \ldots$

6   A term of each sequence is missing. If each sequence is geometric, what is the value of m?
   (a) $1, 4, m, \ldots$ (b) $m, 5, 25, \ldots$ (c) $10, 5, m, \ldots$
   (d) $2, m, 32, \ldots$ (e) $1, \dfrac{-1}{3}, m, \ldots$ (f) $a, m, b, \ldots$

7   Each sequence is geometric. What are the missing terms?
   (a) $15, 5, x, y$ (b) $x, y, 10, 20$ (c) $1.6, 4, 10, x, y$

8   $1, 3, 9, \ldots, 2187$ is a geometric sequence.
   (a) Which term is shown by 2187?
   (b) How many terms are in the sequence?

9   Find the number of terms in each of these geometric sequences.
   (a) $2, 10, 50, \ldots, 156\ 250$ (b) $16, -8, 4, \ldots, \dfrac{1}{4}$ (c) $36, 18, 9, \ldots, \dfrac{9}{128}$
   (d) $-\dfrac{1}{10}, 1, -10, \ldots, 10^6$ (e) $2, 6, 18, \ldots, 1458$

B   Remember: You must know the meaning of each variable in the nth terms of sequences. Review them.

10   Determine a and r, given

(a) $t_3 = 18$ and $t_7 = 1458$.   (b) $t_4 = \dfrac{3}{8}$ and $t_8 = \dfrac{3}{128}$.

11   Find the missing term of each of the following.

(a) $t_3 = \dfrac{1}{9}$, $t_7 = 9$, $t_4 = ?$ (b) $t_5 = 8$, $t_{10} = \dfrac{1}{4}$, $t_3 = ?$

(c) $t_8 = -\dfrac{1}{8}$, $t_3 = -4$, $t_2 = ?$ (d) $t_3 = 27$, $t_8 = -\dfrac{1}{9}$, $t_4 = ?$

12   The fifth term of a geometric sequence is $\frac{4}{27}$ and the eighth term is $\frac{4}{729}$. Find the first three terms of the sequence.

13   The tenth term of a geometric sequence is 2560 and the fifth term is 80. Find the twelfth term.

14   The terms $x + 1$, $x + 7$, and $2x + 14$ are of a geometric sequence. Find x.

15   Find an integer x so that x, $x + 4$, and $4x + 10$ form a geometric sequence.

16   A sequence is defined as follows: $t_1 = 3$, $t_k = 2(t_{k-1})$. Show that the sequence is geometric.

17   Prove that the sequence defined by the recursive relationship $t_1 = a - b$, $t_{n-1} = 3t_n$, $n > 1$, is geometric.

18   Find the geometric mean for each of the following.
(a) 4, 16   (b) 5, 20   (c) 5, 125   (d) 6, 150

19   (a) Find three geometric means between 3 and 48.
(b) Find four geometric means between 3 and 96.

20   Find four numbers between 2 and 6250 so that the six numbers are in geometric sequence.

C 21   For a geometric sequence, $t_2 + t_3 = 24$ and $t_7 + t_8 = 5832$. Find the first three terms of the sequence.

22   For any two positive numbers, prove that the arithmetic mean is not less than the geometric mean.

Problem Solving: Making Decisions

To solve a problem with sequences, an important step is to decide what type of sequence is involved.

23 For each sequence
    (i) decide what type of sequence occurs.
    (ii) determine the number of terms.

(a) $3, 6, 12, \ldots, 192$ (b) $-2, 2, 6, \ldots, 58$ (c) $1, \dfrac{1}{2}, \dfrac{1}{4}, \ldots, \dfrac{1}{256}$

(d) $17, 11, 5, \ldots, -103$ (e) $3, 5, 7, \ldots, 23$ (f) $5, 10, 20, \ldots, 640$

24 Determine x, $x \in I$, in order that x, $x + 8$, and $8x + 4$ form
    (a) a geometric sequence.   (b) an arithmetic sequence.

25 Determine $y \in I$, in order that $y - 2$, $5y + 10$, and $y - 50$ form
    (a) a geometric sequence.   (b) an arithmetic sequence.

26 A sequence is defined by the recursive formula $t_1 = 4$, $t_k = 2(t_{k-1})$, $k \in I$, $k > 1$.
    (a) What type of sequence is it?   (b) Find the tenth term.

27 (a) What type of sequence is given by the recursive formula
        $$t_1 = 2x + 3y \qquad t_{n-1} = 4t_n?$$
    (b) Find an expression for the nth term.

28 To completely define a sequence, the nth term must be given. For each sequence
    • decide whether the sequence is arithmetic, geometric, or neither.
    • write the nth term if the sequence is arithmetic or geometric.

(a) $2, 8, 32, \ldots$ (b) $5, 9, 12, 16, 19, 23, \ldots$ (c) $\dfrac{1}{16}, \dfrac{1}{8}, \dfrac{1}{4}, \ldots$

(d) $3, 5, 7, 9, 11, 13, \ldots$ (e) $-3, 1, -\dfrac{1}{3}, \ldots$ (f) $9, 3, 1, \ldots$

29 The word *arithmetic* or *geometric* has been omitted from each of the following problems. Make a decision as to which type of sequence more likely occurs. Then solve the problem
    (a) For a sequence, the first term is 2. If the fifth term is 162, find the first three terms of the sequence.
    (b) For the sequence, $2, 8, 14, \ldots$, what term is equal to 128?
    (c) The first term of a sequence is 2 and the twentieth term is 40. Find the first four terms.
    (d) The sixth term of a sequence is 7 and the tenth term is 19. Find the first term.

10.5 Problems Involving Geometric Sequences

Collectors of coins or stamps expect a collection to increase in value each year. For example, if a stamp is worth $20, and appreciates 12%/a, what will be its value in 5 years?   current value   Increase in value is given by

12% of 20 = 0.12(20)

$$\text{Value, in dollars, after 1 year} = 20 + 0.12(20)$$
$$= 20(1 + 0.12)$$
$$= 20(1.12) \longleftarrow \text{new value}$$

Next year, the new value becomes the current value

$$\text{Value, in dollars, after 2 years} = 20(1.12) + \overbrace{0.12(20(1.12))}^{\text{increase in value}}$$
$$= 20(1.12)(1 + 0.12)$$
$$= 20(1.12)^2 \longleftarrow \text{This new value becomes the}$$
current value for the next year.

$$\text{Value, in dollars, after 3 years} = 20(1.12)^2 + 0.12(20(1.12)^2)$$
$$= 20(1.12)^2(1 + 0.12)$$
$$= 20(1.12)^3$$

The values, in dollars, form a geometric sequence.

$$20, \quad 20(1.12), \quad 20(1.12)^2, \quad 20(1.12)^3, \quad \dots$$

In general, if an amount, P, appreciates at the rate of $i\%$ per annum, then its value, A, after n years is given by

$$A = P(1 + i)^n$$

Example   A coin appreciates in value each year by 8%. If the value today is $165, what will the coin be worth in 5 years?

Solution   Use $A = P(1 + i)^n$ where $P = 165$, $i = 0.08$, $n = 5$

$$A = 165(1.08)^5$$
$$A = 242.44$$

Thus, the coin will be worth $242.44 in 5 years.

10.5 Exercise

A 1   A company increases sales by 15%/a. Initial sales amount to $2 300 000. The amounts below are in millions of dollars. What does each represent?
(a) $2.3(1.15)^2$ (b) $2.3(1.15)^5$

2   A club consists of 250 members. The membership committee plans to increase
     its membership by 25%/a. What do each of the following represent?
     (a) $250(1.25)^3$ (b) $250(1.25)^8$

3   A school population is 1200. It is expected that this population will increase
     by 10%/a for 2 years. Write an expression to show the expected population
     (a) after 1 year.   (b) after 2 years.

4   An object is thrown from a height of 200 m. It bounces back to a position
     0.6 of its previous height. Write an expression to show how high the ball is
     after
     (a) 3 bounces.   (b) k bounces.

5   A baseball player's batting average is 0.260. He expects to increase his
     average by 6%/a for 3 years. What is his expected average
     (a) the next year?   (b) after 3 years?

6   In a village the number of deaths each year was 40. If this number
     increased by approximately 10%/a over a period of 3 years, how many
     people died
     (a) the first year?   (b) the third year?

7   A piece of duplicating equipment costs $6900. If it depreciates 10%/a, write
     an expression to show how much it is worth after
     (a) 1 year   (b) 3 years   (c) 5 years

B   Remember: To solve the following problems, you need to use your skills
     with sequences. Review your skills. Then solve the problems.

8   A car valued at $7500 depreciates 15%/a. Find the value of the car at the
     end of 4 years.

9   The population of a city of 300 000 increases each year by 2%. Find the
     population after 5 years.

10   In a certain bacterial strain, the number of bacteria doubles every half-second.
     Starting with one of them, how many bacteria would there be after 6 s?

11   Steve buys a stereo system for $1200. If the system depreciates 30% the
     first year and then by 20% each year thereafter, how much is the system
     worth after 5 years?

12   A chain letter starts with one person sending out ten letters. Each of these
     recipients sends out ten letters, and so on. How many letters will be in
     the mail after four mailings?

13 A colour television set is purchased for $720. It is estimated that it depreciates 18% of its previous year's value each year for 5 years. How much is it worth after 5 years?

14 Five years ago the cost of a hamburger, french fries and soft drink was $1.50. If food prices have been rising at an average rate of 11%/a, what is the current cost for this meal?

15 A company had sales increase by 10%/a over a four-year period. If there were a million dollars in sales one year, how many were there 4 years later?

16 A pool table cost $620. It depreciated by 12%/a. How much was it worth after 5 years?

17 A tennis club wants to increase it membership by 20%/a. If 400 people belong to the club now, what will be the membership after 6 years?

18 A football club wants to increase the number of season ticket holders by 15%/a. If there are 7000 season ticket holders now, how many will there be after 7 years (to the nearest hundred)?

C 19 A town becomes a city and in its third year has a population of 220 000. Three years later the population has risen to 292 820. If the population can be represented by a geometric sequence, find the city's population after 10 years.

Problem Solving

In order to develop a method of solving a problem, you often look for a pattern.

The 3×3 square has squares of different areas, some of which are hidden. Derive a method that gives the total number of squares for any $n \times n$ squares. Study the pattern carefully.

3 × 3

2 × 2

1 × 1

14

5

1

Number of squares in all.

10.6 Introduction to Series: Skills and Concepts

For the *sequence* 1, 2, 4, 8, 16, 32, 64 there is an associated sum called a **series**.

$$1 + 2 + 4 + 8 + 16 + 32 + 64$$

The Greek symbol $\sum$ (sigma) is used to write the series in compact form.

$$\underbrace{1 + 2 + 4 + \cdots + 64}_{} = \underbrace{\sum_{n=1}^{7} 2^{n-1}}_{}$$

The terms form a geometric sequence with $a = 1, r = 2$ $t_n = 1(2)^{n-1}$.

This symbol is read as "the sum of the terms of the sequence given by $t_n = 2^{n-1}$ from $n = 1$ to $n = 7$".

The symbol S_n is also used to represent the sum of n terms of a sequence. Thus, the meaning of S_7 is given by

$$S_7 = \sum_{n=1}^{7} 2^{n-1}$$

The number 7 shows that there are 7 terms in the sum.

A series can be shown for any type of sequence, whether arithmetic or geometric.

Example 1 Find each sum.

(a) $S_4 = \sum_{n=1}^{4} n^2$ (b) $S_5 = \sum_{n=1}^{5} (3n + 2)$

Any variable can be used when you write a series in sigma notation. Each of these has the same meaning.

$$\sum_{n=1}^{4} n^2 \qquad \sum_{h=1}^{4} h^2 \qquad \sum_{p=1}^{4} p^2$$

Solution To find each sum you need to find the terms of the series by substitution.

(a) $\sum_{n=1}^{4} n^2 = (1)^2 + (2)^2 + (3)^2 + (4)^2$

$n = 4$

$$= 1 + 4 + 9 + 16 = 30$$

The sum of the series is 30.

(b) $\sum_{n=1}^{5} (3n + 2) = 5 + 8 + 11 + 14 + 17 = 55$

$3n + 2$
$= 3(1) + 2$
$= 5$

$3n + 2$
$= 3(4) + 2$
$= 14$

The sum of the series to five terms is 55.

Summation symbols can also be used to represent algebraic sums with any variable.

Example 2   Show each sum in expanded form.

(a) $\displaystyle\sum_{k=1}^{5} kn^k$ (b) $\displaystyle\sum_{k=1}^{4} (k+1)(n^{k-1})$

Solution   (a) $\displaystyle\sum_{k=1}^{5} kn^k = n + 2n^2 + 3n^3 + 4n^4 + 5n^5$

(b) $\displaystyle\sum_{k=1}^{4} (k+1)(n^{k-1}) = 2 + 3n + 4n^2 + 5n^3$ $(k+1)(n^{k-1}) = (4+1)(n^{4-1})$
$= 5n^3$

$(k+1)(n^{k-1}) = (1+1)n^{1-1}$
$= 2n^0 = 2$

To write a series in compact form, you can use sigma notation, and the general terms of a sequence, as shown in the following example.

Example 3   Write each series in sigma notation.

(a) $2 + 5 + 8 + 11 + 14$

(b) $-3 + 6 - 12 + 24 - 48 + 96 - 192$

Solution   (a) Write the general term of the series. It is arithmetic.

$$a = 2 \qquad d = 3$$
$$t_n = 2 + (n-1)(3)$$
$$= 2 + 3n - 3$$
$$= 3n - 1$$

Thus, $2 + 5 + 8 + 11 + 14 = \displaystyle\sum_{k=1}^{5} (3k-1)$.   There are five terms.

(b) The series is geometric. $a = -3 \qquad r = -2$
$$t_n = -3(-2)^{n-1}$$
There are seven terms.

Thus, $-3 + 6 - 12 + 24 - 48 + 96 - 192 = \displaystyle\sum_{k=1}^{7} -3(-2)^{k-1}$.

In working with series, you will prove various properties of $\sum$ notation.

Example 4   Prove that $\displaystyle\sum_{n=1}^{4} an = a \sum_{n=1}^{4} n$.

Solution $\text{LS} = \displaystyle\sum_{n=1}^{4} an$ $\text{RS} = a \displaystyle\sum_{n=1}^{4} n$ $\text{LS} = \text{RS}$

$= a + 2a + 3a + 4a$ $= a(1 + 2 + 3 + 4)$ Thus, $\displaystyle\sum_{n=1}^{4} an = a \sum_{n=1}^{4} n$.

$= 10a$ $= 10a$

10.6 Exercise

A In the exercise you will learn other properties of $\sum$ notation.

1 Write the series represented by each of the following.

(a) $\displaystyle\sum_{j=2}^{6} j$　(b) $\displaystyle\sum_{i=1}^{5} i^2$　(c) $\displaystyle\sum_{k=1}^{4} 2k^2$　(d) $\displaystyle\sum_{i=1}^{5} (3i+1)$　(e) $\displaystyle\sum_{j=1}^{5} 2^j$

2 Write each of the following sums explicitly.

(a) $\displaystyle\sum_{i=1}^{5} (3i-1)$　(b) $\displaystyle\sum_{k=1}^{4} 4^k$　(c) $\displaystyle\sum_{k=1}^{6} \cos(kx)$

3 For each of the following ● find the nth term.
● express in sigma notation.

(a) $2+3+4+5+6+7$　(b) $2+5+8+11+14$
(c) $4+8+16+32+64+128$　(d) $2+4+8+16+32$

4 Express each of the following using sigma notation (summation notation).

(a) $3^2+4^2+5^2+6^2+7^2$　(b) $10^3+11^3+12^3+13^3$
(c) $x_1+x_2+x_3+x_4+x_5$　(d) $3y^4+3y^5+3y^6+\cdots+3y^{12}$

5 Write each of the following in summation notation.

(a) $2-2+2-2+2-2+2$　(b) $3-6+12-24+48-96+192$
(c) $-3+6-12+24-48+96-192$
(d) $1+2a+3a^2+4a^3+\cdots+12a^{11}$
(e) $1-2a+3a^2-4a^3+\cdots-12a^{11}$
(f) $a+(a+d)+(a+2d)+\cdots+(a+(n-1)d)$
(g) $a+ar+ar^2+\cdots+ar^{n-1}$

6 Find each sum.

(a) $\displaystyle\sum_{k=1}^{5} k$　(b) $\displaystyle\sum_{k=3}^{6} 2k$　(c) $\displaystyle\sum_{n=1}^{3} (2n+1)$
(d) $\displaystyle\sum_{i=1}^{9} (-1)^i$　(e) $\displaystyle\sum_{j=1}^{8} (-1)^j$　(f) $\displaystyle\sum_{k=1}^{4} (k^2+1)$

7 For the series $S_n = \displaystyle\sum_{k=1}^{n} (k^2+2)$ find　(a) S_1　(b) S_8　(c) S_{k-1}　(d) S_{m+1}

8 What value is represented by each of the following?

(a) $\displaystyle\sum_{k=1}^{3} 3^{k-1}$　(b) $\displaystyle\sum_{n=2}^{5} |n-4|$　(c) $\displaystyle\sum_{k=1}^{6} (-1)^k(3k)$
(d) $\displaystyle\sum_{n=-1}^{3} 3^n$　(e) $\displaystyle\sum_{k=1}^{5} (2k-1)$　(f) $\displaystyle\sum_{k=2}^{4} (2k-1)$

9   Express each of the following series so that the lower bound reads $n = 1$.

   (a) $\displaystyle\sum_{n=4}^{8} (n + 3)$ (b) $\displaystyle\sum_{n=2}^{3} (2n - 1)$

B 10   The following shows the importance of brackets. Show that

   (a) $\displaystyle\sum_{n=1}^{4} (3n + 2) = \left(\sum_{n=1}^{4} 3n \right) + 8.$ (b) $\displaystyle\sum_{n=1}^{k} (3n + 2) = \left(\sum_{n=1}^{k} 3n \right) + 2k.$

11   Show that each of the following is true.

   (a) $\displaystyle\sum_{k=1}^{n} a = na$ (b) $\displaystyle\sum_{i=1}^{n} af(i) = a \sum_{i=1}^{n} f(i)$

   (c) $\displaystyle\sum_{i=1}^{n} [f(i) + g(i)] = \sum_{i=1}^{n} f(i) + \sum_{i=1}^{n} g(i)$

12   Prove that

   (a) $\displaystyle\sum_{j=3}^{6} 5(j^2 + 1) = 5 \sum_{j=3}^{6} (j^2 + 1).$ (b) $\displaystyle\sum_{j=1}^{n} 5(j^2 + 1) = 5 \sum_{j=1}^{n} (j^2 + 1).$

13   Prove that

   (a) $\displaystyle\sum_{k=5}^{15} k = \sum_{k=1}^{15} k - \sum_{k=1}^{4} k.$ (b) $\displaystyle\sum_{i=m}^{n} yi = \sum_{i=1}^{n} yi - \sum_{i=1}^{m-1} yi.$

   (c) $\displaystyle\sum_{i=m}^{n} x_i = \sum_{i=m-p}^{n-p} x_{i+p}.$

14   Prove each of the following.

   (a) $\displaystyle\sum_{k=5}^{9} k^2 = \sum_{k=1}^{5} (k + 4)^2$ (b) $\displaystyle\sum_{n=1}^{10} (2n^2 + 3n) = \sum_{n=1}^{10} 2n^2 + \sum_{n=1}^{10} 3n$

15   Use the properties developed in the previous questions to rewrite each of the following using a single summation symbol.

   (a) $\displaystyle\sum_{k=1}^{5} k^2 - 4 \sum_{k=1}^{5} k$ (b) $\displaystyle\sum_{k=1}^{6} x^2 - \left(2 \sum_{k=1}^{6} kx \right) + 6$

   (c) $\displaystyle\sum_{n=1}^{5} n^2 + \left(6 \sum_{n=1}^{5} n \right) + 75$ (d) $\displaystyle\sum_{i=1}^{5} 2i + \sum_{k=1}^{5} 7k$

   (e) $\displaystyle\sum_{k=1}^{n} (5k - 1) + \sum_{k=1}^{n} (5k - 1)$ (f) $\displaystyle\sum_{n=1}^{7} (2n - 1) + \sum_{k=1}^{7} (2k - 1)$

16   If $\displaystyle\sum_{i=1}^{n} i = \frac{n(n + 1)}{2}$, find the value of each of the following.

   (a) $\displaystyle\sum_{i=1}^{20} i$ (b) $\displaystyle\sum_{i=1}^{50} 5i$ (c) $\displaystyle\sum_{i=1}^{200} (4 + i)$ (d) $\displaystyle\sum_{i=1}^{300} (3i - 13)$ (e) $\displaystyle\sum_{i=500}^{1000} i$

10.7 Arithmetic Series: A Strategy

The diagram shows a strategy that is often used in mathematics.

- Step A

Solve a simple numerical example.

- Step B

Use the method in Step A and apply it to develop a general solution.

This strategy can be applied to your work with arithmetic series.

Step A: Develop a method to find the sum of a *specific* arithmetic series, as given in the following example.

Example 1 Find the sum of the arithmetic series $5 + 12 + 19 + 26 + 33 + 40 + 47$.

Solution $a = 5, d = 12 - 5 = 7$ S_7 is the sum of the seven terms.

$$S_7 = \ \ 5 + 12 + 19 + 26 + 33 + 40 + 47 \qquad ①$$

Reverse order $\quad S_7 = 47 + 40 + 33 + 26 + 19 + 12 + \ \ 5 \qquad ②$

Add ① and ② $\quad 2S_7 = \underbrace{52 + 52 + 52 + 52 + 52 + 52 + 52}_{7 \text{ terms}}$

$$= 7 \times 52$$
$$= 364$$

$$S_7 = \frac{364}{2} = 182$$

Thus, $5 + 12 + 19 + 26 + 33 + 40 + 47 = 182$.

Step B: Apply the method in Step A to develop a general method, as follows.

An arithmetic series can be represented, in general, by

$$a + (a + d) + (a + 2d) + (a + 3d) + \cdots + (a + (n - 1)d)$$

Represent the sum of n terms of an arithmetic series by S_n.

$$S_n = \qquad a \qquad + \quad (a + d) \quad + \cdots + [a + (n - 2)d] + [a + (n - 1)d] \ ①$$
$$S_n = [a + (n - 1)d] + [a + (n - 2)d] + \cdots + \quad (a + d) \quad + \qquad a \qquad ②$$

$$\uparrow\text{---}(a + d) + [a + (n - 2)d]$$

$$2S_n = \underbrace{[2a + (n - 1)d] + [2a + (n - 1)d] + \cdots + [2a + (n - 1)d]}_{n \text{ terms}}$$

$$2S_n = n[2a + (n - 1)d]$$

$$S_n = \frac{n}{2}[2a + (n - 1)d]$$

The previous formula can now be written using the first and last terms of an arithmetic series to obtain another form of the formula for the sum of n terms of an arithmetic series S_n.

$$S_n = \frac{n}{2}[2a + (n-1)d]$$

$$= \frac{n}{2}[a + \underbrace{a + (n-1)d}]$$

first term of
the arithmetic series

last term of
the arithmetic series

$$= \frac{n}{2}(a + t_n)$$

> The sum of n terms S_n of an arithmetic series is given by
>
> $$S_n = \frac{n}{2}[2a + (n-1)d] \quad \text{or} \quad S_n = \frac{n}{2}(a + t_n)$$

Once the general method of finding the sum of an arithmetic series is obtained, it can be applied to any arithmetic series, as shown in the following examples.

Example 2   Find the sum of 100 terms of the arithmetic series $1 + 4 + 7 + 10 + \cdots$.

Solution $a = 1 \qquad d = t_2 - t_1 \qquad n = 100$

Since $\qquad S_n = \frac{n}{2}[2a + (n-1)d]$

then $\qquad S_{100} = \frac{100}{2}[2 + (100-1)3]$

Always record the formula you are using to find the sum of the series. For an arithmetic series

$$S_n = \frac{n}{2}[2a + (n-1)d] \quad \text{or}$$

$$= 50[2 + 3(99)]$$
$$= 50(299)$$
$$= 14\,950$$

$$S_n = \frac{n}{2}(a + t_n)$$

Thus, the sum of 100 terms is 14 950.

Example 3   How many terms are in the series $\quad 3 + 8 + 13 + \cdots + 248$ if its sum is 6275?

Solution   Use $\qquad S_n = \frac{n}{2}(a + t_n) \qquad\qquad a = 3, d = 5, S_n = 6275, t_n = 248$

$$6275 = \frac{n}{2}(3 + 248)$$

$$= \frac{n}{2}(251) \quad \text{or} \quad \frac{2 \times 6275}{251} = n$$

$$50 = n$$

Thus, there are 50 terms in the series.

10.7 Exercise

A Throughout the exercise, all series referred to are arithmetic.

1 For the series $5 + 11 + 17 + 23 + \cdots$ find   (a) t_{20}.   (b) S_{20}.

2 For each series, find t_{10} and S_{10}.
   (a) $5 + 10 + 15 + \cdots$ (b) $10 + 7 + 4 + \cdots$
   (c) $100 + 85 + 70 + \cdots$ (d) $2 + 10 + 18 + \cdots$

3 Find the sum of the following arithmetic series.
   (a) $1 + 2 + 3 + \cdots + 25$ (b) $1 + 2 + 3 + \cdots + 50$
   (c) $1 + 2 + 3 + \cdots + 100$ (d) $1 + 2 + 3 + \cdots + n$

4 Find the sum of each of the following series.
   (a) $3 + 7 + 11 + \cdots$ to 16 terms.   (b) $1 + 6 + 11 + \cdots$ to 10 terms.
   (c) $100 + 85 + 70 + \cdots$ to 20 terms.   (d) $2 + 10 + 18 + \cdots$ to 11 terms.

5 Find S_{20} for the following series.
   (a) $1 + 5 + 9 + \cdots$ (b) $-21 - 19 - 17 - \cdots$
   (c) $7 + 2 - 3 - \cdots$ (d) $\sqrt{3} + 2\sqrt{3} + 3\sqrt{3} + \cdots$

6 Sum each of the following series.
   (a) $1 + 5 + 9 + \cdots + 77$ (b) $4 + 7 + 10 + \cdots + 34$

   (c) $15 + 11 + 7 + \cdots + (-37)$ (d) $\dfrac{1}{6} + \dfrac{1}{3} + \dfrac{1}{2} + \cdots + \dfrac{5}{3}$

7 (a) For an arithmetic series $a = 2$ and $d = 5$. Find t_{20} and S_{20}.
   (b) For an arithmetic series $a = 5$ and $d = -3$. Find t_{30} and S_{30}.
   (c) For an arithmetic series $a = 3x$ and $d = x + y$. Find t_{30} and S_{30}.

8 Evaluate.   (a) $\displaystyle\sum_{k=1}^{12} (2k - 1)$ (b) $\displaystyle\sum_{k=1}^{14} (5 - 2k)$

9 Find the sum shown for each of the following.
   (a) S_{16} $7 + 10 + 13 + \cdots$ (b) S_{15} $2 - 1 - 4 - \cdots$
   (c) S_{20} $3.5 + 3.7 + 3.9 + \cdots$ (d) S_{19} $15 + 10 + 5 + \cdots$

   (e) S_{21} $a + (2a + b) + (3a + 2b) + \cdots$ (f) S_{18} $\dfrac{2}{3} + 1 + \dfrac{4}{3} + \cdots$

10 Find S_{20} for each series.
   (a) $a = 5, d = 3$ (b) $a = -2, d = 5$ (c) $a = 1.2, d = 0.6$

11 (a) An arithmetic series has $t_1 = -5$, $d = 2$, and $S_n = 112$. Find n.
    (b) For the arithmetic series $2 + 5 + 8 + \cdots$, $S_n = 495$. Find n.
    (c) An arithmetic series has $t_1 = -8$, and $S_{11} = 242$. Find t_{11}.

12 An arithmetic series is defined by $t_1 = 3$, $\quad t_n = t_{n-1} + 8$, $\quad n \in N, n > 1$.
    (a) Find the sum of five terms.   (b) Find the sum of ten terms.

B 13 For an arithmetic series, the first term is 2 and the tenth term is 29. Find
       the sum of ten terms of the series.

14 An arithmetic series has a common difference of 3 and a thirteenth term
    of 25. Find the sum of thirteen terms of the series.

15 If the second term and twelfth terms of an arithmetic series are -1 and
    19 respectively, find the sum of thirteen terms of the series.

16 (a) In an arithmetic series $t_{12} = 15$ and $S_{15} = 105$. Find the first three
        terms of the series.
    (b) For an arithmetic series $t_1 = 95$ and $S_{12} = 876$. Find S_{22}.

17 (a) For an arithmetic series $t_6 = 4$ and $S_{18} = 261$. Find the first term and
        the common difference.
    (b) An arithmetic series has $t_{15} = 43$ and $S_{15} = 120$, find S_{20}.

18 Find n if
    (a) $28 + 26 + 24 + \cdots + t_n = 154$.   (b) $8 + 2 + (-4) + \cdots + t_n = -300$.

19 (a) Find the sum of all whole numbers less than 200 which end in 9.
    (b) Find the sum of all two-digit odd numbers.
    (c) Find the sum of six terms of the arithmetic series.
    $$(a + b)^2 + (a^2 + b^2) + (a - b)^2 + \cdots$$

20 (a) Prove that $9 + 16 + 23 + \cdots + 212 = 3315$.
    (b) Prove that the sum of the first n natural numbers $1 + 2 + 3 + \cdots + n$
        is given by $\dfrac{n(n + 1)}{2}$.

21 (a) The terms of an arithmetic series are given by $t_n = 10 - \frac{5}{2}n$. Find S_8
        and S_n.
    (b) For an arithmetic series $S_n = \dfrac{3n^2 - n}{2}$, find the first three terms of the
        series and S_{20}.

C 22 For an arithmetic series $t_1 = -3a + 2b$ and $t_4 = 5b$. Find S_n in terms of
       a, b, and n.

10.8 Solving Problems: Arithmetic Series

There are many situations that require your knowledge of arithmetic series in order to find a solution.

Example 1

In an auditorium there are twenty-five seats in the front row. Each row after that has two more seats. How many seats are there in all if the auditorium has fifteen rows?

Solution

The rows form the terms of an arithmetic series.

$$\overbrace{25 + 27 + 29 + \cdots}^{15 \text{ rows}}$$

$$S_n = \frac{n}{2}(2a + (n-1)d) \qquad a = 25 \qquad \begin{aligned} d &= t_2 - t_1 \\ &= 27 - 25 \\ &= 2 \end{aligned} \qquad n = 15$$

$$S_{15} = \frac{15}{2}[2(25) + (15-1)2]$$

$$= \frac{15}{2}(50 + 28) \quad \text{or} \quad \frac{15}{2} \times 78$$

$$= 585$$

Thus, there are 585 seats in the auditorium.

Example 2

(a) A small electronics firm needs to sell a certain number of circuit boards in order to make a profit. If the company sells only one circuit board (the prototype) it loses $350.00. For each additional circuit board sold, the loss decreases by $25.00. How many circuit boards must the company sell to break even?

(b) After the break-even point, the profit increases by $25.00 for each item sold. How many circuit boards must the company sell to make a profit of at least $10 000?

Solution

(a) The terms represent those of an arithmetic series.

$$S_n = \frac{n}{2}[2a + (n-1)d] \qquad a = -350 \qquad d = 25$$

$$= \frac{n}{2}[2(-350) + (n-1)25]$$

$$= \frac{n}{2}(-700 + 25n - 25)$$

$$= \frac{n}{2}(25n - 725) \rightarrow \begin{bmatrix} \text{Think:} \\ \text{Required: to find} \\ n, \text{ if } S_n = 0 \end{bmatrix} \rightarrow \frac{n}{2}(25n - 725) = 0$$

$$25n - 725 = 0 \qquad \text{or} \qquad \frac{n}{2} = 0$$

$$25n = 725 \qquad\qquad n = 0$$

$$n = 29 \qquad\qquad \nearrow$$

$$\text{inadmissible.}$$

Thus, in order to break even, the firm must sell 29 circuit boards.

(b) To compute the number of circuit boards the company must sell to make $10 000 use $S_n = 10\ 000$.

$$\frac{n}{2}(25n - 725) = S_n$$

Use the quadratic formula.

$$n = \frac{-b \pm \sqrt{b^2 - 4ac}}{2a}$$

$$\frac{n}{2}(25n - 725) = 10\ 000$$

$$n(25n - 725) = 20\ 000$$

For $a = 1$, $b = -29$, and $c = -800$,

$$25n^2 - 725n - 20\ 000 = 0$$

$$n^2 - 29n - 800 = 0$$

$$n = \frac{+29 \pm \sqrt{(-29)^2 - 4(-800)}}{2}$$

$$= \frac{29 \pm \sqrt{4041}}{2} \quad \text{Use a calculator.}$$

$$= \frac{29 \pm 63.6}{2} \qquad \lceil\text{inadmissible}$$

$$n = 46.3 \quad \text{or} \quad n = {}^{\downarrow}-17.3$$

Thus, to make at least $10 000 the manufacturer must sell 47 items.

10.8 Exercise

B 1 In a lecture hall there are 11 seats in the first row. The next 6 rows increase by 2 seats each. Each of the remaining rows increase by 3 seats. If there are 9 rows in all, how many seats are in the lecture hall?

2 A pyramid of bodies has 15 people in the bottom row and one fewer person in each succeeding row above. How many people are used if the top row contains 8 people?

3 Billiard balls are arranged to form a triangle; one at the top, 2 in the second row, 3 in the third row, and so on until there are 7 in the final row. How many billiard balls are there?

4 Carl Friedrich Gauss solved the following problem without any written calculations, in less than one minute. He was 10 years old at the time. Can you solve it? Find the sum $1 + 2 + 3 + 4 + \cdots + 100$.

5 A pile of logs has 25 logs in the bottom row, 24 logs in the next row, and so on. If there are 12 logs in the top row, how many logs are there in all in the pile?

6 To belong to a club there are two possible ways of paying your membership. Pay 10¢ the first week, 15¢ the second week, 20¢ the third week and so on, or pay a fixed flat rate of $12.00. If a person belonged for 20 weeks, which would be the better plan?

7 A mosaic consists of 20 rows of designs starting with one design in the first row, 2 designs in the second row, and so on. How many designs are there altogether?

8 A chorus line at Radio City Music Hall in New York City stretched a record 48 m long. The front line contained 36 dancers. Each succeeding row contained one less dancer than the row in front of it. How many dancers were on the stage if the last row contained 30?

9 Terry purchased a used car for $6000. Once driven off the lot it depreciated by 20%. For each subsequent year it depreciated by $200 compared to the previous year. What was the total depreciation over 6 years?

10 When Dar Robinson jumped off the C.N. Tower, it was found that he fell 4.9 m in the first second, 14.7 m in the second second, 24.5 m in the third second, and so on in the same pattern until his back-up crew applied the brakes to his cable. How far did he fall during his 10.5 s jump?

11 Larry's new snowmobile cost $3200. It depreciates by 15% the first year and by $60 each subsequent year.
(a) Find the total depreciation over 4 years.
(b) What was the value of the machine at that time?

C 12 A rock group charges its recording company a set fee for each album produced by the group. The group also receives royalties of $1.20 for each record sold. For one record the group received $250 000 and for another record it received $340 000. If the total number of records sold was 450 000, what is the set fee?

Calculator Tip

The value of π is given by expression $\pi - 4\left(1 - \frac{1}{3} + \frac{1}{5} - \frac{1}{7} + \cdots\right)$

How many terms are needed in the above expression to obtain the value of π accurate to 3 decimal places? (Remember: Use a calculator. Refer to the manual about the $\boxed{M+}$ $\boxed{MS}$ and $\boxed{MR}$ feature of your calculator.)

Math Tip

It is important to clearly understand the vocabulary of mathematics when solving problems.

• Make a list of all the words you have met in this chapter.
• Provide a sample example to illustrate each word.

10.9 Geometric Series

In mathematics, you often apply the same strategy more than once to solve a problem. For example, the strategy used to find the general formula for the sum of an arithmetic series, can be applied to develop a formula for the sum of a geometric series. Remember, the terms of a geometric sequence are given as

$$a, \quad ar, \quad ar^2, \quad ar^3, \quad \ldots$$

where a is the first term, and r is the common ratio.

A **geometric series** is obtained by adding the terms of a *geometric sequence*.

To find a formula for the sum of a geometric series, examine the sum of a specific geometric series to identify a method that can be extended to finding the sum of any geometric series.

Example 1 Find the sum of the geometric series $6 + 18 + 54 + 162 + 486 + 1458$.

Solution $a = 6$ and $r = \dfrac{t_2}{t_1} = \dfrac{18}{6} = 3$

Now, S_6 is the sum of the six terms.

$$
\begin{aligned}
S_6 &= 6 + 18 + 54 + 162 + 486 + 1458 &\quad① \\
3S_6 &= 18 + 54 + 162 + 486 + 1458 + 4374 &\quad②
\end{aligned}
$$

Multiply each term by the common ratio, r, in this case, $r = 3$.

Subtract ② − ①. $3S_6 - S_6 = -6 + 0 + 0 + 0 + \cdots + 4374$
$$2S_6 = 4368$$
$$S_6 = 2184$$

Thus, $6 + 18 + \cdots + 1458 = 2184$.

The previous strategy can now be used to find an expression for the sum of n terms of the general geometric series.

$$
\begin{aligned}
S_n &= a + ar + ar^2 + ar^3 + \cdots + ar^{n-1}. &\quad① \\
rS_n &= ar + ar^2 + ar^3 + \cdots + ar^{n-1} + ar^n. &\quad②
\end{aligned}
$$

$$
\begin{aligned}
S_n - rS_n &= a + 0 + 0 + \cdots - ar^n \qquad \text{Subtract ① − ②.} \\
S_n - rS_n &= a - ar^n \\
(1 - r)S_n &= a - ar^n
\end{aligned}
$$

For $1 - r \neq 0$, $S_n = \dfrac{a - ar^n}{1 - r} = \dfrac{a(1 - r^n)}{1 - r}, \quad r \neq 1.$

The sum of n terms of a geometric series is

$$S_n = \frac{a(1 - r^n)}{1 - r}, \quad r \neq 1.$$

To find the sum of a geometric series, you need to first find how many terms there are, as shown in the following example.

Example 2 A geometric series is given by $\quad 10 + 5 + \dfrac{5}{2} + \cdots + \dfrac{5}{64}$. Find the sum, S_n.

Solution *Step 1:* Find the number of terms.

$$a = 10 \qquad r = \frac{1}{2} \qquad t_n = \frac{5}{64}$$

For a geometric series $t_n = ar^{n-1}$.

Thus, $\quad 10\left(\dfrac{1}{2}\right)^{n-1} = \dfrac{5}{64}$

$$\left(\frac{1}{2}\right)^{n-1} = \frac{1}{128}$$

$$\frac{5}{640} = \frac{1}{128}$$

$$\left(\frac{1}{2}\right)^{n-1} = \left(\frac{1}{2}\right)^7$$

$$n - 1 = 7$$
$$n = 8$$

Step 2: Find the sum.

Find the sum of 8 terms.

$$S_n = \frac{a(1 - r^n)}{1 - r} \quad n = 8, a = 10, r = \frac{1}{2}$$

$$S_n = \frac{10\left(1 - \left(\frac{1}{2}\right)^8\right)}{1 - \frac{1}{2}}$$

$$= \frac{10\left(1 - \dfrac{1}{256}\right)}{\dfrac{1}{2}}$$

$$= 20\left(\frac{255}{256}\right) = \frac{1275}{64} \quad \text{or} \quad 19\frac{59}{64}$$

Thus, the sum of the geometric series is $19\dfrac{59}{64}$.

10.9 Exercise

A 1 For each geometric series find S_4 and S_n.

(a) $2 + 6 + 18 + 54 + \cdots$ (b) $2 + \dfrac{2}{3} + \dfrac{2}{9} + \dfrac{2}{27} + \cdots$

(c) $24 - 12 + 6 - 3 + \cdots$

2 (a) Find S_7 for the series $30 - 5 + \dfrac{5}{6} - \cdots$.

(b) Find S_6 for the series $24 - 18 + \dfrac{27}{2} - \cdots$.

3   For each geometric series, find the sum indicated.
    (a) S_8 $3 + 6 + 12 + \cdots$ (b) S_7 $5 - 10 + 20 - \cdots$
    (c) S_6 $81 + 27 + 9 + \cdots$ (d) S_9 $1 - 2 + 4 - \cdots$
    (e) S_5 $0.02 + 0.002 + 0.0002 + \cdots$ (f) S_8 $\sqrt{2} - 2 + 2\sqrt{2} - \cdots$

4   Evaluate.
    (a) $\displaystyle\sum_{k=1}^{6} 2^k$ (b) $\displaystyle\sum_{n=1}^{8} 9\left(\frac{1}{3}\right)^{n-1}$

5   Find each sum.
    (a) $\displaystyle\sum_{k=1}^{n} -2(-3)^k$ (b) $\displaystyle\sum_{k=1}^{n} 18\left(\frac{2}{3}\right)^{k-1}$

6   For each geometric series, find an expression for the sum of n terms.
    (a) $1 + x + x^2 + \cdots$ (b) $x^2 + x^4 + x^6 + \cdots$
    (c) $y - y^2 + y^3 - \cdots$ (d) $3b + 6b^2 + 12b^3 + \cdots$

B 7   What is the sum of each geometric series?
    (a) $5 + 10 + 20 + \cdots + 1280$ (b) $1 + \dfrac{5}{2} + \dfrac{25}{4} + \cdots + \dfrac{15\,625}{64}$
    (c) $6 - 12 + 24 - 48 + \cdots - 768$

8   A geometric series has a common ratio of 2 and a tenth term of 16. Find the sum of ten terms.

9   If the sum of seven terms of a geometric series is 1093 and the common ratio is $\dfrac{1}{3}$, find   (a) the first term.   (b) the fourth term.

10   For a geometric series the seventh term is 192. If the first term is 3, find the sum of eight terms of the series.

11   For a geometric series, the first term is -9 and the last term is $-\dfrac{1}{9}$. If the common ratio is $-\dfrac{1}{3}$, find the sum of the series.

12   For a geometric series the common ratio is -2. If five terms have a sum of -33, find   (a) the first term.   (b) the general term.

13   The sum of the geometric series $4 + 12 + 36 + 108 + \cdots + t_n$ is 4372. How many terms are in the series?

14   Find the value n if $3 + 3^2 + 3^3 + \cdots + 3^n = 9840$.

15 Show that for a geometric series, with first term a and common ratio r

$$S_n = \frac{t_n r - a}{r - 1}, \quad r \neq 1.$$

16 The sum of five terms of a geometric series is 186 and the sum of six terms is 378. If the fourth term is 48, find
(a) the first term.   (b) the common ratio.
(c) the tenth term.   (d) the sum of ten terms.

17 For a geometric series, $S_4 : S_8 = 1:17$. Find the common ratio for the series.

18 The numbers a, b, and c form a geometric sequence so that $a + b + c = 35$ and $abc = 1000$. Find a, b, and c.

19 (a) Show that $\quad 1 + \dfrac{1}{2} + \dfrac{1}{4} + \cdots + \dfrac{1}{2^{n-1}} = \dfrac{2^{n-1} - 1}{2^{n-1}}.$

(b) What is the significance of your result in part (a)?

20 Show that the sum of n terms of the series $4 + 2 + 1 + \dfrac{1}{2} + \dfrac{1}{4} + \cdots + t_n$ is always less than 8 regardless of the value of n.

For the following problems, the word *arithmetic* or *geometric* has been omitted. Make a decision as to which type of series more likely occurs. Then solve the problem.

21 (a) Find S_{10} for the series $1 + 2 + \cdots$
(b) Find S_5 for the series $30 - 15 + \cdots$

22 Find t_n and S_n for each series.
(a) $6 + 18 + 54 + \cdots$ (b) $1 + 5 + 9 + \cdots$ (c) $-1 + 3 - 9 + \cdots$
(d) $\dfrac{1}{27} + \dfrac{1}{9} + \dfrac{1}{3} + \cdots$ (e) $-5 - 2 + 1 + \cdots$ (f) $-18 + 6 - 2 + \cdots$

23 Find each sum.
(a) $2 + 8 + 14 + \cdots + 50$ (b) $2 + 6 + 18 + \cdots + 1458$
(c) $2 + 1 + \dfrac{1}{2} + \cdots + \dfrac{1}{128}$ (d) $28 + 22 + 16 + \cdots + (-32)$
(e) $4 + \dfrac{7}{2} + 3 + \cdots + 0$ (f) $1 + 3 + 9 + \cdots + 729$

C 24 For the geometric series given by $a + ar + ar^2 + ar^3 + \cdots$, show that
(a) $rt_n = a - S_n(1 - r).$ (b) $r = \dfrac{S_n - a}{S_n - t_n}.$

10.10 Solving Problems: Geometric Series

How far does a ball travel up and down as it bounces?

Example A ball is dropped from a height of 10 m. It bounces to $\frac{5}{8}$ of its height after each bounce. How far has it travelled when it touches the ground on the third bounce? Express your answer to one decimal place.

Solution To represent the problem sketch a diagram.

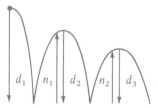

Find the sum of the downward distances. The terms d_1, d_2, and d_3 form a geometric sequence with $a = 10$ and $r = \frac{5}{8}$.

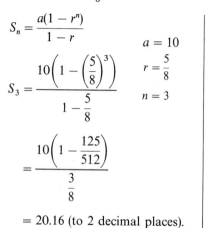

$$S_n = \frac{a(1 - r^n)}{1 - r}$$

$a = 10$

$r = \frac{5}{8}$

$n = 3$

$$S_3 = \frac{10\left(1 - \left(\frac{5}{8}\right)^3\right)}{1 - \frac{5}{8}}$$

$$= \frac{10\left(1 - \frac{125}{512}\right)}{\frac{3}{8}}$$

$$= 20.16 \text{ (to 2 decimal places).}$$

Find the sum of the upward distances

$$n_1 = 10\left(\frac{5}{8}\right) \qquad n_2 = 10\left(\frac{5}{8}\right)^2$$

Since there are only two terms, add to find the sum.

$$n_1 + n_2 = 10\left(\frac{5}{8}\right) + 10\left(\frac{5}{8}\right)^2$$

$$= \frac{25}{4} + \frac{125}{32}$$

$$= 10.16 \text{ (to 2 decimal places)}$$

The total distance travelled by the ball is 30.3 m.

10.10 Exercise

B 1 A basketball bounces to 0.6 of its initial height when dropped on a hard floor. If the ball falls from a 4 m high basket,
(a) what is the height after the fourth bounce?
(b) what distance has the basketball travelled when it touches the floor for the fifth time?

2 The profits of a company in the first year of production were a million dollars. The company expects to increase profits by 10%/a.
(a) Find the profit after 6 years.
(b) Find the total profit after 10 years of operation.

3   In a lottery the first prize is $1 000 000. Each succeeding prize is $\frac{1}{2}$ of the preceding prize.
(a) How much is the sixth prize?
(b) How much money is allotted in 7 prizes?

4   Chitra is training for a marathon which takes place in 4 months. This week she ran 45 km. She intends to increase her distance by 90 m each week. How far will she have run after 10 weeks?

5   In a lottery there are 10 prizes. The last prize is $25 and each prize is double the preceding prize. What is the total amount of prize money awarded?

6   The Johnsons receive yearly payments from a pension. On each anniversary of the pension they received 90% of the preceding year's amount. If the first payment is $6350, how much in all will be paid out in 8 years?

7   Sunil climbed 60 m up a cliff in the first hour of climbing. In each of the next 4 h he climbed only 75% of the distance of the previous hour. How far had he climbed after 5 h?

8   A company has gone on strike and the employees must be notified. A phone system has been arranged in which the chief negotiator calls three employees. Each of these makes three calls and so on. How many employees have been alerted after the seventh level of calls?

9   When you shut off a circular saw it continues to turn. Each second, the speed is $\frac{2}{3}$ of the speed of the previous second. After the first 8 s, the saw has turned 258 times. What was the speed of the saw before the motor was shut off?

10   One third of the water in a tank is removed with each stroke of a vacuum pump. What fraction of the original amount of water has been removed from the tank after the fifth stroke?

11   A sweepstakes gives away $1 000 000 in the following manner: $25 is given away the first week, $75 in the second week, $225 in the third week, so on. How many weeks will it take to give away the entire prize?

12   Under conditions favourable to growth, certain bacteria can divide into two every 20 min. How many times the original number of bacteria will there be at the end of a 3-h period?

13   The largest number of twins born to a mother is sixteen. The mother was Fyodor Vassilet (1816–1872) of Russia. If each twin had one set of twins and each of these twins had one set of twins, and so on, how many twins would have been descendants of Vassilet after 7 generations?

Practice and Problems: A Chapter Review

1 (a) Find the first six terms of the sequence $f(n) = 1$ if n is odd and $f(n) = n$ if n is even.

 (b) Find the first six terms of the sequence if $f(1) = -1$, $f(2) = -2$, $f(3) = -3$, and $f(n) = f(n - 3)$ for $n > 3$, $n \in N$.

2 A sequence has a first term of -5 and each succeeding term is three less than the preceding term. Find

 (a) the first four terms.　　 (b) t_n.

 (c) a recursive definition.　 (d) the hundredth term.

3 The speed of sound is given for different temperatures.

Temperature (°C)	1	2	3	4
Speed of Sound (m/s)	332.1	332.7	333.3	333.9

 (a) Write an expression for the nth term of the sequence.

 (b) Define the sequence recursively.

 (c) Find the 15th term of the sequence.

 (d) What is the speed of sound at a temperature of $10°C$?

4 For the following sequences, the word arithmetic or geometric has been omitted. Decide which type each sequence is, and find the term indicated.

 (a) For the sequence $3, 6, 12, \ldots$, what term is 384?

 (b) For a sequence, $t_6 = 21$ and $t_{10} = 37$. Find t_{22}.

5 (a) A computer valued at \$6200 depreciates 18% each year. Find the value of the computer after 5 years.

 (b) An exercise club has 250 members and wants to increase its membership by 25% each year. What will the membership be in 4 years?

6 (a) The terms of an arithmetic series are given by $10 + \frac{3}{2}n$. Find S_4 and S_n.

 (b) When Jennifer began to work, she initially earned \$18 000 a year, and was guaranteed a raise of \$1800 each year for the next 6 years. How much in all will she receive in these years?

7 A ripe dandelion plant produces on average, 3000 seeds each year. From each seed a new plant may begin. It has been found that only an average of five survive to give root to new plants. How many plants grow as a result of a single dandelion plant after 7 years?

Test for Practice

1 For the sequence defined recursively as $t_1 = 1$, $t_2 = 1$, $t_n = t_{n-1} + t_{n-2}$, $n > 2$, find the first six terms.

2 (a) The general term of a sequence is given by $t_n = 2n + 1$. Find the first 3 terms.

   (b) Define the sequence in (a) recursively.

3 Refer to Question 3 on the previous page.

   (a) The speed of sound on a summer day is 347.1 m/s. What is the temperature?

   (b) The speed of sound one evening was about 350 m/s. What was the approximate temperature?

4 For a sequence, $t_2 = \frac{2}{3}$, and $t_6 = 54$.

   (a) What type of sequence do you think this is?

   (b) Find t_8.

5 Find each sum.

   (a) $\sum_{k=1}^{5} (k^2 - 1)$ (b) $\sum_{k=1}^{6} (-1)^k(2k)$

6 Find the sum of all whole numbers less than 200 which are multiples of 9.

7 For a rock concert, the seats are arranged in semi-circles. The number of seats in each semi-circle increases by 8 seats. If the front row has 75 seats, how many seats are there in all for 38 semi-circles?

8 For a geometric series, the seventh term is 384. If the first term is 6, find the sum of eight terms of the series.

9 A super rubber ball is dropped from a height of 12 m. It bounces back 80% of the distance after each previous bounce.

   (a) How much has the ball travelled after it touches the fourth time?

   (b) How many times does the ball need to bounce to travel 45 m?

Maintaining Skills: Linear Systems

Solve each of the following systems.

(a) $y + 4 = 3x$
$3 + 2y = x$

(b) $3a - 5b = 7$
$b + 3 = a$

(c) $3x + y = 50$
$x + y = 26$

(d) $2m = 4 + 5n$
$2m + 2 = 8n$

(e) $2x - y = 14$
$3x + 4y = -23$

(f) $m + 5n = -80$
$2m - n = 5$

(g) $2m - n = 0$
$m - 2n = -30$

(h) $4a + 12b = 7$
$4a - 8b = -9$

(i) $2x + 3y = -3$
$5x - y = 35$

(j) $3x - 12 = -2y$
$2x - y = 1$

(k) $10 - y = 4x$
$y = 2 - 2x$

(l) $3m + n - 11 = 0$
$2m = -1 + n$

(m) $\dfrac{a}{6} = 3 + \dfrac{b}{2}$

$\dfrac{5a}{6} - (b + 3) = 6$

(n) $\dfrac{3}{a} + \dfrac{1}{b} = 2$

$\dfrac{4}{a} - \dfrac{1}{b} = 12$

(o) $a - \dfrac{2}{3}b = -2$

$b - 4a = -5$

(p) $\dfrac{1}{m} = \dfrac{3}{n} - 12$

$\dfrac{4}{m} - 27 = -\dfrac{3}{n}$

(q) $2(x - 1) = 3(1 - y) - 7$
$x - 5y = -1$

(r) $2(x + 2) + 3(y - 1) = 8$
$3(5 - x) - (y + 2) = 6$

(s) $2(3x - 2) + 3(y - 1) = 1$
$6x + 5 + 4(y - 3) = 5$

(t) $\dfrac{x + y}{3} + \dfrac{x - y}{5} = -2$

$x + 4y = 0$

(u) $\dfrac{x + 2y}{3} + \dfrac{x + 2y}{2} = -5$

$\dfrac{2x - y}{7} - \dfrac{3x + 2y}{2} = 6$

11 Mathematics of Investment

principles of interest, compound interest, nominal and effective rates of interest, skills with amounts and present value, ordinary and deferred annuities, amortization of loans and mortgages, amortization tables and schedules, buying and selling bonds, market values, applications, strategies and problem solving

Introduction

To solve a problem in mathematics, often you may require a combination of skills you have learned. As you learn different strategies and skills to solve problems, you improve your ability to solve a problem you have never met before. However, basic to solving any problem is understanding clearly the answers to these two questions.

A: What information are you asked to find?
B: What information are you given in the problem?

In this chapter, you will learn about the nature of financial decisions based on applying skills and concepts of mathematics to make wise decisions.

As a consumer or as an investor you need to obtain always the maximum return on hard-earned dollars. By doing so, you will acquire funds to allow you to take that trip to Hawaii, or provide for your education, or, in general, provide you with an improved standard of living.

By investing $10 a week for 8 years you could buy the boat in the picture. You need to know how invested money grows and how to get the best return on your investment to do so. Read on!

11.1 Principles of Interest

A glance at the financial page of a newspaper will reveal the various financial institutions that want your money for deposit or want you to borrow money from them. However, most of their calculations are based on compound interest which you will learn about in the next section.

When you deposit money, in a financial institution, simple interest, I, is paid to you for the use of your money and is calculated as follows.

$$I = P \times r \times t$$

P, principal or the amount of money you deposit r, annual rate of interest t, length of time your money is deposited in years.

Similarly, when you want to borrow money the same formula is used to calculate the simple interest, I, you will pay as follows.

$$I = P \times r \times t$$

amount of loan   rate of interest   time, in years

Simple Interest Formula $I = Prt$ where P is principal,
r is annual rate of interest
t is time in years

For example, Jennifer borrowed $500 at 12% per annum and wanted to pay off the loan in 2 years. The interest she will pay for the use of the money is as follows.

Information	Calculation	Statement
$I = ?$, $P = 500$,	$I = Prt$	Thus, Jennifer paid
$r = 12\%$ or 0.12, $t = 2$	$I = 500(0.12)(2)$	$120 interest on
	$I = 120$	the loan.

However, if you borrow money, then at the end of your contract you agree to repay the original loan amount, (principal), P, plus the interest, I. This total is called the *accumulated amount*, A.

$$A = P + I$$
$$A = P + Prt$$
$$A = P(1 + rt)$$

Example   Lucy borrowed $2500 to purchase a micro computer at the simple interest rate of $10\frac{1}{2}\%$ for 3 years 6 months. What is the accumulated amount of the loan?

Record the given information to help you sort out what the problem asks you to do.

Solution $P = 2500,\quad r = 10\frac{1}{2}\%$ or 0.105, $t = 3.5,\quad A = ?$

A diagram is often used to visualize the given information of the problem.

Now	1 year	2 years	3 years	3 years 6 months

$2500

$$A = P(1 + rt)$$
$$A = 2500(1 + 0.105 \times 3.5)$$
$$A = 3418.75$$

Thus, the accumulated amount of the loan is $3418.75.

11.1 Exercise

A   Use simple interest to do the following questions. Round your answers to the nearest cent.   Use a calculator when necessary.

1   John deposited $680 for 3 years at 10%.
   (a) Draw a diagram to illustrate the information given in the problem.
   (b) Find the amount of the investment.

2   Jennifer invested $550 for 2 years 6 months at 8%.
   (a) Draw a diagram to illustrate the information given in the problem.
   (b) Find the accumulated amount.

3   Find the amount of each investment at the following rates of interest.

	Principal Invested	Time	Rate
(a)	$450	3 years	8%
(b)	$692	6 months	$9\frac{1}{2}\%$
(a)	$196.18	3.5 years	$11\frac{1}{4}\%$
(d)	$4326	2 years 3 months	$10\frac{1}{2}\%$

4 Find the annual rate of simple interest.

	Principal	Time	Amount
(a)	$680	2 years	$802.40
(b)	$96.50	8 months	$102.93
(c)	$320.80	$3\frac{1}{2}$ years	$438.69
(d)	$7270.40	2 years 8 months	$9548.46

5 Find the time needed for the principal to accumulate to each amount.

	Principal	Rate	Amount
(a)	$420	9%	$571.20
(b)	$75.20	$10\frac{1}{2}\%$	$77.83
(c)	$892.45	$10\frac{3}{4}\%$	$1132.26
(d)	$3007.22	$11\frac{1}{4}\%$	$4106.73

6 For each investment find the missing information.

	Principal of Investment	Time	Rate	Amount of Loan
(a)	$700	2 years	8%	?
(b)	$1200	3 years	?	$1410
(c)	$624.34	?	9.25%	$941.97
(d)	?	4 years 3 months	$10\frac{1}{2}\%$	$2598.98
(e)	$3014.22	7.25 years	?	$5445.38

7 For each problem,
   • clearly identify the principal, interest rate, and time.
   • clearly identify whether you need to find the principal, interest rate, or time.

   (a) What principal should Glenn invest in order to have $75.00 interest in $2\frac{1}{2}$ years? The simplest rate of interest is 11%.

   (b) How long should $1407.32 be invested at $10\frac{3}{4}\%$ in order to obtain $624.00 interest? Express your answer to the nearest month.

   (c) What interest rate is used for an investment of $3973.25 to earn $2170.39 interest in 5 years 9 months?

   (d) How much interest does $1979.00 accumulate in 6 years at $11\frac{3}{4}\%$?

   (e) What amount of money will Ernie have at the end of $4\frac{1}{2}$ years if he invests $2217.30 at $9\frac{1}{2}\%$?

   (f) If Betty invests $7927.26 at $11\frac{3}{8}\%$, how much money does she have at the end of a 7 year 3 month term?

8   A West Coast fishing company obtains a loan of $14 500.00 to purchase new equipment. If the interest rate is $9\frac{1}{2}\%$ annually, how much money is paid back after $6\frac{1}{2}$ years?

9   Lori borrows $2770.00 from a bank. How much interest will be paid in 3 years if the interest rate is $10\frac{1}{4}\%$ per annum?

10   Chris wants to buy a scooter for $1150.00. He can put $750.00 in the bank now at an interest rate of $10\frac{1}{2}\%$ per annum. In how many years, to the nearest year, will he be able to buy the scooter?

11   Phil wants to buy a windsurfer for his cottage off Vancouver Island. He has $800. What interest rate, to 1 decimal place, must his principal of $800 earn in order to reach the required cost of $1100 in $3\frac{1}{2}$ years?

12   Jim borrows $1947.34 to buy a personal computer. How much interest, at $9\frac{1}{2}\%$, will Jim have paid in 3 years?

13   Elaine borrows $2300 to buy herself a motorcycle. If the interest rate is $8\frac{3}{4}\%$, how much money will she pay the bank after a 4-year term?

14   Fred and his dad need $1600.00 for a fly-in fishing trip on Great Bear Lake. If they invest $900.00 at $10\frac{1}{4}\%$, in how many years will they be able to take the trip, to the nearest year?

15   Jeff wants to buy a new ski-boat. The engine alone will cost $3995.00. If Jeff invests his $3000 summer earnings, what rate of interest, to 1 decimal place, will allow him to buy the motor in 3 years?

16   Jane borrows $2595 to buy a jet ski. The interest rate is $9\frac{1}{2}\%$ and she borrows the money for 4 years. How much is she really paying for the jet ski?

17   Shari needs $700 for her expenses at school. If, on June 1, she invests $520, what must be the rate of interest, to 1 decimal place, to accumulate the required amount by September 1?   Do you think she will be able to do so in time?

Math Tip

Often when you see quotes for interest rates you see the following

12%	9.5%
compounded	compounded
quarterly	semi-annually

Interest rates are quoted *per annum* unless otherwise indicated.

11.2 Working with Compound Interest

In any form of investment, calculations with interest are made.
For example, if you deposit $100 in a financial institution, at the rate of
9% per annum, then at the end of the year you will receive interest.

Principal	$100
Interest paid	$9
Balanced at end of first year	$109

If you leave the money in the account, then at the end of 2 years you will
have the following balance or amount in your account.

Principal	$109.00
Interest paid	$9.81
Balance at end of second year	$118.81

Thus, by leaving the money in the account for 2 years, the original amount
of $100 has *compounded* to $118.81.

Calculations with compound interest occur when borrowing or investing
money. To calculate compound interest, the interest for each time period is
added to the principal before the interest is calculated for the next period
of time. The balance at the end of the period, in this case, 2 years, is called
the *compound amount*. When the interest rate is 12% compounded
semi-annually, then interest is calculated every 6 months. The period of
time between each calculation of interest is called the *conversion period*.
The following example shows the significance of compound interest and
how the amount of money grows.

Example 1 Joanne placed $100 into a term deposit that pays interest at the rate of 12%
compounded annually. Find the value of the investment at the end of 3 years.

A chart is used to
organize the calculations.

Solution

Conversion period (one year)	Principal at start of conversion period	Calculation	Amount at the end of period
1	$100	$100 + 100(0.12) = 112$	$112
2	$112	$112 + 112(0.12) = 125.44$	$125.44
3	$125.44	$125.44 + 125.44(0.12) = 140.49$	$140.49

Thus, the value of the investment
is $140.49 after 3 years.

The amount calculated occurs at the
end of 3 conversion periods, since the
interest rate was compounded annually.

The calculations in the previous example can be expressed in the form of a geometric sequence as follows.

Conversion period (years)	Principal at start of conversion period	Calculation
1	100	$100 + 100(0.12) = 100(1 + 0.12)$ $= 100(1.12)$
2	$100(1.12)$	$100(1.12) + 100(1.12)(0.12) = 100(1.12)^2$
3	$100(1.12)^2$	$100(1.12)^2 + 100(1.12)^2(0.12) = 100(1.12)^3$
$\vdots$	$\vdots$	$\vdots$
n	$100(1.12)^{n-1}$	$100(1.12)^{n-1} + 100(1.12)^{n-1}(0.12)$ $= 100(1.12)^n$

From the chart you see how the principal, P, of $100 invested at the interest rate, i, of 12% compounded annually for n years is given by the expression

$$A = 100(1.12)^n$$ Note: how the exponent n is related to the number of conversion periods, in this case, n years.

Thus, to calculate the compound amounts, A, you can see that:

$$A = P(1 + i)^n \quad \text{for any principal, } P, n \text{ conversion periods, and}$$
interest per conversion period, i.

Example 2 A Trust company advertises investments as shown. If $100 is deposited for 3 years, find the compound amount to the nearest cent.

> **Super Deposit Account**   12% compounded quarterly

Solution Use the formula
$$A = P(1 + i)^n$$
$$P = 100, \quad i = \frac{12\%}{4} = 3\%$$

n = number of conversion periods
$\quad$ = number of years $\times$ number of conversion periods per year
$\quad$ = 3×4
$\quad$ = 12

Now $\quad$ 1 $\quad$ 2 $\quad$ 3 $\quad$ 10 $\quad$ 11 $\quad$ 12
$100(1.03)$ $100(1.03)^2$ $100(1.03)^3$ $100(1.03)^{10}$ $100(1.03)^{11}$ $100(1.03)^{12}$

$A = P(1 + i)^n$
$A = 100(1 + 0.03)^{12}$
$\quad = 100(1.03)^{12}$
$\quad = 100(1.425761)$
$\quad = 142.58$ (to the nearest cent)

A time diagram can be used to represent the given information.

To calculate $(1.03)^{12}$ you can use a calculator.

Thus, the compound amount of $100 invested for 3 years compounded quarterly is $142.58.

If you compare the results of Example 1 and Example 2 you will note that the same interest rate is used for different conversion periods. However, there is a difference in the compound amounts obtained.

$100 invested at
12% compounded annually
grows to $140.49.

$100 invested at
12% compounded quarterly
grows to $142.58.

———— Compare ————

Thus, when you make an investment, you should be aware that you can improve your return on your investment by having more conversion periods. Note that rates are quoted per annum.

Compound Interest Formula

The compound amount, A, is given by

$$A = P(1 + i)^n$$ where P is the principal amount in dollars
i is the interest rate per conversion period
n is the number of conversion periods

11.2 Exercise

A   Round answers when appropriate to the nearest cent. The variables that occur are based on the compound interest formula $A = P(1 + i)^n$.

1   Each of the following expressions occur in finding the answer to a compound interest problem. Calculate.

Use a calculator.

(a) $(1.06)^6$ (b) $(1.08)^2$ (c) $(1.01)^{24}$ (d) $(1.025)^8$

(e) $(1.03)^{24}$ (f) $(1.05)^8$ (g) $(1.04)^{12}$ (h) $(1.015)^{30}$

(i) $(1.035)^{30}$ (j) $(1.045)^{26}$ (k) $(1.075)^4$ (l) $(1.06)^{18}$

2   Find the missing entries in the table.

	Rate per year	Number of years	Conversion period	n	i
(a)	$8\frac{1}{2}\%$	4	semi-annually	?	?
(b)	?	2	?	24	0.01
(c)	8%	?	quarterly	28	?
(d)	?	2	?	4	0.045
(e)	$9\frac{3}{4}\%$	?	annually	10	?
(f)	?	?	monthly	48	0.0125

3   Write an expression for the amount A of each of the following in the form $A = P(1 + i)^n$.
   (a) $600 for 2 years at 9% compounded annually.
   (b) $900 for 4 years at $8\frac{1}{2}$% compounded semi-annually.
   (c) $1000 for 5 years at 12% compounded monthly.
   (d) $1400 for 17 years at $10\frac{1}{4}$% compounded quarterly.

4   Each expression is the result of applying the compound interest formula. For each, what is the principal, rate of interest, and time?
   (a) $300(1.09)^{23}$, semi-annually   (b) $700(1.045)^{24}$, quarterly
   (c) $627(1.01)^{12}$, monthly   (d) $526(1.02125)^8$, semi-annually
   (e) $221(1.0075)^6$, monthly   (f) $323(1.03)^{12}$, quarterly
   Find the value of each of the above expressions.

5   For each of the following
      • Construct a time diagram.   • Then calculate the amount.

   (a) $2750 for 6 years at 8% compounded annually.
   (b) $3272 for 3 years at 9% compounded semi-annually.
   (c) $1475 for 5 years at 12% compounded quarterly.

6   Find the amount of each deposit.

	Principal	Rate per year	Conversion period	Term
(a)	$2200	9%	annually	3 years
(b)	$1750	8%	quarterly	8 years
(c)	$325	9.5%	semi-annually	4 years
(d)	$1617	12%	monthly	2 years 3 months

7   Each principal is invested at the following terms. Find each amount.
   (a) a deposit of $450 at $8\frac{1}{2}$% compounded annually after 6 years
   (b) a loan of $15 000 at $8\frac{1}{2}$% compounded semi-annually after 7 years 6 months.
   (c) an investment of $6600 at 12% compounded quarterly after 4 years 9 months
   (d) an account has $4247 at 12% compounded monthly after 2 years 5 months

8   A deposit is made of $3500. Calculate the amount after 4 years if the money is invested at 10% compounded
   (a) annually.   (b) semi-annually.   (c) quarterly.

B Round your answers to the nearest cent.

9 Refer to the advertisement.

Golden Seniors Account

9% compounded monthly

(a) Agnew deposited $6300 into the account and did not disturb it for a year. What is the balance of the account at the end of the year?

(b) Carl cashed a Canada Savings Bond and placed the proceeds of $1938.75 into the account. If he needs $2500 in 3 years for a vacation, will he have enough money in his account?

10 Find the amount of money needed to pay out a loan of $6500 after 3 years if the terms of the loan include the rate of interest of 9% per annum compounded semi-annually.

11 Jeremiah invested $400 at 10.5% compounded semi-annually on his birthday at age 17.

(a) How much money will he have when he is 20?

(b) What assumption did you make in obtaining your answer in (a)?

12 Marshall invested $6500 at 9% compounded semi-annually for 3 years.

(a) How much interest did he actually earn at the end of the 3 years?

(b) How much interest did he earn in the second year?

13 Predict who will have the most money in 4 years? Then verify your prediction.

A Johnny invested $600 at 12% compounded semi-annually.

B Maryrose invested $400 at 12% compounded monthly.

C Melanie invested $700 at 10% compounded annually.

14 Today, Jeff began to save money for his university studies. He invested his summer earnings of $1250 at 8% compounded quarterly. If Jeff needs $3200 in 3 years, how much will he need to borrow from his parents at that time?

15 The Shaws deposited $12 500 in an account that pays 9% compounded monthly. If they withdraw $1000 at the end of every 6 months, how much will be in their account at the end of 2 years?

16 An auditor, in examining an account, noted that an investment of $3500 amounted to $5509.84 after 5 years.

(a) What was the interest rate compounded yearly?

(b) Find the interest rate if it actually compounded semi-annually.

17 Darrin borrowed $12 000 from a bank at 10% calculated semi-annually. He then invested the money in a venture that paid him 12% compounded quarterly. Calculate the expected profit at the end of one year.

18 A bank pays interest at the rate of 9% compounded monthly on the minimum monthly balance of an account. The interest is added at the end of each month. Find the balance of the account on June 1, if the following transactions were made in the account.

Date	Item	Withdrawal	Deposit	Balance
Mar 1	BAL			$635.85
Mar 12	DEP		$65.80	
Mar 31	INT			
Apr 6	WD	$23.90		
Apr 10	DEP		$46.70	
Apr 30	INT			
May 2	WD	$119.50		
May 4	DEP		$48.50	
May 9	WD	$23.60		
May 31	INT			
June 3	DEP		$123.25	

C 19 Dean and his sister decide to begin a gardening business and will need $4000. To do so, Dean invests $800 compounded quarterly at 10% and Susan invests $1000 compounded semi-annually at 8%. How long will it take them to accumulate the money needed for the business?

Calculator Tip

When using a calculator, you should always ask yourself "Is there a more efficient way to do the calculation?" For example, in your work with investments you need to evaluate expressions like the one below.

Step A: First calculate the expression. Show your answer accurate to 2 decimal places. Record the steps used.

$$\frac{1700}{1.08} \frac{\left(1 - \left(\frac{1}{1.08}\right)^{10}\right)}{\left(1 - \frac{1}{1.08}\right)}$$

Step B: Now calculate the expression, but use the steps as follows. Can you improve the efficiency of the steps?

$\boxed{\text{CE/C}}$ 1.08 $\boxed{1/x}$ $\boxed{+/-}$ $\boxed{+}$ 1 $\boxed{=}$ MS 1.08 $\boxed{1/x}$ $\boxed{y^x}$ 10
$\boxed{=}$ $\boxed{+/-}$ $\boxed{+}$ 1 $\boxed{=}$ $\boxed{\times}$ 1700 $\boxed{\div}$ 1.08 $\boxed{\div}$ $\boxed{\text{MR}}$ $\boxed{=}$?

11.3 Nominal and Effective Rates of Interest

The statement for a credit card owner shows that a service charge of 2% per month is used. On the surface 2% seems little, but if it is converted to an annual rate, will it still seem little?

INTEREST is charged at the rate of 2% per month or at such other rates as may be notified to you from time to time. No interest is charged on purchases paid in full before the due date on the statement showing them. Interest shall be accrued and calculated to each statement date on cash advances from the date of advance and on the unpaid balance of other Indebtedness from the date of the monthly statement on which such Indebtedness is first shown.

Different annual rates with different conversion periods can yield the same compound amount at the end of the year as shown below.

Interest A (for one year)
$100 is invested at 12%.
Compounded quarterly,

$$A = P(1 + i)^n$$
$$= 100(1.03)^4$$
$$= 112.55$$

The $100 has compounded to $112.55.

Interest B (for one year)
$100 is invested at 12.55%.
Compounded annually,

$$A = P(1 + i)^n$$
$$= 100(1 + 0.1255)^1$$
$$= 112.55$$

The $100 has become the amount of $112.55.

Two annual rates of interest with different conversion periods are called **equivalent** if they give the same compound amount at the end of one year. Thus, the interest rates shown in the previous calculations are equivalent.

A: 12% compounded quarterly is called the **nominal annual interest rate** or just the **nominal rate**.

B: 12.55% compounded, annually is called the **effective annual interest rate** or just the **effective rate**.

To find the effective rate of interest, $1 is invested for a year as shown in the following example.

Example What is the effective rate, to 1 decimal place, that is equivalent to a nominal rate of 2% compounded monthly?

Solution Use $A = P(1 + i)^n$ $\qquad P = 1, i = 2\%, n = 12$
$$= 1(1 + 0.02)^{12}$$
$$= 1.268\ 242$$

Thus, $1 yields $1.268. The interest paid on $1 is $0.268 or 26.8¢. Thus, the effective rate of interest is 26.8%.

2% compounded monthly is equivalent to 26.8% compounded annually.

In everyday financial decisions, the effective rate can be used to compare the interest rates offered by different institutions for either borrowing or investing money. By comparing the effective rates of interest, you can then decide which is the "best deal."

▶ When you borrow, you want the *lowest* effective rate.
▶ When you invest, you want the *greatest* effective rate.

11.3 Exercise

A Round answers to 2 decimal places, unless indicated otherwise.

1 Complete the following chart.

	Nominal Rate	Effective Rate
(a)	12% compounded quarterly	?
(b)	8% compounded semi-annually	?
(c)	12% compounded monthly	?
(d)	9% compounded semi-annually	?
(e)	8% compounded quarterly	?
(f)	10% compounded quarterly	?

2 A loan of $1200 is made at 10% compounded semi-annually.
   (a) What is the nominal rate of interest?
   (b) What is the effective rate of interest?
   (c) What is the amount of the loan in 3 years?

3 The balance of a chequing savings account is $850. The account pays a rate of interest of 6% compounded quarterly.
   (a) What is the nominal rate?
   (b) What is the effective rate?
   (c) What is the balance of the account in 1 year?

4 (a) What is worth more, A or B? By how much?
      A $2100 compounded quarterly at 12% for 2 years.
      B $2100 compounded semi-annually at 12% for 2 years.
   (b) What are the effective annual rates?

B Be sure you clearly understand the meaning of nominal and effective rates.

5 What would the effective rate of interest be for money invested at 8% for one year compounded
   (a) annually?   (b) semi-annually?   (c) quarterly?

6   Which is the best effective rate?

A: 10% compounded annually.   B: 9% compounded semi-annually.
C: 8% compounded quarterly.

7   Shirley deposited money into an account that pays 9% compounded semi-annually. Lara deposited the same amount of money into an account that pays $8\frac{1}{2}$% compounded quarterly. Who made the better investment?

8   American Express indicates a service charge of $1\frac{1}{2}$% per month on the unpaid balance of your account. Your unpaid balance is $1680.56.

(a) What is the effective rate of interest?

(b) What is the service charge on an unpaid balance for 6 months?

(c) What assumption do you make in obtaining your answer in (b)?

9   (a) Find the nominal rate if an investment of $350 with interest compounded semi-annually will amount to $665 in 18.5 years.

(b) Percy invested $640 and saw it grow to $1150 in $15\frac{1}{2}$ years. If the interest rate was compounded semi-annually, what is the nominal rate?

10   The following statement occurs on the monthly statement of a department store.

> If you do not pay your account in full, a CREDIT SERVICE CHARGE will be added to your account based on your previous month's balance calculated at the rate of 28.8% per annum (2.40% per month).

(a) Christine's balance was $169.50. For 12 consecutive months she made no purchases and did not make any payments on her account. Calculate the balance of her account at the end of this time.

(b) What is the effective rate of interest?

(c) Do you agree with the information given in the statement? Give reasons for your answer.

C 11   Betty invested $1000 into an account. The interest for the first 4 years was calculated at 8% compounded annually. The interest for the next 4 years was 8% compounded semi-annually.

(a) Calculate the balance at the end of the 8 years.

(b) What would be the effective annual rate of interest after the 8 years?

Computer Tip

Write a BASIC program to calculate the expression for input values of P, n, and i.

$$\frac{P}{1+i} \cdot \frac{\left(1 - \left(\frac{1}{1+i}\right)^n\right)}{\left(1 - \frac{1}{1+i}\right)}$$

11.4 Applications with Present Value

You may want to place money aside today for a trip, a special event, or something you have always wanted to buy like a stereo, sailboat, to be purchased in the future.

For example, suppose that in 4 years, you want to go on a vacation such as the one described in the advertisement at the right. You estimate that in 4 years the trip will cost $2000. How much should you invest today so that you will have the $2000 in 4 years time?

The present value (PV) of an amount such as $2000, is the amount of money that must be invested now to give you the required amount ($2000) at a later date (4 years), as shown in the following example.

Example Find the present value of $2000 invested at 9% compounded annually for 4 years.

Solution Sketch a diagram to show the given information.

Let PV, in dollars, represent the amount deposited today.

Use the formula. $A = P(1 + i)^n$

List the information, before you substitute.

Substitute. $2000 = PV(1.09)^4$ $P = PV, n = 4, i = 0.09, A = 2000$

Solve the equation for the variable PV.

$$PV = \frac{2000}{(1.09)^4}$$

$$= \frac{2000}{1.411\,582}$$

$$= \$1416.85$$

Thus, $1416.85 is the principal you need to invest in order for it to grow to $2000 in 4 years compounded annually at 9%.

In general, the previous example shows

> The **present value**, PV, of a future amount, A, is given by the formula
>
> $$PV = \frac{A}{(1 + i)^n},$$
>
> where
> i is the interest rate for the time or conversion period
> n is the number of time or conversion periods, for the interest rate, i

The diagram compares the two situations.

Finding the *compound amount*, A Finding the *present value*, PV

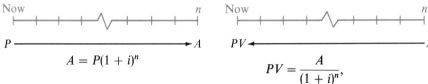

$$A = P(1 + i)^n$$

$$PV = \frac{A}{(1 + i)^n},$$

11.4 Exercise

A   Round answers when appropriate to the nearest cent. The variables that occur are based on the present value formula $PV = \dfrac{A}{(1 + i)^n}$.

1.   Each of the following expressions occur in finding the answer to a present value problem. Calculate to 6 decimal places.

   (a) $\dfrac{1}{(1.045)^6}$ (b) $\dfrac{1}{(1.065)^{14}}$ (c) $\dfrac{1}{(1.075)^{12}}$ (d) $\dfrac{1}{(1.075)^{24}}$

   (e) $\dfrac{1}{(1.01)^{24}}$ (f) $\dfrac{1}{(1.015)^{22}}$ (g) $\dfrac{1}{(1.0625)^{16}}$ (h) $\dfrac{1}{(1.08)^3}$ (i) $\dfrac{1}{(1.0925)^{11}}$

2.   (a) What do each of A, PV, i, and n represent in the formula $PV = \dfrac{A}{(1 + i)^n}$?

   (b) Find the missing entries in the table.

	Rate per year	Number of years	Conversion period	n	i
(i)	8%	3	quarterly	?	?
(ii)	?	2	?	24	0.01
(iii)	$8\frac{1}{2}\%$	?	semi-annually	6	?
(iv)	?	?	monthly	36	0.0125
(v)	9%	?	semi-annually	8	?

3 Write an expression for the present value PV of each of the following in the form $PV = \dfrac{A}{(1 + i)^n}$.

(a) $1400 in 4 years at 8%/a compounded annually.
(b) $1700 in 6 years at 9%/a compounded semi-annually.
(c) $1600 in 5 years at 10%/a compounded quarterly.

4 Each expression is the result of applying the present value formula for the given conversion period. For each, what is the amount, the annual rate of interest, and the time?

(a) $\dfrac{700}{(1.01)^{12}}$, monthly

(b) $\dfrac{1844}{(1.045)^8}$, semi-annually

(c) $\dfrac{1372}{(1.025)^{26}}$, quarterly

(d) $\dfrac{622}{(1.02125)^{20}}$, quarterly

Find the value of each of the above expressions.

5 Calculate the amount of money that should be deposited now in order that the account's balance be $1000 for each of the following terms.

	Time	Rate of Interest
(a)	2 years	9%/a compounded annually
(b)	4 years	11%/a compounded semi-annually
(c)	$3\frac{1}{2}$ years	8%/a compounded quarterly
(d)	3 years 2 months	6%/a compounded monthly

6 For each of the following problems about present value,
▶ Construct a time diagram.   ▶ Then calculate the present value.
(a) $1600 in 3 years at $9\frac{3}{4}$%/a compounded annually
(b) $4200 in 7 years at $10\frac{1}{2}$%/a compounded semi-annually
(c) $830 in 8 years at 8%/a compounded quarterly
(d) $7100 in 3 years 3 months, at 12%/a compounded monthly
(e) $1080 in 2.5 years at $8\frac{1}{2}$%/a compounded semi-annually

7 Each amount was obtained at the following terms. Find the present value of each amount.
(a) an investment of $1900 at $10\frac{1}{2}$%/a compounded annually for 6 years
(b) a loan of $4350 at 11%/a compounded semi-annually for 4 years
(c) a term deposit of $1797 at 12%/a compounded monthly for 2 years 4 months

8 Five years ago, an amount was deposited into an account. Today it is worth $6000. Find the amount deposited, if it was compounded at 8%/a
(a) annually.   (b) semi-annually.   (c) quarterly.

B 9 (a) You invest $1250 at 8%/a compounded quarterly for 3 years. Find the compound amount.

(b) An amount of $1585.30 is due in 3 years. You are being charged 8%/a compounded quarterly. Find the present value of your loan.

10 Sharon has a debt of $650 payable in 2 years. Find the present value of $650 if money is worth 10.5%/a compounded quarterly.

11 When Kevin was born, his father invested enough money in a trust so that on Kevin's 16th birthday he received $4500.00. The rate of interest on the trust was 5%/a compounded semi-annually. How much did Kevin's father invest?

12 Sarah estimates that she will need $8000 to take an engineering course in 4 years. How much money should she invest today at 9%/a compounded semi-annually to achieve her objective?

13 Erin agreed to pay off a loan in 4 years at a cost of $4800. How much could she save if the loan were paid off today? Money is presently worth 9.5%/a compounded semi-annually.

14 Derek purchased a micro computer and paid $750 immediately and agreed to pay $3500 at the end of 3 years. If money is worth 12%/a compounded quarterly, find the cash value of the micro computer today.

15 In 12 years, Bruce wants to purchase a cottage near Grand Beach Provincial Park in Manitoba. He estimates it will cost him $42 000. How much would he need to invest now if the rate of interest is $8\frac{1}{2}$%/a compounded semi-annually?

16 Rob bought his new car with a loan that cost 10%/a interest compounded quarterly. The loan has 3 years to run and the amount due is $4500. Today he received his income tax refund and can pay off the loan.

(a) What is the present value of the loan?

(b) How much money will he save if he pays off the loan?

C 17 Conrad borrowed money from his sister to purchase a sidewinder boat. He agreed to pay her back according to the following terms.

● $500 due in 3 years and $2000 due in 6 years

Conrad is able to discharge his debt sooner than he thought by a single payment that he will make at the end of 4 years. If money is worth 9%/a compounded semi-annually, how much is Conrad's payment to his sister?

11.5 Amount of an Ordinary Annuity

Often people will work out a program to save a certain amount of money each year. For example, Justine has decided to save $1000 each year from her part-time job. She does this for 5 years and invests the amount each year at 9% per annum compounded annually. How much will she have saved at the end of the 5th year? To solve the problem, you can interpret the information visually. Draw a time line.

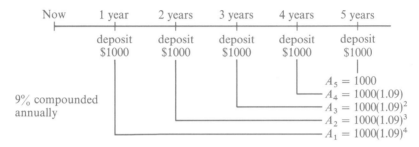

At the end of the fifth year, the amount of money accumulated is given by

$$S_5 = 1000 + 1000(1.09) + 1000(1.09)^2 + 1000(1.09)^3 + 1000(1.09)^4$$

The above series is a geometric series. The formula is used to find the sum. Use $a = 1000$, $n = 5$, and $r = 1.09$.

$$S_n = \frac{a(r^n - 1)}{r - 1}$$

$$S_5 = \frac{1000[(1.09)^5 - 1]}{1.09 - 1}$$

$$= \frac{1000(1.538\ 624 - 1)}{0.09}$$

From a calculator $(1.09)^5 = 1.538\ 624$

$$= 5984.71 \text{ (to 2 decimal places)}$$

Thus, she has saved $5984.71 (to the nearest cent).

The above problem is often referred to as an annuity problem, since fixed amounts of money are invested or paid out over a specified period of time at regular intervals. The sequence of payments is referred to as an annuity, even though the payments may be made at intervals other than yearly. An **annuity** is a sequence of equal payments made at regular intervals, (such as annually, semi-annually, quarterly). The amount of the annuity is calculated by finding the sum of the fixed amounts of money, including the interest. You receive the first payment at the end of the first period.

In another context, an annuity often provides a number of equal payments at regular time intervals for a specified amount of time as shown in the following example.

Example A personal injury fund is set up to invest $2000 at the end of each year for 3 years. What is the accumulated value of the money at the end of the fourth year? Money is worth 12% per annum compounded annually.

Be sure to read the problem carefully! Every word must be translated accurately.

Solution Construct a diagram to show the problem.

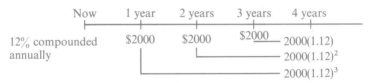

Accumulated amount, A, is given by

$$A = 2000(1.12) + 2000(1.12)^2 + 2000(1.12)^3$$

This is a geometric series.

$$S_n = \frac{a(r^n - 1)}{r - 1}.$$

Use $a = 2000(1.12)$, $n = 3$, and $r = 1.12$.

$$A = \frac{2000(1.12)(1.12^3 - 1)}{1.12 - 1}$$

$$= \frac{2000(1.12)(1.404928 - 1)}{0.12}$$

$$= 7558.66 \text{ (to 2 decimal places)}$$

Thus the accumulated value of the money is $7558.66.

The type of annuity above is called an **ordinary annuity**, since payments are made at the end of each time interval. A **deferred annuity** is another type of annuity where the first payment is delayed (deferred) until some later predetermined date. To study annuities you must know the meanings of these words.

Term is the time interval from the beginning of the first to the end of the last interval.

Periodic payment is the amount of money paid at each interval.

Payment interval is the time occurring between each payment.

11.5 Exercise

A Round your answers, where needed, to the nearest cent. Use a calculator.

1 Calculate each of the following. Express your answer to 6 decimal places.
   (a) $(1.09)^8$ (b) $(1.12)^6$ (c) $(1.095)^{12}$ (d) $(1.04)^{12}$
   (e) $(1.02)^{24}$ (f) $(1.035)^{30}$ (g) $(1.005)^{25}$ (h) $(1.0125)^{20}$

2   Use the information in each diagram. Find the amount of the annuity.
All amounts are in dollars.
(a) The rate of interest is 9% per annum compounded annually.

Now	1 year	2 years	3 years	4 years	5 years	6 years	7 years
	$500	$500	$500	$500	$500	$500	$500

(b) The rate of interest is 8% per annum compounded semi-annually.

Now	1 year		2 years		3 years		4 years		5 years
	$100	$100	$100	$100	$100	$100	$100	$100	$100	$100

(c) The rate of interest is 7% per annum compounded semi-annually.

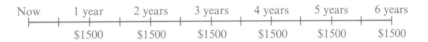

Now	1 year	2 years	3 years	4 years	5 years	6 years
	$1500	$1500	$1500	$1500	$1500	$1500

3   Construct a time diagram for each of the following annuities, then find the
amount of the annuity.
(a) $600 is deposited at the end of each year in a savings account paying
8%/a annually. Eight deposits are made.
(b) $750 is invested at the end of each year in a real estate development
paying 11%/a compounded semi-annually. Ten payments are made.

4   Find the amount of each annuity. Calculate the amount to the last payment
(including the last payment).
(a) $250 is invested each year for 5 years at 10%/a compounded annually.
(b) $625 is placed into a retirement fund at the end of each year for 10
years at 8%/a compounded annually.

5   (a) What is the value of $25 deposited at the end of each month for 2
years at 12%/a compounded monthly?
(b) What is the value of $50 deposited at the end of every 3 months for
4 years at 8%/a compounded quarterly.

B   For each problem, record the given information on a diagram, then solve
the problem.

6   To buy gifts, Ramon deposited $50 in an account at the end of each month
for 8 months. Calculate the amount he has at the end of 8 months if money
is worth 9%/a compounded monthly.

7   Find the amount in a special deposit account at the end of 5 years if $1500 is deposited at the end of each year for 5 years and money is worth 10.5%/a compounded annually.

8   At the end of each month Joya deposits $30 into her Daily Interest Savings account. If the account pays 6%/a compounded monthly, what should the balance be at the end of 2 years?

9   The Johnson family saves $400 every year for their children's education. They deposit this money at the end of each year, at a fixed rate of $8\frac{1}{2}$%/a compounded annually. How much will they have saved after 18 years?

10   Rabher Corporation sets aside $10 000 each year for 10 years to provide funds for an expansion program. What is the fund worth at the end of the 10th year invested at 11%/a compounded annually?

11   If your great-grandparents made annual deposits of $10 at $3\frac{1}{2}$%/a compounded semi-annually starting 25 years ago, how much money would they have saved for you?

12   (a) Use the ad. Find the accumulated value of ten $500-bonds purchased each year for 10 years.
     (b) What assumption(s) do you make in finding your answer in (a)?

Canada Savings Bonds
pays 12%
Compounded Annually

13   Lori spends $450 a year for tennis club dues (payable at the start of the year). If she had saved this money at 10%/a compounded quarterly, how much would she have saved at the end of 5 years?

14   Who will have accumulated more money in 15 years?
     A   John who makes annual deposits of $100 compounded annually at 7.5%/a
     B   Balraj who makes annual deposits of $90 compounded semi-annually at 7%/a.   _____

C 15   At the age of 60, Rod decides he wants to retire and receive a lump payment of $25 000 from the company's deposit plan. This money will be reinvested so that he will receive equal payments semi-annually for 10 years. What is the amount of each payment if money is worth 14%/a compounded semi-annually?

16   (a) Review the meaning of effective annual rate of interest in Section 11.3.
     (b) Calculate the effective annual rate of interest for each ordinary annuity in Questions 8, 11, and 13.

11.6 Present Value of an Annuity

In your earlier work, you found the present value of an amount. This skill can be applied to find the present value of an annuity. For example:
You win a lottery of $50 000. You do not want to spend it all now. Instead, you would like to spend some of it and invest the rest so that you will receive $2500 each year for 5 years.
The problem suggests finding present value. This is developed in the following example.

Example How much money should be invested now to provide $2500 at the end of each year for 5 years? Money is worth 10% compounded semi-annually

Solution Construct a time-line diagram.

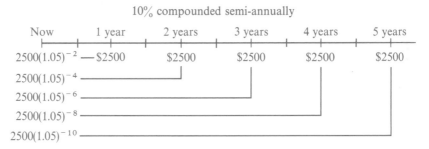

10% compounded semi-annually

| Now | 1 year | 2 years | 3 years | 4 years | 5 years |

$2500(1.05)^{-2}$ — $2500 $2500 $2500 $2500 $2500
$2500(1.05)^{-4}$
$2500(1.05)^{-6}$
$2500(1.05)^{-8}$
$2500(1.05)^{-10}$

The present value, PV, of the annuity is given by

$$PV = \frac{2500}{(1.05)^2} + \frac{2500}{(1.05)^4} + \frac{2500}{(1.05)^6} + \frac{2500}{(1.05)^8} + \frac{2500}{(1.05)^{10}}$$

Use $a = \dfrac{2500}{(1.05)^2}$

$n = 5$.

$r = \dfrac{1}{(1.05)^2}$

$$= \frac{2500}{(1.05)^2} \cdot \frac{\left[1 - \left(\frac{1}{1.05^2}\right)^5\right]}{\left[1 - \left(\frac{1}{1.05^2}\right)\right]}$$

Calculate. Use a calculator.

$$= \frac{2500(1 - 0.613913)}{1.1025(1 - 0.907029)}$$

$$= 9416.71 \text{ (to 2 decimal places)}$$

Thus $9416.71 should be invested now to provide an annuity of $2500 for 5 years.

You can also interpret the answer in a different way: an amount of $9416.70 invested at 10% compounded semi-annually will give you an annuity of $2500 paid each year for 5 years.
You have probably heard of lottery winners who somehow manage to spend $250 000 in a very short period of time. Often, people who win large amounts of money in a lottery, mismanage their funds.

11.6 Exercise

A Express your answer to the nearest cent when necessary.

1 Calculate each of the following. Express your answer to 6 decimal places.

(a) $\dfrac{1}{(1.06)^8}$ (b) $\dfrac{1}{(1.10)^{10}}$ (c) $\dfrac{1}{(1.085)^{12}}$ (d) $\dfrac{1}{(1.02)^{20}}$

(e) $\dfrac{1}{(1.015)^{30}}$ (f) $\dfrac{1}{(1.035)^{25}}$ (g) $\dfrac{1}{(1.005)^{30}}$ (h) $\dfrac{1}{(1.0125)^{25}}$

2 Use the information in each diagram. Find the present value of each annuity.

(a) Interest is calculated at the rate of 9% per annum compounded annually.

(b) Interest is calculated at the rate of 11% per annum compounded semi-annually.

3 Construct a time diagram to show the following information, then find the present value of each annuity.

(a) $1700 payable annually for 10 years with interest calculated at 8% per annum compounded annually.

(b) $2500 payable semi-annually for 8 years, with interest calculated at 11% per annum compounded semi-annually.

4 Find the present value of an annuity of 16 quarterly payments of $1200 if the interest rate is 10% per annum compounded quarterly.

5 (a) What is the present value of $50 deposited at the end of each month for 2 years calculated at 12% per annum compounded monthly?

(b) What is the present value of $125 deposited at the end of each quarter for 4 years at 8% per annum compounded quarterly?

B For each problem, record the given information on a diagram, then solve.

6 Calculate the present value of each.
   (a) 10 payments of $500 paid at the end of each year; 8% per annum compounded annually
   (b) 6 payments of $250 paid at the end of each quarter, 10% per annum compounded quarterly

7 Find the equivalent cash value of $10 000 paid at the end of each year for 5 years if money is worth 11% per annum compounded semi-annually.

8 How much money should you invest now so that at the end of each year you will receive $1000 for 20 years? Money is presently worth 9% per annum compounded semi-annually.

9 Jeremey planned on depositing payments of $500 at the end of each year for 5 years. The money will be compounded annually at the rate of 7.5% per annum. Find the present value of this annuity.

10 A colour T.V. may be purchased for $65 a month for 12 months at 18% per annum compounded monthly. How much is the cost of the T.V. at today's prices?

11 A scholarship fund is set up so that $500 is given out each year for 10 years. How much money should be invested now at 8.5% per annum compounded annually to set up the fund?

12 L. C. Company sponsored a sale on television sets on the following deal.

   • pay $250 down now
   • pay $28.75 per month for the next 10 months

   If money is worth 9% per annum compounded monthly, calculate the cash value of the television set.

13 The annual costs for maintaining a fishing camp are about $1900 paid at the end of each year. Sheila plans to set aside an amount today to pay for these annual costs for the next 5 years. If money is worth 8% per annum compounded annually, what amount should Sheila deposit today?

C 14 The Jacksons left Jennifer a trust fund in the sum of $25 000. Jennifer would like to receive equal payments at the end of every semi-annual period for the next 10 years. What is the value of each payment, if interest is calculated at the rate of 9% per annum compounded semi-annually?

Applications: Deferred Annuities

For an ordinary annuity it is understood that you receive the first payment one period from now. When the first payment of an annuity is delayed for a later time, the annuity is called a **deferred annuity**. For example, Jeremy is to receive a deferred annuity payable yearly for 10 years in the amount of $1000. The first payment is to be received 5 years from now. Find the present value of the annuity if money is worth 12% per annum compounded annually.

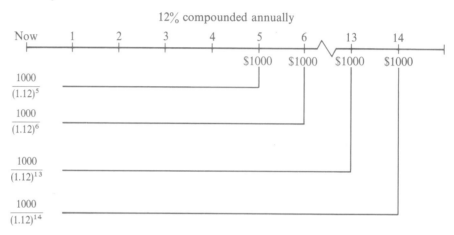

The present value, PV, of the deferred annuity is given by the value of the expression

$$PV = \frac{1000}{(1.12)^5} + \frac{1000}{(1.12)^6} + \cdots + \frac{1000}{(1.12)^{14}}$$

15 Refer to the above deferred annuity.
(a) Calculate the value of the expression PV.
(b) What is the present value of the deferred annuity?
(c) What is the amount of the annuity on the day of the 5th payment (including the 5th payment)? Money is worth 10.5% per annum compounded annually.

16 Jeremy is to receive a semi-annual annuity of $1500 for 8 years. The first payment is deferred for 4 years. Money is worth 9.5% per annum compounded semi-annually.
(a) Calculate the present value of the deferred annuity.
(b) Calculate the value of the annuity on the day of the last payment.

17 Because of an inheritance, Stacy invested $25 000 and 4 years later began to withdraw yearly equal payments. If money is worth 8.5% per annum compounded annually and she wants to withdraw 10 equal payments, how much money will she receive each year?

11.7 Amortization of Loans and Mortgages

It is often necessary to borrow money in order to buy a major item. For example, if you buy a car, you sign a document and agree to pay back the amount borrowed over a period of time. In other words you agree, in a sense, to pay the loan company an annuity. In the agreement you sign, you often pledge the car as collateral. (You guarantee payment to the loan company or it can sell your car to pay off the loan.) The principal of the loan is the present value of the annuity.

Most people do not have all the cash to buy a house. So they finance the purchase. One way of financing the purchase is to obtain a mortgage. A **mortgage** is a signed document for the loan and indicates that if the person who is obtaining the mortgage (the **mortgagee**) fails to make the proper payments as agreed upon, **the mortgager** (the person who gave you the mortgage) can sell the house and use the proceeds to pay off the mortgage. However, in simple terms, a mortgage is a form of an annuity.

When you obtain a loan or a mortgage, you agree to pay the lender a fixed amount of money for a period of time. The word **amortization** means "the repaying of a loan or mortgage by a sequence of periodic payments."

The industry engaged in providing loans and mortgages and the vocabulary generated by the various financial institutions is a study in itself. However the mathematical principles involved are based on the mathematics you have learned thus far involving sequences, series, amount of an annuity and present value of an annuity. These principles are illustrated in the following examples, as well as by the problems in the exercise.

Example Anne-Marie purchased an antique car for $14 000. She put down $2000 as a down payment, and agreed to make a payment every 3 months for 4 years. If the interest rate agreed upon was 12% per annum compounded quarterly, calculate the amount of each payment.

Solution Let x represent the equal payments. Draw a time-line.

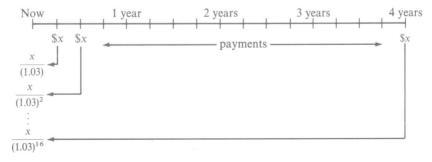

An equation is then written to solve the problem, as follows.

The present value of the payments is $12 000. Find x.

$$\frac{x}{1.03} + \frac{x}{(1.03)^2} + \cdots + \frac{x}{(1.03)^{16}} = 12\ 000$$

Geometric series with

$$x\left(\frac{1}{1.03} + \frac{1}{(1.03)^2} + \cdots + \frac{1}{(1.03)^{16}}\right) = 12\ 000 \qquad a = \frac{1}{1.03}, r = \frac{1}{1.03}, n = 16$$

$$x\left(\frac{\frac{1}{1.03}\left(1 - \left(\frac{1}{1.03}\right)^{16}\right)}{1 - \frac{1}{1.03}}\right) = 12\ 000 \longleftarrow \qquad \text{Use } S_n = \frac{a(1 - r^n)}{1 - r}$$

$$= \frac{12\ 000}{\dfrac{\frac{1}{1.03}\left(1 - \left(\frac{1}{1.03}\right)^{16}\right)}{\left(1 - \frac{1}{1.03}\right)}} \qquad \text{Use your calculator.}$$

$$= 955.33 \text{ (to 2 decimal places)}$$

Thus, each equal payment is $955.33 to the nearest cent.

If you do a simple calculation of 16 payments of $955.33 you find that you have paid $16 \times \$955.33 = \$15\ 285.28$ plus $2000 downpayment for a total of $17 285.28 for your $14 000 car. The extra $3285.28 is the interest charges you have incurred.

Exactly the same principles are involved in calculating the payments needed to amortize a mortgage. In the next section you will learn various other terms related to mortgages, as well as the financial sources that offer mortgages.

11.7 Exercise

A   Express your answers to the nearest cent when necessary.

1   For each of the following, find the amount at the end of the given time period.

(a) $1000 paid annually at a rate of 10%/a compounded annually for 10 years

(b) $2200 paid semi-annually at a rate of 10.5%/a compounded semi-annually for 5 years

(c) $1400 paid semi-annually at 9.5%/a compounded quarterly for $7\frac{1}{2}$ years

(d) $250 paid monthly at 9%/a compounded monthly for 2 years 3 months

2 Find the present value of the following.
   (a) $2300 paid annually at 12%/a compounded quarterly for 4 years
   (b) $600 paid quarterly at $9\frac{1}{4}$%/a compounded monthly for $1\frac{1}{2}$ years

3 Find the equal payments that will amortize each of the following debts.
   (a) $15 000 borrowed at 11%/a compounded semi-annually; agreement is to repay the loan in 6 years with semi-annual payments.
   (b) $25 000 borrowed at 12%/a compounded quarterly; agreement is to repay loan in 10 years, with payments every 3 months.

4 Calculate the periodic payments needed to pay each of the following.
   (a) a mortgage of $115 000 paid by equal monthly payments for 10 years at 12%/a compounded monthly
   (b) a loan of $10 000 paid by equal quarterly payments for 5 years at 10.5%/a compounded quarterly
   (c) a second mortgage of $45 000 paid by equal semi-annual payments for 8 years at 16%/a compounded quarterly
   (d) a loan of $15 000 paid by equal annual payments for 6 years at $8\frac{1}{2}$%/a compounded semi-annually

B For each problem, use a diagram to help you record the given information and solve the problem.

5 Shirley purchased a compact car for $7900 with $600 down, and the remainder to be paid in 36 equal monthly installments.
   (a) If the interest rate is 12% per annum compounded monthly, calculate what the equal payments are.
   (b) How much of the total amount paid is interest?

6 The Mateus family purchased a home for $120 000 and used $80 000 cash as a down payment from their previous home. They agree to take a mortgage for the balance and amortize it in equal semi-annual payments. Money is worth 12% per annum compounded semi-annually. Find the amount of the equal payments if they are to pay it in 8 years.

7 The Roberto family bought a vacation home for $40 000 with a down payment of $15 000. It decided to amortize the mortgage by making equal semi-annual payments for 10 years. Money is worth 11.5% per annum compounded quarterly. What were the equal payments?

8 Alexandra purchased a motorcycle worth $2500 and paid $800 down. She agrees to make equal semi-annual payments for 5 years. If money is worth 11% per annum compounded semi-annually. calculate how much the equal payments are?

9   The Drews purchased a backsplit home for $135 000 with a down payment of $75 500 obtained from the sale of their previous home. They secured a 5-year mortgage from the Credit Union for the balance and agreed to amortize the balance in equal semi-annual payments at a rate of 13% per annum compounded semi-annually.

(a) Find the amount of each equal payment.

(b) If they did amortize the mortgage in 5 years, how much money in interest did they pay?

10   A real estate sales person informs you of a terrific buy. The terms of the sale are that you pay $9000 down and pay equal monthly payments of $680.00 for 20 years.

(a) If money is worth 12% per annum compounded monthly, what is the equivalent cash price of the house?

(b) How much would you pay in interest charges?

11   Refer to the newspaper advertisement.

Drew Fibreglass Inboard/Outboard

Buy your boat at TOWN BOATS for the best deal. Model HP 1030 priced at

$8900 with down payment of $600
lowest rate of interest
10% per annum compounded quarterly

Calculate the equal quarterly payments if you agree to pay the amount in 4 years. The first payment is in 3 months.

Problem Solving

Often a problem may seem difficult because you do not know the meaning of the words. Read the problem.

Find the present value of an annuity of $1500 paid in perpetuity. (The current rate of interest is 7% compounded annually).

To solve the problem, you must know the meaning of **present value**, **annuity**, and **annuity in perpetuity**. Find the meaning of annuity in perpetuity and solve the problem. (If your answer is $21 428.57, you have researched well.)

11.8 Working with Mortgages: Shoppers Beware!

In the previous section you saw that your skills in mathematics can be applied to amortize a mortgage. A mortgage is a major expenditure of your lifetime. Most financial institutions place advertisements in newspapers which inform you of what they have to offer. In the previous section you were given the meaning of various terms essential to the understanding of mortgages. When you read a newspaper, or visit various financial institutions, to obtain information about their mortgages these words will occur.

Fixed Rate The financial institution will guarantee the rate of interest for a certain period of time. This period of time is used to calculate the payments needed to amortize your mortgage and will vary from institution to institution.

Variable Rate Some lenders will use a rate of interest that is related to some indicator, such as the Bank of Canada rate. The advantage of a variable rate is, if the rate of interest drops, you will benefit, since the total interest you need to pay will decrease. If the interest rate increases, the total interest you will pay to amortize your mortgage will also increase.

First Mortgage When only one mortgage is agreed upon to pay the balance of the purchase of your home, it is called a first mortgage.

Second Mortgage Often a purchaser does not have the required down payment to purchase the home, and lenders will not issue a mortgage to pay the balance of the price of the home. However, if the purchaser is capable of paying additional monthly payments, he or she can obtain a second mortgage. If a purchaser defaults on the mortgage payment, the lender can force the sale of the house. The proceeds of the sale are then used to pay back, first, the first mortgage lender, and then, the second mortgage lender. If there are not sufficient funds to pay back both lenders, then the second mortgage lender will lose money. For this reason, a lender of a second mortgage on a home is more at risk and thus charges a higher rate of interest when calculating the equal periodic payments.

In the previous section you learned that in amortizing a mortgage you are really paying back the debt by an acceptable schedule of payments agreed upon between you, the mortgagee, and the lender, the mortgagor. When you make one of your equal periodic payments you are in effect paying a blend of principal owed and interest owed. Whether you have taken out a loan or a mortgage you can calculate an amortization schedule which gives you a clear picture of how much of each payment consists of principal or interest and how much you still owe after you have made a number of payments as shown in the following example.

Example The Wrights decide to invest in a cottage property worth $28 000. They put down $8000 and take out a first mortgage for the balance at the agreed rate of interest of 10% per annum compounded annually. They agree to amortize the mortgage in 5 years. Calculate each equal annual payment.

Solution Let $x be the equal yearly payment.

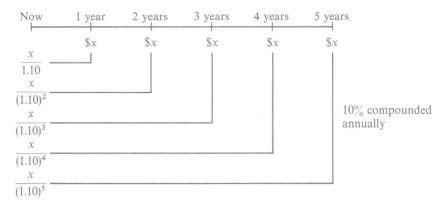

$$\frac{x}{1.10} + \frac{x}{(1.10)^2} + \frac{x}{(1.10)^3} + \frac{x}{(1.10)^4} + \frac{x}{(1.10)^5} = 20\,000$$

$$\underbrace{x\left(\frac{1}{1.10} + \frac{1}{(1.10)^2} + \frac{1}{(1.10)^3} + \frac{1}{(1.10)^4} + \frac{1}{(1.10)^5}\right)}_{\text{This is a geometric series}} = 20\,000$$

$$x\left(\frac{\frac{1}{1.10}\left[1 - \frac{1}{(1.10)^5}\right]}{1 - \frac{1}{1.10}}\right) = 20\,000$$

$$x = 5275.96 \text{ (to 2 decimal places)}$$

Thus, the equal yearly payment is $5275.96 for 5 years.

Once you have obtained the amount you pay each year, you can then organize a schedule of payments that show how the mortgage is amortized.

Amortization Table

Year	Principal of mortgage owed	Interest payment 10% per annum	Total payment	Payment on principal	Unpaid principal at end of the year
1	$20 000	$2000	$5275.96	$3275.96	$16 724.04
2	$16 724.04	$1672.40	$5275.96	$3603.56	$13 120.48
3	$13 120.48	$1312.05	$5275.96	$3963.91	$9156.57
4	$9 156.57	$915.66	$5275.96	$4360.30	$4796.27
5	$4 796.27	$479.63	$5275.96	$4796.33	0

From the table you can then do problems related to your own situation.

- At the end of year 3 you have acquired some extra money and you would like to pay off the principal. Based on the table, you can see that the principal owed is $9156.57.

- At the end of the second year, you decide that you would like to take longer to pay off the mortgage and you still owe $13 120.48 on the mortgage. With this information, you seek out a lender who will lend you this amount, and then work out with you a new schedule of periodic payments to amortize your new principal of $13120.48.

Once you are armed with the amortization table you have a clear picture of your personal financial picture and thus are able to make financial decisions related to your interests. Above all you can only make wise financial decisions if you *shop around* and know the meaning of the words such as the following.

Closed, Open Mortgage   Usually, when you agree to amortize your mortgage, you obtain a contract that stipulates equal payments. In this way you can budget for the rest of your daily expenditures. However, it may happen that you receive an unexpected sum of money and want to pay it towards the mortgage. Thus, you make a payment on your mortgage that reduces the principal you owe. A mortgage agreement that allows you to do this is called an **open mortgage**. Often in some mortgages there is an initial period of time in which you cannot make other cash payments. The mortgage at this time is said to be **closed**. In securing a mortgage you must shop around to determine which financial institution has the most convenient terms for your needs. For example, some institutions will make you pay a penalty if you make a payment on your mortgage other than the equal periodic payments you agreed to.

Conventional Mortgage   Some lenders will only mortgage a home up to a certain percentage of the property value. Often, the financial institution will lend you 75% of the appraised value of your home. As well, the lender will set a limit on the mortgage based on your ability to pay off the mortgage. When you apply for a mortgage, the lender will appraise your home and determine what amount will be set on the mortgage limit. As well, the lender will ask you to complete a questionnaire about your financial picture: how much you earn, your savings, your other debts, how much your spouse earns, and so on.

High Ratio Mortgage   In buying your home, you may discover that the down payment you have is not enough to qualify for a conventional mortgage, but you may still want to purchase a home. In this case, you approach a lender who will lend you a higher percentage of the appraised value of your home, say 90%. For this feature of your mortgage you will have to pay a greater interest rate when the equal periodic payments are calculated. Again, be sure to compare the rates of interest offered before you sign on the dotted line.

11.8 Exercise

A Round your answers to the nearest cent, where needed.

1   Calculate the equal periodic payments needed to amortize each mortgage.
   (a) a first mortgage of $25 000 amortized over 10 years, at the current interest rate of 11% per annum; compounded semi-annually; equal payments to be made semi-annually.
   (b) a second mortgage of $18 000 amortized over 5 years at the current second mortgage rate of 14% per annum compounded quarterly; equal payments to be made quarterly.

2   Prepare an amortization table for the following second mortgage. The terms of the mortgage are as follows: amount of mortgage $14 500; rate of interest 13% per annum calculated semi-annually; mortgage to be amortized over 6 years; equal payments to be made annually.

3   Refer to the amortization table in Question 2. At the time of the fourth payment, the mortgagee decides to refinance the mortgage by making a cash payment of $2000. Use the same terms for an additional 5-year period to calculate the equal periodic payment needed to amortize the mortgage.

4   Refer to the amortization table in Question 2. After shopping around, the mortgagee finds that the principal owing at the end of the first year, can be discharged for the new terms of 10% per annum compounded annually. The mortgage is to be discharged in 10 years. Find the value of the equal yearly payments.

B 5   In purchasing their home, the Bavasis obtain an open first mortgage for $68 000 with the following terms.

   • mortgage to be amortized in 10 years, equal payments are made annually
   • interest rate is 11.5% per annum compounded annually

   (a) Prepare an amortization schedule.
   (b) After fourth year, the Bavasis pay a lump sum of $8000 off the principal. Calculate the new equal annual payments for the remainder of the amortization schedule of payments.

6   The Pearsons obtain a high ratio mortgage of 90% on the appraised value of $92 000 on their home. The balance of the purchase is paid by cash. The mortgage is open after 3 years. Prepare an amortization table, if the rate of interest is 12% per annum compounded semi-annually. They also pay an additional 1% premium for this high ratio mortgage and will make equal semi-annual payments for 12 years.

7 (a) Refer to Question 6. After 4 years, the Pearsons negotiate a conventional mortgage on the remaining balance with another financial institution. If they wish to pay off the mortgage in 10 years, calculate the annual payment if money is worth 11% per annum compounded annually.

   (b) Calculate the cash payment needed to discharge the mortgage in (a) after the fifth year. There is a prepayment penalty of 0.5% of the principal owing on this mortgage. (The Pearsons did not do the best job possible in shopping around for this mortgage.)

8 The appraised value of a home purchased by the Hallidays was $85 000. They obtain a conventional mortgage after they made a $5000 down payment.

   (a) What is the principal of the conventional mortgage?

   (b) To amortize the mortgage in (a) in 10 years, the terms agreed upon are 11% per annum compounded semi-annually. Calculate the equal periodic semi-annual payments.

   (c) The balance of the money owed on the purchase is obtained through a second mortgage. The terms of this mortgage are 14% per annum compounded quarterly and amortized in 5 years. Calculate the equal periodic payments to be made every 3 months.

9 Refer to your results in Question 8.

   (a) In shopping around after the purchase, the Hallidays discovered that they could have obtained the second mortgage in Question 8(c) with an interest rate of 12% per annum compounded quarterly. How much money would they have saved?

   (b) In 3 years, the Hallidays will pay $10 000 off on the open first mortgage of Question 8(b) they have acquired and will refinance the remaining principal for the same terms. Calculate the remaining equal periodic payments to amortize this mortgage.

Problem Solving

Shopper Beware!

Before signing a contract, you must answer some important questions. Ask yourself: What am I getting into? Do I understand the terms of the contract? Are there any words I don't understand? and so on. Obtain a copy of a mortgage or loan agreement. Does the contract answer these questions? What are the terms of the contract (rate of interest, length of time, amount of payment, and so on)? Are there any penalties for paying before it's due? Is it renewable? Are there any parts you don't understand?

Remember: Shopper Beware!

Applications: Amortization Schedule For Personal Debt

Earlier, you learned about amortizing a debt. You can apply the skills required to prepare an amortization schedule for a mortgage to the preparation of a schedule for amortizing a personal debt. Note the similarity between the headings below and those in your previous work.

Amortization Table (schedule)

Year	Principal of loan owed	Interest payment	Total payment	Payment on principal	Unpaid principal at end of the year

Once you prepare a schedule for your loan, you know exactly, *at any time,*

A   the total amount of interest you have paid on the loan.
B   the total amount of principal payments you have made.
C   the total amount you owe on the loan.

With the information of A, B, and C, you can make wise investment decisions at any time.

10   Paul has incurred a debt of $1250 by purchasing a micro-computer, payment at 12% per annum interest compounded annually. He wishes to amortize the debt in 5 years in 5 yearly equal payments (the first payment to be due at the end of the first year).

(a) Calculate the payment Paul makes yearly.

(b) Prepare an amortization schedule for the loan.

(c) After he makes 3 payments, he decides to discharge (pay off) the loan. How much will he owe if there are no penalties for doing so?

11   Carolyn purchased a life-time gift for her parents anniversary and borrowed $3500 to do so. She wants to amortize the debt by equal semi-annual payments in 3 years. Money is worth 11% per annum compounded semi-annually.

(a) Prepare an amortization schedule for loan.

(b) Calculate the total amount of money she will pay in carrying charges (interest) for the loan.

12   Darryl has borrowed $2500 on his insurance policy at 6% per annum compounded quarterly. He agrees to pay back the loan in 8 equal quarterly payments. He also agrees to a penalty of 0.5% of the outstanding principal if he discharges the loan early.

(a) Prepare an amortization schedule of the loan.

(b) After 5 payments he is able to discharge the debt. How much will he pay?

11.9 Bonds: A Form of Investment

Many of the mathematical skills you have learned about other investments can be applied to working with bonds. A newspaper often provides advertisements, which contain information about bonds.

> Issue of
> **$200 000 000**
> NON-CALLABLE
> ## GOVERNMENT OF CANADA
> ## BONDS
> DATED 19XX
>
> The Bank of Canada is authorized by the Minister of Finance to receive subscriptions for a loan to be issued for cash as follows:
>
> **20 year 11% bonds due 19XX**
> **Issue price: 99.00 %yielding about ■% to maturity**
>
> The new bonds will be available in denominations of $1000, $5000. $25 000. $100 000 and $1 000 000
> The Bank of Canada has agreed to acquire a minimum of $400 million of the new bonds
> Proceeds of the offering will be used for general purposes of the Government of Canada
>
> Applications for the new bonds may be made, subject to allotment. through any investment dealer eligible to act as a primary distributor or through any bank in Canada.
>
> DEPARTMENT OF FINANCE   MINISTERE DES FINANCES
> CANADA   CANADA
> AP3

Often, a major company, a government agency, or even a city, may advertise the desire to obtain funds to pay for a building program, or to refinance a current debt. Usually, such a large sum of money, is obtained from many sources (individuals, financial institutions, etc). The contract between the lender and the borrower will indicate

- how much is borrowed
- the interest rate to be paid
- the terms of payment of interest
- the date by which time the loan will be repaid

Such a contract is called a **bond**. There are various features of bonds that you will read about as you read the various advertisements about bonds, some of these features occur as follows.

Registered Bond   The bond can only be transferred by the consent of the owner and the proper paper work needs to be completed to do so. The interest is paid directly to the registered owner by cheque.

Unregistered Bond   The owner of the bond is not recorded on the bond. This means the bond certificate can be transferred from one person to another.

Coupon Bond   Some bonds have coupons attached to the actual bond, are individually dated, and indicate the amount payable to the owner of the bond at specified dates. The coupons are clipped and then presented for payment at the appropriate times.

Face Value   Bonds are issued with different principal amounts determined by the institution issuing the bonds. The amount of a bond can vary from as little as $100 to amounts exceeding a million dollars! Thus, the face value is the sum of money borrowed and indicated on the face of the bond. The **par value** of the bond is another name for the face value of the bond.

Premium Bond   Bonds often sell at prices that are greater than the face value shown on the bond. The bond is said to sell at a premium, and is sold at its **premium value**.

Discount Bond   Bonds often sell at prices less than the face value. The bond is said to sell at a discount and is sold at its **discounted value**.

Market Value   The bond market prices are listed in the financial pages and a quick glance at them indicates that bonds seldom sell at the face value of the bond. The selling or buying price of a bond is dictated by the financial climate that occurs at the particular time you want to sell or buy bonds. These values are called the **market values** of the bonds.

Redemption Date   This is the date, which is stated on the bond, by which the loan (face value on the bond) will be repaid.

Bond Rate   Since you have lent money, you are paid interest based on the face value of the bond. If the bond rate is 12% per annum you will be paid $12 interest each year on a $100 bond. This rate of interest is called the bond rate. Some bonds have a compound feature built into the bond rate. For example, for Canada Savings Bonds, you can purchase *Regular* or *Compound* interest bonds.

> If you purchase a Regular interest bond you are paid simple interest each year. If you purchase a Compound bond you are paid compound interest to the date you cash the bond.

Obtaining a bond as a form of investment involves a certain degree of risk. For this reason the rates of interest provided are high enough to attract investors. Most bonds sell at prices other than the face value before they reach the redemption date depending on the financial climate. Often when a bond is put up for sale, it may be offered at a price less than the face value to attract a buyer. For this reason, a bond with a face value of $1000 might be offered for sale at $950. If the bond rate is 10%, then the actual money you will make on your investment is higher than 10%. For this reason, when you are investing in bonds, there are 2 interest rates you must examine.

- The **bond rate** is the rate quoted on the face or par value of the bond.

- The **yield rate** is the rate of interest you actually realize on your bond.

The following example illustrates the method of calculating a yield rate on your bond.

Example 1 Joanne received as a gift a 12% $2000 bond with a redemption date 5 years from now. The bond was actually purchased for $1925 and the interest is payable yearly.
(a) How much interest will Joanne receive each year?
(b) Calculate the actual yield rate in the first year, to 2 decimal places.
(c) In the next year the bond increased to a premium value and sold for the year at $2090. Calculate the yield rate to 2 decimal places.

Solution (a) A 12% $2000 bond pays yearly interest calculated as

$$12\% \text{ of } \$2000 = 0.12 \times \$2000$$
$$= \$240$$

(b) Joanne has made $240 on an actual investment of $1925.00.

Principal = $1925, Interest received = $240, Rate of Interest = $x\%$
Solve $x\%$ of $1925 = 240$

$$x = \frac{240}{1925} \times 100$$

$x = 12.47$ (to 2 decimal places)
The yield rate is 12.47%. Note that the yield rate is greater than the bond rate.

(c) Joanne makes $240 interest on a bond worth $2090.

Principal = $2090, Interest received = $240, Rate of Interest = $x\%$
Solve $x\%$ of $2090 = 240$

$$x = \frac{240}{2090} \times 100$$

$x = 11.48$ (to 2 decimal places)
The yield rate is 11.48%. Note that the yield rate is less than the bond rate.

In the exercise your skills with present value are needed to calculate the present value of a bond.

11.9 Exercise

A 1 What is meant by each of the following terms related to bonds? Give an example of each to illustrate the meaning.

(a) Registered   (b) Face Value   (c) Premium   (d) Market Value

(e) Discount   (f) Unregistered   (g) Par Value

(h) Coupon   (i) Redemption Date   (j) Bond Rate

2   (a) You purchase a bond at a discount. Will your yield rate be more or less than the bond rate? Give reasons for your answer.

    (b) You purchase a bond at a premium. Will your yield rate be more or less than the bond rate? Give reasons for your answer.

3   Calculate the value of the coupon that would be attached to each bond.

    (a) $500, Bell Canada Bond, $10\frac{1}{2}\%$ (b) $5000, Abitibi, 8.75%

4   Calculate the yield rate of each of the following bond purchases.

    (a) face value $2000, discount value $1880, bond rate $9\frac{1}{2}\%$

    (b) face value $4000, premium value $4365, bond rate $11\frac{1}{4}\%$

5   Sarah has purchased two 5-year 11% bonds with a face value of $1000 each. Her total purchase price was $1965.

    Identify the following information for the purchase

    (a) face value   (b) discounted value

    (c) bond rate   (d) yield rate for the first year

B   When you purchase a bond you often need to pay a commission on the purchase price. The commission charged varies from sale to sale based on the commission structure established by the firm selling the bonds. The public are not usually charged a commission on a new issue of bonds.

6   For each purchase, calculate the yield rate for the year.

    (a) A bond with face value $2000 is purchased for $1940. The bond rate is $10\frac{1}{4}\%$. A commission of $\frac{1}{4}\%$ is charged on the sale.

    (b) A bond with face value $5000 is at a premium price of $5320. The bond rate is $14\frac{1}{2}\%$. A commission of $\frac{1}{2}\%$ is charged on the sale.

7   The $100 New Brunswick $7\frac{3}{4}\%$ bond sells at a discount price of $79\frac{7}{8}$. What is the yield rate if you pay $\frac{1}{4}\%$ commission on the price of the bond?

8   B.C. Electric issued bonds called the 2 Jan 00 issue, at a rate of interest of 10%. If a face value of $5000 costs $91.75 per hundred, calculate the yield rate, if a commission of $100 is charged.

9   The New Brunswick government issued the $100 $13\frac{1}{4}\%$ 1 Nov 04 issue. Presently, the bonds sell at a premium of $112\frac{1}{8}$. Calculate your yield if you buy $1200 face value of the bonds at the selling price. (You also pay a $25 commission.)

10   Which investment has the better yield?

    (a) Winnipeg Municipal issue 1 Feb 98 paying $9\frac{3}{4}\%$ at a price of $89\frac{3}{4}$ per face value of $100.

    (b) Algoma Steel $17\frac{3}{8}\%$ bond (issue 15 May 97) selling at $121\frac{5}{8}$ per face value of $100

11.10 Bonds and Market Values

As has been mentioned, the market value of bonds fluctuates often, day to day, depending on the financial climate that occurs at the time. The yield rate of a bond over a longer period of time, can only be calculated approximately and so the term **average yield rate** is introduced.

$$\text{Average Yield Rate} = \frac{\text{average income}}{\text{average principal}} \times 100\%$$

The face value of a bond is fixed, but the market value fluctuates. Thus to calculate the approximate or average yield rate, you define the **average principal** for any transaction to be

$$\text{Average Principal} = \frac{\text{face value} + \text{purchase price}}{2}$$

If you purchase a 10.5% bond, maturing in 10 years, with face value $500 for only $450, then in addition to the interest you make you will also make $50 income when you cash the bond at maturity. Over the 10 years you will receive $\frac{\$50}{10}$ or $5 income per year in addition to the interest. Thus for this discounted bond, the **average income** is given by

$$\text{Average income} = \text{yearly interest} + \frac{\text{face value} - \text{purchase price}}{\text{number of years to maturity}}$$

$$= \$52.50 + \frac{\$500 - \$450}{10}$$

10.5% of 500

$$= \$57.50$$

Thus, the average yield to 2 decimal places, for the bond above is given by

$$\text{Average yield rate} = \frac{\text{average income}}{\text{average principal}} \times 100\%$$

$$= \frac{\$57.50}{\$475} \times 100\% \qquad \frac{\$450 + \$500}{2}$$

$$= 12.11\%$$

In general, for a bond maturing in n years, the average income is given by

$$\text{Average income} = \text{yearly interest} + \frac{\text{face value} - \text{purchase price}}{n}$$

11.10 Exercise

A   Express your answers to 2 decimal places.

1   Find the approximate yield rate for each bond. (All interest rates are annual.)

	Face value	Purchase price	Rate of interest	Maturity
(a)	$100	$95	$9\frac{1}{2}\%$	in 10 years
(b)	$100	$110	$8\frac{1}{2}\%$	in 8 years
(c)	$1000	$1150	$10\frac{1}{4}\%$	in 20 years
(d)	$1000	$965	$15\frac{3}{4}\%$	in 15 years

2   A $1000 Alberta Government $8\frac{3}{4}\%$ bond, maturing in 6 years is bought for $930. Calculate the approximate yield.

3   British Columbia Hydro issued $14\frac{1}{2}\%$ bonds due in 30 years. A $1000 bond sells for $1220. Calculate the approximate yield rate.

4   Each $100 New Brunswick Electric $12\frac{1}{2}\%$ bond due in 10 years sells for $106.50. If you have 20 of these bonds, what is your approximate yield rate?

5   Each $100 Government of Canada $9\frac{1}{4}\%$ bond (15 May 97 issue) due in 10 years is worth $89.75. If you own 15 of these bonds, what is your average yield rate?

B   The Financial Section of the newspaper carries the quotations of the various daily market values of bonds. A part of the table is shown.

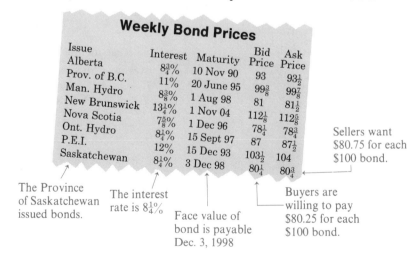

Issue	Interest	Maturity	Bid Price	Ask Price
Alberta	$8\frac{3}{4}\%$	10 Nov 90	93	$93\frac{1}{2}$
Prov. of B.C.	$11\frac{1}{2}\%$	20 June 95	$99\frac{3}{8}$	$99\frac{7}{8}$
Man. Hydro	$8\frac{3}{8}\%$	1 Aug 98	81	$81\frac{1}{4}$
New Brunswick	$13\frac{1}{4}\%$	1 Nov 04	$112\frac{1}{8}$	$112\frac{5}{8}$
Nova Scotia	$7\frac{5}{8}\%$	1 Dec 96	$78\frac{1}{4}$	$78\frac{3}{4}$
Ont. Hydro	$8\frac{1}{4}\%$	15 Sept 97	87	$87\frac{1}{2}$
P.E.I.	12%	15 Dec 93	$103\frac{1}{2}$	104
Saskatchewan	$8\frac{1}{4}\%$	3 Dec 98	$80\frac{1}{4}$	$80\frac{3}{4}$

Weekly Bond Prices

The Province of Saskatchewan issued bonds.

The interest rate is $8\frac{1}{4}\%$

Face value of bond is payable Dec. 3, 1998

Sellers want $80.75 for each $100 bond.

Buyers are willing to pay $80.25 for each $100 bond.

6 Refer to the data in the Weekly Bond Prices.

(a) You purchased $1000 of the Manitoba Hydro at $81.25. If the bond matures in 20 years, calculate the approximate yield rate (you will also receive 20 interest payments).

(b) For his birthday, Brent received $500 of the Ontario Hydro Bonds, at Bid Price. If the bond will mature in 10 years, calculate the approximate yield rate.

(c) For her education, Joanne received $2000 of the Province of New Brunswick bonds at the Ask Price. If the bond will mature in 25 years, calculate the present approximate yield rate. (Joanne can later sell her bonds at the going market value.)

7 The Government of Canada 15 Oct 93 pays $11\frac{3}{4}\%$ interest.

(a) Allan purchased $3000 of them at the market value of $105\frac{1}{8}$. Calculate the average yield rate if the bond matures in 5 years.

(b) Because of the financial climate, 2 years later, the bonds sold at $96\frac{1}{4}$. Calculate the average yield rate.

8 Edmonton issued $12\frac{1}{4}\%$ bonds (14 June 03 issue). The current bid price is $103\frac{1}{4}$ and you purchase $5000 of them.

(a) Calculate the average yield rate if the bond matures in 15 years.

(b) A year later the bid price as $96\frac{1}{2}$. Predict whether the average yield rate will increase or decrease. Then calculate the average yield rate.

9 Algoma Steel required funds for capital expansion and issued $10\frac{3}{8}\%$ bonds (1 June 94 issue). The current ask price is $95\frac{3}{8}$.

(a) Calculate the approximate yield rate if you purchase $2000 bonds with them due in 8 years.

(b) If the market value does not change, calculate the amount of your investment in 5 years, if money is worth $8\frac{1}{2}\%$ compounded annually.

Problem Solving

Regardless of what form of an investment you make, your investment will be affected by **inflation**. Simply put, inflation describes the decline in the value of money in relation to the goods and services it will buy. Inflation has been a problem-solving activity for many economists for years. Explore the following.

A   Obtain information about how inflation is caused.

B   What is the current rate of inflation in the major countries?

C   What are the effects of inflation?

D   What skills in mathematics are used to study inflation?

11.11 Paying for Bonds: Present Value

The newspaper weekly bond prices tells you what the seller wants for a bond. Thus, you will know how much you need to pay for a bond.

Often there is a rate of return that you know that you at least want to make on an investment. You can use your skills with present value to acquire another piece of information which will help you make a wise financial decision.

When you buy a bond, you know

A you will receive the face value at the end of the term of the bond.
B you will receive certain interest payments given at a predetermined interest rate.

What are the typical calculations you need to make to find the present value of a bond? For example, the $16\frac{1}{2}\%$ Quebec Hydro bond will mature in 10 years. What price should you pay if you want your approximate yield to be 12%?

To find your answer, you essentially need to do two calculations as shown by the diagram.

PV Interest

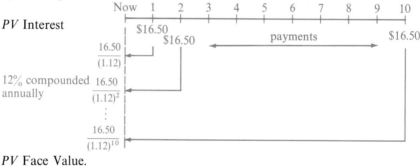

PV Face Value.

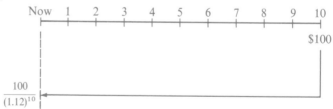

Based on the diagram above, all you need to do is the following.

$$\binom{\text{Price you pay}}{\text{for the bond}} = \binom{\text{Present value of}}{\text{interest payments}} + \binom{\text{Present value of}}{\text{principal}}$$

The calculations you need to complete, to obtain the answer for this new problem, have been performed by you many times.

11.11 Exercise

A   Remember: The calculator is a useful tool in working with investment.

1   Refer to the diagram on the previous page. Calculate the present value of
(a) the interest payments.   (b) the face value.
(c) What is the price you should pay to obtain an approximate rate of
return of 12%?

2   Find the price you would want to pay to achieve the following expected
rate of return.

	Face value of bond	Rate of interest	Term left	Your expected rate of return
(a)	$2000	$11\frac{1}{2}\%$	10 years	9.5%
(b)	$1500	$10\frac{1}{4}\%$	5 years	$11\frac{1}{2}\%$
(c)	$1800	$9\frac{3}{4}\%$	20 years	13%
(d)	$3500	$12\frac{1}{2}\%$	25 years	12.5%

B   Express your answer to the nearest cent in each of the following problems.

3   The Province of Saskatchewan Bonds (2 Dec. 99 issue) pays 10% annually.
You want to purchase $1000 face value of the bonds.
(a) If you expect to receive 11.5% as your rate of return for the remaining
15 years, how much should you pay per $100 bond?
(b) The next day, you increase your expected rate of return to 13%.
Calculate what you should pay per bond now.

4   The municipality of Ottawa-Carlton issued $9\frac{3}{8}\%$ bonds maturing in
12 years. Calculate the amount Michelle should pay for $1000 of the bonds
maturing in 10 years to achieve a yield of 10.5%.

5   Ashland Oil issued the $10\frac{3}{8}\%$ Bonds to mature 1 Nov 96. If you expect to
achieve a yield rate of 12.5%, calculate the price you will pay for a $1000
bond if the bond matures in 8 years.

6   The Canadian Tire $10\frac{3}{4}\%$ Bonds mature in 10 years. As a seller, you know
that people expect a rate of return of approximately 11.95%. Calculate the
price you should set to sell each $100 bond you own.

11.12   Investigating Stocks

To invest means to commit money in order to earn financial gain. You have already explored investment instruments such as bonds, term deposits and compound interest. Another investment tool available to the investor is the buying of stocks.

Before you invest you should know your investment objectives. In order to make a list of your investment goals, a financial advisor would ask the following types of questions:

A   Is the capital you invest secure?

B   Does the investment provide income?

C   Are you seeking a long-term or short-term financial growth?

Before you invest, you need to list the following:

Assets   These include cash in bank accounts, bonds, term deposits, value of your home, and personal effects, real estate investments, business interest. In other words: — **what you are worth**

Liabilities   These include money you owe in loans, credit card accounts, personal debts, mortgage. In other words: — **what you owe**

Now you can calculate you net worth.   **Net Worth = Assets − Liabilities**

Once you know your net worth, you can seek financial advice on whether or not to invest in stocks. To do this you must have a current working knowledge of the vocabulary, and an understanding of the terms used in buying stocks. When you buy stock, you are buying a **share** of a company. In so doing, you expect to receive a **share of the profits** of this company. This will be paid in the form of a **dividend**. If the company's profit increases, you will receive increased dividends, if its profit decreases then the dividend may decrease. Thus, if you are considering investing in a company, you need to investigate its financial state. You can do this by studying the **Financial** or **Annual Report** of the company.

Stocks of publicly-owned companies are listed on one of the *Stock Exchanges* such as Toronto, Vancouver or Montreal. You can purchase or sell stocks by using the services of a **stockbroker** who arranges the business transaction for you (at one of the Stock Exchanges) and charges a **commission** for the service provided. A newspaper provides information about stock prices.

Bid : The price people are willing to pay for a share.

Ask : The price people are asking for a share.

High Low: The highest and lowest price the stock has reached during the last 52 weeks.

Stock	Vol	Bid	Ask	Last Price	Chge	High	Low
Slater A	4000	$12¾	12½	12¾ +	¼	14⅝	9¾
Slater B f	2300	$12¾	12¼	12¼ −	¼	14¼	9¼
Slat Stl 1p	100	$12	12	12 −	½	12½	12
Slater B pr	450	$13½	13½	13½		14½	13
Sobeys A f	14575	$16½	16	16¼ −	¼	17½	6½

Last price: The last price paid on a transaction.

Change: The difference in price since the last transaction

Preferred stocks are certain shares of the company which have a preference over the other shares of the company, called **common stock**. A preferred stock pays a fixed dividend, whereas common stock allow you the opportunity of participating in the actual profit picture of the company. Thus, the owners of preferred stock may receive a dividend before the owners of the common stock. As a company increases in value so does the value of its shares. Thus, the purchase of stocks can increase your net worth while being paid a dividend. The following investigations explore various aspects of buying stock. Remember: Buyer Beware!

Investigation A   Vocabulary of Stocks

1   What is meant by each of the following?

(a) common stock   (b) preferred stock   (c) dividends

(d) loss   (e) shareholder   (f) stockbroker

(g) stock exchange   (h) profit   (i) commission

(j) fixed dividend   (k) company earnings

2   (a) Which investment has less risk: preferred stock or common stock?

(b) What are the advantages and disadvantages of purchasing preferred stock? common stock?

3   (a) From the yellow pages, find the name of a stockbroker and obtain a list of the current commission rates used for selling or buying stocks.

(b) Inquire as to what printed reading materials are available to a person who wishes to invest in the stock market.

Investigation B   Stock Prices

4   Refer to the current listings on the Toronto Stock Exchange. What is the Ask and the Bid price for each of the following?

(a) 100 shares of Hard Crp C   (b) 50 shares of Stelco A

(c) 1000 shares of Wcoast T   (d) 100 shares of BC Tel

(e) How much commission would you pay to buy each stock in (a)–(b)?

(f) How much commission would you pay to sell each stock in (c)–(d)?

5   To calculate the yield rate for your investment, use

$$\text{Yield Rate} = \frac{\text{amount of dividends paid yearly}}{\text{price of stock}} \times 100\%$$

(a) Calculate the yield rate for each stock in Question 4.

(b) When you earn income you need to pay income taxes. For each $100 Jennifer earns in dividends, she pays $38 in income taxes. To calculate her yield rate after taxes use

$$\frac{\text{Yield Rate}}{\text{(after taxes)}} = \frac{\text{amount of yearly dividend} - \text{income tax}}{\text{price of stock}} \times 100\%$$

Calculate Jennifer's yield rate after taxes for each stock in Question 4.

Investigation C   Buying Low, Selling High

6   (a) Choose a stock listed on the Toronto Stock Exchange. You bought
       1000 shares at the low price shown. What is the total purchase price
       including commission?
    (b) You sold the stock in (a) at the high price shown. How much will you
       receive in all after commissions are paid?
    (c) How much money did you make in completing the transactions (a)
       and (b)?
    (d) Repeat Steps (a) to (c) for another stock of your choice.

7   (a) Choose a stock of your own and record the daily Bid and Ask prices
       in a chart.

Day	1	2	3
Bid Price			
Ask Price			

28	29	30

    (b) Draw a line graph to show the fluctuations in price for 30 d.
    (c) Contact a Stockbroker. Obtain a graph of the stock's past performance.
       Can you predict the high and low prices for the stock, based on these
       graphs?

Investigation D   Annual or Financial Reports

Obtain a financial report of a company listed on the Toronto Stock Exchange.

8   Locate each of the following sections in the Annual Report.
    (a) Balance Sheet   (b) Income Statement
    (c) What is this company's total assets? total liabilities?
    (d) What are the current Bid, Ask prices of the stocks of this company?

9   What do you think is meant by each of these terms found in an Annual
    or Financial Report? What is the dollar value listed for each?
    (a) Cash Assets   (b) Accounts Receivable
    (c) Accounts payable   (d) Inventories
    (e) Net fixed assets   (f) Mortgage bonds
    (g) Accrued expenses payable   (h) Income taxes payable

10 (a) What is the total value of the stocks issued for the company:
       preferred stock? common stock?
    (b) What is the total value of the capital surplus? retained earnings?
    (c) What types of graphs are used in the report to display information?
       Do the graphs display the information accurately?
    (d) What is the value of Net Sales? Operating expenses? Total income?
       Net profit?

11 (a) What is the net earnings per share listed on the Financial Report?
    (b) What are the dividends and the yield rate for this stock?

12 (a) Obtain an Annual Report of another Canadian Company. Compare the two companies with respect to the dollar amounts shown in Questions 8–11.

(b) Which company would you interpret to be "in better financial shape"

Investigation E Stocks and Income Tax
Refer to a copy of the General Income Tax Guide (Revenue Canada).

13 (a) What is meant by each of these items in your income tax return?
   (i) interest, dividends, capital gains deductions
   (ii) taxable capital gains
   (iii) taxable amount of dividends from taxable Canadian Corporations

(b) What is the maximum deduction you can claim for (i)?

(c) How are taxable capital gains calculated?

(d) How are (i) to (iii) related to your buying and/or selling stock?

14 (a) What is meant by "The current rate of inflation is 8.5%."?

(b) The buying power of the Canadian dollar has decreased by 36.9% since the early sixties. Your income is $18 500. What is its actual buying power as compared to the sixties?

(c) "Buying stock is often considered to be a hedge against inflation." What do you think is meant by this statement?

Exploring Life Insurance
When you buy life insurance, you pay a premium now to provide money for the future, to protect you and your family against financial hardship. If you die, your beneficiaries receive the money; if you live a certain period of time, you, the insured, receive the money. Life insurance can also provide money for retirement, used as a savings plan, and has many other uses. You must discuss your insurance needs with a qualified person. Explore the following vocabulary and information about life insurance.

1 (a) For what reasons can you purchase life insurance?

(b) How old do you need to be to purchase life insurance?

(c) How does a life insurance company decide whether they will provide you with life insurance?

(d) How are premiums determined for life insurance policies? What factors affect the amount of the premium?

2 What is meant by the following terms?

(a) insured	(b) mortality table	(c) 10 year payment life
(d) premiums	(e) ordinary life	(f) 25 year endowment
(g) the policy	(h) straight life	(i) insurance claim
(j) whole life	(k) beneficiary	(l) term insurance
(m) cash value of a life insurance policy		
(n) loan value of a life insurance policy		

Practice and Problems: A Chapter Review

1   Each principal is invested at the following terms. Find each compound amount.
   (a) a term deposit of $1740 at 8% per annum compounded quarterly after 11 years 6 months.
   (b) a loan of $6500 at $9\frac{1}{2}$% per annum compounded semi-annually after 5 years.

2   Examine the information given in the two advertisements.

A:	**Chequing/Savings Account**	B:	**Super A Account**
	6% Interest Compounded Monthly		6.5% Interest of Minimum Monthly Balance

   (a) In A, interest is added at the end of each month. In B, accumulated interest is added every 6 months to the account. Which is the better rate?
   (b) If you maintain a minimum monthly balance of $750.00, which account will pay you more at the end of 6 months? How much more?

3   Marsha won $20 000 in a lottery. In 8 years she wants to have $9500 available for the trip of her life. How much money should she invest now at 10.5% per annum compounded semi-annually to achieve her dream?

4   The annual costs for maintaining a vacation property are about $2300 paid at the end of each year. Trent plans to set aside an amount today to pay for these annual costs for the next 8 years. If money is worth 9% per annum compounded annually, what amount should Trent deposit today?

5   In purchasing their home, the Hasbros obtain an open first mortgage for $73 000 with the following terms.
   • mortgage to be amortized over 10 years
   • interest rate is 12.5% per annum compounded annually
   • equal payments are made annually

   (a) Prepare an amortization schedule.
   (b) After the fifth year, the Hasbros pay $8000 off the principal. Calculate the new equal annual payments for the remainder of the amortization schedule of payments.

6   Calculate the approximate yield rate for each of the following.
   (a) Northern Telecom issued $12\frac{3}{4}$% bonds due in 12 years. A $100 bond sells for $83.50.
   (b) A $1000 Telecon 10.5% bond due in 5 years is sold for $1112.

Test For Practice

1　The Trust Company pays 11% per annum interest compounded semi-annually in their SC Account.

  (a) How many interest periods are there in 3 years?

  (b) Find the amount at the end of 3 years if $1650 is the initial and only deposit?

2　Money is presently worth 8% per annum as an effective interest rate. Find the equivalent nominal rate compounded monthly.

3　Brian has a debt of $3000 payable in 30 months. If the terms of the loan are 14.5% per annum compounded semi-annually, what is the present value of the loan?

4　Find the amount of each annuity.

  (a) $75 is deposited at the end of every 6 months for 4 years at 13.5% per annum compounded semi-annually.

  (b) $1500 is invested at the end of every year for 6 years at 9.75% per annum compounded quarterly.

5　Rana is planning a trip to Europe after she graduates. She deposits $60 at the end of each month for 5 years. This money will earn 8.5% per annum compounded semi-annually. What is the present value of the money she will have at the end of 5 years?

6　Tim purchases a cottage worth $27 000.00. He has agreed to pay $600.00 monthly for 5 years. If the interest rate charged is 12% per annum compounded quarterly, how much of a down payment must Tim have in order to make the purchase?

7　The $100 Government of Canada $9\frac{1}{4}$% Bond is selling at a discount price of 95\frac{1}{2}$. A company fund purchases $100 000 of the bonds. If the commission is $125, calculate the yield rate.

8　The Baldwins put down $30 000 towards the purchase of a $95 000 house. They agreed to make equal monthly payments for 15 years. The interest rate on the mortgage is 12.5% per annum compounded semi-annually.

  (a) Find the amount of the monthly payments.

  (b) Construct an amortization table to find the outstanding principal at the end of 1 year.

Year-End Review

One of the most important skills for solving problems is to identify which skills are needed to solve the problem. Throughout this book you have acquired different skills and strategies for solving problems occurring in the various sections, as well as in the problem-solving tips. Solve each of the following problems.

1   Draw a sketch of $y = 2x^2 + 8x - 6$. Write the equation of the axis of symmetry and the co-ordinates of the vertex.

2   If A(0, 1) and B(-2, -3) are points on the graph defined by $y = ax^2 + b$, find the values of a and b.

3   The hypotenuse of a right-angled triangle is 1 m more than the length of the second largest side. If the perimeter is 56 m, find the length of the other sides.

4   The point $(-4, -9)$ is on the line $(k^2 - 3)y = \frac{1}{2}x - (3k + 1)$. Find the value of k.

5   Find the point on the y-axis which determines a line perpendicular to the line $x + 2y = 7$ when joined to $(-2, 4)$.

6   Write the expression $\dfrac{(x^m)^2(x^n)^2(x^p)^2}{x^{m+n}x^{n+p}x^{p+m}}$ with a single base.

7   Simplify.

(a) $\dfrac{1 - 3y}{2y + 1} \div \dfrac{1 - 9y^2}{4y^2 - 1}$

(b) $\dfrac{4 - x}{x^2 - 4} \div \dfrac{x^2 - 16}{x^2 + 2x - 8}$

(c) $\dfrac{4k^2 - 36k + 72}{k^2 - 36}$

(d) $\dfrac{1}{y + 3} - \dfrac{3y - 1}{y^2 - 9} + \dfrac{4}{3 - y}$

8   Find the ratio $x:y$ for each of the following.

(a) $3x = 2y$ (b) $3y - 2x = 5y$

(c) $\dfrac{2y}{3} = \dfrac{2x}{5}$ (d) $\dfrac{3x - 2y}{5x + y} = \dfrac{4}{3}$

(e) $(x + 7)(y + 4) = (x + 14)(y + 2)$

9   Lines are given by $2x + y = 1$, $3x + 2y = 12$.

(a) What are the slopes and intercepts?

(b) Find the intersection point.

(c) If $3x + 2ky = -1$ is perpendicular to $2x + y = 1$, find the value of k.

10 The membership fee of a local golf club is partly constant and partly varies inversely with the number of members. For 500 members, the fee is $800 per member, but if there are 700 members, the fee would be only $700. What would be the membership fee if there were only 350 members?

11 If 1296 is added to the square of one number, the result is the square of the second number. If the numbers are in the ratio $13:5$, find the numbers.

12 Points $A(-3, 5)$ and $B(1, -3)$ are on the same line. What is the value of k if $(k, -7)$ is a point on this line?

13 A polynomial, increased by $2(y^2 - 6y + 11)$, is equal to $4y^2 - 8y + 5$. Write the polynomial.

14 If $a = -9$, $b = 3$, find the value of each of the following.

(a) ab^3 (b) a^3b (c) a^3b^3 (d) $(ab)^3$ (e) $\dfrac{a^3}{b}$ (f) $\left(\dfrac{a}{b}\right)^3$

15 In a newspaper contest, the last two numbers of a combination to open a safe add up to 44. As an additional clue, the product of the two numbers is a maximum. What are the last two numbers?

16 Boyle's Law states that at the same temperature, the volume of a gas is inversely proportional to the pressure. If the volume of the gas is 30 L when the pressure is 8 units, find the pressure when the gas expands to 80 L.

17 Solve each of the following.
(a) $3x^2 + 5x - 2 = 0$ (b) $1 - 5x = 6x^2$

18 Ned jogged 15 km from his home at a steady pace and then jogged back 2 km/h slower. Find his average speed on the first part of his route if his time was 2 h 45 min.

19 Two numbers have the property that
• the ratio of one number to the other is $4:5$
• the sum of the numbers is 243.
Find the numbers.

20 Solve $\dfrac{2m}{2n + 1} = \dfrac{3 - 2m}{4n + 2} = \dfrac{m + 1}{2n + 3}$ for m and n.

21 Find the co-ordinates of C if AB, given by $A(-1, -2)$ and $B(7, 10)$, is divided externally in the ratio $5:4$.

22 GF is divided internally by X in the ratio $3:8$. If GF is 62 cm, what are the lengths of GX and XF?

23   The greatest hoard of gold, valued at $30 000, was recorded off the coast
      of Florida and dates back to a Spanish bullion fleet of 1715. This treasure
      contained 20 k (20 karat) gold coins and 12 k gold coins. How much of
      each coin would have to be melted and struck to produce a 24 g coin of
      18 k gold?

24   (a) Household ammonia consists of nitrogen, hydrogen, and oxygen
          combined in the ratio 14:5:16 by mass. What mass of hydrogen can
          be obtained from 105 g of ammonia?

      (b) The hydrogen in (a) is used to create vinegar which consists of hydrogen,
          carbon, and oxygen in the ratio 1:6:8 by mass. How much vinegar
          can be obtained if there is sufficient oxygen and carbon?

25   (a) Prove that the points P(-4, -3), Q(0, -1), and R(4, 1) are collinear.

      (b) Use *another* strategy to prove the result in (a).

26   The path of a meteor is represented by the line $3x + 4y + 7 = 0$. If the
      earth is situated at (4, -1) and each unit of distance is equivalent to
      20 000 km, find the closest approach the meteor makes with the earth.

27   A rectangle ABCD has vertices A(-3, -4), B(3, 5), C(6, 3) and D(0, -6).
      Are the diagonals AC and BD perpendicular? Why or why not?

28   To determine the number of trout in a fishing area, 40 are tagged and
      released. After a sufficient time 90 are netted and of those 5 are found to
      have been tagged. Based on this information, estimate the total number
      of trout.

29   (a) Find the equation of the locus of all points that are equidistant from
          S(-4, 0) and T(0, 6).

      (b) Describe the locus in (a).

30   James travelled 50 km from camp in search of a lost friend. He used skis
      on one part of the journey averaging 10 km/h and then used snowshoes
      for the rest of the trip averaging 4 km/h. If the journey took 8 h, how far
      did he travel on snowshoes? (Note: He found his friend.)

31   Find the equation of the line passing through the intersection of the lines
      $3x = 5 - 2y$, $15x + 4y = 1$ and passing through (-3, 5).

32 (a) The lines $3x + 2y - 8 = 0$ and $2x + y = k$ have equal y-intercepts. Find the value of k.

   (b) Show why the triangle with vertices given by $(-6, -2)$, $(-1, 0)$ and $(1, -5)$ is right-angled.

   (c) At which vertex is the right angle in (b)?

33 A single-engine plane starts out with a high tailwind and makes a trip of 500 km in 2 h. On the return trip, the pilot is forced to land after 45 min having travelled only 75 km. What was the rate of the plane in still air? What was the rate of the wind?

34 The length of the hypotenuse of a right-angled triangle is x. The other sides are $x - 1$ and $x - 2$. Find the perimeter of the triangle.

35 At a given speed, the distance that a car travels varies directly as the amount of gasoline consumed. A driver notices that on a certain day he drove 200 km at a certain speed and used 40 L of gasoline. How much gasoline will he need for a night run of 300 km at the same speed on roads that have no gas stations open?

36 The height of a high-rise office tower is directly proportional to the square of its base length. An office tower 400 m high, has a base of 100 m. How high could it be with a base of 110 m?

37 Five milkshakes and 2 fries cost $5.85 at a small truck stop. Three milkshakes and 4 fries cost $5.05. What is the price of a milkshake?

38 Find the equation of the line passing through the intersection of the lines $2x + 5y = 46$ and $x + 4y = 32$ and having the same slope as $4x = 10y + 5$.

Math Tip

The Next Step

A: Many of the strategies and suggestions for solving problems can be used in your work later in mathematics. Summarize a list of them.

B: When you solve a problem, you must organize planning and thoughts. Summarize the steps for solving problems you have used. You can extend these steps in your later work in mathematics.

C: Throughout this book you were encouraged to record the meaning of words in mathematics and to illustrate their meaning with an example. Keep all of these for your future work in the study of mathematics.

Answers

Answers to Chapter Reviews, Chapter Tests, Maintaining Skills, Cumulative Reviews and Year-End Review will be included in the Teacher's Edition of the text.

CHAPTER 1

1.1 Exercise, page 12

1.a)$3, x$ **b)**$-4, x^2$ **c)**$2, y^2$ **d)**$-16, xy$ **e)**$-25, mn$
f)$\frac{1}{3}, mn$ **g)**$25, p^2$ **h)**$\frac{2}{3}, mn$ **2.a)**6 **b)**4 **c)**9 **d)**34
3.a)$3, 5, 7, 9$ **b)**$14, 11, 8, 5$ **c)**$2, -1, 2$ **d)**$-4, -3,$
-2 **e)**$0, -1, 0$ **4.a)**$0, 3, 8, 15$ **b)**$18, 6, 0, 0$ **c)**$5, 1,$
$-1, -1$ **5.a)**2 **b)**-2 **c)**-1 **d)**7 **e)**-3 **f)**1 **g)**2 **h)**-1
i)4 **6.a)**$\frac{15}{2}$ **b)**7 **c)**T **7.a)**$\frac{7}{2}$ **b)**$\frac{7}{2}$ **c)**F **8.a)**T **b)**F **c)**F **d)**T
e)T **9.a)**72 kg **b)**168 cm **10.a)**177 cm **11.a)**165 kg

1.2 Exercise, page 16

1.a)m^5 **b)**p^7 **c)**p^9 **d)**x^5 **e)**w^8 **f)**2^4 **g)**10^5 **h)**$(-1)^5$
i)$(-1)^9$ **j)**$(-2)^5$ **k)**$(-x)^{10}$ **l)**$(-y)^4$ **m)**x^{4p} **n)**y^x **o)**m^{5x}
2.a)3^6 **b)**2^6 **c)**a^6 **d)**y^8 **e)**1^6 **f)**a^6 **g)**m^2y^2 **h)**m^4y^2 **i)**m^3y^6
j)$\frac{a^6}{b^3}$ **k)**$\frac{b^2}{a^4}$ **l)**$p^{12}q^8$ **m)**$w^9x^3y^6$ **n)**k^8 **o)**$\frac{x^6y^3}{z^3}$ **p)**$\frac{p^{12}}{q^4r^{16}}$
3.a)y^4 **b)**x^{10} **c)**m^{10} **d)**y^{12} **e)**p^2 **f)** $\frac{1}{s^3}$ **4.a)**3^2 by 1
b)3^4 by 17 **c)**2^5 by 7 **d)**equal **e)**3^5 by 118 **5.b)**2^3
c)2^6 **d)**2^7 **e)**2^9 **f)**2^3 **g)**2^{3m} **h)**2^{5p} **i)**2^{11} **j)**$2^{3p\ +\ 3}$ **k)**2^{3m}
l)2^m **m)**$2^{4k\ +\ 2}$ **n)**$2^{8p\ -\ 4}$ **o)**$2^{12p\ -\ 2}$ **6.a)**-2 **b)**4 **c)**4
d)4 **e)**-8 **f)**-8 **7.a)**-32 **b)**$-\frac{1}{2}$ **c)**-8 **d)**-8 **e)**-6
f)$-\frac{2}{3}$ **8.a)**A: $\frac{9}{2}$ B: $\frac{9}{2}$ **9.b)**$\frac{16}{9}$ **10.a)**T **b)**T **c)**T **d)**F
e)F **f)**T **g)**F **h)**T **i)**T **j)**T **k)**F **l)**F **m)**T **n)**F **o)**T
11.a)3^{11} **b)**5^3 **c)**2^4 **d)**10^1 **e)**$2^{2x\ +\ 1}$ **f)**$3^{2y\ +\ 1}$
12.a)$p^{2x\ +\ y}$ **b)**$y^{2x\ -\ 2p}$ **c)**p^{5x} **d)**$p^{x\ -\ 1}$ **e)**p^m **f)**a^{-m}
g)$x^{2a\ +\ 2b}$ **h)**$y^{a\ -\ b\ -\ 2c}$ **13.a)**-8 **b)**12 **c)**-128
d)$-32\ 768$ **e)**$-131\ 072$ **f)**-2048 **14.a)**a^5 **b)**m^3 **c)**a^{5k}
d)x^p **e)**$m^{3k\ +\ 5}$ **f)**p^{6k} **15.a)**64 **b)**$\frac{1}{4}$ **c)**$-\frac{1}{2}$ **16.**$A = 8$,
$B = 2$; $A > B$ **17.a)**$b^{5\ -\ p}$ **b)**$p^{2b\ -\ 3}$ **c)**$64, -1$
18.a)$4, 2, 1$ **b)**decreases **19.**11 **20.a)**0.016 units **b)**9
21.a)4.3 units, 2.7 units, 1.7 units **b)**decreases **22.**23

1.3 Exercise, page 20

1.a)1 **b)**$\frac{1}{64}$ **c)**1 **d)**1 **e)**$\frac{1}{16}$ **f)**1 **g)**0.0001 **h)**1
i)$0.000\ 000\ 81$ **2.a)**2 **b)**$\frac{1}{9}$ **c)**$\frac{1}{16}$ **d)**$\frac{9}{100}$ **e)**1 **3.a)**m^4
b)x^9 **c)**p^5 **d)**2 **e)**100 **f)**1 **g)** $\frac{1}{729}$ **h)** $\frac{1}{a^6}$ **i)**a^4b^2 **j)**x^5y^5 **k)** $\frac{64}{a^6}$
4.a) $\frac{2}{3}$ **b)** $\frac{5}{6}$ **c)**5 **d)**4 **e)** $-\frac{9}{4}$ **5.a)** $\frac{b^9}{a}$ **b)** $\frac{1}{m}$ **c)** $\frac{1}{x^{5k}}$ **d)** $\frac{1}{x^p}$
e) $\frac{a^4}{b^4}$ **f)**a^2 **g)** $\frac{1}{p^{7k}}$ **6.a)**4 **b)**2 **c)**4 **d)** $\frac{1}{4}$ **e)**4 **f)** $\frac{1}{16}$ **g)**16 **h)**16
i)16 **j)**64 **7.a)** $\frac{a^3}{b^2}$ **b)** $\frac{3am^2}{4b^2}$ **c)** $\frac{a^2bc^2}{3}$ **d)** $\frac{bc^2}{5a}$ **e)** $\frac{m}{a^3b^2}$ **8.**A

1.4 Exercise, page 23

9.a)-1 **b)**-1 **c)**-1 **d)**1 **e)**1 **f)**-1

1.5 Exercise, page 25

1.a)$4m$ **b)**$6x$ **c)**$6y$ **d)**$-6y$ **e)**$12p$ **f)**$-6q$ **g)**$3p$ **h)**$3r$
2.a)$7x - 3y$ **b)**$9a - 2b$ **c)**$8x^2 - 2x$ **d)**$5xy - y^2$
e)$5x - 3y$ **f)**$4x - 4y$ **g)**$8x + 3y$ **h)**$4m + 2p$ **i)**$2p$
3.a)$2x + 5y$ **b)**q **c)**$2m - 5n$ **d)**$5u - w$
e)$-p - q + 7r$ **f)**$-x$ **g)**$-2x^2$ **4.a)**$-a - 4b$
b)$-a - 4b$ **5.a)**-19 **b)**-14 **c)**-11 **d)**-8
6.a)$3x - 15$ **b)**$2 - 4y$ **c)**$15 - 9a$ **d)**$12 - 4y$
e)$6y - 3x$ **f)**$4x + 10y$ **g)**$6x^2 - 9x + 15$
h)$18 + 15a - 6a^2$ **7.a)**$2x^2 - 2x$ **b)**$6a - 3a^2$
c)$2m^3 - 4m^2$ **d)**$-3y^3 - 12y^2$ **e)**$2t + 4t^2 - 2t^3$
f)$6m^3 - 3m^2 + 15m$ **g)**$6a^3b + 12a^2b^2$
h)$-3x^3y - 3xy^2$ **8.a)**$-x - 8y$ **b)**$-x - 8y$
9.b)$-15x + 12y$ **10.a)**$\times$ **b)**$+$ **c)**$\times$ **d)**$\times$ **e)**$+$ **f)**$\times$
12.a)$2x - y$ **b)**$-x^2 - x + 1$ **c)**$7a - 4ab - 1$
d)$-2x^2 - 4xy - 3y^2$ **13.a)**$13 + 2x - x^2$
b)$-11 + 6x - 4x^2$ **14.a)**$10x - 2y$ **b)**$16x$
c)$12x + 9y$ **15.a)**$14x + 4$ **b)**$4a - 2b$
c)$-8a + 18b - 38$ **d)**$-5x + 7y - 12$
e)$-3x^2 + 7x + 6$ **f)**$7a^2 + 4a - 2$
16.a)$38 + 4y - 5y^2$ **b)**$18 - 21y - y^2$
c)$-3 + 16y - 2y^2$ **17.a)**$-2a$ **b)**$a + 11b$ **c)**$4a - 9b$
d)$a + 11b$; (b), (d) are equivalent **18.a)**$8x - 25$
b)$-15y - 30$ **c)**$15b + 28$ **19.a)**90 **b)**3 **20.**B **21.**A
22.C **23.a)**3900 m **b)**3510 m **24.a)**440 m
b)26 s and 27 s **25.a)**2160 m **b)**397 m **c)**421 m
26.a)10.45 m **b)**24.50 m **c)**no

1.6 Exercise, page 31

1.a)a^3b^3 **b)**$6a^4b^5$ **c)** $-16x^3y^5$ **2.a)**$6x^3y^4$ **b)**-96
3.a)$16x^2y^2$ **b)**576 **4.a)**$2x^2y^2 + 3x^3y, 4$ **b)**$aby - a^3b^2y,$
6 **c)**$-3m^2n - 4mn, 3$ **d)**$-x^3y^3 - 2xy^5, 6$
e)$2v^4w^2x^2 - 5v^2w^3x^5, 10$ **5.a)**$-5p^4r^3 - 10p^5r^4$ **b)**120
6.a)$p^2q + 2pqr + p^2r, 3$ **b)**$-3m^3n^3 + 9m^2n^2 - 6m^2n,$
6 **c)**$4a^2bc - 6ab^2c + 8abc^2, 4$
d)$w^3x^2 + 3w^2x^3 - \frac{3}{2}w^2x^2 + 2w^3x^3, 6$
e)$15p^3 + 45p^4r^2 + 15p^2r - 5pr, 6$ **7.a)**$-6xy$ **b)**$-12x^3$
c)$24x^4y^5$ **d)**$2ab - 6a^2b^2$ **e)**$6x^3y^3 - 8x^3y^2$
f)$3p^2q^3 - p^3q^2 - 4p^4q^3$ **g)**$9x^3y^3$ **h)**$2a^3b^2$ **i)**$3m^4n^2 - 3m^3n^3$
j)$-3p^4q^2 + 6p^3q^2 - 3p^2q^2$ **8.a)**-648 **b)**-72
c)$73\ 872$ **d)**-864 **e)**84 **f)**$123\ 120$ **9.a)**-24 **b)**-4374
c)$-38\ 700$ **10.a)**$8x^3y^5$ **b)**$81m^4n^2$ **11.** 243

1.7 Exercise, page 35

1.a)$x^2 + 8x + 15$ **b)**$2x^2 - 11x - 6$ **c)**$6a^2 - 7a - 5$
d)$9a^2 - 6ab + b^2$ **e)**$1 - 4x + 4x^2$ **f)**$4a^2 - b^2$
g)$a^2 - 6ab + 9b^2$ **h)**$x^2y^2 - 11xy + 18$ **i)**$42 - p - p^2$
j)$x^2 - 7xy + 12y^2$ **k)**$y^4 + 6y^2 - 16$ **l)**$3x^2 + \frac{23}{2}xy - 2y^2$
2.a)$9y^2 - 1$ **b)**$x^4 - 9$ **c)**$16x^2 - 4xy - 6y^2$
d)$24 - 14y + 2y^2$ **e)**$9k^2 - 15k + 6$ **f)**$9y^2 - 12y + 4$

g)$1 - 6x + 9x^2$ h)$m^2 - 5my + 6y^2$ i)$6y^4 + y^2 - 1$
j)$a^2b^2 + 4ab - 12$ k)$4x^2 - 6x + \dfrac{9}{4}$ l)$x^2y^2 - xy - 30$
3.a)$2y^2 - 10y + 8$ b)$3y^2 + 3y - 90$ c)$18x^2 - 12x + 2$
d)$-3x^2 + 6xy - 3y^2$ e)$3x^3 - 3xy^2$ f)$-9m^2 - 15mn + 6n^2$
g)$4x^2 - x - \dfrac{3}{2}$ h)$-3m^3 + 3mn^2$ i)$-18a^2 + 24ab - 8b^2$
4.a)$3a^2 - 12ab + 12b^2$ b)$9a^2 - 12ab + 4b^2$
5.a)$5x^2 - 18xy - 45y^2$ b)$x^2 - 18xy - 99y^2$
6.a)$-20x^2 + 34x + 19$ 7.a)$10x^2 + 18x - 16y^2$
8.a)$-2y^2 + 6y$ b)$5x^2 + 14x - 96$ c)$4x^2 + 5xy - 3y^2$
d)$-5a^2 + 4ab - 98b^2$ e)$-2m^2 + 6mn - 19n^2$
f)$7c^2 + 12cd + 13d^2$ g)$3x^3 - 8x^2y - 5xy^2 - 8y^3$
9.a)$-x^2 - 12$ b)$-y^2 - 18y + 27$ c)$m^2 - 21m + 36$
d)$-x^2 + 6xy - 5y^2$ e)$9a^2 - 2ab - b^2$ 10.$2x^2 - 24x + 3$
11.$6x^2 - 8x + 17$ 12.$5x^2 - 6xy + 5y^2$
13.a)-2 b)0 c)4 d)-1 e)0 f)$-\dfrac{1}{2}$ g)3 h)0 14.a)-3 b)7
15.a)$(2x - 5)^2 - (x - 1)^2$ b)24 units²
16.a)$14x^2 + 12x - 3$ b)$5x^2 + 3x + 4$ 17.a)9 b)43
c)97 18.a)14 b)25 c)34 d)41
e) 14   25   34   41   46   49   50
    11   9   7   5   3   1

1.8 Exercise, page 38
1.a)a^2 b)$4a^2$ c)$4a^3$ d)x^2y e)$-2xy$ f)$-4x^2y$ g)$4m^5n$
h)$-5q^2$ 2.a)$-3xy$ b)6 3.a)-18 b)-36 c)36 d)6
e)12 f)4 g)4 h)12 4.a)36 b)-72 c)144 d)$\dfrac{8}{3}$ e)$\dfrac{16}{3}$
f)$-\dfrac{8}{3}$ g)36 h)1 5.b)$4m + 3n$ 6.b)$9a^4b^4$ 7.a)$-4x$
b)$3mn$ c)$-5a^2b$ d)$-8x^2y$ e) $-6pq$ f)$-8m^3$ 8.a)$-\dfrac{1}{2}$
b)-9 c)-27 d)$-\dfrac{2}{3}$ e)9 f)-18 9.a)$a - b + b^2$
b)$-2y - 4$ c)$-7mn + 2$ d)$-3b + 4$ e)$-4ab + a^3b^2$
f)$-p + p^2 + 3q$ g)$-3mn + 2n + 6m$ h)$-b + 2a - 3a^2$
10.a)3 b)12 c)-43 11.a)$-\dfrac{a}{5}$ b)$8b$ c)$8mn$ d)$-2b$
e)$-3a^8b$ f)$-3x$ g)$6a - 1$ h)$-2a^3b$ i)$-\dfrac{3}{4}a^2b$ j)a^4b^3
k)$-3x^2 + 6xy + 2y$ l)$xy - 4x^2y^2$ 12.(a) 13.A

1.9 Exercise, page 42
1.a)$m^3 + m^2 - 11m + 3$ b)$y^4 + y^3 + 2y^2 - 4y - 3$
c)$p^3 + p^2y^2 + pq - 3$ d)$-x^5 + x + 4 + \dfrac{1}{x}$ 2.b)$3q + 1$
3.b)$m^2 - 4$ 4.a)$(p + 5)R - 2$ b)$2m + 5$ c)$2x + 1$ R2
5.a)-8 b)0 6.a)$3x + 7$ b)$p - 5$ c)$4m - 3$ d)$3x - 8$
7.a)$m^2 + 3m + 1$ b)$x + 4$ R 10 c)$3p^2 + p + 1$
8.a)$-p^2 - p + 1$ b)$3x^2 + 2x - 5$ c)$7m - 1$
d)$4p^2 - 3p - 2$ 9.a)$p^2 + p - 2$ b)$a^2 + 3$ c)$w^3 + 1$
d)$k^4 - 3k^2 + 1$ e)$x^2 + x - 1$ 10.$p = 9$
11.a)$k = 2$ b)$2m^2 + 3m + 2$ 12.$4x + 12$

1.10 Exercise, page 44
1. 4.8×10^{-13} 2. $395.93 3. 22.83 m²

CHAPTER 2

2.1 Exercise, page 49
1.a)$2b$ b)$2x$ c)$2y^2$ d)ac e)$2a^2b$ 2.a)a b)$8ab$ c)y
d)$2x^3$ e)$3a^2$ f)3 3.a)$2xy(x - 3y)(x - y)$ 4.a)$2m$ b)a
c)$3x$ d)$-2mn$ e)$2\pi m$ 5.a)$-13a$ b)$5xy$ c)$4m$ d)3 e)x
f)$2xy$ g)$2ab^2$ h)$3m^2n^2$ 6.a)$4x(a - 2b)$ b)$9y^3(2y - 3)$
c)$7xy(7 - 2xy)$ d)$5ab(5 - 2b)$ e)$y(3y^2 - y + 1)$
f)$-3m(2m + m^2 + 3)$ g)$2a^3(4 + a + 4a^2)$
h)$a(a^2 - ab + b^2)$ i)$2xy^2(xy - 3x + y)$
j)$3x^2(3x^2 - 2xy + 4y^2)$ 7.a)18 b)18 d)39.7
8.a)$P = 2(l + w)$ b)$S = n(n + 1)$ c)$S = n(4n + 3)$
d)$E = I(r + R)$ e)$S = 180(n - 2)$ f)$S = \dfrac{n}{2}(n + 1)$
g)$A = 2\pi r(h + r)$ h)$S_n = \dfrac{n}{2}(3n - 1)$ 9.a)1660 cm²
b)383 cm² c)344 cm² 10.a)420 b)$S_n = n(n + 1)$, 420

2.2 Exercise, page 52
1.b)$(x + 2y)(a - b)$ 2.a)$(a + b)(x + y)$ b)$(a + b)$
$(x + y)$ 3.a)$(2x + y)(a + b)$ b)$(3m - k)(x - y)$
c)$(3y - 2)(m - n)$ d)$(2m + n)(y + 3)$
e)$(3x + 2y)(3m - 2n)$ f)$(4m - 3n)(4a - 2b)$ 4.a)2
b)$-3a$ c)$2xy$ d)$7mn^2$ e)$6x^2y$ f)$3de^2$ 5.a)$(a + b)(x + y)$
b)$(a - b)(2x - y)$ c)$(a - b)(a + c)$ d)$(b-3a)(3n-2m)$
e)$(ac + b)(ac + d)$ f)$(y + 1)(y^3 + 2)$
6.a)$(a - c)(a + b)$ b)$(x - 1)(x - y)$
c)$(k + 1)(m^2 + m + n^2)$ d)$(2v - w)(5 - 3q + 2p)$
e)$(5 - z)(x + y + 2)$ f)$(3d^2 + 2d + 1)(4g - e)$
7.a)$(2p + q)(5a + 2b)$ b)$(21p^2 + 3)(m^2 - 2n)$
c)$y^2(2y^2 + x)(xy + 1)$ 8.a)$3x(y - 2)(m - n)$
b)$(x + y)(-2p + 2r - q)$ c)$2gh(g + 2h^3)(h + 2g^2)$
d)$4v(v - 2w)(3u + 2x^2)$ e)$\dfrac{1}{8}(m - n)(2p^3 - 3q)$

2.3 Exercise, page 56
1.a)$x + 5$ b)$y - 2$ c)$a - 2$ d)$m - 3$ 2.a)$+2,+4$
b)$-2,-10$ c)$-4,+2$ d)$+10,-3$ 3.b)$(3x + 1)(2x - 3)$
4.a)$+1, +9$ b)$(3y + 1)(y + 3)$ 5.a)$-21,$
$+2$ b)$(3x + 2)(x - 7)$ 6.a)$(y - 1)(2y + 1)$
b)$(x - 3)(3x - 2)$ c)$(2n - 1)(n - 3)$ d)$(x - y)(2x - 3y)$
7.a)$(x + 7)(x + 6)$ b)$(3m + 1)(m + 2)$
c)$(x - 2)(x + 1)$ d)$(y + 3)(y - 1)$ e)$3(m + 2)(m + 1)$
f)$(5m + 1)(m + 2)$ g)$(2y + 1)(2y - 3)$
h)$2(a + 2)(a + 2)$ 8.a)$(5x - 1)(3x - 5)$
9.a)$(a + 2)(a + 1)$ b)$(a + 6)(a - 2)$ c)$(x - 7)(x + 8)$
d)$(6x + 7)(x - 1)$ e)$2(5 - x)(5 - x)$
f)$(4x + 1)(5x - 6)$ g)$(4m - n)(4m - n)$
h)$(x - 12y)(x - 12y)$ i)$x(x - 3)(x - 3)$ j)$(3x + 1)(x - 1)$
k)$(7x + 2)(4x + 5)$ l)$3(a + 3)(a + 3)$
m)$3(x + 3)(x + 4)$ n)$(5x + 1)(x - 6)$
10.a)$(x + 3)(x + 5)$ b)$(a - 9)(a + 8)$ c)$(b + 4)(b + 2)$
d)$(2x - 7)(2x - 1)$ e)$(2x + 1)(2x + 3)$
f)$(a + 4)(a + 4)$ g)$(5t - 1)(5t - 1)$ h)$2(x + 5)(x - 1)$
i)$(2x - 3)(3x - 7)$ j)$(3x + 2)(x - 3)$

k)$(2x + 1)(x + 10)$ **l)**$(3x − 5)(x − 2)$ **11.a)**5, 8, 9
b)8,18 **c)**2, 14 **d)**5, 7 **e)**4, 6 **f)**7, 12, 15, 16
12.a)$(2y + 1)(y + 5)$ **b)**$(3 − 2m)(1 + 2m)$
c)$(6x + 5)(x − 4)$ **13.a)**$(4m + 5)(5m + 2)$
b)$(10m + 1)(m + 2)$ **14.a)**$(3x − 1)(2x + 1)$
b)$(4y + 1)(y − 3)$ **c)**$(3m − 1)(m − 3)$
d)$3(7k + 2)(k + 1)$ **e)**$(6a − 5b)(4a + b)$
f)$(5p + 2)(2p − 5)$ **g)**$(4x − 7y)(2x − 3y)$
h)$(8p + 9q)(5p + 2q)$ **i)**$(9r + 5s)(3r − 2s)$

2.4 Exercise, page 61
1.a)$p^2 + 8p + 16$ **b)**$9m^2 − 12m + 4$ **c)**$x^2 + 4xy + 4y^2$

d)$a^2 − a + \dfrac{1}{4}$ **e)**$4g^2 − 20gk + 25k^2$

f)$49w^2 + 14wv^2 + v^4$ **2.a)**$a^2 − 25$ **b)**$4x^2 − 9$
c)$x^2 − 9y^2$ **d)**$9x^2 − b^2$ **e)**$a^4 − 4b^4$ **f)**$x^2y^2 − 1$
g)$x^2 + 2xy + y^2 − z^2$ **h)**$a^2 + 4ab + 4b^2 − y^2$
3.a)y^2 **b)**$4a^2$ **c)**$9x^2$ **d)**1 **e)**$36x$ **f)**$24a$
4.a)$(3a − b)(3a + b)$ **b)**$(m − 4n)(m + 4n)$
c)$(5x − 7y)(5x + 7y)$ **d)**$(x − y − 4a)(x − y + 4a)$
e)$(10m − 2a − b)(10m + 2a + b)$ **5.a)**$(m + 3)^2$
b)$(a − 4)^2$ **c)**$(2x + 1)^2$ **d)**$(3y − 2)^2$ **e)**$(5a − 4b)^2$

f)$(2 − 5m)^2$ **g)**$(2p + 3q)^2$ **h)** $\left(\dfrac{1}{2}w − 3v\right)^2$ **i)**$(m^2n + 2)^2$

j)$(3c − 2de)^2$ **k)**$(7g + h)^2$ **l)**$(a^2b^2c − 2)^2$ **m)**$2(2y − 5)^2$
n)$n(2m − 7n)^2$ **o)**$2xy(x + 2y)^2$ **6.a)**9 **b)**22
c)36 **d)**1 **e)**12 **f)**16 **7.b)**$(2x + y − c)(2x + y + c)$
c)$(x + 3 − 2y)(x + 3 + 2y)$
d)$(2x − a − b)(2x + a + b)$
e)$(3y − 2a + b)(3y + 2a − b)$
f)$(4x − m − 3n)(4x + m + 3n)$
g)$(5y − 1 + 3x)(5y + 1 − 3x)$
h)$(a − b − x − y)(a − b + x + y)$
8.b)$(2k + x)(2k − x),(2a + 2b + x)(2a + 2b − x)$
9.b)$(p + 3k)(p − 3k), (p − 3q − 3r)(p + 3q + 3r)$
10.a)$(3a − b − x)(3a − b + x)$ **b)**$(1 − y − 2x)$
$(1 − y + 2x)$ **c)**$(3a + 1 − 3b)(3a + 1 + 3b)$
d)$(10x − m − 1)(10x + m + 1)$
e)$(7x − 2m − 1)(7x + 2m + 1)$
f)$(5y − 1 + 3x)(5y + 1 − 3x)$
g)$(x + y − a + b)(x + y + a − b)$
h)$(−x + y − 1)(7x − y − 1)$
11.a)$(m^2 + 1)(m + 1)(m − 1)$
12.a)$(x + 1)(x − 1)(x + 2)(x − 2)$
14.a)$(y + 4)(y − 4)$ **b)**$(m + 10)(m − 10)$
c)$(6 + x)(6 − x)$ **d)**$2(3y + 1)(3y − 1)$
e)$(3 + 2k)(3 − 2k)$ **f)**$(6x + y)(6x − y)$
g)$(5m − 4a)(5m + 4a)$ **h)**$(1 − 5y)(1 + 5y)$
i)$(ab + 1)(ab − 1)$ **j)**$m(1 − 4m)(1 + 4m)$
k)$(3m + 11)(3m − 11)$ **l)**$2a(7 − 6a)(7 + 6a)$
m)$(2a − 3b^2)(2a + 3b^2)$ **n)**$(4m^2 − 3n)(4m^2 + 3n)$
o)$(xy + 2)(xy − 2)$ **15.a)**$(n + 6)(n − 6)$
b)$(3h + 7m)(3h − 7m)$ **c)**$(15m + 1)(15m − 1)$
d)$(xyz + 3)(xyz − 3)$ **e)**$(6m + 1)(6m − 1)$
f)$(x + y + 3)(x + y − 3)$ **g)**$(x + y − m)(x + y + m)$

h)$(y^2 + 9)(y + 3)(y − 3)$ **i)**$2(2x + 5y)(2x − 5y)$
j)$(y + a + h)(y − a − h)$
k)$(x − 3y − 2a)(x − 3y + 2a)$
l)$(3m − 2x + 2y)(3m + 2x − 2y)$
m) $\left(\dfrac{1}{2}x − \dfrac{1}{3}y\right)\left(\dfrac{1}{2}x + \dfrac{1}{3}y\right)$ **n)**$(a^2 + b^2)(a + b)(a − b)$

o)$(y + 0.4x)(y − 0.4x)$ **p)**$2\left(x − 2y + \dfrac{1}{2}m\right)\left(x − 2y − \dfrac{1}{2}m\right)$

q)$(x − y − 2p + 2q)(x − y + 2p − 2q)$
r)$(x + y − 3z − 2k)(x + y − 3z + 2k)$
s)$(x + y − 3a − 3b + 3c)(x + y + 3a + 3b − 3c)$
16.a)$(a − b − m)(a − b + m)$ **b)**$(k − m + n)(k + m − n)$
c)$(a − y − 2x)(a − y + 2x)$ **d)**$(a − b − c^2)(a − b + c^2)$
e)$(x − y − z)(x + y + z)$ **f)**$(m^2 − x + y)(m^2 + x − y)$
g)$(x + y − a − b)(x + y + a + b)$
h)$(x + y − a + b)(x + y + a − b)$
i)$(x + w − y − z)(x + w + y + z)$
17.a)$(4x − y)(4x + y)$ **b)**$(x − 7y)(x + 7y)$
c)$(2x + 1)(2x − 1)$ **d)**$(2x + 5)(2x − 5)$ **e)**$(x + 8)(x − 2)$
f)$(x + y + 3)(x − y + 3)$ **g)**$2(x + 3)(x − 3)$
h)$3(x + 5)(x − 5)$ **i)**$(a − b + 2c)(a + b − 2c)$
j)$(9 − x)(5 + x)$ **k)**$6(x + 3y)(x − 3y)$
l)$3(3x + y)(3x − y)$ **m)**$(3a + 3m − 1)(3a − 3m − 1)$
n)cannot be factored **o)**$(m + 1)(m − 1)(m + 4)(m − 4)$
p)$(x + y − 3)(x − y + 7)$ **q)**cannot be factored
r) $\dfrac{1}{4}\left(\dfrac{x}{2} + \dfrac{y}{3}\right)\left(\dfrac{x}{2} − \dfrac{y}{3}\right)$
s)$(2a + 1)(2a − 1)(a + 3)(a − 3)$
t)$(9m^4n^2 + y^4)(3m^2n + y^2)(3m^2n − y^2)$
u)$(a − b − 3x − 3y)(a − b + 3x + 3y)$
v)$(m − n − p − q)(m − n + p + q)$
18.a)24 **b)**6 **c)**24 **d)**10 **e)**40 **f)**36
19.a)$(x^2 + 1 − x)(x^2 + 1 + x)$
b)$(a^2 + 4 − a)(a^2 + 4 + a)$
c)$(a^2 + 2 − 2a)(a^2 + 2 + 2a)$
d)$(m^2 − n^2 − 3mn)(m^2 − n^2 + 3mn)$
20.a)$(2y^2 − 1 − 3y)(2y^2 − 1 + 3y)$
b)$(a^2 + 3b^2 − 2ab)(a^2 + 3b^2 + 2ab)$
21.a)$(y^2 + 5 + 3y)(y^2 + 5 − 3y)$
b)$(x^2 + 3 + 2x)(x^2 + 3 − 2x)$
c)$(a^2 + 2 − a)(a^2 + 2 + a)$
d)$(y^2 + x^2 − 5xy)(y^2 + x^2 + 5xy)$
e)$(4x^2 − 1 − 2x)(4x^2 − 1 + 2x)$
f)$(3m^2 + 1 + 2m)(3m^2 + 1 − 2m)$
g)$(3a − 4b)(a + 2b)(3a + 4b)(a − 2b)$
h)$(2m^2 − 3 − 2m)(2m^2 − 3 + 2m)$

2.5 Exercise, page 65
1.$x^2(4x + 1)$ **2.**$3x(1 − 3y)$ **3.**$6x(x^3 − 2)$
4.$(3x^2 − 4y)(3x^2 + 4y)$ **5.**$(x + 4)(x + 5)$
6.$5(x + y)(x − y)$ **7.**$(y − 6)(y − 7)$ **8.**$(2x − 5)(3x + 1)$
9.$(x + 4y)(x − 3y)$ **10.**$(3x + 1)(3x + 8)$
11.$(5x + 2)(5x − 2)$ **12.**$(y − 2)(y^2 + 2y + 3)$
13.$3y^2(1 − 3y)$ **14.**$(x + 5)(x + 1)$ **15.**$(9x + 1)(2x − 3)$
16.cannot be factored **17.**$2(3x + 1)(x − 5)$
18.$(x^2 + 8)(x^2 − 8)$ **19.**$(m^2 + 2 − m)(m^2 + 2 + m)$

20.$(y^2 + 3x)(y^2 - 3x)$ 21.$(x^2 + 1)(x - 2)(x + 2)$
22.$(5x + 1)(2x + 1)$ 23.$(2x^3 - y^3)(2x^3 + y^3)$
24.$(x + 7)(x - 3)$ 25.$(2x^2 + 1)(x^2 - 2)$
26.$(y^2 + 3 - 2y)(y^2 + 3 + 2y)$ 27.$2x(x - 2y + 4)$
28.$(x + 11)(x - 11)$ 29.$2(x^2 - x - 14)$
30.$(2x + y - z)(2x + y + z)$ 31.$(m^2 + 3)(m - 3)(m + 3)$
32.$(2y^2 - 3 - 2y)(2y^2 - 3 + 2y)$ 33.$(x^2 + 5)(x^2 - 3)$
34.$(2y + 1)(4y^2 - 2y + 1)$ 35.$(3x^5 - 2)(3x^5 + 2)$
36.$2(y + 10)(y + 2)$ 37.$5(x + 2)(x - 2)$
38.$3(x - 6)(x - 3)$ 39.$(x^2 + 15y)(x^2 - 15y)$
40.$4(x - 8)(x + 1)$ 41.$(x^3 + y^3)(x^3 - y^3)$
42.$3x(x^2 + 4)(x^2 + 1)$ 43.$3(2x^2 - 5)(2x^2 + 5)$
44.$3xy(xz^3 + 6y)$ 45.$(y + 4)(y - 4)(y + 1)(y - 1)$
46.$(x - 3y)(3x - y)$ 47.$(7x + 2y)(-5x - 4y)$
48.$(m + 3 - 2n)(m + 3 + 2n)$
49.$(4y - a - 3b)(4y + a + 3b)$ 50.$(x - 2)(x + 3)(x - 3)$

2.6 Exercise, page 67

1.a)-5 b)$2, -5$ c)$-\frac{1}{2}$ d)$\frac{2}{3}, -\frac{1}{2}$ e)$3, -4$ f)$-5, 6$
g)$3, -\frac{2}{3}$ h)$\frac{1}{2}, \frac{2}{3}$ 2.a)$3, -2$ b)$5, -5$ c)$\frac{2}{3}, -3$ d)$0, 5$
e)$3, -\frac{1}{2}$ f)$0, 5$ 3.a)$(x + 5)(x + 3) = 0; -3, -5$
b)$(m + 10)(m - 3) = 0; -10, 3$ c)$(m + 5)(m - 5) = 0;$
$5, -5$ d)$(5x + 2)(x + 3) = 0; -\frac{2}{5}, -3$
e)$(3y + 1)(y + 3) = 0; -\frac{1}{3}, -3$ f)$(3 + 5y)(2 - y) = 0;$
$-\frac{3}{5}, 2$ 4.b)$3, 4$ 5.a)$\{-3, 7\}$ 6.a)$8, -6$
b)$\frac{5}{3}, -6$ c)$-\frac{1}{3}, \frac{3}{2}$ d)$\frac{3}{2}, 2$ e)$-\frac{5}{2}, 3$ f)$3, -10$
7.b)$4, -3$ 8.a)$-2, -4$ b)$-8, 9$ c)$\frac{3}{2}, \frac{7}{3}$ d)$-2, -3$
e)$-\frac{5}{2}, 3$ f)$\frac{5}{3}, 2$ 9.b)$-\frac{11}{2}, 3$ 10.a)$3, -2$ b)$5, -3$
c)$-4, -5$ d)$6, 7$ e)$0, 8$ f)$-\frac{5}{2}, -7$ g)$-4, 4$
h)$-2, 7$ i)$-\frac{1}{3}, 5$ j)$-7, 3$ k)$-\frac{7}{5}, -1$ l)$\frac{5}{4}, -\frac{5}{4}$
11.a)$7, -3$ b)$-9, 2$ c)$\frac{5}{3}, -3$ d)$\frac{7}{2}, 1$ e)$7, -6$ f)$\frac{6}{5}, 4$
g)$0, 9$ h)$-6, 6$ 12.a)$4, -2, 2$ b)$-3, 3, -1$
c)$-3, 3, 4$ 13.a)$1, 2, 3$ b)$0, 1, -3$ c)$0, -2, -3$
d)$0, -5, \frac{3}{2}$ e)$0, -3, \frac{5}{3}$ f)$0, 7, -3$ 14.a)$3, -3, 1,$
-1 b)$\{2, -2, 3, -3\}$ 15.a)$-\frac{1}{5}, 4$ b)$\frac{5}{3}, -3$ c)$4, -4$
d)-1 e)$\frac{3}{4}, -\frac{5}{2}$ f)$\frac{1}{5}, -\frac{1}{5}$ g)-5 h)$\frac{1}{6}, 1$ i)$\frac{10}{3}, -3$
j)-2 k)$\frac{3}{2}, -1$ l)$0, 4, -4$ m)$\frac{3}{4}, -\frac{5}{3}$ n)$\frac{1}{3}$ o)$-\frac{4}{5}, \frac{4}{5}$
p)$0, 6, -2$ q)$0, 9$ r)-5 s)$3, -3, 16$ t)$2, -2, 7$
16.a)$(2x - 5)(2x + 1) = 0; \frac{5}{2}, -\frac{1}{2}$ b;$2x^2 + x - 21 = 0;$
$3, -\frac{7}{2}$ c)$3x^2 + 8x - 3 = 0; (3x - 1)(x + 3) = 0$

d)$(3x - 1)(x - 3) = 0; 3, \frac{1}{3}$ 17.a)$x^2 - x - 6 = 0$
b)$x^2 + 10x + 24 = 0$ c)$2x^2 - 7x + 3 = 0$
d)$3x^2 + 7x - 6 = 0$ e)$x^2 - 4x = 0$
f)$6x^2 + x - 1 = 0$ 18.a)-12 b)$\frac{2}{3}$ 19.a)$p = -2; \frac{1}{3}$
b)$p = -5; -\frac{1}{2}$ c)$p = 25; \frac{1}{4}$ d)$p = 5; -5$

2.7 Exercise, page 71

1.a)$x \neq 0$ b)$x \neq 0$ c)$y \neq 2$ d)$x \neq \frac{1}{5}$ e)$x \neq -\frac{5}{2}$
f)$x \neq 0, -1$ g)$k \neq 2, -1$ h)$x \neq y, -y$
i)$x \neq 2y$ j)$m \neq -\frac{1}{2}$ k)$x \neq 0$ l)$m \neq 0$ m)$m \neq 1,$
-1 2.equivalent (a), (c), and (d) 3.a)1 b)-1 c)1
d)1 e)1 f)-1 4.a)$x \neq 0; \frac{1}{2x}$ b)$p \neq 0; \frac{2}{p}$ c)$y \neq 0;$
$\frac{y + 2}{5y}$ d)$m \neq 0, n \neq 0; -5n$ e)$x \neq -1; x + 1$
f)$m \neq 1, -1; \frac{2(m - 1)}{m + 1}$ g)$x \neq -4; 4$ h)$k \neq -3, 0;$
$\frac{1}{k}$ i)$w \neq 3, -1; \frac{w + 1}{w - 3}$ j)$d \neq \frac{1}{2}, 3; \frac{d - 2}{2d - 1}$
5.a)$-(2p + 3q); q \neq \frac{2p}{3}$ b)$\frac{-3}{1 + 2a}; a \neq \frac{1}{2}, -\frac{1}{2}$
c)$\frac{2(1 - a)}{1 + a}; a \neq -1$ d)$\frac{5x^4}{5 - 2x}; x \neq \frac{1}{3}, \frac{5}{2}$
e)$\frac{p - 7}{p - 3}; p \neq \pm 3$ f)$\frac{1}{4}(x + 3); x \neq 5$ g)$\frac{y + 5}{y + 2};$
$y \neq 5, -2$ h)$\frac{y - 5}{y + 2}; y \neq -2, 3$ i)$\frac{x + 1}{5x}, x \neq 0, 5$
6.a)$\frac{3 - 2x}{3x + 1}; x \neq -\frac{1}{3}, -1$ b)$\frac{m - n}{m + n}; m \neq -n$
c)$\frac{x(x + 3)}{x + 5}; x \neq -4, -5$ d)$\frac{4}{x^2}; x \neq 0, -4$
e)$\frac{2x - 5y}{2x + 5y}; x \neq -\frac{3}{2}y, -\frac{5}{2}y$ f)$\frac{2}{(w^2 + 9)(3 - w)};$
$w \neq 3, -3$ g)$\frac{-(4 + 3x)}{x + 1}; x \neq -1, \frac{4}{3}$
h)$\frac{4x^2(3x + 1)}{x + 1}; x \neq \pm 1$ 7.a)$\frac{x - 2}{2x - 1}; x \neq -5, \frac{1}{2}$
b)$\frac{2 - k}{2k + 3}; k \neq -2, -\frac{3}{2}$ c)$\frac{x}{x - 1}; x \neq -\frac{11}{6}, 1$
d)$\frac{a - 14b + 2c}{a + 2c}; a \neq 0, -2c$ e)$\frac{5}{6 - y}; y \neq 6, -3$
f)$\frac{1}{2p + 1}; p \neq 5, -2, -\frac{1}{2}$ g)$x^2 + 4y; y \neq -\frac{x^2}{4}$

2.8 Exercise, page 74

1.a)$-a - b; a \neq b$ b)$2x + y; y \neq 2x$ c)$1 - x;$
$x \neq 1$ 2.a)$\frac{1}{4}$ b)$\frac{b}{5x}$ c)$-\frac{y}{t}$ d)$\frac{45x^3}{128y^2}$ e)$-\frac{2m^3}{9}$ f)2
g)$-\frac{x^{11}}{4}$ h)$2x^5y^2$ 3.a)-2 b)$-\frac{1}{2}$ c)$\frac{1}{3(x + 1)}$
d)$\frac{y}{(y - 1)^2}$ 4.a)$\frac{x(x + 2)}{(x - 1)(x + 7)}; x \neq \pm 1, -7$
b)$\frac{x + 3}{x - 1}, x \neq \pm 1, 3, -4$

c) $\frac{(x-1)(x-3)}{2(x+3)}$, $x \neq -3, 2$

d) $\frac{2x-1}{2(x+4)}$, $x \neq \pm 4, 3, 5$ **5.a)**3 **b)**$-\frac{2}{5}$

c)0 **d)**1 **6.a)**$\frac{(m+4)(m+5)}{2(m-2)}$

b)$\frac{x-2}{2x+1}$ **c)**$\frac{a-5}{a-3}$ **d)**$\frac{1}{(a-1)(a+3)}$

e)$x(x-2)(x+1)$ **7.b)**decreases from $-\frac{4}{3}$ to $\frac{-20}{3}$

c)factor **d)**decreases from $-\frac{7}{8}$ to -2 **8.a)**1, 1 **b)**$-\frac{9}{2}$

9.a)-3 **b)**0 **c)**-1 **d)**$-\frac{24}{5}$ **e)**-14

2.9 Exercise, page 77

1.a)$\frac{b+4}{b-4}$ **b)**$\frac{-a^2}{3(1+a)}$ **c)**$\frac{k+1}{k-1}$ **2.a)**$4-y$ **b)**$x-y$

c)$\frac{-1}{x+3}$ **d)**$\frac{-(2a+1)}{(a+1)}$ **e)**x **f)**$\frac{-m}{5+m}$ **3.a)**x^2+x

b)$3a+6$ **c)**$-(2-m)^2$ **d)**$2y^2-3y+1$

4.a)$\frac{3}{x+1}-\frac{2}{x+1}$ **b)**$\frac{1}{x+1}$

5. $\frac{2y}{y-3}$ **6.a)**$\frac{4-y}{20}$ **b)**$\frac{3a}{4}$ **c)**$\frac{2}{3x}$ **d)**$\frac{2-3y}{2y^2}$

e)$\frac{3a-1}{a(a+1)}$ **f)**$\frac{3p+1}{p(p+1)}$ **g)**$\frac{11-x}{(x+1)(x-2)}$

h)$\frac{x-11}{12}$ **i)**$-\frac{3(a^2+b^2)}{ab}$ **j)**$\frac{3(a^2+b^2)}{(2a-3b)(3a+2b)}$ **k)**2

7.a)$\frac{2y-3x}{xy(x-y)}$; $x \neq 0, y \neq 0, x \neq y$

b)$\frac{7a-15}{(a+3)(a-3)}$; $a \neq -3, 3$ **c)**$\frac{7}{2y-1}$; $y \neq \frac{1}{2}, -\frac{1}{2}$

d)$\frac{x(4x+15)}{(x+1)(x+2)(x+3)}$; $x \neq -1, -2, -3$

8.a)$\frac{x^2-4xy+y^2}{(x+y)(x-y)}$; $x \neq y, x \neq -y$ **b)**$\frac{-2(a+8)}{(a+3)(a-3)}$;

$a \neq \pm 3$ **c)**$\frac{-4ab}{(a-b)(a+b)}$; $a \neq b, a \neq -b$ **d)**$\frac{-3}{xy}$; $x \neq 0$,

$y \neq 0, x \neq y$ **e)**$\frac{x^2-8x+31}{4(x-4)}$; $x \neq 4$ **9.a)**$\frac{4(y+1)}{1-y}$

b)0 **10.a)**$\frac{3x+2}{(x-2)(x+3)(x-6)}$ **b)**0 **11.a)**1 **b)**$-\frac{4}{3}$

12.a)$-\frac{11}{5}$ **b)**$\frac{26}{77}$ **13.**$-\frac{4}{65}$ **14.**no change **15.**decreases

in value from $\frac{5}{2}$ to $\frac{5}{3}$ **16.**decreases in value from $\frac{5}{2}$ to 2

2.10 Exercise, page 80

1.$\frac{1-6x}{1-9x^2}$ **2.**$\frac{7x^2-2x-8}{x(x^2-4)}$ **3.**$\frac{-9}{x^2-9}$ **4.**$\frac{2-x^2}{x^2-16}$

5.$\frac{-7x-3}{x^2-9}$ **6.**$\frac{6}{x-3}$ **7.**$\frac{-x^2-3x+6}{x^2+7x+6}$

8.$\frac{2x^3+x^2-3x+18}{(x-3)(x+2)(x+5)}$ **9.**$\frac{4x^2+20x+27}{2x+5}$

10.$\frac{x+5}{3(x+1)(x+8)}$ **11.**$\frac{15y-27}{4}$ **12.**$\frac{20y-5}{20y+6}$

CHAPTER 3

3.1 Exercise, page 86

1.rational: (a), (c), (f), (h), (j), (n), (o)
irrational: (b), (d), (e), (g), (i), (k), (l), (m)

2.a)0.25 **b)**0.375 **c)**-0.4 **d)**0.46 **e)**$-0.0\overline{9}$ **f)**$0.\overline{2}$

g)$1.\overline{2}$ **h)**-2.125 **i)**0.53 **j)**$-0.4\overline{6}$ **k)**$0.\overline{428\ 571}$

l)$1.\overline{6}$ **m)**-3.125 **n)**$0.\overline{523\ 809}$ **o)**$-0.538\ 461$

3.a)$0.3\overline{6}$, $0.346\ \overline{153\ 8}$ **b)**$\frac{11}{30}$ **4.a)**$\frac{6}{29}$ **b)**$-\frac{3}{13}$ **c)**$\frac{11}{57}$

5.a)6, 1 **b)**6, 1 **c)**36, 2 **d)**8,1 **e)**16, 2 **f)**162, 3

g)382, 3 **h)**045, 3 **i)**142 857, 6 **6.a)**2 **b)**2 **c)**3 **d)**3

e)0 **f)**1 **g)**5 **h)**5 **i)**1 **j)**9 **k)**3 **l)**3 **7.a)**$\sqrt{3}$ **b)**2

11.a)rational **b)**irrational **12.a)**$\frac{1}{4}$ **b)**$\frac{7}{9}$ **c)**$-\frac{25}{99}$ **d)**$\frac{13}{99}$

e)$2\frac{2}{15}$ **f)**$\frac{13}{999}$ **g)**$-3\frac{19}{30}$ **h)**$2\frac{424}{495}$ **13.a)**$\frac{9}{50}$ **b)**$\frac{2}{11}$ **c)**$\frac{17}{90}$ **d)**1

e)$\frac{1}{5}$ **f)**$\frac{3}{25}$ **15.a)**$\frac{1}{2}$ **b)**$\frac{1}{2}$ **c)**equal **d)**$\frac{3}{4}$ **16.a)**$0.25, 0.24\overline{9}$

b)$0.375, 0.374\overline{9}$ **c)**$-1.125, -1.124\overline{9}$ **d)**$0.15, 0.14\overline{9}$

e)$0.625, 0.624\overline{9}$ **f)**$-0.24, -0.23\overline{9}$ **17.a)**$\frac{2}{9}$ **b)**$\frac{1}{15}$ **c)**$\frac{4}{9}$ **d)**$\frac{25}{99}$

3.2 Exercise, page 90

1.a)$-\frac{1}{9}$ **b)**$\frac{1}{9}$ **c)**-1 **d)**1 **e)**$\frac{4}{3}$ **f)**$\frac{1}{12}$ **g)**9 **h)**$-\frac{1}{9}$ **2.a)**$\frac{1}{8}$

b)$\frac{1}{4}$ **c)**$\frac{1}{25}$ **d)**-1 **e)**9 **f)**1 **g)**$\frac{2}{3}$ **h)**$\frac{8}{9}$ **i)**32 **j)**$\frac{9}{4}$ **3.a)**$\frac{1}{x^2}$

b)$\frac{1}{y^3}$ **c)**$\frac{1}{a^7}$ **d)**$\frac{1}{b^5}$ **e)**x^2 **f)**a **g)**c^4 **h)**$\frac{2}{x^4}$ **i)**$\frac{a}{b^5}$ **j)**$\frac{y^4}{x^3}$ **k)**$\frac{4}{a^2}$

l)$\frac{3y^2}{2x^4}$ **4.a)**x^{-3} **b)**xy^{-4} **c)**$3ab^{-3}$ **d)**$4a^3$ **e)**$3a^2b$

f)$3(x+y)^2$ **5.a)**a^2 **b)**$\frac{1}{m^6}$ **c)**a^{13} **d)**$\frac{1}{3a}$ **e)**x^6 **f)**$\frac{1}{xy^2}$ **g)**$\frac{1}{a^2}$

h)$\frac{1}{b^{12}}$ **6.a)**$\frac{1}{100}$ **b)**24 **c)**$\frac{17}{4}$ **d)**36 **e)**0 **f)**6 **7.a)**-6 **b)**$\frac{1}{17}$

c)$\frac{26}{17}$ **d)**$-\frac{1}{9}$ **8.a)**2^{18-6n} **b)**3^{2-5m} **9.a)**1 **b)**$\frac{16}{9}$ **c)**-1 **d)**$\frac{1}{3}$

3.3 Exercise, page 93

1.a)1 **b)**2 **c)**$\frac{1}{2}$ **d)**3 **e)**$\frac{1}{3}$ **f)**1 **g)**-1 **h)**-10 **i)**$-\frac{1}{10}$

j)1 **k)**5 **l)**$\frac{1}{5}$ **2.a)**5 **b)**5 **c)**$\frac{1}{5}$ **d)**16 **e)**$\frac{1}{2}$ **f)**$\frac{1}{16}$ **g)**2 **h)**2

i)-2 **j)**$-\frac{1}{3}$ **k)**-3 **l)**-3 **3.a)**2 **b)**4 **c)**8 **d)**2 **e)**4 **f)**8 **4.a)**$\frac{1}{5}$

b)8 **c)**10 **d)**$\frac{1}{2}$ **e)**-3 **f)**4 **g)**4 **h)**16 **i)**$\frac{1}{8}$ **j)**-2 **k)**25

l)-9 **5.a)**$3=\sqrt[3]{27}$ **b)**$3=\sqrt[5]{243}$ **c)**$-1=\sqrt[5]{-1}$

d)$2=\sqrt[4]{16}$ **e)**$-2=\sqrt[5]{-32}$ **f)**$4=\sqrt[3]{64}$ **g)**$5=\sqrt[4]{625}$

h)$7=\sqrt[4]{2401}$ **i)**$0.2=\sqrt{0.04}$ **6.**(a), (c), (d) **7.a)**m^4

b)x^9 **c)**p^5 **d)**2 **e)**10^2 **f)**1 **g)**$\frac{1}{3^6}$ **h)**$\frac{1}{2^6}$ **i)**$\frac{1}{a^6}$ **j)**a^4b^2 **k)**x^5y^5

l)$\frac{64}{a^6}$ **8.a)**2 **b)**-5 **c)**$\frac{1}{2}$ **d)**2 **e)**$\frac{5}{6}$ **f)**$-\frac{3}{5}$ **g)**$\frac{1}{32}$ **h)**2

i)-10 **j)**$\frac{1}{9}$ **k)**-25 **l)**4 **m)**$-\frac{1}{4}$ **n)**$\frac{4}{5}$ **o)**32 **p)**$\frac{1}{8}$ **q)**8

r)-3 **s)**-3 **t)**3 **9.a)**2^{-1} **b)**-8 **c)**8^{-1} **d)**2^{-1} **e)**125^{-1}

f)-2 **g)**4^{-1} **h)**4 **i)**2 **j)**-3^{-1} **k)**6×7^{-1} **l)**144

m)5×7^{-1} **n)**1 **o)**-8

.4 Exercise, page 95

.a)15 b)6 c)$15\frac{26}{27}$ d)$-\frac{1}{4}$ e)68 2.a)$3\frac{1}{2}$ b)$3\frac{2}{3}$

)$-\frac{17}{20}$ d)$-\frac{177}{40}$ 3.a)$\frac{2}{3}$ b)$\frac{8}{3}$ c)$\frac{8}{9}$ d)1 e)1 f)$\frac{256}{9}$

.a)5 b)4 c)$-\frac{9}{4}$ d)$\frac{15}{2}$ e)-4 f)$\frac{1}{4}$ 5.a)$x^{\frac{11}{12}}$ b)x

)$\frac{1}{2y^{\frac{1}{2}}}$ d)1 e)$\frac{27}{2x^{\frac{1}{4}}}$ f)xy g)$x^{\frac{2}{9}}y^{\frac{1}{6}}$ h)x^n i)$\frac{a^8x^{\frac{7}{2}}}{b^8y^{\frac{15}{2}}}$

5.a)$\frac{b^9}{a}$ b)$\frac{(-1)^k}{a^{3k}x^{2k}}$ c)$\frac{1}{x^p}$ d)$\frac{a^4}{b^4}$ e)a^2 f)1 7.a)4 b)2 c)4

d)$\frac{1}{4}$ e)4 f)$\frac{1}{16}$ g)16 h)16 8.a)$\frac{a^3}{b^2}$ b)$\frac{3bc}{a}$ c)$\frac{3am^2}{4b^2}$

d)$\frac{a^2bc^2}{3}$ e)$\frac{bc^2}{5a}$ 9.a)$x \geqq -\frac{1}{3}$ b)$y \geqq \frac{3}{2}$ c)$|m| \geqq 5$

d)no restriction e)$y \geqq -1$ 10.a)0 b)$\frac{1}{3}$c)3 d)5 e)1 11.A

3.5 Exercise, page 99

1.a)$\pm 0.000\ 05$ m b)± 0.0005 m c)± 0.005 m
d)± 0.05 m e)± 0.005 m f)± 0.005 kg g)± 0.05 km
h)± 5 kg i)± 0.0005 m j)0.005 km k)$\pm 0.000\ 005$ g
l)0.000 005 g 2.b)21.31 kg $\pm$ 0.005 kg c)0.251 m $\pm$
0.0005 m d)27 000 m $\pm$ 500 m e)386.4 g $\pm$ 0.05 g
f)1.0001 L $\pm$ 0.000 05 L g)526.02 mL $\pm$ 0.005 mL
h)1798.7 g $\pm$ 0.05 g i)0.000 02 m $\pm$ 0.000 005 m
j)89 625 000 mL $\pm$ 500 mL k)15.0 m $\pm$ 0.05 m
l)6.032 g $\pm$ 0.0005 g m)889.8264 kg $\pm$ 0.000 05 kg
3.a)0.01 m b)0.1 kg c)0.0001 kg d)100 m e)1 000 000 g
f)0.001 L g)0.000 01 g h)1 mm i)0.01 mL j)1 L k)10 g
l)0.1 m 4.a)0.01 L, ± 0.005 L b)0.1 mL, ± 0.05 mL
c)0.001 kg, ± 0.0005 kg d)0.1 m, ± 0.05 m e)1 g, ± 0.5 g
f)0.000 01 km, $\pm 0.000\ 005$ km g)0.01 g, ± 0.005 g
h)0.01 km, ± 0.005 km i)0.0001 mm, $\pm 0.000\ 05$ mm
j)0.01 km, ± 0.005 km k)0.001 L, ± 0.0005 L
l)0.000 001 g, $\pm 0.000\ 000\ 005$ g 5.a)0.0061%
b)0.0036% c)8.3% d)0.000 001 6% e)0.13% f)0.13%
g)0.000 051% h)0.13% i)0.00050% j)0.000 001 3%
k)0.13% l)0.000 013% 6.a)2 b)3 c)2 d)8 e)3 f)4 g)5
h)6 i)10 j)7 k)6 l)4 7.a)100 b)0.001 03 c)0.039
d)11 500 e)0.020 000 f)120 000 8. 0.326 g

3.6 Exercise, page 102

1.a)3.62×10^7 b)$7.38 \times 10^\circ$ c)7.80×10^{10} d)3.82×10^6
e)5.86×10^{-5} f)3.62×10^3 g)5.75×10^{-5}
h)7.30×10^{-10} 2.a)2.80×10^4 b)2.38×10^{-3}
c)7.80×10^3 d)6.32×10^8 e)7.50×10^{-1} f)8.77×10^8
g)7.38×10^{-5} h)4.23×10^{-8} i)9.00×10^{-7} 3.a)6.3×10^{11}
b)4.8×10^{-10} c)3.8×10^{12} d)5.3×10^{-17} e)8.0×10^{-6}
f)4.6×10^{-8} 4.a)72 100 b)3600 c)0.007 31 d)0.000 458 1
e)567 000 000 f)0.0002 g)0.000 008 7 h)2 100 000
i)36 200 000 j)753 k)7 500 000 000 l)38 600 m)0.058 64
n)728 5.a)6.4×10^6 m b)6.4×10^6 m c)1.5×10^{11} m
d)1.7×10^{-24} g e)$1.5 \times 10^7 {}^\circ$C f)4.0×10^{-13} cm
g)7.0×10^8 km 6.a)150 000 000 km b)384 000 km
c)0.000 000 000 000 000 000 000 001 66 g

d)0.000 000 000 000 000 000 000 000 000 000 000 904 g
e)5 980 000 000 000 000 000 000 000 000 kg
7.a)3.20×10^{11} b)1.79×10^{-1} c)7.55×10^7
d)4.78×10^7 e)2.13×10^9 f)1.09×10^3 8.a)1.0×10^4
b)7.1×10^2 c)1.7×10^5 d)3.3×10^{-3} 9.a)2.6×10^9
b)1.3×10^6 c)3.5×10^9 d)$5.7 \times 10^\circ$ 10.a)8.85×10^{-12}
b)$3.45 \times 10^\circ$ c)1.11×10^{-4} d)1.20×10^4 11.a)1.1×10^{-1}
b)5.1×10^{-5} c)1.1×10^{-9} d)4.4×10^{-37} 12.2.42:1
13.86 h 40 min 14.1.29 parsecs 15.4.64×10^{22} km
16.1.51×10^{14} km 17.a)7.1×10^{18} km b)3.1×10^{16} km
c)9.3×10^{18} km 18.a)2.998×10^{10} cm/s b)3.0×10^{10} cm/s
19.a)1.08×10^9 km b)9.45×10^{12} km

3.7 Exercise, page 107

1.a)$\{5\}$ b)$\{5\}$ c)$\{4\}$ d)$\{6\}$ e)$\{3\}$ f)$\{3\}$ 2.a)5 b)3 c)2
d)4 3.a)4 b)-2 c)8 d)2 e)2 or 3 f)1 or 5 4.a)-5
5.equivalent (b) (c) 6.a)$\{-1, 5\}$ b)$\{-1, 3\}$ c)$\{-2\}$ 7.a)8
b)-6 c)-7 d)8 e)2 f)2 g)4 h)6 8.a)-1 or 5 b)1 or -2
c)1 or 2 d)1 or 4 9.a)$x = 4, y = 2$ b)$x = 0, y = 1$

CHAPTER 4

4.1 Exercise, page 116

1.a)6:1 b)8:1 c)15:2 d)8:1 e)4:1 f)20:1 2.a)1:2 b)$2a$:1
c)a:2b d)$-x$:2 e)3:1 f)1:2 g)18:pq h)xy:27 i)$(x + 2y)$:x
j)a:b k)$(p - q)$:1 l)$(a + b)$:1 m)$(a^2 + b^2)$:$(a + b)$

3.a)$\frac{3}{2}$ b)$\frac{3}{2}$ c)1 d)$\frac{7}{4}$ e)$\frac{5}{4}$ 4.a)$\frac{35}{2}$ b)10 c)$\frac{28}{15}$ d)$\frac{27}{4}$ e)$\frac{5}{2}$

f)$\frac{12}{7}$ 5.a)30 b)$\frac{27}{4}$ c)$\frac{36}{5}$ d)$\frac{6}{7}$ 6.a)3:4 b)-2:5 7.a)3:2

b)5:4 c)3:1 d)4:3 e)3:4 f)5:1 g)-3:1 8.a)$x = 6, y = 15$

b)$m = 15, n = \frac{4}{5}$ c)$p = 24, q = 20$ 9.a)$-\frac{1}{2}$ b)$-\frac{1}{3}$ c)$-\frac{1}{5}$

d)-5 10.a)5 b)$\frac{15}{2}$ c)$-\frac{1}{5}$ 11.a)-5 b)-13 c)$-\frac{2}{5}$ d)0 e)1

f)-23 12.a)0 b)-21 c)5 d)6 e)2 f)-2 13.a)2:1 b)3:1
c)3:8 d)-3:2 14.a)1:1 or 3:1 b)-5:1 or 2:1 c)1:2 or 3:1
d)2:5 or 1:2 15.a)± 6 b)± 9 c)$\pm mn$ d)$\pm 6m^2$ e)$\pm 4ab$
f)$\pm 8p^3$ g)± 3 h)$\pm 2a\sqrt{a}$ 16.a)16 b)20 c)32 d)1

17.a)3 b)4 c)$\frac{1}{2}$ d)$\frac{3}{5}$ e)3 18.12:49 19.-8:9

4.2 Exercise, page 120

1. 35 cm 2.c)75 3. $21 270 4. 8.8 mL 5. 204 cm
(nearest centimetre) 6. 205 7. 56, 84 8.Tony 12,
Colin 42, Andre 18 9.Jane $240, Karen $180,
Rose $120 10.8, 12 11.6, 10 12.20, 25 or -20,
-25 13.14, 4 or -14, -4 14.26, 8 or -26, -8
15. 19 16. 9 17. Ann 12 h, Bill 20 h, Chris 18 h
18.Bill 120 shares, Brad 80 shares, Bob 100 shares
21. 40 g 22. 8 g 23. 48 g 24. 324 g 25. 9.5 g 26. 21 g
27. 71 g 28. 45 g 29. 45 g

4.3 Exercise, page 124

1.a)2:3:4 b)3:-1:2 c)a:$2b$:3 d)$(a + b)$:1:$(a - b)$

e)$(x + y):1:(x − y)$ **2.a)**$a = 2, b = 24$ **b)**$a = 1,$ $b = 2$ **c)**$a = 2, b = 10$ **d)**$a = 6, b = 5$ **e)**$a = 10,$ $b = 12$ **f)**$a = 6, b = 15$ **3.a)**3:1:4 **b)**3:−1:−4
4.a)$a = 2, b = 5$ **b)**$a = 2, b = 4$ **c)**$a = 0, b = 9$ **d)**$a = −4, b = −5$ **5.a)**$m = \frac{4}{3}, n = \frac{4}{7}$ **b)**$m = −3,$ $n = −\frac{2}{5}$ **6.**12, 6, 3 **7.**40°, 40°, 100° **8.**90, 60, 150
9.to the nearest gram protein 194 g, carbohydrates 278 g, water 28 g **10.**Jenny $20 000; Lori $30 000; Alex $50 000 **11.** 12, 18, 30 **12.** 9, 12, 15 **13.** 13.3 g
14. 22.6 kg **15.** 6, 8, 12 **16.** 64.3 g **17.** 212 **18.**Carbon 21 g; Oxygen 24 g **19.a)**3 **b)**$−\frac{3}{13}$ **20.a)**2 **b)**$\frac{19}{10}$
21.phosphoric acid 21 kg, potash 18 kg **22.**nitrogen 8 kg, phosphoric acid 2 kg **23.**1 kg **24.**nitrogen 1.3 kg, potash 2.7 kg **25.**3.9 kg, 0.6 kg, 0.6 kg **26.**0.9 g, 1.2 g, 0.8 g

4.4 Exercise, page 128
1.a)9 **b)**6 **c)**$x = 10, y = 6$ **d)**$x = 4, y = 3$ **e)**$x = 20, y = 12$ **f)**$x = 12, y = 10$ **2.**15 **3.**$\frac{15}{4}$ **4.a)**15 **b)**$\frac{16}{3}$
5.$x = 15, y = 6$ **6.**4.6 m, 4.2 m **7.**26.2 m **8.**10.5 m **9.** 10.5 m **10.** 225 m **11.** 63.6 m **12.** 147 m

4.5 Exercise, page 131
1.a)$\frac{A}{W} = k$ **b)**900 **2.a)**$\frac{H}{A} = k$ **b)**58.9 **3.a)**$\frac{1}{6}$ **b)**12 **c)**15 **d)**10 **e)**2 **4.a)**(3, 12) **b)**(3, 18) **c)**(10, 150) **d)**(5, 60), (10, 120) **5.a)**$k = 200, V = 7.5$ **b)**$k = 50,$ $d = 600$ **c)**$k = 36, h = 720$ **6.a)**675 **b)**12 **c)**53.2 **d)**81.6 **7.a)**$p = kl$ **b)**$C = kr$ **c)**$m = kd^3$ **8.a)**175 **b)**12 s **9.a)**$m = kl$ **b)**250 kg **10.a)**21 g **b)**3.3 cm **11.**333.3 km **12.**1027 cm³ **13.**2 h **14.**$32.50 **15.**450 km **16.**45 units

4.6 Exercise, page 135
1.$\frac{1}{2}$ **2.a)**$s = kp^2$ **b)**25 **3.**30 **4.a)**16 **b)**20 s **5.a)**$m = kd^2$ **b)**100 g **6.**25 units **7.**375 m **8.a)**400 mg **b)**$123.48 **9.**80 min **10.**8.5 cm **11.a)**5 **b)**9 km **12.a)**$d \, α \, t^2$ **b)**488 m **13.a)**44 m **b)**78 m **c)**34 m **14.a)**34 m **b)**44 m **c)**9.8 m (to 1 decimal place) **15.a)**$d \, α \, v^2$ **b)**18 m **16.**90 km/h **17.**50.6 m **18.**no **19.**1261 kg

4.7 Exercise, page 139
1.a)50 **b)**64 **c)**96 **2.a)**A, C **b)**A, B **c)**A, B, C **3.a)**324 **b)**18 **c)**6 **4.a)**$H = \frac{k}{S}$ **b)**21 **5.a)**25 **b)**10 **c)**8 **6.a)**5 **b)**5 **c)**12.5 **7.a)**$V = \frac{k}{t}$ **b)**$f = \frac{k}{l}$ **c)**$V = \frac{k}{p}$ **8.**2.5 h **9.**3 units **10.**2.25 s **11.**160 units **12.**1 h **13.**20 m

4.8 Exercise, page 142
1.384 **2.**4 **3.a)**5400 **b)**216 **c)**6 **4.**150 **5.**3 **6.a)**33.75

b)2.56 **c)**$\frac{5}{2}$ **d)**75 **7.**5 cm **8.**49 mg **9.**833 g
10. 1.6 min **11.** 12 cm **12.** $7.03 **13.** 84 cm³

4.9 Exercise, page 145
1.a)$V = kTQ$ **b)**$R = \frac{kT}{P}$ **c)**$U = \frac{kT^2}{S}$ **d)**$E = kMv^2$ **e)**$Q = \frac{kM}{P^2}$ **2.a)**$\frac{J_1P_1}{T_1} = \frac{J_2P_2}{T_2}$ **b)**$\frac{P_1R_1^2}{Q_1} = \frac{P_2R_2^2}{Q_2}$ **c)**$\frac{A_1}{B_1C_1^2} = \frac{A_2}{B_2C_2^2}$ **d)**$\frac{R_1S_1^2}{G_1} = \frac{R_2S_2^2}{G_2}$ **3.a)**20 **b)**125 **4.a)**$\frac{R_1D_1^2}{L_1} = \frac{R_2D_2^2}{L_2}$ **b)**1.75 **5.**equivalent (a) (d) **6.**6 **7.**15 **8.**$Q_2 = 2520$ **9.**180 **10.**121 cm² **11.**27 units **12.**3 m/s **13.**20 000 units

4.10 Exercise, page 147
1.$m = 3, p = 13$ **2.**$k = 40, p = 20$ **3.a)**150 **b)**$405 **c)**301 **4.**$85.80 **5.**$1075 **6.**2 **7.**$1850 **8.**$21.00 **9.**4.5 h

4.11 Exercise, page 149
1.a)direct variation **b)**$44.10 **2.a)**inverse squared variation **b)**$\frac{1}{4}$ **3.a)**inverse variation **b)**1250 **4.**10 cm **5.**74 L **6.**$259.20 **7.**15 min **8.**50 625 km **9.**$2.75 **10.**3 m **11.**80 cm² **12.**5 s **13.**$10.20 **14.**200 **15.**12 km/L **16.**2.8 m

CHAPTER 5

5.1 Exercise, page 157
1.linear (a) (c) (d) (e) **2.a)**$x = −3$ **b)**$x = 5$ **c)**$x = 2$ **3.a)**$y = 1$ **b)**$y = −4$ **c)**$y = −3$ **4.a)**$2x − y + 1 = 0$ **b)**$x − 3y − 15 = 0$ **c)**$2x − 3y − 1 = 0$ **d)**$x − 2y − 15 = 0$ **e)**$3x − 2y − 36 = 0$ **f)**$2x − 3y − 6 = 0$ **g)**$3x − 2y + 41 = 0$ **h)**$2x − 3y − 9 = 0$ **5.a)**$\frac{2}{3}, −2$ **b)**$5, −2$ **c)**$−\frac{1}{6}, 1$ **d)**$−6, 12$ **e)**$\frac{1}{2}, −\frac{1}{3}$ **f)**5, no y-intercept **g)**no x-intercept, $−6$ **h)**$\frac{1}{3}, \frac{1}{4}$ **i)**$\frac{1}{3}, −1$ **j)**$\frac{1}{2}, −\frac{1}{3}$
6.a)$\{y \, \epsilon \, R| − 15 \leq y \leq −6\}$ **b)**$\{y \, \epsilon \, R| −5 \leq y \leq −3\}$ **c)** $\{y \, \epsilon \, R| \frac{1}{3} \leq y \leq \frac{4}{3}\}$ **d)**$\{y \, \epsilon \, R| −\frac{29}{2} \leq y \leq −\frac{11}{2}\}$ **7.a)**1 **b)**$−2$ **c)**$−17$ **d)**4 **8.**$−\frac{1}{2}$ **9.**4 **10.**6 **11.**2
13.a)$3, \frac{3}{2}$ **b)**$−2, 4$ **c)**$2, −6$ **d)**$4, 8$ **e)**$−2, 6$ **f)**$\frac{5}{3}, −5$

5.2 Exercise, page 161
1.Satisfy (a), (d) **2.**on the graph (a), (c), (d), (f) **3.a)**A, B **b)**A, C **c)**B, C **4.a)**$−3$ **b)**$−6$ **5.a)**3 **b)**7 **c)**4 **d)**10 **e)**$−11$ **f)**5 **6.**A, C **7.**slope 3, parallel **8.**same y-intercept **9.**pass through (0, 5) **10.**slope 2 **11.a)**3, 9 **b)**6, −4 **c)**5, 3 **d)**9, −3 **e)**4, −4 **f)**$\frac{1}{3}, −\frac{1}{2}$ **g)**$\frac{3}{2}, −3$ **h)**$\frac{3}{2}, −1$
12.a)$\{y \, \epsilon \, R| −3 \leq y \leq 3\}$ **b)**$\{y \, \epsilon \, R| −9 \leq y \leq −3\}$ **c)**$\{y \, \epsilon \, R| −11 \leq y \leq 21\}$ **d)**$\{y \, \epsilon \, R| −11 \leq y \leq −5\}$

5.3 Exercise, page 163
1.Arnold, Hazel **2.**Cherokee, Starcraft **3.**Golden, Calgary, Banff **4.**Red Deer, Calgary **5.a)**$(4, 3)$ **b)**$(-6, -3)$ **c)**$(-3, 2)$ **6.a)**$(3, 2)$ **b)**$(-3, 4)$ **c)**$(-1, -1)$ **d)**$(4, -3)$ **e)**$(-6, -2)$ **f)**$(-1, 4)$ **7.a)**$(-1, 6)$ **b)**$(2, 3)$ **c)**$(2, 3)$ **d)**$(-3, 5)$ **e)**$(m, t) = (3, 4)$ **f)**$(3, -2)$ **8.**$A(-3, 3)$, $B(3, 2)$, $C(2, -2)$, $D(-5, 1)$ **9.**$(2, 3)$ **10.a)**$(3, 2)$ **b)**tugboat **c)**cruiser **11.**$(-1, 6)$ **12.**I (b) (e); II (a) (c) (f); III (d)

5.4 Exercise, page 167
1.b)same solution of $(3, -2)$ **2.b)**same solution **3.a)**P, S **b)**P, S **c)**Q: $(-2, -3)$ R: $(3, 2)$ **4.**$x + 5y = 11$, $3x + 2y = -6$; $3x + 2y = -6$, $3x - 2y = -18$ **5.a)**$x + 2y = -5$, $x = 3$; $x + 2y = -5$, $y = -4$; $x = 3$, $y = -4$ **b)**$x = 3$, $y = -4$ **6.c)**coincide **8.d)**same intersection $(2, 1)$ **9.**same intersection $(-4, 3)$ **10.a)**$2x + y = 5$ **b)**$3x - y = -5$ **c)**$3x - y = -16$ **11.a)**add equations **b)**subtract equations **c)**add equations

5.5 Exercise, page 170
1.b)more than one solution **2.b)**do not intersect, no solution **4.a)**inconsistent **b)**consistent, independent **c)**consistent, dependent **d)**inconsistent **e)**consistent, independent **f)**consistent, dependent

5.6 Exercise, page 173
1.a)$y = -3x + 4$ **b)**$y = -5x + 8$ **c)**$y = 3x + 8$ **d)**$y = 2x - 6$ **e)**$y = 2x - 4$ **f)**$y = -3x + 4$ **g)**$y = -2x + 7$ **h)**$y = 2x + 5$ **i)**$y = \frac{4}{3}x$

2.a)$x = -3y + 8$ **b)**$x = 2y + 6$ **c)**$x = -y + 5$ **3.a)**$x = 1$, $y = 1$ **4.a)**$x = 3$, $y = -1$ **b)**$x = -2$, $y = 5$ **c)**$a = -2$, $b = 0$ **d)**$a = -4$, $b = -3$ **e)**$m = 1$, $n = 3$ **f)**$a = -1$, $b = -2$ **5.b)**$x = 0$, $y = 1$ **6.a)**$x = -3$, $y = 1$ **b)**$x = 2$, $y = 1$ **c)**$x = 1$, $y = 0$ **d)**$x = 4$, $y = 0$ **7.a)**$x = -1$, $y = 3$ **b)**$x = 3$, $y = -7$ **c)**$x = 0$, $y = -1$ **8.b)**$x = 4$, $y = -4$

5.7 Exercise, page 174
a)$n = 2m - 6$ **b)**$x = 3y - 8$ **c)**$b = 4a - 6$ **d)**$y = 3x + 8$ **e)**$x = 3y - 8$ **f)**$b = -5a + 8$ **g)**$m = -\frac{3}{2}n + \frac{5}{2}$ **h)**$y = -\frac{4}{3}x$ **2.a)**$a = \frac{1}{2}$, $b = \frac{3}{2}$ **3.a)**$m = 1$, $n = 0$ **b)**$x = -1$, $y = -1$ **c)**$m = 3$, $n = 0$ **d)**$m = 1$, $n = 0$ **e)**$x = 1$, $y = -1$ **f)**$a = -1$, $b = 1$ **4.a)**$(1, 0)$ **b)**$(-1, 1)$ **c)**$(-3, 2)$ **5.a)**$x = 1$, $y = -3$ **b)**$x = 1$, $y = -3$ **6.a)**$a = 3$, $b = -1$ **b)**$x = -1$, $y = 3$ **c)**$a = -1$, $b = -3$ **d)**$x = \frac{2}{3}$, $y = 7$ **e)**$x = -2$, $y = 3$ **f)**$m = 1$, $n = -1$ **7.a)**$x = -3$, $y = 0$ **b)**$x = 6$, $y = 1$ **c)**$a = 3$, $b = 4$ **d)**$a = 3$, $b = 6$ **e)**$m = 3$, $n = -2$ **8.a)**$x = 6$, $y = 5$ **b)**$(6, 5)$ **9.**$(2, 3)$ **10.**$(3, 4)$ **11.**$(-1, 1)$ **12.a)**$(2, 3)$ **b)**$(-4, -3)$

5.8 Exercise, page 179
1.a)multiply by 2 **b)**multiply by 3 **c)**multiply by $\frac{1}{2}$ **d)**multiply by -2 **e)**multiply by -3 **2.a)**$2 \times$ ① 2,

5.3 Exercise (cont.)
b)$3 \times$ ② **3.a)**y **b)**$x = -2$, $y = -3$ **4.a)**a **b)**$a = 0$, $b = -2$ **5.a)**$m = -1$, $n = 1$ **b)**$x = 2$, $y = 0$ **c)**$a = -3$, $b = -2$ **d)**$p = 4$, $q = -2$ **e)**$x = -3$, $y = -3$ **f)**$m = 5$, $n = -1$ **6.a)**$x = -1$, $y = 3$ **b)**$m = 4$, $n = 2$ **c)**$a = -3$, $b = 0$ **7.a)**$a = 2$, $b = 1$ **b)**$m = 3$, $n = 0$ **c)**$p = 1$, $q = 1$ **d)**$a = 1$, $b = 3$ **e)**$m = -\frac{3}{2}$, $n = 2$ **f)**$p = 0$, $q = 0$ **g)**$x = 1$, $y = 2$ **h)**$x = 9$, $y = 1$ **i)**$x = 2$, $y = \frac{1}{2}$ **8.b)**$x = 4$, $y = -3$ **9.b)**$a = 2$, $b = -3$ **10.a)**$a = 4$, $b = -6$ **b)**$x = 1$, $y = 8$ **c)**$x = 3$, $y = 1$ **d)**$x = 2$, $y = -1$ **e)**$a = 8$, $b = 1$ **f)**$m = 2$, $n = -1$ **11.**$(-8, 3)$ **12.a)**$(2, 3)$ **b)**$(3, -2)$ **c)**$(2, 6)$ **d)**$(2, 3)$ **e)** $\left(2, -\frac{1}{2}\right)$ **f)** $\left(-2, \frac{1}{2}\right)$ **13.**$P(-5, 3)$, $Q(3, 6)$, $R(5, -2)$

5.9 Exercise, page 182
2.b)$x = 5$, $y = 3$ **3.b)**$x = -2$, $y = 3$ **4.a)**$x = -6$, $y = 1$ **b)**$x = 2$, $y = -7$ **c)**$x = -3$, $y = -2$ **d)**$x = \frac{7}{12}$, $y = -\frac{1}{3}$ **5.a)**$x = -3$, $y = 0$ **6.a)**$x = 0$, $y = -\frac{1}{3}$ **b)**$x = -7$, $y = -3$ **7.b)**$x = 1$, $y = 2$ **8.a)**$x = -1$, $y = 4$ **b)**$x = \frac{7}{4}$, $y = \frac{1}{11}$ **9.a)**$x = \frac{2}{5}$, $y = \frac{3}{5}$ **b)**$x = \frac{1}{4}$, $y = -\frac{1}{5}$ **10.a)**$A = 3$, $B = -4$, $C = 8$, $D = 1$, $E = 5$, $F = 8$ **c)**$x = 3$, $y = 1$ **11.a)**$x = -2$, $y = 3$ **b)**$x = 2.5$, $y = -2.3$ (to 1 decimal place); exact answer $x = \frac{5}{2}$, $y = -\frac{7}{3}$ **c)**$x = -3$, $y = 1$ **d)**$x = 2$, $y = 0.75$ **e)**$x = 3$, $y = 3$ **f)**$x = 4$, $y = 8$ **12.a)**$x = \frac{5a - 6}{ab + 6}$, $y = \frac{-2(b + 5)}{ab + 6}$ **b)**$x = \frac{bf - ed}{bc - ad}$, $y = \frac{ce - af}{ad - bc}$ **13.**$x = 3$, $y = 2$

5.10 Exercise, page 186
1.a)60 **b)**$10t$ **c)**$20m$ **d)**$25k + 50$ **e)**$10t + 25k$ **f)**$25s + 10t$ **g)**$5a + 25b$ **h)**$d + 25e$ **2.a)**$0.08s + 0.09y$ **b)**$0.15k + 0.10y$ **c)**$0.10y + 0.12m + 0.02$ **3.a)**$14y$ km **b)**$12m$ km **c)**$\frac{3}{2}x$ km **4.a)**$b + 3f = 160$ **b)**$0.09m - 0.12n = 190$ **c)**$2w + \frac{1}{2}l = 126$ **d)**$40y + 65x = 480$ **5.**236 girls, 184 boys **6.**39, 14 **7.**Alex \$700, Sam \$1300 **8.**950 **9.**18 \$1-bills, 6 \$2-bills **10.**pike 3500, salmon 5500 **11.**\$1.69 **12.**220 kg **13.**40 \$10-bills, 36 \$5-bills **14.**30 quarters, 40 nickels

5.11 Exercise, page 189
1.a)$0.502 (r + p)$ **b)**regular 4000 L, premium 6000 L **2.a)**$a + b$, $0.8(a + b)$ **b)**A 100 kg, B 50 kg **3.**\$1400 at 9%, \$400 at 6% **4.**\$4000 at 10%, \$6000 at 11% **5.**regular 600 L, premium 400 L **6.**4% on \$2900, 5% on \$1300 **7.** 14-k gold 0.8 kg; 6-k gold 2.4 kg **8.** 3.5 kg **9.** 18-k gold 7.5 g; 11-k gold 10 g **10.**216 kg **11.a)**21 g **b)**10.5 g

5.12 Exercise, page 192

1.b)240 L of 50% solution; 60 L of 30% solution
2.b)11 L 3.20 kg of 20% mix, 80 kg of 40% mix
4.4 L 5.$83\frac{1}{3}$ mL 6.$3\frac{1}{3}$ mL 7.60 kg of $2.20/kg
mixture; 40 kg of $2.40/kg mixture 8.300 mL
9.125 g of 50% alloy, 375 g of 70% alloy

5.13 Exercise, page 194

1.b)Grant 5.0 m/s; John 4.8 m/s 2.b)Train x
137 km/h; Train y 113 km/h 3.110 km/h, 120 km/h
4.9 m/s, 11 m/s 5.20 km/h, 21 km/h 6.17.5 km/h
7.helicopter 140 km/h; wind 20 km/h 8.plane
365 km/h; wind 35 km/h 9.canoeist 13.5 km/h;
current 3.5 km/h 10.kayak 23 km/h; current 17 km/h

5.14 Exercise, page 197

1.a)(600, 400) 2.a)(90, 50 000) b)$0 < n < 90$;
$n > 90$ c)$88 500 3.a)Demand > Supply
b)Supply > Demand

CHAPTER 6

6.1 Exercise, page 203

All variables represent real numbers.
1.a)$\{-2 \leq x \leq 4\}$ b)$\{-1 \leq y \leq 5\}$ 2.a)$\{-6 \leq x \leq 2\}$
b)$\{-3 \leq y \leq 1\}$ 3.a)(i) {2, 3, 4, 5} (ii) {3, 4, 5, 6}
b)(i) {3, 4} (ii){1, 5, 6, 8} c)(i){6, 7, 8} (ii){0, 1}
d)(i){0, 1, 2, 3} (ii){2, 4, 6, 8} e)(i) {−1, 0, 1}
(ii) {3, 4, 5, 6} f)(i) {2, 4, 6} (ii) {−1, −2, −3}
4.a){−1, 0, 1, 2}; {−2, −1, 0} 5.b){0, 1, 2, 3};
{1, 2, 3, 4} 6.a)(0, −1), (1, 2), (2, 5), (3, 8), (4, 11)
b){−1, 2, 5, 8, 11}

6.2 Exercise, page 207

All variables represent real numbers.
1.a)$x \, \epsilon \, R$ b)$\{y \leq 3\}$ c)yes 2.a)$\{-4 \leq x \leq 0\}$
b)$\{-4 \leq y \leq 4\}$ c)no d)x-axis e)y-axis
3.a)yes; $\{-3 \leq x \leq 3\}$; $\{0 \leq y \leq \ \}$ b)yes; $x \, \epsilon \, R$; $y \, \epsilon \, R$
c)no; {1, 2, 3, 4}; {1, 2, 3, 4}
d)no; {−3, −2, −1, 0, 1}; {−1, 0, 1, 2, 3} e)no;
$\{-2 \leq x \leq 0\}$; $\{-2 \leq y \leq 2\}$ f)yes; $\{-2 \leq x \leq 2\}$,
$\{0 \leq y \leq 2\}$ g)yes; $\{-4 \leq x \leq 3\}$; $\{3 \leq y \leq 5\}$ h)no;
$\{-2 \leq x \leq 1\}$; $\{-3 \leq y \leq 5\}$ i)yes; $\{-5 \leq x \leq 2\}$;
$\{-2 \leq y \leq 3\}$ 4.a){−5, −6, −7, −8}; {5, 6, 7, 8}; not
a function b){1, 2, 3, 4, 5}; {−2, −3, −5}; function
c){2, 4, 6, 8}; {1, 3, 5, 7}; function 5.a)no b)yes c)no
d)yes 6.a)$y \, \epsilon \, R$ b)no 8.a){−5, −2, 1, 10} b){5, 3, 1, −5}
c){4, 1, 0, 9} d){1, −2, −3, 6} e) $\left\{-\frac{1}{2}, \, -1, \, \frac{1}{3}\right\}$

f) $\left\{-\frac{1}{7}, \, -\frac{1}{4}, \, -1, \, \frac{1}{8}\right\}$ 9.b)$x \, \epsilon \, R$; $\{y \geq 1, y \, \epsilon \, R\}$ c)yes
10.b)$\{x \, \epsilon \, R, x \neq 0\}$; $\{y \, \epsilon \, R, y \neq 0\}$ c)yes
11.b)$\{x \geq -3, x \, \epsilon \, R\}$; $y \, \epsilon \, R$ c)no

6.3 Exercise, page 211

1.a)5 b)3 c)11 2.a)14 b)50 c)5 3.a)0 b)3 c)8 d)0
e)15 f)$\frac{5}{4}$ 4.a)8, −17 b)9, 11 c)7, 7 5.a)$\frac{1}{2}$ b)$-\frac{1}{2}$ c)$\frac{1}{2}$
6.a)−1 b)−3 c)−2 d)$-\frac{1}{2}$ e)$-\frac{11}{2}$ 7.a)5 b)7 c)20 d)49
e)−10 f)17 g)50 h)199 8.a)0 b)42 c)12 d)30 e)54
f)−30 9.a)−5 b)17 c)12 d)3 e)1 f)4 g)−21 h)$\frac{7}{2}$
10.a)30 b)225 c)225 11.a)5 b)2 c)$\frac{8}{3}$ 12.a)−1 b)3
c)12 13.a)3 b)−1 14.−5 15.−1 17.$-\frac{1}{4}$

6.6 Exercise, page 221

1.a)many-to-one b)one-to-many c)one-to-many d)one-to-one 2.(a), (b) (d) 3.yes; no; yes 4.a)0 b)0
5.(a), (b), (c), (f), (g), (h)

6.7 Exercise, page 224

1.a)increasing b)decreasing c)increasing
2.a)$-\frac{7}{2} \leq x \leq 1$ b)$3 \leq x \leq 4$ c)$-5.5 \leq x \leq 3.5$,
$1 \leq x \leq 3$, $4 \leq x \leq 6$ 3.a)A: $-3 \leq x \leq 0$,
$3 \leq x \leq 6$ B: $-6 \leq x \leq -3$, $0 \leq x \leq 3$
b)A: $-2 \leq x \leq 2$, $6 \leq x \leq 8$ B: $-4 \leq x \leq -2$,
$2 \leq x \leq 6$ 4.a)$x \, \epsilon \, R$; $y \geq -1$ b)x-intercepts 1, 3;
y-intercept 3 d)$x \geq 2$ 5.a)$-6 \leq x \leq 0$, $6 \leq x \leq 9$
b)$0 \leq x \leq 6$ c)$-10 \leq x \leq -6$ 6.a)increasing for
all x b)decreasing $x \leq 0$; increasing $x \geq 0$ c)decreasing
$x \geq 0$; increasing $x \leq 0$ d)increasing for all $x \geq 0$
e)increasing for all x, $|x| \geq 1$ f)decreasing for all x,
$x \neq 0$ 12.a)9 b)increases by 9 13.a)$2x + 1$
b)changes by 2 14.a)10 b)6 c)f 15.a)$6x + 3$ b)$4x + 2$
c)f 16.a)f b)f c)f

6.8 Exercise, page 228

1.a)(1, 4) b)(2, −3) c)(−5, −4) d)(−3, 6) e)(4, 0)
f)(0, −5) 2.a)yes b)no c)no 3.f^{-1}, h^{-1}
4.a)A: {−3, −2, −1, 0, 1, 2, 3}, {0, 1, 2, 3, 4};
inverse {0, 1, 2, 3, 4}, {−3, −2, −1, 0, 1, 2, 3}
b)A: {−5, −4, −3, −2, −1, 0, 1, 2}, {1, 2, 3};
inverse {1, 2, 3}, {−5, −4, −3 −2, −1, 0, 1, 2}
c)A: {−3, −2, −1, 0, 1, 2, 3}, {−1, 0, 1};
inverse {−1, 0, 1}, {−3, −2, −1, 0, 1, 2, 3}
5.a)f: $\{x \, \epsilon \, R, x \geq 0\}$, $\{y \, \epsilon \, R, y \geq 0\}$
f^{-1}: $\{x \, \epsilon \, R|, x \geq 0\}$, $\{y \, \epsilon \, R|y \geq 0\}$, both functions
b)f: $\{x \, \epsilon \, R| x \leq 0\}$ $\{y \, \epsilon \, R|0 \leq y\}$; f^{-1}: $\{x \, \epsilon \, R|0 \leq x\}$,
$\{y \, \epsilon \, R|y \leq 0\}$; both functions c)$f$: $\{x \, \epsilon \, R|-3 \leq x \leq 3\}$,
$\{y \, \epsilon \, R| 0 \leq y \leq 3\}$; f^{-1}: $\{x \, \epsilon \, R|0 \leq x \leq 3\}$, $\{y \, \epsilon \, R|$
$-3 \leq y \leq 3\}$; f is a function, f^{-1} is not 6.a)B: f and
f^{-1} are functions C: f: $\{x \, \epsilon \, R|0 \leq x \leq 2\}$,
$\{y \, \epsilon \, R|0 \leq y \leq 2\}$; f^{-1}: $\{x \, \epsilon \, R|0 \leq x \leq 2\}$
$\{y \, \epsilon \, R| 0 \leq y \leq 2\}$ b)B: f, f^{-1} are functions C:
f, f^{-1}: $\{x \, \epsilon \, R| x \geq 0\}$, $\{y \, \epsilon \, R|y \geq 0\}$ c)B: f, f^{-1} are

functions C: $\{x \in R | x \leq 0\}$, $\{y \in R | y \leq 0\}$ **d)**B: f, f^{-1} are functions C: $f: \{x \in R | -5 \leq x \leq 0\}$, $\{y \in R | 0 \leq y \leq 4\}$; $f^{-1}: \{x \in R | 0 \leq x \leq 4\}$, $\{y \in R | -5 \leq y \leq 0\}$ **e)**B: f is a function, f^{-1} is not a function C:

$f: \left\{x \in R | -\dfrac{3}{2} \leq x \leq \dfrac{3}{2}\right\}$, $\{y \in R | 0 \leq y \leq 2\}$;

$f^{-1}: \{x \in R | 0 \leq x \leq 2\}$, $\left\{y \in R | -\dfrac{3}{2} \leq y \leq \dfrac{3}{2}\right\}$ **f)**B: f

is not a function, f^{-1} is a function C: $f: \{x \in R | 0 \leq x \leq 2.5\}$, $\{y \in R | -2.5 \leq y \leq 2.5\}$; $f^{-1}: \{x \in R | -2.5 \leq x \leq 2.5\}$, $\{y \in R | 0 \leq y \leq 2.5\}$ **7.**(c) **8.**(a) (b) **9.**C **10.**B

6.9 Exercise, page 232

1.b)$y = 2x + 3$, $y = \dfrac{x-3}{2}$ **c)**$f^{-1}: x \to \dfrac{x-3}{2}$

2.(b) **3.b)**$y = 2x^2 - 1$ **c)**$x = 2y^2 - 1$ **4.**(a)

5.a)$f^{-1}(x) = \dfrac{3-x}{2}$, $x \in R$, $y \in R$ **b)**$f^{-1}(x) = \sqrt{\dfrac{x}{3}}$;

$x \geq 0$, $x \in R$; $y \geq 0$, $y \in R$ **c)**$f^{-1}(x) = \dfrac{1}{2x}$; $x \in R$,

$x \neq 0$; $y \in R$, $y \neq 0$ **d)**$f^{-1}(x) = \sqrt[3]{2x}$; $x \in R$, $y \in R$
6.a)$y = 2x + 4$; f: x-intercept 4, y-intercept -2; f^{-1}:

x-intercept -2, y-intercept 4 **b)**$y = \sqrt[3]{4 - \dfrac{x}{2}}$;

g: x-intercept $\sqrt[3]{4}$, y-intercept 8; g^{-1}: x-intercept 8,

y-intercept $\sqrt[3]{4}$ **c)**$y = \dfrac{x^2 + 1}{2}$; h: x-intercept $\dfrac{1}{2}$,

y-intercept does not exist; h^{-1}: x-intercept does not

exist, y-intercept $\dfrac{1}{2}$ **d)**$y = \dfrac{1}{1-x}$; f: x-intercept 1,

y-intercept does not exist; f^{-1}: x-intercept does not

exist, y-intercept 1 **7.b)**f: x-intercept $\sqrt{3}$, y-intercept

-3; f^{-1}: x-intercept -3, y-intercept $\sqrt{3}$ **c)**f: $\{x \in R |$ $x \geq 0\}$, $\{y \in R | y \geq -3\}$; f^{-1}: $\{x \in R | x \geq -3\}$,

$\{y \in R | y \geq 0\}$ **d)**$y = \sqrt{x+3}$ **9.a)**$y = \dfrac{1}{3}(x + 2)$, $x \in R$,

$y \in R$ **b)**$y = \dfrac{1}{2}(x^2 + 1)$, $x \geq 0$ $x \in R$, $\left\{y \in R | y \geq \dfrac{1}{2}\right\}$

c)$y = \sqrt{x+3}$, $\{x \in R | x \geq -3\}$, $\{y \in R | y \geq 0\}$
d)$x = 2 - y^2$, $y \leq 0$, $\{x \in R | x \leq 2\}$, $\{y \in R | y \leq 0\}$
e)$x = \sqrt{9 - y^2}$, $y \geq 0$, $\{x \in R | -3 \leq x \leq 3\}$,

$\{y \in R | 0 \leq y \leq 3\}$ **f)**$y = \dfrac{1}{x+1}$, $\{x \in R | x \neq -1\}$,

$\{y \in R | y \neq 0\}$ **10.a)**no restrictions, $f^{-1}: x \to \dfrac{x+7}{2}$

b)no restrictions, $y = \dfrac{4x + 2}{3}$ **c)**no restrictions,

$f^{-1}(x) = \dfrac{x+6}{3}$ **d)**$x \geq 0$, $f^{-1}: x \to \pm \sqrt{x}$ **e)**no

restrictions, $y = \sqrt[3]{x}$ **f)**$y \geq 0$, $y = x^2$ **g)**$x \geq 1$,

$f^{-1}(x) = \pm\sqrt{x} + 1$ **h)**$x \geq 0$, $y = \pm \sqrt{\dfrac{x+3}{2}}$ **i)**$x \geq 0$,

$f^{-1}: x \to \dfrac{x^2}{4} + 3$ **j)**$x \geq 3$, $f^{-1}: x \to \sqrt{\dfrac{x-2}{2}} + 3$

11.a)$x \geq 0$ or $x \leq 0$ **b)**$x \geq 0$ **c)**$x \geq 0, y \geq 0$ or $x \geq 0, y \leq 0$ or $x \leq 0, y \geq 0$ or $x \leq 0, y \leq 0$ **d)**$x \geq 0, y \geq 0$

CHAPTER 7

7.1 Exercise, page 240

1.(a), (c) **2.a)**$\{x | x \in R\}$, $\{y \in R | y \geq -4\}$ **b)**$(4, -4)$
c)$x = 4$ **d)**$x = 2$ and $x = 6$ **e)**2 and 6 **f)**minimum
point **g)**opens upwards **3.a)**$\{x | x \in R\}$, $\{y \in R | y \leq 3\}$,
$(0, 3)$, $x = 0$, maximum value 3 **b)**$\{x | x \in R\}$,
$\{y \in R | y \geq 3\}$, $(0, 3)$, $x = 0$, minimum value 3
c)$\{x | x \in R\}$, $\{y \in R | y \geq -5\}$, $(4, -5)$, $x = 4$,
minimum value -5 **d)**$\{x | x \in R\}$, $\{y \in R | y \leq -3\}$,
$(-3, -3)$, $x = -3$, maximum value -3 **e)**$\{x | x \in R\}$,
$\{y \in R | y \leq 3\}$, $(2, 3)$, $x = 2$, maximum value 3
f)$\{x | x \in R\}$, $\{y \in R | y \geq -2\}$, $(-3, -2)$, $x = -3$,
minimum value -2 **4.a)**$y = 3x^2 - 6x + 3$

b)$y = 2x^2 + 4x + 2$ **c)**$y = -2x^2 + 12x - \dfrac{58}{3}$

d)$y = \dfrac{1}{2}x^2 - 4x + 13$ **5.a)**B **b)**A **c)**B **d)**A, B

e)neither **6.b)**A minimum point; B maximum point
c)A **7.a)**U **b)**D **c)**U **8.b)**$(0, -3)$ **c)**minimum point
$(0, -3)$ **9.b)**$\{x | x \in R\}$, $\{y \in R | y \geq 2\}$, $(0, 2)$, $x = 0$
10.b)minimum value -3 **c)**$(0, -3)$ **11.a)**A, C
b)$x = 0$ **c)**$(-1, 1)$, $(2, 7)$ **12.a)**1.8 m **b)**1.1 m
13. 1.2 s **14.** 3 s **15.** 8 min 20 s **16.**3 s **17.a)**5.9 m **b)**yes

7.2 Exercise, page 244

1.b)12.5 m **2.a)**8 m **b)**8 m **3.a)**12 m **b)**12 m
c)12.5 m **d)**10.5 m **4.** 4 s **5.b)**80 m **c)**55 m **6.b)**1.5,
-0.9 **7.b)**3.2, -2.7 **8.**-0.5, -1.2

7.3 Exercise, page 245

1.b)$y = 2x^2$ **c)**$y = -2x^2$ **2.a)**P, R **c)**4, -4 **d)**4, -4
e)opens upwards **3.a)**A, B **c)**$x = 0$ **d)**$(0, -2)$
e)upwards **4.b)**$y = x^2 - 3$ **c)**$y = -x^2 + 3$ **5.f)**same
vertex, same axis of symmetry, open upwards
6.g)same vertex, same axis of symmetry, all open
downwards **7.a)**upwards **b)**downwards **c)**minimum
point **d)**maximum point 8 **e)**$(0, 0)$, $(0, -1)$, $(0, 1)$
f)$x = 0$ **9.e)**$(0, 0)$, $(0, -1)$, $(0, 1)$ **f)**$x = 0$ **12.b)**-5
c)$x = 3$ **d)**$(3, -5)$ **13.b)**4 **c)**$x = -2$ **d)**$(-2, 4)$

7.4 Exercise, page 248

12.b)3, -1 **13.b)**3 **c)**-1, -3 **14.a)**A, D open
upwards; B, C open downwards **b)**A: minimum point
$(1, -3)$; B: maximum point $(-4, -1)$; C: maximum
point $(-3, 2)$; D: minimum point $(2, -5)$

7.5 Exercise, page 251

All variables represent real numbers.
1.a)$(0, 3)$, $x = 0$ **b)**$(0, -8)$, $x = 0$ **c)**$(-1, 3)$,
$x = -1$ **d)**$(1, -8)$, $x = 1$ **e)**$(3, -6)$, $x = 3$

f)$(3, 8)$, $x = 3$ **g)**$(1, -7.2)$, $x = 1$ **h)**$(-1, -3.6)$, $x = -1$ **2.a)**upwards, $\{y|y \geq -3\}$ **b)**downwards, $\{y|y \leq 6\}$ **c)**downwards, $\left\{y|y \leq -\dfrac{1}{2}\right\}$ **d)**upwards, $\{y|y \geq 5\}$ **e)**upwards, $\{y|y \geq -0.5\}$ **f)**downwards, $\{y|y \leq 1.6\}$ **3.a)**$(1, 6)$ **b)**$x = 1$

6.a)$y = -3(x + 2)^2 + 3$ **b)**$y = -2(x - 6)^2 + 3$ **c)**$y = 2(x + 3)^2 - 2$ **d)**$y = -10x^2 - 3$

e)$y = \dfrac{1}{2}(x + 8)^2 - \dfrac{1}{2}$ **f)**$y = -\dfrac{3}{2}(x - 3)^2 - 4$

g)$y = 0.5(x - 4)^2 - 3$ **h)**$y = -1.5(x - 6)^2 - 2$
7.a)1 **b)**minimum value 6 **c)**$y = (x - 2)^2 + 6$
8.a)-1 **b)**maximum value 5 **c)**$y = -(x - 3)^2 + 5$
9.a)$a = 2$, $b = 3$ **b)**$(0, 3)$ **10.a)**$y = -2x^2 + 1$
b)parabola, opens downwards, axis of symmetry $x = 0$, vertex $(0, 1)$ **11.a)**$y = 3(x - 2)^2 + 5$
b)parabola, opens upwards, axis of symmetry $x = 2$, vertex $(2, 5)$ **12.**$y = \dfrac{11}{4}x^2$ **13.**$a = -1$, $b = 6$

14.a)$a = -\dfrac{5}{2}$, $q = 1$ **b)**$f(x) = -\dfrac{5}{2}(x - 1)^2 + 1$

7.6 Exercise, page 255

1.a)4 **b)**4 **c)**9 **d)**16 **e)**$\dfrac{25}{4}$ **f)**$\dfrac{9}{4}$ **g)**2 **h)**3 **i)**$\dfrac{25}{8}$ **j)**$\dfrac{25}{2}$

k)$\dfrac{25}{2}$ **l)**$\dfrac{27}{8}$ **2.a)**1 **b)**16 **c)**9 **d)**25 **e)**$\dfrac{9}{4}$ **f)**$\dfrac{81}{4}$ **g)**$\dfrac{121}{4}$

h)$\dfrac{25}{4}$ **i)**$\dfrac{25}{16}$ **3.a)**$p = -2$, $q = -4$ **b)**$p = 3$, $q = -9$

c)$p = \dfrac{9}{2}$, $q = -\dfrac{81}{4}$ **d)**$p = -\dfrac{5}{2}$, $q = -\dfrac{25}{4}$

4.a)$a = 2$, $p = -2$, $q = -4$ **b)**$a = -3$, $p = -2$,
$q = 17$ **c)**$a = \dfrac{1}{2}$, $p = 3$, $q = \dfrac{1}{2}$ **d)**$a = -1$,

$p = -3$, $q = 13$ **e)**$a = -2$, $p = 1$, $q = 0$
5.a)$y = (x + 3)^2 - 9$ **b)**$y = (x + 3)^2 - 13$

c)$y = 2\left(x - \dfrac{3}{4}\right)^2 + \dfrac{31}{8}$ **d)**$y = -\left(x + \dfrac{3}{2}\right)^2 + \dfrac{41}{4}$

e)$y = -2(x - 2)^2 + 13$ **f)**$y = -3\left(x + \dfrac{1}{2}\right)^2 + \dfrac{63}{4}$

g)$y = 4\left(x - \dfrac{5}{4}\right)^2 - \dfrac{37}{4}$ **h)**$y = \dfrac{2}{3}\left(x - \dfrac{9}{4}\right)^2 + \dfrac{45}{8}$

6.a)$x = 1$; $(1, -2)$; -2, minimum **b)**$x = -1$;
$(-1, 5)$; 5, maximum **c)**$x = 1$; $\left(1, -\dfrac{3}{2}\right)$; $-\dfrac{3}{2}$,

minimum **d)**$x = -2$; $(-2, 6)$; 6, maximum **e)**$x = 3$;
$(3, 0)$; 0, maximum **f)**$x = -5$; $\left(-5, -\dfrac{3}{2}\right)$; $-\dfrac{3}{2}$,

minimum **7.a)**$y = (x - 1)^2 - 4$ **b)**$x = 1$ **c)**$(1, -4)$
d)-4, minimum **e)**$\{y|y \geq -4\}$ **9.a)**$x = -2$,
$(-2, -1)$ **b)**$x = 3$, $(3, -4)$ **c)**$x = 1$, $(1, -4)$

d)$x = 1$, $(1, -1)$ **e)**$x = -2$, $(-2, 2)$ **f)**$x = 1$, $(1, -3)$

11.a) $\left(\dfrac{1}{6}, \dfrac{1}{12}\right)$ **b)**$x = \dfrac{1}{6}$ **12.a)**yes **b)**no **c)**yes **d)** $\left(\dfrac{1}{3}, \dfrac{2}{3}\right)$

e)$x = \dfrac{1}{3}$ **13.a)**yes at $(-5, 400)$ **b)** $\left(\dfrac{5}{3}, 0\right)$ **c)**$x = \dfrac{5}{3}$

7.7 Exercise, page 258

1.a)minimum $-\dfrac{5}{4}$ **b)**minimum 2 **c)**minimum -6

d)maximum $\dfrac{13}{12}$ **e)**minimum -1 **f)**maximum -2

g)minimum -1 **h)**maximum -4 **2.a)**$x = \dfrac{3}{2}$, $\left(\dfrac{3}{2}, -\dfrac{21}{4}\right)$

b)$x = \dfrac{3}{4}$, $\left(\dfrac{3}{4}, \dfrac{7}{8}\right)$ **c)**$x = \dfrac{1}{3}$, $\left(\dfrac{1}{3}, \dfrac{2}{3}\right)$ **d)**$x = -\dfrac{1}{6}$,

$\left(-\dfrac{1}{6}, \dfrac{61}{12}\right)$ **e)**$x = -1$, $(-1, -2)$ **f)**$x = 1$, $(1, 1)$

g)$x = 1$, $(1, 4)$ **h)**$x = 1$, $(1, 2)$

7.8 Exercise, page 259
1.a)parabola opens downwards

2.a)$y = -\dfrac{1}{25}(x + 3)^2 + 1$ **b)**$y = -x^2 + 4$

c)$y = \dfrac{1}{4}(x + 1)^2 - 3$ **d)**$y = \dfrac{7}{32}(x - 2)^2 - \dfrac{1}{2}$

e)$y = -\dfrac{7}{50}(x - 3)^2 - \dfrac{3}{2}$ **3.a)**$f(x) = -5(x + 3)^2 + 5$

4.a)$y = -\dfrac{1}{32}(x - 3)^2 - \dfrac{1}{2}$ **5.a)**$y = \dfrac{1}{2}(x - 3)^2 - 2$

6.a)$y = -\dfrac{4}{9}(x - 4)^2 + 4$ **b)**$y = 3(x + 5)^2 - 3$

c)$y = -\dfrac{3}{16}(x + 4)^2$ **d)**$y = (x - 3)^2 - 4$

8.$y = -\dfrac{8}{25}(x - 5)^2 + 8$ **9.**$y = -0.004(x - 100)^2 + 40$
10.$y = -0.19(x - 10)^2 + 19$ **11.**$y = 0.0889(x - 15)^2 - 20$
12.$y = -0.025(x - 20)^2 + 10$

7.9 Exercise, page 263

1.a)$-\dfrac{3}{2}$ minimum **b)**$\dfrac{12}{5}$ maximum **c)**-25 maximum

d)16 minimum **2.a)**$\dfrac{40}{3}$ **b)**$\dfrac{2}{3}$ **3.a)**$\dfrac{31}{8}$ **b)**$\dfrac{3}{4}$ **4.a)**1 **b)**$\dfrac{3}{4}$

5.a)$\dfrac{3}{4}$ **b)**1 **6.**$\dfrac{7}{2}$, $-\dfrac{7}{2}$ **7.**$\dfrac{13}{2}$, $-\dfrac{13}{2}$ **8.**$x = 7$, $y = 21$

9.$y = 28.9$, $x = 5.7$ **10.a)**6.5 m **b)**3 s **11.a)**32 m
b)4 s **12.** 9 km by 18 km **13.** 7.5 m by 15 m **14.** 900 m^2
15. 11.0 m **16.** 45.1 m **17.** 10.9 m **18.a)**about 42 m
b)2.9 s **19.**1.5 s **20.**8.0 s

7.10 Exercise, page 268

1.a)$f^{-1}(x) = \pm\sqrt{\dfrac{x}{9}}$ **b)**$f^{-1}(x) = \pm\sqrt{\dfrac{x - 6}{3}}$

c)$f^{-1}(x) = \pm\sqrt{x+1} - 1$ **d)**$f^{-1}(x) = 2 \pm \sqrt{\dfrac{5-x}{3}}$

2.b)f: domain $\{x \in R | x \geq 0\}$, range $\{y \in R | y \geq -8\}$
f^{-1}: domain $\{x \in R | x \geq -8\}$, range $\{y \in R | y \geq 0\}$
4.b)$y = \pm\sqrt{x+16}$ **c)**no **5.b)**$y = \pm\sqrt{25-x}$ **c)**no

7.11 Exercise, page 270

3.b)A, C **4.b)**Region R **9.a)**$y > x^2 - 4x + 2$

b)$y < -x^2 - 6x - 7$ **c)**$y \leq \dfrac{1}{3}x^2 + 2x + 1$

d)$y \geq -2x^2 + 8x - 5$ **e)**$y \geq 2x^2 - 4x + 3$

f)$y > -\dfrac{1}{2}x^2 - 2x + 3$

7.12 Exercise, page 273

1.a)minimum 5, $x = 3$ **b)**maximum -25, $x = 2$
c)minimum 6, $a = 2$ **d)**maximum 8, $m = 3$
e)maximum 16, $m = 4$ **f)**minimum -3, $y = 2$

g)minimum -16, $d = \dfrac{2}{3}$ **h)**minimum $-\dfrac{8}{3}$, $a = 9$

2.a)minimum 3, $x = -3$ **b)**minimum $\dfrac{119}{32}$, $m = \dfrac{3}{16}$

c)minimum 5, $m = 1$ **d)**maximum $\dfrac{129}{4}$, $a = -\dfrac{9}{2}$

e)maximum $\dfrac{137}{8}$, $a = -\dfrac{3}{4}$ **f)**minimum $-\dfrac{4}{3}$, $m = \dfrac{2}{3}$

g)minimum $-\dfrac{67}{8}$, $y = \dfrac{1}{4}$ **h)**maximum 25, $m = 3$

i)maximum $\dfrac{521}{32}$, $y = \dfrac{3}{8}$ **3.a)**minimum $-\dfrac{4}{3}$, $x = \dfrac{2}{3}$

b)maximum $\dfrac{49}{3}$, $x = -\dfrac{1}{3}$ **c)**minimum 4, $t = 1$

d)maximum $\dfrac{69}{5}$, $t = \dfrac{3}{5}$ **e)**maximum 66, $m = -5$

f)minimum $\dfrac{5}{4}$, $y = \dfrac{3}{2}$ **4.a)**$y = 28 - 2x$ **b)**$x(28 - 2x)$

c)$x = 7$, $y = 14$ **5.**$x = 8$, $y = 32$ **6.** $\dfrac{3}{2}$, $-\dfrac{3}{2}$ **7.** $-\dfrac{7}{2}$, $\dfrac{9}{2}$

8.$x = 31.6$, $y = 142.1$ **9.** $\dfrac{9}{2}$, $-\dfrac{9}{2}$ **10.** 30, 30 **11.** 22, 22

12. 2500 m^2 **13.** 20 000 m^2 **14.** 6 m^2 **15.** 60.5, 60.5
16. 12 km by 24 km by 12 km **18.** $3.50 **19.** $1.50
20. $49.50 **21.** $6.20 **22.** $54.00 **23.** $97.00

7.13 Exercise, page 277

1.$\dfrac{1}{2}$ **2.** $\dfrac{25}{2}$, $\dfrac{25}{2}$ **3.** $\dfrac{25}{2}$, $-\dfrac{25}{2}$ **4.** $\dfrac{11}{2}$, $-\dfrac{11}{2}$ **5.** $\dfrac{29}{2}$, $\dfrac{29}{2}$
6.10, 10 **7.**8, 8 **8.**15, 16, 17 **9.**$a = 150$, $b = 75$
10.$25 each **11.**225 m by 150 m **12.a)**1406.25 m^2
b)150 **13.a)**5 m or 40 m **b)**30 times or 60 times
14.a)maximum 79 **b)**(20, 79) **15.a)**162 cm^2
b)base 18 cm, height 18 cm **16.**125 m by 125 m
17. 20 m **18.** 19.2 m **19.** 9 m

CHAPTER 8

8.1 Exercise, page 285
1.a)$(x - 2)(x - 6)$ **b)**$(x - 3)(x + 2)$
c)$(a - 2)(a + 7)$ **d)**$(2b + 1)(b + 3)$
e)$(3p + 4)(p - 5)$ **f)**$(3y - 1)(2y + 1)$
2.a)$(x - 3)(x - 5)$ **b)**$(x + 2)(x - 4)$
c)$(x + 9)(x - 6)$ **d)**$(3x + 1)(x + 2)$
e)$(2m + 1)(m - 7)$ **f)**$(8x - 7)(x + 1)$ **3.a)**0, 6

b)-2, -7 **4.a)**1, -3 **b)**4, $-\dfrac{1}{2}$ **c)**2, $-\dfrac{1}{3}$ **d)**$\dfrac{1}{4}$, $\dfrac{6}{7}$

e)$\dfrac{1}{3}$, -4 **f)**$\dfrac{1}{2}$, $\dfrac{1}{3}$ **g)**$\dfrac{3}{4}$, $\dfrac{1}{2}$ **h)**$-\dfrac{2}{3}$, $\dfrac{2}{5}$ **5.a)**2, -6

b)3, -8 **c)**$\dfrac{2}{3}$, $-\dfrac{1}{2}$ **d)**$-\dfrac{2}{5}$, $-\dfrac{4}{3}$ **e)**4, $-\dfrac{3}{2}$ **f)**1, $-\dfrac{1}{2}$

g)$\dfrac{1}{2}$, 0 **h)**2, 0 **6.**(a) (d) (e) **7.a)**3, -7 **b)**5, 2

c)3, $-\dfrac{5}{2}$ **d)**$\dfrac{1}{3}$, $-\dfrac{7}{2}$ **e)**$\dfrac{2}{3}$, $\dfrac{1}{2}$ **f)**$\dfrac{6}{5}$, 0 **8.a)**4, 1 **b)**4, 1

9.a)$\dfrac{1}{2}$, -4 **b)**$\dfrac{1}{2}$, -4 **10.a)**3, -2 **b)**5, -8 **c)**-2, 3

d)3, $-\dfrac{1}{2}$ **e)** $-\dfrac{5}{4}$, $\dfrac{3}{2}$ **f)**-7, $\dfrac{3}{2}$ **11.a)**x-intercepts $\dfrac{5}{2}$, -2,

y-intercept -10 **b)**x-intercepts 3, $-\dfrac{1}{2}$, y-intercept -3

c)x-intercepts -5, $-\dfrac{3}{2}$, y-intercept 15

d)x-intercepts $\dfrac{3}{2}$, $-\dfrac{2}{3}$, y-intercept -6 **12.**(a) and(f);

(b) and (d); (c) and (e) **13.a)**$x^2 + 6x - 27 = 0$

b)3, -9 **14.a)**$\dfrac{4}{3}$, $-\dfrac{1}{2}$ **b)**3, 3 **c)**4, -2 **d)**4, $-\dfrac{3}{2}$

e)-1, -7 **f)**$\dfrac{1}{2}$, $\dfrac{1}{2}$ **g)**-4, -5 **15.a)**$\dfrac{4}{3}$, -1 **b)**$\dfrac{9}{2}$, $-\dfrac{1}{3}$

c)$-\dfrac{1}{4}$, $\dfrac{3}{2}$ **d)**7, 3 **e)**3, -2 **f)**1, $\dfrac{5}{2}$ **16.a)**2, -3

b)2, -3 **17.a)**10, -3 **b)**4, 1 **c)**1, $-\dfrac{1}{5}$ **18.a)**$x \neq 3$,

$x \neq -2$ **b)**$-\dfrac{3}{4}$, 2 **19.a)**3, -1; $x \neq -\dfrac{2}{3}$ **b)**$\dfrac{1}{3}$, 2;

$x \neq 0$ **c)**2, $-\dfrac{3}{7}$; $x \neq \pm 1$ **20.a)**4, -3 **b)**4, -3

c)(4, 0), (-3, 0) **d)**4, -3 **21.a)**$\dfrac{1}{2}$, -2 **b)**$\dfrac{1}{2}$, -2

c) $\left(\dfrac{1}{2}, 0\right)$, ($-2$, 0) **d)**$\dfrac{1}{2}$, -2 **22.a)**3, -5 **b)**3, 0

c)5, $-\dfrac{1}{2}$ **23.a)**5, -8 **b)**$-\dfrac{1}{2}$, $\dfrac{4}{3}$ **c)**0, 4 **24.**(a) and (d)

25.a)(-3, 0), (-5, 0) **b)**(-8, 0), (8, 0)
c)(0, 0), (1, 0)

8.2 Exercise, page 290

1.a)3, −2 b)5, −3 c)7, 3 d)$\frac{1}{2}$, −1 e)$\frac{4}{3}$, 1 f)3, $\frac{5}{2}$

2.a)1 ± $\sqrt{3}$ b)2 ± $\sqrt{5}$ c)1, −3 d)$\frac{2 \pm \sqrt{5}}{3}$ e)$\frac{2 \pm \sqrt{6}}{4}$

f)$\frac{4 \pm 3\sqrt{10}}{12}$ 4.a)5 ± $\sqrt{21}$ 5.a)$\frac{3 \pm \sqrt{5}}{2}$ b)$\frac{5 \pm \sqrt{17}}{4}$

c)$-\frac{1}{2}$, 2 d)$\frac{-5 \pm 3\sqrt{5}}{2}$ 6.a)$\frac{-5 \pm \sqrt{37}}{2}$ b)3, −5

c)$\frac{1}{3}$, −3 d)$\frac{-4 \pm \sqrt{14}}{2}$ e)$\frac{2}{3}$, 5 f)$\frac{1}{6}$, −1 7.a)$\frac{3 \pm \sqrt{5}}{2}$

b)x-intercepts 8.a)−4 ± $\sqrt{13}$ 9.$\left(\frac{2}{5}, 0\right)$, (−1, 0)

10.a)$\frac{5}{2}$, −1 11.a)1 ± $\sqrt{7}$ b)−3, 1 c)$\frac{5 \pm \sqrt{33}}{4}$

d)$\frac{-1 \pm \sqrt{37}}{6}$ 12.a)8, 6 b)10, 4 c)9, 5 13.a)8 b)15

c)30 14.a)$k = 2 + \sqrt{19}$ or $2 - \sqrt{19}$ b)$\frac{4}{3}$, −1

c)3, −1 16.a)−1 ± $\sqrt{1-c}$ b)$\frac{-b \pm \sqrt{b^2 + 12}}{2}$

c)$\frac{-2 \pm \sqrt{4-a}}{a}$ d)$\frac{-b \pm \sqrt{b^2 - 4c}}{2}$

8.3 Exercise, page 294
1.a)−4.5, 1.5 b)0.5, 5.7 c)−2.1, 6 2.a)0.4, 2.6
b)0.4, 2.6 3.a)5.3, −1.3 4.a)2 + $\sqrt{11}$, 2 − $\sqrt{11}$

b)5.3, −1.3 5.b)1.1, −3.1 c)$\frac{-2 \pm 3\sqrt{2}}{2}$ d)1.12,

−3.12 6.a)−0.4, −5.6 b)−3 ± $\sqrt{7}$ c)−5.6, −0.4

7.a)2.7, −0.2 b)$\frac{5 \pm \sqrt{33}}{4}$ c)2.69, −0.19

8.a)−0.21, − 4.79 b)5.41, 0.09 c)1.63, −1.63
9.(−0.13, 0), (−3.87, 0) 10.a)5.16, −1.16
b)1.70, −4.70 c)1.18, −0.43 11.a)5.1 s, 0.5 s
b)41.2 m 12. 86 m/s

8.4 Exercise, page 297
1.a)$a = 3$, $b = -2$, $c = -7$ b)$a = 2$, $b = -6$,
$c = 11$ c)$a = 4$, $b = 5$, $c = 1$ d)$a = -3$, $b = -1$,
$c = -10$ e)$a = 2$, $b = 0$, $c = -11$ f)$a = 3$,
$b = 8$, $c = 0$ 2.a)$a = 2$, $b = -3$, $c = -2$
b)$a = 1$, $b = -4$, $c = -2$ c)$a = 3$, $b = -4$,
$c = 2$ d)$a = 2$, $b = -5$, $c = -1$ e)$a = 2$,
$b = -3$, $c = -1$ f)$a = 3$, $b = -2$, $c = -5$
3.a)$2x^2 + 8x - 4 = 0$, $a = 2$, $b = 8$, $c = -4$
b)$x^2 - 8x + 6 = 0$, $a = 1$, $b = -8$, $c = 6$
c)$2x^2 - 2x - 3$, $a = 2$, $b = -2$, $c = -3$
d)$2x^2 + 2x = 0$, $a = 2$, $b = 2$, $c = 0$
e)$2x^2 - 7x + 4 = 0$, $a = 2$, $b = -7$, $c = 4$
f)$2x^2 - 6x + 1 = 0$, $a = 2$, $b = -6$, $c = 1$

4.a)1, $\frac{2}{3}$ 5.a)3, 2 b)$\frac{1}{2}$, $-\frac{1}{3}$ c)3, −3 d)0, 6

6.a)$\frac{-5 \pm \sqrt{41}}{4}$ 7.a)2 ± $\sqrt{5}$

8.a)1, −4 b)3, −4 c)2, −1.5 d)3, $-\frac{5}{3}$

9.a)$\frac{-3 \pm \sqrt{7}}{2}$ b)you know x-intercepts 10.a)$\frac{7 \pm \sqrt{37}}{6}$

b)$\frac{9 \pm \sqrt{65}}{4}$ c)$\frac{-5 \pm \sqrt{41}}{4}$ 11.a)2, $-\frac{1}{2}$ b)1, $-\frac{3}{4}$

c)$\frac{-3 \pm \sqrt{7}}{2}$ 12.a)2 ± $\sqrt{5}$ b)$\frac{-5 \pm \sqrt{17}}{2}$ c)$\frac{7 \pm \sqrt{57}}{2}$

d)$\frac{3}{2}$, −1 e)$\frac{-7 \pm \sqrt{41}}{4}$ f)$\frac{3 \pm \sqrt{19}}{5}$ 13.a)$\frac{-3 \pm \sqrt{89}}{8}$

b)$\frac{3 \pm \sqrt{41}}{8}$ c)4 ± $\sqrt{22}$ d)$\frac{-3 \pm \sqrt{137}}{8}$ e)$\frac{2 \pm \sqrt{22}}{3}$

f)$\frac{3 \pm \sqrt{17}}{4}$ g) $-\frac{4}{3}$, 1 14.a)$\frac{-3a + \sqrt{9a^2 + 8}}{4}$

b)$\frac{-1 \pm \sqrt{1-3a}}{2a}$ c)$\frac{2 - 3m^2}{8m}$ d)$-a \pm \sqrt{a^2 + b^2}$

e)$\frac{1}{2}$, $-\frac{1}{m}$

8.5 Exercise, page 300
1.a)5.7, 2.3 b)5.73, 2.27 2.a)2 ± $\sqrt{5}$ b)4.2, −0.2
3.a)$\frac{-1 \pm \sqrt{13}}{2}$ b)1.30, −2.30 4.a)$\frac{-1 \pm \sqrt{5}}{4}$

b)0.31, −0.81 5.a)$\frac{1 \pm \sqrt{7}}{3}$ b)1.22, −0.55

6.a)(i)−0.4, −2.6 (ii)−0.38, −2.62 7.a)3.4, −0.4;
3.44, −0.44 8.a)0.6, −3.6 b)2.8, −1.8 c)2.3, 0.2
d)0.8, −1.6 e)0.7, −0.4 f)−0.4, −0.8
10.a)$a^2 - 6a - 3 = 0$, 6.5, −0.5 b)$k^2 - k - 1 = 0$,
1.6, −0.6 c)$4t^2 - 9t - 6 = 0$, 2.8, −0.5
d)$13x^2 - 2x - 1 = 0$, 0.4, −0.2 e)$6n^2 - 4n - 5 = 0$,
1.3, −0.6 f)$4a^2 + 16a - 11 = 0$, 0.6, −4.6
11.12.6 cm 12.5.4 cm 13.20 m 14.a)450 m b)29.0 km/h
15.a)6.8 m b)45 km/h

8.6 Exercise, page 304
1.a)$n^2 + (n + 4)^2 = 208$ b)− 12, 8 d)8 and 12;
−8 and −12 2.24.1 cm 3.10 cm, 24 cm, 26 cm
4.Ordinary 70 km/h, super 90 km/h 5.14 and 15;
−14 and −15 6.base 8 cm, height 24 cm 7.5 m
8.7 m 9.30 cm, 40 cm 10.10 cm 11.3.3 m
12.a)Mark 4 km/h, Tina 4.8 km b)Mark 15 h,
Tina 13 h 13.30 cm by 50 cm

8.7 Exercise, page 306
1.d)first day 80 km/h, second day 70 km/h 2.house
12 m by 12 m, garage 6 m by 6 m 3.a)John 4 km/h,
Petra 4.5 km/h b)John 45 min, Petra 40 min 4.1,3,5
or 3, 5, 7 5.6 cm by 6 cm, 4 cm by 4 cm 6.6 h
7.100 m 8.8 guitars per month 9.8.8 cm

8.8 Exercise, page 309

1.a)(i)49 (ii)100 (iii)25 (iv)121 **b)**real, unequal, rational **2.a)**(i)17 (ii)33 (iii)41 (iv)8 **b)**real, unequal, irrational **3.a)**(i)0 (ii)0(iii)0 (iv)0 **b)**real, equal, rational **4.a)**(i) -32 (ii) -19 (iii) -71 (iv) -12 **b)**not real, unequal **5.a)**real, unequal, rational **b)**real, unequal, irrational **c)**unreal, unequal **d)**real, unequal, irrational **e)**real, equal, rational **f)**real, unequal, rational **g)**real, unequal, rational **h)**unreal, unequal **i)**real, unequal, irrational **j)**real, unequal, rational **6.a)**28; real, unequal, irrational **b)**3 $\pm \sqrt{7}$ **7.a)**21; real, unequal, irrational **b)**16; real, unequal, rational **c)**16; real, unequal, rational **d)**44; real, unequal, irrational **e)** -80; unreal, unequal **f)**520; real, unequal, irrational **8.a)** $2k \pm k\sqrt{2}$ **b)**1, $-\dfrac{1}{k}$ **9.a)**0

b) $9k^2 - 8k$ **c)**0 **d)** $k^2 + 4k + 4$ **10.a)**real, unequal, irrational **b)**real, unequal, irrational **c)**unreal, unequal **d)**real, unequal, irrational **11.a)**real, unequal, irrational **b)**real, unequal, irrational **c)**unreal, unequal

d)unreal, unequal **12.a)** $\dfrac{1}{4}$ **b)**16, 4 **13.a)** $k < \dfrac{3}{8}$

b) $k < -4$ or $k > 4$ **14.a)** $k > \dfrac{25}{24}$ **b)** $k > 1$

15.a) $m > -\dfrac{1}{4}$ **b)** $m < \dfrac{9}{16}$ **16.**All $k \in R$ **17.**All $k \in R$

18. $p = -\dfrac{1}{4}$ **23.**0 **24.** $a^2c^2 + 10abc + b^2 = 0$

8.9 Exercise, page 314

1.a) $-\dfrac{5}{3}$, $-\dfrac{2}{3}$ **b)**B **2.a)**yes **b)**yes **c)**no **d)**yes

3.a) -5, 2 **b)** -6, 9 **c)** $-\dfrac{2}{3}$, $-\dfrac{7}{3}$ **d)** $\dfrac{3}{5}$, $-\dfrac{1}{5}$ **e)** $-\dfrac{19}{11}$,

$-\dfrac{7}{11}$ **f)** $-\dfrac{\sqrt{6}}{2\pi}$, $-\dfrac{4}{\pi}$ **g)** $\dfrac{11}{3}$, 3 **h)** $-\dfrac{3}{2}$, 0 **4.a)** $\dfrac{2e}{d}$, $-\dfrac{3f}{d}$

b) $\dfrac{3g}{4p}$, $\dfrac{5}{4p}$ **5.a)** $x^2 - 12x + 27 = 0$ **b)** $x^2 - 9 = 0$

c) $16x^2 + 8x - 3 = 0$ **d)** $3x^2 - 10x + 3 = 0$
e) $x^2 - 6x + 6 = 0$ **6.a)** $9x^2 - x - 3 = 0$

b) $\dfrac{(1 \pm \sqrt{109})}{18}$ **7.a)** -8 **b)**2 **8.a)** -3 **b)** -10 **c)** -2 **d)**3

e) $\dfrac{1}{3}$ **9.a)** -6 **b)**3 $+ \sqrt{3}$ **10.** -2 **11.**12 **12.**16

13.a) -1.2 **b)** $\dfrac{1}{4}$ **c)** $\pm\dfrac{\sqrt{10}}{5}$ **d)**24 **e)** -3 **f)** $\dfrac{4}{3}$ **14.a)** $-\dfrac{1}{2}$

b) -3 **c)**1 **15.a)** $a = -c$ **16.** $3q^2 = 16pr$ **17.** $\dfrac{13}{4}$

CHAPTER 9

9.1 Exercise, page 321

1.a)4 **b)**8 **c)**5 **d)**5 **e)** $2\sqrt{2}$ **f)** $2\sqrt{5}$ **g)** $\sqrt{85}$ **h)** $\sqrt{113}$

2.a)10 **b)** $\sqrt{65}$ **c)** $\dfrac{5}{4}$ **d)**2 **e)**1 **3.a)**10 **b)** $\sqrt{10}$ **c)** $\sqrt{146}$

d) $2\sqrt{26}$ **e)** $\sqrt{65}$ **f)**20 **4.a)** $\sqrt{13}$ **b)** $\sqrt{13}$ **c)** $\sqrt{13}$ **d)**all the same **5.a)**12 **b)**36 **c)**60 **d)**56 **6.a)**5 $+ \sqrt{13} + 2\sqrt{10}$ **b)**Scalene **7.a)**AB = CD = $4\sqrt{10}$, AD = BC = $2\sqrt{10}$ **b)**AC = $10\sqrt{2}$ **8.** 29 **9.** yes, PC = QC **10.** (4, 0) **11.** 10 **13.** yes **15.** Plane A **16.** Boat B **17.a)** $15\sqrt{2}$ **b)** $12\sqrt{2}$ **18.**Campsite A **19.**Yes, fly to airport

9.2 Exercise, page 326

1.a)internal **b)**external **c)**internal **d)**external **2.a)**2:4 or 1:2 internally **b)**2:7, internally **c)**6:4 or 3:2 externally **d)**9:3 or 3:1 externally **e)**3:4, internally **f)**3:7, externally **g)**2:9, externally **h)**4:6 or 2:3 externally **i)**7:3, externally **j)**9:7, externally **k)**3:6 or 1:2 internally **l)**6:3 or 2:1 internally **3.a)**5:3 **b)**2:3 **c)**3:2 **d)**5:2 **4.a)**1:12 **b)**2:7 **c)**11:3 **d)**14:11 **e)**7:7 or 1:1 **f)**4:3 **5.a)**N **b)**P **c)**M **d)**N **e)**M **f)**R **6.**10 cm, 18 cm **7.**17.5 cm, 7.5 cm **8.**32 cm, 12 cm **9.**16.8 m, 11.2 m **10.**40 cm, 24 cm **11.**20 cm, 12 cm, 32 cm **12.a)**4:1:2.5 **b)**48 cm, 12 cm, 30 cm **13.a)**4:2 or 2:1 **b)**5:6 **c)**1:1 **d)**6:4 or 3:2 **14.a)**5:2 **b)**5:7 **15.a)**3:10 **b)**3:7 **c)**7:10 **16.a)**4:7 **b)**4:3 **c)**3:7 **17.**RP = 14 cm, PQ = 10 cm, QR = 6 cm

9.3 Exercise, page 330

1.a) $\left(6, 5\dfrac{1}{2}\right)$ **b)** $(-8, 3)$ **c)** $\left(9\dfrac{1}{2}, -13\right)$ **d)** $(26, 11)$

e) $(0, 8)$ **f)** $(10, 9)$ **2.**Internally, 1:3 **3.a)**AC:CB = $-5:4$; C divides AB externally in the ratio 5:4

4. $\left(-2, \dfrac{11}{2}\right)$ **5.** $\left(2, 3\dfrac{1}{5}\right)$ **6.a)** $-7:10$ **b)**A divides CB externally in the ratio 7:10 **7.**(1, 2) **8.** $\left(\dfrac{4}{5}, \dfrac{1}{5}\right)$ **9.**3:2

10. $m = 6$, $n = 0$ **11.** $p = -1$, $q = -7$ **12.** $(-4, 5)$, (0, 2) **13.a)**P(6, 10), Q $\left(9\dfrac{1}{2}, 7\right)$, R $\left(5\dfrac{1}{2}, 5\right)$

b)T $\left(7, 7\dfrac{1}{3}\right)$ **c)**2:1, 2:1

9.4 Exercise, page 333

1.AB: $\left(6\dfrac{1}{2}, 5\right)$, CD: $\left(4, -\dfrac{1}{2}\right)$, EF: $\left(7\dfrac{1}{2}, 2\right)$,

GH: $\left(-2, -1\dfrac{1}{2}\right)$, IJ: $\left(1\dfrac{1}{2}, -4\right)$, KL: $\left(-7\dfrac{1}{2}, -\dfrac{1}{2}\right)$,

MN = $\left(-11, \dfrac{1}{2}\right)$ **2.a)**(4, 6) **b)** $(-7, 6)$ **c)** $(-1, -4)$

d)(1, 1) **e)** $\left(1, 1\dfrac{1}{2}\right)$ **f)**(0, 0) **g)** $\left(\dfrac{a}{2}, \dfrac{b}{2}\right)$ **h)** $(a, 2b)$

3. $(-3, 1)$ **4.** $\left(-8, \dfrac{1}{2}\right)$ **6.** $(10, -9)$ **7.** $x = 3$, $y = 6$

8. $x = 8$, $y = 8$ **9.** $(-7, -6)$, $(-4, 4)$, $(-1, 14)$
10.A $(-8, 1)$, P(2, 3)

1.a)$x^2 + y^2 = 9$ b)$x^2 + y^2 = 3$ c)$x^2 + y^2 = 20$
d)$x^2 + y^2 = 4r^2$ 2.a)A:4, B:$5\sqrt{2}$ b)A:±4, B: $\pm5\sqrt{2}$
c)A: ±4, B: $\pm5\sqrt{2}$ d)A: $\{x|\ -4 \le x \le 4, x \in R\}$
B: $\{x|\ -5\sqrt{2} \le x \le 5\sqrt{2}, x \in R\}$ e)A: $\{y|\ -4 \le$
$y \le 4, y \in R\}$ B: $\{y|\ -5\sqrt{2} \le y \le 5\sqrt{2}, y \in R\}$
3.a)±8 b)±6 c)0 d)±10 e)$\pm5\sqrt{3}$ f)$\pm5\sqrt{2}$
4.(b), (e), (f) 5.a)$x^2 + y^2 = 36$ b)$x^2 + y^2 = 9$
c)$x^2 + y^2 = 25$ d)$x^2 + y^2 = 3$ 6.a)centre (0, 0);
domain $\{x|\ -2 \le x \le 2, x \in R\}$
range $\{y|\ -2 \le y \le 2, y \in R\}$; x-intercepts ±2;
y-intercepts ±2 b)centre (0, 0); domain
$\{x|\ -4 \le x \le 4, x \in R\}$; range $\{y|\ -4 \le y \le 4, y \in R\}$;
x-intercepts ±4; y-intercepts ±4 c)centre (0, 0);
domain $\{x|\ -10 \le x \le 10, x \in R\}$;
range $\{y|\ -10 \le y \le 10, y \in R\}$;

x-intercepts ±10; y-intercepts ±10 7.a)$x^2 + y^2 = \dfrac{1}{4}$

b)$x^2 + y^2 = \dfrac{1}{9}$ c)$x^2 + y^2 = 2$ 8.b)$\dfrac{1}{2}$

9.a)$x^2 + y^2 = 64$ b)$x^2 + y^2 = 25$ c)$x^2 + y^2 = 7$
d)$x^2 + y^2 = 25$ e)$x^2 + y^2 = 16$ 10.a)$\pm3\sqrt{3}$ b)$\pm\sqrt{30}$
11.a)$2\sqrt{13}$ b)diameter 12.$x^2 + y^2 = 40$ 13.2

9.6 Exercise, page 339
1.a)(0, 0), 7 b)(0, 3), 4 c)(3, 0), 7 d)(0, 2), 8
e)(5, −3), 4 f)(−4, 2), 10 2.a)$x^2 + y^2 = 4$
b)$x^2 + (y + 2)^2 = 25$ c)$(x - 4)^2 + y^2 = 9$
d)$(x - 3)^2 + (y - 2)^2 = \dfrac{4}{9}$ e)$(x - 5)^2 + (y + 3)^2 = 8$

f)$(x - h)^2 + (y - k)^2 = p^2$ 3.P, Q 4.N, S
5.−4 6.a)$x^2 + y^2 = 16$ b)$x^2 + y^2 - 6x + 4y = 13$
c)$x^2 + y^2 - 4x - 6y = 7$ 7.a)(0, 3), $2\sqrt{3}$
b)(5, 0), $\sqrt{26}$ c)(2, 1), 2 d)(−3, 4), $\sqrt{6}$ e)(3, −5),
$\sqrt{\dfrac{2}{3}}$ or $\dfrac{\sqrt{6}}{3}$ 8.a)$x^2 + y^2 - 8x + 6y + 5 = 0$
b)$x^2 + y^2 + 6x + 8y - 16 = 0$
9.$x^2 + y^2 - 8y - 9 = 0$
10.a)$x^2 + y^2 - 8x + 10y + 21 = 0$ b)(4 + 2√5, −5),
(4 − 2√5, −5) 11.$x^2 + y^2 - 4x - 4y - 18 = 0$

9.7 Exercise, page 343
1.a)(4, 3), (−4, −3) b)(−1, 3), (3, 1) 2.b)(8, 6),
(−8, −6) c)(8, 6), (−8, −6) 3.a)(0, 5), $\left(4\dfrac{4}{5}, 1\dfrac{2}{5}\right)$

4.a)(3, −1) b)The line is a tangent to the circle.

5.a)(4, 3), (−4, −3) b) $\left(\dfrac{3 + 3\sqrt{11}}{10}, \dfrac{-1 + 9\sqrt{11}}{10}\right)$,

$\left(\dfrac{3 - 3\sqrt{11}}{10}, \dfrac{-1 - 9\sqrt{11}}{10}\right)$ c) $\left(\dfrac{8 + \sqrt{29}}{5}, \dfrac{4 - 2\sqrt{29}}{5}\right)$

$\left(\dfrac{8 - \sqrt{29}}{5}, \dfrac{4 + 2\sqrt{29}}{5}\right)$

6.a)(−3, −1), (1, 3) b)(6, 2), (−2, −6)
c)(−9, −3), (3, −9) d) $\left(-1 + \dfrac{\sqrt{2}}{2}, \dfrac{\sqrt{2}}{2}\right)$,
$\left(-1 - \dfrac{\sqrt{2}}{2}, -\dfrac{\sqrt{2}}{2}\right)$ e)(−3, −3), (3, 3)
7.(1, −3), (3, 1) 8.a)(−8, 5), (1, 6) b)(−8, 5),
(1, 6) 9. $\left(\dfrac{-1 + 5\sqrt{649}}{26}, \dfrac{203 - \sqrt{649}}{26}\right)$,

$\left(\dfrac{-1 - 5\sqrt{649}}{26}, \dfrac{203 + \sqrt{649}}{26}\right)$ 10.a)P(−4, −3), Q(3, 4)

b)$7\sqrt{2}$ c) $\left(-\dfrac{1}{2}, \dfrac{1}{2}\right)$ d)90° e)$\dfrac{\sqrt{2}}{2}$ 11.$\dfrac{\sqrt{106}}{2}$

12.(−2.39, −4.39), (4.39, 2.39) 13.14 cm, 48 cm
14.2, −7 15.−5, −11 or 11, 5 16.5 m, 12 m
17.35 m by 35 m; 25 m by 25 m 18.a)$m^2(a^2 + 1) > b^2$
b)$m^2(a^2 + 1) = b^2$ c)$m^2(a^2 + 1) < b^2$

9.8 Exercise, page 346
1.b)M(4 − 2√2, 2√2 c)$y = (1 + \sqrt{2})x$ 2.b)$y = x$
3.a)(−1, −1) b)slope OM = 1, slope PQ = −1
5.b)not defined c)0 d)$y = 0$ e)(2, 0) f)(2, 0)

11.a)$y = -(x + 2)$ 13.b)$y = -\dfrac{1}{5}x$ c)$y = -\dfrac{3}{2}x$

d)(0, 0) 14.6.36 units (correct to 2 decimal places)

15.a)$x + 2y = 26$, $2x - 3y = 0$ b) $\left(\dfrac{78}{7}, \dfrac{52}{7}\right)$

9.9 Exercise, page 350

1.b)-2 c)$\dfrac{1}{2}$ d)$x - 2y = 10$ 2.b)$8x + 7y = -113$

3.$3x + 2y = -13$ 4.$8x - 9y = -145$ 5.b)$\dfrac{3}{4}$

c)$3x - 4y = 30$ 6.$9x + 10y = -193$
7.$3x + y = -24$ 8.a)$4x - 3y = -25$
b)$4x - y = 17$ c)$2x + y = 0$ d)$5x - y = 14$
e)$7x + y = 25$ f)$2x + 3y = -11$

g)$10x + 9y = 159$ h)$x - y = 3$ 10. $\dfrac{9\sqrt{5}}{5}$ 11.$2\sqrt{5}$

9.10 Exercise, page 353
3.a)$y = \dfrac{3}{4}x + \dfrac{5}{2}$, $y = \dfrac{3}{4}x - \dfrac{5}{2}$ 5.a)$y = x + 3 + 3\sqrt{2}$,

$y = x + 3 - 3\sqrt{2}$ b)$y = -8$, $y = \dfrac{40}{9}x - \dfrac{104}{3}$

6.$y = 3x + 4\sqrt{5}$, $y = 3x - 4\sqrt{5}$ 7.correct to 3
decimal places $y = -0.790x - 3$, $y = 1.306x - 3$
8.b)$x + 2y = -9$ 9.a)$\dfrac{24\sqrt{13}}{13}$

b)$(x + 3)^2 + (y - 4)^2 = \left(\dfrac{24\sqrt{13}}{13}\right)^2$ or
$13x^2 + 13y^2 + 78x - 104y - 251 = 0$
10.$y = \dfrac{-10x - 188}{9}$, $y = \dfrac{-10x + 174}{9}$

11.c)$x + 4y = 6$, $x + 4y = -28$

9.11 Exercise, page 356

1. $5\sqrt{3}$ **3.a)** $2\sqrt{3}$ **b)** $2\sqrt{21}$ **c)** $3\sqrt{2}$ **d)** $4\sqrt{3}$ **e)** $2\sqrt{3}$ **f)** $\sqrt{3}$
g) $2\sqrt{10}$ **h)** $2\sqrt{7}$ **i)** $\sqrt{43}$ **j)** $3\sqrt{2}$ **4.** $10\sqrt{3}$ **5.a)** $5x + y = 26$
b) $x - 5y = 26$ **c)** $(6, -4)$ **d)** $\sqrt{26}, \sqrt{26}$

6.a) $\left(-\dfrac{17}{3}, -2\right)$ **7.a)** $3x - 5y = -34$,

$3x + 5y = 34$, $x = 6$, $3x - 5y = 34$, $3x + 5y = -34$,
$x = -6$

9.12 Exercise, page 359

1.a) $\left(-\dfrac{11}{13}, -\dfrac{16}{13}, \dfrac{4}{13}\right)$ **2.a)** $(1, 2, 3)$ **b)** $(-1, 0, 3)$

c) $\left(-\dfrac{3}{2}, \dfrac{3}{4}, 1\right)$ **3.** $(-1, 2, 1, 3)$

CHAPTER 10

10.1 Exercise, page 366

Variables represent natural numbers. $n, k \in N$.
1.a) $3, 6, 9, 12$ **b)** $0, -1, -2, -3$ **c)** $2, 4, 8, 16$
d) $1, 3, 9, 27$ **e)** $2, 8, 18, 32$ **f)** $10, 20, 40, 80$

g) $5, 8, 11, 14$ **h)** $2, 5, 8, 11$ **i)** $3, 2, \dfrac{5}{3}, \dfrac{6}{4}$ **2.a)** $-1, 1,$

$3, 5$ **b)** $-2, 4, -8, 16$ **c)** $2, 1, \dfrac{2}{3}, \dfrac{1}{2}$ **d)** $1, 2, 4, 8$

e) $1, 3, 6, 10$ **f)** $\dfrac{2}{3}, \dfrac{2}{9}, \dfrac{2}{27}, \dfrac{2}{81}$ **g)** $\sqrt{2}, \sqrt{3}, 2, \sqrt{5}$

h) $1, 4, 9, 16$ **3.a)** $k - 1$ **b)** $3k + 1$ **c)** $2 - k$
d) $k^2 + 4k + 3$ **4.a)** $2, 4, 8, 16$ **b)** $3, 7, 13, 21$
c) $-2, -7, -14, -23$ **d)** $2, 7, 22, 67$ **5.a)** 11 **b)** -17
c) 2 **6.a)** 102 **b)** 64 **c)** 28 **d)** $1\ 358\ 381$ **8.a)** $9, 11, 13;$

$t_n = 2n - 1$ **b)** $-2, 0, 2; t_n = 2n - 12$ **c)** $\dfrac{4}{5}, -\dfrac{5}{6}, \dfrac{6}{7};$

$t_n = (-1)^n \dfrac{n}{n + 1}$ **9.a)** $47, 95, 191; t_1 = 2,$

$t_n = 2t_{n-1} + 1, n > 1$ **b)** $16, 32, 64; t_1 = 1,$
$t_n = 2t_{n-1}, n > 1$ **c)** $-1, 1, -1; t_1 = -1, t_n = -t_{n-1},$
$n > 1$ **10.a)** $t_n = 2(3^{n-1})$ **b)** $t_n = 3[2^{n+1} - n - 2]$
c) $t_n = 2^{2n-1}$ **d)** $t_n = 2^{n+2} - 3$ **11.a)** $t_1 = 5, t_n = t_{n-1} + 1,$
$n > 1$ **b)** $t_1 = 2, t_n = \dfrac{1}{t_{n-1}}, n > 1$ **c)** $t_1 = 2, t_n = (t_{n-1})^2 + 1,$

$n > 1$ **d)** $t_1 = 1, t_2 = 0, t_n = t_{n-1} - (-1)^{n-1}, n > 2$
e) $t_1 = 5, t_n = 2t_{n-1} + 1, n > 1$ **f)** $t_1 = 2,$
$t_n = -2t_{n-1} + 1, n > 1$ **12.a)** $10, 20, 40, 80, 160,$
$320, 640, 1280, 2560, 5120$ **b)** $t_n = 10(2^{n-1})$
c) $t_1 = 10, t_n = 2t_{n-1}, n > 1$ **13.a)** $1, r, r^2, r^3, r^4,$
$r^5,$ **b)** $t_n = r^{n-1}$ **c)** $t_1 = 1, t_n = r(t_{n-1}), n > 1$
14.a) $1, 2, 4, 8, 16, 32, 64, 128$ **b)** $t_n = 2^{n-1}$
c) $t_1 = 1, t_n = 2t_{n-1}, n > 1$ **15.a)** $-3, -1, 1, 3$
b) $t_n = 2n - 5$ **c)** $t_1 = -3, t_n = t_{n+1} + 2, n > 1$
d) 95 **16.a)** $3n + 1$ **b)** $9 - 2n$ **c)** $3n - 5$ **17.a)** The nth

triangular number, t_n, is given by $t_n = \dfrac{n(n + 1)}{2}$

b) $15, 55$ **18.a)** The nth square number, S_n, is given by

$S_n = n^2$ **b)** $S_1 = 1, S_n = t_n + t_{n-1}$, where t_n is the
n^{th} triangular number, $n > 1$ **19.b)** $t_n = 3n - 2$ **c)** $25,$

88 **20.b)** $t_n = \dfrac{n(n - 1)}{2}$ **c)** 55 **d)** 190 **21.a)** 2 **b)** 5 **c)** 8 **d)** 21

e) 34 **f)** 55 **22.a)** 5 **b)** 10 **c)** 13 **d)** 16 **e)** 19 **f)** 21 **23.a)** $t_1 = 1,$
$t_2 = 1, t_n = t_{n-1} + t_{n-2}, n > 2$ **24.b)** Fibonacci

10.2 Exercise, page 371

1.a) yes **b)** yes **c)** yes **d)** no **e)** yes **f)** yes **2.a)** 3 **b)** -4

c) 7 **d)** -2 **e)** $\dfrac{1}{6}$ **f)** -7 **3.a)** $13, 16$ **b)** $-2, -5$ **c)** $4, 7$

d) $2, 3$ **e)** $\dfrac{1}{2}, \dfrac{7}{12}$ **f)** $a + 6b, a + 8b$ **4.** (a), (b)

5.a) $11, 14; t_n = 3n - 1$ **b)** $1, -1; t_n = 9 - 2n$
c) $34, 40; t_n = 6n + 10$ **d)** $2\sqrt{2}, \sqrt{2}; t_n = 6\sqrt{2} - \sqrt{2}n$
e) $a + 6b, a + 8b; t_n = a + 2b(n - 1)$

f) $3x - 11, 3x - 14; t_n = 3x - 3n + 1$ **g)** $\dfrac{8}{x}, \dfrac{10}{x};$

$t_n = \dfrac{2n}{x}$ **6.a)** $8, 5, 2$ **b)** $\dfrac{1}{2}, \dfrac{1}{6}, -\dfrac{1}{6}$ **c)** $2m, 3m^2 - 1,$

$4m - 2$ **d)** $2, 6, 10$ **e)** $-2, 1, 4$ **7.a)** 1 **b)** 22 **c)** $3n + 1$
d) 3 **8.b)** arithmetic **9.a)** 35 **b)** -21 **c)** $x + 29y$ **d)** $153a$
10.a) $a = 2, d = 3; t_n = 3n - 1$ **b)** $a = 10,$
$d = -2; t_n = 12 - 2n$ **c)** $a = -8, d = 4;$

$t_n = 4n - 12$ **d)** $a = 8, d = \dfrac{-31}{7}; t_n = \dfrac{-31n + 87}{7}$

e) $a = 2, d = 6; t_n = 6n - 4$ **11.** $2, 6, 10;$
$t_n = 4n - 2$ **13.a)** $-4, -1, 2$ **b)** 113 **c)** 30 **d)** $3n - 10$
e) -3 **f)** 60 **14.a)** 3 **b)** $1,$ or 4 **15.a)** 10 **b)** 12 **c)** 15 **d)** 12
e) 10 **f)** 11 **16.a)** 1 **b)** 50th **17.a)** 15 **b)** -7 **18.** $9, 13, 17,$
$21, 25$ **19.** $2, 12$ **20.** $a = 2, x = 7, b = 12$ **21.** 7

10.3 Exercise, page 375

1. \$124.50 **2.** 40 m **3.** \$145 **4.** \$17.14 **5.** 3.974 billion
6. 310.4 m/s **7.** 175 m **8.** \$50 **9.** 17 years **10.** 7 years
11. 9 years **12.** \$35 000 **13.a)** 44.1 m **b)** 9.8 m **14.** \$22 000
15. \$2033.33 **16.a)** 60 km/h **b)** 9.8 **17.a)** 6424.30

b) $12\dfrac{1}{2}$ years **18.a)** 1100 **b)** 78 **19.** \$440 **20.** \$16 896

10.4 Exercise, page 378

1.a) yes, $r = 3$ **b)** no **c)** no **d)** no **e)** yes, $r = y^2$ **f)** yes,
$r = 2$ **g)** no **h)** yes, $r = 0.1$ **2.a)** geometric; 24, 48
b) arithmetic; 13, 15 **c)** geometric; 2, -2 **d)** geometric;

$\dfrac{1}{4}, \dfrac{1}{16}$ **e)** arithmetic; $-11, -13$ **f)** geometric; $-8, 16$

g) arithmetic; 2, $\dfrac{5}{2}$ **h)** geometric; $\dfrac{1}{2}, \dfrac{1}{4}$

i) geometric; $8m^4, 16m^5$ **j)** geometric; 1, 3
k) arithmetic; $7p, 9p$ **l)** geometric; $9, 9\sqrt{3}$ **3.a)** 32

b) 128 **c)** $t_n = 2^n$ **4.a)** 3 **b)** 48 **c)** $3(-2)^{2k-1}$ **d)** $-\dfrac{1}{2}$

5.a) 128 **b)** $\dfrac{2}{2187}$ **c)** $-\dfrac{32}{3}$ **d)** 2^{22} **e)** $\dfrac{p^{11}}{512q}$ **f)** $16\sqrt{3}$

6.a) 16 **b)** 1 **c)** $\dfrac{5}{2}$ **d)** ± 8 **e)** $\dfrac{1}{9}$ **f)** $\pm\sqrt{ab}$ **7.a)** $x = \dfrac{5}{3},$

$y = \dfrac{5}{9}$ **b)** $x = \dfrac{5}{2}, y = 5$ **c)** $x = 25, y = 62.5$

8.a)8th term b)8 9.a)8 b)7 c)10 d)8 e)7

10.a)$a = 2, r = \pm 3$ b)$a = 3, r = \frac{1}{2}$ 11.a)$\pm\frac{1}{3}$

b)32 c)-8 d)-9 12.12, 4, $\frac{4}{3}$ 13.10 240 14.5

15.2 or $-\frac{8}{3}$ 18.a)± 8 b)± 10 c)± 25 d)± 30 19.a)6,

12, 24 b)6, 12, 24, 48 20.10, 50, 250, 1250

21.2, 6, 18 23.a)geometric; 7 b)arithmetic; 16

c)geometric; 9 d)arithmetic; 21 e)arithmetic; 11

f)geometric; 8 24.a)4 or $-\frac{16}{7}$ b)$\frac{12}{7}$ 25.a)0 or $\frac{19}{3}$

b)-9 26.a)geometric b)2048 27.a)geometric

b)$t_n = (2x + 3y)\left(\frac{1}{4}\right)^{n-1}$ 28.a)geometric; $t_n = 2(4)^{n-1}$

b)neither c)geometric; $t_n = 2^{n-5}$

d)arithmetic; $t_n = 1 + 2n$ e)geometric; $t_n = (-1)^n$

3^{2-n} f)geometric; $t_n = 3^{3-n}$ 29.a)geometric,

2, ± 6, 18 or arithmetic 2, 42, 82 b)arithmetic, 22

c)arithmetic 2, 4, 6, 8 d)arithmetic, -8

10.5 Exercise, page 382
1.a)amount of sales after 2 years; $3 041 750

b)amount of sales after 5 years; $4 626 122

2.a)membership after 3 years; 488 members

b)membership after 8 years, 1490 members

3.a)$1200(1.10)$ b)$1200(1.10)^2$ 4.a)$200(0.6)^3$ metres

b)$200(0.6)^k$ metres 5.a)0.276 b)0.310 6.a)44 b)53

7.a)$6900(0.9) b)$6900(0.9)^3$ c)$6900(0.9)^5$

8. $3915.05 9. 331 224 10. 4096 11. $344.06

12. 10 000 13. $266.93 14. $2.53 15.$1 464 000

16.$327.19 17.1194 18.18 600 19.428 718

10.6 Exercise, page 387
1.a)$2 + 3 + 4 + 5 + 6$ b)$1 + 4 + 9 + 16 + 25$

c)$2 + 8 + 18 + 32$ d)$4 + 7 + 10 + 13 + 16$

e)$2 + 4 + 8 + 16 + 32$ 2.a)$2 + 5 + 8 + 11 + 14$

b)$4 + 16 + 64 + 256$ c)$\cos x + \cos 2x + \cos 3x +$

$\cos 4x + \cos 5x + \cos 6x$ 3.a)$t_n = n + 1$, $\sum_{j=1}^{6} (j + 1)$

b)$t_n = 3n - 1$, $\sum_{i=1}^{5} (3i - 1)$ c)$t_n = 4(2^{n-1})$, $\sum_{n=1}^{6} 4(2^{n-1})$

d)$t_n = 2^n$, $\sum_{m=1}^{5} 2^m$ 4.a) $\sum_{j=1}^{5} (j + 2)^2$ b) $\sum_{k=1}^{4} (k + 9)^3$

c) $\sum_{n=1}^{5} x_n$ d) $\sum_{n=1}^{9} 3y^{n+3}$ 5.a) $\sum_{r=1}^{7} 2(-1)^{r-1}$ b) $\sum_{i=1}^{7} 3(-2)^{i-1}$

c) $\sum_{j=1}^{7} -3(-2)^{j-1}$ d) $\sum_{r=1}^{12} ra^{r-1}$ e) $\sum_{p=1}^{12} p(-a)^{p-1}$

f) $\sum_{m=1}^{n} [a + (m - 1)d]$ g) $\sum_{b=1}^{n} ar^{b-1}$ 6.a)15 b)36 c)15

d)-1 e)0 f)34 7.a)3 b)220 c)$3 + 6 + 11 + \ldots$

$+ [(k - 2)^2 + 2] + [(k - 1)^2 + 2]$ d)$3 + 6 + 11 + \ldots$

$+ [m^2 + 2] + [(m + 1)^2 + 2]$ 8.a)13 b)4

c)9 d)$40\frac{1}{3}$ e)25 f)15 9.a) $\sum_{n=1}^{5} (n + 6)$ b) $\sum_{n=1}^{2} (2n + 1)$

15.a) $\sum_{k=1}^{5} (k^2 - 4k)$ b) $\sum_{k=1}^{6} (x^2 - 2kx + 1)$

c) $\sum_{n=1}^{5} (n^2 + 6n + 15)$ d) $\sum_{j=1}^{5} 9j$

e)$2 \sum_{k=1}^{n} (5k - 1)$ f)$2 \sum_{t=1}^{7} (2t - 1)$ 16.a)210 b)6375

c)20 900 d)131 550 e)375 750

10.7 Exercise, page 391
1.a)119 b)1240 2.a)50, 275 b)$-17, -35$ c)$-35, 325$

d)74, 380 3.a)325 b)1275 c)5050 d) $\frac{n(n + 1)}{2}$

4.a)528 b)235 c)-850 d)462 5.a)780 b)-40

c)-810 d)$210\sqrt{3}$ 6.a)780 b)209 c)-154 d) $\frac{55}{6}$

7.a)97, 990 b)$-82, -1155$ c)$32x + 29y, 525x + 435y$

8.a)144 b)-140 9.a)472 b)-285 c)108 d)-570

e)$231a + 210b$ f)63 10.a)670 b)910 c)138 11.a)14

b)18 c)52 12.a)95 b)390 13.155 14.91 15.117

16.a)$-7, -5, -3$ b)1166 17.a)$a = -11, d = 3$ b)410

18.a)$n = 7$ or 22 b)12 19.a)2080 b)2475

c)$6a^2 - 18ab + 6b^2$ 21.a)$-10, S_n = \frac{n(35 - 5n)}{4}$

b)1, 4, 7; $S_{20} = 590$ 22.$S_n = \frac{n^2}{2}(a + b) - \frac{n}{2}(7a - 3b)$

10.8 Exercise, page 394
1.174 2.92 3.28 4.5050 5.259 6.first plan 7.210

8.231 9.$2400 10.705.6 m 11.a)$660 b)$2540

12.$25 000

10.9 Exercise, page 397
1.a)80, $S_n = 3^n - 1$ b)$2\frac{26}{27}$, $S_n = 3 - 3^{1-n}$

c)15, $S_n = 16 + (-1)^{n+1} \cdot 2^{4-n}$ 2.a)$25\frac{5555}{7776}$ b)$11\frac{35}{128}$

3.a)765 b)215 c)$121\frac{1}{3}$ d)171 e)0.022 222 f)$15\sqrt{2} - 30$

4.a)126 b)$13\frac{121}{243}$ 5.a)$S_n = \frac{1}{2}(3 + (-3)^{n+1})$

b)$S_n = 54\left[1 - \left(\frac{2}{3}\right)^n\right]$ 6.a)$S_n = \frac{x^n - 1}{x - 1}$

b)$S_n = \frac{x^{2n+2} - x^2}{x^2 - 1}$ c)$S_n = \frac{y + (-y)^{n+1}}{y + 1}$

d)$S_n = \frac{3b[1 - (2b)^n]}{1 - 2b}$ 7.a)2555 b)$406\frac{15}{64}$ c)-510 8.$31\frac{31}{32}$

9.a)729 b)27 10.765 11.$-6\frac{7}{9}$ 12.a)-3, $t_n = 3(-1)^n(2)^{n-1}$

13.7 14.8 16.a)6 b)2 c)3072 d)6138 17.$r = \pm 2$ 18.$a = 5$,

$b = 10, c = 20$ 21.a)55 b)$20\frac{5}{8}$

22.a)$t_n = 2(3)^n$, $S_n = 3^{n+1} - 3$ **b)**$t_n = 4n - 3$,
$S_n = n(2n - 1)$ **c)**$t_n = (-1)^n (3^{n-1})$,
$S_n = \dfrac{(-3)^n - 1}{4}$ **d)**$t_n = 3^{n-4}$, $S_n = \dfrac{3^n - 1}{54}$

e)$t_n = 3n - 8$, $S_n = \dfrac{n}{2}(3n - 13)$

f)$t_n = 2(-1)^n (3^{3-n})$, $S_n = \dfrac{-27 - (-3)^{3-n}}{2}$

23.a)234 **b)**2186 **c)**$3\dfrac{127}{128}$ **d)**-22 **e)**18 **f)**1093

10.10 Exercise, page 400
1.a)0.5 m **b)**14.4 m **2.a)**$1 610 510 **b)**$15 937 400
3.a)$31 250 **b)**$1 984 375 **4.**454 km **5.**$25 575
6.$36 165.33 **7.**183 m **8.**3279 employees **9.**about 89.5
turns per second **10.**$\dfrac{211}{243}$ of the amount removed

11. After the 10th week $738 100 has been given away.
The prize for the 11th week is the remaining money,
namely $261 900. **12.**512 times **13.**2032 descendants

CHAPTER 11
Throughout Chapter 11, answers involving money are
expressed to the nearest cent, unless otherwise
indicated, and rates of interest are expressed to 2
decimal places, unless otherwise indicated. Answers
found using a calculator may vary in the last places of
the decimal.

11.1 Exercise, page 407
1.b)$884 **2.b)**$660 **3.a)**$558 **b)**$724.87 **c)**$273.43
d)$5348.02 **4.a)**9% **b)**10% **c)**10.5% **d)**11.75%
5.a)4 years **b)**4 months **c)**2.5 years **d)**3.25 years
6.a)$812 **b)**5.83% **c)**5.5 years **d)**$1797.05 **e)**11.13%
7.a)$272.73 **b)**4 years, 1.5 months **c)**9.5%
d)$1395.20 **e)**$3165.20 **f)**$14 464.77 **8.**$23 453.75
9.$851.78 **10.**5 years **11.**10.7% **12.**$554.99
13.$3105.00 **14.**8 years **15.**11.1% **16.**$3581.10
17.138.5%

11.2 Exercise, page 412
1.a)1.418 519 **b)**1.1664 **c)**1.269 735 **d)**1.218 403
e)2.032 794 **f)**1.477 455 **g)**1.601 032 **h)**1.563 080
i)2.806 794 **j)**3.140 679 **k)**1.335 469 **l)**2.854 339
2.a)8, 0.0425 **b)**12%, monthly **c)**7, 2% **d)**9%, semi-
annually **e)**10, 0.0975 **f)**15%, 4
3.a)$A = 600(1 + 0.09)^2$
b)$A = 900(1 + 0.0425)^8$
c)$A = 1000(1 + 0.01)^{60}$
d)$A = 1400(1 + 0.025 625)^{68}$

4.

	P	r	t	Amount, A
a)	$300	18%	11½ years	$2177.36

Continued at top of the next column.

b)	$700	18%	6 years	$2013.21
c)	$627	12%	1 year	$706.52
d)	$526	4¼%	4 years	$622.36
e)	$221	9%	6 months	$231.13
f)	$323	12%	3 years	$460.52

5.a)$4363.90 **b)**$4261.00 **c)**$2664.01 **6.a)**$2849.06
b)$3297.95 **c)**471.10 **d)**2115.37 **7.a)**$734.16
b)$28 004.78 **c)**$11 573.14 **d)**$5667.64 **8.a)**$5124.35
b)$5171.09 **c)**$5195.77 **9.a)**$6890.98 **b)**$2537.14, yes
10.$8464.69 **11.a)**$543.74 **12.a)**$1964.69 **b)**$653.21
13.A: $956.31, B: $644.89, C: $1024.87; Melanie
14.$1614.70 **15.**$10 671.54 (assuming that $1000 was
also withdrawn at the end of 2 years) **16.a)**9.5% per
annum **b)**9.3% per annum **17.**$276.11 **18.**$644.35
19.approximately 9 years

11.3 Exercise, page 416
1.a)12.55% **b)**8.16% **c)**12.68% **d)**9.20% **e)**8.24%
f)10.38% **2.a)**10% **b)**10.25% **c)**$1608.11 **3.a)**6%
b)6.14% **c)**$902.16 **4.a)**A: $2660.22, B: $2651.20;
A is worth $9.02 more **b)**A: 12.55%, B: 12.36%
5.a)8% **b)**8.16% **c)**8.24% **6.**A: 10%, B: 9.2%,
C: 8.24%; A is the best **7.**Shirley: 9.20%, Lara: 8.77%
Shirley made the better investment. **8.a)**19.56%
b)$157.04 **9.a)**3.50% compounded semi-annually
b)3.8% compounded semi-annually **10.a)**$225.30
b)32.92% **11.a)**$1861.92 **b)**8.08%

11.4 Exercise, page 420
1.a)0.767 896 **b)**0.414 100 **c)**0.419 854 **d)**0.176 277
e)0.787 566 **f)**0.720 688 **g)**0.379 085 **h)**0.793 832
i)0.377 889 **2.b)**(i) 12, 0.02 (ii) 12%, monthly (iii) 3,
0.0425 (iv) 15%, 3̶(v̶)4, 0.045 **3.a)**$PV = \dfrac{1400}{(1.08)^4}$
b)$PV = \dfrac{1700}{(1.045)^{12}}$ **c)**$PV = \dfrac{1600}{(1.025)^{20}}$

4.

	A	r	t	Value
a)	$700	12%	1 year	$621.21
b)	$1844	9%	4 years	$1296.67
c)	$1372	10%	6.5 years	$721.99
d)	$622	8.5%	5 years	$408.46

5.a)$841.68 **b)**$651.60 **c)**$757.88 **d)**$827.35
6.a)$1210.34 **b)**$2051.82 **c)**$440.43 **d)**$4816.42
e)$877.09 **7.a)**$1043.71 **b)**$2834.46 **c)**$1360.03
8.a)$4083.50 **b)**$4053.39 **c)**$4037.83 **9.a)**$1585.30
b)$1250 **10.**$528.31 **11.**$2041.97 **12.**$5625.48
13.$1488.62 **14.**3204.83 **15.**$15 467.63
16.a)$3346.00 **b)**$1154.00 **17.**$2223.13

11.5 Exercise, page 424
1.a)1.992 563 **b)**1.973 823 **c)**2.971 457 **d)**1.601 032

e)1.608 437 f)2.806 794 g)1.132 796 h)1.282 037
2.a)$4600.22 b)$1200.61 c)$10 763.12 3.a)$6381.98
b)$12 725.66 4.a)$1526.28 b)$9054.10 5.a)$674.34
b)$931.96 6.$410.66 7.$9249.24 8.$762.96
9.$15 729.20 10.$167 220.09 11.$391.09
12.a)$87 743.68 13.$3055.60 14.John 15.$2359.82

11.6 Exercise, page 428
1.a)0.627 412 b)0.385 543 c)0.375 702 d)0.672 971
e)0.639 762 f)0.423 147 g)0.861 030 h)0.733 034
2.a)$2767.41 b)$4193.93 3.a)$11 407.14
b)$26 155.41 4.$15 666.00 5.a)$1062.17 b)$1697.21
6.a)$3355.04 b)$1377.03 7.$36 679.44 8.$8998.33
9.$2022.94 10.$708.99 11.$3280.67 12.$525.99
13.$7586.15 14.$1921.90 15.a)$3590.82 b)$3590.82
c)$6166.16 16.a)$11 959.57 b)$34 774. 17.$4866.72

11.7 Exercise, page 432
1.a)$15 937.42 b)$27 996.40 c)$29 773.52
d)$7451.17 2.a)$6905.62 b)$3330.79 3.a)$1740.44
b)$1081.56 4.a)$1649.92 b)$649.07 c)$5136.08
d)$3312.02 5.a)$242.46 b)$1428.56 6.$3958.09
7.$2150.10 8.$225.54 9.a)$8276.73 b)$23 267.30
10.a)$70 757.20 b)$101 442.80 11.$635.77

11.8 Exercise, page 438
1.a)$2091.98 b)$1266.50

2.

Year	Principal of mortgage owed	Interest owed	Total payment	Payment on principal	Unpaid principal at the end of the year
1	$14 500.00	$1946.26	$3670.00	$1723.74	$12 776.26
2	$12 776.26	$1714.89	$3670.00	$1955.11	$10 821.15
3	$10 821.15	$1452.47	$3670.00	$2217.53	$8603.62
4	$8603.62	$1154.82	$3670.00	$2515.18	$6088.44
5	$6088.44	$817.22	$3670.00	$2852.78	$3235.74
6	$3235.74	$434.32	$3670.06	$3235.74	0

3. At the time of the 4th payment, interest and principal owed is $9758.44. A payment of $2000 is made (but not the $3670); new equal payments are $2228.62 **4.**$2079.28

5.a)

Year	Principal of mortgage owed	Interest owed	Total payment	Payment on principal	Unpaid principal at the end of the year
1	$68 000.00	$7820.00	$11 789.65	$3969.65	$64 030.35
2	$64 030.35	$7363.49	$11 789.65	$4426.16	$59 604.19
3	$59 604.19	$6854.48	$11 789.65	$4935.17	$54 669.02
4	$54 669.02	$6286.94	$11 789.65	$5502.71	$49 166.31
5	$49 166.31	$5654.13	$11 789.65	$6135.52	$43 030.79
6	$43 030.79	$4948.54	$11 789.65	$6841.11	$36 189.68
7	$36 189.68	$4161.81	$11 789.65	$7627.84	$28 561.84
8	$28 561.84	$3284.61	$11 789.65	$8505.04	$20 056.80
9	$20 056.80	$2306.53	$11 789.65	$9483.12	$10 573.68
10	$10 573.68	$1215.97	$11 789.65	$10 573.68	$0

6.

Year	Principal of mortgage owed	Interest owed	Total payment	Payment on principal	Unpaid principal
1	$82 800.00	$5382.00	$6905.33	$1523.33	$81 276.67
	$81 276.67	$5282.98	$6905.33	$1622.35	$79 654.32
2	$79 654.32	$5177.53	$6905.33	$1727.80	$77 926.52
	$77 926.52	$5065.22	$6905.33	$1840.11	$76 086.41
3	$76 086.41	$4945.62	$6905.33	$1959.71	$74 126.70
	$74 126.70	$4818.24	$6905.33	$2087.09	$72 039.61
4	$72 039.61	$4682.57	$6905.33	$2222.76	$69 816.85
	$69 816.85	$4538.10	$6905.33	$2367.23	$67 449.62
5	$67 449.62	$4384.23	$6905.33	$2521.10	$64 928.52
	$64 928.52	$4220.35	$6905.33	$2684.98	$62 243.54
6	$62 243.54	$4045.83	$6905.33	$2859.50	$59 384.04
	$59 384.04	$3859.96	$6905.33	$3045.37	$56 338.07
7	$56 338.07	$3662.01	$6905.33	$3243.32	$53 095.35
	$53 095.35	$3451.20	$6905.33	$3454.13	$49 641.22
8	$49 641.22	$3226.68	$6905.33	$3678.65	$45 962.57
	$45 962.57	$2987.57	$6905.33	$3917.76	$42 044.81

Continued at top of the next column.

9	$42 044.81	$2732.91	$6905.33	$4172.42	$37 872.39
	$37 872.39	$2461.71	$6905.33	$4443.62	$33 428.77
10	$33 428.77	$2172.87	$6905.33	$4732.46	$28 696.31
	$28 696.31	$1865.26	$6905.33	$5040.07	$23 656.24
11	$23 656.24	$1537.66	$6905.33	$5367.67	$18 288.57
	$18 288.57	$1188.76	$6905.33	$5716.57	$12 572.00
12	$12 572.00	$817.18	$6905.33	$6088.15	$6483.85
	$6483.85	$421.45	$6905.30	$6483.85	$0

7.a)$11 453.04 **b)**$42 540.92 **8.a)**$63 750 **b)**$5334.57
c)$1143.37 **9.a)**$1022.22 **b)**$4291.77 **10.a)**$346.76
b) **c)**$586.05

Year	Principal of loan owed	Interest payment	Total payment	Payment on principal	Principal owed at end of year
1	$1250.00	$150.00	$346.76	$196.76	$1053.24
2	$1053.24	$126.39	$346.76	$220.37	$832.87
3	$832.87	$99.94	$346.76	$246.82	$586.05
4	$586.05	$70.33	$346.76	$276.43	$309.62
5	$309.62	$37.15	$346.77	$309.62	$0

11.a) **b)**$703.75

Year	Principal of loan owed	Interest payment	Total payment	Payment on principal	Principal owed
1	$3500.00	$192.50	$700.63	$508.13	$2991.87
	$2991.87	$164.55	$700.63	$536.08	$2455.79
2	$2455.79	$135.07	$700.63	$565.56	$1890.23
	$1890.23	$103.96	$700.63	$596.67	$1293.56
3	$1293.56	$71.15	$700.63	$629.48	$664.08
	$664.08	$36.52	$700.60	$664.08	$0

12.a) **b)**$977.42

Year	Principal owed	Interest payment	Total payment	Payment on principal	Principal owed at end of year
1	$2500.00	$37.50	$333.96	$296.46	$2203.54
2	$2203.54	$33.05	$333.96	$300.91	$1902.63
3	$1902.63	$28.54	$333.96	$305.42	$1597.21
4	$1597.21	$23.96	$333.96	$310.00	$1287.21
5	$1287.21	$19.31	$333.96	$314.65	$972.56
6	$972.56	$14.59	$333.96	$319.37	$653.19
7	$653.19	$9.80	$333.96	$324.16	$329.03
8	$329.03	$4.94	$333.97	$329.03	$0

11.9 Exercise, page 443
2.a)more b)less 3.a)$52.50 b)$437.50 4.a)10.11%
b)10.31% 5.a)$2000 b)$1965 c)11% d)11.20%
6.a)10.54% b)13.56% 7.9.68% 8.10.67% 9.11.60%
10.a)10.86% b)14.29%; (b) has the better yield

11.10 Exercise, page 446
1.a)10.26% b)6.90% c)8.84% d)16.27% 2.10.28%
3.12.40% 4.11.48% 5.10.83% 6.a)10.28%
b)10.21% c)11.99% 7.a)10.46% b)12.74%
8.a)11.84% b)12.71% 9.a)11.21% b)$2868.23

11.11 Exercise, page 449
1.a)$93.23 b)$32.20 c)$125.43 2.a)$2251.15
b)$1431.57 c)$1389.05 d)$3500.00 3.a)$89.51
b)$80.61 4.$932.33 5.$896.25 6.$93.20

11.12 Exercise, page 451
The answers obtained in the investigations of this section will vary, since stock prices continually fluctuate. Also, calculations involving commission rates will vary depending on the price of the stock. The *Teachers Edition* that accompanies this text includes additional resources that can be used to explore the answers required in these investigations.

Index